Lecture Notes in Computer Science 12807

More information about this subseries at http://www.springer.com/series/7409

Leona Chandra Kruse · Stefan Seidel ·
Geir Inge Hausvik (Eds.)

The Next Wave
of Sociotechnical Design

16th International Conference on Design Science Research
in Information Systems and Technology, DESRIST 2021
Kristiansand, Norway, August 4–6, 2021
Proceedings

Springer

Editors
Leona Chandra Kruse 🆔
University of Liechtenstein
Vaduz, Liechtenstein

Stefan Seidel 🆔
University of Liechtenstein
Vaduz, Liechtenstein

Geir Inge Hausvik 🆔
University of Agder
Kristiansand, Norway

ISSN 0302-9743 ISSN 1611-3349 (electronic)
Lecture Notes in Computer Science
ISBN 978-3-030-82404-4 ISBN 978-3-030-82405-1 (eBook)
https://doi.org/10.1007/978-3-030-82405-1

LNCS Sublibrary: SL3 – Information Systems and Applications, incl. Internet/Web, and HCI

This Springer imprint is published by the registered company Springer Nature Switzerland AG
The registered company address is: Gewerbestrasse 11, 6330 Cham, Switzerland

Preface

The recent global events remind us of the potential of digital technologies to shape society's future. They can help redesign our lives for the better and attain the sustainable development goals. But we can also observe the unintended harmful consequences of digital technologies, if not designed and used mindfully. Security breaches, hate speech, and the digital divide are among those consequences that have been debated in the media and research. Essentially though, these technologies are first and foremost design artifacts. What can we, the community of practitioners and researchers, do to promote the design of digital technology that serves people, organizations, and society in a beneficial and sustainable way?

Our community is in a unique position to not only be aware of but also proactively shape the key developments in the digital age. The design science research (DSR) field has traditionally focused on sociotechnical design to improve the human condition, simultaneously considering tasks, technologies, people, and social structures at the individual, organizational, and societal levels. As the field matured, the "design first and people will adapt" approach gave way to methods and frameworks that embrace the evolving needs of users as well as contextual changes over time. Broadly speaking, DSR scholars have taken three approaches. Some work closely with stakeholders and practitioners. They use action design research and related approaches to gain a deeper understanding into their needs, wishes, and challenges as they deeply engage with development and use contexts. Others focus on designing novel and innovative artifacts to assist specific target users in pursuing their aims. Others find ways to make the knowledge created through their DSR projects reusable across contexts and time. Designers can then build on this knowledge and focus attention on developing methods and artifacts of increasing usefulness. What these three approaches have in common is their cognizance of the sociotechnical nature of design.

It is against this background that the 16th International Conference on Design Science Research in Information Systems and Technology (DESRIST 2021) pursued the motto "The Next Wave of Sociotechnical Design." The intention of this year's conference was to take a step back and revisit the roots of sociotechnical design to make it relevant in the context of the current and coming social and technological developments, including diminishing boundaries of organizations, platformization, and the productive use of artificial intelligence. We hope that DESRIST 2021 helped the DSR community to define its role in this new era by clarifying and strengthening the meaning and scope of DSR.

This volume contains 24 full research papers, 6 short research papers, and 7 prototype papers. The acceptance rate was 47%. The accepted papers reflect the conference's motto well. They address topics related to impactful sociotechnical design, emerging DSR methods and frameworks, the new boundaries of DSR, design knowledge for reuse, and DSR governance.

The COVID-19 pandemic has heavily influenced our organization of this year's DESRIST. We were optimistic in planning for an on-site conference to be held at the University of Agder, Norway, during August 4–6, 2021, while also exploring a hybrid conference model. Our final decision was ultimately made with the interest of the DSR community in mind. We thank all the contributors who helped make DESRIST 2021 a success. We are grateful for the enthusiasm and commitment of our Program Committee members as well as reviewers. We also thank all authors for submitting their work to DESRIST. We believe that our community is thriving. We were thrilled to include interdisciplinary keynote presentations. Their insights will enrich our approach to design and innovation. Our special thanks go to the local organizers at the University of Agder. Their commitment and flexibility in these challenging times were remarkable.

August 2021

Leona Chandra Kruse
Stefan Seidel
Geir Inge Hausvik

Organization

Conference Chairs

Carl Erik Moe   University of Agder, Norway
Kai R. Larsen   University of Agder, Norway and University of
     Colorado Boulder, USA

Program Chairs

Leona Chandra Kruse   University of Liechtenstein, Liechtenstein
Stefan Seidel   University of Liechtenstein, Liechtenstein

Doctoral Consortium Chairs

Bengisu Tulu   Worcester Polytechnic Institute, USA
Gondry Leroy   University of Arizona, USA

Prototypes Chairs

Alexander Mädche   Karlsruhe Institute of Technology, Germany
Sofie Wass   University of Agder, Norway

Proceedings Chair

Geir Inge Hausvik   University of Agder, Norway

Panel Coordinator

Amir Haj-Bolouri   University West, Sweden

General Chairs

Maung Kyaw Sein   University of Agder, Norway
Matti Rossi   Aalto University, Finland
Oliver Müller   Paderborn University, Germany
Leif Skiftenes Flak   University of Agder, Norway

Website

Amna Drace   University of Agder, Norway

Program Committee

Ahmed Abbasi	University of Notre Dame, USA
David Agogo	Florida International University, USA
Nicholas Berente	University of Notre Dame, USA
Daniel Beverungen	Paderborn University, Germany
Samir Chatterjee	Claremont Graduate University, USA
Oscar Diaz	University of Basque Country, Spain
Brian Donnellan	Maynooth University, Ireland
Kaushik Dutta	University of South Florida, USA
Ahmed Elragal	Luleå University of Technology, Sweden
Dominik Gutt	Rotterdam School of Management, The Netherlands
Riitta Hekkala	Aalto University, Finland
Konstantin Hopf	University of Bamberg, Germany
Dirk Hovorka	The University of Sydney Business School, Australia
Juhani Iivari	University of Oulu, Finland
Christian Janiesch	University of Würzburg, Germany
Eduan Kotzé	University of the Free State and University of South Africa, South Africa
Christine Legner	University of Lausanne, Switzerland
Roman Lukyanenko	HEC Montréal, Canada
Monika Malinova	Vienna University of Economics and Business, Austria
Munir Mandviwalla	Temple University, USA
Martin Matzner	University of Erlangen – Nuremberg, Germany
Stefan Morana	University of Saarland, Germany
Matthew Mullarkey	USF Muma College of Business, USA
Jeffrey V. Nickerson	Stevens Institute of Technology, USA
Peter Axel Nielsen	Aalborg University, Denmark
Jeffrey Parsons	Memorial University, Canada
Ken Peffers	University of Nevada, USA
Sandeep Purao	Bentley University, USA
Marthie Schoeman	University of South Africa, South Africa
Jonas Sjöström	Uppsala University, Sweden
Armin Stein	University of Muenster, Germany
Veda C. Storey	Georgia State University, USA
Rangaraja Sundrajan	Indian Institute of Technology Madras, India
Matthias Söllner	University of Kassel, Germany
Monica C. Tremblay	William & Mary, USA
Tuure Tuunanen	University of Jyväskyla, Finland
Judy van Biljon	University of South Africa, South Africa
Amy van Looy	Ghent University, Belgium
Debra VanderMeer	Florida International University, USA
Jan vom Brocke	University of Liechtenstein, Liechtenstein
Barbara Weber	University of St. Gallen, Switzerland
Robert Winter	University of St. Gallen, Switzerland

Reviewers

Ireti Amojo
Alisa Ananjeva
Wasana Bandara
Christian Bartelheimer
Sihem Belabbes
Katrin Bergener
Lina Bouayad
Alfred Benedikt Brendel
Maxime De Bruyn
Marcel Cahenzli
Arturo Castellanos
Alfred Castillo
Friedrich Chasin
Dongwook Chun
Nico Clever
Niall Connolly
Jeremías P. Contell
Djordje Djurica
Katharina Drechsler
Paul Drews
Thomas Ejnefjäll
Edona Elshan
Jasper Feine
Vincent Ford
Michael Gau
Gunther Gust
Amir Haj-Bolouri
Fatima Hajjat
Moez Hamedani
Danielle Hartigan
Thomas Haskamp
Hossam Hassanien
Philipp Zur Heiden
Marlien Herselman
Alexander Herwix
Fabian Hunke
Joschka Hüllmann
Rehan Iftikhar
Gloria Ejehiohen Iyawa
Hemant Jain
Clemens Kerschbaum
Kimia Keshanian
Gregor Kipping

Pavel Krasikov
Jan H. Kroeze
John Lalor
Arto Lanamäki
Kai R. Larsen
Gondy Leroy
Aron Lindberg
Juuli Lintula
Yulia Litvinova
Peter Loos
Carl-Mikael Lönn
Lukas Malburg
Shane McLoughlin
Nita Mennega
Michael Zur Muehlen
Anik Mukherjee
Pavankumar Mulgund
Mudassir Imran Mustafa
Frederik Möller
Per Rådberg Nagbøl
Long Nguyen
Jacob Nørbjerg
Ahmed Osman
Danielly de Paula
Esko Penttinen
Juan Antonio Pereira
John Persson
Lukas Pfahlsberger
Daniel Pienta
Henri Pirkkalainen
Geert Poels
Andre van der Poll
Martin Poniatowski
Tero Päivärinta
Xinxue Qu
Arindam Ray
Annika Reinelt
Aya Rizk
Jaana Räisänen
Hani Safadi
Burcin Sari
Philipp Scharfe
Marius Schmid

Thorsten Schoormann
Ronny Seiger
Dominik Siemon
Deepti Singh
Vivek Singh
Sriram Somanchi
Nicola Staub
Carlo Stingl
Karthikeyan Umapathy
Elin Uppström
Sriram V

Fanny Vainionpää
John Venable
Maxim Vidgof
Nishant Vishwamitra
Gerit Wagner
Florian Weber
Manuel Weber
Sven Weinzierl
Axel Winkelmann
Bastian Wurm
Aleksi Aaltonen

Contents

Problem and Contribution Articulation

Design Knowledge for Reuse

Emerging Methods and Frameworks for DSR

DSR and Governance

The New Boundaries of DSR

Impactful Sociotechnical Design

KlimaKarl – A Chatbot to Promote Employees' Climate-Friendly Behavior in an Office Setting

Kirsten Hillebrand[1]([⊠]) [iD] and Florian Johannsen[2] [iD]

[1] Bern University of Applied Sciences, Bern, Switzerland
`kirsten.hillebrand@bfh.ch`
[2] University of Applied Sciences Schmalkalden, Schmalkalden, Germany
`f.johannsen@hs-sm.de`

Abstract. Environmental protection is a central challenge these days. At the same time, digital technologies have experienced tremendous technical progress in recent years and their potentials to support firms' sustainability strategies and corporate social responsibility efforts are intensively discussed. In this respect, companies search for efficient ways to trigger a change of employee behavior in terms of climate-friendly practices. We propose chatbots as a promising technology to promote the climate-friendly behavior of employees. Following a Design Science Research (DSR) procedure, we develop a chatbot prototype called KlimaKarl to sensitize the workforce to behave in a more climate-conscious way in the everyday office life. We show that chatbots may be a suitable instrument to promote employees' climate-friendly behavior.

Keywords: Chatbot · Green office · Sustainability · Digital technologies

1 Introduction

Environmental and climate protection are crucial challenges of our time. The United Nations recognizes the importance of these challenges as part of the Agenda 2030, which was passed by the member states in 2015 [48]. The core of the Agenda 2030 are 17 global goals – the sustainable development goals (SDGs). Given the little time left to reach the SDGs by 2030, enterprises should use the disruptive potential of digital technologies [1, 8] to meet their corporate social responsibility (CSR) and thereby to support the achievement of the SDGs. Innovative technologies comprise various solutions and tools and their possible application fields to promote sustainability are manifold [e.g., 12, 41]. One promising technology that has attracted a lot of attention from practitioners in recent years are chatbots. In a business context, chatbots have a variety of uses for external communication purposes (e.g., customer service, sales, marketing), but also for promoting the communication within a company (e.g., employee training, knowledge management) [32]. Given their interactive and communicative character [6], chatbots have the potential to encourage employees to behave in a climate-friendlier way in everyday office life. Nevertheless, the literature about chatbots to promote sustainability within companies is scarce yet. Hence, we strive for the design and development of a

© Springer Nature Switzerland AG 2021
L. Chandra Kruse et al. (Eds.): DESRIST 2021, LNCS 12807, pp. 3–15, 2021.
https://doi.org/10.1007/978-3-030-82405-1_1

chatbot to endorse employees' "green behavior" [14] in this paper. Designing a chatbot to motivate climate-friendly behavior serves companies' CSR measures for two reasons. First, human behavior is the main source of negative environmental influences, and hence, the most important mechanism for achieving ecological sustainability [33, 47, 51]. Second, the commitment of employees is supportive for implementing a company's sustainability strategy. A chatbot could familiarize employees with sustainable measures and behavioral patterns in a playful way. During the interaction with the chatbot, users may additionally promote their own ideas for more climate protection within a company. Generally, chatbots have proven as highly effective for supporting communication processes [33], and we believe this potential of chatbots is also given for the domain of sustainability, which motivates us to conduct the study.

This paper illustrates how a chatbot-based mobile app can be used to reach environmental and climate protection goals within an enterprise. The following research question guides our DSR project: *What can a chatbot to promote employees' eco-friendly behavior in everyday office life look like?* We consider DSR as a suitable approach, because on the one hand, we contribute to the scientific knowledge base on how chatbots may promote climate-friendly office behavior [2, 18, 20] and on the other hand, we create a corresponding IT-artifact for the problem domain described [21, 31]. The paper is structured as follows: In the next section, we provide theoretical foundations. Subsequently, we show the research methodology and the requirements on our prototype. After a description of the prototype development, demonstration and first evaluation, the paper concludes with a discussion and outlook.

2 Foundations and Related Work

2.1 Digital Technologies and Environmental Sustainability

In the recent past, enterprises have increasingly shown interest in the effects of digital technologies on the environment while their awareness regarding social and environmental challenges has risen tremendously [12, 41]. In this respect, environmental sustainability is seen as an essential feature of CSR these days [12]. On this occasion, digital technologies are judged to be major drivers for ecological sustainability and promoting green behavior within the workforce (green office) [25, 40]. The impact of information technology on the environment is specified by Berkhout and Hertin [3] in more detail, who differentiate between "direct" (e.g., reduced pollution), "indirect" (e.g., substitution of materials by information goods) as well as "structural and behavioral" effects (e.g., changes in peoples' lifestyle or structural changes in the economy). Similar thoughts can be found in Li and Found [29], who propose a series of environmental benefits caused by digital technologies. From the perspective of DSR in particular, Seidel et al. [45] investigate the role of information systems (IS) to implement sustainable work practices within companies and identify functional affordances of IS that are supportive in green transformation projects. Thereby, the authors differentiate between sensemaking and sustainable practicing affordances and develop an integrated model of functional affordances [45]. In a latter publication, design principles for IS that support organizational sensemaking in sustainability transformation projects are derived [44]. In addition, Schoormann et al. [42] define design principles with corresponding design features for tools that enable the development of sustainable business models. Particular these Design Science (DS) research streams are highly relevant for our approach, because they help to derive design requirements for our solution later on. To sum up, a lot of research about digital technologies on environmental sustainability is performed. However, the role of chatbots – to induce a sustainable environmental behavior within the workforce – seems to be an under-researched topic yet.

2.2 Entrepreneurial Chatbot Usage for Internal and External Communication

The first chatbot ELIZA, which was created by Joseph Weizenbaum in the '60s [50], simulated a psychotherapist and triggered the search for further beneficial application fields for chatbots [cf. 10]. These days, chatbots are used in various functional areas for internal as well as external communication purposes. In terms of an organization's external communication with consumers, many companies and institutions have introduced chatbots as a means to support the customer service [e.g., 17]. Horzyk et al. [23] point out that chatbots may also increase the customer experience during online shopping, while the Bank of America uses chatbots to analyze customers' behavior for being able to provide consumer-specific offerings [28]. Other application fields for chatbots include e-government [e.g., 40], education [e.g., 16], healthcare [e.g., 5, 9] and law [e.g., 11]. Moreover, chatbots are increasingly discussed to support the internal communication within organizations [26, 38]. According to a recent interview study by Meyer von Wolff et al. [32], practitioners see internal/external support, human resources, (employee) self-service, employee training and knowledge management as promising areas for chatbots to foster the communication within the workforce [e.g., 27, 37, 52]. However, using chatbots as part of companies' ecological sustainability efforts – generally or within the workforce – is neither covered in current research nor tested by practitioners so far. In this paper, we address this research gap by the design, development and first evaluation of the chatbot KlimaKarl that promotes environmental sustainability within the workforce. While singular chatbots to support environmental education, e.g., AluxBot for school-age children [cf. 34] or to encourage sustainable mobility behavior exist [cf. 13], our target audience is the company employee in particular.

3 Methodology and Research Design

To come to a prototype of our app KlimaKarl, we conduct a DSR project [cf. 18, 21] and follow the procedure of Peffers et al. [35]. Figure 1 summarizes the steps of the design procedure. The problem statement (Step 1) has been formulated in the introduction. In Step 2 (Objectives of a Solution), we derive requirements on our prototype (1) by reviewing corresponding fields of literature, (2) by examining the German B2B market for similar chatbots, (3) by discussing the chatbot usage in an office environment with company representatives at a workshop, and (4) by conducting a survey at a city fair where we asked 98 office employees about their requirements for KlimaKarl. Hence, we consider the existing field of literature (DS rigor cycle) but also the practical application context (DS relevance cycle) [e.g., 20]. Step 3 (Design & Development) includes design-related decisions as well as the implementation of the prototype by help of suitable frameworks and open source solutions. The next step (Demonstration) deals with the demonstration of the prototype at two companies from the energy and retail sector to assess its general practicality. In Step 5 (Evaluation) the usefulness, applicability and usability [cf. 21] of the prototype are to be analyzed in more-depth in a larger field study. Subsequent to the evaluation, the app will be revised and further optimized before a large-scale roll-out across German companies will be performed.

1. Problem	2. Objectives of a Solution	3. Design & Development	4. Demonstration	5. Evaluation	6. Communication
Digital technologies are not yet sufficiently used to promote CSR. Currently, there is a lack of chatbots that motivate green office behavior in special.	Requirements on a chatbot prototype to promote green office behavior are formulated.	An iOS/Android chatbot prototype is designed and implemented.	By referring to an employee contest scenario, the chatbot's functionality is demonstrated and exemplified.	The usefulness, applicability and usability of the prototype are evaluated in field studies.	The app will be rolled out at partner companies and the German B2B market.

☐ : Focus of this paper
☐ : In progress
☐ : Future Work

process iteration

Fig. 1. DSR procedure by Peffers et al. [35] adapted for this research.

4   Objectives of a Solution

To collect and select specific requirements for the chatbot's design and functionalities, we considered different perspectives from research, market, customer, and user. Figure 2 visualizes the collection and selection process.

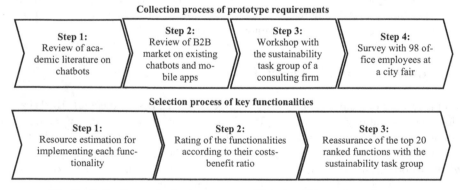

Collection process of prototype requirements

| Step 1: Review of academic literature on chatbots | Step 2: Review of B2B market on existing chatbots and mobile apps | Step 3: Workshop with the sustainability task group of a consulting firm | Step 4: Survey with 98 office employees at a city fair |

Selection process of key functionalities

| Step 1: Resource estimation for implementing each functionality | Step 2: Rating of the functionalities according to their costs-benefit ratio | Step 3: Reassurance of the top 20 ranked functions with the sustainability task group |

Fig. 2. Collection and selection process of functionalities and requirements.

To derive design requirements, we scrutinized the literature [49] about chatbot design at first to find generally acknowledged design propositions concerning the implementation of chatbots [e.g., 4, 15, 22, 24]. Moreover, design principles for IS in green transformation projects were considered [e.g., 44]. In a second step, the B2B market was searched for similar digital technologies and chatbots. Although there are a number of technologies to promote climate protection in companies (e.g., PlanA, Planetly, CoZero), we could not find any chatbots nor innovative solutions to promote green office in particular. While existing innovative technologies enable the analyses of a company's CO_2 emissions based on data, the promotion of employees' behavioral change is not sufficiently covered. When expanding our search from innovative technologies to common mobile apps we found existing services (Changers and Stadtradeln), which offer activity tracking and contest design functionalities. Although the appstore ratings for these apps contain some user reservations, they inspired us in designing gamification and tracking functionalities for our chatbot prototype. In a third step, we gathered additional requirements in a workshop at a multinational consulting company. In total, three company representatives, one of the authors and one research associate participated. All company representatives held the position of a "consultant". The company representatives were selected for the workshop because they were members of a sustainability task group. This group's major aim is to develop measures for integrating climate protection and sustainability efforts within the corporate strategy. In a five-hour-workshop, the participants first brainstormed new ideas on functionalities that were not covered by our initial collection yet. The attendees then jointly ranked the ideas in terms of their perceived value for users. Fourth, a survey was conducted at Breminale, a German city fair. In total, 98 office employees were asked about their personal requirements on a prototype to foster environmental-friendly behavior in an office setting. The city festival which took place in July 2019 in a large German city was chosen for the survey, because it usually attracts a very heterogeneous group of people. Visitors were randomly approached and asked whether they worked in an office environment. If so, they were explained the KlimaKarl project and requested to fill out an online questionnaire that could be accessed via their private mobile phones (by help of QR codes) or via provided iPads.

For realizing a first version of the chatbot KlimaKarl, the 32 initially collected requirements were condensed and prioritized in three steps. First, the authors, a research associate and a developer performed an initial resource estimate for each functionality. Second, this group rated the functionalities according to their ratio of potential value and development effort to come to a distinction between must-have and nice-to-have functionalities. Finally, the resulting ranking of must-have functionalities was rechecked with abovementioned workshop attendees at the consulting company. Lastly, our group came up with a manageable set of 19 must-have design requirements (DR). Table 1 lists and shortly explains the requirements. Thereby, the requirements for the first four categories have been identified as specific for our solution, whereas the requirements considering "user management & backend system" are generally acknowledged for this type of technology at large [e.g., 24].

Table 1. Requirements.

Design requirements	Description
Principal functionalities	
DR 1: Push-notifications with daily information about climate protection topics	Users receive notifications and interesting facts regarding climate protection topics [44]. They have the opportunity to rate the relevance of each notification from their personal point of view by help of a star rating-scale
DR 2: Chat function to document completed tasks related to green office behavior	A chat function is realized, which allows to mark completed tasks (e.g., vegetarian lunch, turning off lights, using public transportation) by help of buttons in the categories of nutrition, energy and mobility. Each button is associated with certain credit points regarding CO_2 savings [44, 45]
DR 3: Calculation of the kilometer distance of a route	The chatbot queries how users have covered a distance, e.g., by bike or train. If desired, the chatbot calculates the number of kilometers of the distance automatically in case the user enters a start and end address
DR 4: Continuous feedback to scores	The chatbot reacts with the total number of points scored and with mimic art to give user feedback [4, 15, 24]. Hence, employees are motivated to continue their climate-friendly behavior
DR 5: Instructions for team challenges	Employees (and teams) are provided with "green" challenges [44–46]. When they complete a challenge, employee teams trigger a green donation from the employer, such as the compensation of distance kilometers or the planting of a tree
DR 6: Employee surveys	The chatbot gives employees the opportunity to submit their own ideas for more climate protection in the company in a weekly survey [42, 44]. For this purpose, an additional button appears in the chat, which leads to a freeform text entry
DR 7: Quizzes	The chatbot conducts a weekly quiz with employees, through which they can earn additional points [39, 46]

(*continued*)

Table 1. (*continued*)

Enterprise dashboard	
DR 8: Ranking and current position of all teams	Employees form teams and the scores of each single employee are aggregated. In a dashboard, the ranking of each team is shown [46]
DR 9: Donations for "green projects"	The total amount of money, which was triggered by all employees and donated by the company for green projects is listed

Team dashboard	
DR 10: Individual ranking	The ranking of each employee within each team is provided [46]
DR 11: Progress indicator for the team challenges	Each employee team can perform challenges [39, 46], which require a particular score of points per category, e.g., nutrition or mobility (see DR 2). The progress of a team's task fulfillment is indicated by the chatbot

User dashboard	
DR 12: Badges	Every employee can collect badges [19]. To receive these badges, they must have completed certain green tasks several times in a row. The more difficult the badge is to reach the more extra points are generated
DR 13: Personal statistics	Each employee receives an overview of personal statistics, e.g., a weekly overview of the points achieved daily, the amount of CO_2 emissions avoided and points achieved per category

User management & backend system	
DR 14: FAQ-section	A section with answers to FAQs is provided
DR 15: Support for finding teams	The chatbot helps to form teams by proposing users that are still in search for a team
DR 16: User data management	The user can modify her/his master data (e.g., nickname, name, password) any time
DR 17: Backend system	The backend system allows to modify the provided content, the chatbot's layout or granted scores amongst others
DR 18: Transition design	The chatbot follows the transition design guidelines [cf. 30] to promote sustainable design
DR 19: Branding	The backend system allows to brand the mobile app with the company logo on the loading and setting screens

5 Design and Development

The prototype's general architecture was developed to be executable via the operating systems iOS and Android. For that purpose, the Google Flutter framework was used for implementing the frontend and the Express framework for the backend. Thereby, the programming languages Dart and TypeScript were applied and we built on the integrated development environments Xcode, Android Studio and Visual Studio Code. Furthermore, the bcrypt solution was used to create the login functionality. The communication between the front- and backend – but also the internal communication within these blocks (front-/backend) – was realized by help of REST (Representational State Transfers) APIs and the standards HTTP and JSON. In addition, MongoDB was drawn upon to establish the database and the database management system. A first design of the user interface, that matched with the design requirements, was discussed and revised by the development team using wireframes. Initial wireframes of the KlimaKarl prototype were sketched by hand and prepared the ground for a more fine-granular design produced via the Adobe XD Design Kit. In the course of the implementation, templates of Google Material Design and icons of Evil Icons were used. As an external service, the Google Distance Matrix API was referenced to realize the calculation of distances (see DR 3). Figure 3 shows three selected design examples of the prototype's principal functionalities. We plan to extend the chatbot's functionalities, e.g., by the capability to give answers to open questions, in future revisions.

(DR 4) Feedback by text and   (DR 10) Individual employee   (DR 12) Badges
mimic art   ranking

Fig. 3. Selected screenshots of the app.

6 Demonstration and First Evaluation

For demonstration and evaluation purposes, the KlimaKarl prototype was field-tested in September 2020 in cooperation with two companies and 74 voluntary office employees to see, whether the artifact is practicable in an entrepreneurial context. One company provides advice on energy efficiency in a German federal state and recruited 21 participants to take part in our field test. The other company is globally operating in the retail sector and recruited 53 participants at its German headquarters. The chatbot was tested as part of the two-week CO_2 saving competition with KlimaKarl. As part of the contest (1) employees entered completed tasks via buttons in the chat and received feedback on the points achieved, (2) they took part twice in an employee survey, (3) they received and rated the daily tips with stars, (4) they could achieve team challenges and thus trigger various donations, (5) they could unlock badges for repeated tasks and (6) they had an overview of their ranking and statistics in the company, team and user dashboard. Finally, the winning team was announced by releasing the ranking and a newsletter to all participants. From a technical point of view, the test of the prototype worked well, except for a few minor details. Two participants stated that the chatbot was not accessible on one day. One participant did not receive any push notifications, although he declared to have activated them. From a content perspective, the field test revealed potentials for improvement, particularly considering the documentation of completed tasks. The rankings, tips, badges and some other features were praised. However, the participants wished for more variety in the dialogue with KlimaKarl. A concrete suggestion was to add more tasks or days on which tasks count double points.

Besides the general demonstration of the prototype's practicability, we further wanted to test its usability and see whether it can promote behavioral change. Therefore, the employees taking part in the field-test were asked to fill out an online survey[1]. Of the 74 employees, 25 filled out the questionnaire. To test the usability, we used the System Usability Scale [7] on a five-point Likert-scale. Participants rated the usability of the prototype with an average score of 3.89 (standard deviation: 0.56; max. score: 5; min. score: 1). Thus, the app was rated as rather easy to handle and user-friendly, but still leaves room for improvement. To check whether employees have the intention to behave in a more climate-friendly in future, we used designated question items for "desire" and "intention" from the expanded Theory of Planned Behavior [36] with a five-point Likert-scale. The 25 respondents rated their desire to behave in a more climate-friendly way after using KlimaKarl as an average of 3.5 (standard deviation: 0.88; max. score: 5; min. score: 1). Their concrete intention to do so was rated as an average of 3.3 (standard deviation: 1.23; max. score: 5; min. score: 1). Hence, the results of the first evaluation indicate the chatbot's potential to increase employees' climate-friendly behavior. To test whether the participating employees behaved in a more climate-friendly way while using the prototype, we asked them to indicate whether they performed a certain set of climate-friendly tasks more frequently than before using KlimaKarl. Figure 4 summarizes the results. Eating habits changed significantly: 18 of 25 respondents (72%) have eaten vegan or vegetarian food more often during the use of KlimaKarl than previously.

---

[1] The questionnaire is available at: https://tinyurl.com/y6mbbwnf.

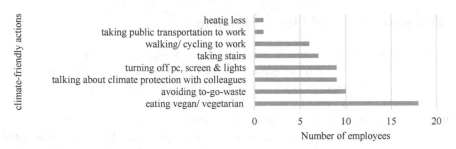

Fig. 4. Climate-friendly activities performed more often while using the prototype.

7 Discussion and Conclusion

Although chatbots have received increasing attention in literature, their use as part of companies' environmental sustainability efforts is not sufficiently covered by current research yet. A review of existing apps and chatbots on the German market shows that companies are already using digital technologies in a business and office context. However, they do not yet sufficiently do so to promote their CSR. Considering that climate protection is one of the most important challenges of our time, our research aims to address this research gap and to trigger a discussion of whether chatbots can promote climate protection or not. We therefore developed a chatbot prototype called KlimaKarl that promotes climate-friendly behavior of employees within companies. Results from the demonstration and first evaluation are encouraging. We could show that our prototype is of rather high usability and may motivate people to behave in a more climate-friendly way. However, this first evaluation of the KlimaKarl prototype has limitations. First, only employees of two particular companies participated. Since corporate cultures and sustainability strategies can differ considerably, additional study participants from more companies have to be recruited in future evaluation steps. More, since the respondents filled out the online survey voluntarily, a self-selection bias could probably be given. Furthermore, future evaluation measures for behavioral change should be based on revealed rather than self-reported behavior, e.g., by means of experiments. However, at this stage of the chatbot development, the goal was not to precisely quantify the desired effects, but to find out whether KlimaKarl has the potential to influence employees' behavior or not. The contribution of this research for practice is twofold. At first, managers will receive a running chatbot solution to motivate their employees for green office behavior and integrate climate protection into the company culture. Therefore, means to support running CSR efforts are given. Second, the use case of KlimaKarl may provide inspiration for managers to examine the appropriateness of other digital technologies to promote climate protection within an enterprise (e.g., big data analytics). We contribute to research by complementing the lively discussion of how chatbots may be purposefully used for internal purposes [e.g., 32]. In this respect, we introduce "green office behavior" [14] as a further application field, that may profit from the chatbot technology. Finally, the results from the evaluation conducted so far may trigger further investigations in the IS community to analyze the sustainability of changes in employee behavior by help of digital technologies.

In future steps, we plan to extend the chatbot's functionalities (e.g., by the possibility to ask open questions) and to run more evaluations at several companies with varying cultures. We also intend to evaluate the app more in-depth in order to maximize the chatbot's ecological impact in the office environment. After a corresponding revision of the prototype, we plan to make the chatbot available to German companies this autumn. Depending on how KlimaKarl will be accepted in practice, we would be happy to translate the app to other languages and make it available on an international level.

References

1. Acemoglu, D., Restrepo, P.: Artificial intelligence, automation and work (No. w24196). National Bureau of Economic Research (2018)
2. Baskerville, R., Baiyere, A., Gregor, S., Hevner, A., Rossi, M.: Design science research contributions: finding a balance between artifact and theory. J. Assoc. Inf. Syst. 19(5), 358–376 (2018)
3. Berkhout, F., Hertin, J.: De-materialising and re-materialising: digital technologies and the environment. Futures 36(8), 903–920 (2004)
4. Berry, D., Butler, L., de Rosis, F., Laaksolahti, J., Pelachaud, C., Steedman, M.: Embodied Believable Agents. University of Edinburgh (2004)
5. Bickmore, T.W., Mitchell, S.E., Jack, B.W., Paasche-Orlow, M.K., Pfeifer, L.M., O'Donnell, J.: Response to a relational agent by hospital patients with depressive symptoms. Interact. Comput. 22(4), 289–298 (2010)
6. Brandtzaeg, P.B., Følstad, A.: Why people use chatbots. In: Kompatsiaris, I., et al. (eds.) INSCI 2017. LNCS, vol. 10673, pp. 377–392. Springer, Cham (2017). https://doi.org/10.1007/978-3-319-70284-1_30
7. Brooke, J.: SUS: A "quick and dirty" usability scale. In: Jordan, P.W., Thomas, B., Weerdmeester, B.A., McClelland, I.L. (eds.) Usability Evaluation in Industry, pp. 189–194. Taylor & Francis, London (1996)
8. Brynjolfsson, E., McAfee, A.: The Second Machine Age: Work, Progress, and Prosperity in a Time of Brilliant Technologies. W. W. Norton & Company (2014)
9. Comendador, B.E.V., Francisco, B.M.B., Medenilla, J.S., Mae, S.: Pharmabot: a pediatric generic medicine consultant chatbot. J. Autom. Control Eng. 3(2), 137–140 (2015)
10. Dale, R.: The return of the chatbots. Nat. Lang. Eng. 22(5), 811–817 (2016)
11. Dale, R.: Law and word order: Nlp in legal tech. Nat. Lang. Eng. 25(1), 211–217 (2019)
12. Dedrick, J.: Green IS: concepts and issues for information systems research. Commun. Assoc. Inf. Syst. 27(1), 11 (2010)
13. Diederich, S., Lichtenberg, S., Brendel, A.B., Trang, S.: Promoting sustainable mobility beliefs with persuasive and anthropomorphic design: insights from an experiment with a conversational agent. In: International Conference on Information Systems (ICIS), Munich, Israel (2019)
14. Fraunhofer IAO: Green Office (2014)
15. Gennermann, H., Hack, S.: Qualitätsstandards für Chatbots in der bibliothekarischen Auskunft in Deutschland. BIT online–Innovative, p. 111 (2011)
16. Goda, Y., Yamada, M., Matsukawa, H., Hata, K., Yasunami, S.: Conversation with a chatbot before an online EFL group discussion and the effects on critical thinking. J. Inf. Syst. Educ. 13(1), 1–7 (2014)
17. Gorelov, Z.: Introducing KAI banking on messaging and MyKAI. http://kasisto.com/introducing-kai-banking-on-messaging-and-mykai/. Accessed 10 Oct 2020

18. Gregor, S., Hevner, A.R.: Positioning and presenting design science research for maximum impact. MIS Q. **37**, 337–355 (2013)
19. Hamari, J.: Do badges increase user activity? A field experiment on the effects of gamification. Comput. Hum. Behav. **71**, 469–478 (2017)
20. Hevner, A.R.: A three cycle view of design science research. Scand. J. Inf. Syst. **19**(2), 87–92 (2007)
21. Bichler, M.: Design science in information systems research. Wirtschaftsinformatik **48**(2), 133–135 (2006). https://doi.org/10.1007/s11576-006-0028-8
22. Hill, J., Ford, W.R., Farreras, I.G.: Real conversations with artificial intelligence: a comparison between human–human online conversations and human–chatbot conversations. Comput. Hum. Behav. **49**, 245–250 (2015)
23. Horzyk, A., Magierski, S., Miklaszewski, G.: An intelligent internet shop-assistant recognizing a customer personality for improving man-machine interactions. In: Recent Advances in Intelligent Information Systems, pp. 13–26 (2009)
24. Johannsen, F., Leist, S., Konadl, D., Basche, M., de Hesselle, B.: Comparison of commercial chatbot solutions for supporting customer interaction. In: European Conference on Information Systems, Portsmouth, England (2018)
25. Knaut, A.: How CSR should understand digitalization. In: Sustainability in a Digital World, pp. 249–256. Springer (2017)
26. Kottorp, M., Jäderberg, F: Chatbot as a potential tool for businesses: a study on chatbots made in collaboration with Bisnode (2017)
27. Kowalski, S., Pavlovska, K., Goldstein, M.: Two case studies in using chatbots for security training. In: Dodge, R.C., Futcher, L. (eds.) WISE 2009/2011/2013. IAICT, vol. 406, pp. 265–272. Springer, Heidelberg (2013). https://doi.org/10.1007/978-3-642-39377-8_31
28. Kusber, R.: Chatbots–conversational UX platforms. In: Innovationen und Innovationsmanagement in der Finanzbranche, pp. 231–244. Springer (2017)
29. Li, A.Q., Found, P.: Towards sustainability: PSS, digital technology and value co-creation. Procedia Cirp **64**, 79–84 (2017)
30. Liedtke, C., Kühlert, M., Huber, K., Baedeker, C.:Transition Design Guide: Design für Nachhaltigkeit; Gestalten für das Heute und Morgen; ein Guide für Gestaltung und Entwicklung in Unternehmen, Städten und Quartieren, Forschung und Lehre (2020)
31. March, S.T., Smith, G.F.: Design and natural science research on information technology. Decis. Support Syst. **15**(4), 251–266 (1995)
32. Meyer von Wolff, R., Masuch, K., Hobert, S., Schumann, M.: What Do You Need Today?-An Empirical Systematization of Application Areas for Chatbots at Digital Workplaces (2019)
33. Osbaldiston, R., Schott, J.P.: Environmental sustainability and behavioral science: meta-analysis of proenvironmental behavior experiments. Environ. Behav. **44**(2), 257–299 (2012)
34. Peniche-Avilés, J., Miranda-Palma, C., Narváez-Díaz, L., Llanes-Castro, E.: AluxBot-a chatbot that encourages the care for the environment. Int. J. Comput. Sci. Issues (IJCSI) **13**(6), 120 (2016)
35. Peffers, K., Tuunanen, T., Rothenberger, M.A., Chatterjee, S.: A design science research methodology for information systems research. J. Manag. Inf. Syst. **24**(3), 45–77 (2007)
36. Perugini, M., Bagozzi, R.P.: The role of desires and anticipated emotions in goal-directed behaviours: broadening and deepening the theory of planned behaviour. Br. J. Soc. Psychol. **40**(1), 79–98 (2001)
37. Piyatumrong, A., Sangkeettrakarn, C., Witdumrong, S., Cherdgone, J.: Chatbot technology adaptation to reduce the information gap in R&D center: a case study of an IT research organization. In: International Conference on Management of Engineering and Technology (PICMET), Portland, USA, pp. 1–9 (2018)
38. Raut, S.: A virtual chatbot for ITSM application. Asian J. Convergence Technol. **4**(I) (2018)

39. Salcu, A.V., Acatrinei, C.: Gamification applied in affiliate marketing. Case study of 2Parale. Manage. Market. **8**(4), 767 (2013)
40. Sandoval-Almazán, R., Gutiérrez-Alonso, M.A.: Virtual assistants for e-government interaction. In: Social and Political Implications of Data Mining: Knowledge Management in E-Government, pp. 255–266. IGI Global (2009)
41. Schneider, S.: The impacts of digital technologies on innovating for sustainability. In: Innovation for Sustainability, pp. 415–433. Springer (2019)
42. Schoormann, T., Stadtländer, M., Knackstedt, R.: Designing business model development tools for sustainability—a design science study. Electron Markets (2021)
43. Seele, P., Lock, I.: The game-changing potential of digitalization for sustainability: possibilities, perils, and pathways. Sustain. Sci. **12**(2), 183–185 (2017). https://doi.org/10.1007/s11 625-017-0426-4
44. Seidel, S., Chandra Kruse, L., Székely, N., Gau, M., Stieger, D.: Design principles for sensemaking support systems in environmental sustainability transformations. Eur. J. Inf. Syst. **27**(2), 221–247 (2018)
45. Seidel, S., Recker, J., Vom Brocke, J.: Sensemaking and sustainable practicing: functional affordances of information systems in green transformations. MIS Q. **37**(4), 1275–1299 (2013)
46. Söbke, H.: A case study of deep gamification in higher engineering education. In: Gentile, Manuel, Allegra, Mario, Söbke, Heinrich (eds.) GALA 2018. LNCS, vol. 11385, pp. 375–386. Springer, Cham (2019). https://doi.org/10.1007/978-3-030-11548-7_35
47. Steg, L., Vlek, C.: Encouraging pro-environmental behaviour: an integrative review and research agenda. J. Environ. Psychol. **29**(3), 309–317 (2019)
48. United Nations (UN): The 2030 Agenda. https://www.un.org/ga/search/view_doc.asp?symbol=A/RES/70/1&Lang=E. Accessed 11 Apr 2021
49. Vom Brocke, J., Simons, A., Niehaves, B., Riemer, K., Plattfaut, R., Cleven, A.: Reconstructing the giant: on the importance of rigour in documenting the literature search process. In: 17th European Conference on Information Systems, Verona, Italy, pp. 1–12 (2009)
50. Weizenbaum, J.: ELIZA—A computer program for the study of natural language communication between man and machine. Commun. ACM **9**(1), 36–45 (1966)
51. Zhao, D., McCoy, A.P., Du, J., Agee, P., Lu, Y.: Interaction effects of building technology and resident behavior on energy consumption in residential buildings. Energy Buildings **134**, 223–233 (2017)
52. Zumstein, D., Hundertmark, S.: Chatbots - An interactive technology for personalized communication transactions and services. IADIS Int. J. Internet **15**(1), 96–109 (2017)

RefineMind: A Mobile App for People with Dementia and Their Caregivers

Beenish Moalla Chaudhry$^{(\boxtimes)}$ ⓘ and Joy Smith ⓘ

University of Louisiana, Lafayette, LA 70504, USA
{beenish.chaudhry,joy.smith1}@louisiana.edu

Abstract. Although there is no cure for dementia, in the earlier disease stages, while symptoms are not very severe, some non-pharmacological treatments aimed towards memory support and social interactions may preserve autonomy and dignity of dementia patients. With this goal in mind, we designed a tablet application called *RefineMind* that refreshes and reminds patients of important details about themselves and others, and aids them with daily life tasks and interactions with caregivers. The app features a photo book, a medication reminder, a daily schedule reminder and a game module with interfaces designed using evidence-based principles. 5 caregivers of dementia patients assessed the app for its usability and provided feedback on the app's usefulness. The app received an average score of 86.5 on the System Usability Scale, which translates to excellent usability. All caregivers agreed that the app can improve interactions with their patients. A usability evaluation of the app is being planned with people with dementia.

Keywords: Dementia · Caregiver · Tablet app · Memory · Autonomy

1 Problem Statement

Though dementia is not a normal part of ageing, it is rapidly becoming prevalent in our older communities. About 5.8 million Americans are currently living with dementia and the number is expected to reach 13.8 million by 2050 [2]. Dementia refers to a range of conditions that progressively result in deterioration of brain function. The symptoms vary depending on the part of the brain impacted but, they typically include trouble following instructions, remembering steps in a process, staying engaged with a task and making choices. These cognitive difficulties are severe enough to interfere with the activities of daily living and negatively impact people's self-worth and autonomy [8].

Caregivers are often required to remind or help patients with their tasks and to address their agitation or discomfort. This reliance is often stressful for both dementia patients and caregivers, and impacts the quality of life of both individuals. Though there is no cure for dementia, in the earlier disease stages, while symptoms are not very severe, some "non-pharmacologic interventions" [6] aimed at promoting autonomy in dementia patients can help prevent caregiver burnout and improve quality of life of both patients

---

The original version of this chapter was revised: The multiple errors in data have been corrected in Abstract and sections 2.1, 2.2, 2.3, 3.1, 3.2, and 4. The name of the first author has been corrected as "Beenish Moalla Chaudhry". The correction to this chapter is available at https://doi.org/10.1007/978-3-030-82405-1_38

© Springer Nature Switzerland AG 2021, corrected publication 2022
L. Chandra Kruse et al. (Eds.): DESRIST 2021, LNCS 12807, pp. 16–21, 2021
https://doi.org/10.1007/978-3-030-82405-1_2

and caregivers. Autonomy is defined as independence and decision-making power. It is central to people's self-determination and feelings of worth [4], in addition to preserving their dignity, integrity and personhood [5]. Research confirms that people with dementia who still live at home strive to be independent and able, and express their sense of self (i.e. strive to maintain their autonomy) [7].

Evidence suggests that technology-based interventions are superior to usual care (without technology) when it comes to producing a positive impact on cognitive functions of people with mild to moderate dementia. This includes working memory and attention that improve with both general and domain-specific, technology-based training [15]. Some evidence also suggest that executive functions are positively affected [14]. It has also been shown that technology-based socialization tools can promote social interaction and encourage reminiscence, which not only benefits patient-caregiver relationships [12] but also improves cognition and quality of life of people with dementia [13].

Motivated by this knowledge, we created a prototype application called *RefineMind* for people in earlier stages of dementia and their caregivers. The goal of the application is to promote autonomy in people with dementia by providing memory support, and opportunities to practice reminiscence and refresh memory with information about self and others. We hypothesize that a memory support tool can reduce dementia patient's reliance on their caregivers and, hence promote autonomy of dementia patients.

2 Design of the Artifact

2.1 Intended User Groups

a) Rachel - Coping with Dementia. Rachel recently received a diagnosis that confirmed she has Alzheimer's. She is still in the early phase of the disease and maintains some of her cognition. Though, she has started experiencing some major changes in her life. Before she was diagnosed, she thrived on being with friends and family, and creating memories by organizing events and activities with them. But, with Alzheimer's, Rachel has started to forget some of her long-term memories. She is having problems recalling many important events of her life and has longer recall time to answer questions about herself. She does not remember and mixes up names of certain people. Other changes such as short-term memory problems have been the hardest to cope with. She can still do her daily routine but often forgets the steps involved in everyday chores such as bathing, cooking, taking medications, etc. She is looking for a tool that can help her keep her memories fresh and give her reminders about daily chores.

b) Dan - Caregiver to Rachel. Dan is Rachel's husband as well as her caregiver. He is looking for resources and tips to improve the quality of time that he is spending with Rachel. Although he is doing a lot for Rachel, he also understands that Rachel should be able to perform some daily tasks on her own so her dependence on him is minimized. For example, he wants her to take her medications correctly on time, go out for walks by herself, not forget who she is, etc. He also wants Rachel to maintain memories of her past for as long as it does not strain her. Moreover, he has noticed that Rachel enjoys playing games and he thinks that mentally stimulating activities will be useful for her. He is hoping for tool that he can customize with what Rachel needs for her daily use.

2.2 Use Cases

a) Learning about Oneself. Dan notices that Rachel is having a hard time remembering who she is today. He encourages Rachel to view important details about herself on *RefineMind*. Rachel opens up the app on her tablet and enters 'All About Me' section, where she reviews important details about herself including her name, birthday, home address, and more. She then decides to test herself by entering the quiz section. There she answers several multiple choice questions and receives the report which shows that she answered more correct answers than the last time she took the quiz.

b) Remembering Shared History. It has been a while since Dan and Rachel spent some quality time together. Today, Rachel seems a little agitated because she has not been able to do anything for herself. Dan wants to make her feel better, so he brings the tablet to her and goes into the special moments section, where he has uploaded family and event photos that Rachel likes. They start looking at some pictures together. Dan clicks on Rachel's 40th birthday picture and the tablet starts playing an audio clip that Rachel had recorded earlier about her birthday party. All of a sudden, Rachel gets excited and adds more details to the story told by the tablet. Dan responds by laughing and sharing his interest. Rachel feels wonderful about the fact that she shared something and made someone laugh. She also feels that talking about her birthday is bringing back happy memories and good feelings, which is wonderful for both her and Dan. Dan adds a star to the birthday picture so it is saved to Rachel's favorites.

c) Getting Reminders. At 11 am, *RefindMind* sends a medication reminder to Rachel's smartwatch. Rachel feels a tingling sensation on her wrist and sees that her smartwatch is blinking. She touches screen of her smartwatch's screen and sees a picture of her medication. She knows that it is time to take her medication. She goes into her kitchen and takes her medication. She then clicks on her smartwatch to record that she has taken her medication. At 1 pm, she feels another tingling sensation on her wrist. She looks at her smartwatch's dial face and sees that she has a 3 pm doctor's appointment. She opens her tablet and reviews additional details. Rachel is happy and begins to get ready for her ride.

2.3 Description of Features

With *RefineMind* [11] (Fig. 1a), users can recall information about themselves and their lives through the use of pictures, video, audio, and text. It also aims to improve the relationship between dementia patients and their caregivers by acting as a conversation starter on topics of interest. Users can receive reminders related to their daily schedules. Caregivers can customize the application according to patient's needs.

a) Photo Book. This feature has three sections: "All about Me", "Family and Friends", and "Special Moments", with photos on the selected topic (Fig. 1c). For example, "Family and Friends" has photos of family members and friends. The user can click a picture to listen to a recorded memory or record a new one.

b) Daily Schedule. The user will be able to see what tasks and events have been planned for the day, including to-do lists, appointments, and reminders. The user can also add new items to the daily schedules and set additional reminders.

c) Medication. This feature allows users to review their medication intake history, prescribed medications along with time and dosage information. Users can also update medication information, and set up intake reminders.

Fig. 1. (a) Home Screen (b) Brain Games Main Screen (c) A PhotoBook Screen

d) Brain Games. Here users can play different games, e.g. quizzes and puzzles (Fig. 1b), to stimulate their minds, and refresh their memories about themselves, life events and people they know.

e) Get Help. Each screen has a Get Help button that allows user to easily access instructions or helpful tips about each screen. If, at any time, the user gets confused, they can turn on help to learn how different screen components work.

f) Edit settings. Each screen has an edit feature that allows the caregiver to set up the app with patient's information. Patients can also use it to customize app's appearance, e.g. adjust text size and background mode.

3 Significance of the Artifact

3.1 Significance to Research

Much of dementia research has focused on the biomedical aspects of the disease [10], knowledge on how to effectively meet the care needs of individuals living at home between the initial diagnosis of dementia and potential institutionalization is rather limited [9]. Support for memory problems and reminiscence is the unmet need most frequently mentioned by people with dementia and their caregivers. Small-scale studies of devices supporting memory in dementia patients appear promising, but a robust evaluation of such tools is still pending. The impact of technology-based cognitive training on mood (e.g., depression, anxiety) and physical abilities (e.g., cooking, walking) of target individuals is less convincing due to inconsistent findings across studies. Moreover, game-based cognitive trainings have not been evaluated in people with dementia. *RefindMind* provides us with the opportunity to explore these areas further.

3.2 Significance to Practice

Several gaming, task list and medicine tracker apps exist but *RefineMind* provides everything in one place. Users do not have to download multiple applications. Other gaming apps in the market usually quiz people with dementia on random questions, which they find difficult to relate to or uninteresting. *RefineMind* game questions are not random, simply to test knowledge, but they are personalized to users and their lives. This helps keep people's mind refreshed on the things they encounter the most. The users are also able to keep all their most important memories, information, pictures, videos, or audio stored and organized in one place for easy access. The app aims to emulate the best practices in caring for people with dementia [3] and apply evidence-based principles in the design of its user interfaces [1]. Hence, people with dementia and their caregivers should be able to immediately apply the app in their daily lives and practice. Caregivers can use it as a talking prompt to improve their interactions with their dementia patients. People with dementia can use it to stimulate their minds and keep themselves engaged and, hopefully, reduce their dependence on others.

4   Evaluation of the Artifact

We assessed the usability (i.e. ease of use) of *RefineMind* with five caregivers of people with dementia to identify technical issues and ease of navigation (i.e. do participants understand what to do and can they do it without assistance). The caregivers were asked to perform specific tasks such as upload a photo, set a reminder, update schedule. Afterwards, participants completed the System Usability Scale (SUS). They then commented on the app's usefulness, and discussed potential use cases.

The prototype received an average score of 86.5 on SUS, which translates to excellent or Grade A usability. Participants found the app easy to navigate and successfully completed all of the assigned tasks during the usability test (Effectiveness: 100%). Everyone agreed that the application was a good idea and concept, and that it has the potential to help people with dementia. Some comments made by the participants are given below.

Participant 1. *"This application could really help and support people with dementia and Alzheimer's. I do think some of the instructions and help text can be a bit clearer and maybe add some cool effects or make the game portion more interactive."*

Participant 2. *"The app is an idea. The helpful tips and larger text are great for older individuals. This design is very simple, which I like! With my experience, people with dementia and Alzheimer need more help and guidance. The photo book concept with the pop up text can really help with recall. A few patients of mine would always mix up name and faces of people, so I think if they used this app it could help with that. The medicine and schedule is a good addition, considering they tend to have trouble remembering those types of things."*

Participant 3. *"Overall I think the application is a great concept. I think it can really help some people who struggle with memory issues. It could help some of my patients with dementia. It can be a fun little tool to use when I'm sitting with them besides just watching television. The brain games with questions on things related to the owner of the app is also a great touch to help their memory."*

Some updates and changes recommended by caregivers included improving the comprehensibility and readability of written text and instructions, revamping the brain games to be "fun" and interactive, and simplifying schedule and medication management tasks. To accommodate these requests, we are planning to conduct participatory design workshops to conduct task analysis with dementia patients.

Even though the prototype has received a high usability rating from the caregivers, it does not represent the feedback of dementia patients. A usability study is currently being planned with dementia patients. In the near future, we will conduct an efficacy trial to assess the impact of the application on the quality of life of the target population. Intended consequences of the app (e.g. instances of missed medications, number of laughs or duration of memory sharing during a reminiscence session, number of completed daily task reminders, perceived carer burden, etc.) will be collected to measure impact.

References

1. Ancient, C., Good, A.: Issues with designing dementia-friendly interfaces. In: Stephanidis, Constantine (ed.) HCI 2013. CCIS, vol. 373, pp. 192–196. Springer, Heidelberg (2013). https://doi.org/10.1007/978-3-642-39473-7_39
2. Association, A.: 2019 alzheimer's disease facts and figures. Alzheimer's Dement. **15**(3), 321–387 (2019)
3. Providing everyday care to dementia patients (2021). https://alzheimer.ca/en/help-support/im-caring-person-living-dementia
4. Fetherstonhaugh, D., Tarzia, L., Nay, R.: Being central to decision making means i am still here!: the essence of decision making for people with dementia. J. Aging Studies **27**(2), 143–150 (2013)
5. Gallagher, A., Li, S., Wainwright, P., Jones, I.R., Lee, D.: Dignity in the care of older people–a review of the theoretical and empirical literature. BMC Nurs. **7**(1), 1–12 (2008)
6. Gitlin, L.N., Kales, H.C., Lyketsos, C.G.: Nonpharmacologic management of behavioral symptoms in dementia. JAMA **308**(19), 2020–2029 (2012)
7. Hedman, R., Hansebo, G., Ternestedt, B.M., Hellstr¨om, I., Norberg, A.: Expressed sense of self by people with alzheimer's disease in a support group interpreted in terms of agency and communion. J. Appl. Gerontol. **35**(4), 421–443 (2016)
8. Knopman, D.S., Boeve, B.F., Petersen, R.C.: Essentials of the proper diagnoses of mild cognitive impairment, dementia, and major subtypes of dementia. In: Mayo Clinic Proceedings, vol. 78, pp. 1290–1308. Elsevier (2003)
9. Mountain, G.A.: Self-management for people with early dementia: an exploration of concepts and supporting evidence. Dementia **5**(3), 429–446 (2006)
10. Steeman, E., De Casterl´e, B.D., Godderis, J., Grypdonck, M.: Living with early-stage dementia: a review of qualitative studies. J. Adv. Nurs. **54**(6), 722–738 (2006)
11. Refinemind: A mobile app for people with dementia (2021). https://youtu.be/xfTeGMkiHjw
12. Astell, A.J., et al.: Using a touch screen computer to support relationships between people with dementia and caregivers. Interact. Comput. **22**(4), 267–275 (2010)
13. Astell, A.J., Smith, S.K., Potter, S., Preston-Jones, E.: Computer interactive reminiscence and conversation aid groups—delivering cognitive stimulation with technology. Alzheimer's Dement. Transl. Res. Clin. Interv. **4**, 481–487 (2018)
14. Burdea, G., et al.: Feasibility study of the brightbrainerTM integrative cognitive rehabilitation system for elderly with dementia. Disabil. Rehabil. Assistive Technol. **10**(5), 421–432 (2015)
15. Nousia, A., et al.: Beneficial effect of multidomain cognitive training on the neuropsychological performance of patients with early-stage alzheimer's disease. Neural Plast **2018** (2018)

Building a Vulnerability Index of Biological and Socioeconomic Risk Factors to Combat COVID-19 Spread

Thomas Roderick[1] (iD), Yolande Pengetnze[1] (iD), Steve Miff[1] (iD),
Monica Chiarini Tremblay[2](✉) (iD), and Rajiv Kohli[2] (iD)

[1] Parkland Center for Clinical Information, Dallas, TX 75247, USA
{thomas.roderick,yolande.pengetnze,steve.miff}@pccinnovation.org
[2] William and Mary, Williamsburg, VA 23185, USA
{monica.tremblay,rajiv.kohli}@mason.wm.edu

Abstract. In early 2020, many community leaders faced high uncertainty regarding their local communities' health and safety, which impacts their response to the pandemic, public health messaging, and other factors in guiding their communities on how to remain healthy. Making decisions regarding resources was particularly difficult in Dallas, Texas, USA where local communities face stark differences in social determinants of health, such as availability of fresh foods and environmental pollution. We use an action design research approach to develop an index to assess vulnerability, which incorporates both long-term COVID-19 community risk measures and ongoing dynamic measures of the pandemic. Community and public health officials utilize the index in making critical policy and strategic decisions while guiding their communities during COVID-19 and in future crises.

Keywords: Index · COVID-19 · Social determinants of health · Action design research

1 Introduction

A pandemic affects a community, which is a geographically interconnected area where people of many backgrounds, demographics, and relative health levels interact. At the beginning of the COVID-19 pandemic, many local leaders faced a lack of information regarding how the disease may play out in their local community. Questions included where to test, whether a full community lockdown was required, whether certain essential services could be shutdown, and which individuals were that faced significant risk to the disease. In Dallas County, Texas (United States) communities faced stark differences in socioeconomic elasticity. The research team, which included researchers from Parkland Center for Clinical Innovation (PCCI), used an action design research approach (ADR) [1] to develop an index to capture community vulnerability index (VI) in order to assist community leaders in strategic planning. PCCI, a healthcare data science non-profit research group associated with Parkland Health Hospital System (PHHS), has partnered

L. Chandra Kruse et al. (Eds.): DESRIST 2021, LNCS 12807, pp. 22–33, 2021.
https://doi.org/10.1007/978-3-030-82405-1_3

with Dallas County Health and Human Services as well as several healthcare systems across North Texas to develop technology and research solutions and to address the needs of the most vulnerable communities using social determinants of health (SDOH). Social determinants of health can have a major impact on people's health, well-being, and quality of life. Some examples of SDOH include: 1) safe housing, transportation, and neighborhoods, 2) racism, discrimination, and violence, 3) education, job opportunities, and income [2].

The VI incorporated factors for both static COVID-19 community risk measures and ongoing dynamic measures in the community. We apply the ADR framework to describe our problem formulation, the building, intervention, and evaluation (BIE) of our index and subsequent reflection and learning.

2 Problem Formulation

When the World Health Organization (WHO) Director-General announced COVID-19 as a pandemic on March 11, 2020, it brought immediate attention to a situation that, for many, was occurring far away [3]. Community and public health leaders, researchers, and the public were bereft of actionable insight and sought answers to questions such as:

- Which communities are most at-risk due to their population demographics?
- where should testing efforts be targeted to ensure access, coverage, and equity, especially when supplies of drugs and equipment are limited?
- When vaccines become available, what programming should be used to ensure community focus on equitable access and correct information to target resources to areas at highest risk?

Cerise et al. [4], authored by Dallas County public health officials and local health leaders, described the need *"to reduce the spread of infection, to identify and engage with those who are considered to be vulnerable and at high risk of contracting the virus, and to plan for community interventions through mapping and hotspotting."*

2.1 Actionable Insight Needed to Combat a Pandemic

As the pandemic reached the North Texas region, the PCCI research group was entrusted to interpret and recommend actionable analysis and intelligence for COVID-19 in the Dallas metro area. The analysis sought to incorporate long-term risk factors, immediate needs, healthcare access, and community equity. We developed the VI, which incorporated community-level factors associated with known COVID-19 risk and ongoing dynamic measures to capture the evolution of the pandemic. The VI assisted the community and public health officials as they made critical policy and strategic decisions while equitably allocating resources in guiding their communities through the crisis.

2.2   Health Outcomes and Social Determinants of Health

The synergistic interaction of socioeconomic, environmental, and biological factors primarily drives health outcomes. Eighty percent of health outcomes depend on social determinants of health compared to only twenty percent on clinical care [5]. As the COVID-19 pandemic swept through the world, the early response experience made it clear that any policy or Public Health intervention would have to carefully consider each community's socioeconomic and biological context to control pandemic impact on the community effectively. The multi-disciplinary team brought clinical area theories as an impetus to our design of VI [6]. The ecological model of disease prevention highlights the importance of people's interaction with their physical and social environments and the interdependence of individual and ecological risk factors in disease prevention programs [7]. Different levels of factors are considered in the ecological model of disease prevention, including intrapersonal factors (e.g., knowledge, attitudes, and beliefs), interpersonal factors (e.g., interactions with other individuals), institutional and organizational factors (e.g., institutional policies and practices), community factors (e.g., community norms about healthcare), and Public Policy factors (e.g., Public Health authority's decision about lockdown, isolation, or quarantine). The ecological model of healthcare was well-suited in the context of the COVID-19 pandemic to guide the building and implementation of the VI in a manner that captured the complex interplay of health status, social determinants of health, response to Public Health containment measures, and advanced age to measure an individual's risk for COVID-19 infection.

COVID-19 is a highly contagious respiratory disease transmitted by droplets or airborne particles. Historically, epidemics of droplet or airborne diseases have disproportionately affected populations in the lower socioeconomic strata for reasons such as personal and social practices in the community, crowded living conditions, and inability to observe effective Public Health measures such as isolation, quarantine, or gathering restrictions [8]. Moreover, low-wage workers lack the economic resilience necessary to miss long stretches of workdays due to isolation, quarantine, or lockdown measures, leading to higher risks for occupational or community exposure to spreading diseases [8]. As a result, COVID-19 morbidity and mortality disproportionately affect low socioeconomic populations and racial and ethnic minorities [9], and COVID-19 outbreaks occur in low-wage occupational settings such as livestock plants [10] where working conditions are tenuous and personal protective equipment scarce.

COVID-19 disease severity and mortality also are exacerbated by biological factors such as advanced age ($>=65$ years old) and underlying chronic diseases, including obesity, diabetes, cardiopulmonary diseases, and hypertension [11–13]. These underlying health conditions also disproportionately affect lower socioeconomic populations and racial/ethnic minorities [9], partly driven by the same social risk factors driving COVID-19 infection and further illustrating the complex interplay between social and biological risk factors.

Our challenge, therefore, was to build and validate a comprehensive index that captures the complex interaction of biological and socioeconomic risk factors to quantify population-level vulnerability to COVID-19 infection. The novel COVID-19 vulnerability index would support a holistic and equitable approach to designing, prioritizing, and evaluating policies and interventions to mitigate the pandemic.

3 Building, Intervention and Evaluation

ADR emphasizes the inseparable influences mutually exerted by the IT artifact and the organizational context [1]. Development of the artifact occurred with active input from the community, public health, and healthcare leaders in the area. Figure 1 shows the outcome of design sessions with external stakeholders in the North Texas healthcare systems and public health offices and identifies the expected risk drivers.

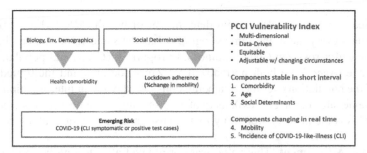

Fig. 1. Model design

The risk of COVID-19 comorbidity is heightened both by pre-existing health conditions and by a person's potential for exposure to the disease: biology, environment, demographics, and social determinants of health impact health comorbidities. Social determinants of health impact both ongoing health comorbidities as well as capacity to adhere to public health guidance (annotated in Fig. 1 as lockdown adherence). Increased comorbidity and incapacity to lock down or otherwise minimize risky behavior during a pandemic heighten a person's potential for exposure to disease. This behavior may be driven by personal and familial situations, which may prevent adhering to public health policy such as recommended lockdowns, social distancing from neighbors and community members, keeping children home from school, and so forth.

The VI can be defined as an organization-dominant BIE, as we generated design knowledge where the primary source of innovation is organizational intervention, in this case, to deal with a public health crisis. With existing connections to several non-profits, data aggregators, and local community organizations, we built the VI identify geographic areas where local communities faced risk in all dimensions. The data sources included the US Census, SafeGraph (mobility data provider)[1], Dallas County Health and Human Services, Dallas/Fort Worth Hospital Council Foundation, and University of Wisconsin Madison Area Deprivation Index (ADI) [14–16].

3.1 Building the Vulnerability Index

Following the initial presentation, we worked with community organizations to determine the distribution of known COVID-19 comorbidity at a geographic level and coordinated with hospital and public health groups to validate the artifact. Our VI is the resulting metric and contains two combined components: static and dynamic.

---

[1] https://www.safegraph.com/.

Static Component. The value for each geographic area is formulated as the product of ranks for each geographic area under consideration. A geographic area here can be a Zip code or a Census Tract. Each factor is normalized and ranked from lowest (0) to highest (1) risk. The static component is then created by the product of the normalized ranks, and highlights areas that have relatively higher vulnerability in all factors. The static component is shown in Eq. (1) below.

$$S_i = rank(SDOH_i) \times rank(Com_i) \times rank(Aged_i) \tag{1}$$

The area deprivation index, social determinant of health ($SDOH_i$), is normalized by definition – everyone in the same geography has the same value and can have that value compared across Zip Codes. Comorbid proportion (Com_i) and population with advanced age ($Aged_i$) are both normalized by Zip Code area and multiplied by the percent of the population over the area being considered, with an interpretation that the resulting values are comparable as density of area and number of people impacted within the area. This is the primary weighting that we use in the evaluation, along with other weighting approaches.

Dynamic Adjustment. This value was formulated after testing became available after the early July 2020 peak to understand the short run components affecting the disease. This is a qualitative overlay to the static VI to highlight where active cases concentrate current risk. Two risk factors were included: (1) "stay-at-home" rate defined as the year-over-year increase in a geographic area's adherence to social distancing; (2) active case-load present in the local community. The Dynamic adjustment was formulated as rank of the product of mobility change multiplied by the active case density weighted by the percent of population in the Zip Code.

Composite Vulnerability Index. The composite VI was implemented after the initial July 2020 peak, containing the Static Component and Dynamic Adjustment normalized to July 2020 to allow for monthly comparison. This is calculated as the product of the two components.

The feedback from public health officials, community leaders, and other health-care research groups was carefully considered and, where appropriate, incorporated into the design of the artifact. The VI now includes a mix of stable and dynamic factors that identifies COVID-19 vulnerability when all factors are relatively higher than neighboring areas. The community responded directly and immediately to prioritization decisions taking into account the risk identified in the VI artifact. The community utilized the VI for decisions 1) to choose COVID-19 testing site location, 2) deployment of mobile testing units, 3) as an input into healthcare workflows to help anticipate COVID-19 risk for upcoming outpatient/ambulatory surgical appointments, 4) for public communication of risk levels in the county, and 5) as input into vaccine education communications and targeted marketing for communities with less internet penetration. This early success led to interest by external healthcare research institutions, community organizations, and innovation groups in the artifact as we shared our preliminary findings, resulting in discussion and feedback from groups across the US regarding use, improvements, and other directions that the VI artifact could be employed as a cohesive pandemic response package in other communities. Formal presentations included the Institute for Healthcare Improvement, SafeGraph COVID-19 Symposium Elevate

Health, United Way Metropolitan Dallas Aspired United 2030, and Dallas healthcare and community leaders. The dynamic components of the VI artifact (discussed above) are updated monthly, and this updated information is distributed to the public and critical healthcare stakeholders in the region. We anticipate that static factors will be evaluated annually as data sources are updated each year.

3.2 Evaluation

This section describes the data used for the artifact and the findings and validation of the VI artifact.

Data definitions and descriptions. The data includes community (Zip Code)-level information. The summary statistics for the data are shown in Table 1.

1. **Cases:** Positive-tested COVID-19 cases at a Zip Code level collected as of May 19, 2020, the date of initial evaluation.
2. **Cases, different bias:** COVID-19-like illnesses (CLI) captured by a local area hospital, aggregated to a Zip Code level as of May 19, 2020 date. This comes from people who felt sick enough to seek medical care within the healthcare system, which avoids potential biases like time capacity for testing or similar selection bias considerations.
3. **Comorbid population:** Proportion of comorbid population living within a Zip Code across Dallas County, as defined by individuals receiving an Inpatient visit in the prior two years from over 80% of the North Texas hospital network. (Data sourced from the Dallas Fort Worth Hospital Council Foundation, a local health information exchange. This captures where the population is located that may be susceptible to COVID-19. The comorbid populations included at the time of initial VI build included ICD10 diagnosis classifications available from the Centers for Medicare and Medicaid Chronic Condition Warehouse (CMS CCW). The conditions include irritable bowel syndrome, rheumatoid arthritis, heart failure, ischemic heart failure, atrial fibrillation, acute myocardial infarction, asthma, hypertension, chronic obstructive pulmonary disease, chronic kidney disease, diabetes, obesity, leukemia, multiple sclerosis, cystic fibrosis, and selected cancers.
4. **Demographic information:** was extracted from the US Census American Community Survey (ACS) population total estimates and population aged 65 and older. For race and ethnicity equity assessment, including Hispanic, black non-Hispanic, white non-Hispanic, and other non-Hispanic estimates are used to define community proportions of the group being considered.
5. **Social Determinants of Health:** Area Deprivation Index (ADI), a social determinants of health measure provided by the University of Wisconsin Madison (version 2, 2015), consisting of the nationwide percentile at a Census Blockgroup level. We aggregate this to the Zip Code level using the ACS 2018 population-weighted average.
6. **Mobility Information:** data from SafeGraph, a private data broker that provides aggregated anonymous information for travel between geographic areas, as well as no-mobile rates (also known as stay-at-home rates). The treatment on this variable was to assess the stay-at-home rate during the height of the pandemic (from 5/1/2020 to 5/14/2020) versus a baseline (from 2/14/2020 to 2/28/2020) of normal activity.

Table 1. Early July 2020, static component data for 94 Dallas County Zip Codes

Variable by Zip Code	Mean	StdDev
Positive cases count (through 5/19/2020)	82.4	78.78
CLI count (through 5/19/2020)	21.59	22.91
Comorbidity proportion	1.1%	0.7%
Total population	32,310	20,462
Population 65+	3,257	2,149
Hispanic population	12,121	12,244
Black, non-Hispanic population	6,822	7,433
White, non-Hispanic population	10,395	8,384
Other, non-Hispanic population	2,972	3,563
ADI	51	21
Mobility stay-at-Home rate increase	13.9%	4.6%

3.3 Evaluation

We conduct three assessments, replicated in Python, R, and Excel, to evaluate the static VI component for relevance to COVID-19, for equity assessment, and for different normalization schema. The first assessment looked at the correlation of community COVID-19 cases to the artifact relative to individual components. Because disease testing bias may be present in confirmed cases (e.g., tests have a time and expense cost, information and access may also be a concern), we compare the Dallas County reported cases, as well as COVID-19-like illnesses (symptomatic diagnoses) collected by a local health system over the same time period. This measure does not face the same testing biases since only symptomatic cases presented are collected.

Table 2. May 19, 2020, COVID-19 pandemic cumulative cases with static component

Rank dorrelation with COVID-19 densities	PHHS COVID-like Illness (CLI)	DCHHS confirmed positive
VI static component	87%	85%
Density of comorbidities	68%	65%
Density of elderly population	64%	63%
Social determinants of health	40%	34%

Table 2 shows the outcomes of these assessments; columns show the Dallas County confirmed cases and the PHHS CLI counts, and each row shows the VI artifact and component correlations to COVID-19 cases. A key result is that our VI artifact performs better than any individual factor in correlating to the Dallas County confirmed cases per Zip Code.

For the second assessment, we compared the artifact to race and ethnicity using partial correlation controlling for factors to understand equity impact (Table 3). This assessment was performed by correlating PHHS CLI cases to the demographic group population-weighted density residing in a specific geography. We implemented controls via partial correlation. This assessment indicates that social determinants of health improved equity of the index. Controlling solely for comorbidity or elderly population increased disparity relative to the uncontrolled correlation, whereas controlling for social determinants of health reduced (but did not eliminate) community differences due to racial and ethnicity composition. Note that controlling for Social Determinants of Health do not eliminate disparity, but substantially reduce disparity.

Table 3. Equity Impact, correlation of population weighted case- and demographic-group densities in Dallas County Zip Codes

Rank correlation, Weighted CLI to group population density	Black, non-Hispanic	Hispanic	Other, non-Hispanic	White, non-Hispanic	Max difference
Full correlation	65%	84%	29%	38%	55%
Control: social determinants of health	63%	85%	61%	78%	24%
Control: comorbidity	31%	68%	−25%	−18%	93%
Control: elderly population density	43%	72%	−32%	−33%	105%

Finally, we compared different factor weighting methods and interpretations as robustness checks for the weighting approach utilized (Table 4). We did not weight Social Determinants of Health (contained in the Area Deprivation Index) because they are already normalized across Zip Codes.

Figure 2 shows the static component's correlation to cumulative caseloads through the dates listed in the horizontal axis, showing both rank and Pearson correlations against COVID-19 caseload in each zip code in Dallas County. The relationship is stable and robust through the pandemic, highlighting that the artifact captured COVID-19 community risk.

The dynamic adjustment does not include a formal assessment, as it is domain expert input to weight areas relative to their active caseloads and known risks (static portion). The first months of deployment and subsequent assessment resulted in a final normalized artifact that allowed a Zip Code to be compared over time and across the geographies. The impact of the use of the static and dynamic components of the VI in County and

Table 4. Comparison of weighting method alternatives

Weighting method	Interpretation	PHH CLI rank correlation	DCHHS positive rank correlation
Raw	Raw factors and raw cases correlated	78.2%	76.0%
Population normalized	Factor percent and case percent of population[a]	41.4%	33.9%
Density and % Of Population	Density and proportion of population in the total area identifies the risk to what proportion of the total population	87.1%	85.2%
Case Burden (inverse, density, and population)	A robustness check; if the same number of cases are observed in a diffuse population, then something is very concerning about the spread in this population	85.9%	74.5%

[a]Note that this is a common public-health approach, to normalize by population. Unfortunately, this does not account for density.

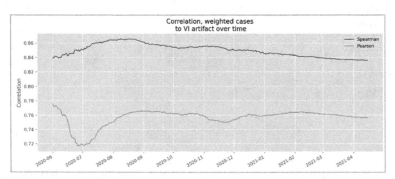

Fig. 2. COVID-19 pandemic cumulative cases with VI static factor index. (Source: Authors' Calculations across cumulative Dallas County confirmed cases over time.)

PHHS planning are documented in Cerise et al. [4], including, but not limited to, testing center placement, vaccine programming, and other community efforts.

4   Reflection and Learning

The factors below detail our approach for building a vulnerability index and can be readily replicated in other geographies. Based upon our experiences, we propose seven design guidelines on how to extend our VI to other geographical areas. In Table 5, we present the guidelines, and the approaches taken to build the VI. We separate stable risks from short-run factors and define stable, long-term risks as attributes associated with COVID-19 mortality that cannot be changed, either permanently or across a timeframe of several years. We define short-run factors as attributes that change frequently and may be especially amenable to policy intervention or community action. G1–G4 constitute the stable risks guidelines, and G5—G7 constitute short run factors.

5   Formalization of Learning

From what we learned building the VI, we have started to incorporate these design guidelines into building new indices, as well as continuously improving the current index as the issues of the pandemic change. This approach has directly or indirectly guided other index developments since early 2020. We formalize the learning from the VI development as:

1. The **continued evolution of the VI** dynamic portion, incorporating vaccination of the COVID-19 susceptible population and removal of the mobility factor after masking became more prevalent in late Summer.
2. **School Vulnerability**: Using a similar design approach and framework, school campuses were evaluated for long term needs in a pandemic, including capacity to switch to virtual learning, ongoing student need such as subsidized meals, access to internet, and neighborhood safety as pre-existing factors. Dynamic factors include caseloads in school catchment areas and mobility measures to school campuses weighted by caseloads to capture potential campus employee vectors.
3. **Social Needs Index**, which follows the static VI component constructive framework to classify community social elasticity risk beyond COVID-19.
4. As an input for the **Proximity Index**, which is a healthcare provider workflow prioritization approach assessing immediate risk of nearby COVID-19 cases with community vulnerability.

Our general finding is that, from an ADR evaluation perspective, the VI artifact approach helps to organize available information, domain understanding, ongoing evaluation, and data-driven policy inputs in situations with high risk where immediate threats can adversely impact healthcare services and community well-being.

Table 5. Guidelines for creating a vulnerability index

	Guideline	Our approach
G1	Define a regional geographic boundary of interest, and subdivisions of this geography	Dallas County zip codes, due to data availability
G2	Identify available static or long-term, hard-to-change factors from available data sources	Social determinants of health, demographic and comorbid health measures for population factors
G3	Rank each factor between 0 and 1, with 0 representing the lowest risk and 1 representing the highest risk within a factor's dimension. Consider population weighting factors, if appropriate	We needed a view that ranked high when all factors were high
G4	Define the metric to rank static risk on a single dimension	If the domain or questions require that all factors be high, take the geometric average or simple product of the scored values. If the domain risk is specified such that any factor having heightened risk is of concern, use the maximum of the factors
G5	Determine short-run factor data sources and apply a similar methodology rank weighting methodology	We used mobility to help determine areas more likely at risk due to population network effects, especially early on
G6	Identify existing quantified risk	We used active cases in an area to ascertain where the absolute risk would be highest. We normalized this using the highest Zip Code caseload during a peak to make monthly comparisons available to a standard reference point
G7	Evolve the short-run factors as needed	As a control item, we used the number of vaccinations that would lower the susceptible population. As more of the population is vaccinated, the level of risk is lower, both due to susceptible population decrease as well as vaccine efficacy

6 Conclusion and Future Work

Continued formalization of the index generation approach through Action Design Research will allow for extensions of the original VI artifact as well as other artifacts and high-level metrics to assess vulnerabilities. As an approach for pandemic response, it informs stakeholders and the public regarding what they can anticipate as their community's risk. Further, the design approach in the space of healthcare ensures that social determinants of health and human behavior considerations are included in public health policy risk assessments and response. Finally, the community risk approach can be used across numerous social health domains and the ADR approach used in creating this artifact ties health, social science, and technology for the improvement of policy creation and understanding of tradeoffs.

Future work in applying ADR to improving community resilience includes expanding to other COVID-19 affected areas, generating a formal behavioral response theory incorporating social determinants of health and similar socioeconomic measures with effectiveness impact on policies implemented during crises, and to evaluation of risk during more common high-risk occurrences such as natural disasters or utilities and infrastructure failures.

References

1. Sein, M.K., Henfridsson, O., Purao, S., Rossi, M., Lindgren, R.: Action design research. MIS Quar. **35**, 37–56 (2011)
2. Office of Disease Prevention and Health Promotion: Social determinants of health (nd). https://health.gov/healthypeople/objectives-and-data/social-determinants-health. Accessed on 2021
3. Cucinotta, D., Vanelli, M.: WHO Declares COVID-19 a pandemic. Acta bio-medica: Atenei Parmensis **91**(1), 157–160 (2020). https://doi.org/10.23750/abm.v91i1.9397
4. Cerise, F.P., Moran, B., Huang, P.P., Bhavan, K.P.: The imperative for integrating public health and health care delivery systems. NEJM Catal. Innov. Care Deliv. **2**(4) (2021)
5. Manatt Health: Medicaid's Role in Addressing Social Determinants of Health. Health Policy in Brief: Robert Wood Johnson Foundation (2019)
6. Chiasson, M.W., Davidson, E.: Taking industry seriously in information systems research. MIS Quar.**29**, 591–605 (2005)
7. National Cancer Institute: Theory at a glance : a guide for health promotion practice
8. Guide for health promotion practice: U.S. Deptartment of Health and Human Services, Public Health Service, National Institutes of Health, National Cancer Institute, Bethesda, Md (1995)
9. Blumenshine, P., Reingold, A., Egerter, S., Mockenhaupt, R., Braveman, P., Marks, J.: Pandemic influenza planning in the United States from a health disparities perspective. Emerg. Infect. Dis. J. **14**(5), 709 (2008). https://doi.org/10.3201/eid1405.071301
10. CDC: COVID-19 Racial and Ethnic Disparities (2020). https://www.cdc.gov/coronavirus/2019-ncov/community/health-equity/racial-ethnic-disparities/disparities-illness.html. Accessed on April 2021
11. Taylor, C.A., Boulos, C., Almond, D.: Livestock plants and COVID-19 transmission. Proc. Natl. Acad. Sci. **117**(50), 31706–31715 (2020). https://doi.org/10.1073/pnas.2010115117
12. CDC: Underlying Medical Conditions Associated with High Risk for Severe COVID-19: Information for Healthcare Providers (2020). https://www.cdc.gov/coronavirus/2019-ncov/hcp/clinical-care/underlyingconditions.html. Accessed on April 2021.
13. Rosenthal, N., Cao, Z., Gundrum, J., Sianis, J., Safo, S.: Risk factors associated with in-hospital mortality in a US national sample of patients With COVID-19. JAMA Netw. Open **3**(12), e2029058 (2020). https://doi.org/10.1001/jamanetworkopen.2020.29058
14. Williamson, E.J., Walker, A.J., Bhaskaran, K., Bacon, S., Bates, C., Morton, C.E., et al.: Factors associated with COVID-19-related death using OpenSAFELY. Nature **584**(7821), 430–436 (2020). https://doi.org/10.1038/s41586-020-2521-4
15. Kind, A.J.H., Buckingham, W.R.: Making neighborhood-disadvantage metrics accessible—the neighborhood atlas. N. Engl. J. Med. **378**(26), 2456–2458 (2018). https://doi.org/10.1056/NEJMp1802313
16. University of Wisconsin School of Medicine and Public Health. Area Deprivation Index, 2 edn (2018)

A Health Service Delivery Relational Agent for the COVID-19 Pandemic

Ashraful Islam[1]([✉]) [iD], Mohammad Masudur Rahman[2] [iD], Md Faisal Kabir[3] [iD], and Beenish Chaudhry[1] [iD]

[1] University of Louisiana at Lafayette, Lafayette, LA 70503, USA
ashraful.islam1@louisiana.edu
[2] Bangladesh University of Engineering and Technology, Dhaka 1000, Bangladesh
[3] Pennsylvania State University-Harrisburg, Middletown, PA 17057, USA

Abstract. State of the art suggests that Relational Agents (RAs) can alleviate escalated demands of health care services during a pandemic. Inspired by these facts, this work presents the design, significance, and initial evaluation of a prototype RA that supports people amid the COVID-19 crisis. The prototype is the end-result of an analysis that investigated interviews of patients (n = 12) and health care professionals (HCPs) (n = 19). The study established three example scenarios (i.e., testing guidance, home care, and post-recovery care) where RA can support people during COVID-19. Furthermore, a user evaluation is conducted with target users (n = 87) to validate the design of the proposed system and explore its acceptance among the target population. Findings from the evaluation indicate that the proposed RA was acceptable to the target users and further development of the prototype is justified.

Keywords: Relational agent · COVID-19 · mHealth · User-centered design

1 Introduction

COVID-19 is a virus that affects the human respiratory system and causes it to malfunction. On March 11, 2020, the World Health Organization (WHO) declared COVID-19 as a pandemic due to its highly contagious nature [1]. As of May 31, 2021, 169,597,415 persons have contracted the COVID-19, while 3,530,582 people have died from the infection globally [1]. Even though millions of people have already been vaccinated in many countries, it is too early to gauge the success of these campaigns. Moreover, with variants springing up in various parts of the world, the number of people who are contracting the infection on a daily basis has not gone down. Hence, the pandemic remains an insurmountable challenge until today.

Recent advances in digital mobile health (mHealth) include relational agents (RAs) that are being viewed as feasible alternatives for in-person provider visits [2]. RA is a computational artifact that has the capacity to maintain a long-term simulated social-emotional interaction with the user. RA's interaction model can be viewed as a computer-human relationship consisting of verbal and nonverbal interactions that can be used for

© Springer Nature Switzerland AG 2021
L. Chandra Kruse et al. (Eds.): DESRIST 2021, LNCS 12807, pp. 34–39, 2021.
https://doi.org/10.1007/978-3-030-82405-1_4

advancing the relationship in a particular direction. It consists of a dialogue manager that can plan conversational strategies that work both for the task completion and for the relationship building that emulate human face-to-face interaction experience [3, 4]. The COVID-19 pandemic necessitates social distancing to decrease viral transmission, which may lead to confinement and social isolation, often associated with negative psychological effects. Therefore, the goal of this work is to design and evaluate a social companion that not only acts as a conversational partner but also maintains a long-term socio-emotional relationship with the user.

We adopted a user-centered design (UCD) approach to develop an RA-based prototype mHealth intervention to support people during the COVID-19 crisis. We conducted a background research to identify three personas who might benefit from an RA-based solution. We then conceptualized interaction scenarios to illustrate the working of the RA for each persona. These scenarios were then used to develop a prototype application to demonstrate the working of the RA. A feasibility and user acceptance study of the developed prototype was then conducted with 87 participants, including both currently infected and recovered COVID-19 patients. The findings indicate that the proposed RA-enabled mHealth intervention has promising prospects as a care delivery tool during COVID-19 pandemic.

2 Design of the Artifact

Following the UCD methodology, we initiated the development of the intervention by conducting a background research consisting of a review of CDC's guidelines on COVID-19 prevention [5], and interviews of patients (n = 12) and HCPs (n = 19) (published in online news portals, e.g., [6]). This led to the identification of three personas. To understand experiences and needs of each persona, we interviewed twelve persons who had made their journey through COVID-19 while experiencing each persona. We then used informed brainstorming to craft scenarios to illustrate how RA can provide support to each persona.

2.1 Personas

We use 'Olivia Smith', a 35 years old female from United States as our persona profile. Olivia has no existing health conditions and is staying at home during the pandemic. She is also an expert smartphone user.

Olivia Smith: Experiencing COVID-19 Symptoms. Olivia Smith has been experiencing fever, cough, and shortness of breath for a past couple of days. She is afraid, she might have contracted the COVID-19 infection but she does not know whether it is true or not. To avoid unnecessary exposures, she does not want to make a trip to a testing center. However, if she does need to visit the center, she wants to inform her mother while she is on her way. She wants to know where the nearest COVID-19 testing site is, what to expect at that site and what precautions she needs to take in order when she arrives there. She owns a smartphone and considers herself an expert smartphone user.

Olivia Smith: COVID-19 Positive with Mild Symptoms. Olivia has been diagnosed with COVID-19 but the symptoms are mild and she does not have any underlying conditions. She has been advised by the doctors to self-isolate at home for at least 14 days. During this time, she must adopt health-promoting behaviors such as consuming a well-balanced diet, taking adequate sleep, and prescription drugs. Even though her symptoms are mild, she still needs someone to tell her what kind of health-promoting activities she should engage in during her self-isolation time. Her doctor had also told her that she would benefit from periodic monitoring of blood oxygen levels and some emergency medical assistance, such as an ambulance or oxygen.

Olivia Smith: Recovering from COVID-19. Olivia has recently recovered from severe symptoms of COVID-19 which required her to be admitted to the hospital and to spend a week in the Intensive Care Unit (ICU). She has recovered from the infection, but it was very difficult for her to go through ICU and survive a near-death experience. Now she is back at home but she is suffering from post-traumatic stress disorder (PTSD) as a result of the stress of the infection and prolonged hospitalization [3, 4]. Her mental health has been greatly influenced by other patients and the overall hospital atmosphere. In addition, she is struggling to heal from the physical damage that the virus caused to her entire body. She thinks that she is losing interest in activities she enjoyed pre-infection. She has trouble sleeping and she keeps having nightmares about the virus and the hospital. She wants to recover soon but requires both emotional and material support.

2.2   Scenarios and Prototype Design

Scenarios based on each of the personas are listed below. In each case, the persona's communications are likely to be carried out on a smartphone. The voice-activated interactive prototype based on these scenarios is built using a conversational design tool called *Botscociety* (https://botsociety.io) and simulated on the same platform.

Scenario 1: Guidance for Testing. Olivia launches the RA app on her mobile and begins interacting with it. The RA recommends her to stay at home for the next few hours based on her responses to a screening questionnaire and captured vital physiological records. Olivia's feedback is regulated by the interface, which presents her with a menu of options for each question. Furthermore, the RA will directly receive physiological measurements from Olivia's smartwatch; if the software is not connected to the smartwatch, Olivia simply needs to press the synchronize button. Olivia can also use a speech-to-text feature to enter her responses. Olivia's health metrics can also be shown on the interface, enabling her to visualize them. After two hours, the RA checks in with Olivia again. Olivia discusses her complications and reports her breathing difficulties. This time, the RA immediately recommends her to go to the closest COVID-19 testing center and provides driving directions. Olivia may even schedule her appointment at the testing center directly via the RA's interface. Also, she can inform any person (i.e her mother) about her visit to the testing center. The hyperlink to the simulated proto-type for this scenario is https://bit.ly/3nUVX7e.

Scenario 2: Helping a Patient Recover at Home. The doctor recommends Olivia to return home since she does not need hospitalization at this time. Olivia continues to communicate with the RA after returning home, and she is now being guided to take the necessary steps (i.e., taking medication and supplementary vitamins on time, hot steam therapy by nasal passage, and monitoring daily sleep and exercise routines) to avoid any worsening of her condition. The RA helps Olivia in the simulated prototype (Hyperlink: https://bit.ly/3ixOc5W) by helping her to maintain the necessary healthy lifestyle habits for a quick recovery from COVID-19.

Olivia's conditions are routinely monitored by the RA to ensure that her condition does not deteriorate. She remains fragile the next day, with severe shortness of breath. She shares her health problems with the RA that quickly dials emergency service and orders an ambulance, which rushes her to the hospital, where she is admitted to the intensive care unit (ICU) due to her serious health issues. The RA's actions as it recognizes Olivia's need for medical attention are seen in the simulated prototype (Hyperlink: https://bit.ly/3p4803b).

Scenario 3: Reducing PTSD in a Recovered Patient. As a consequence of recovering from the near-death condition, Olivia does not involve actively in daily activities like before the COVID-19 infection. RA can serve as Olivia's partner and interact with her on a regular basis to help her improve mental health. In this instance, the RA acts as a companion of Olivia and helps to reduce her PTSD by motivating her to engage in various tasks that she enjoys. The RA recognizes Olivia's current state and deals with her by discussing her mood accordingly. The RA asks Olivia about her situation the next day after her release from the hospital. She is sad and the RA then tries to boost her mood several times. RA's attempts include playing music that she likes, helping Olivia in cooking her favorite food, etc. The simulated prototype (Hyperlink: https://bit.ly/39U IZkG) illustrates some of Olivia's interaction with the RA that complies with reducing the PTSD grown in the patients recovered from the COVID-19 virus with the first two scenarios.

3   Significance to Research

RAs have been found to be efficacious in providing education, advice, and training instructions to patients about health habits by playing the roles of a counselor, a coach, and a companion in various health care settings e.g., counseling about anesthesia at surgery room, coaching for exercises, medication, hospital discharge documents, pregnancy, smoking cessation, interacting in reducing mental health issues like depression, etc. [2, 7, 8]. Earlier explorations in agent-based healthcare interventions utilized the mechanism of embodied conversational agent (ECA) due to ECA's efficacy on building social relationship for a particular goal. Previously, RAs adopted the principles of ECA to use relationship-building strategies with users with the specific goal of maintaining a social relationship and building trust over time through a model of social dialogue. However, these interventions were limited to only communicate using pre-defined verbal and non-verbal dialogues/interfaces. To the best of our knowledge, our proposed RA-enabled mHealth intervention is novel because- (i) no other work has been reported where RA deals with patients during the crisis of COVID-19 as an alternative to HCPs, (ii) it offers real-time communications, such as dealing with emergency situations, engaging the user with tasks according to user's interests, (iii) it combines three different actions (scenarios) and covers all the concerns that can be raised during non-life-threatening COVID-19 circumstances, and (iv) it makes advantage of natural language processing (NLP) applications for formulating a human-like relational history based social companion.

4 Significance to Practice

In the United States alone, 11,134 new positive cases were reported on June 06, 2021 [5]. There is a limited number of skilled workers to provide care for a vast number of sick patients, resulting in a public health crisis. Furthermore, HCPs cannot stop getting into contact with infected people who attend hospitals. People who need to go to clinics or emergency centers for critical care are at a higher risk of contracting the virus from other infected patients. Telehealth is one solution to this issue, as it allows physicians and patients to meet remotely without being exposed to the virus. However, telehealth's usefulness is limited by HCP's availability; for example, patients may be unable to reach a HCP via telehealth during an emergency situation late at night [9]. Since RA eliminates human contact at the provider end, it may be a realistic alternative to telehealth. In the patient-provider partnership, RA serves as a human replacement for caregivers in healthcare environments. In our example, it serves as a substitute for HCP's in highly infectious environments.

5 Evaluation of the Artifact

An online user evaluation study of the prototype was carried out to explore target users' perceptions about the proposed intervention and their willingness to use it in real settings. 87 participants (26 were either currently infected or had recovered and we address them as 'infected' together) completed the survey after interacting with the prototype.

96.15% infected and 78.69% non-infected participants were in agreement with the usefulness of the proposed system. 3.84% infected and 19.67% non-infected were neutral. In terms of the willingness to use, 96.15% infected and 73.77% non-infected were willing whilst 3.84% infected and 24.59% non-infected were unable to make a decision. 1.64% non-infected participants disagreed with the usefulness of the system and expressed unwillingness to use.

Overall, 83.91% participants voted the intervention as useful and 14.94% were neutral in this regard. 54.02% participants believed that it could serve as a substitute for HCPs during COVID-19 non-life-threatening situations whilst 40.22% were undetermined. In terms of using the intervention, 80.46% participants showed willingness and 18.39% were unsure. Motivated by the findings from evaluation, we have been working on developing the next iteration of the proposed intervention. This version will be deployed in-situ for a feasibility evaluation.

References

1. World Health Organization: Coronavirus (2020). https://www.who.int/redirect-pages/mega-menu/health-topics/popular/coronavirus-disease-(covid-19). Accessed on 05 June 2021

2. Kabir, M.F., Schulman, D., Abdullah, A.S.: Promoting relational agent for health behavior change in low and middle - income countries (LMICS): issues and approaches. J. Med. Syst. **43**, 1–11 (2019)
3. Tielman, M.L., Neerincx, M.A., Bidarra, R., Kybartas, B., Brinkman, W.P.: A therapy system for post-traumatic stress disorder using a virtual agent and virtual storytelling to reconstruct traumatic memories. J. Med. Syst. **41**(8), 1–10 (2017)
4. Tielman, M.L., Neerincx, M.A., Brinkman, W.P.: Design and evaluation of personalized motivational messages by a virtual agent that assists in post-traumatic stress disorder therapy. J. Med. Internet Res. **21**(3), e9240 (2019)
5. Centers for Disease Control and Prevention: Coronavirus disease 2019 (covid-19) (2021). https://www.cdc.gov/coronavirus/2019-ncov/communication/guidance.html). Accessed on 05 June 2021
6. Nitkin, K.: Sammy eldin's story (2020). https://www.hopkinsmedicine.org/coronavirus/patient-stories/sammy-eldin.html. Accessed on 05 June 2021
7. Kramer, L.L., Ter Stal, S., Mulder, B.C., de Vet, E., van Velsen, L.: Developing embodied conversational agents for coaching people in a healthy lifestyle: scoping review. J. Med. Internet Res. **22**(2), e14058 (2020)
8. Bhattacharyya, O., Mossman, K., Gustafsson, L., Schneider, E.C.: Using human-centered design to build a digital health advisor for patients with complex needs: persona and prototype development. J. Med. Internet Res. **21**(5), e10318 (2019)
9. Calton, B., Abedini, N., Fratkin, M.: Telemedicine in the time of coronavirus. J. Pain Symptom Manage. **60**(1), e12–e14 (2020)

"BeMyVoice" – An iPad-Based Helper
for Speech Impaired Persons

Alexander Klauer[1] , Florian Johannsen[2]([✉]) , and Susanne Leist[1]

[1] University of Regensburg, Regensburg, Germany
alex@bemyvoice.app, susanne.leist@wiwi.uni-regensburg.de
[2] University of Applied Sciences, Schmalkalden, Germany
f.johannsen@hs-sm.de

Abstract. In the recent past, augmentative and alternative communication (AAC) systems have been introduced as a means to assist speech impaired persons to interconnect with the environment and to increase their communication skills. Considering this, tablet-PC-based AAC systems are getting ever more popular due to reasons of cost efficiency, portability and social acceptance. However, many existing apps do not fully exploit the software and hardware capabilities of topical devices. Moreover, studies on the capabilities of platform-related development environments (e.g., iOS SDK) – in their current versions – to realize tablet-PC-based AAC systems are missing. In this work, we develop an iPad-based AAC prototype, which considers the technical capacities of the device and is offered as an open source solution.

Keywords: Augmented and alternative communication · Speech impairment · Tablet-PC · Open source

1 Introduction

"Perhaps the single quality most central to humanness is the ability to exchange thoughts, ideas, and feelings with others" [1, p. 235]. In this context, speech is seen as a person's most important instrument to be in contact with their human surroundings [2]. However, individuals with severe physical disabilities or brain injury may not be able to control their oral-respiratory musculature sufficiently for speech [3, 4]. This restriction of verbal communication, and hence, the *"separation from the mainstream of society"* [1, p. 235] holds true for people with damages to the vocal tract or other handicaps affecting speech as well [4]. In Germany alone, almost 7,000 out of 317,748 humans who were registered as severely handicapped had a proven speech impediment in 2017 [5]. In this respect, augmentative and alternative communication (AAC) systems have been introduced as a means to assist individuals with communication [1, 6–8]. An AAC system is defined as a technology that consists of a *"group of components, including the symbols, aids, strategies, and techniques used by individuals to enhance communication"* [9, p. 10]. In the past, "non-vocal" communication (unaided AAC), e.g., through the use of sign language or picture modes, has been at the center of AAC research [6]. However, in

© Springer Nature Switzerland AG 2021
L. Chandra Kruse et al. (Eds.): DESRIST 2021, LNCS 12807, pp. 40–51, 2021.
https://doi.org/10.1007/978-3-030-82405-1_5

recent decades, voice output communication aids (VOCA) have gained tremendous popularity due to rapid technological progress [1, 6, 8]. It has been shown that VOCAs have a positive impact on disabled people's communication skills and development [7, 10, 11]. Considering this, the use of tablet-PCs for supporting AAC is judged to be particularly promising [8, 12]. First, the development of AAC systems via tablet-PCs can be realized in a highly cost-effective and user-friendly way [8, 13]. Second, because the technology is widely spread within the population, high social acceptance for tablet-based AAC systems is given [8, 12, 13]. Third, tablet-PCs are more portable, affordable and easy-to-use than many traditional AAC devices [12, 14, 15].

However, the development of AAC systems for tablet-PCs (e.g., [12]) is challenging [16]. For instance, the abilities of current development frameworks to exploit the full capabilities of topical tablet-devices are often unclear [16]. Moreover, the availability of mobile technologies often leads to a premature and overly hasty introduction of AAC systems [17]. Thereby, it is widely acknowledged that the simple provision of an AAC system developed ad hoc will rarely result in effective communication by people who have more complex communication requirements [13]. Accordingly, a clear focus on the aspirations and wants of the user group is central to the successful implementation of a mobile or wearable AAC system [4, 17]. Considering this, typical users of wearable AAC systems are persons with a speech impediment on the one hand but also caregivers or therapists, who configure the system, on the other hand. Thereby, two major skill profiles of speech impaired persons need to be distinguished [18]. Persons with the profile "non-speaking" have sufficient speech comprehension, though their speech production is disabled [18]. Individuals with the profile "non-verbal" have both limited speech comprehension and production, often caused by aphasia and/or multiple disabilities [18]. AAC systems for these groups differ in their vocabulary (cf. [19]); e.g., the composition of a sentence out of singular fragments requires distinct speech comprehension abilities. Hence, this approach is only appropriate for the profile "non-speaking" [20]. In contrast, systems which enable the output of a whole sentence by pushing a certain key are recommended for persons with the profile "non-verbal" [18]. In the work at hand, we focus on the profile "non-verbal" and pose the following research question (RQ): *What can a tablet-PC-based and open source AAC system for "non-verbal" speech impaired persons look like that makes use of the current capabilities of the mobile device?* Generally, this paper describes a first step in our long-term effort to identify how AAC applications on portable devices may impact the communication abilities of patients with speech impediments. Many existing applications in this field are not available on an open source base and they do not keep up with the progress of software and hardware capabilities of tablet-PCs [16]. Accordingly, topical studies that focus on the functionalities of app development environments (e.g., iOS SDK) to come to innovative tablet-PC-based AAC systems are largely missing. The same holds true for works focusing on the applicability of open source components (e.g., freely available symbol libraries, translation services, etc.) to build AAC systems. We contribute to the generation of corresponding insights by implementing a running, open source "symbols to speech" prototype (cf. [12]) that aims at exploiting the current capabilities of an iPad device. The prototype will address "non-verbal" persons in a first step, because the requirements can be specified more precisely for a homogeneous user group (cf. [12, 17]). But since the degree of disability varies within this group, we further narrow the focus on individuals having (1) sufficient motor skills to select symbols on the tablet screen, (2) visual abilities to recognize symbols and (3) intellectual skills to handle the AAC device and to understand the semantics of symbols. The paper is structured as follows: in the next section, we provide theoretical foundations. Subsequently, the research methodology and the requirements on our prototype are shown. After having described the development, the study concludes with a discussion and an outlook.

2 Foundations and Related Work

AAC has been a topic of lively discussion in research (e.g., [1, 8, 21]). In particular, the design and development of new AAC systems and instructional strategies rely on the use of commonly acknowledged theoretical constructs to best serve people with complex communication needs [21]. Important theoretical constructs in AAC research emerge from various scientific fields like natural language processing, machine learning (e.g., [22]), language acquisition (e.g., [23]), communication or social interaction (e.g., [24]). Another essential feature of AAC research is the active participation of people who rely on AAC since they provide evidence about the effectiveness of AAC systems and strategies [21]. Principally, research in the area of AAC has a broad range and seeks to improve the lives of people with complex communication needs [21]. From a general perspective, the positive impact of VOCAs on the interaction between support personnel and disabled persons is shown by Schepis et al. [6] or Brady [25] amongst others. In this context, Ganz et al. [26] conduct a meta-study of 24 case studies dealing with aided AAC for persons with autism spectrum disorders and receive indicators for a strong effect of AAC on the targeted behavioral outcomes. A suggestion for a corresponding AAC system for children with autism is introduced by Sampath et al. [27] for example. Regarding the development of proprietary AAC systems that go along with a proprietary device (e.g., handheld device, etc.), contributions are made by Allen [4], Pollak and Gallagher [2], Hornero et al. [28] or Francioli [29] for instance. Gonzales et al. [30] focus on the advantages and disadvantages of such proprietary AAC devices, whereas Baxter et al. [31] identify factors that impact the provision and usage of these systems. Additionally, a set of symbols to support people with complex communication needs – that may be referenced for the development of AAC systems – is introduced by Krüger and Berberian [32]. Apart from that, Apple devices are also vividly discussed in AAC literature (e.g., [8, 12]). Thereby, Desai et al. [33] show that an iPad-based AAC system may increase communication skills of individuals with a cerebral palsy and autism. In contrast, Flores et al. [34] find out that the communications skills of young people with autism do not necessarily increase by using an iPad-based AAC system in comparison to alternative solutions. A summarizing overview of developments in the AAC discipline over the last decades is provided by Hourcade et al. [1]. In general, tablet-PC-based AAC applications can be classified as "symbols/pictures only", "symbols/text to speech" and "text to speech only" solutions [12]. Thereby, the "symbols/text to speech" solutions use a combination of symbols and/or keyboard capabilities to express sentences [12]. A subgroup of this category are dynamic "symbols to speech" apps, which allow the configuration of multiple patterns of pictures or characters that represent phrases or words [35]. Existing apps of this type differ regarding their "vocabulary strategy" [19]. In case of a "1:1-correspondence" strategy, a certain key represents exactly one word (single word strategy) or a spoken phrase (phrase strategy) [19, 36]. "Semantic coding" strategies classify words according to their semantics [19]. Depending on a sequential selection of certain keys, a key may thus have various semantic meanings, which reduces the number of required keys on a device's display [19, 36]. While several available apps on the market are distributed with a predefined vocabulary, others need to be individually configured at first. Examples of "symbols to speech" AAC systems are "MetaTalk", "GoTalkNow", "Quasselkiste", "TouchSpeak" and "MultiFoXX 24", amongst others. As a common denominator, commercial apps usually comprise features such as the visualization of a raster screen for speech symbols, the production of voice output (based on pre-defined texts), the availability of symbol libraries or the management of different raster screens. However, many of the software and hardware capabilities of modern tablet-PCs are not used by existing apps (cf. [16]). For instance, the software development kit for Apple's iPad includes several frameworks, e.g., for voice output, home and internal process automation or machine learning (ML) that would be potentially useful for AAC system design. Besides these software aspects, most available apps do not fully exploit the hardware capabilities of current tablet-PCs either [16]. A precise localization via GPS data, the application of internet services or the authorization by help of the fingerprint sensor could be mentioned in this respect. Moreover, an analysis of existing apps showed that persons with restricted visual and motor skills may easily produce working errors when working with tablet-PCs, which cannot be reversed by them without further assistance (cf. [16]). Against this background, the development of an easy-to-use and "open source" iPad-based application for persons with speech impediments with the abovementioned characteristics (e.g., profile "non-verbal", etc.; *see introduction*), which makes use of the current capabilities of the iPad device and can be adapted to individuals' needs, is considered promising. Accordingly, we aim at complementing the abovementioned AAC research streams by offering insights on how current development environments and frameworks can be used to create an open source "symbols to speech" prototype, which makes use of the contemporary software and hardware capabilities of an iPad (e.g., use of context information, etc.). Thereby, beneficial results are created for iOS developers in the field of AAC systems (e.g., applicability of pre-defined algorithms).

3 Methodology and Research Design

To arrive at a prototype of our app called "BeMyVoice", we conduct a Design Science Research (DSR) project [37–40] and follow the procedure of Peffers et al. [41].

The problem statement was formulated in the introduction *(Step 1)*. In the second step *("Objectives of a Solution")*, we derive requirements (e.g., [42]) with the help of literature, user stories, an analysis of existing AAC apps that match our research scope ("non-verbal" profile, "symbol to speech", etc.) and interviews with the management of a German software company that focuses on the development of apps for healthcare, amongst others. Based on that, a prioritization of requirements is performed to come to a manageable set for an initial prototype. Afterwards, the prototype is designed and

1. Problem	2. Objectives of a Solution	3. Design & Development	4. Demonstration	5. Evaluation	6. Communication
Many iPad-based AAC apps do not exploit the software and hardware capabilities of the device. Insights about the current potentials of the iPadOS SDK and open source "components "to realize AAC systems are missing.	Requirements for a prototype of a "symbols to speech" app for "non-verbal" speech impaired persons.	Design and implementation of an iPad-based application prototype.	Demonstration of the prototype at a workshop.	Comprising field study to evaluate the usefulness, applicability and usability of the prototype.	Proactive promotion of the app "BeMyVoice".

▭: Focus of this paper
▭: Future work

process iteration

Fig. 1. Procedure by Peffers et al. [41] adapted for this research.

developed in *Step 3*. Thereby, design-related decisions, e.g., the layout of the GUI, have to be made. Moreover, frameworks for technically realizing the prototype need to be selected. Afterwards, a demonstration of the prototype is performed *(Step 4 – "Demonstration")*. In a next step *(Step 5 – "Evaluation")*, the prototype will be subjected to a larger field study with therapists and speech impaired persons to assess its usefulness, applicability and usability (cf. [37]). Then, the app will be revised and promoted as an "open source" app that can be used straight away and further developed to meet individual requirements *(Step 6)*. The purpose of this research (cf. [40]) is to contribute to the knowledge base (cf. [37, 38]) of how to use iPad-based "symbols to speech" AAC systems to support persons with a speech impediment.

4 Objectives of a Solution

As mentioned above, we strive for the development of an iPad-based "symbol to speech" AAC application "BeMyVoice" that targets speech impaired persons that have some motor skills, intellectual aptitudes as well as visual abilities to recognize and select symbols on the tablet screen, but also are able to understand the semantics of the symbols. To arrive at requirements for a corresponding prototype *(*Fig. 1 – *Step 2)*, we followed the suggestions of *Schilling* [42] for mobile app requirements engineering and we emphasize the perspective of people who rely on them to communicate. Accordingly, a review of the market (e.g., "MetaTalk", "GoTalkNow", etc.) was performed first (cf. [42]) to derive common functionalities of mobile AAC apps (e.g., visualization via raster screens, etc. – see Sect. 2). Second, user stories (cf. [42]) of potential app users, called "Felix", "Anita" and "Petra" hereinafter, were set up. Thereby, Felix is characterized by severe mental and physical disability caused by a lack of oxygen at birth. He was diagnosed with aphasia and a spasticity of both arms. He is unable to speak and can only emanate sounds. The sheltered workshop he works at is located near his care facility. He uses a wheelchair and the iPad with "BeMyVoice" is attached to it by help of a mount.

Anita lives and works at a home for disabled people. She has a mental handicap and aphasia, which were caused by a craniocerebral injury. Anita does not depend on a wheelchair, and can hold the iPad in her hands. Petra is Anita's and Felix's therapist and configures the app for them. With the help of the user stories, the objects processed by the app could be itemized and the underlying logic specified more precisely (cf. [42]). Third, interviews (cf. [42]) with the management of a software company were performed. The mentioned firm has long experience in creating apps for education, fitness and healthcare, amongst others. Moreover, creating open source apps is a major principle of

Table 1. Requirements for the prototype.

Functional Design Requirements (DR)	Description
DR 1: Push-to-talk buttons (in form of a raster screen – GUI)	A raster screen of symbols ("push to talk" buttons) is offered, with each symbol representing a word or a sentence that can be individually defined (cf. [33, 43]).
DR 2: Modification and individual design of the raster screen (GUI)	The design of the raster screen can be modified and buttons can be added, deleted or edited. This also includes the definition of the background color of symbols to enable a (visual) clustering of symbols if required (cf. [43]).
DR 3: Folder structures for selecting raster screens	Folders with predefined raster screens can be created. When selecting a certain folder, the user is directed to another (previously defined) raster screen (*/**).
DR 4: Library of predefined symbols	A library of established symbols for AAC (e.g., METAKOM) is provided by the app (cf. [32]).
DR 5: "Dock" for frequently used buttons	Buttons for frequently used sentences (e.g., "I need help") are statically fixed on the display independent of the (currently) selected raster screen (cf. [12]).
DR 6: Intelligent suggestions	The app learns the speaking/communication behavior of the user with the help of machine learning; it proposes buttons the user will most likely use next by considering the time-related and location-related context information (*).
DR 7: Language translator	Users may switch between different languages (cf. [8]).
DR 8: Context-dependent selection of a raster screen	Depending on the location, a suitable raster screen is selected for the user (*/**).
DR 9: Emergency call	A button that sends a mail or SMS to a contact person with the geographical location of the "BeMyVoice" user is provided (*).
DR 10: Smart home control	A button to control smart home devices, e.g., lamps, is added (*).
DR 11: Speech memos	Therapists can record speech memos for family members or caregivers (*/**).
Non-functional Design Requirements (DR)	**Description**
DR 12: High usability and accessibility	The symbols (buttons) need to have a sufficient size for use by persons with restricted motor, intellectual and visual abilities (e.g., [8]). Further, therapists as well as patients should be able to easily handle the app (*/**).
DR 13: Voice output in real-time	The voice output should have no delays when pushing "push to talk" buttons (*/**).
DR 14: Navigation in real-time	Switching between different screens happens in real-time (*/**).
DR 15: High reliability	Since the target group may not be able to undo working errors, the software must be highly reliable and avoid "crashes" (cf. [8]/*).

Legend:				
DR	Considered for the first version of the app	DR	To be realized in an upcoming version.	**Source:** *: management interview; **: user stories; []: literature

the company culture and this expertise helped to identify additional requirements. Fourth, the insights acquired hitherto were complemented by suggestions derived from literature about iPad-based AAC systems (e.g., [8, 33]). Finally, user journeys were specified for the aforementioned user groups to get an understanding for potential usability problems when using the app (cf. [42]).

In summary, the "functional" and "non-functional" design requirements (DR) as shown in Table 1 were defined. After a prioritization in cooperation with the management of the mentioned software company and an initial effort estimation, DR 1 to DR 7 as well as DR 12 to DR 15 were considered to be realized in a first iteration of the DSR process (see Fig. 1).

5 Development and Demonstration

For realizing our app "BeMyVoice" *(*Fig. 1– *Step 3)*, the operating system *iPadOS* and the *iOS SDK* environment were chosen (https://developer.apple.com/). The programming language *Swift* was used for code generation (cf. [44]), *SQLite* as the database management system and *Xcode 11* as the integrated development environment (IDE). The operating system functionalities and frameworks of the *iPadOS Software Development Kit* have the advantage of reducing implementation efforts for programmers, of being constantly updated and of having been tested broadly. Further, the user interface (UI) components are used by the operating system for other applications as well, which largely contributes to a high usability. A first design of the UI, matching the above-mentioned requirements – with the help of wireframes – was discussed and revised in interaction with the management of the software company. Figure 2 shows the wireframe from the discussions as well as a simplified use-case-diagram highlighting the users of "BeMyVoice", namely the speech impaired person and the therapist.

For the symbols, the library of the *Aragonese Centre for Augmentative & Alternative Communication* was referred to (http://www.arasaac.org/), which is provided for free and has established in practice. The voice output functionality was realized with the help of the *AVFoundation Framework* of the *iOS SDK* and the corresponding class *AVSpeechSynthesizer*. With the "guided access" functionality of the operating system, operating errors can be largely eliminated during the app's use. For the implementation of the "intelligent suggestions" requirement, the Naïve Bayes (NB) algorithm was used (e.g., [45]). We did not apply the machine learning (ML) framework *CoreML* of the *iOS SDK*, because it primarily relies on pre-built machine learning models rather than on mechanisms that support model training during device usage. The *Google MLKit Translate API* (https://developers.google.com/ml-kit/language/translation) was used to enable the possibility of voice output in multiple languages. In this respect, considerations about data privacy played a major role during the implementation. With the use of online translation APIs, providers could potentially get profound insights about the user's private life by analyzing "translation requests". *MLKit Translate* however uses offline translation, which means that all translated phrases and words are computed on the device as opposed to a server. Besides this privacy-sensitive approach, the API offers a high-quality translation. Therefore, it was chosen for our prototype.

On the left-hand side in Fig. 3, a screenshot of a sample raster screen with selected "push to talk" buttons is shown. The lower edge of the figure shows a "dock" with frequently used buttons but also with suggestions of buttons that might be used next, which are "intelligently" anticipated by "BeMyVoice". The demonstration *(see* Fig. 1– *Step 4)* of the prototype was done in cooperation with the management of the software company in form of a workshop. So, raster screens were created for the abovementioned persons Felix and Anita by taking the perspective of the therapist Petra.

Then, typical everyday scenarios – that might be supported by the app – were talked through (e.g., visit with a family member, talk with colleagues at work, leisure activities).

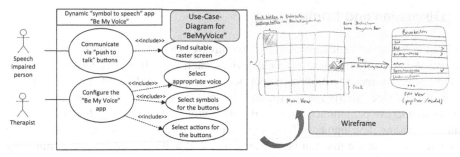

Fig. 2. Partial results of the design stage.

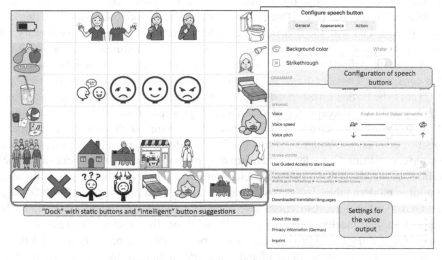

Fig. 3. Screenshots of "BeMyVoice".

To cope with these situations, the following "folders" for raster screens were configured for Felix and Anita based on the results of aphasiological research (cf. [18]): *"professional activities"* (buttons required for the working environment), *"emotions/moods"* (e.g., "I am happy"), *"friends/acquaintances/family"* (information about important persons, e.g., "name", etc.), *"social etiquette"* (greeting, polite expressions, etc.), *"profile"* (buttons for introducing oneself, etc.), *"information related to one's speech impediment"* (e.g., "I can only speak by help of this AAC device", "please be patient", etc.) and *"leisure time"* (buttons regarding leisure activities, e.g., "I'd like to paint"). In the workshop, there was an agreement that the highlighted design requirements in Table 1 were fulfilled and the general applicability of "BeMyVoice" for the targeted user group could be assumed. Moreover, several ideas regarding a further development of "BeMyVoice" came up (e.g., activation of the device's flashlight in case of adverse lightning conditions, etc.) encouraging us to start a comprising evaluation of "BeMyVoice" in everyday scenarios.

6 Discussion and Implications

Most high-tech AAC technologies used to require tremendous learning efforts [2]. Thus, the use of commonly accepted technical devices, such as the iPad, has been increasingly getting attention recently. In this project, we develop an iPad-based AAC "symbol to speech" prototype "BeMyVoice", which helps people with a "non-verbal" speech disability to improve communication with the environment. Considering this, our research and the ongoing development of the app entails several benefits. First, we provide an open source prototype that can be further developed and enhanced by the community to meet individual demands. Accordingly, we provide a cost-effective solution that can be used straight away complementing the market of commercial applications. Second, we contribute to the academic discussion of how technological devices – that are used in peoples' everyday life (e.g., iPad) – can support AAC. More concretely, the demonstration provided us with the first important findings regarding the app's suitability for dealing with typical everyday scenarios. In addition, we obtained insights about the usefulness of the defined symbols as well as raster screens and validated the used theoretical constructs. These findings and their contribution to the underlying theories (see Sect. 2) are to be further investigated in upcoming steps. Additionally, the easy handling, portability and social acceptance of such technologies may foster the wide distribution of AAC solutions and increase the social contact of persons with a speech impairment. In this respect, many existing solutions for the iPad do not exploit its full software and hardware capabilities. Considering this, the study proposes a set of frameworks and functionalities of the iPadOS Software Development Kit, which can be purposefully used for building modern tablet-based AAC software along with propositions for the design of the GUI. Furthermore, restrictions also became evident, e.g., regarding the CoreML package to support machine learning in AAC. Additionally, existing services – e.g., the *Google MLKit Translate API* – turned out to be suitable for building an iPad-based AAC solution. These insights determine the newness and innovativeness of our solution considering that a gap in literature can be observed to this effect. Third, our prototype may serve as a starting point for creating apps for speech impaired persons with other characteristics and "profiles" as well (e.g., "non-speaking"). That way, the requirements for different types of speech disabled persons will become clearer.

Nevertheless, our research is also subject to restrictions. Although we received promising results hitherto, a comprising evaluation is still an open issue. Moreover, we focus on a specific type of speech impaired person as outlined above. This is necessary, for being able to precisely define the requirements matching the particular needs of that group and to avoid creating an "ad-hoc" solution that may not meet expectations (e.g., [17]). Accordingly, our app targets "non-verbal" persons with the characteristics described in Sect. 1 and our insights primarily refer to this group. We used the iPad and its corresponding developer frameworks as a technological base. This of course limits the freedom of design due to platform-dependent reservations. Further, only selected design requirements have been considered hitherto.

7 Conclusion and Outlook

In the work at hand, we introduce "BeMyVoice", an iPad-based "symbol to speech" system targeting speech impaired persons who have some motor, intellectual and visual skills enabling them to handle the app, to recognize symbols and comprehend their semantics. The research provides beneficial insights for developers about the current capabilities of the *iPadOS* and *iOS SDK* as well as freely available services and components (e.g., symbol libraries) to realize an iPad-based "symbols to speech" AAC system, which draws upon the device's present technological maturity. "BeMyVoice" is intended to be an open source app (i.e., the source code is freely available) that can be adapted on demand.

In the future, "BeMyVoice" will thus be subjected to a larger evaluation to get feedback on its applicability. Moreover, the app will be made accessible via GitHub to push collaborative further development. Recently the app has been made available for free via Apple's AppStore and has successfully passed Apple's quality check, an obligatory step for publication.

References

1. Hourcade, J., Everhart Pilotte, T., West, E., Parette, P.: A history of augmentative and alternative communication for individuals with severe and profound disabilities. Focus Autism Other Dev. Disabil. **19**(4), 235–244 (2004)
2. Pollak, V., Gallagher, B.: A fast communication aid for non-verbal subjects with severe motor handicaps. J. Med. Eng. Technol. **13**(1–2), 23–27 (1989)
3. Vanderheiden, G.C.: Non-conversational communication technology needs of individuals with handicaps. Rehabil. World **7**(2), 8–12 (1983)
4. Allen, J.: Designing desirability in an augmentative and alternative communication device. Univ. Access Inf. Soc. **4**(2), 135–145 (2005)
5. Statista. https://de.statista.com/statistik/daten/studie/247950/umfrage/anzahl-der-schwerhoe rigen-in-deutschland-nach-art-der-behinderung/. Accessed on 26 May 2021
6. Schepis, M.M., Reid, D.H., Behrman, M.M.: Acquisition and functional use of voice output communication by persons with profound multiple disabilities. Behav. Modif. **20**(4), 451–468 (1996)
7. Romski, M.A., Sevcik, R.: Augmentative and alternative communication systems: considerations for individuals with severe intellectual disabilities. Augment. Altern. Commun. **4**(2), 83–93 (1988)
8. Bradshaw, J.: The use of augmentative and alternative communication apps for the iPad, iPod and iPhone: an overview of recent developments. Tizard Learn. Disabil. Rev. **18**(1), 31–37 (2013)
9. American Speech-Language-Hearing Association: Report: augmentative and alternative communication. ASHA **33**, 9–12 (1991)
10. Locke, P., Mirenda, P.: A computer-supported communication approach for a child with severe communication, visual, and cognitive impairments: a case study. Augment. Altern. Commun. **4**(1), 15–22 (1988)
11. Romski, M., Sevcik, R., Washburn, D.: Microcomputer communication system implementation in homes and classrooms of nonspeaking youngsters with retardation. Annual meeting of the American Association on Mental Deficiency, Los Angeles (1987)

12. Alliano, A., Herriger, K., Koutsoftas, A.D., Bartolotta, T.E.: A review of 21 iPad applications for augmentative and alternative communication purposes. Perspect. Augment. Altern. Commun. **21**(2), 60–71 (2012)
13. McNaughton, D., Light, J.: The iPad and mobile technology revolution: benefits and challenges for individuals who require augmentative and alternative communication. Augment. Altern. Commun. **29**(2), 107–116 (2013)
14. Brady, L.J.: Apps for Autism: An Essential Guide to Over 200 Effective Apps for Improving Communication, Behavior, Social Skills, and More! Future Horizons (2012)
15. McNaughton, D., Bryen, D.N.: AAC technologies to enhance participation and access to meaningful societal roles for adolescents and adults with developmental disabilities who require AAC. Augment. Altern. Commun. **23**(3), 217–229 (2007)
16. Klauer, A.: Prototypische Entwicklung einer elektronischen Kommunikationshilfe für Menschen mit Behinderung. Report, University of Regensburg (2019)
17. McBride, D.: AAC evaluations and new mobile technologies: asking and answering the right questions. Perspect. Altern. Augment. Commun. **20**(1), 9–16 (2011)
18. Nonn, K., Pässler-van Rey, D.: Unterstützte Kommunikation in der Logopädie. Thieme, Stuttgart (2011)
19. Lüke, C., Vock, S.: Unterstützte Kommunikation bei Kindern und Erwachsenen. Springer, Berlin, Heidelberg (2019). https://doi.org/10.1007/978-3-662-58128-5
20. Beck, A., Fritz, H.: Can people who have aphasia learn iconic codes? Augment. Altern. Commun. **14**(3), 184–196 (1998)
21. Blackstone, S.W., Williams, M.B., Wilkins, D.P.: Key principles underlying research and practice in AAC. Augment. Altern. Commun. **23**(3), 191–203 (2007)
22. Elsahar, Y., Hu, S., Bouazza-Marouf, K., Kerr, D., Mansor, A.: Augmentative and alternative communication (AAC) advances: a review of configurations for individuals with a speech disability. Sensors **19**(8), 1911 (2019). https://doi.org/10.3390/s19081911
23. Bedrosian, J.: Language acquisition in young AAC system users: issues and directions for future research. Augment. Altern. Commun. **13**(3), 179–185 (1997)
24. Lilienfeld, M., Alant, E.: The social interaction of an adolescent who uses AAC: The evaluation of a peer-training program. Augment. Altern. Commun. **21**(4), 278–294 (2005)
25. Brady, N.: Improved comprehension of object names following voice output communication aid use: two case studies. Augment. Altern. Commun. **16**(3), 197–204 (2000)
26. Ganz, J.B., Earles-Vollrath, T.L., Heath, A.K., Parker, R.I., Rispoli, M.J., Duran, J.B.: A meta-analysis of single case research studies on aided augmentative and alternative communication systems with individuals with autism spectrum disorders. J. Autism Dev. Disord. **42**(1), 60–74 (2012)
27. Sampath, H., Indurkhya, B., Sivaswamy, J.: A communication system on smart phones and tablets for non-verbal children with autism. In: Miesenberger, K., Karshmer, A., Penaz, P., Zagler, W. (eds.) ICCHP 2012. LNCS, vol. 7383, pp. 323–330. Springer, Heidelberg (2012). https://doi.org/10.1007/978-3-642-31534-3_49
28. Hornero, G., et al.: A wireless augmentative and alternative communication system for people with speech disabilities. IEEE Access **3**, 1288–1297 (2015)
29. Francioli, F.: Device for communication for persons with speech and/or hearing handicap. Google Patents (2011)
30. Gonzales, C.H., Leroy, G., De Leo, G.: Augmentative and alternative communication technologies. In: Computer Engineering: Concepts, Methodologies, Tools and Applications, pp. 1164–1180. IGI Global (2012)
31. Baxter, S., Enderby, P., Evans, P., Judge, S.: Barriers and facilitators to the use of high-technology augmentative and alternative communication devices: a systematic review and qualitative synthesis. Int. J. Lang. Comm. Disorders **47**(2), 115–129 (2012)

32. Krüger, S., Berberian, A.P.: Augmentative and alternative communication system (AAC) for social inclusion of people with complex communication needs in the industry. Assist. Technol. **27**(2), 101–111 (2015)
33. Desai, T., Chow, K., Mumford, L., Hotze, F., Chau, T.: Implementing an iPad-based alternative communication device for a student with cerebral palsy and autism in the classroom via an access technology delivery protocol. Comp. Ed. **79**, 148–158 (2014)
34. Flores, M., et al.: A comparison of communication using the Apple iPad and a picture-based system. Augment. Altern. Commun. **28**(2), 74–84 (2012)
35. Keller, C.: Fachbuch Außerklinische Intensivpflege. Elsevier Health Sciences (2017)
36. Müller, A., Gülden, M.: Linguistische Aspekte der visuellen Darstellung von Sprache in der Unterstützten Kommunikation. Unterstützte Kommunikation **4**, 17–32 (2016)
37. Hevner, A.R., March, S.T., Park, J., Ram, S.: Design Science in Information Systems Research. MIS Q. **28**(1), 75–105 (2004)
38. Gregor, S., Hevner, A.R.: Positioning and presenting design science research for maximum impact. MIS Q. **37**(2), 337–356 (2013)
39. Hevner, A., Chatterjee, S.: Design research in information systems. Springer US, Boston, MA (2010)
40. Baskerville, R., Baiyere, A., Gregor, S., Hevner, A., Rossi, M.: Design science research contributions: finding a balance between artifact and theory. JAIS **19**(5), 358–376 (2018)
41. Peffers, K., Tuunanen, T., Rothenberger, M.A., Chatterjee, S.: A design science research methodology for information systems research. JMIS **24**(3), 45–77 (2007)
42. Schilling, K.: Apps machen - Der Kompaktkurs für Designer. Hanser (2016)
43. Lopez-Samaniego, L., Garcia-Zapirain, B., Mendez-Zorrilla, A.: Memory and accurate processing brain rehabilitation for the elderly: LEGO robot and iPad case study. Bio-Med. Mater. Eng. **24**(6), 3549–3556 (2014)
44. Mathias, M., Gallagher, J.: Swift Programming. Pearson Technology Group (2016)
45. Forsyth, D.: Applied Machine Learning. Springer International Publishing, Cham (2019). https://doi.org/10.1007/978-3-030-18114-7

Designing an Avatar-Based Virtual Coach
for Obesity Patients

Thure Weimann[1]([✉]) [iD], Hannes Schlieter[1], and Martin Fischer[2]

[1] Chair of Wirtschaftsinformatik, Esp. Systems Development, Technische Universität Dresden,
Dresden, Germany
thure.weimann@tu-dresden.de
[2] Klinikum St. Georg gGmbH, Leipzig, Germany

Abstract. The COVID-19 pandemic reveals that digital health interventions will
be indispensable to care for special patient groups in the long-term successfully.
Current research focuses on embodied conversational agents (ECAs) that promise
patient support by emulating interpersonal communication. Against the background of high relapse rates in obesity care and significant costs for the healthcare
systems, this work presents a prototype of an ECA as a virtual coach for morbidly
obese patients, along with a first evaluation of its acceptability from a patient's
perspective. The results indicate that a virtual coach meets the patients' needs and
motivate further investigations of the technological concept.

Keywords: Embodied conversational agent · Virtual coaching · Obesity

1 Introduction and Motivation

More than 20 years ago, obesity was classified by the world health organization as an
epidemic and global problem [1]. Since then, prevalence rates have steadily increased,
making obesity and associated secondary diseases (e.g., cardiovascular diseases or diabetes) a significant burden for national healthcare systems [2]. Sustainable lifestyle mod-
ifications with changes in nutrition and exercise behavior are mandatory for long-term
treatment success. However, weight loss programs often miss their goal of long-term
weight reduction due to a lack of adherence and resulting in relapses [3]. Current research
focuses on embodied conversational agents (ECAs) as virtual coaches (VCs), i.e., intelligent software systems with an animated avatar that support patients in their daily life
and promise an improvement of therapy adherence [4]. In particular, the COVID-19
pandemic with restrictions in social contacts highlights the need for ECAs to support
traditional healthcare approaches. However, there is a lack of digital health applications that utilize avatar and conversational agent (CA)-technologies for addressing the
needs of obese and especially morbidly obese patients. Previous research investigated
the use of an ECA as unimodal support (i.e., promoting physical activity) for overweight
patients (BMI of 30 kg/m^2) [5] and the use of a disembodied chatbot [6]. However, an
avatar-based VC supporting the recommended multimodal treatment consisting of diet,
exercise and behavioral therapy of morbid obesity (BMI > 40 kg/m^2) is not available

L. Chandra Kruse et al. (Eds.): DESRIST 2021, LNCS 12807, pp. 52–57, 2021.
https://doi.org/10.1007/978-3-030-82405-1_6

yet. Therefore, we introduce an avatar-based VC prototype for morbidly obese patients. This paper continues by describing the design approach, providing a system overview, explaining the components in detail and providing results of an evaluation of its potential usability from a patient's perspective.

2   Design of the Artifact

2.1   Approach and Design Process

When it comes to the design of socio-technical systems that target behavior changes, especially findings from health psychology can inform design decisions. Therefore, our prototype design is informed by the Behavior Change Technique Taxonomy by Michie et al. [7]. A literature review by Asbjørnsen et al. [8] revealed that with respect to weight loss maintenance, self-monitoring, feedback, goal-setting, shaping knowledge as well as social support were significant behavior change techniques applied in existing e-Health applications. We used these findings as a first set of meta-requirements (MRs) to prepare interviews with health professionals and construct questionnaire items for a patient survey. Three guided interviews with a psychologist, a dietary assistant and a physician were conducted to identify and refine requirements. The interview questions were focused on possible use cases, frequently asked patients' questions, and examples of shared therapy goals. In addition, two patient surveys were conducted. The first survey ($n = 27$) focused on self-monitoring using sensor integration and self-reporting scales. In contrast, the second survey ($n = 33$) assessed how helpful goal-setting features, personalized feedback, reminders and asking the coach various therapy-related questions were perceived to prioritize the requirements. Both surveys were unrelated and conducted with patients from a non-surgical obesity treatment program. The program participants have a mean age of 46 years and a mean BMI of 49.5 kg/m^2 [3]. As our survey solely focused on opinions, a formal medical ethical approval was not required. All patients provided their consent. The highly prioritized requirements were then instantiated in a first prototype. Figure 1 depicts the elicited core set of MRs and derived design principles (DPs) based on the structure proposed by Gregor et al. [9].

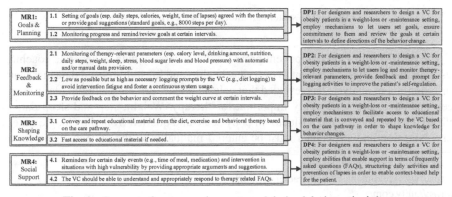

Fig. 1. Core set of meta-requirements and derived design principles

2.2 System Overview

Our implementation of the virtual obesity coach extends and adapts a web-based patient portal for patients with multiple sclerosis [10]. In the following, the main system components (see Fig. 2) are briefly described.

Animation Rendering: This component represents the avatar of the coach rendered via WebGL[1] in the browser. We deliberately chose a cartoonized avatar similar to "Disney Pixar" or Apple "Memojis", as previous research has shown that this might be beneficial to avoid uncanny feelings of the user due to imperfections of too photorealistic representations [11]. Regarding gender, we chose a female avatar for this research. The avatar model was designed with the software "Reallusion Character Creator"[2] and animated, as well as exported (WebGL build) with the gaming engine "Unity"[3]. For animating the avatar, we used animations such as idle, greeting or pointing gestures from the library "mixamo.com". Further, we used a Unity package[4] that allows a lip sync approximation and automated animation of eyes, eyelids and head. The speech data is delivered from the backend and lip sync is generated in real-time. To realize the multimodal behavior of the avatar (e.g., talking while pointing on the weight curve), we build on the behavior markup language (BML) that aims to standardize behavioral control of ECAs. Therefore, we re-used a BML realizer provided by the Horizon 2020 project "RAGE"[5].

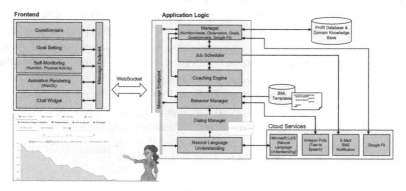

Fig. 2. The system architecture of the virtual coach

The **Self-Monitoring** component provides the necessary data to generate coaching messages and enables the patient to overview health- and lifestyle-related data in a chart. Our requirement analysis has revealed that caloric intake, drinking amount, daily steps, sleep and stress are particularly important for therapy. Weight, step and sleep data is delivered by wearables and a Bluetooth body scale and queried from the Google fitness store. Nutrition and stress data must be entered manually by the patients using forms

---

[1] https://www.khronos.org/webgl/.

[2] https://www.reallusion.com/character-creator/.

[3] https://unity.com/.

[4] https://crazyminnowstudio.com/unity-3d/lip-sync-salsa/.

[5] http://rageproject.eu/bml-realizer/.

or questionnaires. On the backend side, several manager components control the data provision and integration. To avoid intervention fatigue, patients are prompted by the system only twice a week (on randomly selected days) to log their diet.

Goal-Setting: Patients can actively set goals (steps, calories, weight, time of lapses) that were agreed with the therapist. Several time periods and also details on how to achieve the goals are adjustable (e.g., to increase daily steps, the patient is instructed to get off one tram stop earlier on the way to work). The specified goals also serve the coaching engine for message generation and patients can track their progress in a chart.

Coaching-Engine: Our prototype instantiates the just-in-time-adaptive intervention (JITAI) framework [12]. JITAIs refer to an intervention design with the philosophy of providing the right type and amount of support at the right time by continuously adapting to the changing context. A central building block of the JITAI framework are decision rules (if-then) that link tailoring variables (e.g., stress, weight loss or hour of day) with intervention options (e.g., feedback, reminder). For example, patients often relapse after work by turning to unhealthy food. Here, the coach may intervene, for instance: *"Before you reach for unhealthy food, always remember: now you may feel better, but just imagine how you feel on the scale tomorrow! Does this really reduce your stress?"*. To integrate the coach into daily life, we integrated a Job-Scheduler that sends E-Mail and SMS notifications.

For the conversational competencies of the VC, a **Natural Language Understanding** component and a **Dialog-** and **Behavior Manager** are utilized. The user can interact with the coach via a text-based chat widget that uses a combination of constrained input for safety-critical conversations (action buttons with predefined questions/answers) and unconstrained input (free text). Understanding unconstrained text input is realized via the Microsoft language understanding service[6] and may be enriched by automatic speech recognition in a further development of the prototype. The dialog manager keeps track of the conversation flow based on a finite state machine (i.e., rule-based). The behavior manager then generates appropriate non-verbal and verbal behavior based on the dialog state and converts it into a representation that the Animation Rendering component can realize. For verbal-behavior, we used the text-to-speech service Amazon Polly[7] and a voice called "Vicky" similar to the voice of the popular speech assistant "Alexa". For example, the user can ask for practical support in the form of diet suggestions ("What can I eat for lunch?") or other therapy-related questions (e.g., "Why have I gained weight this week?"). If the user reports medical problems and feels unwell, the therapist is notified by the system. The VC also shapes knowledge by providing behavioral guidance in critical situations such as when eating out or when the system has noticed unexpected changes in daily routines. By using unconstrained input for well defined and uncritical intents (e.g., recipe recommendation), the input modalities of the VC go beyond previous work on an ECA for this health context that solely relied on multiple-choice menus [5]. Although language understanding capabilities render a more natural interaction possible, conducting empathic dialogues this way remains a challenge since the advent of ECAs [13] and was solved with constrained input options.

---

[6] https://www.luis.ai/.

[7] https://aws.amazon.com/de/polly/.

3 Evaluation, Significance of Results and Outlook

We evaluated our software artifact with a video demonstration. A one-minute video[8] was presented to $n = 12$ patients (female: 7, male: 5) where the VC introduces herself *"Hello, my name is Lea, I'm your virtual coach..."* and explains the core functions of the system. We assessed perspicuity (pragmatic quality), stimulation and novelty (hedonic quality) based on the user experience questionnaire items (UEQ) [14]. In addition, we asked for verbal feedback regarding the overall impression. Since we used a video, an evaluation of efficiency and dependability was considered inappropriate. Overall, the results indicate a clear positive feedback (see Fig. 3) that is supported by a both-sided Wilcoxon rank sum test against the neutral value of the 7-point scale (all $p < .05$). Although the concept of an avatar-based VC for morbidly obese patients is novel, the ratings for novelty varied. The variance could reflect previous experiences with avatars, e.g., in video games. Regarding the verbal feedback, only one patient criticized the artificial voice of the coach. Implementing pre-recorded voices might be an alternative but would require more resources and restrict adaptability.

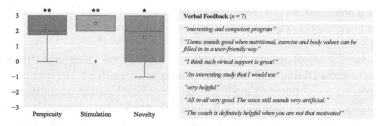

Fig. 3. Evaluation results of perspicuity, stimulation, novelty and verbal feedback

Our research contributes further evidence to the notion that ECAs could help address a gap in medical care and, moreover, introduces a promising first design of an avatar-based VC for obesity patients. The present data suggest that patients not only welcome a VC but may even have a demand for it. This is of particular importance as ECAs could also help reduce healthcare costs and provide the continuous care support required to manage chronic diseases such as obesity. Because ECAs are complex systems that have so far been mostly deployed as desktop installations [4], our study also demonstrates the practical feasibility of a web-based ECA. The web-based implementation enables broad accessibility and adoption of the VC. Additionally, this research presents a core set of MRs and DPs validated with multiple surveys and interviews. However, the current version does not contain elements for the management of diabetes, a condition quite common in the target population (e.g., monitoring blood sugar levels). This will be taken into account in further development. We also plan to port the application to mobile phones to enable more comprehensive just in time support. For example, the VC could then automatically detect if the patient is in a grocery store and provide nutrition advice for maintaining behavior changes or help prevent relapses. The advanced avatar could also be provided with abilities to demonstrate physical exercises. At the same time,

---

[8] Video demonstration of the prototype: https://youtu.be/EwJYHuewe9o.

further usability studies are required to determine, if, for example, an obese "peer buddy" is more suitable as an avatar than a lean one and which gender might be beneficial for this context. Finally, future studies should demonstrate the clinical evidence and investigate long term effects.

References

1. WHO: Obesity: preventing and managing the global epidemic. WHO (2000)
2. Effertz, T., Engel, S., Verheyen, F., Linder, R.: The costs and consequences of obesity in Germany: a new approach from a prevalence and life-cycle perspective. Eur. J. Health Econ. **17**(9), 1141–1158 (2015). https://doi.org/10.1007/s10198-015-0751-4
3. Fischer, M., Oberänder, N., Weimann, A.: Four main barriers to weight loss maintenance? A quantitative analysis of difficulties experienced by obese patients after successful weight reduction. Eur J Clin Nutr. **74**, 1192–1200 (2020)
4. Tropea, P., et al.: Rehabilitation, the great absentee of virtual coaching in medical care: scoping review. J. Med. Internet Res. **21**, e12805 (2019)
5. Watson, A., Bickmore, T., Cange, A., Kulshreshtha, A., Kvedar, J.: An internet-based virtual coach to promote physical activity adherence in overweight adults: randomized controlled trial. J. Med. Internet Res. **14**, e1 (2012)
6. Stein, N., Brooks, K.: A fully automated conversational artificial intelligence for weight loss: longitudinal observational study among overweight and obese adults. JMIR Diabetes **2**, e28 (2017)
7. Michie, S., et al.: The behavior change technique taxonomy (v1) of 93 hierarchically clustered techniques: building an international consensus for the reporting of behavior change interventions. Ann. Behav. Med. **46**, 81–95 (2013)
8. Asbjørnsen, R.A., et al.: Persuasive system design principles and behavior change techniques to stimulate motivation and adherence in electronic health interventions to support weight loss maintenance: scoping review. J. Med. Internet Res. **21**, e14265 (2019)
9. Gregor, S., Chandra Kruse, L., Seidel, S.: Research perspectives: the anatomy of a design principle. J. Assoc. Inf. Syst. **21**, 2 (2020)
10. Voigt, I., et al.: A digital patient portal for patients with multiple sclerosis. Front. Neurol. **11**, 400 (2020)
11. MacDorman, K.F., Green, R.D., Ho, C.-C., Koch, C.T.: Too real for comfort? Uncanny responses to computer generated faces. Comput. Hum. Behav. **25**, 695–710 (2009)
12. Nahum-Shani, I., Hekler, E.B., Spruijt, D.: Building health behavior models to guide the development of just-in-time adaptive interventions: a pragmatic framework. Health Psychol. **34**, 1209 (2015)
13. Bickmore, T.W., Picard, R.W.: Establishing and maintaining long-term human-computer relationships. ACM Trans. Comput.-Hum. Interact. **12**, 293–327 (2005)
14. Laugwitz, B., Held, T., Schrepp, M.: Construction and evaluation of a user experience questionnaire. In: Holzinger, A. (ed.) USAB 2008. LNCS, vol. 5298, pp. 63–76. Springer, Heidelberg (2008). https://doi.org/10.1007/978-3-540-89350-9_6

AMRITA: Designing New Recipes for Phytonutrition

Riccardo Bonazzi$^{(\boxtimes)}$ (iD) and Michael Coimbra Vaz (iD)

University of Applied Sciences Western Switzerland, HES-SO, Sierre, Switzerland
{riccardo.bonazzi,michael.coimbravaz}@hevs.ch

Abstract. In this paper, we describe a prototype, which is aimed at cooking chefs and that generates list of ingredients for recipes made of local plants. We focus on a specific type of cooking recipes based on plants, which are used in cultural food practices worldwide to support wellbeing ("phytonutrition"). Researchers in food technology have been successfully developing food recommenders but there is a gap concerning the notion of phytonutrition changes the set of required functions and the theoretical framework to assess the software. We describe an end-to-end support system for recipe design in compliance with European regulations concerning phytonutrients. Results of a longitudinal test, which was done in a hotel in the Alpine region, show that our software allows chefs to conceive a set of dishes, which increase the satisfaction of customers.

Keywords: Phytonutrition · Nutrition claim · Traditional food innovation

1 Introduction: Description of the Artefact

Problem Statement and Intended User Group. This paper investigates how to extend functionalities of recipes management software for cooking chefs and to include phytonutrition. The term *phytonutrition* refers to the role of substances from plants (phytonutrients) used in cultural food practices and cuisines worldwide to support health; in addition to their phytonutritive role, phytonutrients have a phytotherapeutic role, acting as modifiers of physiological function [1]. On the one hand, phytonutrition allows chefs to develop new recipes with proven effects on the wellbeing, while increasing the authenticity of new dishes rooted in local cultures. On the other hand, a new stakeholder needs to be acknowledged in many countries: authorities that control nutrition claims associated with phytonutrients. *Nutrition claim* means any claim, which states, suggests or implies that a food has particular beneficial nutritional properties due to: (a) the calorific value it provides, provides at a reduced or increased rate or does not provide (b) the nutrients or other substances it contains, contains in reduced or increased proportions or does not contain [2: art.2.2.4]. An example of nutrition claim is "*iron contributes to the reduction of tiredness and fatigue*".

Use Case: Combining Food Recipes Innovation and Customers Satisfaction by Using Food Design Thinking. Scholars have already explored how innovation occurs

© Springer Nature Switzerland AG 2021
L. Chandra Kruse et al. (Eds.): DESRIST 2021, LNCS 12807, pp. 58–64, 2021.
https://doi.org/10.1007/978-3-030-82405-1_7

among professional chefs [3], although the creative process of chefs has been understudied [4]. Such assessment has led to the creation of initial themes based on specific eating situations for use in the early stages of the Food Design process, facilitating the subsequent idea generation phase [4]. In this paper, we focus on the results of a previous study [5], which have shown that the creativity tool SCAMPER (substitute, combine, adapt, modify/magnify, put to other use, eliminate, reverse/rearrange) [6] can be used to support the creative process of chefs. Accordingly, we shall assume that to *substitute* existing ingredients with phytonutrients will enhance chefs' creativity.

Missing Feature in Existing Software: software for cooking chefs mostly focuses on material planning to lower cost, but it does not include features that are mostly used by nutritionists. Figure 1 illustrates how we approach the problem using a *dietetic marketing perspective* [7], which focuses on (a) the health-related potential of a specific food according to authorities, (b) the incorporation of perspectives from social marketing to include the customer and (c) the application of consumer and sensory research methods to assess the performance. There seems to be still a lack of software supporting the innovation process of chefs, and our article is an attempt to close on of those gaps concerning the management of recipes for phytonutrition. Indeed, once authorities are in the loop, regulatory compliance, and scientific results from existing studies in food science need to be taken into account. Hence, we aim at obtaining design guidelines for a software that can (1) integrate nutritional data from existing databases, (2) extract a set of ingredients according to customer's preferences and (3) prove to authorities that the chefs is entitled to make nutrition claim to differentiate the product with respect to competitors. Therefore, our research question is: *how to support cooking chefs develop new recipes for phytonutrition?*

Fig. 1. Stakeholders involv.ed in phytonutrition.

Description of Features. This section illustrates the functions of the mobile service that we developed, whose name (AMRITA), which recalls the Sanskrit name of the food of gods and that is a pseudonymous for *Autonomous Management of Recipes Integrating Touristic Associates.*

F1) Data Collection from Datasets for Regulatory Compliance. In the first part of the code, we collect and manage data from the different datasets available online by using R tidyverse (F1). These are the datasets collected by AMRITA: 999 food values items are gathered from the Food Compendium, 2543 EU nutritional claims come from the EU database, 23 information concerning daily Intakes refer from the Swiss regulation.

F2) List of Ingredients for the Cooking Chef. We filter the data according to the season and the nutritional claim requested by the customer; we use the R package Lpsolve to define the amount of each ingredient that minimizes the set of ingredients, while respecting the required amount of phytonutrients. As an example of IT-based regulation, the software adapts the choice of fruits and vegetables to fulfill the nutritional claims according to the season. The software selects seasonal fruits and vegetables by using the database of an association that focuses on biological products extracts the data concerning seasonal food from the official database of fruits and vegetables, concerning the average nutritional composition of the raw product and the cooked product. Finally, the software extracts a list of ingredients that complies with the claim while minimizing the number of ingredients. For example, Table 1 shows that for the month of February, the software extracts 21 seasonal ingredients such as "Lamb's lattuce" and "Garlic", whose combination leads to high values for Iron and folate. Based on previous studies on creativity of cooking chefs [6], we claim that a list of ingredients to substitute and combine will allow cooking chefs to create new recipes. Thus, our first testable proposition is:

P1: Cooking chefs manage to create new plates starting from a suggestion of ingredients that should replace standard recipes.

F3) Presentation of Results to the Client. Finally, we present the list of the ingredients to the chef by using R markdown. The cooking chef takes the list of the ingredients and adapts it, by adding ingredients and by deciding how to cook them, according to her experience. The recipes are shared on the platform under a creative common license, to support sharing among chefs. In the end, the client receives a detailed list explaining how the dish complies with regulation and the customer an information card that enhance the dining experience by explaining the effect of each ingredient. Hence, our second testable proposition is:

P2: customers are willing to pay more than average for this type of product.

Table 1. Example of list of ingredients to reduce tiredness and fatigue

Ingredients	Qte..gr	Folate	iron..Fe
Garlic	92	févr.76	1.288
Lamb's lettuce..raw	39	62.40	0.819
Five-grain.beer	375	18.75	0.000
TOT	:	83.91	2.107
GOAL (reduction of tiredness and fatigue)	:	30.00	2.100
CHECK	:	1.00	1.000

Extra: Combining F3, F2 and F1 in Reverse Order. AMRITA can assess existing recipes as well. Table 2 shows an existing recipe extracted from the software of a cooking chef. The columns show the current focus on quantity of each product to buy and the cost of each ingredient.

Table 2. Example of list of ingredients in an existing recipe of a cooking chef

Merchandise	Net quantity in kg or L	Cost
Beet, steamed (no salt added)	0,9	6
Beet leaves	0,2	1,2
Vinaigrette (with rapeseed oil)	0,05	0,25
Olive oil	0,03	0,45
Cooking salt with iodine	0,5	1
Pepper	0,001	0,02

AMRITA can assess the nutrients of each ingredient, compare it against the requirement and underline the nutritional claims that the cooking chef can associate to the dish. Figure 2 shows that the chef would be advised to claim that "the dish reduces the tiredness and fatigues" (the last column), since the recipe can assure required levels of calcium and folate. Hence, our second testable proposition is:

P3: the phytonutrients checker increases regulatory compliance.

Nutrient	blood coagulation	energy-yielding metabolism	function of digestive enzymes	maintenance of normal bones and teeth	muscle function and neurotransmission	regulation of cell division and differentiation	"cell membrane permeability"	contribution to the maintenance or achievement of a normal body weight	maintenance of normal blood pressure	reduction of tiredness and fatigue
calcium (Ca)	1	1	1	1,1	1,1	1	1	1	1,1	1
chloride (Cl)	NULL	NULL	NULL	NULL	NULL	NULL	NULL	NULL	NULL	NULL
folate	NULL	NULL	NULL	NULL	NULL	NULL	NULL	NULL	NULL	1

Fig. 2. Ingredients for "Red beets on a bed of salt" and assessment of nutrients

2   Evaluation of the Artefact

We tested our artefact with clients of a hotel located in the Alpine region. Culinary tourism emphasizes unique foods and dishes from the culture of the host region and a community development strategy [8]. The hotel MBH (name changed to respect anonymity) mostly targets couples ranging from 50 to 70 years old and it has a restaurant within the premises. The cooking chef used the system to develop a set of dishes based on seasonal plants, which aimed at reducing stress.

Collected Data. We have collected data from 50 clients of the hotel, who stayed at least 3 days and experience at least one menu of phytonutrition. The survey had two parts: (1) in the first part, we assessed the overall quality of the service with a version of a SERVQUAL that was adapted to restaurants [9], to make sure that clients appreciated the dish instead of just appreciating the overall ambience of the restaurant; (2) in the second part of the survey, we used four performance indicators to assess the performance of the overall service: (a) the willingness to pay for a dish, (b) the willingness to pay for the menu, (c) the willingness to pay for a menu multiple times over one year and (d) the willingness to recommend the service to other people. In the end, we obtained 37 valid surveys completed by clients at the end of their stay (13 surveys had missing values). Fig. 3 shows that clients liked the overall experience (S4), they liked the taste of the dishes (S3) and felt the dishes were good for their well-being (S2).

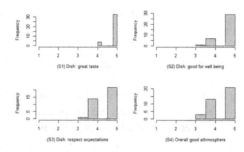

Fig. 3. Four items from the SERVQUAL survey [S1–S4]

As shown in Fig. 4, the willingness to pay of the clients was fairly high, with some most clients willing to pay at least \$30 for a dish (P1) and \$50 for a menu (p2). By multiplying the WTP for a menu and the frequency of purchase (P3), we can have an idea of the *customer lifetime value* over one year. Moreover, the customer referral value can be derived from the willingness to recommend the service to other people (the so-called net promoter score in P4). Finally, we created a definition of Champion by using the median of the customer lifetime value over one year and the cutoff of 8/10 for the Net Promoter Score to assess the customer referral value, as suggested by Kumar et al. [10]. In our dataset, we found 13 Champions out of 37 (35%).

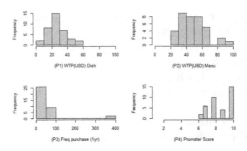

Fig. 4. Four performance indicators [P1–P4]

3 Discussions and Conclusions

The purpose of this study was to design a system to support cooking chefs develop new recipes for phytonutrition. According to Davis [11], "all interesting theories, at least all interesting social theories, then, constitute an attack on the taken-for-granted world of their audience". Consequently, this section is split into two statements regarding what we consider to be interesting.

What Seems To Be a Bad Phenomenon is in Reality a Good Phenomenon. Regulations are often associated to additional costs. Nonetheless, the MBH case has shown that the *"chefs managed to create new plates starting from a suggestion of ingredients that should replace standard recipes"* (proposition P1) and that *"customers are willing to pay for this type of product"* (proposition P2).

What Seems To Be a Single Phenomenon is in Reality Composed Of Assorted Heterogeneous Elements. Nutrition claims should be done by carefully assessing the compliance with existing regulations and that nutrition does not always have positive effects on wellbeing. In other words, a new stakeholder (the authority) should be taken into account while design the software and functions for IT-based regulation should be included. The case of MBH shows that *"the phytonutrients checker increases regulatory compliance"* (proposition P3), since the chef managed to develop dishes that customers liked and that complied with regulations.

In its current stage of development, the software does not make extensive use of machine learning algorithms and it does not take advantage of existing datasets of flavor networks. Moreover, the prototype has been assessed only by measuring the acceptance of the service by the final user, instead of being tested by multiple chefs and by food providers in the region of MBH. Therefore, we will extend the functionalities of the software and to test it more extensively over a larger spectrum of participants.

References

1. Bland, J.S.: Phytonutrition, phytotherapy, and phytopharmacology. Altern. Ther. Health Med. **2**, 73–76 (1996)
2. European Commision: Regulation No 1924/2006 of the European Parliament and of the council. The Official Journal of the **European Union** L 404 (2006)

3. Fauchart, E., Von Hippel, E.: Norms-based intellectual property systems: the case of French chefs. Organ. Sci. **19**, 187–201 (2008)
4. Zampollo, F., Peacock, M.: Food design thinking: a branch of design thinking specific to food design. J. Creat. Behav. **50**, 203–210 (2016)
5. Kudrowitz, B., Oxborough, A., Choi, J., Stover, E.: The chef as designer: classifying the techniques that chefs use in creating innovative dishes. In: Design Research Society Conference 2014, p. 21 (2014)
6. Eberle, R.F.: Developing imagination through scamper. J. Creat. Behav. (1972)
7. Sandvik, P.: Designing healthy foods–a dietetic marketing perspective. Int. J. Food Des. **3**, 125–134 (2018)
8. Green, G.P., Dougherty, M.L.: Localizing linkages for food and tourism: culinary tourism as a community development strategy. Community Dev. **39**, 148–158 (2008)
9. Stevens, P., Knutson, B., Patton, M.: DINESERV: a tool for measuring service quality in restaurants. Cornell Hotel Restaur. Adm. Q. **36**, 5–60 (1995)
10. Kumar, V., Petersen, J.A., Leone, R.P.: How valuable is word of mouth? Harv. Bus. Rev. **85**, 139 (2007)
11. Davis, M.S.: That's interesting! towards a phenomenology of sociology and a sociology of phenomenology. Philos. Soc. Sci. **1**, 309–344 (1971)

Towards Design Principles for the Three Phases of Physicians' Information Seeking Activities

Helena Vallo Hult[1,2]([✉]) [iD] and Christian Master Östlund[1] [iD]

[1] School of Business, Economics and IT, University West, Trollhattan, Sweden
`helena.vallo-hult@hv.se`
[2] NU Hospital Group, Trollhattan, Sweden

Abstract. Healthcare settings involve complex sociotechnical challenges, accentuated by rapidly expanding medical knowledge and technological developments. This entails a need for the professionals to continually seek information to update their skills and knowledge to solve problems in daily clinical practice while at the same time facing an increasingly fragmented health information environment. This research in progress paper addresses the real-life problem of physicians' information seeking activities before, during and after a patient visit. The anticipated contribution is a set of design principles that a system for information seeking through these three phases should support.

Keywords: Design science research · Information seeking · Learning · Healthcare

1 Introduction

Physicians belong to a highly specialized profession, with demands to keep their knowledge current and keep learning throughout their working life. Recent developments in medicine and technology enable fast and easy access to online clinical evidence. Various digital tools have been designed to bring together medical and patient information for supporting decision making at the point of care [1]. At the same time, it is hard to get an overview due to rapidly expanding medical knowledge, along with its overall increased complexity and fragmentation [2]. Furthermore, established role relationships within healthcare are challenged by digitally engaged patients who find other paths to knowledge than through traditional healthcare institutions and increasingly generate and track their own data on health apps and smartphones [3]. Recent research shows that while technology and sources of information retrieval have changed and improved, barriers for information seeking and retrieval still fail to satisfy the needs of physicians [4]. This calls for a design of health information systems that takes into consideration this complexity of on-the-fly decision making.

Therefore, we argue that there is a need for a more design-oriented approach [5, 6] when designing information seeking systems that take the dependency between the context and the IT system into consideration. The practical problem identified and addressed in this study concerns the need for physicians to continually seek new information to

© Springer Nature Switzerland AG 2021
L. Chandra Kruse et al. (Eds.): DESRIST 2021, LNCS 12807, pp. 65–70, 2021.
https://doi.org/10.1007/978-3-030-82405-1_8

update or confirm their knowledge and find answers to clinical questions [7]. The aim of this research in progress paper is to identify and analyze how physicians learn through information-related activities in connection to patient work. The main contribution is a tentative design that supports the process of information seeking activities before, during and after a patient visit.

2 Theoretical Background

Research on information seeking behavior is spread across different disciplines concerned with the design, development, and evaluation of Information Technology (IT). Professional groups and occupations have provided a common structure for such investigations, with an increasing interest in health information systems resulting from the rapid growth of medical information and advances in digital technology [8]. Earlier studies focused on physicians' information needs and use, with emphasis on formal information sources related to either keeping up to date or clinical treatment and patient care [9]. While the technology keeps progressing, searching for information online broadly outlines the same pattern, and physicians still face problems related to information seeking and retrieval [4, 10]. Common barriers identified in the literature include time, accessibility, personal skills and attitudes, institutional characteristics as well as resource features [11]. In the Swedish context, prior research has highlighted the importance of relevance to clinical context for successful training in information seeking, and a recent national report shows that while physicians are positive to the use of digital tools, they face barriers in terms of lack of time, login procedures and technical problems as well as a lack of knowledge about available information sources [12, 13].

A common explanation for user resistance in healthcare is that the introduction of new technologies may change traditional practice and threaten the medical profession, which highlight the importance of adapting information systems to the workflow of clinicians. However, this is not without problems; as Zhou, Ackerman and Zheng [14] point out, medical records have what they describe as a dichotomized purpose of being both practice-centered, to facilitate real-time activities, and patient-centered, to support long-term information reuse. Due to the specific characteristics of the healthcare information environment and the complexity that comes with a design both supporting quick decisions and long-term competence development, a design-oriented approach, where the system will be informed by theories and rooted in practice, was chosen.

3 Method

The research is carried out within the Swedish healthcare system in response to a need for insights into the existing information practices of physicians, as well as practical recommendations for future design and integration of digital learning in clinical practice. The research approach is qualitative, and the study draws from interview data with Swedish physicians and prior work on digital learning and engagement in practice [3] to illustrate and gain more in-depth insights into the phases of information seeking at the point of care which is the focus of this paper. The research design is guided by the general design cycle by Vaishnavi and Kuechler [6], where interviews and workshops with participating physicians [3] were analyzed, and tentative design guidelines derived to be evaluated in the next phase. The overall aim of the research project is to arrive at design principles [15] that will guide future designs of information seeking systems for physicians and other groups with similar needs. The participating physicians were women and men, all resident physicians at the time of the data collection, i.e., practicing as physicians while also in training towards specialist competence. Most of them worked at outpatient clinics to obtain a specialty in general medicine (patient-based medical care provided across specialty boundaries). Other specialties, as well as physicians working in hospital settings, were also represented. Data collection activities are specified in Table 1.

Table 1. Data collection activities

Participants	Data collection	Year
Physicians	15 individual interviews	2015
Researcher, faculty, course participants	Engagement in 2-day workshops in evidence-based information seeking and case-based discussions	2015, 2021
Physicians	Respondent validation (planned)	2021

The analysis was done based on thematic analysis [16] to provide an overview of key events during the information seeking process, guided by theories on information seeking as outlined above, with the purpose to identify and analyze the types of information-related activities described in each phase.

4 Results: Three Phases of Information Seeking

In the analysis, we have focused primarily on how physicians seek information at the point of care, i.e., related to patient care in three phases: prior to meeting patients, during patient meetings and after patient meetings.

Phase 1: Prior to the Patient Meeting. Searching for information beforehand was mentioned as most common in cases where the patient has an unusual symptom or a known but rare disease: *"...then I can read up on that if it is something that I don't know or feel confident about"*. But the physicians also commented that it depends on other factors as well, such as time to prepare and having access to background information about the patient. They described that they often turn to the internet for an initial search: *"...to get an idea of, for example, a specific or unusual diagnosis or treatment, or to check for new updates"*. The importance of trustworthy information was highlighted, especially related to online health information, but they also trust their own judgement: *"...a quick Google search is usually enough to get confirmation"*. Other types of information seeking that was mentioned prior to meeting the patient was to look for updates or specific recommendations: *"I can also search for drugs and possible side effects to prepare myself"*.

Phase 2: During the Patient Meeting. In this phase, the physicians likewise described information seeking activities when the patient has a new symptom, or something comes up during the consultation: *"Then, when the patient comes, and I examine, and it's something I do not know what it is, well then I have to check it out of course."* They also described that it has become more common to include the patients in the information seeking process: *"to find out what information the patient has read"* and how they, when searching for information together with patients, deliberately turn to reliable information sources targeted towards patients that can be printed or shared: *"because there it is well explained [...] which is often appreciated."* A typical case when the physicians themselves search for information during patient visits is for dermatology: *"then you can search for pictures or symptoms, and it is quite easy to get it down to a probable diagnosis."* It was more common in this phase to mention consulting a peer or an expert as the first source of information. But online information seeking was also considered a second step, done after self-consultation: "[for the] *more difficult or unusual things; then you have to go in and search."*

Phase 3: After the Patient Meeting. Finally, the physicians described the need to search for information after having met with the patient, either for a specific question: *"I can also go in afterwards...to look it up before prescribing"* or for a more general update: *"...to see that my knowledge is still correct"*. The physicians, in general, did not find it hard to search for information if they knew what they were looking for: "[then] *it is not so difficult to find, and it's usually easiest to ask the patient, so you get a little more explanation, and then you can usually find the information."* As one of the participants noted, this can make it hard to search in preparation: *"because it can seem to be about one thing, and so when you talk to the patient, it turns out to be something completely different."* Colleagues were also mentioned in this phase, but more seldom for consultation, but rather to discuss cases and new recommendations or treatments brought up by patients: *"...if there is new information on [mentions a Swedish medical site], or if you have had a patient, then you bring this to discuss in the group."*

5   Discussion and Conclusion

This study has described physicians' information seeking in three phases, and how they in this process face barriers but also engage in various types of learning. *The first phase*, prior to the patient meeting, can be characterized as mainly fact-checking to find updates on specific, known information, often through online digital tools provided by the hospital or quick internet searches using freely accessible, yet trustworthy sources. In this phase, the learning is typically for updating or re-learning something that is already known. In *phase two*, during patient meetings, physicians commonly search for information to guide the patient towards more validated sources tailored for laymen. Most often, the questions that arise during this phase are common questions that they already know the answer to from experience or basic medical knowledge. But when there is a need for gaining new knowledge relatively fast, they often use digital tools provided by the hospital. The information seeking done in *the third phase*, after patient meetings, most often regards follow-ups on specific questions, where the physicians need to check that they are updated on clinical guidelines, but also for more in-depth knowledge and reflection when discussing cases with colleagues.

Our findings confirm common barriers to information seeking such as difficulties to remember passwords and websites, and technical issues especially as they sometimes need to log-in at multiple levels while having a lack of time [11, 12]. Barriers were identified in all phases but considered most critical in phase two due to the presence of the patient. This highlights the importance to incorporate and align the technology with the work processes in healthcare, and that information seeking needs to be regarded as a sequential process rather than as separate entities [4, 17]. However, and equally important, findings from this study also illustrate that there are risks involved if too much focus is placed on "fast and easy access", as this may inhibit critical thinking and introduce new errors instead. Thus, stressing the importance of not viewing information seeking as an isolated activity out of context, but rather an activity that is integrated with work. Therefore, we suggest a holistic approach for developing a better understanding of the various strategies undertaken by physicians to overcome barriers to information seeking as they navigate and interact with both people and technologies in the information environment [3, 14].

For this initial step we have chosen to primarily zoom in on the information seeking done in the three phases, which is directed towards patient care, to develop a tentative design that supports the process of information seeking activities before, during and after the patient visit. Viewing the empirical data through the lens of previous research on information seeking among physicians, we arrive at four tentative design principles. The tentative design principles for the three phases of physicians' information seeking activities are as follows:

1. The system should support the validation of sources on the internet so the physicians can confirm what is already known or learn what is not known.
2. The system should provide seamless information so the physicians can access the information with low cognitive effort.
3. The system should enable physicians to consult peers or experts as a readily accessible sounding board during consultations.
4. The system should facilitate reflective peer discussions that leave digital footprints so it can be retrieved and spread throughout the organization.

The next step is to validate these design principles with the physicians through workshops and a survey. The final design principles should then be instantiated in a system that can be evaluated against the final design principles. Future research could follow changes or similarities in the three phases over time to capture continuing learning. It would also be interesting to explore patients' perspective or compare and contrast identified barriers within and across specific medical specialties and diseases.

References

1. Tan, S.S.L., Goonawardene, N.: Internet health information seeking and the patient-physician relationship: a systematic review. J. Med. Internet Res. **19**, e9 (2017)

2. Catillon, M.: Medical knowledge synthesis: a brief overview. Research report. Harvard University and National Bureau of Economic Research (2017)
3. Vallo Hult, H.: Digital Work: Coping with Contradictions in Changing Healthcare. University West, Trollhättan (2021)
4. van der Keylen, P., et al.: The Online Health Information needs of family physicians: systematic review of qualitative and quantitative studies. J. Med. Internet Res. **22**, e18816 (2020)
5. Hevner, A.R., March, S.T., Park, J., Ram, S.: Design science in information systems research. MIS Q. **28**, 75–105 (2004)
6. Vaishnavi, V.K., Kuechler, W.: Design Science Research Methods and Patterns: Innovating Information and Communication Technology. CRC Press, Boca Raton (2015)
7. Cass, H., Barclay, S., Gerada, C., Lumsden, D.E., Sritharan, K.: Complexity and challenge in paediatrics: a roadmap for supporting clinical staff and families. Arch. Dis. Child. **105**, 109–114 (2020)
8. Case, D.O.: Looking for Information: A Survey of Research on Information Seeking, Needs, and Behavior. Bingley, Emerald (2012)
9. Gorman, P.N.: Information needs of physicians. J. Am. Soc. Inf. Sci. **46**, 729–736 (1995)
10. Younger, P.: Internet-based information-seeking behaviour amongst doctors and nurses: a short review of the literature. Health Info. Libr. J. **27**, 2–10 (2010)
11. Aakre, C.A., Maggio, L.A., Fiol, G.D., Cook, D.A.: Barriers and facilitators to clinical information seeking: a systematic review. J. Am. Med. Inform. Assoc. **26**, 1129–1140 (2019)
12. Pettersson, J., Bjorkander, E., Bark, S., Holmgren, D., Wekell, P.: Using scenario-based training to promote information literacy among on-call consultant pediatricians. J. Med. Library Assoc.: JMLA **105**, 262 (2017)
13. Inera: Vägen till vetenskapen - en användarundersökning från Eira och Sveriges sjukhusbibliotek (2019, in Swedish)
14. Zhou, X., Ackerman, M.S., Zheng, K.: The Recording and Reuse of Psychosocial Information in Care. In: Ackerman, M.S., Goggins, S.P., Herrmann, T., Prilla, M., Stary, C. (eds.) Designing Healthcare That Works, pp. 133–148. Academic Press, Cambridge (2018)
15. Chandra, L., Seidel, S., Gregor, S.: Prescriptive knowledge in IS research: conceptualizing design principles in terms of materiality, action, and boundary conditions. In: 2015 48th Hawaii International Conference on System Sciences, pp. 4039–4048. IEEE (2015)
16. Braun, V., Clarke, V.: Using thematic analysis in psychology. Qual. Res. Psychol. **3**, 77–101 (2006)
17. Daei, A., Soleymani, M.R., Ashrafi-Rizi, H., Zargham-Boroujeni, A., Kelishadi, R.: Clinical information seeking behavior of physicians: a systematic review. Int. J. Med. Inform. **139**, 104144 (2020)

Towards Smart Maritime Port Emissions Monitoring: A Platform for Enhanced Transparency

Philip Cammin$^{(\boxtimes)}$ and Stefan Voß

Institute of Information Systems, University of Hamburg, 20146 Hamburg, Germany
{philip.cammin,stefan.voss}@uni-hamburg.de

Abstract. In business-as-usual scenarios, the carbon dioxide (CO_2) foot print from global maritime shipping is estimated to rise up to 50% in 2050; in 2018 levels this accounts for 1,500 Mt [6]. The contribution of smart ports towards reducing air emissions comprises achieving higher operational efficiency. However, since air emissions monitoring is diversified in the maritime ports domain, it is difficult to obtain (comparable) emissions inventories (EIs) and judge upon the quality of air emissions monitoring as a whole of one or many ports. We understand this paper as a contribution to the monitoring component of green and smart ports, for which we propose a shared platform to create EIs frequently, foster standardization, transparency and comparability, and provide the basis for assessing the quality of emissions monitoring quality. The evaluation suggests potentials regarding, e.g., EIs standardization and frequency, and motivates further investigation such as integrating port tenants.

Keywords: Air emissions inventories · Maritime ports · Information systems

1 Introduction

Despite an increasing number of methodologies from research and practice to create emissions inventories (EIs), ports are lacking consistent provision of high-quality EIs to quantify emissions from port activities [3]. However, we consider the interplay of direct measures and long-term monitoring as an important issue for attaining transparency, adapting strategies, and promoting the abatement of emissions which is the most important environmental concern for Europeans [11]. To cope with the issue, port authorities (PAs) as regulators and policymakers design emissions reduction plans that involve stakeholders of the port and different measures regarding landside and seaside emitters. For example, six large Californian ports such as the Port of Long Beach (POLB) have to comply to the at-berth regulation, where terminal operators have to provide the cold-ironing (CI) infrastructure and vessel fleet operators have to use CI to some extent. There is an increasing number of academic works that address the needs of stakeholders, e.g., Wang et al. [16] who propose a framework to optimize government subsidies to ports to maximize at-berth emissions reduction per monetary unit, or Yu et al. [17] who establish a multi-objective optimization model to provide decision support for ship retrofitting.

© Springer Nature Switzerland AG 2021
L. Chandra Kruse et al. (Eds.): DESRIST 2021, LNCS 12807, pp. 71–76, 2021.
https://doi.org/10.1007/978-3-030-82405-1_9

The branch of *direct measures* is supplemented with EI methodologies from academia (for a review see Nunes et al. [10]) and practice (e.g., SPBP [13]). Nunes et al. [10] suggest using more accurate input data and combining different data sources that would increase comprehensive and accurate results, which is believed to standardize a methodology to be universally accepted. Azarkamand et al. [1] review initiatives and methodologies to reduce carbon dioxide (CO_2) emissions and find that each PA and terminal uses different methodologies. Therefore, the authors suggest creating a standardized tool to create EIs which is believed to "establish a benchmark and a potential comparison of results among ports" [1]. Moreover, a case study in ports implies that a tool could mitigate the technical burden from PAs in order to create EIs more frequently and quickly [3].

We perceive the aforementioned suggestions not as competing but rather supplementing: A good number of comprehensive EI methodologies should be supported with a tool so that methodologies could be further improved and evolve to standards, after usage and evaluation in the community of ports. Moreover, the availability of such a tool could promote its usage and afford the availability (frequency) of multi-year and comparable port EIs, not only to PAs but also to the public. Therefore, in this paper, we describe and evaluate a prototypical platform that manifests itself as the aforementioned tool.

The paper is structured as follows. Next, we describe the design of the platform. We proceed with outlining the significance to research and practice in Sect. 3. An evaluation of the platform is presented in Sect. 4. Section 5 outlines the conclusions and provides an outlook to further research.

2   Design of the Artifact

Based on the problem statement, we propose a shared and scalable platform (Port-EI) to create frequent, transparent and comparable EIs and foster the standardization of methodologies in a community of ports, resulting in large volumes of multi-port and multi-year data. The platform should provide a common interface to EI methodologies to access data and store estimated emissions, in this way, only a combination of such a platform and suitable methodologies support the aforementioned aims. A primal platform idea (conceptual system model and an early instantiation) has been presented to mitigate the problems to *assess emissions monitoring* quality and *create EIs* in the first place [2]. Therefore, we do not start from scratch but rather extend this idea by formulating additional goals: To increase the EI *frequency*, *standardization*, and *transparency and comparability*; for the latter, we concretize the existing solution sketch (which is to document the used methodology and input data). Based on these goals, we define five system components (partly presented in Fig. 1). The system is multi-user capable and extendable with methodologies. Two user groups are served: PAs as the primary user group responsible to obtain data from tenants and to provide data to the system, and general stakeholders that view and compare EIs. The system is implemented using Python, the Bottle web application framework, PivotTable.js and an SQLite database:

The **Data upload component** (see Fig. 1a) takes, hashes and stores data from (e.g., spreadsheet) files. Methodology data (e.g., emissions factors, energy factors) is stored as a single instance, whereas port data (e.g., activity data or infrastructure data) comprises instances, referencing a version (e.g., to label forecasts [3]), a time (coverage) and a user (PA) (see Fig. 1c). The **Data quality component** (see Fig. 1b) signals the need for data input or correction. Quality assurance (QA) is realized through data checkers, written by methodology authors, that may assess multi- and intra-port data (e.g., to audit accepted relational increases of activity [3]). The QA results can be shared with the Generation component to avoid repetitive QA on large data sets (e.g., Automatic Identification System (AIS) data). The **Generation component** executes methodologies given the QA passed, and labels the resulting EIs individually, for unique identification to support transparency and comparability, with the following attributes: The used methodology, methodology data hash and port data hash, as well as the version, time and user. All input data can be shared by methodologies to avoid data redundancy. The **Comparability component** provides an overview about the availability of EIs based on the abovementioned attributes. The **Compare component** (see Fig. 1d) visualizes EIs using a pivot table and various diagrams and features predefined views per methodology.

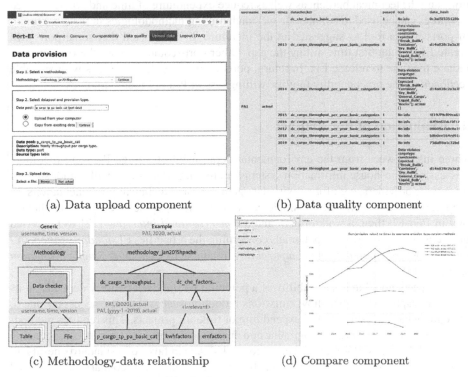

(a) Data upload component   (b) Data quality component

(c) Methodology-data relationship   (d) Compare component

Fig. 1. System components

3   Significance to Research and Practice

EI methodologies prominently follow a bottom-up, activity-based calculation approach that allows the assignment to emitters in order to steer emissions abatement and policy-making [4]. The academic literature provides different methodologies and single- and multi-year EIs, for instance, with a regional or global focus [e.g., 5, 7, 8] or multi-port focus [e.g., 4, 9, 15]. Nunes et al. [10] study 26 activity-based ship EI methodologies to synthesize a scheme of sources and procedures: The works tackle, e.g., social and external costs, analysis of spatial allocation and seasonality, comparison to land-based and other ship EIs or emissions projections for different scenarios. However, it is bur-densome to quickly re-execute those methodologies, caused by the cost of implementing algorithms, data gathering (if still available at all) and preprocessing for a set of ports and years. Implemented in a central platform as designed in Sect. 2, these problems could be mitigated, and, to the best of our knowledge, no such widely accepted approach in the maritime ports domain exists.

In practice, PAs can overcome the use of spreadsheet software for emissions calcula-tions and the technical burden, as well as reduce expenditure of time and costs; released resources can be used to collaborate on standardizing methodologies in the community of ports with a tool as suggested in the literature. It is expected that some ports will create EIs for the first time, filling the gap. Other ports could increase the frequency or reduce the time to release EIs. In return, ports could provide academics with valuable feedback on the practicability (ability, willingness of PAs) of methodologies.

4   Evaluation of the Artifact

Three interviewees from the environmental department of a large PA were recruited, possessing an in-house information system for creating various EIs, with minor support by service providers, e.g., for activity data gathering and technical implementations. In preparation, we implemented a simple cargo-handling equipment (CHE) EI methodol-ogy in Port-EI; then, a walkthrough and a *conversational interview* [12] were carried out, sensitized to investigate potentials concerning the properties EI *standardization, fre-quency*, and *transparency and comparability*, relatable to a *Quick & Simple evaluation strategy* [14].

The peers noted that the viability of a potential EI *standard* majorly depends on its ability to capture data that show emissions reduction success stories, necessary due to huge monetary investments and expenditure of time for projects. This requires method-ologies to cover appropriate geographic and operational scopes; for instance, renouncing the use of the PA's GPS-equipped drayage trucks' data in favor of a standard one-fits-all methodology is unrealistic. Standardization is indicated as a secondary, justified and difficult objective; the interviewees suggested utilizing Port-EI as a tool for discussing and experimenting among ports (given some methodologies implemented) to agree to a multi-tier methodology standard. One peer noted the case of ports using non-fitting methodologies (that require not obtainable data) that would raise concerns towards input data validity and question the *transparency and comparability*, thus creating uncertainty for stakeholders, which advocates the need for a multi-tier standardization approach.

Moreover, stakeholders' different expectations toward transparency and comparability (e.g., EI comparability among ports vs. for a specific port over time) were emphasized: We think this supports the Compare component's predefined views concept for tailoring EI reports to different stakeholders if the methodology allows. The interviewees find that Port-EI fosters consistent and *frequent* EIs creation in general, so ports lacking good tool support (e.g., due to lacking competency or resources) or avoiding external service providers would reduce costs and expenditure of time. However, a major effort lies in data gathering from tenants (who are not supported as active users) and subsequent data correction. Although for simple methodologies, the current data quality view is sufficient, it is suspected that implementing more comprehensive methodologies in Port-EI will reveal weaknesses in scanning diversified and massive amounts of activity data, which increases effort and hinders EI *frequency*.

5 Conclusions and Outlook

This paper describes a prototypical platform (Port-EI) to support the frequent creation of transparent and comparable maritime ports' EIs and to foster standardization, as well as to support the quality assessment of port emissions monitoring. Apart from the practical relevance, we add to the literature by concretizing the existing idea of *a tool* to create standard EIs. Implemented in a community of ports, it could reveal the practicability about the myriad of methodologies to academia available today. The evaluation in a large PA outlines the difficulties and benefits of EI standardization, which Port-EI could help to support. EI frequency could be increased for ports using simple methodologies and lacking resources. We emphasize the need to address a number of tasks based on the problems identified in the evaluation in forthcoming research, which we ordered according to our plans: The integration of comprehensive methodologies to investigate the usability of the Data quality component, the integration of port tenants to support data gathering, and the design of reciprocity mechanisms.

References

1. Azarkamand, S., Wooldridge, C., Darbra, R.M.: Review of initiatives and methodologies to reduce CO2 emissions and climate change effects in ports. Int. J. Environ. Res. Public Health **17**(11) (2020). https://doi.org/10.3390/ijerph17113858
2. Cammin, P., Voß, S.: Towards smart maritime port emissions monitoring: a shift to enhanced transparency (2021, Submitted)
3. Cammin, P., Yu, J., Heilig, L., Voß, S.: Monitoring of air emissions in maritime ports. Transp. Res. Part D: Transp. Environ. **87**, 102479 (2020). https://doi.org/10.1016/j.trd.2020.102479
4. CARB. Draft: 2018/2019 update to inventory for ocean-going vessels: methodology and results. California Air Resources Board (2019). https://ww3.arb.ca.gov/msei/ordiesel/draft2019ogvinv.pdf. Accessed 22 Aug 2019
5. Coello, J., Williams, I., Hudson, D.A., Kemp, S.: An AIS-based approach to calculate atmospheric emissions from the UK fishing fleet. Atmos. Environ. **114**, 1–7 (2015). https://doi.org/10.1016/j.atmosenv.2015.05.011
6. IMO. Fourth IMO GHG study: Final report. International Maritime Organization (2020). https://docs.imo.org/Shared/Download.aspx?did=125134. Accessed 7 Aug 2020

7. Jalkanen, J.-P., Johansson, L., Kukkonen, J.: A comprehensive inventory of the ship traffic exhaust emissions in the Baltic Sea from 2006 to 2009. Ambio **43**(3), 311–324 (2013). https://doi.org/10.1007/s13280-013-0389-3

8. Johansson, L., Jalkanen, J.-P., Kukkonen, J.: A comprehensive modelling approach for the assessment of global shipping emissions. In: Mensink, C., Kallos, G. (eds.) ITM 2016. SPC, pp. 367–373. Springer, Cham (2018). https://doi.org/10.1007/978-3-319-57645-9_58

9. Merk, O.: Shipping emissions in ports. ITF/OECD (2014). http://www.internationaltransportforum.org/jtrc/DiscussionPapers/DP201420.pdf. Accessed 15 Sept 2020

10. Nunes, R.A.O., Alvim-Ferraz, M.C.M., Martins, F.G., Sousa, S.I.V.: The activity-based methodology to assess ship emissions - a review. Environ. Pollut. **231**(Pt 1), 87–103 (2017). https://doi.org/10.1016/j.envpol.2017.07.099

11. Ortiz, A.G., Guerreiro, C., Soares, J., Antognazza, F., Gsella, A., Houssiau, M., et al.: Air quality in Europe - 2019 report. Publications Office of the European Union (EEA report, No. 10/2019), Luxembourg (2019)

12. Patton, M.Q.: Qualitative Research & Evaluation Methods - Integrating Theory and Practice, 4th edn. SAGE , Thousand Oaks (2015)

13. SPBP. San Pedro Bay Ports emissions inventory methodology report - version 1 (2019). San Pedro Bay Ports (2019). http://www.polb.com/civica/filebank/blobdload.asp?BlobID=15032. Accessed 26 Aug 2019

14. Venable, J., Pries-Heje, J., Baskerville, R.: FEDS: A framework for evaluation in design science research. Eur. J. Inf. Syst. **25**(1), 77–89 (2016). https://doi.org/10.1057/ejis.2014.36

15. Wan, Z., Ji, S., Liu, Y., Zhang, Q., Chen, J., Wang, Q.: Shipping emission inventories in China's Bohai Bay, Yangtze River Delta, and Pearl River Delta in 2018. Mar. Pollut. Bull. **151**, 110882 (2020). https://doi.org/10.1016/j.marpolbul.2019.110882

16. Wang, Y., Ding, W., Dai, L., Hu, H., Jing, D.: How would government subsidize the port on shore side electricity usage improvement? J. Clean. Prod. **278**, 123893 (2021). https://doi.org/10.1016/j.jclepro.2020.123893

17. Yu, J., Voß, S., Tang, G.: Strategy development for retrofitting ships for implementing shore side electricity. Transp. Res. Part D: Transp. Environ. **74**, 201–213 (2019). https://doi.org/10.1016/j.trd.2019.08.004

Supporting the Development of Strategic Mobility Agendas for Cities: The Pathway Method

Alexia Athanasopoulou[1]([⊠]) (ID), Rianne Valkenburg[1,2], Elke den Ouden[1,2] (ID), and Oktay Turetken[1] (ID)

[1] Eindhoven University of Technology, 5612AZ Eindhoven, The Netherlands
{a.athanasopoulou,a.c.valkenburg,e.d.ouden,o.turetken}@tue.nl
[2] Lighthouse, 5612AZ Eindhoven, The Netherlands

Abstract. Technological advances trigger a significant increase in the number of mobility solutions. Such solutions can address various mobility challenges that city authorities encounter, especially when planning their long-term strategic objectives. However, it is not always clear how city authorities can choose these solutions towards achieving their strategic goals collectively. Therefore, there is a need for a structured method that helps city authorities to establish their mobility agendas and plan their long-term objectives. We have developed a method that supports cities in creating pathways with strategic ambitions and visions regarding urban mobility that support the choice for current and future mobility solutions suitable for their implementation areas and aligned with their objectives. We did so by following the design science research methodology. We have designed our method by considering the information from existing mobility projects, evaluating and demonstrating it to relevant stakeholders with a paper prototype of the website to be delivered. Our study contributes with a structured stepwise approach that enables cities to create their pathways for urban mobility, starting with a strategy, all the way to solutions that help to reach the strategy.

Keywords: Urban mobility · Design science research · Stepwise approach · Strategic mobility agenda

1 Introduction

European Commission (EC) aims to archive an efficient, safe, secure, integrated, and environmentally friendly transportation system by 2050 [1]. Mobility allows the citizens to travel freely, improves the quality of life, and creates new jobs, leading to economic growth. Considering the various old and contemporary societal challenges, such as climate change, urbanization, population aging, technological change, the geopolitical landscape, and diversifying values and lifestyles [2], local authorities should take initiatives that keep mobility tenable [1].

Technology-enabled initiatives, such as car-sharing or Mobility-as-a-Service (MaaS), can address some of these mobility challenges if adopted by city authorities

© Springer Nature Switzerland AG 2021
L. Chandra Kruse et al. (Eds.): DESRIST 2021, LNCS 12807, pp. 77–88, 2021.
https://doi.org/10.1007/978-3-030-82405-1_10

[3]. However, the implementation of innovations to address the mobility challenges remains slow [4, 5] due to the lack of strategy and governmental policies that cannot be approved, legitimized, and therefore implemented [5]. Benefits, such as efficient vehicle use, optimized transport networks, and smooth citizens' experience, also necessitate new strategy and policy development [6].

The need for integrative and sustainable planning and appropriate policies that deal with these complex challenges has already been acknowledged [7]. Coordinated actions are needed, both from private and public stakeholders, to solve the mobility challenges and meet the emerging mobility demands on top of the transport infrastructure. Contrary to traditional approaches, city authorities need to create plans that consider the techno-logical disruptions and the emerging customer demands towards economic, social, and environmental benefits [8]. These mobility plans require a sustainable and long-term vision of a specific urban area while considering various societal costs and benefits and existing practices considered successful in other areas [7]. However, it is not clear how cities can choose these solutions and make choices to draft their plan (e.g., defining ambitions and visions, locating existing or potential future mobility solutions appropri-ate for their target implementation area) as a pathway to achieve their long-term strategic objectives.

This research aims to develop a step-by-step method that supports city authori-ties in creating pathways with strategic ambitions and visions regarding urban mobility and choosing current and future mobility solutions suitable for their implementation areas and aligned with their urban mobility objectives. This method – entitled the *Path-way Method*-, can accelerate the effective deployment of concrete mobility solutions in urban areas. We deployed the Design Science Research (DSR) methodology [8]. This manuscript addresses the design, development, and a paper-based formative evaluation of the method, supporting city authorities to create pathways of potential mobility solu-tions aiming to address their long-term urban mobility plan. The manuscript seeks to conceptualize and develop a novel framework of a guided stepwise approach that will enable city authorities and policymakers to create their pathways for urban mobility. In the subsequent design cycles, a web application will be developed as an integral part of the proposed artifact to support the execution of the method.

The remainder of this paper is structured as follows. In Sect. 2, we present the background and discuss works that are relevant to our research. Section 3 presents our research design. Section 4 introduces the Pathway Method, while in Sect. 5, we demonstrate our method. Finally, Sect. 6 presents our conclusions and future research directions.

2 Background Related Work

Mobility is defined as '*the ability to move or be moved freely and easily*' [11]. In simple words, mobility refers to pedestrians, car drivers, cyclists, delivery of goods, or people, all using and living in the same urban living environment doing their daily activities, such as commute to and from work [8].

Mobility is essential for a productive and efficient economy. Social and technolog-ical trends increase the expectations and demands on transport infrastructure, driving urban centers to become more open to mobility disruptions [8]. Therefore, there is a growing need for mobility solutions that limit the automotive industry's economic, societal, and environmental effects [12] and allow the design and development of innovative and customized mobility solutions. Mobility services are enabled by advanced mobility technologies such as cooperative-intelligent transport systems (C-ITS), big data analytics, and artificial intelligence that allow optimized transport networks and improved infrastructure utilization while enhancing user experience [6]. While the pace of these innovations grows, more solutions are emerging, challenging mobility's future steps [8]. Yet, governance and decision-making issues impede the pace that innovative mobility solutions are implemented [5].

The European Union (EU) supports urban mobility plans and encourages sustainable incentives to create them [13]. A *sustainable urban mobility plan* is based on a long-term vision, addresses transport-related problems in urban areas. In practice, city authorities can deal with mobility challenges to develop and integrate relevant policies and sustainable mobility plans explicitly inspired by strategies, visions, and solutions that have already been successfully deployed in other cities [14].

A long-term vision considers the societal dimensions, which require relevant knowledge (e.g., existing practices) and directions to support choice making for specific desirable mobility outcomes. In other words, approaches are needed to select and make choices [6]. Keeping directions allows to deliberately design policies to achieve a specific societal goal (based on particular ambitions and visions), favoring change directions over others [15] while stimulating the development of innovations needed for the transformative change [16]. Examples of these ambitions include the desire to have 'a reliable and accurate public transport for a city', the aim to foster 'a green and healthy city with high air quality and noise-free areas' or the become 'a city where mobility is traveler-centric and enables people to have freedom of choice' [17]. Examples of visions include 'having a city that provides a seamlessly connected network', 'a comfortable, accessible, high-quality living environment that encourages outdoor life', or 'an integrated data system across all mobility modes (public and private) that enables easy planning' [3]. Yet, how city authorities can take advantage of the potential directions to make their long-term choices based on their strategic objectives and visions is unclear. Developing step-by-step methods to support cities in making decisions related to their mobility plans can be a viable approach to address this gap.

Within the EU, various projects focusing on urban mobility have been initiated, some of which aim to deliver tangible outcomes, while others target intangible ones. However, despite their differences, these projects provide potentially generalizable use cases, best practices, or successful policies (e.g., *BABLE, CitizenCity, ASSURED, IRIS,* and *MOMENDUM*). A number of these projects also offer customized solutions that fit specific cities (e.g., *CitizenCity, KonSULT,* and *InSMART*). Among offerings include toolkits that city authorities can use to identify potential solutions that fit their target implementation area (e.g., *Streetmix, BABLE, SUNRISE,* and *KonSULT*). Common to these projects is the involvement of local authorities and other stakeholders in developing these tools (such as *SUMI, BABLE, CitizenCity, C-Mobile,* and *GrowSmarter*). Long- and short-planning is another common characteristic of several existing mobility projects (e.g., *CH4LLENGE, RiConnect,* and *Streetmix*). Finally, several projects (such as the

KonSULT) propose a set of indicators that report the potential impact of a mobility solution on specific aspects of mobility.

The available projects aim to address urban mobility issues at different levels and with varying outcomes and approaches. However, it is not clear how city authorities can choose suitable solutions or make choices related to their higher strategic ambitions and visions on urban mobility. For instance, while *BABLE* provides a list of potential solutions and examples of how they have been implemented in real-life settings, it lacks a guideline or method that would help cities define their ambitions and visions and tie them to the proposed mobility solutions. Similarly, the *Matchup* and *eHubs* projects provide demonstrations of best practices yet fail to offer guidelines on creating roadmaps that would lead to services aligned with the objectives.

The Pathway Method proposed in this study aims to address this gap by building upon the lessons learned in these projects and advancing in providing support for cities to develop a mobility roadmap starting with the strategic ambitions and visions to specific services suitable for a particular implementation in a target area.

3   Research Design

We have followed the DSR methodology [18], leveraging the process proposed by Peffers et al. [10] to structure our efforts. Accordingly, our research involved the following research steps: problem identification, defining the objectives of the solution, design, and development of the method, demonstration, and evaluation in a proper context [10, 17, 18]. For the demonstration and formative evaluation, we have developed a conceptual model of the model. Additionally, we developed paper prototypes of the method, which were demonstrated to an expert group to acquire evidence for the validity and utility of the proposed method [20, 21].

Figure 1 presents the process we followed to develop the proposed solution. First, we have identified the problem by performing a theoretical review [22], collecting a representative sample of finalized projects' deliverables from 2014 to 2020. We only included projects focused on improving the mobility of people (from a societal approach) that took place in European countries and have working websites. Thirty-three projects were included in our final list. By reviewing the aims and goals of these projects, we identified the existing gap. More specifically, we determined that currently, there is a lack of support for city authorities and other stakeholders to navigate from their high-level strategic ambitions to hands-on solutions to reach these ambitions.

We communicated the intermediate versions of the method through demonstrations to experts in the mobility domain. The group consisted of 8 experts (5 from academic institutions and 3 from public authorities) with 8 to 35 years of experience in the domain - particularly on urban mobility, transportation modeling, mobility services- and working experience in many projects/initiatives mentioned in Sect. 2. We set up eight focus group sessions of one hour from September to December 2020 with the expert group to gather their feedback regarding the validity and utility of the artifact. All sessions were held online, starting with a short presentation of how the feedback concerning the method and the conceptual model has been incorporated. Due to the online setting and for convenience *Miro*, an online collaboration whiteboard was used to brainstorm the objectives (Objx) the method should meet.

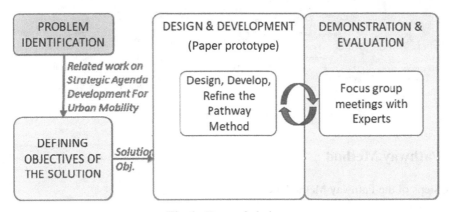

Fig. 1. Research design.

The focus group meetings provided valuable feedback that was incorporated in the design of the method. We initiate the design of the Pathway Method and its steps based on the results of the *Roadmaps for Energy (R4E)* project that focused on developing a method for new types of strategic development roadmaps for the development and implementation of energy solutions [23]. Based on the results of this project, feedback received from the experts, and the literature review, we defined the following objectives -aligned with our main goal - for the Pathway Method to guide its design:

Obj1: The method should incorporate a stepwise approach to help cities to create their pathways for urban mobility, starting with a strategy, all the way to mobility solutions that help to reach the strategy.
Obj2: The stepwise approach should be supported, where necessary, with available insight from existing research and practice (e.g., existing or future mobility solutions appropriate for their target implementation area).
Obj3: The method should allow users to define their target implementation area's characteristics so that appropriate mobility solutions aligned with these characteristics (as well as the defined ambitions and vision) can be located.

After iterations and changes at the initial Pathway, Method steps, a consensus was reached regarding the design of the method.

The method incorporates 5 steps, as depicted in Fig. 2. We performed a 'sanity check' between the sessions to test if the final process is rational. To do so, we used the results from previous EU-funded projects, such as *BABLE*, *Roadmaps for Smart Mobility*, and *UNaLab*, and relevant research as the content of the sanity check. More specifically, for each Strategic Ambition, we went through the process and checked if we can reach a set of solutions for this specific ambition. We did the same backward checking if each Solution can lead back to a Strategic Ambition.

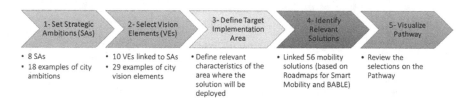

Fig. 2. The pathway method steps.

4 Pathway Method

The steps of the Pathway Method are:

Step 1. Set Strategic Ambitions (SAs): In the first step, city authorities define the future of urban mobility for their city concerning their overall ambitions. The city authorities can choose from a predefined list, the strategic ambition that fits best with their city (e.g., energy neutrality, healthy city, smart city ambitions, ambitions to be the frontrunner in specific domains), and their goals set their urban mobility planning. They can derive from their city strategic plans for all fields related to urban mobility, such as strategic energy action plans, covenants, coalition agreements, etc. To do so, we focused on European Union initiatives. More specific the strategic ambitions all refer to the strategic objectives defined in the current European Institute of Innovation & Technology's (EIT) Urban Mobility (UM) strategic plan [24]. In this way, when the pathway is created, the set of solutions' impacts can be directly referenced to the EIT-UM strategic objectives. We provide the cities with 8 predefined strategic ambitions derived from past projects. Additionally, we provide 18 example descriptions of city ambitions as an inspiration.

Step 2. Select Vision Elements (VEs): In the second step, city authorities define the city's desired future urban mobility scenario. Vision elements (VEs) operationalize strategic ambitions and describe how the city will look once the urban plan is implemented in the future. The cities need to decide on key elements that are part of the desired future (e.g., sustainable healthy behavior). Like SAs, we provide the cities with ten predefined VEs derived from relevant past projects. The VEs are linked to specific SAs so that when stakeholders choose a certain SA, they are provided with a set of relevant VEs that can be taken as a basis. Additionally, we provide 29 example descriptions of city visions with which stakeholders can be inspired.

Step 3. Define Target Implementation Area in the City: In Step 3, authorities can select the most suitable area and the underlining challenges in realizing their SA and VE(s). More specifically, a target implementation area is a specific location that the cities selected to address a particular challenge related to their vision is a specific location. We used the Urban Mobility Assessment Model (UMAM) to support the stakeholders in describing the target implementation area they want to improve. It contains relevant characteristics of that area that are used to identify suitable solutions. This will be a selection step to provide the cities with relevant solutions that suit both the ambition (content) and the target area (context variables).

Step 4. Identify Relevant Solutions: Based on the characteristics of the implementation area (e.g., size, geography, technology diffusion, etc.), the VEs, and related challenges, the authorities are provided with a list of potential mobility solutions to be implemented. These solutions are presented to the cities as inspiration to choose from. This set is based on the current urban mobility solutions already implemented in Europe and reported in the Energy project [25] and the *BABLE* initiative. The solutions are clustered into categories that share common characteristics. In this way, city authorities can identify relevant solutions and solution categories, searching for relevancy for their situation. The solution categories serve as a filtering tool. Currently, 56 solutions are incorporated into the method. To keep the link with the original implementations in cities from which the solutions are driven, the method also includes the use-cases as example implementations of the solutions in cities as a source of inspiration for future implementations.

Step 5. Visualize Pathway: When city authorities have completed the first four steps of the approach and finally chose solutions to be implemented, the visual representation of the pathway can be created. The pathway presents all the selections and decisions that the authorities made in the steps. This is visualized as a 'roadmap.' On the right side of a path, the selected VE(s) and SA(s) are presented, describing the desired future scenario the city would like to achieve. On the left side, the description of the implementation area and the mobility challenge is positioned, describing the current situation. The chosen solutions can be organized between the current state and the intended future state, visualizing the city's path to reach the strategy.

5   Demonstration and Evaluation

This manuscript focuses on demonstrating and formative evaluating that the method works [20] to improve the Pathway Method and its outcomes [9]. We have developed the conceptual model that represents the core concepts of the Pathway Method and their interrelationships. Following an iterative process, we have defined all the concepts' attributes and their relations in the conceptual model. In describing the conceptual model, we have also considered existing mobility-related tools and platforms (e.g., BABLE) to allow for a more efficient tool implementation and integration. Figure 3 illustrates the conceptual model as a UML diagram.

Based on the conceptual model and facilitating the communication and application of the conceptual model, we have developed paper prototypes representing concepts in visual forms. Figure 4 presents a number of examples of strategic ambitions, vision elements, and solutions in the form of the paper prototype.

Although the Pathway Method has been designed and developed in close collaboration with expert practitioners, we considered that the proof-of-concept implementation of the method in the form of a paper prototype can also serve as a means to evaluate its validity, given also that the method is a highly novel artifact [21]. We assessed the conceptual models and the paper prototype in close collaboration with 8 experts. To do so, we presented and discussed the conceptual model and the paper prototype in design sessions with the experts (same participants). We gather their feedback regarding the conceptual model and the paper prototype, and the need for an implementable version of the Pathway Method. The experts are the implementors of a software version (to be developed) of the paper prototype. After every focus group meeting, we gathered and processed the feedback and implement it for the next focus group. After the eighth

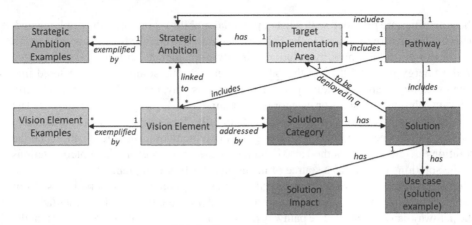

Fig. 3. Conceptual model.

meeting, the experts' group agreed that the conceptual model and the paper prototype are valuable and demonstrate what the Pathway Method aims to do. Additionally, as the implementors of the method, the experts agreed that the Pathway Method was consistent. The materials developed are implementable and meaningful and can be used to achieve the objectives we set forth.

Although the process and content of the Pathway Method are not yet tested and validated with real users (i.e., city authority stakeholders), the experts' analysis identified the expectations and motivations that the Pathway Method could fulfill and the challenges to be tackled. The main findings of this expert analysis identify important user aspects to be tested in practice related to the objectives.

According to the experts, a coherent process should be presented that provides sufficient guidance and supporting information through each step to facilitate decision-making and help build a robust strategic case. With user feedback, we need to validate the interrelations of the artifacts in each step and the supporting examples (Obj1).

The focus group indicated that a tool version of the Pathway Method needs to be populated with valuable content at each step of the process (Obj2). They indicated real-life examples, concrete use cases, and additional information at the solution level. Additionally, collecting user feedback can determine what type of content is valuable and focus our efforts.

Finally, the participants indicated that real-life examples should inspire and help the users (Obj3). The experts suggest that the Pathway Method can provide a streamlined user experience with straightforward actions and clear instructions and present supporting information incrementally without overburdening the user.

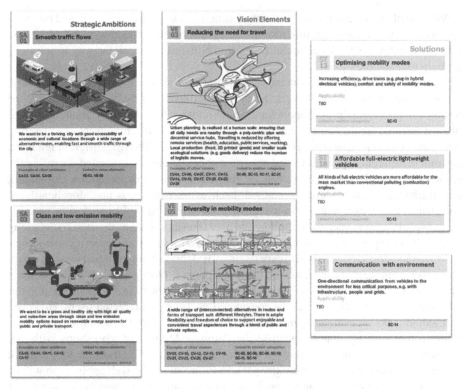

Fig. 4. Examples of Strategic Ambitions, Vision Elements, and Solutions in a Paper Prototype (Follow the link for the full list of Strategic Ambitions, Vision Elements and Solutions: https://drive.google.com/file/d/1Cyx9r39PtJlicJoYHtU8WVehZLqP7hGX/).

6 Conclusions

The Pathway Method introduced in this paper aims to help city authorities create a step-by-step plan of future mobility solutions aligned with their strategic and vision objectives regarding urban mobility. We discussed the conceptualization, development, and initial evaluation of the guided stepwise method. Following a DSR methodology, we identified three objectives for our artifact. Accordingly, our method incorporates a stepwise approach to help city authorities to create pathways for urban mobility (addressing Obj1). The stepwise approach includes existing insights -where available- that originate from an existing initiative in the domain (addressing Obj2). The method also facilitates city authorities to define the characteristics of the implementation area they target to locate and present mobility solutions applicable and potentially serve to achieve that area's mobility vision and strategic ambitions (addressing Obj3).

Our work provides initial evidence that the proposed method can support users to accelerate the effective deployment of concrete mobility solutions in their urban areas. It can support their decision-making for the next step with guidance, inspiration, and examples stemming from cities that have completed the process steps.

We contribute to research by providing a structured stepwise method based on existing literature that allows practitioners (i.e., city authorities and other stakeholders) to create their pathways for urban mobility, starting with a strategy, all the way to solutions that help to reach their plan.

Although the process and content of the paper prototype are not yet validated with real users, the preliminary demonstration and evaluation with the experts showed that the method can provide helpful support for cities to address their mobility challenges. The Pathway Method (in the form of an artifact) can be used by different users - such as city managers, consultants, or other governmental agencies - each having different interests, resulting in different expectations and needs. Further elaboration is needed regarding the primary and secondary user groups and the goals, motivations, expectations, challenges, and limitations of each operating method, such as user personas and storyboards, to formulate a target user and relevant scenarios on which to build the design process. Further specification is needed regarding the user interface design (through focus group meetings with experts and design methods such as user journey and user flow mapping).

We demonstrated our method to experts (involved throughout the design and development process) through a conceptual model and a paper prototype of the web application to be developed. Our evaluations with experts provided us with initial evidence that our proposed method is valid and can be considered useful by its targeted users. However, our method lacks an evaluation in a practical setting and with the actual target group. In future research, we plan to evaluate the Pathway Method in workshops with city representatives regarding the extent to which the method can be used for the intended purpose and its usefulness and usability [21]. In future steps, the web application will be designed and developed. A detailed analysis will be conducted to identify the target user groups, the users' needs, and the functional and non-functional requirements. An online mockup will be developed and evaluated by a more extensive set of experts that were not involved in the development and implementation, following the framework proposed by Venable et al. [9].

Furthermore, the design and development of the Pathway Method (and therefore the artifact) were influenced by [23] and other EU-funded projects. However, we did not compare our outcomes with the results of the previous projects. In the future, after developing and evaluating the digital artifact, we plan to benchmark our results with existing ones.

Another limitation of our study is related to the extent to which the artifact is actionable. The method's final step produces a static single-page report presenting the specific selections of the users in every step. Further research should include a dynamic timeline for the city per implementation area and the grouping of solutions into project plans, including additional elements, such as financing options and suitable business models.

Acknowledgments. This research received funding by EIT Urban Mobility.

References

1. EU. Roadmap to a single European transport area — towards a competitive and resource-efficient transport system, Luxembourg (2011). https://doi.org/10.2832/30955

2. EEA. Drivers of change of relevance for Europe's environment and sustainability. European Environment Agency (EEA), Copenhagen, Denmark, pp 1–138 (2019)
3. Lu, M., et al.: Cooperative Intelligent Transport Systems (C-ITS) deployment in Europe: challenges and key findings (2018)
4. Turetken, O., Grefen, P., Gilsing, R., Adali, O.E.: Service-dominant business model design for digital innovation in smart mobility. Bus. Inf. Syst. Eng. **61**(1), 9–29 (2018). https://doi.org/10.1007/s12599-018-0565-x
5. Aparicio, Á.: Streamlining the implementation process of urban mobility innovations: lessons from the ECCENTRIC project in Madrid. Transp. Policy **98** (2020). https://doi.org/10.1016/j.tranpol.2019.12.005
6. Wong, Y.Z., Hensher, D.A., Mulley, C.: Mobility as a Service (MaaS): charting a future context. Transp. Res. Part A Policy Pract. **131** (2020). https://doi.org/10.1016/j.tra.2019.09.030
7. Wefering, F., et al.: Guidelines-developing and implementing a sustainable urban mobility plan. www.eltis.org. Accessed 07 June 2021
8. Casady, C.B.: Customer-led mobility: a research agenda for Mobility-as-a-Service (MaaS) enablement. Case Stud. Transp. Policy **8**(4) (2020). https://doi.org/10.1016/j.cstp.2020.10.009
9. Venable, J., Pries-Heje, J., Baskerville, R.: FEDS: a framework for evaluation in design science research. Eur. J. Inf. Syst. **25**(1), 77–89 (2016). https://doi.org/10.1057/ejis.2014.36
10. Peffers, K., Tuunanen, T., Rothenberger, M.A., Chatterjee, S.: A design science research methodology for information systems research. J. Manag. Inf. Syst. **24**(3), 45–77 (2007). https://doi.org/10.2753/MIS0742-1222240302
11. Cambridge Dictionary. Mobility. Cambridge Dictionary (2020)
12. Butler, L., Yigitcanlar, T., Paz, A.: Barriers and risks of Mobility-as-a-Service (MaaS) adoption in cities: A systematic review of the literature. Cities (2020). https://doi.org/10.1016/j.cities.2020.103036
13. EU.: Action plan on urban mobility, Brussels (2009)
14. Rupprecht, S., Brand, L., Böhler-Baedeker, S., Brunner, L.: Guidelines for Developing and Implementing a Sustainable Urban Mobility Plan, 2nd (edn.). Ruppercht Consult, Koln (2019)
15. Salas Gironés, E., Van Est, R., Verbong, G.: The role of policy entrepreneurs in defining directions of innovation policy: a case study of automated driving in The Netherlands. Technol. Forecast. Soc. Change **161** (2020). https://doi.org/10.1016/j.techfore.2020.120243
16. Schot, J., Steinmueller, W.E.: Three frames for innovation policy: R&D, systems of innovation and transformative change. Res. Policy **47**(9) (2018). https://doi.org/10.1016/j.respol.2018.08.011
17. Grefen, P., Gilsing, R., Adali, E., Ozkan B.: Business-model innovation in the smart mobility domain. In: Cooperative Intelligent Transport Systems: Towards High-Level Automated Driving, vol. 25, pp. 63–86. IET (2019)
18. Hevner, A.R., et al.: Design science in information systems research. Manag. Inf. Syst. Q. **28**, 75 (2004)
19. Pries-Heje, J., Baskerville, R., Venable J.: Strategies for design science research evaluation (2008)
20. Venable, J., Pries-Heje, J., Baskerville, R.: A comprehensive framework for evaluation in design science research. In: Peffers, K., Rothenberger, M., Kuechler, B. (eds.) DESRIST 2012. LNCS, vol. 7286, pp. 423–438. Springer, Heidelberg (2012). https://doi.org/10.1007/978-3-642-29863-9_31
21. Gregor, S., Hevner, A.R.: Positioning and presenting design science research for maximum impact. MIS Q. Manag. Inf. Syst. **37**(2), 337–355 (2013). https://doi.org/10.25300/MISQ/2013/37.2.01

22. Paré, G., Trudel, M.C., Jaana, M., Kitsiou, S.: Synthesizing information systems knowledge: a typology of literature reviews. Inf. Manag. **52**(2), 183–199 (2015). https://doi.org/10.1016/j.im.2014.08.008
23. Den Ouden, E., Valkenburg, R.: Ambition setting. Eindhoven (2015)
24. EIT UM. EIT urban mobility strategic agenda mobility for liveable urban spaces (2020)
25. Van Galen, W., Den Ouden, E., Valkenburg, R.: Timelines for the topics in smart mobility. European Commission (2017)

Towards Design Principles for Safety Training in Virtual Reality: An Action Design Research Case

Amir Haj-Bolouri[1]([⊠]) [iD] and Matti Rossi[2] [iD]

[1] School of Economics, Business, and IT, University West, Trollhättan, Sweden
amir.haj-bolouri@hv.se
[2] Information Systems, Aalto University, Espoo, Finland
matti.rossi@aalto.fi

Abstract. Virtual Reality (VR) technology has progressed and become viable for the purpose of education, learning, and training. Organizations adopt and employ VR technologies to enhance employees' skills, competency, and readiness through safety training that prepare the employees towards work-specific situations that are dangerous, hazardous, and uncertain. This research in progress paper reports early results from an Action Design Research case on VR safety training. The empirical work of this study is on-going and is set in the domain of rail industry. Early results are reported as tentative design implications for safety training in VR, which are based on a first round of data analysis. The implications are proposed with the ambition of extending them into design principles for safety training in VR. Subsequently, steps for future research are outlined and discussed to advance the design implications into principles.

Keywords: Virtual Reality · Safety training · Action design research · Design principles

1 Introduction

The progress of immersive technologies has resulted in the introduction of high-end consumer-grade Virtual Reality (VR) hardware products such as the Oculus Rift and HTC Vive [1]. As a consequence, organizations are keen to adopt and employ VR within different areas of use, including education, teaching, and training in various application domains [2–4]. In this paper, we focus on VR for the domain of safety training, a domain which emphasizes how organizations can employ VR to design, organize, and perform training scenarios that increase their employees' skills in managing hazardous situations at work [5–7]:

As VR technologies have now matured to a point where both hardware and software are powerful enough to allow sophisticated forms of collaboration and learning to take place in the industry, scholars such as Wohlgenannt et al. [8] point out that there is an urgent need to provide 'prescriptive design knowledge' [9] such as design principles [10] or design theories [11]. As a consequence, the design of VR applications becomes highly

© Springer Nature Switzerland AG 2021
L. Chandra Kruse et al. (Eds.): DESRIST 2021, LNCS 12807, pp. 89–95, 2021.
https://doi.org/10.1007/978-3-030-82405-1_11

situated and less generalizable for use in other safety training contexts. Subsequently, as a response to address this issue, and to advance the knowledge about VR and safety training through Design Science Research (DSR) in Information Systems (IS) [12–14], we explore in this RIP paper the following research question: *how to design VR environments for the purpose of safety training?*

We are fully aware of the fact that we cannot answer the research question in its entirety through a research in progress work. Instead, we will address the research question by outlining our study as a case of Action Design Research (ADR) [15], where we propose tentative outcomes in form of domain specific implications for VR and safety training. Consequently, we frame the implications as 'nascent' outputs [16] for future development of design principles that can provide organizations insights on how to design, organize, and perform safety training in VR.

The rest of the paper is structured according to the identified meta-requirements: firstly, we propose an overview of the meta-requirements. After that, we go through the reviewed literature and show how and where we identified the proposed meta-requirements. Finally, we conclude the paper and shortly propose further research opportunities.

2 Virtual Reality and Safety Training

VR is a set of technologies that give people an immersive experience of a virtual world beyond the physical reality. VR technologies are conceptually characterized through three main features: *presence, interactivity,* and *immersion* [17]. *Presence* is typically understood as the feeling of being physically somewhere other than where one actually is [4], whereas *interactivity* influences presence and refers to the extent to which users can manipulate their virtual environment in real time [1]. Finally, *immersion* is attributed as the feeling of becoming completely absorbed and surrounded by enclosing VR space, which increases the sensations of embodiment and presence among users [3]. Consequently, the three mentioned features are also prevalent to take into consideration when organizing and conducting safety training in VR [4, 5].

Safety training in VR is a growing application domain because it resolves many of the issues with safety training in general, including how to manage dangerous activities under secure circumstances with low-cost features that increase employees' safety performance [5]. VR has also been proven to offer organizations low-cost training features that project realistic scenarios for safety training [6], by resolving many of the challenges that organizations face through traditional safety training (e.g., social sustainability, employees' safety). Examples of areas where VR has frequently employed for safety training include: construction workers [18], mine personnel [19], community-based pedestrians [20], and rail industry personnel [21].

Outcomes of safety training in VR, generate knowledge that enhances employees' safety knowledge, risk perception, safety motivation, and overall safety performance, which directly influences the likelihood of reducing accidents and workplace injuries [18, 19]. In order to map safety training scenarios sufficiently with dangerous real-life situations, it is critical that the design of such scenarios incorporate the working environments and lived experiences of safety training participants [7]. Hence, design plays a crucial role. However, most seminal studies within IS that relate to VR have mostly been studying virtual worlds or virtual environments (e.g., [22–24]), rather than the design of immersive VR in general, or design of safety training with VR in particular [8]. Nevertheless, the current on-going publication trend on VR research is clearly showing positive signs in IS; e.g., conferences such as the *Hawaii International Conference on Systems Sciences (HICSS)* [25] and journals such as the *Journal of Management Information Systems (JMIS)* [26] have encouraged IS researchers to investigate VR with dedicated tracks and special issues. We thus position this research in progress paper as a contribution to that ongoing trend.

3   A Case of VR Safety Training in Rail Industry

This study is designed and framed according to Sein et al.'s [15] ADR method because the long-term goal of the subsequent research case is to: design, implement, use, and evaluate immersive VR-environments for safety training. The ADR method provides a framework (shown in Fig. 1) with four interrelated stages: (i) problem formulation, (ii) building, intervention, and evaluation, (iii) reflection and learning, and (iv) formalization of learning outcomes into design principles. Moreover, the ADR method balances practice-oriented research with generalizable outcomes in order to produce solutions and knowledge that are relevant for both organizations and academia. Finally, the generalizable outcomes of an ADR cycle are typically produced as design principles, which capture crucial knowledge and encapsulate it for extensive application in other similar project settings. In so, we utilize the ADR framework to outline the research case and discuss implications for advancing the research project accordingly.

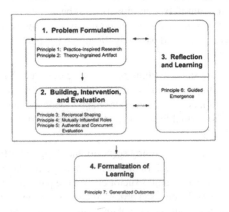

Fig. 1. Action design research: stages and principles (adapted from [15])

The research project at hand was initiated in April 2020 and is still on-going. The stakeholders of the case are Sweden's biggest rail industry organization, and the empirical setting emphasizes VR for fire safety training among personnel that work onboard trains (e.g., conductors, train drivers). Currently, the case has undergone the three first stages of ADR (problem formulation, building, intervention, and evaluation, reflection and learning) and is now in the phase of formalizing research outcomes from the first ADR cycle.

During the **problem formulation** stage, data was collected through meetings with responsible stakeholders, documents that describe the organization's virtual training platform, and audio/video clips that explicate the VR safety training module. Outcomes of this stage were identified as challenges in terms of mapping learning theories and training scenarios in VR, with realistic objectives that match a dangerous fire situation on a train. This led to the stage of **building, intervention, and evaluation**, where focus was mainly on evaluating the training sessions through a mixed methods approach for data collection. The approach consisted of three components: (i) 5 group interviews with instructors and participants of the training sessions; (ii) a web-survey that evaluates participants' overall learning experience; and (iii) observations of all 5 training sessions (see Figs. 2 and 3 for photos from the safety training session). The data was consequently processed during the **reflection and learning** stage through a first round of transcriptions and open coding to extract domain specific implications for principles that support the design of safety training in VR. Here, we reviewed literature on VR and safety training [2–7] [7, 27–29] to guide the data analysis, which resulted into identifying four design implications for designing VR environments that support safety training. The implications are depicted in Table 1.

Table 1. Tentative design implications of safety training in VR

Component	Description
Risk perception	During safety training scenario, the design of VR environment needs to provide participants interactive signs which indicate the level of safety/unsafety. Participants must be able to experience the risk perception both directly and passively; directly through their own experience, and passively through other participants' experience [5, 6, 7]
Multimodal feedback	During safety training scenario, the design of VR environment needs to able to provide instant feedback to the participants based on their performance. This includes haptic feedback, visual feedback, audio-textual feedback, and summative/formative immediate feedback [7, 27]
Safety cognition	During safety training scenario, the design of VR environment needs to provide feedback to the participants' performance, and after the performance, an instructor checks the participants' performance and corrects the errors. Through recording of the training performance, the safety knowledge is explained and confirmed for further reflection [27, 28]
Hazard inspection	During safety training scenario, the design of VR environment needs to afford the participants the possibility to inspect the unsafety conditions and unsafety safety sequences of activities that are specific for the participants' profession [29]

Fig. 2. VR Fire extinguisher

Fig. 3. VR Safety training

Further research will focus on a second round of data analysis and extraction of design principles. The design principles will encapsulate knowledge on how to design VR environments for the purpose of safety training by explicating specific prototype features and mapping with the proposed design implications of this study. The results of future research will also focus the users' experience of safety training sessions, and investigate the meaningfulness of training outcomes.

4 Concluding Remarks

In this research in progress paper, we have reported early outcomes of an ongoing research project that studies safety training in VR. We have outlined the research project as a case of ADR in the context of safety training for personnel in the Swedish rail industry. Consequently, the study reports four tentative design implications of safety training, which were extracted through reviewed literature along with a round of data analysis. The contribution of this work is thus nascent and in progress, representing an initial understanding about how to proceed towards developing future design principles for safety training in VR.

References

1. Anthes, C., Garcia-Hernandez, R.J., Wiedemann, M., Kranzlmuller, D.: State of the art of virtual reality technology. In: 2016 IEEE Aerospace Conference, pp. 1–19 (2016)
2. Carruth, D.W.: Virtual reality for education and workforce training. In: 2017 15th International Conference on Emerging eLearning Technologies and Applications (ICETA), pp. 1–6. IEEE (2017)
3. Feng, Z., González, V.A., Amor, R., Lovreglio, R., Cabrera-Guerrero, G.: Immersive virtual reality serious games for evacuation training and research: a systematic literature review. Comput. Educ. **127**, 252–266 (2018)
4. Jensen, L., Konradsen, F.: A review of the use of virtual reality head-mounted displays in education and training. Educ. Inf. Technol. **23**(4), 1515–1529 (2017). https://doi.org/10.1007/s10639-017-9676-0

5. Wang, P., Wu, P., Wang, J., Chi, H.L., Wang, X.: A critical review of the use of virtual reality in construction engineering education and training. Int. J. Environ. Res. Public Health **15**(6), 1204 (2018)

6. Pena, A.M., Ragan, E.D.: Contextualizing construction accident reports in virtual environments for safety education. In: 2017 IEEE Virtual Reality (VR), pp. 389–390. IEEE (2017)

7. Leder, J., Horlitz, T., Puschmann, P., Wittstock, V., Schütz, A.: Comparing immersive virtual reality and powerpoint as methods for delivering safety training: impacts on risk perception, learning, and decision making. Saf. Sci. **111**, 271–286 (2019)

8. Wohlgenannt, I., Simons, A., Stieglitz, S.: Virtual reality. Bus. Inf. Syst. Eng. **62**(5), 455–461 (2020)

9. Gregor, S.: The nature of theory in information systems. MIS Q. **30**(3), 611–642 (2006)

10. Chandra, L., Seidel, S., Gregor, S.: Prescriptive knowledge in IS research: conceptualizing design principles in terms of materiality, action, and boundary conditions. In: 2015 48th Hawaii International Conference on System Sciences, pp. 4039–4048. IEEE (2015)

11. Walls, J.G., Widmeyer, G.R., El Sawy, O.A.: Building an information system design theory for vigilant EIS. Inf. Syst. Res. **3**(1), 36–59 (1992)

12. Hevner, A., Chatterjee, S.: Design science research in information systems. In: Design Research in Information Systems. ISIS, vol. 22, pp. 9–22. Springer, Boston (2010). https://doi.org/10.1007/978-1-4419-5653-8_2

13. Gregor, S., Hevner, A.R.: Positioning and presenting design science research for maximum impact. MIS Q. **37**, 337–355 (2013)

14. Baskerville, R., Baiyere, A., Gregor, S., Hevner, A., Rossi, M.: Design science research contributions: finding a balance between artifact and theory. J. Assoc. Inf. Syst. **19**(5), 358–376 (2018)

15. Sein, M.K., Henfridsson, O., Purao, S., Rossi, M., Lindgren, R.: Action design research. MIS Q. **35**, 37–56 (2011)

16. Heinrich, P., Schwabe, G.: Communicating nascent design theories on innovative information systems through multi-grounded design principles. In: Tremblay, M.C., VanderMeer, D., Rothenberger, M., Gupta, A., Yoon, V. (eds.) Advancing the Impact of Design Science: Moving from Theory to Practice. LNCS, vol. 8463, pp. 148–163. Springer, Cham (2014). https://doi.org/10.1007/978-3-319-06701-8

17. Walsh, K.R., Pawlowski, S.D.: Virtual reality: a technology in need of IS research. Commun. Assoc. Inf. Syst. **8**(20), 297–313 (2002)

18. Sacks, R., Perlman, A., Barak, R.: Construction safety training using immersive virtual reality. Constr. Manag. Econ. **31**(9), 1005–1017 (2013)

19. Zhang, H., He, X., Mitri, H.: Fuzzy comprehensive evaluation of virtual reality mine safety training system. Saf. Sci. **120**, 341–351 (2019)

20. Schwebel, D.C., Combs, T., Rodriguez, D., Severson, J., Sisiopiku, V.: Community-based pedestrian safety training in virtual reality: a pragmatic trial. Accid. Anal. Prev. **86**, 9–15 (2016)

21. Randeniya, N., Ranjha, S., Kulkarni, A., Lu, G.: Virtual reality based maintenance training effectiveness measures–a novel approach for rail industry. In: 2019 IEEE 28th International Symposium on Industrial Electronics (ISIE), pp. 1605–1610. IEEE (2019)

22. Chaturvedi, A.R., Dolk, D.R., Drnevich, P.L.: Design principles for virtual worlds. Manag. Inf. Syst. Q. **35**(3), 673–684 (2011)

23. Davis, A., Murphy, J., Owens, D., Khazanchi, D., Zigurs, I.: Avatars, people, and virtual worlds: foundations for research in metaverses. J. Assoc. Inf. Syst. **10**(2), 90–117 (2009)

24. Pannicke, D., Zarnekow, R.: Virtual worlds. Bus. Inf. Syst. Eng. **2**, 185–188 (2009)

25. Parvinen, P., Hamari, J., Pöyry, E.: Introduction to minitrack: mixed, augmented and virtual reality. In: Proceedings of the 51st Hawaii International Conference on System Sciences, Big Island (2018)
26. Cavusoglu, H., Dennis, A.R., Parsons, J.: Special issue: immersive systems. J. Manag. Inf. Syst. **36**(3), 680–682 (2019)
27. Bahari, A.: Computer-mediated feedback for L2 learners: challenges versus affordances. J. Comput. Assist. Learn. **37**(1), 24–38 (2021)
28. Morélot, S., Garrigou, A., Dedieu, J., N'Kaoua, B.: Virtual reality for fire safety training: influence of immersion and sense of presence on conceptual and procedural acquisition. Comput. Educ. **166**, 104145 (2021)
29. Buttussi, F., Chittaro, L.: Effects of different types of virtual reality display on presence and learning in a safety training scenario. IEEE Trans. Vis. Comput. Graph. **24**(2), 1063–1076 (2017)

Problem and Contribution Articulation

Design Science Research Problems … Where Do They Come From?

Sandeep Purao[✉]

Department of Information and Process Management, Bentley University, Waltham, MA, USA
spurao@bentley.edu

Abstract. Effective and impactful design science research requires appropriate research conduct, and an appropriate research *problem*. Scholars in the DSR community continue to clarify the foundations for appropriate research conduct. In contrast, few guidelines or guardrails have been proposed to identify and develop research problems. Without such guidance, DSR efforts run the risk of pursuing problems that are either un-important or not-well-formulated. In this paper, I draw on writings beyond the DSR community to develop considerations that DSR scholars can use to *identify* and *develop* research problems, acknowledging their evolving ontological status. The paper describes an approach, articulates these considerations, and develops arguments that can help the identification and development of research problems for DSR efforts.

Keywords: Design science research · Research problem · Problem formulation

1 Motivation

Since its recognition as a distinct research genre within the IS discipline (Hevner et al. 2004), several scholars in the design science research (DSR) community have explored a number of fundamental questions. These have included explicating and distinguishing it from behavioral science (Hevner et al. 2004), approaches to conducting DSR (Vaishnavi and Kuechler 2008; Pfeffers et al. 2007); methods for pursuing DSR with authentic collaboration (Sein et al. 2011); clarifications to the nature of design principles (Chandra et al. 2015; Purao et al. 2020), and the role of theory and theorizing (Gregor and Jones 2007; Iivari 2020; Lukyanenko and Parsons 2020). Through these contributions, the DSR community is starting to signal a consensus about what constitutes design science research (Baskerville 2008), different genres of DSR (Kaul et al. 2015), and possibilities for accumulation of knowledge (Rothe et al. 2020). These efforts are useful to DSR scholars because they provide the infrastructure necessary for research conduct, and well-reasoned arguments to defend and justify choices (similar to other research genres such as case studies (Lee 1989), critical research (Myers and Klein 2011), and qualitative inquiry (Sarker et al. 2013)).

Such norms for research conduct are necessary (Parsons 2015) but may not be sufficient for effective and impactful design science research. That goal requires another

© Springer Nature Switzerland AG 2021
L. Chandra Kruse et al. (Eds.): DESRIST 2021, LNCS 12807, pp. 99–111, 2021.
https://doi.org/10.1007/978-3-030-82405-1_12

important ingredient: research-worthy problems (Weber 2003). This concern is particularly important for DSR because design science scholars strive to produce prescriptive knowledge about the design of a class of *future* IT artifacts. Other professional fields and academic disciplines with a focus on the future have struggled with similar concerns, e.g. computer science (Brooks 1987; Regli 2017) and engineering design (Mosyjowski et al. 2017) as well as science and technology studies (Laudan 1984). If these concerns are not addressed, the promise of relevance and impact from DSR remains at the risk of remaining merely an ideology (Chatterjee 2000). Within the IS field, senior scholars have reflected on such concerns, sometimes describing these as Type III errors (Rai 2017). Within the DSR community as well, a nascent body of work is emerging with reflections and empirical investigations about problems and problematizing (Nielsen 2020, Maedche et el. 2019; Thuan et al. 2019).

The concerns – pursuing the right problems, framing them appropriately, and developing these in a manner that allows research contributions as well as broader impacts – are also of personal interest to all researchers. Effective responses to these concerns can influence speed of research completion (Pries-Heje et al. 2014), determine the type and quality of job opportunities, guide one's research trajectory, and shape one's academic reputation (Jensen 2013). Few sources provide help in this regard beyond broad recommendations, which are often aimed at doctoral students (Horan 2009; Luse 2012). However, researchers face these challenges throughout the career; and the skills needed to make these choices remain scarce and valuable (Jensen 2013).

In spite of this perceived importance of addressing important problems, it remains difficult for DSR scholars to figure out how to get there. Within the DSR community, "the problem of the problem" has been acknowledged (Nielsen 2020), efforts to structure the problem space have been proposed (Maedche et al. 2019), and reflective accounts are starting to appear (Twomey et al. 2020). Together, these efforts are providing DSR scholars new perspectives to explore "the problem of the problem." Our intent in this paper is to suggest a broader lens that includes not just problem framing, formulation and development (Jones and Venable 2020; Nielsen 2020' Twomey et al. 2020) but also initial problem identification and awareness. In Sect. 2, we review the core concern and how it has been addressed elsewhere. Section 3 develops key considerations for problem identification and formulation across four phases with particular attention to DSR scholarship. In Sect. 4, we summarize the challenges and offer a hopeful message to pursue more effective and impactful design science research.

2   Background

The core concern – how to *choose* a research problem – is particularly difficult to explore because of three reasons. First, this phase of research is rarely reported[1]. The stylized reporting in conference and journal publications often provides the motivation by citing industry or societal statistics but does not reveal how the research idea was generated. Second, researchers appear to attribute this phase to individual creativity and brilliance

---

[1] As Nielsen (2020, p. 265) points out problem analysis and problem presentation is often very brief and sometimes even missing completely.

that remains hard to describe. Apprenticeship models, commonplace in doctoral programs, further emphasize this perspective. Third, the vision of the individual inventor persists in spite of the shift to partnering (see, e.g. (Sein et al. 2011)) and the recognition of collaborations (Schneiderman 2016). In spite of these obstacles, several scholars have provided thoughtful reflections about this phase. An example is Jensen (2013) who puts forward, concisely, three principles for a worthy research problem: novelty, significance[2], and tractability. The empirical investigation by Barr (1984) supports this articulation. Table 1 summarizes.

Table 1. Key dimensions to assess research-worthiness

Dimension	Description
Novelty	Pushing the frontier of knowledge; creating something that is new (to the world)
Significance	Ensuring that the answers and solutions are of interest to the stakeholders, and contribute to societal welfare
Tractability	Having the ability to answer the question posed or develop the solutions in response to the problem within reasonable time and resources

Novelty. Sometimes described as originality, the interpretation of this dimension can vary. Barr (1984) describes this as "the integration of ideas that lead to a new or novel extension along a research path" (Chemistry) or "using a new framework or perspective in addressing a piece of literature or literary area" (English) or "use of a new theoretical perspective or new combination of perspectives as a framework for observing some group or system or use of a [new] methodology in studying a set of data" (Political Science and Sociology). In the IS discipline, Rai (2017) points out that answers that are "derivative to current understanding," or "taking what is well known and reiterating it in a different context" does not meet this burden[3]. Embedded in this idea is a consideration of "the size of the inventive step[4]" (Jensen 2013).

Significance. Sometimes described as importance, this dimension points out that the outcomes one produces "must be of interest (and relevance) to the profession or for the welfare of society" (Jensen 2013), but it is often tough to answer the question 'why should anyone care' [ibid]. Barr (1984) describes significance in terms of "contribution to knowledge" beyond what is already known. This may include "indicating that previous research was of little or no value" (English) or "both field and practical significance" (Political Science and Sociology). Note that these descriptions allude to the *outcomes* of research instead of a focus on choosing a research problem.

---

[2] Described as 'importance' in the original (Jensen 2013).

[3] Describing it as "affirming that gravity works in my kitchen" (Rai 2017).

[4] Refers to *non*-obvious-ness; too small a step will prevent granting of a patent (Moir 2013).

Tractability. Sometimes described as solvability, this dimension refers to the ability to devise solutions to the research problem. If the problem is too large (scope), mere scale may make it un-solvable with available techniques or data within reasonable resource constraints (see also Rai (2017)). If the problem is addressed in a particular manner the researcher may encounter an intractable solution space compared to another research direction, which may be more efficient (and improve the probability of finding a solution) (Regli 2017). These dimensions are useful to assess whether a research problem is worthy. However, the first two (novelty and significance) are often easier to assess only in retrospect (e.g. by reviewers and readers). The third (tractability) may be considered by the researcher as s/he embarks on the research effort. Additional considerations are, therefore, necessary for *choosing* worthy research problems. The investigation by Mosyjowski et al. (2017), prescriptive suggestions by Luse et al. (2012), and the empirical investigation by Barr (1984) in diverse disciplines (Chemistry, English, Political science, and Sociology); along with the investigation by Thuan et al. (2021) suggests these elements. Table 2 summarizes.

Table 2. Additional criteria that influence selection of research problems

Dimension	Description
Identity	Personal identification with a research area and affinity to a certain mode of research
Experience(s)	Experiences prior to and during the academic career that shape the world-view and preferences of the researcher
Data availability	Ability to access primary or secondary sources that make available data about the phenomenon of interest
Influence from others	Influence from mentors and peers, as an early indication of the key dimensions of research worthiness (see Table 1)
Career outlook	Perceptions of how the choice of a research problem would contribute to greater career opportunities

We may argue that finding a worthy research problem for DSR is no different from other disciplines (see Tables 1 and 2). However, many DSR scholars (e.g. Hevner et al. (2004)) have argued that the DSR paradigm is different from behavioral science. This distinction makes it incumbent upon us to explore whether these criteria and elements are adequate for DSR scholars. Consider, for example, how behavioral science researchers identify research problems by systematically examining prior work (Webster and Watson 2002) to identify gaps (Sandberg and Alvesson 2011) that can point to opportunities for further research. Contrast this with DSR. As Brooks (1996) describes: "hitching our research to someone else's driving problems, and solving those problems on the owners' terms, leads us to richer … research." These ideas have been developed within the DSR community by Sein et al. (2011) who emphasize the important of collaboration. This distinction between *discipline-generated* and *practice-generated* problems (Welke 1998; Rai 2017) is the first indication that problem formulation may require new considerations for DSR. DSR scholars (Nielsen and Persson 2016; Nielsen 2020; Maedche et al. 2019; Twoney et al. 2020, Jones and Venable 2020) acknowledge this distinction as they address "the problem of the problem." I build on these to suggest a broader lens that includes problem identification *and* problem formulation.

3   How to Identify and Develop Research Problems for DSR

My proposal consists of an approach to identify and develop research problems for DSR. It is reminiscent of other research approaches (Saunders et al. 2007; Creswell 1994) with phases such as (a) topic selection, and (b) topic development, and builds on contemporary work about problem formulation such as: the reflective account from Twomey et al. (2020); the efforts from Maedche et al. (2019) to structure the problem space; Venable et al.'s (2017) checklist of business needs; and Nielsen's (2020) account of problematization that acknowledges that a problem 'is not just given as though it exists objectively' [ibid]. The approach I suggest consists of interlocking phases that start with initial awareness of the problem (Kuechler and Vaishnavi 2008) but continue ongoing engagement with problem formulation (Sein et al. 2011; Rittel and Webber 1973; Nielsen 2020). Figure 1 summarizes the approach that I elaborate next.

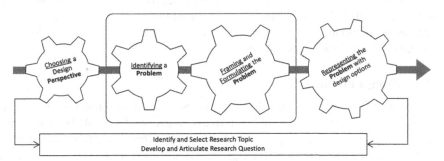

Fig. 1. An approach to develop research problems for DSR

3.1   Choosing a Design Perspective

The first stage in this journey is to choose a design perspective (as opposed to, say, an empirical perspective) when faced with a problem situation[5]. Brooks (1996) describes it as a 'toolsmith' perspective, where researchers take their inspiration by "partner[ing] with those who will use our tools" [ibid]. This ensures that we (a) aim at relevant, not toy-scale problems, (b) remain honest about success and failure, and (c) face the whole problem, not just the parts easily amenable to analysis [ibid]. Echoes of these ideas are found in ADR (Sein et al. 2011), which emphasizes partnering with external stakeholders to identify a specific (instead of abstract) problem (see, e.g. (Lee et al. 2008)).

---

[5] The former points to a desire to change the current situation; the latter, a desire to develop further understanding of the current situation.

However, the need for a design perspective is not always apparent nor necessary in all situations. Consider the case reported by Purao and Karunakaran (2020), where initial awareness of the problem situation was articulated as 'the need to better support complex knowledge-work in organizations.' Developing a concise statement of the problem situation, however, required them to invest considerable effort; and eventually lead them to identify different aspects such as (i) what artifacts do actors use to support knowledge work, (ii) what strategies do organizations use to develop the artifacts, and (iii) how can knowledge embedded in these artifacts be extracted and managed. The first two require empirical investigations; the third requires a design perspective.

A corollary to the above is to ensure that the problem specification respects both, the specific problem faced by the external partners as well as the more general version of the problem. Rai (2017) (citing (Weber 2003)) describes an emphasis on the former at the expense of the latter as myopic[6], where researchers "formulate the problem with a sole focus on an immediate practical problem … but do not evaluate how the problem relates to a more generic, archetypal problem." This distinction between a problem instance and a class of problems has been acknowledged in the DSR community (Kuechler and Vaishnavi 2008) as well as elsewhere acknowledging the importance of partnering for grounding the problem (Van de Ven 2007), while emphasizing the need to generate and respond to a more general version of the problem. We note that for the DSR scholar, it is often important to address the idiosyncratic details of the problem, a theme acknowledged by Majchrzak et al. (2016) who emphasize the need to acknowledge a theory of the problem as an important part of the contribution. These challenges (outlined above) persist and resurface through the other phases.

3.2 Identifying a Problem

Continuing the ideas outlined so far, the source of the research problem for DSR efforts is not likely to be an effort at gap-finding (Alvesson and Sandberg 2013). Instead, the impetus is likely to be a situation perceived in practice. This distinction, described as discipline-generated research vs. practice-generated research (Welke 1997; see also Rai 2017) is evident in a recent empirical investigation of the source of research questions for DSR. Thuan et al. (2021) find that problems from practice accounted for 51 out of 63 conference papers, 18 out of 21 papers from MIS Quarterly, and 11 out of 20 dissertations (in total, 77% of the 104 research manuscripts they examined). Based on the results, they find overwhelming evidence that compared to gap-finding (or problematization) (Alvesson and Sandberg 2013) the dominant mode for DSR scholarship remains problem-solving (Pries-Heje and Baskerville 2008), where the researchers attempt to address a practical and/or knowledge problem by creating IS artifacts.

More detailed investigations of sources of technological problems and how inventions are generated are the domain of scholars in the fields of science and technology studies (STS) and research policy. Here, I draw on Laudan (1984) to suggest a taxonomy (albeit incomplete) for types of technological problems that DSR scholars can

---

[6] For instance, evaluating how intelligent wearable devices can persuade diabetic patients to make necessary behavioral changes (specific version) may map to how information systems can persuade patients with chronic diseases to make behavioral changes to comply with therapy (general version) (Rai 2017).

draw upon. For example, a problem situation may be described in terms of an imminent problem that would lead to the potential failure of a technology (presumptive anomaly). As another example, a problem situation may be described as one that requires some technology layers or components to work effectively with other, currently incompatible layers or components (technological imbalances). Table 3 summarizes.

Table 3. Types of technological problems

Source	Description
Perceived from the environment	A problem in the environment not yet solved by any technology (Example: monitoring use of different services by disadvantaged populations such as the homeless)
Functional failure of technology	Functional failures can occur when a technology is subject to greater demands or when it is applied in new situations (Example: breakdowns of websites when faced with high and bursty traffic loads)
Presumptive anomalies	Potential rather than actual failures predicted by some observations or trends (similar to Problematization (Alvesson and Sandberg 2013)) (Example: unstable usage patterns of users requiring dynamic personalization)
Cumulative improvement	Extrapolation from past technological successes (Example: need to improve allocation or classification performance of algorithms)
Technological imbalances	Effective operation of a particular technology hindered by lack of an adequate complementary technology (Example: need to map faster analytic algorithms in response to speed of big data streams)

The typology suggests one possibility for moving to a class (a *technological* problem type). Although it is difficult to provide such a taxonomy of problem types for the larger socio-technical problem; it is possible that the DSR scholars would describe the problem they are dealing with using phrases at different levels of abstraction (e.g. decision support, knowledge management, therapy compliance and others) to signal the readers the specific stream(s) of work that define the problem space, and avoid falling prey to a myopic problem formulation (Rai 2017) described earlier.

A final consideration during this stage is to ensure that the problem is not one that "can be readily structured and solved by applying extant knowledge from IS or from other disciplines" (Rai 2017). For DSR scholars, such problems are described as routine design that requires "the application of existing knowledge" as opposed to innovative design, where the solution will produce "a contribution to the ... knowledge base of foundations and methodologies" (Hevner et al. 2004).

3.3   Framing and Formulating the Problem

The research problem identified would need to be narrowed down with a particular focus, as well as developed with support from ongoing work, similar to the idea of a 'rigor cycle' (Hevner 2007). The apparatus suggested by Maedche et al. (2019) can be useful here to structure the problem space with concepts such as needs, goals, requirements, stakeholder and artifact. This stage is also important because the researcher must further explore how to place the practice-generated problem in one or more prior research streams, and explore the 'research front,' reflecting current research thinking in relation to the chosen research focus (Horan 2009). Here, the idea of a 'research front' encompasses an examination of what has been tried before, addressing known obstacles to progress, and using prior work as a catalyst for refining the research idea (Barr 1984). By clearly articulating the research front, the researcher can ensure that the planned research will produce new knowledge beyond what is already known.

Another consideration during this phase is to ensure that the research problem matters. Researchers are often drawn to problems they consider interesting[7]. Beyond personal interest is the realm of important and significant, i.e., "problems where the answers will matter in important ways" (Rai 2017). By mapping the research interest to larger business or societal challenges, the researcher can ensure that the problem is relevant (Hevner 2007). Horan (2009) describes several suggestions, e.g. identifying the audience, developing rationale, and other that can be useful towards this end. Ideas such as 'grand challenges' identified by different disciplines, government agencies and research groups[8] can add to this significance. The researcher can use 'backward reasoning' to explore how their chosen research focus can contribute to the grand challenges. Without this effort, the researchers may be swayed by the 'streetlight effect' (Rai 2017), driven by available datasets or tools. Finally, the researchers must decide problem scope with the so-called Goldilocks principle, deciding what to emphasize and what to place in the background (Rai 2017). Venable et al.'s (2017) checklist of business needs provides one possible approach that DSR scholars can use for this purpose.

A related consideration during this phase is to establish that the problem is solvable. Unlike empirical research, where researchers are encouraged to: "choose topics where the result is interesting no matter what answer you get" (Barrett 2013); design science scholarship requires that the researcher would repeatedly develop and evaluate the artifact until positive results are achieved (Thuan et al. 2021). A part of this effort may include characterizing the expected outcomes with the typology suggested by Gregor and Hevner (2013), where a move from improvement to exaptation to invention would indicate increasing levels of difficulty. Another possibility to explore solvability *ex-ante* would be to follow the Heilmeier questions[9], which include queries such as: (a) what is new in the approach and why the researcher thinks it will be successful, (b) what are the

---

[7] "Almost any problem is interesting if it is studied in sufficient depth" (Medawar 1979; cited in Van de Ven 2007 and Rai 2017).

[8] See https://grandchallenges.org/; https://obamawhitehouse.archives.gov/administration/eop/ostp/grand-challenges; and https://en.wikipedia.org/wiki/Grand_Challenges.

[9] Attributed to George Heilmeier, Director of ARPA in the 1970's. These questions, which he expected every new research program to answer, continue to survive at DARPA. See a version here: https://john.cs.olemiss.edu/~hcc/researchMethods/notes/HeilmeierQuestions.html.

risks and the payoffs, and (c) what are the midterm and final exams to check for success. In their apparent simplicity, they allow the to reflect on the solvability of the research problem (Shapiro 1994).

This phase can lead to the construction of *initial* versions of research questions. Their nature and format will be different from behavioral and natural sciences (which may focus more on causality and explanation). As Thuan et al. (2021) describe, the research questions may take forms such as: "how can we develop X?" or "how can we develop X to resolve Y?", i.e., they will not posit conjectures for falsification.

3.4 Representing the Problem with Design Options

The "problem of the problem," however, continues because design involves re-design, which in turn, requires refining the problem. Hevner et al. (2004) capture this as: "knowledge and understanding of a problem domain and its solution are achieved in the building and application of the designed artifact." Purao (2013) uses the phrase "evolutionary ontology" to characterize the problem, describing it as the following: "as ... the artifact begins to take shape ... [it] ... influences the researcher's stance towards the problem. It ceases to be independent of the researchers' efforts. Instead, it is interpreted in conjunction with the properties of the artifact." These descriptions emphasize a key characteristic of all design problems (including problems considered by DSR scholars): they are "wicked problems" that defy "a definitive formulation" (Rittel and Webber 1973, p. 161). For example, approaches to design science research describe phases such as problem awareness (Kuechler and Vaishnavi 2008, Figure 3), problem identification and motivation (Peffers et al. 2007, Figure 1, p. 54), and problem formulation (Sein et al. 2011, Figure 1, p. 41) and even acknowledge the need to return to the problem formulation stage as the research unfolds. However, they do not suggest pathways or specific ways to do this. In the absence of these, DSR scholars are tempted to rely on a more linear process (see, e.g. Feine et al. (2020)).

Returning to the original conceptualization of wicked problems (Rittel and Webber 1973, 1984), and its contemporary descriptions (Sweeting 2018), I note that an attempt to solve a wicked problem creates new problems. In other words, instead of moving from problem to solution, the "process of formulating the problem and of conceiving a solution (or re-solution) are identical" (Rittel and Webber 1973, p. 161). It is, therefore, important to recognize that problem formulation cannot stop after initial awareness; instead, the DSR efforts lead to continuing problem re-definition. The account by Twomey et al. (2020) provides a contemporary narrative that reflects similar ideas. Simon (1988) suggests a more specific perspective by describing problem-solving as a "change in representation[10]" to "make evident what was previously true but obscure," i.e., problem-solving involves representing the problem in such a way that it "makes the solution transparent" [ibid]. He acknowledges that even if this is considered an exaggerated view, different representations can provide not only a path towards a solution but

---

[10] The first example he provides is how arithmetic became easier with Arabic numerals and place notations (instead of Roman numerals), and points out that there appears to be no 'theoretical' explanation of this.

also a greater understanding of the problem itself. In the absence of a taxonomy of representation for socio-technical problems, the argument I advance here merely emphasizes the role of representation in continued problem (re-)formulation.

Devising and evaluating design options is, therefore, an important contributor to developing the problem[11]. As Regli (2017) points out, outmoded or inappropriate representations remain obstacles to progress. Partnering with domain experts (similar to the arguments in Sein et al. (2011)) can provide opportunities to DSR scholars to develop novel representations and digital abstractions that can transform the outcomes.

4 Discussion and Next Steps

The concerns I have explored in this paper are difficult, partly because many of us may believe we already know the answer, and partly because it remains difficult to peel back the layers of uncertainty that DSR scholars face as they engage in DSR efforts. Although it is recognized that DSR is inherently different from behavioral science (Hevner et al. 2004), scholars engaged in DSR have sometimes remained trapped in the expectations they have inherited, e.g. "clearly articulate your research questions before starting the research project." Contemporary investigations (Nielsen 2020; Twomey et al. 2020) have started to explore these differences, drawing on specific DSR (and allied) methods as well as prior work related to information systems design (Lanzara and Matthiassen 1985; Schön 1983). Others, such as Maedche et al. (2019) and Jones and Venable (2020) have proposed new structuring devices for problem formulation.

Table 4. Identifying and developing research problems for DSR: key challenges

Phase	Key challenges
Choosing a design perspective	• Choose a problem-solving/design orientation • Articulate specific and generic problem
Identifying a problem	• Consider technological problem type • Ensure the problem is not routine
Framing and formulating the problem	• Select a specific research focus • Identify the research front • Establish problem significance • Explore solvability of the problem
Re-presenting the problem with design options	• Acknowledge the wicked nature of the problem • Experiment with different representations

My investigation here has drawn upon a *different* set of foundations, such as research methodologies in other disciplines (Regli 2017), work related to design foundations

---

[11] Regli (2017) describes it by pointing to a standard exercise called the eight queens problem. A naïve representation of the problem means the solution can take hours. In contrast, a clever representation results in an instant solution for vastly larger problems.

(Rittell and Weber 1984), and foundational work in science and technology studies (Laudan 1984). The approach I have outlined, therefore, addresses a set of concerns that overlaps with contemporary investigations in the DSR community but points to new opportunities for investigation. Table 4 summarizes these.

I hope that the DSR scholars will find the echoes of their struggles within the challenges outlined, and that we can continue this dialog to identify (choose) and develop (formulate) research problems towards more impactful outcomes.

References

Barrett, C.B.: Publishing and collaborations: Some Tips. Seminar. University of Melbourne, 23 April (2013)

Baskerville, R.L., Kaul, M., Storey, V.C.: Genres of inquiry in design-science research. MIS Q. **39**(3), 541–564 (2015)

Baskerville, R.: What design science is not. Eur. J. Inf. Syst. **17**(5), 441–443 (2008). https://doi.org/10.1057/ejis.2008.45

Brooks, F.P., Jr.: The computer scientist as toolsmith II. Commun. ACM **39**(3), 61–68 (1996)

Chandra, L., Seidel, S., Gregor, S.: Prescriptive knowledge in IS research: conceptualizing design principles in terms of materiality, action, and boundary conditions. In: Proceedings of 48th HICSS, pp. 4039–4048. IEEE (2015)

Chatterjee, S.: Personal communication. Differences between design science and behavioral science. Georgia State University (2000)

Creswell, J.W.: Research Design, Qualitative & Quantitative Approaches. Sage, Thousand Oaks (1994)

Gregor, S., Hevner, A.R.: Positioning and presenting design science research for maximum impact. MIS Q. **37**, 337–355 (2013)

Gregor, S., Jones, D.: The anatomy of a design theory. J. Assoc. Inf. Syst. **8**, 313–335 (2007)

Horan, C.: Research topic selection & development: suggested guidelines for the student researcher, Chapter 2. In: Hogan, J., et al. (eds.) Approaches to Qualitative Research: Theory and its Practical Application. Oak Tree Press (2009)

Iivari, J.: A critical look at theories in design science research. J. Assoc. Inf. Syst. **21**(3), 10 (2020)

Jensen, P.H.: Choosing your PhD topic (and why it is important). Aust. Econ. Rev. **46**(4), 499–507 (2013)

Jones, C., Venable, J.R.: Integrating CCM4DSR into ADR to improve problem formulation. In: Hofmann, S., Müller, O., Rossi, M. (eds.) DESRIST 2020. LNCS, vol. 12388, pp. 247–258. Springer, Cham (2020). https://doi.org/10.1007/978-3-030-64823-7_23

Lanzara, G.F., Mathiassen, L.: Mapping situations within a system development project. Inf. Manag. **8**, 3–20 (1985)

Laudan, R.: Introduction. In: Laudan, R. (ed.) The Nature of Technological Knowledge, pp. 1–26. D. Reidel Publishing Co. Boston (1984)

Lee, A.S.: A scientific methodology for MIS case studies. MIS Q. **13**(1), 33–50 (1989). https://doi.org/10.2307/248698

Lee, J., Wyner, G.M., Pentland, B.T.: Process grammar as a tool for business process design. MIS Q. **32**(4), 757–778 (2008). https://doi.org/10.2307/25148871

Lukyanenko, R., Parsons, J.: Design theory indeterminacy: what is it, how can it be reduced, and why did the polar bear drown? J. Assoc. Inf. Syst. **21**(5), 1 (2020)

Luse, A., et al.: Selecting a research topic: a framework for doctoral students. Int. J. Dr. Stud. **7**, 143 (2012)

Maedche, A., Gregor, S., Morana, S., Feine, J.: Conceptualization of the problem space in design science research. In: Tulu, B., Djamasbi, S., Leroy, G. (eds.) DESRIST 2019. LNCS, vol. 11491, pp. 18–31. Springer, Cham (2019). https://doi.org/10.1007/978-3-030-19504-5_2

Majchrzak, A., Markus, M.L., Wareham, J.: Designing for digital transformation: lessons for information systems research from the study of ICT and societal challenges. MIS Q. **40**(2), 267–277 (2016)

Moir, H.V.: Empirical evidence on the inventive step. European Intellectual Property Review, April (2013)

Mosyjowski, E.A., et al.: Drivers of research topic selection for engineering doctoral students. Int. J. Eng. Educ. **33**(4), 1283 (2017)

Myers, M.D., Klein, H.K.: A set of principles for conducting critical research in information systems. MIS Q. **35**(1), 17–36 (2011). https://doi.org/10.2307/23043487

Nielsen, P.A., Persson, J.S.: Engaged problem formulation in IS research. Commun. Assoc. Inf. Syst. **38**(1), 35 (2016)

Nielsen, P.A.: Problematizing in IS design research. In: Hofmann, S., Müller, O., Rossi, M. (eds.) DESRIST 2020. LNCS, vol. 12388, pp. 259–271. Springer, Cham (2020). https://doi.org/10.1007/978-3-030-64823-7_24

Parsons, J.: Personal communication about the role of DESRIST in clarifying norms of research conduct, 21–22 May, Clontarf Castle, Dublin, Ireland (2015)

Pries-Heje, J., Baskerville, R.: The design theory nexus. MIS Q. 731–755 (2008)

Pries-Heje, J., et al.: RMF4DSR: a risk management framework for design science research. Scand. J. Inf. Syst. **26**(1), Article no. 3 (2014)

Purao, S.: Truth or dare: the ontology question in design science research. J. Database Manag. **24**(3), 51–66 (2013)

Purao, S., Karunakaran, A.: Designing platforms to support knowledge-intensive organizational work. In: vom Brocke, J., Hevner, A., Maedche, A. (eds.) Design Science Research. Cases. PI, pp. 207–227. Springer, Cham (2020). https://doi.org/10.1007/978-3-030-46781-4_9

Rai, A.: Avoiding type III errors: formulating IS research problems that matter. MIS Q. **41**(2), iii–vii (2017)

Regli, W.: Wanted: toolsmiths. Comm. ACM **60**(4), 26–28 (2017)

Rittel, H., Webber, M.: Dilemmas in a general theory of planning. Policy Sci. **4**, 155–169 (1973)

Rittel, H., Webber, M.: Planning problems are wicked problems. In: Cross, N. (ed.) Developments in Design Methodology, pp. 135–144. Wiley (1984)

Romme, A.G.L., Endenburg, G.: Construction principles and design rules in the case of circular design. Organ. Sci. **17**, 287–297 (2006)

Rothe, H., Wessel, L., Barquet, A.P.: Accumulating design knowledge: a mechanisms-based approach. J. Assoc. Inf. Syst. **21**(3), 1 (2020)

Sandberg, J., Alvesson, M.: Ways of constructing research questions: gap-spotting or problematization? Organization **18**(1), 23–44 (2011)

Sarker, S., et al.: Guest editorial: qualitative studies in information systems: a critical review and some guiding principles. MIS Q. **37**(4), iii–xviii (2013)

Saunders, M.N.K., Lewis, P., Thornhill, A.: Research Methods for Business Students, 3rd edn. Pitman Publishing, London (2007)

Schön, D.: The Reflective Practitioner: How Professionals Think in Action. Basic Books (1983)

Seidel, S., et al.: Design principles for sensemaking support systems in sustainability transformations. Eur. J. Info. Syst. **27**(2), 221–247 (2018)

Sein, M.K., Henfridsson, O., Purao, S., Rossi, M., Lindgren, R.: Action design research. MIS Q. **35**, 37–56 (2011)

Sein, M.K., Rossi, M.: Elaborating ADR while drifting away from its essence. Eur. J. Inf. Syst. **28**(1), 21–25 (2019)

Shapiro, J.: George H. Heilmeier. IEEE Spectr. **31**(6), 56–59 (1994)

Shneiderman, B.: The New ABCs of Research: Achieving Breakthrough Collaborations. Oxford University Press (2016)

Thuan, N., et al.: Construction of Design Science Research Questions, Communications of the Association for Information Systems (forthcoming), (2021, in press)

Twomey, M.B., Sammon, D., Nagle, T.: The tango of problem formulation: a patient's/researcher's reflection on an action design research journey. J. Med. Internet Res. **22**(7) (2020)

Van de Ven, A.H.: Engaged Scholarship: A Guide for Organizational and Social Research. Oxford University Press, New York (2007)

Weber, R.: Editor's comment: the problem of the problem. MIS Q. **27**(1), iii–ix (2003)

Venable, J., et al.: Designing TRiDS: treatments for risks in design science. Australas. J. Inf. Syst. (2019)

Webster, J., Watson, R.T.: Analyzing the past to prepare for the future: writing a literature review. MIS Q. xiii–xxiii (2002)

Welke, R.: Personal communication about problem-finding by going beyond a literature review. Georgia State University (1997)

Yu, L., et al.: A decision support system for finding research topic. In: PACIS 2013 Proceedings, 190 (2013). http://aisel.aisnet.org/pacis2013/190

MyResearchChallenge.digital - A Participatory Problem Discovery System for Citizen Design Science Research

Anke Greif-Winzrieth[1]($\boxtimes$) (iD) and Michael Gau[1,2] (iD)

[1] Karlsruhe Institute of Technology (KIT), Karlsruhe, Germany
{anke.greif-winzrieth,michael.gau}@kit.edu
[2] University of Liechtenstein, Vaduz, Liechtenstein
michael.gau@uni.li

Abstract. To solve societal problems, it is essential to engage with actual problem owners in society in a scalable way. In this paper, we follow a Citizen Design Science Research (CDSR) paradigm proposing to more actively involve society in DSR projects. Specifically, we present MyResearchChallenge.digital, a prototypical system that supports participatory problem discovery by enabling the involvement of citizens in problem awareness in a scalable way. The system allows researchers and citizens to cooperate on the exploration of a given problem space, leveraging the creativity and wisdom of the crowd for identifying and describing relevant DSR problems. The evaluation of the prototype with 30 representative citizens points to the system's strengths and opportunities related to its ease of use and the problem articulation feature but also reveals weaknesses and threats concerning the problem exploration features and issues about platform abuse.

Keywords: Design science research · Citizen science · Problem identification

1 Introduction

Design Science Research (DSR) targets to solve real-world problems in business and society. From a societal perspective, engaging with citizens to understand problems and provide solutions is critical and constitutes a prerequisite for responsible research and innovation in IS and beyond [1, 2]. Citizen Science, "the (large-scale) involvement of citizens in scientific endeavors not only as participants but as co-researchers" [3, p. 273] is a prominent approach to foster extensive public participation in research projects with the aim to close the gap between scientific and public perspectives on real-world problems [3]. Thus there are recent calls for leveraging the potential of Citizen Science in IS [3, 4]. Related to Citizen Science, crowdsourcing is an increasingly important approach in practice as well as in research and is heavily used in the field of open innovation and co-creation to access the knowledge and resources of the crowd. [5] provide a framework describing the input-process-output aspects in crowdsourcing. One essential part of crowdsourcing systems is to define a problem or task that should be solved by

L. Chandra Kruse et al. (Eds.): DESRIST 2021, LNCS 12807, pp. 112–117, 2021.
https://doi.org/10.1007/978-3-030-82405-1_13

the crowd. Furthermore, providing existing ideas or problems expanding the problem space can increase the originality of generating ideas or problems [6].

In DSR, as in any other research domain, an appropriate understanding of the problem to be investigated as well as a thorough formulation of the research questions is a key success factor [7] – put differently "coming up with the right answer to the wrong question does not create value" [8, p. ii]. Identifying and formulating problems that matter requires substantial engagement with the stakeholders [9]. However, scholars rarely involve those affected by their research [1, 10]. Approaches to leverage creativity, wisdom, and experience of the society for identifying relevant research problems are still scarce. One example of such an attempt is presented by [11], who proposed "Theory Garden", a visualization tool enabling individuals to develop theories about phenomena of their interest.

Some recent studies have applied the DSR paradigm to provide innovative solutions for Citizen Science [4, 12–14]. However, not much has been done at the intersection of DSR and Citizen Science from an integrative point of view. We propose to connect the two fields towards Citizen Design Science Research (CDSR). In this paper, we present a prototype that specifically focuses on the problem awareness phase and showcases the potential of this connection. By leveraging a Citizen Science paradigm, we present a tool that provides a scalable approach supporting DSR researchers to involve citizens in the identification and description of problems in specific fields of interest. Furthermore, the tool supports the prioritization of specific problems by citizens. We develop an initial set of design requirements and derive design features based on the requirements. These are instantiated in the prototypical implementation of a system called *MyResearchChallenge.digital*.

2 Design Requirements

Based on the existing DSR, Citizen Science, and crowdsourcing literature introduced above, we derive an initial set of design requirements (DR) for our participatory problem discovery system following a CDSR paradigm. As argued by [1] and [2] the identification of relevant real-world problems requires the involvement of those affected already in the initial problem identification phase which is crucial for the success of a DSR project [7]. We thus articulate the first and second design requirements as follows:

DR1: The system should enable the cooperation between researchers and citizens to jointly explore the problem space of a DSR project.
DR2: The system should enable researchers to identify the most relevant classes of problems in the problem space of a DSR project.
Due to the heterogeneity of contributors ensuring data quality is a main issue in Citizen Science and crowdsourcing [4]. Further, a clear definition of the task given to the crowd is essential in any crowdsourcing system [5]. To enable an appropriate understanding and description of the problem space in DSR [7] proposed a conceptual model consisting of four key concepts: (1) Needs informing (2) Goals that are satisfied by (3) Requirements while (1)–(3) are contextualized and influenced by different (4) Stakeholders. This leads to the third requirement:

DR3: The system should ensure data quality by enforcing structured and complete problem specifications.

As the main goal of the proposed system is to involve society into the initial phase of DSR projects on a large scale which nowadays comes with challenges faced by any (social) platform, the fourth and fifth requirements are:

DR4: The system should be scalable in terms of the number of projects launched by researchers and in terms of the number of contributing citizens.

DR5: The system should ensure data and process transparency.

3   Prototypical System Implementation

In this section we introduce an initial set of design features (DF) based on the design requirements derived above and describe the prototypical implementation of MyResearchChallenge.digital. The following Table 1 provides an overview of the initial set of design features.

Table 1. Overview of the initially derived design features.

Design feature	Description	Related DR
DF1	Researchers can define and describe the problem space boundaries	DR1
DF2	Citizens can submit specific classes of research problems in the problem space	DR1
DF3	Citizens can explore and prioritize existing problems	DR2
DF4	Citizens are provided with problem description templates	DR3
DF5	Researchers can structure and aggregate problems	DR4
DF6	The system can host several problem space campaigns	DR4
DF7	The system can be accessed from any device	DR4
DF8	User authentication and non-anonymous sharing of content is required	DR5
DF9	The system provides a conversational agent to guide citizens in the structured problem description phase	DR3

MyResearchChallenge.digital is implemented as a web application using python built on top of the web framework django[1] and uses a central database. This allows citizens to access the platform via any device providing a web browser (DF7).

For each research topic to be launched on the platform a problem space campaign must be started by the researcher (DF1). In the template for campaigns, the researcher enters the title of the campaign, the time frame for participation (e.g., a certain month) and a brief description of the research topic defining the boundaries of the problem

---

[1] https://www.djangoproject.com/.

space which is then presented to the citizens on the campaign's main page. Furthermore, campaigns are used to structure the submitted problems by aggregating the problems to the corresponding campaign in the system (DF5). The platform can host several campaigns and implements the user management incorporating different roles (e.g., admin, researcher, citizen) and associated rights (e.g., launching and managing campaigns (researchers), submitting, editing and prioritize problems (citizens)) (DF6). Users need to login to the system via e-mail address and password before they can submit problems that are published under their username (DF8).

Fig. 1. Campaign's main page on MyResearchChallenge.digital.

Via the campaign's main page (Fig. 1) citizens can access the **"Campaign View"** and the **"New Problem View"**. The main elements of the Campaign View illustrated in Fig. 2 implement DF3 and DF4. It provides basic information about the problem space as well as guidelines on how to formulate and submit new problems (called "challenges" in the prototype). The guidelines introduce the four concepts needs, goals, requirements and stakeholders of the DSR problem space model according to [7]. Further, the Campaign View allows citizens to explore and prioritize existing problems following [6]. The list of submitted problems presents a summary of the problem descriptions, a "vote" button and a counter of votes for each problem. Details on the problem descriptions can be retrieved by clicking on a problem title.

Fig. 2. Main elements of the Campaign View: introduction to the topic (left), guidelines (middle), list of submitted problems (right).

The New Problem View implements DF2 and allows citizens to enter new problems related to a campaign. To engage citizens and provide real-time guidance in articulating a research problem, we integrated a conversational agent (CA) asking questions regarding needs, goals, requirements, and stakeholders of the DSR problem space (DF9). Citizens can interact with the CA and create new problem descriptions by answering the questions of the CA. All problems created by citizens in a campaign are publicly available (DF8) and can be accessed and edited by the author via the Campaign View.

The "**Admin View**" implements DF5 and allows researchers or platform managers responsible for a campaign to structure and organize the submitted problem descriptions. For example, in the case of duplicates or similar problem descriptions they can be aggregated to one overarching problem description containing various single problem descriptions provided by the citizens.

4 Evaluation

For a first evaluation of the prototype, we launched the platform on prolific[2], an online recruiting platform for researchers, and invited 30 citizens (mean age 27.9 years, 47% female, 50% male, 3% other) who were given the tasks to log in to the system, read through the main page of the campaign (exemplary topic: home office), explore and rate existing problems, submit at least one problem (min. 10 min of interaction with the system required), and afterwards provide feedback in form of a SWOT analysis. Overall, participants submitted 32 challenges, gave 101 votes, and provided 63 strengths, 44 weaknesses, 45 opportunities, and 33 threats. It took on average 17.87 min (SD 3.25) to complete all tasks.

Two researchers grouped the strengths, weaknesses, opportunities, and threats into 12 categories (and the additional category *other* for statements that could not be grouped with any other statement). We find that most strengths (18) relate to *ease of use/efficacy* (e.g., "easy to use"). Weaknesses are dominated by issues with the *problem exploration & organization* (8) (e.g., "no ranking of top challenges with most likes" or "unclear if similar problems are submitted repeatedly"). Opportunities are most pronounced in statements related to the system's *problem submission* feature for citizens (18) (e.g., "more transparency for the problems of the citizens"). Threats most frequently deal with *trolls/platform abuse* (10) (e.g., "no 'censorship' of swear words, insults or confidential data [...]").

5 Summary and Outlook

In this prototype paper, we presented MyResearchChallenge.digital, a prototypical implementation that supports participatory problem discovery by involving citizens in a scalable way in the problem identification phase of DSR projects. From the evaluation of the requirements and design features, we learned about strengths, weaknesses, opportunities, and threats of the prototype on which we can base the further development. As a next step, we plan to analyze the problems submitted with DSR experts to evaluate

---

[2] https://www.prolific.co/.

the usefulness of the system from the researchers' perspective. Additionally, we plan to further elaborate and refine the design requirements and formulate design principles which we will evaluate in a next design cycle.

References

1. McCarthy, S., Rowan, W., Lynch, L., Fitzgerald, C.: Blended stakeholder participation for responsible Information Systems Research. Commun. Assoc. Inf. Syst. **47**, 716–742 (2020). https://doi.org/10.17705/1CAIS.04733
2. Davison, R., Hardin, A., Majchrzak, A., Ravishankar, M.: Responsible IS research for a better world: a special issue of the information systems journal (Call for Papers). Inf. Syst. J. (2019). https://onlinelibrary.wiley.com/pb-assets/assets/13652575/Responsible%20IS%20Research%20for%20a%20Better%20World%20SI%20CFP%2020210219-1550758914320.pdf
3. Weinhardt, C., Kloker, S., Hinz, O., van der Aalst, W.M.P.: Citizen science in information systems research. Bus. Inf. Syst. Eng. **62**(4), 273–277 (2020). https://doi.org/10.1007/s12599-020-00663-y
4. Lukyanenko, R., Parsons, J., Wiersma, Y.F., Maddah, M.: Expecting the unexpected: effects of data collection design choices on the quality of crowdsourced user-generated content. MIS Q. **43**, 623–647 (2019). https://doi.org/10.25300/MISQ/2019/14439
5. Ghezzi, A., Gabelloni, D., Martini, A., Natalicchio, A.: Crowdsourcing: a review and suggestions for future research. Int. J. Manag. Rev. **20**, 343–363 (2018). https://doi.org/10.1111/ijmr.12135
6. Wang, K., Nickerson, J., Sakamoto, Y.: Crowdsourced idea generation: the effect of exposure to an original idea. Creat. Innov. Manag. **27**, 196–208 (2018). https://doi.org/10.1111/caim.12264
7. Maedche, A., Gregor, S., Morana, S., Feine, J.: Conceptualization of the problem space in design science research. In: Tulu, B., Djamasbi, S., Leroy, G. (eds.) DESRIST 2019. LNCS, vol. 11491, pp. 18–31. Springer, Cham (2019). https://doi.org/10.1007/978-3-030-19504-5_2
8. Rai, A.: Avoiding type III errors: formulating is research problems that matter. MIS Q. Manag. Inf. Syst. **41**, iii–vii (2017)
9. Rai, A.: Editor'scomments: engaged scholarship: research with practice for impact. Manag. Inf. Syst. Q. **43**, iii (2019)
10. Nielsen, P.A., Persson, J.S.: Engaged problem formulation in IS research. Commun. Assoc. Inf. Syst. **38**, 720–737 (2016). https://doi.org/10.17705/1CAIS.03835
11. Boland, R.J., Goraya, T., Berente, N., Hansen, S.: IT for creativity in problem formulation. In: ICIS 2009 Proceedings (2009)
12. Fegert, J., Pfeiffer, J., Christian, P., Anna, G., Christof, W.: Combining e-participation with augmented and virtual reality: insights from a design science research project. In: ICIS 2020 Proceedings (2020)
13. Nielsen, P.A., Persson, J.S.: IT management in local government: engaged problem formulation. In: ICIS 2010 Proceedings (2010)
14. Crowston, K., Prestopnik, N.R.: Motivation and data quality in a citizen science game: a design science evaluation. In: 2013 46th Hawaii International Conference on System Sciences, pp. 450–459. IEEE (2013). https://doi.org/10.1109/HICSS.2013.413

Externalities of Design Science Research: Preparation for Project Success

Alan R. Hevner[1] (iD) and Veda C. Storey[2(✉)] (iD)

[1] School of Information Systems and Management, Muma College of Business, University of South Florida, Tampa, FL, USA
ahevner@usf.edu
[2] Computer Information Systems, J. Mack Robinson College of Business, Georgia State University, Atlanta, GA, USA
vstorey@gsu.edu

Abstract. The success of design science research (DSR) projects depends upon substantial preparation and foresight. The externalities of DSR projects, however, are too often overlooked or given short shrift as the research team wants to 'hit the ground running' to design and build creative solutions to interesting, real-world problems. Frequently, this rush leads to an incomplete understanding of the opportunities and constraints in the project problem, solution, and evaluation spaces, resulting in significant changes and rework. In this research, we propose a model of four essential externalities for DSR projects. Attention to each externality is vital and requires important preparatory activities that entail attention to external impacts of the project's results. The implications of the DSR Externalities Model are discussed and future research directions suggested.

Keywords: Externalities · Design science research · Knowledge bases · Governance · Operational intervention · Resources · DSR externalities model

1 Introduction

Design science research (DSR) projects address complex problems in the real world that involve the development of an impactful artifact and growth of theory surrounding the artifact, bounded by a well-defined application context [1]. These projects require considerable knowledge of both the problem environment and the scientific foundations underlying solution opportunities. Successful projects require substantial preparation and foresight. DSR *externalities*, or considerations outside of the boundaries of the actual project, may be easily overlooked because of the inherent, wicked nature of the project and the effort it takes to address such wickedness. However, understanding and incorporating relevant externalities into the preparation for a DSR project should lead to more successful development of useful artifacts by minimizing lost time for backtracking and rework (iterations).

L. Chandra Kruse et al. (Eds.): DESRIST 2021, LNCS 12807, pp. 118–130, 2021.
https://doi.org/10.1007/978-3-030-82405-1_14

We identify four externalities that are essential for DSR project success: *resources*; *governance*; *knowledge bases*; and *operational intervention*. These externalities are chosen based on the authors' experiences in performing many DSR projects and the hard lessons learned by not addressing them adequately in project preparation. While other important externalities exist, we find these four to be particularly interesting and relevant to DSR success. Thus, the contributions of this paper are to: 1) identify, define, and discuss four key externalities as important, prerequisite considerations for DSR success; and 2) propose an agenda for future research that explicitly studies issues of DSR externalities, so researchers can avoid initiating a DSR project without proper preparation and foresight.

2   Design Science Research Externalities

Design science research projects progress from a problem space to a solution space with iterative cycles of artifact construction and evaluation [2, 3] as shown in Fig. 1. A detailed understanding and description of the research problem and its positioning in the problem space are essential to demonstrate the relevance of the research project. There are two key components that describe the problem space: the application context and the goodness criteria for solution acceptance. The application context information provides a rich description of the problem in context. What is the problem domain? Who are the key stakeholders in the problem space who will impact, and be impacted by, the design solution? Overall, the application context of a DSR project defines an idiographic basis for the dissemination of design knowledge [4].

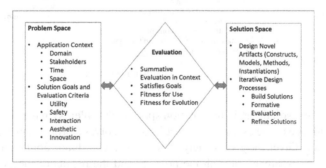

Fig. 1. Design science research process model

The second key design knowledge component in the problem space addresses the solution goals and requirements for how well the new design solves the problem in context. When describing the goodness criteria for the problem, we must recognize the sociotechnical aspects of any practical design solution. Thus, design requirements for satisfactory solutions should include a rich mix of goals from the categories of technology (e.g., security, reliability, performance), information quality (e.g., accuracy, timeliness), human interaction (e.g., usability, user experience) [5], and societal needs (e.g., accessibility, fairness) [6]. The description of these *solution goals and evaluation criteria* provides a rigorous set of acceptance criteria for the evaluation of potential design solutions and establishes guidance for both formative and summative evaluation [7, 8].

The solution space produces artifacts to solve problems. It specifically includes both the results and activities of DSR. Results of DSR can take different forms, such as designed artifacts (i.e., constructs, models, methods, and instantiations) as well as design principles or design theories in the form of nascent theories and midrange theories that generalize an understanding of how and why artifacts satisfy the goals of the problem space. Novel knowledge in the solution space can also refer to design processes that encompass build activities that contribute to creating, assessing, and refining the DSR results in iterative build-evaluation cycles. Information on goodness criteria from the problem space is used to guide a goal-driven search to maximize value that is nevertheless constrained by the availability and feasibility of resources.

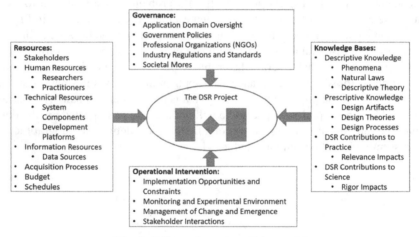

Fig. 2. DSR project externalities model

Evaluations link solutions (in the solution space) to problems (in the problem space) and provide evidence of the extent to which a solution solves a problem using the chosen evaluation method. Given the great variety of different methods and application scenarios for evaluations, transparency of both the process and the results of the evaluation are important issues. Two distinct types of design evaluations are fitness for use and fitness for evolution [9]. *Fitness for use* evaluations assess the ability of a design artifact to perform in the current application context with the current set of goals in the problem space. *Fitness for evolution* evaluations assess the ability of the solution to adapt to changes in the problem space over time. This type of evaluation is critical for application environments in which rapid technology or human interaction changes are inevitable and successful solutions must evolve.

Before commencing the DSR project as seen in Fig. 1, however, essential preparation is needed to reduce the risk of unnecessary design iterations and rework. We propose that there are four key DSR externalities as shown in Fig. 2: *resources*, *governance*, *knowledge bases*, and *operational intervention*, as explored below.

3 Resources Externality

The basic premise of any project management plan is a comprehensive understanding of required resources to complete a successful project [10]. This begins with cataloging available resources (e.g., budget, schedule, human, technical, data) and identifying project stakeholders. Stakeholders have goals, objectives, and values that must be managed via trade-offs to define a set of requirements for system functions and qualities that will lead to an innovative design solution and implementation that meets stakeholder needs. A key activity to prepare for the DSR project is the acquisition of sufficient additional resources in the form of human capabilities, data repositories, and system technologies to achieve both practice and research contributions.

Effective resource identification for DSR projects is often difficult due to the wicked nature of the problem and the emergent behaviors of the solution. The number of iterative diagnosis cycles in the problem space and the number of iterative design and implementation cycles in the solution space are difficult to predict during initial planning [11]. Action design research projects provide additional challenges via requirements to integrate practitioner resources and schedules [12]. An insightful approach to manage the resources externality for DSR projects is to consider the feasibility dimensions of information systems as proposed by Valacich and George [13]. Table 1 summarizes the feasibility dimensions for project resources, identifying the specific considerations needed for managing design science research resources. We specifically add *Innovation Feasibility* to support the scientific knowledge contributions of a DSR project.

4 Governance Externality

Who is looking over your shoulder on the DSR project and who will be impacted by the results? The full range of governance stakeholders in the application domain must be identified and effectively managed. The role of governance provides multiple levels of independent oversight for the development and operations of the desired information systems and clarifies issues of responsibilities and accountabilities. Drawing from governance models by Shneiderman [14–16], we propose a five-level governance hierarchy for DSR project planning.

1. User Governance: The eventual users of the project results will provide requirements on system capability, usability, utility, understandability, and support needs. User focus groups, committees, and embedded practitioners on the DSR project team are sources of user governance needs.
2. Developer Governance: The developers of the technical systems bring rigorous software engineering practices for the building of reliable systems. Good governance supports the effective use of audit trails, static and dynamic analysis tools, verification and validation testing methods, and explainable user interfaces.

Table 1. Feasibility dimensions for DSR project resources

Feasibility dimensions	Description	Manage DSR resources
Technical feasibility	Capabilities of systems technology (hardware, software, infrastructure) and personnel	Capture a complete model of the problem space resources Anticipate resources needed to design novel solution
Economic feasibility	Cost-benefit analysis	Analyze economic constraints and opportunities
Operational/organizational feasibility	Impact of project on organizational structure and work practices	Propose intervention environment for evaluation of solution Operational considerations
Schedule feasibility	Timeframe realistic given skills and availability of participants	Bound DSR project goals and deliverables to match schedule constraints
Legal and contractual/governance feasibility	Legal and regulatory issues and constraints Contracts and legal implications	Incorporate governance and regulatory issues and constraints into artifact designs
Political feasibility	Power structure of stakeholders Impact on organizational environment	Understand design trade-offs to achieve balanced stakeholder satisfaction
Innovation feasibility	Consumption and production of domain knowledge Innovation opportunities Scientific contributions	Structure research questions Communicate new scientific knowledge via publications

3. Management (Inside) Governance: The organization provides a level of governance that promotes safety, privacy, and accountability of the system. Based on the application domain best practices, the organization establishes standard operating procedures for logging system interactions, reporting failures and violations, hiring and training operators, and supporting maintenance and evolution.
4. Independent (Outside) Governance: Depending on the application domain, the new system will fall under a number of independent, outside governance agencies. Attention must be paid to oversight actions and certifications from government regulations, accounting audits, insurance requirements, NGO stakeholders, and professional organizations such as research institutes.
5. Societal Governance: Global issues of ethical behaviors, fairness, diversity, and social consciousness must play a significant role in the design of solutions. Attention to these societal concerns will permeate decisions across all levels of the governance hierarchy.

Identifying stakeholders at all the governance levels during project preparation is time-consuming, but essential, for achieving the goals of usable, reliable, safe, trustworthy, and ethical systems design.

5   Knowledge Bases Externality

A DSR project must appropriately consume existing knowledge and produce new knowledge in the application domain knowledge bases [1, 17]. Depending upon the project research questions, extensive and rigorous interactions with external knowledge bases must be considered and planned early in the project execution. Archival knowledge bases that ground DSR projects include the research literature, data bases, and repositories of IT artifacts and systems. Identifying the appropriate knowledge sources is essential preparation for an effective DSR project. To support effective attention to this externality, six modes of DSR knowledge consumption and production are seen in Fig. 3, and adapted from Drechsler and Hevner [2].

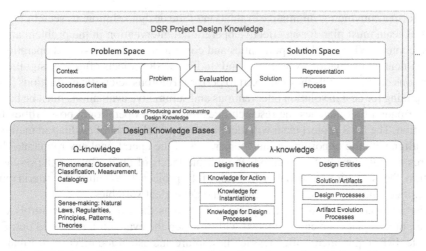

Fig. 3. Modes of DSR project and knowledge bases interactions (Adapted from [2])

Basic knowledge can be represented by two major types: 1) research activities which primarily grow Ω-knowledge (comprising descriptive, explanatory and predictive knowledge), and, 2) research activities which primarily grow λ-knowledge (comprising design knowledge) [17]. The λ-knowledge is divided into two sub-categories. *Design Entities* collect the prescriptive knowledge as represented in the tangible artifacts and processes designed and applied in the solution space. The growing of design theories around these solutions is captured in *Design Theories*. We can describe the interactions of a DSR project with the extant knowledge bases in the following consuming and producing modes:

- **Modes 1 and 2 – Use and Add Ω-Knowledge:** Ω-knowledge informs the understanding of a problem, its context, or the development of a design entity in Mode 1.

Mode 2 involves the testing and building of Ω-knowledge enhancing our descriptive understanding of how the world works given the new design knowledge.

- **Modes 3 and 4 – Use and Add Design Theory:** Solution knowledge, in the form of growing design theory, informs the development of a design entity in Mode 3. Effective principles, features, actions, or effects of a design entity are generalized and codified in solution design knowledge in Mode 4.
- **Modes 5 and 6 – Use and Add Design Entities:** Existing designs and design processes are re-used to inform novel designs of new design entities in Mode 5. Mode 6 contributes new design entities to the knowledge base.

These six modes of producing and consuming knowledge illustrate the multi-faceted opportunities for knowledge accumulation and evolution over time [18] and the importance of how the DSR project interacts with the external knowledge bases.

6   Operational Intervention Externality

To perform a convincing summative evaluation of the design solution, as seen in Fig. 1, the DSR team must plan for an effective operational intervention in the problem application context. What are the opportunities and constraints in the real-world operational environment for evaluation experiments and studies? DSR projects often face significant limitations on the controls they can exert to perform rigorous scientific evaluations [19].

Planning for design solution interventions and summative evaluations must be based on information that matches the research questions to the operational possibilities for evaluation. The DSR project team will identify an appropriate set of evaluation methods [3] to align with the opportunities and constraints of the operational environment. This requires matching evaluation methods to multiple facets of DSR. Besides the research question, the evaluation must match the goals of the project. The evaluation criteria must be specified with respect to the hypotheses and dependent variables.

The application environment impacts and restricts the experimental controls that can be put into place, given the context within which the evaluation is carried out. For example, IRB requirements often restrict the capture and use of identifying information related to a participant. Intentional (and unintentional) capture of identity and supporting information creates an ethical burden for disclosure on the part of the researchers that cannot be trivialized. The stakeholders within the application domain must sign off on experimental evaluation within that domain.

The availability of data sources affects the ability to carry out a proper evaluation. Data might be qualitative or quantitative; primary or secondary. These types and sources of data influence the kind of data analysis that can be conducted as part of the evaluation. Finally, the evaluation skills and availability of evaluation tools impact a project team's ability to perform an appropriate evaluation. In summary, early due diligence on summary evaluation opportunities and constraints must be part of the DSR project's preparation.

7 Exemplar Case Study

During the past decade, one of the co-authors participated in a highly visible DSR project that faced the externalities described in this research [20]. The project's context was a large-scale, multi-disciplinary research program - Uppsala University Psychosocial Care Programme (U-CARE), funded primarily by grants from the Swedish Research Council. The multi-disciplinary program involved researchers and practitioners from the fields of psychology, medicine, information systems, the caring sciences, and economics. The objective of the project is the implementation of a sophisticated software system for online psychosocial care with comprehensive support for online clinical trials. Stakeholder (e.g., patient, provider) privacy concerns make the development and use of the U-CARE system challenging with highly sensitive privacy and accountability requirements. The following sections briefly illustrate how the DSR team managed the four identified DSR externalities.

7.1 Resources

While resource issues of budget and schedule were important for the initiation and continuation of the U-CARE project, we focus here on the challenges of managing the human resources needed to ensure project success. Identifying the stakeholders for such a large, national healthcare endeavor was critical. Based on stakeholder feedback, we quickly realized that no existing software platform would satisfy the needs of the U-CARE community. Thus, the decision was made to design and develop an innovative information system to support online psychosocial care. This required us to build a software development team that included both researchers and professional developers.

The development approach followed Scrum agile methods including bi-weekly sprint meetings with various stakeholders from the U-CARE context. These meetings included researchers, medical doctors, nurses, patient groups, and psychologists who provided feedback on the emerging software design. This process served as formative evaluations of the emerging software; in total, we held 100 + workshops between 2011 and 2015. Psychologists contributed ideas on how to deliver stepped care online, including self-help, cognitive behavior therapy, and peer interaction in forums and chat. Researchers contributed with ideas on how to support randomized controlled trials (RCTs) online, i.e., designing questionnaires, launching them according to study-specific rules, and sending SMS and email reminders to patients and stakeholders to improve adherence to the study. Also, various features to monitor progress in studies and enable therapist decision-making are built into the system to support interactions among psychologists, researchers, and developers.

7.2 Governance

Governance of public healthcare projects was the highest priority externality for the U-CARE project. Early in the project we modeled four groups of stakeholders and their governance requirements for privacy and accountability which we termed *scrutiny*: Societal institutions (e.g., government agencies), Principals (e.g., healthcare providers), Agents (e.g., the staff operating on behalf of principals), and Clients (e.g., community members, including patients). We defined a scrutiny mode for each of the four governance levels. A fundamental proposition is that violation of privacy should be: (i) well-motivated based on organizational responsibility; or (ii) accounted for by someone.

Societal scrutiny explains the processes in society that shape and force stakeholders to comply with ethics and legislative regulations regarding privacy and accountability. In order for the organization to be ready to respond to such external scrutiny, there is a need for ongoing Organizational scrutiny. Such scrutiny requires the organization to stay updated about the external requirements and to set up internal processes to log and monitor use (and misuse) of sensitive information about individuals. Agent scrutiny occurs when staff members responsibly monitor community activity following organizational policies and external requirements. Client scrutiny refers to the community members' peer controls for monitoring system interactions. For example, community members should have the ability to personalize their visibility, to block others' activities, and report unauthorized content.

7.3 Knowledge Bases

The U-CARE DSR goals were to design, build, and evaluate a delivery platform for psychosocial care with support for clinical trials of care protocols. We grounded our research on descriptive and prescriptive theories of privacy and accountability (e.g. [21, 22]). The *technological* research contributions consist of a rich depiction of a process of designing for privacy and accountability, a software system design, and a naturalistic evaluation of the U-CARE platform enacted in practice. We also asserted *theoretical* contributions surrounding a design theory of scrutiny. The project is the first comprehensive, longitudinal DSR study to develop and evaluate a design theory for the development of sensitive online healthcare systems. A full discussion of how we consumed and produced healthcare knowledge is presented in [20].

7.4 Operational Intervention

The intended purpose of the U-CARE platform is to deliver online healthcare to remote locations throughout Sweden. Additionally, it is designed to support clinical trials of experimental healthcare protocols. Thus, from the beginning, we developed a plan for summative evaluations of the platform in actual use with clients, agents, administrators, and regulatory bodies. It was this detailed plan that generated the system requirements for supporting experimental clinical trials. The U-CARE system was used in practice by researchers, psychologists, and patients in 11 research trials for three years (April 2013–September 2016), during which time experimental data were gathered and analyzed. Approximately 3000 patients participated in studies using the software. The practical use of the system over the three years provided a basis for a rigorous naturalistic evaluation of the artifact and its use in practice.

8 Discussion

The DSR Project Externalities Model provides a helpful, albeit incomplete, framework for attending to important externalities in DSR projects. From this starting point, we now propose guidelines and research directions for recognizing and managing externalities. In Fig. 4, we introduce the *prerequisite space* as a project entity, analogous to the problem space and solution space that are well-documented in DSR. The prerequisite space envelopes the DSR project with the essential externalities addressed in the project planning to achieve the research goals. Every project must identify the externalities that apply and commit the resources to manage those externalities throughout the project. Although this might appear to add extra complexity, specifically incorporating this space supports the successful completion of a project, because it acknowledges the substantial preparation and foresight needed by focusing attention on important activities that entail responsiveness to external impacts of the project's results. Table 2 identifies research that considers the prerequisite space and the externalities.

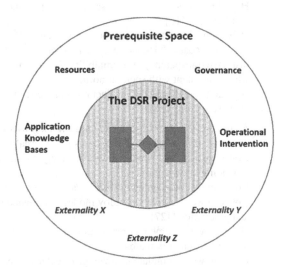

Fig. 4. Externalities addressed in a prerequisite space

Table 2. Future research directions in the prerequisite space

Externality	Research topics
Resources	How do we identify a generic list of resources that might be needed for DSR projects?
	What type of resource management can help ensure innovative artifacts?
	How, specifically, are resources impacted due to DSR's wicked nature of the problem and emergent behaviors of the solution?
	What resources are needed to incorporate innovation feasibility?
	Will a practice-oriented approach, which identifies the relationships between "practices and their material conditions" and ontological foundations for artifacts help? [23, 24]
	How can the sociotechnical aspects be recognized?
	How do we engage stakeholder participation? [12]
Governance	Can we operationalize the five-level governance hierarchy for DSR project planning proposed in this research?
	Conducting DSR experiences many novel forms of risk. How should the risks inherent in design science research be prioritized and treated? [25]
	How do we ensure reliability, safety and reporting, trustworthy certification? [16]
	How do we identify who performs governance activities and what are its boundaries? How do we create social and ethical algorithms that have transparency, accountability, fairness and lack of bias, while consistent with societal norms [16]?
	How do we manage DSR project risks proactively in formative or ex ante evaluation? [26]
Knowledge bases	Analogous to knowledge bases for design knowledge, do we need, or can we produce, knowledge bases for externalities?
	How do we know when we have effectively consumed and produced grounding knowledge?
	How can we focus on naturalistic evaluations?
	How can we effectively employ modes of knowledge consumption and production? [27]
	How can we document consumption and production of knowledge bases in different domains?
	How can we accumulate knowledge of externalities and make it assessable?
	How can we track design knowledge growth over time? [18]
	How do we generate prescriptive knowledge by designing and developing an artifact that meets organizational issues and challenges [28] as suggested by Simon [29]?

(*continued*)

Table 2. (*continued*)

Externality	Research topics
Operational intervention	How do we introduce an artifact into an organizational or societal context and identify the potential resulting organizational/societal impact?
	How can we obtain the foresight needed to assess how artifact introduction could have deliberate organizational/societal affects? [27, 30]
	How can summative evaluations be performed? [8]
	How do we identify the "hidden" contextual factors that might exit? [31]

9 Conclusion

Much research on design science research has focused on the development of an appropriate artifact to solve a real-world problem. We propose a model that encompasses four externalities necessary for DSR project success: *resources*; *governance*; *knowledge bases*; and *operational intervention*. Such externalities require substantial preparation and foresight prior to beginning investigations into the problem and solution spaces of the project. Recognizing these externalities may well lead to less jumping into projects without careful considerations of the problem space and the environment, which can potentially restrict the solution space. It can also result in fewer required iterations to arrive at innovative solution artifacts and novel design theories. A set of research questions and challenges emerge, which provide areas for future research.

References

1. Baskerville, R., et al.: Design science research contributions: finding a balance between artifact and theory. J. Assoc. Inf. Syst. **19**(5), 3 (2018)
2. Drechsler, A., Hevner, A.R.: Utilizing, producing, and contributing design knowledge in DSR projects. In: Chatterjee, S., Dutta, K., Sundarraj, R.P. (eds.) DESRIST 2018. LNCS, vol. 10844, pp. 82–97. Springer, Cham (2018). https://doi.org/10.1007/978-3-319-91800-6_6
3. Hevner, A.R., et al.: Design science in information systems research. MIS Q. **28**, 75–105 (2004)
4. Baskerville, R.L., Kaul, M., Storey, V.C.: Genres of inquiry in design-science research. MIS Q. **39**(3), 541–564 (2015)
5. Adam, M.T., et al.: Design science research modes in human-computer interaction projects. AIS Trans. Hum. Comput. Interact. **13**(1), 1–11 (2021)
6. Hevner, A., et al.: A pragmatic approach for identifying and managing design science research goals and evaluation criteria. In: AIS SIGPrag Pre-ICIS Workshop on "Practice-based Design and Innovation of Digital Artifacts" (2018)
7. vom Brocke, J., Hevner, A., Maedche, A. (eds.): Design Science Research. Cases. Springer International Publishing, Cham (2020)
8. Venable, J., Pries-Heje, J., Baskerville, R.: FEDS: a framework for evaluation in design science research. Eur. J. Inf. Syst. **25**(1), 77–89 (2016)

9. Gill, T.G., Hevner, A.R.: A fitness-utility model for design science research. ACM Trans. Manage. Inf. Syst. (TMIS) **4**(2), 1–24 (2013)
10. Avison, D., Torkzadeh, G.: Information Systems Project Management. Sage, Thousand Oaks (2009)
11. Mullarkey, M.T., Hevner, A.R.: An elaborated action design research process model. Eur. J. Inf. Syst. **28**(1), 6–20 (2019)
12. Sein, H., et al.: Action design research. MIS Q. **35**(1), 37 (2011). https://doi.org/10.2307/230 43488
13. Valacich, J.S., George, J.F., Valacich, J.S.: Modern Systems Analysis and Design, vol. 9. Pearson, Boston (2017)
14. Shneiderman, B.: Human-centered artificial intelligence: three fresh ideas. AIS Trans. Hum. Comput. Interact. **12**(3), 109–124 (2020)
15. Shneiderman, B.: Human-centered artificial intelligence: reliable, safe & trustworthy. Int. J. Hum.Comput. Interact. **36**(6), 495–504 (2020)
16. Shneiderman, B.: Bridging the gap between ethics and practice: guidelines for reliable, safe, and trustworthy human-centered AI systems. ACM Trans. Interact. Intell. Syst. **10**(4), 1–31 (2020)
17. Gregor, S., Hevner, A.R.: Positioning and presenting design science research for maximum impact. MIS Q. **37**, 337–355 (2013)
18. vom Brocke, J., et al.: Special issue editorial–accumulation and evolution of design knowledge in design science research: a journey through time and space. J. Assoc. Inf. Syst. **21**(3), 9 (2020)
19. Maedche, A., Gregor, A., Parsons, J.: Mapping design contributions in information systems research: the design research activity framework. Commun. Assoc. Inf. Syst. (2021)
20. Sjöström, J., Agerfalk, P., Hevner, A.: A design theory of scrutiny for enforcing privacy in sensitive online systems. J. Assoc. Inf. Syst. (2021)
21. Bélanger, F., Crossler, R.E.: Privacy in the digital age: a review of information privacy research in information systems. MIS Q. **35**, 1017–1041 (2011)
22. Weitzner, D.J., et al.: Information accountability. Commun. ACM **51**(6), 82–87 (2008)
23. Källén, M.: Towards higher code quality in scientific computing. Acta Universitatis, Brno (2021)
24. Nicolini, D.: Practice Theory Work and Organization: An Introduction. OUP, Oxford (2012)
25. Venable, J.R., Vom Brocke, J., Winter, R.: Designing TRiDS: treatments for risks in design science. Austral. J. Inf. Syst. **23**, 1–36 (2019). https://doi.org/10.3127/ajis.v23i0.1847
26. Venable, J., Pries-Heje, J., Baskerville, R.: A comprehensive framework for evaluation in design science research. In: Peffers, K., Rothenberger, M., Kuechler, B. (eds.) DESRIST 2012. LNCS, vol. 7286, pp. 423–438. Springer, Heidelberg (2012). https://doi.org/10.1007/978-3-642-29863-9_31
27. Drechsler, A., Hevner, A.: A four-cycle model of IS design science research: capturing the dynamic nature of IS artifact design. In: Breakthroughs and Emerging Insights from Ongoing Design Science Projects. 11th International Conference on Design Science Research in Information Systems and Technology, St. John's, Canada (2016)
28. Cloutier, M., Renard, L.: Design science research: issues, debates and contributions. Project. Proyéctica/Projectique **20**(2), 11 (2018). https://doi.org/10.3917/proj.020.0011
29. Simon, H.A.: The Sciences of the Artificial. MIT Press, Cambridge (1969)
30. Pandza, K., Thorpe, R.: Management as design, but what kind of design? an appraisal of the design science analogy for management. Br. J. Manag. **21**(1), 171–186 (2010)
31. Engström, E., et al.: How software engineering research aligns with design science: a review. Empir. Softw. Eng. **25**(4), 2630–2660 (2020)

Journaling the Design Science Research Process. Transparency About the Making of Design Knowledge

Jan vom Brocke[1], Michael Gau[1,2(✉)] [iD], and Alexander Mädche[2]

[1] University of Liechtenstein, Vaduz, Liechtenstein
{jan.vom.brocke,michael.gau}@uni.li
[2] Karlsruhe Institute of Technology (KIT), Karlsruhe, Germany
{michael.gau,alexander.maedche}@kit.edu

Abstract. Design Science Research (DSR) is a highly context-dependent and iterative process. Design processes in DSR projects represent the actual strategy and execution of design knowledge inquiry and are typically unique. However, details of the actual design process are often lost as there is a lack of transparency in published DSR projects. In this research in progress paper, we present the idea of "journaling" the DSR process. We introduce the concept, showcase it with a conceptual framework, present practical applications, discuss implications and outline future research.

Keywords: Design Science Research · Process Journal · Open Science

1 Introduction

Design Science Research (DSR) is an established field for developing innovative solutions to real-world problems [2]. In recent years, many methodological contributions have increased the maturity of the DSR paradigm, including guidelines on how to conduct DSR [10], templates on how to plan and document DSR projects [4], as well as the conceptualization of the design process, such as the process suggested by Peffers et al. [18].

One major leap in the development of DSR methodology is the understanding that DSR is a highly context-dependent and iterative process [2]. While phased models provide important guidance on what kind of activities comprise a DSR project and how they would relate to one another, it is well understood today that every single DSR project follows its own process on the instance level, and it actually should do, taking into account both specific opportunity and constraints of design. Extant research has emphasized the evolutionary nature of DSR [14]. In an iterative manner DSR seeks to understand and conceptualize the problem space, analyze the solution space and, over the course of multiple iterations, would gradually develop an understanding of both problem and solution space, while also developing and evaluating design knowledge [22]. Contributions to the evaluation of DSR have developed the idea of concurrent evaluation [20] as well

© Springer Nature Switzerland AG 2021
L. Chandra Kruse et al. (Eds.): DESRIST 2021, LNCS 12807, pp. 131–136, 2021.
https://doi.org/10.1007/978-3-030-82405-1_15

as design and evaluation sprints [21]. Vom Brocke, Winter, Hevner, and Maedche have used the analogy of DSR as a "journey through space and time" in order to emphasize and further conceptualize the importance of knowledge accumulation and evolution in DSR [2].

When publishing DSR, it is difficult to account for the evolutionary and accumulative nature of design research. One very obvious reason is the lack of space to report on the process in detail. Often, the "making of" a DSR project and the "making of" the design knowledge presented in a paper gets rather lost in a brief account of the research methodology of the peer. This is problematic, as the design process is the actual strategy of inquiry used to arrive at the design knowledge presented in a paper, so – according to the goal of rigor – this process should be transparent to fellow researchers [13].

Also the discourse on research transparency calls for openness regarding the research process [7]. Open Science practices stress the importance of making the research process and its results more transparent and verifiable. For example, the recently proposed Transparency and Openness Promotion (TOP) guidelines are being increasingly adopted by journals and organizations [16]. A recent editorial in Management Information Systems Quarterly [5] discusses research transparency in IS and calls for contributions taking into account the nature of respective IS sub-communities. In fact, the extent to which a study establishes transparency about the specific design process is also described as an important quality criterion for DSR [2].

In this research in progress paper, we present the idea of keeping a journal of the DSR project to increase transparency and on this basis enable a fruitful discourse in DSR. In other disciplines methods of journaling or keeping a diary are well established [11], however DSR, today, lacks standards and guidelines on how to keep and present a journal of this kind. We conceptualize journaling the DSR process, showcase forms such journals may take, and discuss avenues for further research.

2 Related Work

The processes of conducting DSR have been studied extensively in the DSR literature, such as Nunamaker et al., Walls et al., Hevner, Kuechler & Vaishnavi, and Peffers et al. [10, 12, 17, 18, 23]. Furthermore, there exists tool support for researchers to document and structure such DSR processes, for example, developed in the collaborative DSR research project MyDesignProcess.com [3].

More recently, the discussion on the DSR process has very much focused on the evolutionary and accumulative nature of DSR and more iterative way of designing and evaluating design artifacts. Sonnenberg and vom Brocke [20], for instance, have introduced the idea of concurrent evaluation and design of intermediate artifacts; Abraham et al. argue in favor of failing "early and often" [1]. Winter and Albani, building on Hevner's "three-cycle view of DSR" [9] and referring to ADR [19], develop a one-cycle view of DSR, where every single iteration of the cycle allows for reshaping the DSR knowledge base. Vom Brocke et al. have used the metaphor of DSR as a journey through space and time, and discussed various specific directions this journey can take.

Drawing from the current discourse, we know that DSR does not follow strictly a standardized reference process, instead the activities taken need to be individually decided upon. Hence, we believe it is important to document the entire research process in order to make it accessible for fellow researchers. Indeed, we value the transparency of the research process as a key quality criterion in DSR, and put forward the concept of journaling the DSR process to support such transparency.

3 A Conceptual Framework for Journaling the Design Science Research Process

We use the term "research process" to refer in general to the set of activities conducted in order to fulfill a research objective. Thus, journaling the research process means taking notes concurrently to describe the performed research process. The key characteristic of journaling is the concurrency with which the process is documented. Unlike ex post descriptions, journaling the research process specifically means taking notes on the process as it unfolds, like keeping a log file or a personal diary.

Keeping a journal can relate to different aspects of the DSR process, and we outline such aspects in Fig. 1. DSR has been differentiated on two layers, comprising design processing and design theorizing [4], so that beyond documenting the activities conducted in the design process, a journal could also take notes reflecting on ideas for potential theoretical contributions along this process [11]. Obviously, in the design processing layer, the journal can relate to the phases identified for DSR processes, such as proposed by [18]. Researchers have also suggested one-page representation for DSR, such as [6] and [4], so—before going into details of documenting single DSR activities—a research journal might also include notes on such consideration referring to the overall research design. Hevner and Gregor have presented guidelines on how to publish DSR research [8], so that in preparation for publishing a DSR study specific aspects (such as appropriate ways to structure the presentation of the project) may be supported by the journal.

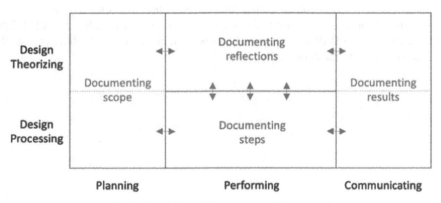

Fig. 1. DSR journaling conceptual framework

The framework presented in Fig. 1 structures potential aspects of a DSR journal according to two dimensions: the progression of a DSR project—planning, performing, and communicating—and the level it refers to, the processing or theorizing level. When planning a DSR project, journaling such items as problem space and solution spaces plays an important role, for example with regard to considerations on the overall process, key concepts, as well as input knowledge and output knowledge. When performing the process, more detailed notes on design activities, such as interviews or sketches of potential solution artifacts, may be noted. To support theorizing, memos could be taken that conceptualize, group, and link up observations. Communicating results, checking for completeness, making supplementary remarks, and providing evidence and reasoning for design decisions are some examples of features that would be of interest for the journal.

4   Practical Examples of Journaling the Design Science Research Process

To illustrate the idea of journaling a DSR process further, we refer to practical example of journals from exemplary DSR projects. In very simple terms, a journal could be kept using a researcher's conventional office environment, so comprising hand-written notes as well as notes using diverse office products. While the flexibility of using such tools is positive, it is also a challenge organizing and structuring the various forms of notes. Such shortcomings are addressed by distinct tools that have been designed for the purpose of documenting the research process, such as the tool MyDesignProess.com [3]. In order to demonstrate the idea of journaling the design process, we used the tool MyDesignProcess.com and reconstructed a journal for a DSR project that has already been published [15]. Figure 2 illustrates the researcher view of a DSR project journal, and the full journal can be accessed via a publicly available link[1].

In the planning phase, an overview of the DSR project is captured in the Design Canvas, available in the project navigation, and mainly filled to organize and structure the project. The performing aspect of the project is expressed through the different activities executed and captured during the project. Such activities can also contain sub-activities in order to structure and organize the process of a DSR project [3]. The complete journal of a DSR project, or only parts of it, can be made publicly accessible and communicated to the community.

---

[1] https://mydesignprocess.com/public/191/ Further journals of projects can be accessed here https://mydesignprocess.com/#projects-section.

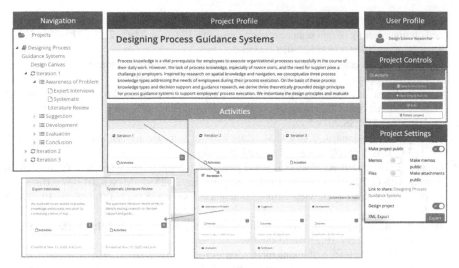

Fig. 2. Example of a DSR journal

5 Implications and Future Research

Journaling the research process makes important contributions to DSR. First, it supports DSR researchers in better planning, communicating, and reflecting upon their research activities. Second, journaling allows for more rigor in DSR, as the research process is highly situational, and all design knowledge derived is only the result of a specific design process. So, disclosing the specific DSR process should be a key quality criterion in DSR. Third, journaling the DSR process makes an important contribution to the discourse of open science and research transparency in DSR [5, 16]. Such transparency will allow for more re-use of design knowledge and increased discourse on design processes in DSR.

Future research will advance our understanding of journaling DSR processes. We intend to undertake further iterations in refining our problem understanding and solution design, while also advancing our knowledge of how journaling of this kind can be applied to support DSR researchers in their practice.

References

1. Abraham, R., et al.: Fail early, fail often: towards coherent feedback loops in design science research evaluation. In: Proceedings of the International Conference on Information Systems - Building a Better World through Information Systems. Association for Information Sytems, AIS Electronic Library (AISeL) (2014)
2. vom Brocke, J., Winter, R., Hevner, A., Maedche, A.: Special issue editorial –accumulation and evolution of design knowledge in design science research: a journey through time and space. J. Assoc. Inf. Syst. **21**(3), 520–544 (2020). https://doi.org/10.17705/1jais.00611
3. vom Brocke, J., Fettke, P., Gau, M., Houy, C., Morana, S.: Tool-Support for Design Science Research: Design Principles and Instantiation. SSRN Electronic Journal (2017). https://doi.org/10.2139/ssrn.2972803

4. vom Brocke, J., Maedche, A.: The DSR grid: six core dimensions for effectively planning and communicating design science research projects. Electron. Mark. **29**(3), 379–385 (2019). https://doi.org/10.1007/s12525-019-00358-7

5. Burton-Jones, A., et al.: Editor's comments: advancing research transparency at MIS Quarterly a pluralistic approach. Manage. Inf. Syst. Q. **45**(2), iii–xviii (2021)

6. Chandra Kruse, L., Nickerson, J.V.: Portraying Design Essence. In: Proceedings of the 51st Hawaii International Conference on System Sciences, Hawaii January 3 (2018). https://doi.org/10.24251/HICSS.2018.560.

7. Davenport, J.H., Grant, J., Jones, C.M.: Data without software are just numbers. Data Sci. J. **19**, 1–3 (2020). https://doi.org/10.5334/dsj-2020-003

8. Gregor, S., Hevner, A.R.: Positioning and presenting design science research for maximum impact. MIS Q. **37**(2), 337–355 (2013). https://doi.org/10.25300/MISQ/2013/37.2.01

9. Hevner, A.: A three cycle view of design science research. Scand. J. Inf. Syst. **19**, 87–92 (2007)

10. Hevner, A.R., et al.: Design science in information systems research. MIS Q. **28**(1), 75–105 (2004). https://doi.org/10.2307/25148625

11. Jepsen, L.O., et al.: Back to thinking mode: diaries for the management of information systems development projects. Behav. Inf. Technol. **8**(3), 207–217 (1989). https://doi.org/10.1080/01449298908914552

12. Kuechler, B., Vaishnavi, V.: On theory development in design science research: anatomy of a research project. Eur. J. Inf. Syst. **17**(5), 489–504 (2008). https://doi.org/10.1057/ejis.2008.40

13. Lukyanenko, R., Parsons, J.: Design theory indeterminacy: what is it how can it be reduced and why did the polar bear drown? J. Assoc. Inf. Syst. **21**, 1–59 (2020)

14. Markus, M., et al.: A design theory for systems that support emergent knowledge processes. MIS Q. **26**, 179–212 (2002). https://doi.org/10.2307/4132330

15. Morana, S., Kroenung, J., Maedche, A., Schacht, S.: Designing process guidance systems. J. Assoc. Inf. Syst. **20**, 499–535 (2019). https://doi.org/10.17705/1jais.00542

16. Nosek, B.A., et al.: Promoting an open research culture. Science **348**(6242), 1422–1425 (2015). https://doi.org/10.1126/science.aab2374

17. Nunamaker, J.F., et al.: Systems development in information systems research. J. Manage. Inf. Syst. (1990). https://doi.org/10.1080/07421222.1990.11517898

18. Peffers, K., et al.: A design science research methodology for information systems research. J. Manage. Inf. Syst. **24**(3), 45–77 (2007). https://doi.org/10.2753/MIS0742-1222240302

19. Sein, M.K., et al.: Action design research. MIS Q. **35**(1), 37–56 (2011). https://doi.org/10.2307/23043488

20. Sonnenberg, C., vom Brocke, J.: Evaluation patterns for design science research artefacts. In: Helfert, M., Donnellan, B. (eds.) EDSS 2011. CCIS, vol. 286, pp. 71–83. Springer, Heidelberg (2012). https://doi.org/10.1007/978-3-642-33681-2_7

21. Venable, J., et al.: FEDS: a framework for evaluation in design science research. Eur. J. Inf. Syst. **25**(1), 77–89 (2016). https://doi.org/10.1057/ejis.2014.36

22. Venable, J.: The role of theory and theorising in design science research. In: First International Conference on Design Science Research in Information Systems and Technology (2006)

23. Walls, J.G., et al.: Building an information system design theory for vigilant EIS. Inf. Syst. Res. **3**, 36 (1992). https://doi.org/10.1287/isre.3.1.36

The Primary Scientific Contribution is Hardly a Theory in Design Science Research

Mikko Siponen[1]([⊠])(iD) and Tuula Klaavuniemi[2]

[1] Faculty of IT, University of Jyvaskyla, 40100 Jyvaskyla, Finland
mikko.t.siponen@jyu.fi
[2] Oncology Department, Mikkeli Central Hospital, 50100 Mikkeli, Finland

Abstract. Generally, to publish a paper in a top IS journal, making a new theory contribution is, so we are told, required. Such a requirement also exists in Design Science Research (DSR) literature. We review a number of claims about the necessity of theory as it applies to DSR. We find these claims wanting. For example, medical research and engineering are both called "design science" in (Simon 1996) *Sciences of the Artificial*. However, most articles in the top medical, computer engineering, and network engineering journals do not develop new theories. Unless the proponents of theories, as the primary vehicle of scientific DSR knowledge, can offer a satisfactory argument for why theories are the primary scientific contribution, we do not have to regard 'theory' as the primary outcome of good scientific research in DSR. If we are correct, then theory is not valuable in its own right in (applied) science, as theory serves higher purposes.

Keywords: Theory · Design Science Research

1 Introduction: The Necessity of Theory

Theory is generally considered important in Information Systems (IS). For instance, the former editor-in-chief of *MIS Quarterly* noted how a "required element" for any excellent paper is that it "sufficiently uses or develops theory" (Straub 2009, p. vi). The supposed necessity of theory has also found its way into Design Science Research (DSR): "it is of vital importance to investigate how design knowledge can be expressed as theory" (Gregor and Jones 2007, p. 314). Venable (2013 in Iivari 2020, p. 504) reported, "Since theory is a key output of rigorous academic research, one would expect the production of DT [design theory] to be a key element of DSR." It has been claimed that developing a theory is how academics differ from practitioners (Gregor 2006, 2014). As a final example, "it has proven difficult to publish novel design artefacts as purely empirical contributions without substantial theoretical contribution" (Ågerfalk 2014, p. 595).

Given such emphasis on theory in IS and DSR, Iivari (2020, p. 503) found "theory fetish" in DSR, which for him is an "excessive emphasis on" theory building and theory "as if they were the only remarkable scientific contribution." According to Iivari (2020, p. 504), DSR "has fallen into the theory trap." A fundamental question before us is whether the primary remarkable scientific contribution in DSR is developing a theory.

© Springer Nature Switzerland AG 2021
L. Chandra Kruse et al. (Eds.): DESRIST 2021, LNCS 12807, pp. 137–146, 2021.
https://doi.org/10.1007/978-3-030-82405-1_16

In our attempt to answer this question, we review the following claims for the necessity of theory in IS and DSR: 1) Theory is the only remarkable scientific contribution (Iivari 2020). 2) Theory is the primary scientific contribution (Iivari's 2020 view slightly revised). 3) Theory separates academics from practice (Gregor 2006, 2014). 4) Mature disciplines have built solid theories.

We find all of these arguments wanting. The chief difficulty is that most scientists rarely develop a new theory, even in the most prestigious scientific journals. For example, Simon (1996) dubbed medical research "design sciences." However, most articles in the top medical journals, such as the *New England Journal of Medicine* (NEJM), do not claim to develop new theories (Siponen and Klaavuniemi 2019). In fact, one can find thousands of articles in the NEJM that do not even contain the word "theory" (Siponen and Klaavuniemi 2019). Or when they use "theory," they mean a speculative guess.

Other problems abound. In IS/DSR, there is an ambition to assert a demarcation tenet—namely, that *theory* (and theory development) is what separates true scientists from mere practitioners (see Gregor 2006; 2013). To defend this argument, one needs a demarcation taxonomy. The taxonomy must not include non-scientific practitioners' outcomes as a scientific theory—the issue of inclusion. It remains debatable whether theory frameworks in IS can satisfy such inclusion requirements. In this paper, we focus on Gregor's (2006) theory taxonomy. We suggest that it is vulnerable to the problem of inclusion. For example, a piece of programming code could (and as we shall later demonstrate, does) pass Gregor's (2006) DSR theory test with flying colors!

2 Theory in DSR and the Theory Fetish Arguments

In this section, we consider the arguments about whether a theory is the main source of scientific knowledge in sciences and DSR. Iivari (2020, p. 512) warned about conceptual confusions in DSR and wished that "scientific discourse should be conceptually as clear as possible." Against this background, it is important to clarify what the arguments vindicating the need for theory amount to.

Two extremes should be avoided. In the first extreme, called *no theory*, we should not argue that scientists never develop theories, because there are plenty of cases where scientists have developed something they referred to as theories. We need only mention the names Newton, Darwin, Einstein, and Kohlberg. Thus, we do not need to waste any time on this 'no theory' theory, i.e., that theories have zero importance in science.

As for the second extreme, we do not wish to consider what we call the *theory only* view. According to this tenet, theories and their development are "the only remarkable scientific contribution" (Iivari 2020, p. 503). We find "only" too restrictive, as one can find some cases in top IS journals (e.g., method articles) where the contribution is not claimed to be a theory. In other words, even the most devoted theory advocates in IS may reject this claim as formulated. Thus, we suggest slightly revising Iivari's interesting argument into something along the following lines: The primary scientific contribution is the development of a theory.

However, there are other pitfalls we need to watch out for. First, it is important to note what counts as a measure of scientific contributions. As most readers probably know, resolving this matter involves complex issues that go beyond one paper's ability to solve.

At the same time, it is necessary to say something about this definition, as otherwise we would run the risk of talking over each other's heads. As one concern regarding theory in IS is publishing a paper in a top journal (e.g., Straub 2009; Ågerfalk 2014), we use this as a "measure." The argument, then, which we wish to challenge in this paper, runs as follows: The primary remarkable scientific contribution—in top scientific journals at least—is developing a new theory. Thus, the term "primary" captures the following spirit: *For most articles*, a new theory contribution is required. We refer to this argument as *theory as a primary contribution*. With these clarifications, we consider the existing arguments in IS for theories, as summarized in Table 1.

Table 1. Summary of the theory arguments, whose merits we review in this paper.

Theory argument	Brief description
Theory separates science from practice	"Developing theory is what we are meant to do as academic researchers and it sets us apart from practitioners and consultants"
Theory as primary contribution	The primary remarkable scientific contribution—in top scientific journals—is developing a new theory
Mature discipline Theory argument	Mature disciplines have already developed theories

In the next sections, we discuss these arguments. However, this paper is far from being a complete treatment of all theory arguments in IS. For example, a number of relevant theory arguments (e.g., Avison and Malaurent 2014a, 2014b; Hirschheim 2019; Schlagwein 2021), albeit they merit discussion, cannot be covered in this paper.

Moreover, it has been asked to what extent the arguments discussed in this paper have been covered by IS literature in general or our previous work in particular. The theory arguments in Table 1 are, of course, presented in the literature. The new contribution of this paper is to *challenge these arguments, including showing how they are problematic in various ways*. As far as we know, this part of challenging these arguments (Table 1) is new in IS literature. In addition, regarding our previous work on IS philosophy, Siponen and Tsohou (2018, 2020) criticized "positivism" in IS, not theory in IS. In turn, Siponen and Klaavuniemi (2020) questioned the claim that most IS research follows the hypothetico-deductive (H-D) method. One reason is that the H-D method in the philosophy of science assumes that hypotheses or theories are guessed. Siponen and Klaavuniemi (2020) do not discuss any of these claims in Table 1. Moreover, Siponen and Klaavuniemi (2021) discussed questionable natural science beliefs in IS, and included relevant material for theories, but did not discuss any of these arguments (Table 1) we try to challenge in this paper. In summary, those papers have zero overlap with the arguments discussed in this paper. With that said, we present evidence in Sects. 2.1.1 and 2.2 from the NEJM and *Cell*, which are also mentioned in Siponen and Klaavuniemi (2019).

2.1 Theory is What Academics Do, and How Academics Differ from Practice

Gregor (2006, p. 613) famously noted: "developing theory is what we are meant to do as academic researchers and it sets us apart from practitioners and consultants." She reiterated the argument in Gregor (2014). Answering this claim requires saying something about what is meant by "developing theory." We discuss two interpretations. According to the first interpretation, called *named theory*, a theory is simply whatever scholars call a theory. To be more precise, developing a theory means proposing a specific theory or named theory. We now examine this interpretation in more detail.

Named Theory Counterargument. Iivari (2020) discussed how "editorial statements" in some physics and economics journals do not manifest the importance of theory. However, as he noted, this information alone makes it hard to draw any conclusions about the status of the theories in the articles. Unfortunately, he does not present any evidence from the articles. Fortunately, we can present some evidence.

In IS, Simon (1996) is noted as the seminal account of design theory (e.g., Gregor and Jones 2007; Gregor and Hevner 2013). Simon himself listed medical research and not physics as a prime example of Design Science Research. Arguably, the most prestigious journal in medical research is the NEJM (impact factor 74.7). The NEJM can hardly be excluded from the list of top medical journals. Yet a reader of NEJM quickly discovers that most of the articles do not develop any theories (Siponen and Klaavuniemi 2019). As we reported in Siponen and Klaavuniemi (2019), NEJM published about 1000 cancer-related articles between January 2012 and January 2017. In this sample, no new theories were proposed. None of these studies tested a specifically named theory. At least, they did not claim to do so. So, where does this lead us?

With the named theory interpretation and Gregor's argument, the evidence from the NEJM comes down to this. Most cancer scholars—even those who publish in the best medical journals (e.g., the NEJM)—are "practitioners and consultants," and not "academic researchers" (cf., Gregor 2006, p. 613). Moreover, following this interpretation, they are not doing what they "are meant to do as academics." This is because most of them never claim to develop a theory. The *named theory* interpretation puts Gregor's argument in jeopardy. We should not believe that cancer researchers publishing in the best medical journals such as the NEJM are "practitioners and consultants," and not "academic researchers," simply because they are not developing theories.

2.2 Gregor's Taxonomy May not Separate Science from Practice

There is another alternative interpretation of the claim that "developing theory is what we are meant to do as academic researchers and it sets us apart from practitioners and consultants" (Gregor 2006, p. 613). The argument runs as follows. We accept that, "Okay, scientists might not use the term 'theory.'" "That being said," the argument continues, "even if they do not mention 'theory,' we can still find elements of theories in their papers." We call this the *theory can be inferred* argument. In other words, although the authors do not call them theories, we would be justified in calling most contributions in journals such as *Cell*, *Nature*, and NEJM theories. Is this argument successful?

The obvious critique is, what is this supposed to demonstrate about *the importance of theory*? If the scientists themselves do not bother to call their contributions theories, then this suggests that the "theory" is not important to them! It also showcases that the whole rhetoric of theory is not important for acceptance by top journals, such as *Cell*, *Nature*, and the NEJM. Why should we call something a theory when many scientists themselves do not bother to call it such?

Even if we ignore this counterargument, there are other problems with the *theory can be inferred* claim. Anyone making such an inference must provide a criterion of what makes a theory. Aside from Gregor's theory taxonomy, not many criteria are available in IS. For DSR, Gregor (2006) might be the only one. Bacharach's (1989) theory account has the status of "general agreement" (Rivard 2014) and "general consensus" theory account in IS (Hirschheim 2019). But it does not talk about DSR.

Moreover, the mere existence of a theory taxonomy is not enough. Remember that we discuss the argument that "developing theory is what we are meant to do as academic researchers and it sets us apart from practitioners and consultants" (Gregor 2006, p. 613). To successfully use this argument with the *theory can be inferred* argument, any theory taxonomy must satisfy (at least) the following requirements:

(1) The theory taxonomy must not exclude something that arguably presents genuine scientific theories.
(2) The theory taxonomy must not include outcomes that hardly anyone would deem theories, but something that "practitioners and consultants" do.

A failing of either of these would be problematic. Consider the first requirement, *the problem of exclusion*. If the theory taxonomy excludes key characteristics of scientists' theories, then it cannot be used to support the claim that "developing theory is what we are meant to do as academic researchers and it sets us apart from practitioners and consultants" (Gregor 2006, p. 613).

The second requirement, the *problem of inclusion*, also causes trouble. The *problem of inclusion* can be demonstrated with the following scenario. Consider a case where the typical activities of practitioners, as defined by a theory taxonomy, later turn out to fulfill the requirements of that theory taxonomy. In such a circumstance, it would fail to support the claim that only academics develop theories, which is what supposedly makes them different from practitioners and consultants. The *problem of inclusion* and the *problem of exclusion* are widely known in the philosophy of science. For example, Carl Hempel's deductive model of explanation (Hempel and Oppenheim 1948) was later attacked on both grounds, and the model is currently deemed a failure. Can Gregor's (2006) taxonomy handle inclusion and exclusion attacks? In this paper, we can give only a few examples, and more detailed debate is beyond the scope of this paper. We also examine only the problem of inclusion. The problem of exclusion is omitted.

Gregor's Taxonomy and the Problem of Inclusion. Gregor's (2006) taxonomy, as we see it, includes cases that we should not generally deem a theory. For example, we can pick a piece of programming code and try to argue that it meets Gregor's design theory features. This attack, we argue, seems to work even with a single line of code. If our argument is successful, it would mean that any professional programmer has written thousands of design theories, if the criterion is Gregor's theory type V (2006)!

Consider writing "hello, you" in some programming language—in our case, C. Can this satisfy the features of design and action in Gregor's theory? Gregor's (2006) design theory "says how to do something ....The theory gives explicit prescriptions (e.g., methods, techniques, principles of form and function)." One can easily meet this requirement. If you want to display "hello, you" in C, then simply write:

```
main(){printf("hello, you\n");}
```

This "says how to do something." It even gives "explicit prescriptions (e.g., methods, techniques, principles of form and function)." But Gregor (2006) has other elements, such as scope, means of representation, testable propositions, and a prescriptive statement. Our example can handle these easily, as demonstrated in Table 2.

Table 2. Theory elements found in a one-line program.

Gregor's (2006) theory elements	Does our simple one-line code meet it?
Scope	Yes, in almost any computer, smart phone, tablet
Means of representation	Yes, "words" (Gregor 2006)
Testable propositions	Yes: writing the code gives "hello, you"
Prescriptive statement:	To write "hello, you" in C, write: main(){printf("hello, you\n");}

If we are correct here, then what happens to the claim that "developing theory is what we are meant to do as academic researchers and it sets us apart from practitioners and consultants" (Gregor 2006, p. 613)? It fails, *if* the criterion for theory is Gregor's theory for DSR (theory type V).

2.3 Mature Discipline Theory Argument

Iivari (2020) presented the mature discipline theory argument (MDTA). The argument runs as follows: "[M]ore mature disciplines such as physics and economics … have already built solid theories" (p. 504). It is not clear whether Iivari himself endorsed this view. However, we are concerned only about the merit of the argument, not who endorses it.

We deem the MDTA problematic for several reasons. First, unfortunately, Iivari (2020) did not tell us what a "mature discipline" is. If we assume that a mature discipline is one that already has solid theories, then we run into a circular argument: Solid theories define a mature discipline which is defined as a discipline that has solid theories.

Some IS readers may hedge their bets by replying that physics or cancer research is arguably more mature than IS. For example, cancer research is mature as it has a track record of successfully treating hundreds of different types of cancers. This may be true, but that is not the point here. What is being challenged is not whether cancer research or physics is more mature than IS. What we challenge is the following: *Even if* we intuitively deem that physics or cancer research is more mature than IS, then *how do we know that the reason for their maturity is that "they have already built solid theories"?* When we are given absolutely no characterization of what counts as "mature," "immature," and "solid theory," it is hard to evaluate these arguments. Iivari's (2020, p. 512) wise advice that "scientific discourse should be conceptually as clear as possible" is needed here. As a result, there is a serious risk of guessing in the dark. Yet despite these deficiencies, something can be said about this argument.

Solid Theories in the Mature Discipline Theory Argument. First, let us start with the concept of *solid theories* in the MDTA, according to which, "mature disciplines… have already built solid theories" (Iivari, 2020 p. 504). Putting aside the fact that "solid" is not defined, we are not quite convinced of this solid theory claim. As Iivari (2020) mentions physics, let's start with that. We do not have degrees in physics. However, reading the philosophy of physics in the philosophy of science suggests a different conclusion. Consider, for example:

> Every theory we have proposed in physics, even at the time when it was most firmly entrenched, was known to be deficient in specific and detailed ways. (Cartwright 1980, p. 160)

> All our current best theories, including General Relativity and the Standard Mode of particle physics, are too flawed and ill-understood to be mistaken for anything close to Final Theory. (Hoefer 2016)

We cannot help wondering how these can be interpreted to support the claim that physics has already built solid theories. If it is true that "all current best theories" and "every theory" in physics are *known* to be deficient and flawed, then this seems to imply the opposite conclusion (in physics): No theory is solid. Other issues lead us to doubt the solid theories tenet in MDTA. Consider, for example, why many philosophers have moved from viewing science as infallible knowledge to viewing science as fallible knowledge. Laudan (1980, p. 180), for example, reported that most "17th- and 18th-century" philosophers were infallibilists. This roughly means that *scientific* theories are literally true and offer knowledge that is 100% certain (Laudan 1980). However, things changed, so that fallibilism rather than infallibilism is now the ruling view. Laudan (1983, p. 115) claimed that "most thinkers had by the mid-nineteenth century" accepted "that science offers no apodictic certainty, that all scientific theories are corrigible and may be subject to serious emendation." One reason is that, over time, the once glorious scientific theories were often found to be wanting (Laudan 1983).

We take it that most philosophers today accept some form of fallibilism. In that case, how does the argument that mature sciences "have already built solid theories" fit into the picture of fallibilism, holding that "our best theories are usually false" (Niiniluoto 1998) and "may be subject to serious emendation" (Laudan 1983, p. 115)?

MDTA and the Argument of "Theory Separates Science from Practice." We also want to point that out that Iivari's (2020) MDTA and Gregor's (2006, 2014) argument are incompatible. *If* the MDTA were to hold, then mature sciences have already developed theories—and do not develop any more of them. But if this assumption were to be granted, then according to Gregor's (2006) argument, mature scientists have turned into "practitioners and consultants" and have stopped being scientists.

If MDTA Were to Be Accepted, Where Would It Lead Us? As noted, we have deemed the MDTA problematic all along. However, let us, *for the sake of argument*, discard all the stated difficulties and accept the present MDTA, according to which mature sciences have already built solid theories. This immediately raises the question of what mature sciences are to do now. Why haven't they stopped publishing, if they have already built solid theories? Why, for example, did *Cell* publish 990 cancer-related articles between 2012 and 2017 (Siponen and Klaavuniemi 2019)? Why did the NEJM publish 985 cancer-related articles between January 2012 and January 2017 if all the solid theories have already been developed (Siponen and Klaavuniemi 2019)? *If* (for the sake of argument) we accept the MDTA, then mature sciences have already built solid theories, and they do not need any more theories. Then why do they still do science? As noted, we do not accept the MDTA. But *if* some accept the MDTA, it leads to the following corollary: Something other than theory is important for mature sciences. Then, granting the MDTA is true, we in IS have missed this something else, i.e., much of what is going on in mature science, if we mainly focus on theories.

3 Conclusive Discussion

Currently, the argument that a primary scientific contribution in the best scientific journals is a new theory seems to fail. Scientists have developed theories. Hardly anyone disputes this fact. Yet neither should we deem theory and theory development as "the *only* remarkable scientific contribution" (Iivari 2020, p. 503, emphasis added). As we see it, what is being challenged is the following claim: The primary scientific contribution, at least in the best scientific journals, is developing a (new) theory. It turns out that most papers in many of the best scientific journals do not develop theories. If many so-called design science disciplines per Simon—e.g., computer engineering, cancer research, network engineering—rarely develop a new theory in their best journals, then why should we?

Moreover, those advocating the criticality of theory in DSR and who wish to demarcate science from practice by *theory* should proffer a satisfactory account of what theory amounts to. It is not clear to what extent such accounts exist for DSR. Such accounts must withstand attacks of exclusion and inclusion. In this paper, we focused on the problem of inclusion. Whatever merits Gregor's (2006) theory taxonomy has, it seems to be open to *the problem of inclusion*. This mean that it cannot demarcate scientific theories from non-scientific accounts. If our analysis of the *problem of inclusion* is correct, then in many cases, the taxonomy may not separate science from practice, as our simple programming example demonstrates.

What we should do with the "theory"? The problem in IS, we take it, is deeming 'theory' as valuable as such, and theory has been becoming the end itself. However, perhaps *theory* is not per se intrinsically valuable in science. In this view, perhaps *theory* serves some higher purposes, which are more important than theory structures. In medical research, for example, roughly speaking, one higher purpose is an improved treatment effect, or similar treatment effect with fewer side effects. In this case, ultimately the importance not the structure of the theory. Instead, what matters is how one can improve on the existing interventions.

If our thinking here is correct, then IS and DSR research, instead of asking 'do you have a theory?', must return to the various aims of science. These various aims of science might be more important than 'theory'. Outlining these various aims of science must, however, be left for future research and other papers.

Acknowledgements. We thank professor Juhani Iivari for providing a number of counterarguments, which we have discussed in this paper. We also thank anonymous DESRIST 2021 reviewers for their comments.

References

Avison, D., Malaurent, J.: Is theory king?: questioning the theory fetish in information systems. J. Inf. Technol. **29**(4), 327–336 (2014)

Avison, D., Malaurent, J.: Is theory king?: a rejoinder. J. Inf. Technol. **29**(4), 358–361 (2014)

Ågerfalk, P.: Insufficient theoretical contribution: a conclusive rationale for rejection? Eur. J. Inf. Syst. **23**, 593–599 (2014)

Bacharach, S.B.: Organizational theories: some criteria for evaluation. Acad. Manag. Rev. **14**(4), 496–515 (1989)

Cartwright, N.: The truth doesn't explain much. Am. Philos. Q. **17**(2), 159–163 (1980)

Gregor, S.: The nature of theory in information systems. MIS Q. **30**(3), 611–642 (2006)

Gregor, S.: Theory – still king but needing a revolution. J. Inf. Technol. **29**, 337–340 (2014)

Gregor, S., Hevner, A.: Positioning and presenting design science research for maximum impact. MIS Q. **37**(2), 337–355 (2013)

Gregor, S., Jones, D.: The anatomy of a design theory. J. Assoc. Inf. Syst. **8**(5), 312–335 (2007)

Hempel, C., Oppenheim, P.: Studies in the logic of explanation. Philos. Sci. **15**, 135–175 (1948)

Hirschheim, R.: Against theory: with apologies to Feyerabend. J. Assoc. Inf. Syst. **20**(9), 1338–1355 (2019)

Hoefer, C.: Causal determinism. In: Zalta, E. N. (ed.) The Stanford Encyclopedia of Philosophy, Stanford (2016)

Iivari, J.: A critical look at theories in design science research. J. Assoc. Inf. Syst. **21**(3), 502–519 (2020)

Laudan, L.: Why was the logic of discovery abandoned? In: Nickles, T. (ed.) Scientific Discovery, Logic, and Rationality, pp. 173–183. D. Reidel Publishing Company, Dordrecht (1980)

Laudan, L.: The demise of the demarcation problem. In: Cohen, R.S., Laudan, L. (eds.) Physics Philosophy and Psychoanalysis: Essays in Honour of Adolf Grünbaum, pp. 111–127. D Reidel Publishing Company, Dordrecht (1983)

Niiniluoto, I.: Verisimilitude: the third period. Br. J. Philos. Sci. **49**(1), 1–29 (1998)

Rivard, S.: The ions of theory construction. MIS Q. **38**(2), iii–xiii (2014)

Simon, H.: The Sciences of the Artificial, 3rd edn. MIT Press, Cambridge, MA (1996)

Schlagwein, D.: Natural sciences, philosophy of science and the orientation of the social sciences. J. Inf. Technol. **36**(1), 85–89 (2021)

Siponen, M., Klaavuniemi, T.: How and why "theory" is often misunderstood in information systems literature. In: Proceedings of the Fortieth International Conference on Information Systems, Munich (2019)

Siponen, M., Klaavuniemi, T.: Why is the hypothetico-deductive (H-D) method in information systems not an H-D method? Inf. Organ. **30**(1), 100287 (2020). https://doi.org/10.1016/j.inf oandorg.2020.100287

Siponen, M., Klaavuniemi, T.: Demystifying beliefs about the natural sciences in information system. J. Inf. Technol. **36**(1), 56–68 (2021)

Siponen, M., Tsohou, A.: Demystifying the influential IS legends of positivism. J. Assoc. Inf. Syst. **19**(7), 600–617 (2018)

Siponen, M., Tsohou, A.: Demystifying the influential IS legends of positivism: response to Lee's commentary. J. Assoc. Inf. Syst. **21**(6), 1653–1659 (2020)

Straub, D.: Why top journals accept your paper. MIS Q. **33**(3), iii–x (2009)

Design Knowledge for Reuse

Generation of Design Principles as Knowledge Conversion - Elucidating Dynamics

Sofie Wass[1]([⊠]) [iD], Lise Amy Hansen[2], and Carl Erik Moe[1]

[1] University of Agder, Kristiansand, Norway
sofie.wass@uia.no
[2] The Oslo School of Architecture and Design, Oslo, Norway

Abstract. In this paper we apply the perspective of knowledge conversion with recent identified core elements for developing design principles to elucidate the dynamics of design principles. In the paper, the elements of influence, actors, and formulation are integrated in a knowledge conversion process of socialization, externalization, combination, and internalization – through which tacit knowledge is made explicit, shared, and turned into action. We exemplify this process with three empirical cases using action design research (ADR) to develop IT artifacts and generate design principles. Our paper shows the dynamics across a process of generating design principles. Viewing the generation of design principles as knowledge conversion may ensure the active utilization of influences, engagement of actors, and purposeful formulation to serve both practical and academic knowledge creation.

Keywords: Knowledge conversion · Design principles · Action design research

1 Introduction

The generation of design principles is an important form of knowledge abstraction in design science research [1, 2]. Design principles provide prescriptive research knowledge [1, 3, 4] and are reported to be purposely incorporated in the design process by designers [5]. Prior studies have contributed with an understanding of the content and structure of design principles [6], highlighting the importance of materiality, action, and boundary conditions [3] and aspects such as application level, type, utility interest, and criteria [7]. Recently, the main components of design principles have been identified as aim, actors, context, and mechanism [6]. While such prior efforts have advanced the notion and anatomy of design principles, ongoing discussions also focus on how design principles are generated and changed during a design process [8, 9].

Recent studies have highlighted this dynamic aspect [6, 8, 9] and provided structured steps to develop design principles [9] as well as dimensions that can assist in the generation of design principles - reflecting on the input and outcome, when, and by whom design principles should be generated [8]. A common concern for these studies is the aspect of temporality in different forms and that design principles can be influenced by different actors, generated at different times, and derived from different sources [8,

© Springer Nature Switzerland AG 2021
L. Chandra Kruse et al. (Eds.): DESRIST 2021, LNCS 12807, pp. 149–161, 2021.
https://doi.org/10.1007/978-3-030-82405-1_17

9]. This is in line with Gregor et al. [6], who finds that design principles are formalized only as relatively stable after reflection/abstraction and application/experimentation have occurred in cycles. To the best of our knowledge, there seems to be a lack of empirical examples that extend the understanding of how the dynamics and temporality of design principles unfold in practice.

Design science research implies the need to draw on prior theory and create knowledge in collaboration with designers, practitioners, and end users [1, 2]. This form of collaboration between researchers, designers, and practitioners can be viewed as a space for knowledge conversion [10], where tacit knowledge converted, combined, and extended with explicit knowledge to generate design principles. Therefore, in this study we seek to answer the following research question: How may the perspective of knowledge conversion contribute to understanding the generation of design principles? With this perspective, we contribute beyond a snapshot of design principles with an elucidation of the dynamic and temporal aspects of design principles.

We explore the generation of design principles through a reflective approach based on insights from three empirical action design research [1, 2] projects, the theoretical perspective of knowledge conversion [10–12], and recent research on design principles [6, 8, 9]. The author team has been lead researchers in the three empirical cases, closely engaged in research activities, the design of IT artifacts, and generation of design principles, giving us extensive insights into the knowledge conversion processes. The reflection was characterized by identifying key activities and work products in each case, mapping them to the knowledge conversion processes [10–12] and recent work on design principles [6, 8, 9].

In Sect. 2 we introduce the perspective of knowledge creation and knowledge conversion. Building upon the notion that design principles are influenced by different actors, generated at different times, and derived from different sources [6, 8, 9] we exemplify the generation of design principles through knowledge conversion [10–12] across three empirical cases in Sect. 3. Section 4 presents our discussion and limitations, and in Sect. 5 we conclude and present future possibilities for research.

2 Knowledge Creation and Knowledge Conversion

In this section we introduce knowledge creation and knowledge conversion as described by Nonaka et al. [10–12]. To define knowledge, a distinction between data, information and knowledge is instrumental. On a continuum, data represents facts, information represents processed data and knowledge represents know-how and understanding of information [13]. The human mind is described as the key difference when distinguishing knowledge from information. Knowledge is therefore personal and needs to be shared in ways which makes it useful and interpretable by others [14]. Tacit knowledge includes cognitive understandings connected to senses, movement, physical experiences, intuition, and know-how of specific contexts [10]. Explicit knowledge includes knowledge that is communicated in language or symbolic forms [11]. Knowledge conversion is used to describe how tacit and explicit knowledge interact and complement each other to create new knowledge [10, 11].

This conversion of knowledge is described as a creative process where tacit knowledge moves along a continuum (losing some of its tacitness) to become more explicit and possible to turn into action [10]. The process includes individuals' socialization around tacit knowledge, externalization or codification of tacit knowledge, combinations of explicit knowledge, and internalization of explicit knowledge [10–12]. Nonaka describes this as four "processes" representing knowledge creation through sharing, use, and conversion of knowledge between individuals, in a group, or across organisations.

The socialization process is characterized by conversion of tacit knowledge through interaction and shared experiences between people. Direct contact among people and face-to-face meetings are crucial to transfer feelings, emotions, experiences, and mental models. The externalization entails dialogue and converting mental models and skills into common concepts and terms. During this process, knowledge is shared with others through dialogue and reflection by making knowledge more explicit. The contextual space of this process is more conscious, in the sense that individuals with the relevant knowledge need to be included in the process (i.e., persons knowledgeable of the specific social practices and contexts). The combination process is a space for sharing and combining existing explicit knowledge with new information and new knowledge. An important element in this process is the use of information systems to support systematization and interaction among individuals. The internalization process focuses on converting explicit knowledge, in real life settings or simulated settings, to make it tacit. During this process, individuals use the explicit knowledge and turn it into action and reflect through action [10].

Each knowledge conversion process is closely connected to interaction in contextual spaces where knowledge and relationships can be created, shared, and interpreted - described as physical, mental, and virtual *ba* [12]. Drawing on the described knowledge conversion processes we hope to exemplify and contribute to an understanding of how the generating of design principles can be viewed as knowledge conversion processes - providing a visualization of the generation and life of design principles.

3   Generation of Design Principles across Three Cases

In this section we apply Nonaka's model of knowledge creation [10–12] in combination with recent work on design principles [6, 8, 9] to exemplify the generation of design principles. We draw on three empirical cases where ADR [1] has been used to design IT artifacts to enable a transition from attending school to finding, securing, and entering work life for young people with intellectual and developmental disabilities (IDD). Table 1 provides a summary and overview of the generation of design principles in the three cases.

Table 1. Generation of design principles across the three cases. [1] sharing of tacit knowledge through direct contact, [2] dialogue to make knowledge explicit and to establish common concepts and terms, [3] sharing and combining existing explicit knowledge with new information and new knowledge, [4] explicit knowledge turned into action and made tacit in a setting.

Overview of Generation of Design Principles in the three Cases												
Knowledge conversion	Socialization[1]			Externalization[2]			Combination[3]			Internalization[4]		
Elements of design principles	Case 1	Case 2	Case 3	Case 1	Case 2	Case 3	Case 1	Case 2	Case 3	Case 1	Case 2	Case 3
Influences Practitioner and/or user insights	x	x	x	x			x			x	x	x
Prior research	x			x								
Kernel theory					x	x	x	x		x	x	x
Design practices							x	x	x	x		
Artifact evaluation		x	x							x	x	x
Actors End users	x	x	x	x						x	x	x
Domain experts	x	x		x			x					
Researchers	x	x	x	x	x	x	x	x	x	x	x	x
External researchers					x		x					
Practitioners					x		x	x	x	x	x	x
Formulation Thematic problem and solution spaces	x											
Design brief		x	x									
Concept				x								
Prototype					x	x	x		x			
Redesigned prototypes										x		
IT artifact								x				
Redesigned artifact											x	
Design principles				x	x	x						
Refined principles							x	x		x	x	x
New solution space												x

3.1 Self-reflective Career Tool (Case 1)

Our first case focuses on the design and development of a self-reflective career tool for adolescents with IDD. The aim of the tool is to assist adolescents to identify and reflect on their preferences, skills, and abilities, preparing them to secure a position and enter the workforce (for a more detailed description of the artifact see [15]). For an overview of how influences, actors, and formulations play a role in the knowledge conversion process in this case, see Table 1.

In the first process of *socialization*, the knowledge conversion process and generation of design principles were influenced by practitioner and user insights by 'life in a day' observations of end users and focus group interviews with a diverse set of practitioners to understand experiences and feelings connected to the transition from school to work. We attended school and work activities together with people with IDD and performed journey mapping with practitioners. Combined with prior research, this resulted in thematic problem and solution spaces, guiding our further work. The activities in the next process of *externalization* were ideation and concept workshops drawing on the knowledge of the lead research team as well as allowing for discussions to reach a common understanding. Brainstorming activities, mood boards, and future state scenarios supported reflection among the actors that participated in the data gathering activities. These two initial processes involved end users and actors from the entire support network of the end user; including employment services, assisted living carers, teachers, and parents. Initial design principles were generated out of the workshops in the form of concepts showing affordances and requirements of the IT artifact and solution space. *"An information space that provides a coherent mapping of the youths' skills and abilities. The artifact follows the students and his/her development towards working life. In education it is used as a support to promote self-perception and self-representation."* These were based on key quotes of user insights and prior research positioned from the concepts.

The activities in the process of *combination* were iterative design workshops such as "crazy eight sessions" [16] and domain specific dissemination such as research conferences and practitioner seminars. The design workshops allowed us to incorporate design and software development knowledge from practitioner experts into the design principles. The research team rephrased the design principles into what the designers described as 'everyday speak' in their native language coupled with a shorter guiding version of the principles with fictive quotes from a user perspective (Table 2). In addition, visual concept development over shared digital whiteboards were used to combine existing explicit knowledge with new information.

Table. 2. Example of the first version of one of the design principles and the 'user activity'.

Design principle	User activity
Provide features for self-assessment and goal setting so that the system supports cognitive impaired users to make conscious and autonomous employment decision	Who am I and what would I like to become?

The feedback from domain specific dissemination assured the relevance for practice and research areas outside of design science by engaging selected external researchers in disability studies. This process allowed the lead researchers to refine the design principles alongside the prototype development. Participatory user evaluation of the prototype was the main activity of the next process of *internalization*. During this process, the explicit knowledge - designed into the prototype - was turned into action by adolescents with IDD and evaluated by researchers and designers. Through several user tests with students with IDD at two local high schools, we gained knowledge on how features, phrasing and design elements were applied in a school setting. This allowed for a redesign of the prototype, as well as adjusting the design principles.

3.2 Communication Support App (Case 2)

The second case focuses on the redesign of an existing smartphone application. The initial version of the application enabled adolescents with IDD to share and take part of daily moments through photos. The redesigned version enables the users to collect and reflect on memories to support autonomy and storytelling of one's lived experiences.

The knowledge creation process of *socialization* was influenced by practitioner and user insights through proxy-supported interviews, observations, and workshops on application use. The gathered insights provided an understanding of the emotions and social practices connected to using the application and resulted in a design brief with potential theory to support development. For an overview of how influences, actors, formulations play a role in the knowledge conversion process in this case, see Table 1 below. We learned through the process that there are multiple transitions within a day as well as in one's life and for our group of users, technology can both constrain and enable autonomy and storytelling. The *externalization* process consisted of ideation and concept development in workshops, engaging design and software practitioners in activities specified to the IT artifact introduced and theoretically framed by the kernel theory of life-stories [17]. Through "crazy eight sessions", informed by design principles, we established dialogues and reflection around elements of storytelling such as coherence, change, retelling in social settings and creativity. These activities resulted in the creation of prototype sketches and a set of initial design principles.

The next process of *combination* was characterized by iterative design workshops, using shared digital whiteboards. Design and software practitioners provided design knowledge to the prototype sketches made by the researchers and produced a beta version of the IT artifact along with refined design principles. The last knowledge conversion process, *internalization,* is planned to include participatory user evaluation performed in real context i.e., community-based housing and assisted work settings where the application is studied as an intervention to improve storytelling.

3.3 Transportation Support Tool (Case 3)

The third case focuses on the design and development of a transport tool supporting independent travel. In the *socialization* process we gained end user insights through photovoice interviews [18], where people with IDD were asked to take photos of things or places that were important, difficult or which make them feel happy, calm, insecure, sad, scared, and/or stressed. The day after we conducted interviews focusing on the experiences that they had captured. This enabled us to understand social practices and emotions connected to transportation for people with IDD. For instance, some participants struggled with social interaction and anxiety while others preferred social settings. Existing artifacts for transport support was also evaluated, resulting in a design brief. In the *externalization* process iterative design workshops were held among the researchers to design prototype sketches, reaching a common understanding, along with formulation of design principles based on theory about disabilities (Cattell–Horn–Carroll (CHC) theory).

During the *combination* process, design practitioners contributed with their knowledge and a prototype was designed (for a more detailed description see [19]). The prototype was evaluated in the *internalization* process through participatory user evaluation. The evaluation took place through enactive workshops in a real setting (a rented bus for performing realistic scenarios) and an arranged, fictional setting (thematic drama class at a school). This allowed us to see how the explicit knowledge was enacted in realistic and fictional settings and emotions connected to these experiences [20]. Through this, the researchers identified an underlying challenge and redirected the solution space to address stress management and travel preparations, thus the second design focused on managing unforeseen events in a more sustainable manner through emotion regulation [21]. Table 3 presents an overview of the design activities in each case.

Table 3. Overview of design and data gathering activities and the knowledge conversion processes in the three cases.

Overview of Design and data gathering activities				
	Socialization	Externalization	Combination	Internalization
Case 1	Observations & focus group interviews	Ideation & concept workshops	Iterative design workshops & domain specific feedback	Participatory user evaluation
Case 2	Interviews, observations & workshops	Ideation & concept workshops	Iterative design workshops & domain specific feedback	Participatory user evaluation
Case 3	Photovoice interviews	Iterative design workshops	Iterative design workshops	Participatory user evaluation

4   Discussion

The generation of design principles is influenced by different actors, generated at different times, and derived from different sources [6, 8, 9]. We build on that work and have through the perspective of knowledge conversion exemplified how we generated design principles in three empirical cases. Figure 1 exemplifies the dynamic process of generating design principles in Case 1. Here we apply the knowledge conversion perspective with recently identified core elements for developing design principles. The figure visualises the complexity and dynamics in how design principles are initiated, refined, and delivered towards implementation.

The left column of Fig. 1 shows different influences, actors, and formulations in generating design principles and their active utilization, engagement, and purposefulness through the processes of socialization, externalization, combination, and internalization (i.e., knowledge conversion from tacit to explicit to new tacit knowledge). The different elements are visualized as 'active' in the knowledge conversion process through different colours. Influences are visualized on the orange spectrum, actors on the blue spectrum and formulation on the green spectrum. In the following section, we discuss the dynamic aspects of influences, actors, and formulation of design principles through the knowledge conversion perspective.

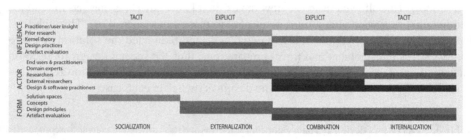

Fig. 1. The dynamic process of generating design principles in Case 1.

4.1 Influences

When design sciences researchers embark on a design journey that requires generating design principles for invention [22] (such as in Case 1), we recognize the need for a *socialization* process to discover tacit knowledge [10]. These design efforts tend to be characterized by limited understanding of the problem space and call for curiosity, imagination, and creativity [22]. The inherent role of tacit knowledge in social practices and innovation - the need to be guided by experienced practitioners to understand skills, values, beliefs and norms and the need for diverse knowledge and perspectives to foster creativity [10] points to this argument of socialization.

With no existing instantiated artifact to evaluate, as in our Case 1, we see that early influences of the design principles need to be based on practitioners' and users' tacit knowledge. However, we do not exclude the important influences of prior theory or design efforts as suggested [8, 9]. In line with the knowledge conversion process, tacit knowledge (i.e., giving an understanding of social practices) needs to be combined with explicit knowledge (i.e., providing reliability to the insights and spanning the knowledge beyond individual perspectives) [10]. While prior theories were discussed as influences among the researchers early in the process, this was found to be less useful without a shared mental understanding of the problem and solution spaces between researchers, practitioners, and users. Therefore, it seems necessary to *externalize* knowledge in order to *combine* kernel theories with tacit knowledge of users and practitioners. As shown in Case 1 and Case 2, the practitioner and user insights contributed to and confirmed the relevance of prior theory and how it could be combined with other concepts in later stages of generating design principles. In Case 3, the externalization process did not involve end users due to time constraints. In hindsight, we see that the prototype development could have benefited from earlier end user design insights.

When the knowledge contribution is in the form of exaptation, extending known solutions to new problems (such in Case 2) or improvement, new solutions to known problems (such as in Case 3) [22], it seems possible to rely on influences such as evaluation of existing IT artifacts and on prior theories [8, 9]. In these cases, the *socialization* process seems less vital as the understanding of the problem space is clearer. However, there might be instances where the life of the end user group is further away from the life experiences and research domain of the researchers (such as people of IDD in our cases), calling for a need to understand their tacit knowledge. During the *internalization* process we see that user insights and kernel theories play an interdependent role. While research shows different ways to evaluate design principles e.g., expert feedback, instantiation, argumentation [9], we found that to ensure an understanding of how explicit knowledge is turned into action (internalization) it needs to be evaluated through an enactment of the design principles. Without this we would find it difficult to evaluate aspects of materiality, action and boundary conditions and unintended consequences as suggested by Gregor et al. [22].

4.2 Actors

When design principles focus on inventive design efforts, we recognize the importance of a *socialization* process that engages an inclusive and extensive scope of actors as they provide pivotal knowledge and expertise towards the problem space. One example was in Case 1 where we saw a need to extend the scope of actors beyond researchers engaged in generating design principles. As previously acknowledged, practitioners with domain expertise can be critical in the development of design principles [8]. When the problem space is more known to information systems researchers, focusing on theories and contexts know to the field and/or less marginalized groups of users, domain expertise plays a less critical role in generating design principles.

The *combination* process for Case 1 and the *externalization* process for 2, indicated the importance of spending time on dialogues with designers on how to make the suggested design principles explicit. This enabled the research team to reach a common understanding, rephrasing the design principles into what the designers described as 'everyday speak' coupled with a shorter guiding version of the principles that translated the principles into fictive quotes from a user perspective. In addition, researchers external to the research team, knowledgeable in disability studies, proved to have an important role in the refinement of the design principles. External researchers can provide valuable knowledge of prior theories [8], however we experienced that it can be challenging for researchers outside of design science to understand the notion and prescriptive practice of design principles. While practitioners and users did not *document* the design principles, they could confirm their relevance in the *combination* process (feedback and domain specific dissemination) and *internalization* processes (prototype and design principle evaluation).

In line with the guideline of mutual influential roles in action design research [1] (the approach we applied in our cases), we highlight that generation of design principles through a knowledge conversion process need to be based on knowledge of professional designers and developers (user insights and guidelines), domain experts (practices and theories) and researchers (user insights and theories) (See Fig. 1). However, our cases also demonstrate the need for lead researchers to drive the development and ensure the relevance of the principles as the design effort proceeds (e.g., use the design principles as a frame when planning workshops, evaluations, design elements, discussions).

4.3 Formulation

The structure and anatomy of design principles is perhaps the most explored dimension in prior studies [3, 6], with Gregor et al. [6] developing a schema including aim for the user, context, mechanism and rationale or justification of design principles. Distinctions have been made between knowledge contributions in the form of design guidelines (aimed at and identified by practitioners) and design principles (aimed at and identified by academics) [7]. Following our discussion on temporality, influences and actors we argue that this distinction between design guidelines and design principles is problematic and might be challenging to make as they are intertwined - at times overlapping and at times taking on different forms. In our cases the design principles took the form of concepts, sketches, prototypes, fictive quotes from a user perspective, coupled with theoretically articulated design principles. This was apparent during the *externalization* and *combination* process [10] to ensure a shared meaning and to build on the explicit knowledge of academics and practitioners. Our three cases support the claim made [6, 8], that the researcher team needs to adapt and decomposition the articulation of design principles towards different contexts, actors, and design efforts. This seems to be especially important when working with marginalized groups that tend to be excluded from research activities [23]. The practice-inspired and iterative approach of design science research [1, 2] requires design principles to be materialised as concepts and prototypes and formulated as both design guidelines and academically formulated design principles. Concepts, prototypes, and design guidelines can ensure that practitioners and end users engage in generating the design principles in a dynamic process. We argue that this is vital to ensure knowledge conversion that combines academic and practitioner knowledge.

4.4 Limitations

Due to the nature of our cases, being linked by a common theme and setting, we wish to clarify the ensuing limitations of our contribution in this paper. The paper builds on three cases carried out by the same lead researchers within a similar problem and solution space - that of supporting young people with IDD in the transition from school to entering the workforce. As such, lifting the variation between the cases may provide a limited view of how to generate design principles. We are aware that there are other approaches to carry out a design effort and so also generating design principles. The aim of our elucidation is therefore not to provide an optimal approach to generate design principles, but rather to unfold the dynamic and temporal aspects. We also acknowledge that the reflective approach in this paper may result in researcher bias, preventing us to see alternative elucidations. However, we hope that the theoretical perspective of knowledge creation and knowledge conversion and ongoing discussion among the authors have contributed to a more nuanced and structured understanding of the co-creation of design of IT-artifacts involving researchers, developers, domain experts and end-users.

5 Conclusion and Future Work

Our study contributes with an elucidation of a dynamic process of the generation and life of the design principles. We show the need for a shared mental understanding between practitioners and academics in order to ensure relevant use of theory in design principle generation. In addition, we found it to be vital to evaluate design principles through enactments to maintain a shared understanding of how explicit knowledge is turned into action. Our cases also show the need for lead researchers to drive the generation of design principles and safeguard the relevance of the principles as the efforts proceed. However, it is important that practitioners and domain specific researchers are able to apply the design principles to guide their actions. It is therefore vital that knowledge conversion combines academic and practitioner knowledge. In our cases, concepts, prototypes, and design guidelines ensured that practitioners and end users engaged in generating design principles. Thus, it requires design principles to be materialised and formulated as both design guidelines and academically formulated design principles. Viewing the generation of design principles as knowledge conversion may ensure the active utilization of influences, engagement of actors and purposeful formulation to serve both practical and academic knowledge creation. Through this we contribute to a more nuanced understanding of the dynamic and temporal aspects of design principles.

Further work is needed to understand if and how the perspective of knowledge conversion can continue to play a generative role beyond the finalisation of a design science research project. The knowledge creation may continue a) within the organisation that implements the IT artefacts - altering and amending the practices of the organisation and b) among the practicing domain experts, designers, and software developers - altering their practices informed and influenced by the design principles. We see this as an exciting avenue for future research to better understand the impact and knowledge contribution of design principles beyond academia. We hope that this paper will contribute to further discussions on the dynamic and longitudinal aspects of design principles.

Acknowledgement. This research was supported by the Research Council of Norway, grant number 269019.

References

1. Sein, M., Henfridsson, O., Purao, S., Rossi, M., Lindgren, R.: Action design research. MIS Q. **35**(1), 37–56 (2011)

2. Hevner, A.R., March, S.T., Park, J., Ram, S.: Design science in informationsystems research. MIS Q. **28**(1), 75–105 (2004)
3. Chandra, L., Seidel, S., Gregor, S.: Prescriptive knowledge in IS research: conceptualizing design principles in terms of materiality, action, and boundary conditions. In: 48th Hawaii International Conference on System Sciences, pp. 4039–4048. IEEE (2015)
4. Seidel, S., Chandra Kruse, L., Székely, N., Gau, M., Stieger, D.: Design principles for sense-making support systems in environmental sustainability transformations. Eur. J. Inf. Syst. **27**(2), 221–247 (2018)
5. Chandra Kruse, L., Seidel, S., Purao, S.: Making use of design principles. In: Parsons, J., Tuunanen, T., Venable, J., Donnellan, B., Helfert, M., Kenneally, J. (eds.) DESRIST 2016. LNCS, vol. 9661, pp. 37–51. Springer, Cham (2016). https://doi.org/10.1007/978-3-319-392 94-3_3
6. Gregor, S., Chandra Kruse, L., Seidel, S.: Research perspectives: the anatomy of a design principle. J. Assoc. Inf. Syst. **21**(6), 1622–1652 (2020)
7. Hansen, M.R.P., Haj-Bolouri, A.: Design principles exposition: a framework for problematizing knowledge and practice in DSR. In: Hofmann, S., Müller, O., Rossi, M. (eds.) DESRIST 2020. LNCS, vol. 12388, pp. 171–182. Springer, Cham (2020). https://doi.org/10.1007/978-3-030-64823-7_16
8. Purao, S., Kruse, L.C., Maedche, A.: The origins of design principles: where do... they all come from? In: Hofmann, S., Müller, O., Rossi, M. (eds.) DESRIST 2020. LNCS, vol. 12388, pp. 183–194. Springer, Cham (2020). https://doi.org/10.1007/978-3-030-64823-7_17
9. Möller, F., Guggenberger, T.M., Otto, B.: Towards a method for design principle development in information systems. In: Hofmann, S., Müller, O., Rossi, M. (eds.) DESRIST 2020. LNCS, vol. 12388, pp. 208–220. Springer, Cham (2020). https://doi.org/10.1007/978-3-030-64823-7_20
10. Nonaka, I., von Krogh, G.: Perspective—tacit knowledge and knowledge conversion: controversy and advancement in organizational knowledge creation theory. Organ. Sci. **20**(3), 635–652 (2009). https://doi.org/10.1287/orsc.1080.0412
11. Nonaka, I.: A dynamic theory of organizational knowledge creation. Organ. Sci. **5**(1), 14–37 (1994)
12. Nonaka, I., Konno, N.: The concept of "Ba": building a foundation for knowledge creation. Calif. Manage. Rev. **40**(3), 40–54 (1998)
13. Davenport, T.H., Prusak, L.: Working Knowledge: How Organizations Manage What They Know. Harvard Business Press, Boston, MA (1998)
14. Alavi, M., Leidner, D.E.: Knowledge management and knowledge management systems: conceptual foundations and research issues. MIS Q. **25**(1), 107–136 (2001)
15. Wass, S., Hansen, L.A., Safari, C.: Designing transport supporting services together with users with intellectual disabilities. In: Hofmann, S., Müller, O., Rossi, M. (eds.) DESRIST 2020. LNCS, vol. 12388, pp. 56–67. Springer, Cham (2020). https://doi.org/10.1007/978-3-030-64823-7_6
16. Google Design Sprints homepage, https://designsprintkit.withgoogle.com/methodology/pha se3-sketch/crazy-8s. Accessed 02 Apr 2021
17. McAdams, D.P.: Personal Narratives and The Life Story. Sage Publications, California (2008)
18. Povee, K., Bishop, B.J., Roberts, L.D.: The use of photovoice with people with intellectual disabilities: Reflections, challenges and opportunities. Disabil. Soc. **29**(6), 893–907 (2014)
19. Wass, S., Hansen, L.A., Stuve, E.K.: Me, myself and I - supporting people with intellectual disabilities towards self-determination. In: Hofmann, S., Müller, O., Rossi, M. (eds.) DESRIST 2020. LNCS, vol. 12388, pp. 420–425. Springer, Cham (2020). https://doi.org/10.1007/978-3-030-64823-7_40
20. Sanders, E.B.N.: Staging Co-Design Within Healthcare: Lessons From Practice. Edward Elgar Publishing, London (2020)

21. Gross, J.J.: Emotion Regulation. Handbook of Emotions, 3rd edn. The Guilford Press, New York (2008)
22. Gregor, S., Hevner, A.R.: Positioning and presenting design science research for maximum impact. MIS Q. **37**(2), 337–355 (2013)
23. Frauenberger, C., Good, J., Alcorn, A., Pain, H.: Supporting the design contributions of children with autism spectrum conditions. In: Proceedings of the 11th International Conference on Interaction Design and Children, pp. 134–143. Association for Computing Machinery, New York, NY (2012)

Communication of Design Research: A Use-Case Agnostic Framework and Its Application

Marcel Cahenzli[✉], Jannis Beese, and Robert Winter

University of St. Gallen, Müller-Friedbergstrasse 8, 9000 St. Gallen, Switzerland
`marcel.cahenzli@unisg.ch`

Abstract. Existing guidance for communicating design research projects commonly focusses on specific communication instance types such as journal paper writing. However, the diversity of design research endeavours and the variety of communication situations within each such project requires broader and more adaptable guidance. This study therefore proposes a use-case agnostic framework for the communication of DSR. The design of this framework was continuously evaluated and refined by using it in University lectures. It guides design researchers by helping them characterize specific communication situations, based on which an informed communication design process can be formulated.

Keywords: Design science research · Research communication · Communication of complex projects

1 Introduction

Communication is an integral part of the Design Science Research (DSR) methodology [1]. However, communication of DSR is not straight forward, with issues ranging from challenging requirements to publish DSR in top-tier IS journals [2, 3] and communication issues with practitioner audiences (e.g. evaluation partners) who are interested in completely different aspects of the research [4]. Despite the fact that design researchers need to communicate their projects throughout the entire DSR process [4], most guidance (e.g., [1, 2]) takes a rather narrow view confined to a specific use case (i.e., 'paper writing') at the final stages of a DSR project. Hence, extant literature mostly addresses a specific sub-class within the broader problem class of 'communicating DSR'. Most communication sub-classes (e.g., presenting research designs at an early stage of the overall DSR project) are not covered by existing approaches, and even for the sub-class of paper writing, guidance is insufficient [3].

In this research paper, we argue that the difficulties we face as design researchers are neither (1) limited to the writing of journal papers, nor (2) limited to summative communication in mature stages of DSR projects. After all, a summative journal paper is only one of many communication situations on the journey of a DSR project, which also include, for example, initial proposals for funding, pitch meetings with potential partners, or intermediate research-in-progress publications. These situations are characterized by diversity in many dimensions, including a varying degree of project maturity as

© Springer Nature Switzerland AG 2021
L. Chandra Kruse et al. (Eds.): DESRIST 2021, LNCS 12807, pp. 162–173, 2021.
https://doi.org/10.1007/978-3-030-82405-1_18

well as different stakeholder types and needs. Consequently, communication guidance should cater to such situational factors. Preparing and implementing context-sensitive communication is crucial to the success of DSR projects [4] and yet there is little to no prescriptive knowledge on how this sub-process in the DSR methodology should look like—both at a use-case level and, more crucially, at an abstract, use-case agnostic level. We use the term 'communication use case' to refer to a specific sub-class (e.g., writing a journal paper, presenting a research design to peers, presenting a project to evaluation partners) of the general problem class 'communication of DSR'.

This paper presents a DSR-specific artefact that is use-case agnostic and context-sensitive yet decontextualized, to lay the foundation for creating concrete, actionable guidance for various use-cases (and, ultimately, contextualized instances). Specifically, we describe the development of a use-case agnostic DSR communication framework as our primary artefact, along with one specific use-case (pitching early research designs within a research methods course) in which the artefact was instantiated as actionable guidance. We also present our problem understanding and explicate the requirements for the development of our solution proposal.

2 Related Work

How to communicate science-related contents to various audiences is addressed in literature on general science communication [5, 6]. However, such existing knowledge is not easily transferrable as its implied focus on descriptive research (identifying valid analytical, explanatory and/or predictive statements, mostly based on a research model) may not fit design-oriented research (focus on utility, based on problem understanding, requirements, finding of a useful design, proof of concept and of design) [1]. The problem therefore also resides in the particular case of DSR and not scientific projects in general. This section discusses both general science communication as a starting point and specific guidance for DSR communication. Each sub-section merely presents excerpts that appear most relevant to this study.

2.1 Science Communication

Focal to our research is not communication per se (e.g. message production and processing, persuasion, emotion expression, cf. [7]), but the communication of research projects (i.e., science, including results, procedures, rationales, etc. cf. [8]). Science communication (SciCom) is concerned with the "exchange of scientific information with target audiences" [9]. Definitions of the term vary in aspects such as the perspective used (expert-expert vs. expert-laymen), the scope (internal vs. external communication), their focus (e.g., on target groups, functions of communication, means of communication), or underlying assumptions and aims [10]. A summarizing, high-level definition is provided in Burns et al. [8]: SciCom covers *"the use of appropriate skills, media, activities, and dialogue to produce one or more of the following personal responses to science: awareness, enjoyment, interest, opinion, and understanding"*.

As competition for publication space, funding, and support increases, effective communication of scientific findings, projects, or plans for investigations becomes increasingly relevant to scientists [10, 11]. They communicate with other experts in the field, but also with non-scientists such as policymakers, resource managers, or practice partners [9, 12]. "Audiences differ with respect to demography, background knowledge, personality, worldview, cultural norms, and preferences" [6] and communicators should account for this diversity [9]. While most descriptions of SciCom audiences are categorical (e.g., experts, scientific colleagues, laypeople, politicians [6, 8–10, 12]), others suggest to account for more fine-grained characteristics, such as state of knowledge, interests, informational needs, expectations on the level of granularity [8, 10], demography, personality, cultural norms, and preferences [6].

Other dimensions that may affect the communication include the mode (e.g., oral, audio-visual, written), means (slide-show, video, website), and format (TV interview, lecture, journal paper, conference presentation) [6, 10, 13]. A further relevant circumstantial aspect is the direction of communication, characterized by either a deficit approach (assuming the audience lacks knowledge, the communication is geared toward providing information in a one-way direction) or a dialogue approach (assuming that the audience has local knowledge, an understanding and interest in the problems to be solved and wants to engage in an exchange) [14]. Finally, the nature of the project itself influences how it can be communicated. This may refer to, e.g., whether a non-disclosure agreement has been signed, or the current phase of the project [10].

For our work, we conclude that communicators must account for audience- and study-specific characteristics along various dimensions such as stakeholder needs, relation with the audience, approach to communication, mode, means, and format.

2.2 Existing Guidance for DSR Communication

Parts of the problem that we address in this paper have been discussed in the past. This includes reflections on how the DSR community may cope with the difficulties to publish in prestigious journals [3], literature reviews that analyse the structure and contents of published DSR [15], and a recent EJIS special issue that addresses problems related to the diversity in DSR projects with a focus on improving communication [16]. Other literature addresses the need for actionable guidance by providing some specific guidance. We discuss three notable publications here.

First, Peffers et al. [1] present a general purpose DSR methodology, including principles to define what DSR is, practice rules, and a process for carrying out and presenting it. They argue that the absence of an established DSR process model requires publications in IS journals to rely on ad hoc arguments to support their validity [1]. Their proposed artefact should facilitate planning, executing, and presenting DSR. "Researchers might use the structure of this process to structure the paper, just as the nominal structure of an empirical research process is a common structure for empirical research papers" [1]. However, while the overall methodology has found widespread adoption as a reference approach to conduct DSR [15], it does not explicate how to structure the communication of resulting knowledge (the sixth phase in their process model [1]), nor does it address the communication throughout a DSR endeavour.

Second, Gregor and Hevner [2] recognized the difficulty in conveying DSR studies such that rigour and relevance become apparent, the employed methodology becomes clear, and the contents are selected and presented convincingly [16]. They propose a "publication schema for a DSR study" to support writing journal papers. As in Peffers et al. [1], Gregor and Hevner [2] propose a set of headlines and commentary as to what may be presented in each section. The structure is closely related to the nominal structure of an empirical research process [1]. This limits its usefulness, as the latter is sequential rather than iterative, and DSR projects—being by nature iterative—can hardly be presented as suggested. Furthermore, the suggestions focus on journal publications and may therefore not address informational needs of, for example, practice-facing audiences or shorter communication formats such as conference presentations.

Third, vom Brocke and Maedche [4] lay out six essential core dimensions (*problem, research process, solution, input knowledge, concepts*, and *output knowledge*) that can help to describe, coordinate and communicate DSR projects. They focus on a high-level project representation that captures essential aspects of a project to improve communication between stakeholders. Adaptations to such guidance may be necessary, depending on the purpose and context of communication. Their framework provides a partial solution for a use-case agnostic representation of DSR studies, which may be useful in identifying informational needs of different audiences.

3   Our Research Approach

With the goal of designing actionable guidance for concurrent and summative communication of DSR, we follow Hevner's [17] three cycle view. We have conducted three design cycles, during which the problem understanding and the artefact evolved.

3.1   Design Cycle 1: Local Problem Identification and Solution

The authors are involved with a research methods course for master students in business innovation at a Swiss university. In small groups, students develop a research design for an explanatory or a DSR project. They present their research designs in four instances (early feedback; formal presentation of results; extended documentation of results (Voice-over-PowerPoint); abstract). Such communication situations constitute our 'research design feedback' use case. We *identified a problem*: the groups that opted for DSR had difficulties with identifying which contents to present, in what order, and how.

Accordingly, we *built a solution* to satisfy their main concerns. Based on our understanding of the topic and SciCom, we designed a use case-specific solution in the form of a checklist, outlining which contents to present, in what order, and how.

We *evaluated* this checklist by integrating it into the course materials and using it over five semesters with about 350 students in total. The initial checklist was useful for groups that presented explanatory research, being based on the nominal structure of an empirical research process. However, students that opted for design research proposals remained uncertain about various aspects, including how to explicate iterations, when and how to present detailed versus abstract procedures, or which contents to focus on.

3.2   Design Cycle 2: Global Problem Identification and Solution

We *identified the remaining problem* to be representative of a larger problem class. An adequate solution may therefore be at a higher level of abstraction (communication of DSR), and thereafter be specialized to our use case (research design feedback).

To *build a solution* for this problem class, we first needed to gain a better understanding of its intricacies. To that end, we identified and analysed literature on SciCom and DSR (see Sect. 2). Based on these discussions, we designed an initial framework for the communication of DSR. The resulting artefact consists of two parts: a characterization of communication use cases and an abstract communication instance design process (as in the final artefact, see Fig. 1).

Considering that this artefact was mainly informed by literature, we decided to *evaluate* it with professional design researchers by conducting interviews (see Sect. 4.1).

3.3   Design Cycle 3: Iteration of the Solution and Instantiation

Based on our generalized *understanding of the problem* and aspects of the initial framework, we decided to initiate a third design cycle. The problem understanding as well as the *designed artefact* are described in more detail in Sect. 4. The *evaluation* of that final artefact is currently ongoing, by means of a controlled experiment with our students, in which we test an instantiation (also a checklist) for the same use case presented in cycle 1. This time, the instantiation was derived from our general framework. Hence, we have applied the framework to come up with a use case-specific solution.

The remainder of this paper focuses on the interview study, the framework that emerged from it and an example on how we situated the artefact to a specific use case.

3.4   The Interview Study and Plans for Evaluation of the Final Artefact

We conducted semi-structured expert interviews to identify, confirm, reject or append to the constituents of our initial framework, and to improve our understanding of the problems, requirements for a solution, design decision in communication, and existing approaches. Specifically, we have sought active design researchers at different career stages by using our personal networks within the DSR community. Finally, we interviewed 11 design researchers at different career stages (4 PhD students, 4 experienced design researchers, and 3 well-known senior scholars). The interview guideline covered (1) descriptions of communication situations, (2) descriptions of the interviewees' communication design processes, (3) a discussion on desired outcomes, (4) notable intricacies of DSR communication, and (5) their coping strategies. Several open questions were used for each of these topic areas, yielding an interview guideline of two pages in length. All interviews were conducted by the first author via video call during November and December 2020, lasting approximately 60 min. Afterwards, all interviews were transcribed, yielding 110 pages of transcript. Thereafter, we applied hybrid-coding in Atlas.ti, using both a literature-derived set of categories (the 5 topic areas) and open coding within these categories. The resulting 719 codes were condensed to 130 code categories (axial coding) and 11 topic streams (selective coding) [18].

Based on the analysis of the interviews, we updated our framework (results from the interview study: Sect. 4.1, updated framework: Fig. 1). To evaluate the latter, we situated it to the research methods course presented above. Student groups that choose to develop a DSR-based research design are part of a condition of the evaluative experiment. Based on experience from past courses, we expect to see at least 15 out of 36 groups to opt for DSR-based projects. The manipulation they receive is our instantiated guidance on how to present DSR research design drafts (resulting from Design Cycle 3, see above), as integrated into the lectures and course materials. The data we use are the Voice-over-Powerpoint presentations. Hence, their communication can be evaluated ex-post. Non-co-authoring fellow researchers who are otherwise not involved in this research endeavour will do so. The same people will also be asked to evaluate a comparable number of student groups' Voice-over-Powerpoint presentations from the year before (from the same course, with the same course materials and lectures, but without the latest instantiation). Since the evaluators are unaware of the experimental conditions, this experiment allows us to test the effectiveness of our guidance. We expect groups with the latest instantiation to perform better in the outcome evaluation.

4 A Use Case-Agnostic Framework for Communicating DSR

Based on the interviews, we have gained a deep understanding of the problem, derived design requirements, and finalized the framework. These aspects are described below.

4.1 Problem Understanding and Derived Requirements

The interviewees' accounts of a self-selected design research project contained on average more than ten different communication situations. They confirm that communicating their projects is indeed a relevant concurrent sub-process of DSR, and that they face DSR project-related and stakeholder-related challenges in doing so.

Some of the central *project-related issues* arise from the sheer amount of content created throughout the project, as *"the initial parts are papers for themselves"* (interviewee 2) and *"if you want to present the whole process it can get huge quite fast"* (interviewee 6). This conflicts with limited availability of presentation time or space, be it facing practitioners or academic audiences. Design researchers are forced to either remove parts they suspect the audience to be familiar with (or not care much about), or cut contents so short that it becomes hard to signal rigor. There is general agreement that one cannot communicate all the phases of the project in depth, and that there is no need to do so either, as the audience is usually not interested in the entire project and all procedures (e.g., *"You have to cut it down. If you had more than 30 pages (...) nobody would read it, right? (...) The question is: How do you summarize the project?"* interviewee 2). Hence, the contents must be shortened based on what interests the audience [3], since stakeholders must be *"addressed very much differently from each other"* (interviewee 1) [6, 9]. This includes using adequate presentation, vocabulary, metaphors, examples, and illustrations [12].

The mode (oral-only, audio-visual or written) and means (e.g., slides, video, text, pictures etc.) of communication do not really affect the core of a storyline, but it may affect how well the information comes across, based on specific strengths [12]. This was summarized by interviewee 4: *"You should be taken through the messages and taken through the arguments – whether it's with slides or just talking. The big difference lies in the purpose (of communicating) and the purpose is based on the stakeholder needs."* However, in DSR communication there is unclarity about these needs and interests (be it practitioners or academics), and how to operationalize knowledge on these needs and interests. Based on these findings, we formulate four requirements:

R1 The artefact must accommodate different application situations along the design research process.

R2 The artefact must support the definition of a stakeholder needs-based purpose.

R3 The artefact must support the selection of contents and the design of a presentation based on the purpose of a specific communication situation.

R4 The artefact must support the operationalization of knowledge about specific stakeholder needs.

Practice-facing concerns include the alignment of terminology (e.g.: ensuring that one talks about the same things), capturing and maintaining interest (especially when it comes to abstract views), or selling a project (e.g. gain commitments of time or money).

While academia-facing concerns also include stakeholder needs-driven issues, they also arise from the role of DSR in IS outlets. Notably, there is a general worry that DSR papers do not fit most IS journals. Since a theoretical contribution is central for many academic outlets, the need for an artefact, its requirements and development become secondary to an investigation of some cause-effect relation. Given the low attributed value of the artefact and its practical utility, it remains unclear how to publish papers that combine theoretical contribution and practical utility in a more balanced fashion.

Another major concern in academia-facing communication is the richness of procedural guidance that has been created on how to conduct 'good' design research: "*With all good intentions, we continue to put out these frameworks. But they just make it harder, because now you have all these boxes to check. Like doing design guidelines; presenting a kernel theory; doing two design cycles etc. Well that's like a 100-page paper*" (interviewee 11). Ignoring some of these check boxes or barely scratching the surface of all of them are coping mechanisms that increase the risk of rejection. Other coping-strategies are to exclude the design part of a study (i.e. presenting the artefact primarily to investigate a behavioral question), targeting specific outlets with less restrictive page limitations (disqualifying many IS journals and conferences), only submitting to outlets with a possibility to extensively use appendices (disqualifying most IS conferences), and abandoning the idea of publishing DSR papers altogether (doing DSR out of interest and publishing behavioral studies for professional advancement).

Lastly, finding an adequate level of abstraction in the communication of DSR is difficult. As critically reflected by interviewee 6: "*We don't really know at what level of abstraction we should communicate the design knowledge (…) I don't know whether we as a community are going into the right direction, for example when it comes to these design principles everyone wants to formulate. Often, they are so trivial (…) practitioners would just laugh at you*" (interviewee 6). Requirement 5 captures this concern:

R5 The artefact should help set an adequate abstraction level to present and discuss a design research project.

4.2 Presentation of the Framework

Taking the findings and requirements outlined above into account, we have created a framework that consists of two parts: A characterization of communication situations, and a communication design process. The framework is use case agnostic (meaning that it can be used for any communication use case along any DSR project). However, it must take specific characteristics of the communication situation into consideration (see e.g.: R1). This is being operationalized by specifying various characteristics and 'recycling' knowledge on these characteristics. For example: If the audience in a specific communication situation has the role of evaluators (e.g., lecturers listening to student presentations), then they have an increased need for understanding the research problem and the methodology. Collaborators from practice may care less about methodological considerations, but it may be important to raise their interest for the topic.

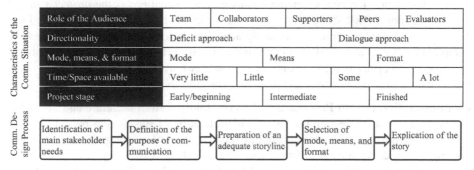

Role of the Audience	Team	Collaborators		Supporters		Peers	Evaluators
Directionality	Deficit approach				Dialogue approach		
Mode, means, & format	Mode		Means			Format	
Time/Space available	Very little	Little			Some		A lot
Project stage	Early/beginning		Intermediate			Finished	

Identification of main stakeholder needs → Definition of the purpose of communication → Preparation of an adequate storyline → Selection of mode, means, and format → Explication of the story

Fig. 1. Framework of DSR communication

The characterization of the communication situation therefore allows to gain key insights for the communication design process. The latter should integrate knowledge on the situation in order to yield communication that is adequate for the respective situation. To pick up the example of the audience: Knowledge on the audience's typical needs directly informs the first step of the communication design process.

Characteristics of the Communication Situation. The *audience*, whose needs are a main determinant of the purpose of communication, can be categorized. Categories identified in the interviews comprise the research team, collaborators from practice, supportive colleagues, peers, and evaluators/reviewers. Each of these types comes with a set of characteristic needs, which inform the communication design process.

Regarding the *direction of communication*, we can draw some implications for the communication design, and in particular for the storyline of the latter, based on whether the communication follows a deficit or a dialogue approach. The deficit approach requires a high level of completeness and specificity in its explications. There is a need to increase the amount of justification and explanation compared to a dialogue approach. This is most notable in case of severe time or space restrictions: In a dialogue approach to communication, a lot of information can be omitted based on the assumption that the audience would request further elaboration if needed.

We have summarized the *mode, means,* and *format* of communication in one dimension to illustrate that they are interlinked. For example, an oral presentation may directly imply that certain means of communication (such as a website) do not apply, and that the format is possibly a lecture, but certainly not a journal paper. Each characteristic comes with certain strengths and weaknesses and, while one cannot necessarily choose these characteristics (e.g., IS conferences tend to not accept videos to illustrate an artefact), the given characteristics may inform the step of explication of the story.

Time and space availability not only changes the amount of information that can be provided, but also the explication of the latter. For instance: Examples are helpful for improving the understanding of contents, to illustrate the relevance of a problem, or to convince audiences. With too restrictive limitations, examples may need to be removed. Another implication is that one may have to decide on either shortening all sections, or to drop entire sections from the narrative. Depending on the audience's needs, the latter can be done without adverse consequences (e.g., drop methodology for practitioners).

The last dimension characterizing communication situations is the *project's stage*. The progress of a DSR study affects how the project is presented. For example: One may present the study more convincingly and provide less open questions once it is completed, whereas at an early stage, given the high uncertainty, one may communicate more openly. Furthermore, the contents themselves may change from problem- and requirements-focused, to prototype-focused, to artefact evaluation-focused.

Communication Design Process. Based on our findings from literature and the interviews, we propose a five-step process: (1) identification of stakeholder needs; (2) definition of the purpose of communication; (3) preparation of an adequate storyline; (4) selection of mode, means, and format; and (5) explication of the story.

Identification of stakeholder needs is the elicitation and specification of needs. Since communication should be tailored to a needs-based purpose, this first step is crucial.

The second step is the *definition of the purpose* of communication, which is to be drafted by selecting the needs that are to be satisfied through a communication situation.

By *storyline* we understand (i) the general milestones that are to be achieved during the communication (e.g.: the audience understands how features map to principles), (ii) the sequential order in which those milestones are to be achieved (the thread running through the communication), and (iii) an argument explaining how each milestone leads to the next. We differentiate the storyline form the story (the sum of all explicated contents of the communication) since the storyline does not depend on the mode, means, or format of communication. This should simplify the design process.

Once the storyline is clarified, the *mode, means, and format* of communication can be specified further. In many instances these are already given. If there is freedom of choice, however, these may be specified with the purpose in mind.

During the *explication of the story* (i.e. the formulation of contents) the insights on the communication situation gained thus far come into play. These provide the boundaries, within which the communication can be formulated.

Next, we present how we used the framework to design a solution for our course.

5   Situating the Framework to a Communications Use Case

Characterization of the Communication Situation: The audience of the students' presentations are the lecturers, who take on the role of *unrelated evaluators*. Since the presentations are handed in as recordings, the information needs to be presented following a *deficit approach*. These *Voice-over-Powerpoint* presentations (means) are *audio-visual* (mode) *group presentations* (format). The students have a maximum of 15 min for their presentations, which should be long enough to present their research designs, but short enough to require them to succinctly phrase their argumentation.

Communication Design Process: Or our students, the main stakeholders are the professors that evaluate and grade their course performance. These evaluator's needs remain the same for all groups (i.e.: understand the research problem, understand the proposed procedures, understand the line of argumentation justifying the procedures, being enabled to evaluate whether the students understood the course's contents).

The *purpose* of communication for our students is to convince the audience of the quality of the research design and therewith that the group understood the core contents of the course. That purpose hinges on the creation of understanding (rather than, e.g., entertainment or emotional relatability of the problem).

The *milestones* we propose for the students' presentations are: Ensuring that the audience understands (1) the research problem (situation, stakeholders and their goals, contextual factors, relevance), (2) the specific focus (justified specification of a research question), (3) the research design (consisting of (3.1) reference approach, (3.2) short summary, (3.3) existing solutions, (3.4) requirements elicitation, (3.5) design process, (3.6) validation strategy), (4) possible implications and limitations.

In the course setting, the mode, means, and format are given. Thereby, students may benefit form the opportunity to use visualizations that underline the central aspects, while using speech to efficiently explain what can be seen (*mode*). Best-practices in Powerpoint apply (students are familiar with these, e.g.: little text per slide, adequate resolution and font-size, no text blocks; *means*) and the university supplies formal requirements for the exam *format* of group presentations (e.g.: equal participation).

To guide students through the process of designing this communication, and lastly to help *explicating* it, we provided them with a checklist-like set of questions and half-sentences that is structured according to the milestones. (The half-sentences should help identify an adequate level of abstraction.) Therewith, and relying on their existing training in how to do Powerpoint-based group presentations, we expect the groups to have less difficulties in designing their DSR research design presentations, resulting in clearer and more focussed audience-specific presentations.

6   Discussion and Outlook

Our proposed framework aims to facilitate the resolution of common issues in the communication of DSR studies. Through a series of semi-structured interviews, we found that most communication issues in DSR arise from a combination of a large scope (i.e. the quantity of the content to be communicated) and limited space (e.g. page and time limitations) in individual communication instances, as well as a large variation between DSR studies and between communication instances within such studies. Concerning the latter, interviewees particularly pointed out the difficulty to adequately address a variety of different stakeholders with fundamentally different needs and concerns. The framework, built to satisfy the requirements we outlined, comprises both a classification schema for DSR communication instances and a communication design process to support content selection and preparation in a given instance.

The classification schema provides a straight-forward approach to describe a DSR communication instance by using the proposed dimensions. These are deemed to be important in terms of content-selection and communication instance preparation, supported by general SciCom literature [10] and by reflections of the interviewed experts. For instance, the preparatory steps that design researchers take for longer direct discussions with practitioner collaborators in the early phases of a DSR study are vastly different to the activities that lead to the creation of an academic publication after the study's conclusion. The proposed classification schema helps to specify relevant characteristics that distinguish one DSR communication instance from another. This also helps to ensure that a significant variety of different DSR communication use cases and specific instances are covered by the overall framework.

The other part of the framework is constituted by a step-by-step process to consciously design a specific communication instance. As highlighted by our interviews and requirements analysis, this process starts with (and thereby emphasizes) the identification of the needs of the main stakeholders involved in the communication instance and clarifying the targeted outcomes of the communication. Subsequently, we then recommend focussing on crafting a clear storyline, which is relatable for the involved stakeholders and in line with the purpose. Only once this is completed, the mode, means, and format of communication become relevant, before explicating the story within the boundaries of purpose suitability and mode, means, and format.

While this overall framework seems both useable and useful, a formal evaluation is still outstanding and the addressee view on communication is currently only partially and indirectly included (through literature and perceptions by design researchers). To address this limitation, we plan on conducting a controlled experiment, in which several communication instances of DSR (as audio-visual presentations of students) are supported by the proposed framework. Subsequently, these communication instances will be evaluated (by unrelated evaluators who are unaware of the experimental conditions) against communication instances that were created in the same way, but without the use of this instantiation. We expect presentations based on our new framework will be judged significantly better, which would demonstrate the framework's usefulness.

References

1. Peffers, K., Tuunanen, T., Rothenberger, M., Chatterjee, S.: A design science research methodology for information systems research. J. Manag. Inf. Syst. **24**(3), 45–77 (2007)
2. Gregor, S., Hevner, A.R.: Positioning and presenting design science research for maximum impact. MIS Q. **37**(2), 337–355 (2013)
3. Tremblay, M.C., VanderMeer, D., Beck, R.: The effects of the quantification of faculty productivity: perspectives from the design science research community. Commun. Assoc. Inf. Syst. **43**(1), 34 (2018)
4. vom Brocke, J., Maedche, A.: The DSR grid: six core dimensions for effective capturing of DSR projects. Electron. Mark. **29**, 379–385 (2019)
5. Pollock, T.G., Bono, J.E.: Being Scheherazade: the importance of storytelling in academic writing. Acad. Manag. J. **56**(3), 629–634 (2013)
6. Cooke, S.J., et al.: Considerations for effective science communication. FACETS **2**(1), 233–248 (2017)

7. Berger, C.R., Roloff, M.E., Ewoldsen, D.R.: The Handbook of Communication Science. Sage, Thousand Oaks (2010)
8. Burns, T.W., O'Connor, D.J., Stocklmayer, S.M.: Science communication: a contemporary definition. Public Underst. Sci. **12**(2), 183–202 (2003)
9. Wilson, M.J., Ramey, T.L., Donaldson, M.R., Germain, R.R., Perkin, E.K.: Communicating science: sending the right message to the right audience. FACETS **1**(1), 127–137 (2016)
10. Mauelshagen, C., Jakobs, E.-M.: Science meets public: customized technology research communication. In: International Professional Communication Conference (IPCC), Austin, Texas, USA, pp. 1–9. IEEE (2016)
11. Van Eperen, L., Marincola, F.M., Strohm, J.: Bridging the divide between science and journalism. J. Transl. Med. **8**(1), 25 (2010)
12. Putortì, E.S., Sciara, S., Larocca, N.U., Crippa, M.P., Pantaleo, G.: Communicating science effectively: when an optimised video communication enhances comprehension, pleasantness, and people's interest in knowing more about scientific findings. Appl. Psychol. **69**(3), 1072–1091 (2020)
13. Lee, A.S.: Editor's comment: MIS quarterly's editorial policies and practices. MIS Q. **25**(1), iii–vii (2001)
14. Miller, S.: Public understanding of science at the crossroads. Public Underst. Sci. **10**(1), 115–120 (2001)
15. Engel, C., Leicht, N., Ebel, P.: The imprint of design science in information systems research: an empirical analysis of the AIS senior scholar's basket. In: International Conference on Information Systems, ICIS, Munich, Germany (2019)
16. Peffers, K., Tuunanen, T., Niehaves, B.: Design science research genres: introduction to the special issue on exemplars and criteria for applicable design science research. Eur. J. Inf. Syst. **27**(2), 129–139 (2018)
17. Hevner, A.R.: A three cycle view of design science research. Scand. J. Inf. Syst. **19**(2), 87–92 (2007)
18. Bortz, J., Döring, N.: Forschungsmethoden und Evaluation. Springer, Heidelberg (2006). https://doi.org/10.1007/978-3-540-33306-7

Knowledge Contribution Diagrams for Design Science Research: A Novel Graphical Technique

David G. Schwartz[1](✉) [iD] and Inbal Yahav[2] [iD]

[1] Bar-Ilan University, Ramat-Gan, Israel
david.schwartz@biu.ac.il
[2] Tel-Aviv University, Tel-Aviv, Israel

Abstract. We extend Gregor and Hevner's knowledge contribution framework (KCF) to cover complex IS artifacts comprised of multiple sub-artifacts. Drawing from the work of Lee, Thomas, and Baskerville which advocates a return to the IS artifact in design science research, we initially extend knowledge contribution evaluation to include distinct information, social, and technology artifacts, by adding graphical elements to create a Knowledge Contribution Diagram (KCD). Additional artifact types are added to show extensibility and expressive power. We demonstrate the approach on four research articles, two from the original set classified by Gregor and Hevner, and two from more recent publications. KCD create an expressive visual evaluation tool. Better articulation of multiple knowledge contributions from complex information system artifacts can improve the appreciation of DSR knowledge contributions in the field. The proposed technique is intuitive, extensible, and can add expressiveness to all design science research reporting.

Keywords: Design science · Knowledge contribution · IS artifact · Graphic

1 Introduction

Knowledge contribution (KC) is a measure for assessing the value of individual research projects, as well as the overall direction taken by an academic discipline [1–3]. Knowledge contribution is often insufficiently articulated by authors resulting in lower potential acceptance of a research manuscript, and underappreciation of the value of a manuscript once published. Expressing the knowledge contribution of a new design is inherently challenging [4–6]. In fact, a meta-analysis of Design Science Research (DSR) research efforts reports that less than half of DSR articles effectively report knowledge contribution, showing only a modest increase over time [7]. Gregor and Hevner [8] explicitly address the challenges of presenting DSR for maximum impact, by analyzing 13 articles published in MISQ ([8] pg 348, Table 2), placing particular emphasis on expressing the contributions of artifact abstraction, and positioning such contributions within a formal and structured DSR Knowledge Contribution framework (KCF, Fig. 1). They focus their efforts on the "role of the IT artifact as a basis for appreciating levels of artifact abstractions that may be DSR contributions" ([8] pg 339). It is the focus on singular IT artifact knowledge

© Springer Nature Switzerland AG 2021
L. Chandra Kruse et al. (Eds.): DESRIST 2021, LNCS 12807, pp. 174–187, 2021.
https://doi.org/10.1007/978-3-030-82405-1_19

contribution that we address in this paper. Gregor and Hevner footnote that they use the term 'IT artifact' as synonymous with 'IS artifact', and there is nothing in their presentation that precludes the use of their framework to map multiple artifacts. DSR projects are recognized as complex and can offer multiple varied contributions to design knowledge [9]. Yet the original analysis of 13 articles addresses a singular one-dimensional artifact and contribution from each paper. While some have questioned the efficacy and completeness of the framework [10], we believe that taking an expanded view of 'IT artifact', and graphically presenting knowledge contribution, will lead to a more effective use of KCF uncovering more and varied contributions, to the benefit of the field.

Academic discourse in the IS field has long considered the 'information technology (IT) artifact' as the atomic-level item of interest in DSR. This approach has been challenged by Lee, Thomas, and Baskerville [11] who advocate unpacking the IT artifact into a separate 'information artifact', 'technology artifact', and 'social artifact' which, when taken together, comprise an 'information system (IS) artifact', a position hotly debated [12]. We contribute to this debate by taking the

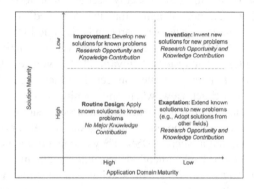

Fig. 1. The DSR knowledge contribution framework (from [8])

ideas espoused by Lee et al. and using them to expand the DSR Knowledge Contribution framework of Gregor and Hevner [8]. In doing so we achieve two significant outcomes: a compelling empirically-grounded argument in favor of the IS-artifact approach; and the introduction of Knowledge Contribution Diagrams (KCD) which adds significant expressiveness to the presentation of DSR. After a brief review of the two primary building blocks for our work – the KCF and the IS-artifact approach, we introduce KCD through an example from Cascavilla et al. [13] where the technique is first demonstrated. This is followed by analysis of four DSR articles - two revisited from the set analyzed by Gregor and Hevner in their original work, and two from recent DESRIST proceedings. A series of examples drawn from the article set illustrates the additional expressive power of the approach.

1.1   The Knowledge Contribution Framework

The KCF is meant to assess contribution relative to x:problem maturity (also referred to as *application domain maturity*) and y:solution maturity. Scaling regions of high and low for each axis gives the four quadrants of: *Routine design* (high, high) applying known solutions to known problems; *Exaptation* (low, high) extending known solutions to new problems; *Improvement* (high, low) developing new solutions to known problems; and *Invention* (low, low) inventing new solutions for new problems. Of the original thirteen articles analyzed, 10 (77%) were classified as *improvement*, 3 (23%) as *exaptation*, and none as either *routine design* or *invention*. At first this may seem surprising as one would expect DSR work to regularly report some form of invention and incorporate, to a lesser extent, routine design. However, when we look at the component breakdown, as will be shown later, we see a very different picture.

1.2 The IS-Artifact Approach

There has been considerable debate around the question of artifacts and their centrality to DSR. Much of DSR work describes information technology (IT) artifacts, which Orlikowski and Iacono [14, 15] define as "bundles of material and cultural properties packaged in some socially recognisable form such as hardware and/or software". However, not all agree that the "bundled" IT artifact should be the focal point of information systems research in general and DSR in particular. Lyytinen and King [16] note that IT artifacts do not deliver value in their own right and must be viewed in the context of a system. Schwartz [17] advocates the decomposition of IT artifacts into several distinct yet interconnected artifacts. Lee Thomas, and Baskerville [11] suggest a multi-artifact view when approaching DSR, arguing that the IT artifact is just one element within a broader Information Systems artifact, which should be viewed as a construct incorporating information, social, and technology artifacts – and must be addressed as such in DSR. They define a framework comprised of three major elements (not to the exclusion of other potential elements, as they discuss) as follows: (1) A *Social artifact* is an artifact embodying relationships or interactions among multiple individuals; (2) An *Information artifact* is an instantiation of information produced by a human participant either directly (as their own creative output) or indirectly (through an individual's invocation of a software program or other automated information production process); (3) A *Technology artifact* is a human-created tool used to solve a human-defined or perceived problem. All three interact within a broader systems framework achieving a result that is greater than the sum of its parts, comprising the IS artifact. But as Lee et al. ([11], pg 6) state *"An examination of the larger system of which any IT artifact is necessarily a part quickly expands the focus from IT artifacts to include artifacts that are not IT and artifacts that are created by people who are not IT designers. We may conceptualize these different artifacts as enabling, interacting with and even transforming one another."* By following their analytical approach, the precise contribution of each element in DSR comes into sharper focus. For a discussion of the applicability and value of the IS-artifact framework the reader is referred to [11, 13]. We will refer to the approach defined by Lee, Thomas, and Baskerville as the IS-artifact framework. We give a motivating example illustrating the use of three artifact types in the IS-artifact framework, then extend this to diverse DSR knowledge contributions such as *design principles* [18], *design theory* [19], and a potpourri of others [7]. In this manner we add component level analysis to the existing systems level analysis.

1.3 Motivating Example

The first use of an enhanced graphical KCD to present an information system artifact appears in [13], which we repeat here by way of introduction. That work describes an IS-artifact that consists of five distinct modules as part of an *information system* artifact to Detect Unintentional Information Leakage (DUIL). In their DSR analysis of the DUIL artifact the authors examine knowledge contribution by applying the KCF which, accordingly, classifies their artifact in the *improvement* quadrant owing to low *problem maturity* and high *solution maturity* of the overall system. However, the

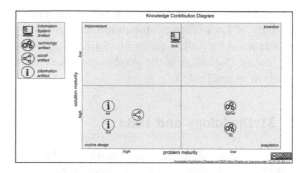

Fig. 2. KCD for "The insider on the outside: a novel system for the detection of information leakers in social networks" [13]

authors go a step further by breaking down the overall IS-artifact into **five component artifacts** following the IS-artifact framework. The result is two *information artifacts* - articles of interest (AoI); comments of interest (CoI); two *technology artifacts* - network analysis (Egonet); and visualization (Viz); and one *social artifact* - users of interest (UoI). Each of these artifacts were then assessed for knowledge contribution according to KCF and assigned their own symbology as shown in Fig. 2. This allowed the authors to present and discuss the specific contributions of each module, showing some elements could be considered *routine design* and others *exaptation*, leading to a higher level artifact exhibiting *improvement*, bordering on *invention*. This six-fold contribution analysis of what would have been a single DSR artifact stands in sharp contradistinction from the currently accepted single contribution approach.

2   Knowledge Contribution Diagrams

We define a Knowledge Contribution Diagram as *a graphical representation of one or more design science artifacts on a knowledge contribution grid to present the contribution of each artifact in terms of problem maturity and solution maturity.* A KCD template consists of a 2 × 2 grid on the axes of *problem maturity* and *solution maturity* alongside a palette presenting a library of information technology-related artifacts that can be drawn upon to complete the diagram. The choice of artifacts to include in the palette is wholly subjective and extensible. Following Lee et al. [11] our initial KCD template included only

Table 1. Artifacts and icons

Artifact	Acronym	Icon
Information Systems Artifact	ISA	
Technology artifact	TA	
Social artifact	SA	
Information artifact	IA	
Policy artifact	PA	
Guideline artifact	GA	
Theory artifact	ThA	
Principle artifact	PrA	

information system, technology, information, and *social* artifacts; however given the diversity of knowledge contribution found in DSR articles, we have extended this to include icons for *policy, guideline, design theory,* and *design principle* [7]. To simplify our textual discussion of the graphic-analytical framework we refer to the artifacts by acronym as per Table 1.

3 Methodology and Data

Using a purposeful sampling approach [20, 21] we conducted qualitative text analysis of four DSR articles listed below, two from the original set discussed in Gregor and Hevner and two from DESRIST proceedings. According to Patton, *"The logic and power of purposeful sampling lie in selecting information-rich cases for study in depth. Information-rich cases are those from which one can learn a great deal about issues of central importance to the purpose of the inquiry, thus the term purposeful sampling. Studying information-rich cases yields insights and in-depth understanding rather than empirical generalizations* ([20, 21] p. 230).*"* We followed the content extraction process detailed by [7] to identify and extract information such as a research summary, artifact description, and any knowledge contribution declared by the authors. The use of key quotes from the target manuscripts to identify knowledge contributions follows the approach of [8].

The following four articles were selected:

1. Abbasi, A., Zhang, Z., Zimbra, D., Chen, H., and Nunamaker, J., Detecting Fake Websites: The Contribution of Statistical Learning Theory, MISQ, 2010 [22].
2. Adipat, B., Zhang, D., and Zhou, L., The Effects of Tree-View Based Presentation Adaptation on Mobile Web Browsing, MISQ, 2011 [23].
3. Hönigsberg, S., A Platform for Value Co-creation in SME Networks, DESRIST, 2020 [24].
4. Brahma, A., Chatterjee, S., & Li, Y., Designing a Machine Learning Model to Predict Cardiovascular Disease Without Any Blood Test, DESRIST 2019, [25].

4 Results

Content analysis of the four DSR articles yielded 15 identifiable sub-artifacts with independent knowledge contribution (MAX = 5; MIN = 3; AVG = 3.75). Seven technology artifacts, three information artifacts, two guidelines, one theory, one principle, and one social, were identified. Knowledge contribution was spread across all four quadrants: six exaptation, four improvement. three invention, two routine design. Detailed analysis of each article in a table documenting component decomposition and knowledge contributions, along with the resulting KCD, follows.

4.1 Case 1

In this case, the identification of two technology artifacts and one information artifact gives us the first indication that there are component-level aspects to this project that

Table 2. Analysis of "Detecting Fake Websites: The Contribution of Statistical Learning Theory" [22]

System artifact	Original KC	Basis
Fake website detection	Improvement	"Systems grounded in SLT can more accurately detect various categories of fake web sites" (p. 435)

Component decomposition

Component artifact	Component-level KC	Basis
TA: custom kernel functions	Exaptation	"Custom kernels have been devised for many classification problems... studies have noted that fake website detection could greatly benefit from the use of custom kernel functions, although none have been proposed..." (p. 442)
IA: fake fraud cues	Routine Design	"The set of fraud cues required to represent these design elements for accurate fake website detection may encompass thousands of attributes." (p. 442)
TA: page level linkage display	Improvement	"although component 1 sufficiently conveys the system's classification results, additional components... illustrate why a particular website is considered legitimate or fake" (p. 449)

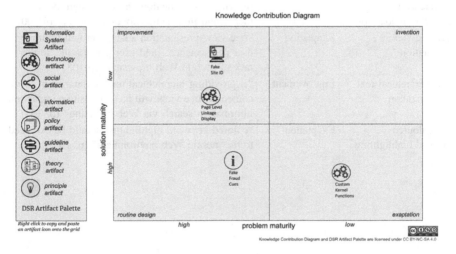

Fig. 3. KCD for "A fake website detection system" [22]

could be of interest to the reader and there is potential contribution beyond that found at the systems level (Table 2 and Fig. 3).

Table 3. Analysis of "The Effects of Tree-View Based Presentation Adaptation on Mobile Web Browsing" [23]

System artifact	Original KC	Basis
A mobile web browser	Exaptation	"Presentation adaptation has been studied in the desktop environment and been proven beneficial… However, research on adaptation of Web content presentation for mobile handheld devices is still rare." (p. 100)

Component decomposition

Component Artifact	Component-level KC	Basis
Theory artifact: adaptation research model	Invention	"There are three types of artifacts created in this research…. research model that relates presentation adaptation to user performance" (p. 100)
Guideline artifact: approaches to presentation adaption	Exaptation	"identify and integrate several approaches to presentation adaptation based on cognitive fit theory and information foraging theory" (p 100)
TA: tree-view presentation	Exaptation	"tree-view presentation adaptation will improve user performance…and user perception…in the task of mobile Web browsing" (p 103)
TA: hierarchical text summarization	Improvement	"…providing hierarchical text summaries of Web content in tree view will have a positive impact on information search via Web browsing" (p. 104)
TA: coloured keyword highlighting	Exaptation	"colored keyword highlighting should be extended to the mobile Web environment" (p. 104)

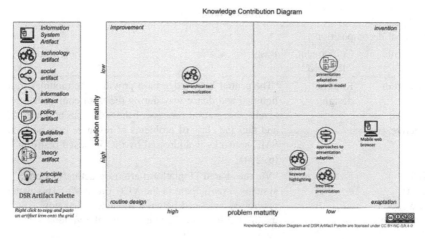

Fig. 4. KCD for "Tree-View Based Presentation Adaptation on Mobile Web Browsing" [23]

4.2   Case 2

This case presents the opportunity to identify both *theory* and *guideline* artifacts, the former contributing an invention and the latter an exaptation. In addition, there are three technology artifacts, two of which provide exaptation and one an improvement (Table 3 and Fig. 4).

Table 4. Analysis of "A Platform for Value Co-creation in SME Networks" [24]

System artifact	Original KC	Basis
Digital value cocreation platform	Exaptation	"Our research contribution can be seen as an exaptation since we transfer the known artifact type of VCC platforms into the still under-researched context of SME networks" (p. 294)
Component decomposition		
Component artifact	Component - level KC	Basis
Technology artifact: analytics component	Exaptation	"The implemented pattern is that new requests are compared with known solutions in the network… examined for optimization potentials and new (re-) configurations are learned" (p. 294)

(continued)

Table 4. (*continued*)

Component decomposition		
Component artifact	Component - level KC	Basis
Information artifact: Centralized knowledge base	Routine design	"The central knowledge base provides the modules in a liquified and dense way during the third configuration level... integration process of the VCC can be improved and thus the class of problems of resource integration in SME networks is addressed by the proposed platform" (p. 294)
Social artifact: service configuration	Exaptation	"Via the shared IT platform arbitrary actors/service systems... participate in the VCC process"; "This pattern, previously practiced between the actors, has now manifested itself in the platform via the various components" (p. 295)
Principle artifact: VCC design principles	Invention	"During the development and feedback loops with the company representatives, we were able to derive design principles (DP) that link the DR to the DF" (p 291)

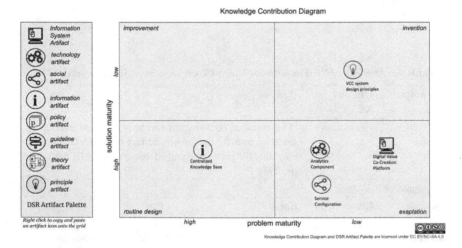

Fig. 5. KCD for "A Platform for Value Co-creation in SME Networks" [24]

4.3   Case 3

In this case, the overall system is described as an exaptation KC, yet the breakdown shows exaptation contributed by the Service Configuration and Analytics sub-artifacts. Here we see the first example of identifying and reporting knowledge contribution of a *principle artifact*, which can be mapped to the invention quadrant (Table 4 and Fig. 5).

Table 5. Analysis of "Designing a Machine Learning Model to Predict Cardiovascular Disease Without Any Blood Test" [25]

System Artifact	Original KC	Basis
Machine-learning model	Invention	"This research has led to the design and development of a high performing CVD predictor artifact that does not require any blood test or invasive patient data, based on machine learning approach." (p. 138)

Component decomposition

Component artifact	Component-level KC	Basis
Guideline artifact: selection methodology	Improvement	"This research has developed a unique and custom feature selection methodology that allowed selection and reduction of features" (p. 137)
TA: front-end user interface	Improvement	"while meeting the goal of a small predictive feature set of only 16 which will make the user interface practical, operationally acceptable, and easily adoptable" (p 134)
IA: predictive features dataset	Invention	"A new set of 16 predictive features capable of CVD prediction" (p. 134)

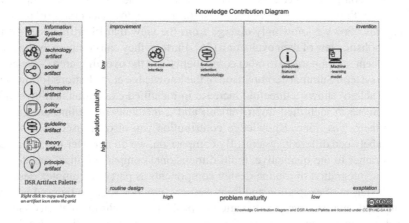

Fig. 6. KCD for "Designing a Machine Learning Model to Predict Cardiovascular Disease Without Any Blood Test [25]

4.4   Case 4

In this case we see a pattern emerge with no *exaptation* and no *routine design* - all KC is found concentrated in the *improvement* and *invention* quadrants. While our study is limited to identification of KC and does not attempt to use KCD to measure knowledge contribution *value,* we

Table 6. Knowledge contribution at original system level and subsequent component level post KCD analysis

Knowledge Contribution	Routine Design	Exaptation	Improvement	Invention	Total
Original in each DSR article (n=4)	0	2	1	1	4
Subsequent KCD analysis (n=4)	2	6	4	3	15

hypothesize that projects populating these upper quadrants may have higher overall value - an important focus of future research (Table 5 and Fig. 6).

5   Discussion

Knowledge contribution of DSR is not one-dimensional and need not be distilled to a single artifact when undertaking a complex project. By drawing attention to the KC of each component of their designs, authors can provide valuable insights relevant to a wider range of readers. In espousing this view we knowingly diverge from the view that IS artifacts are systems requiring a holistic view of their evaluation [26]. Further, they can compare the novelty of each component in comparison to other components, and the overall 'pareto'-like novelty of the entire system. Summary comparison of the knowledge contributions following our approach (Table 6) shows a threefold increase in identified exaptation and invention, a fourfold increase in identified improvement, and 2 incidents of routine design where previously there was none. Knowledge contribution can also be used as a basis for comparison between different systems. By comparison, we do not refer to a quantitative 'score' but rather to the qualitative, multi-dimensional comparison that considers both novelties, the integration of routine-design components as part of a complex design, the level and deviation of exaptation and improvement, etc. For KCD to be used as a comparison method, an objective quantification of problem and solution maturity should be developed. We plan to develop a set of objective questions that together 'place' a component within each quadrant of the KCD. To do so, we will recruit multiple domain experts that will be asked a set of objective questions about a component in an artifact (e.g., 'are you familiar with the method used?'), and then to rate the two-dimensional maturity level of the component. We will then learn the relationship between the objective questions and the experts' mean perceived maturity. We believe this will enable a more precise placement of each artifact within its quadrant which will be an improvement over the current subjective positioning. Our work has shown representation of knowledge contribution from 8 different artifact types. Dwivedi et al. [7] identify 9 different forms of knowledge contribution in DSR research, ranging from *guideline* to *generative mechanism*. Each of these can potentially be incorporated in a KCD. Researchers use a plethora of artifact types, each with its expressive ability and contribution to the art. We see no reason that the valuable contributions of each artifact within a complex system should be lost in the interest of singular system-centric contributions. Graphical representations have been employed for other DSR uses such as project planning and characterization [9], and creating Design Knowledge Maps [27]. Our work builds on the spirit of Design Knowledge Maps to position DSR contributions in problem and solution spaces, by providing guidance on how to use KCD in presenting DSR results.

5.1 Practical Implications

There are three main practical implications of this work. First, manuscripts presenting DSR can and should use the KCD template to help elucidate and amplify the knowledge contribution of their work. Second, our approach of identifying and presenting multiple forms of knowledge contribution of complex DSR projects can raise the perceived and actual impact of DSR. Finally, researchers who identify additional forms of artifact can extend the KCD approach to incorporate new research insights based on these artifacts.

5.2 Limitations and Future Research

Our analysis is based on post-publication interpretation of articles describing DSR which may not coincide with the original intent and/or interpretation of the authors of those articles. The articles analyzed were purposefully sampled to demonstrate the proposed technique and do not provide a random or representative sample. We note that while in most cases, a single Information System artifact will appear on the KCD, some DSR investigates systems of systems (e.g. [28]) in which case multiple instantiation of IS artifacts would be placed on the KCD. In such cases the component artifacts of each IS would need to be identified as connected to the correct IS, possible by the use of color or framing. Extending KCD for systems of systems should be the subject of future research. While this study has focused on *evaluation* and *presentation* of DSR research to enhance knowledge contribution, the component-level analysis of DSR knowledge contributions can be useful in the process of envisioning, designing, or executing a DSR project. Applying KCD at earlier stages of the DSR process may yield great benefits to the challenges faced by DSR and this potential should be explored.

6 Conclusions

Viewing Gregor and Hevner's knowledge contribution framework in juxtaposition with Lee et al. information system artifact decomposition adds depth to knowledge contribution analysis. Visually intuitive Knowledge Contribution Diagrams can improve presentation of DSR knowledge contribution, elucidating multiple knowledge contributions of a single DSR initiative, leading to greater impact. KCD are extensible for new design artifact types, adding further expressiveness. We believe that our technique to express multi-layered DSR knowledge contribution in graphical form can give a much needed boost to DSR research reporting of all kinds, and should also be investigated for possible uses in earlier stages of DSR project planning and execution. We hope that the explanations presented and examples given can help guide researchers in effectively presenting their DSR knowledge contribution leading to fuller appreciation of potential impact. The KCD template used to produce the graphs in this manuscript is available at http://bit.ly/3cdt3fI.

References

1. Katerattanakul, P., Han, B., Rea, A.: Is information systems a reference discipline? Commun. ACM **49**, 114–118 (2006)
2. Katerattanakul, P., Hong, S.: Quality and knowledge contributions of MISQ: a citation analysis. Commun. Assoc. Inf. Syst. **11**, 15 (2003)
3. Xiao, B., Cheung, C., Thadani, D., Assessing the quality and knowledge contribution of top is journals: a comparative citation analysis. In: ECIS Proceedings 227 (2011)
4. Baskerville, R.L., Kaul, M., Storey, V.C.: Genres of inquiry in design-science research: justification and evaluation of knowledge production. MIS Q. **39**, 541–564 (2015)
5. Beck, J., Sosa-Tzec, O., Carroll, J.M.: Communicating design-related intellectual influence: towards visual references. In: 37th ACM International Conference on the Design of Communication, p. 13. ACM (2019)
6. Wiberg, M., Stolterman, E.: What makes a prototype novel? A knowledge contribution concern for interaction design research. In: Proceedings of the 8th Nordic Conference on Human-Computer Interaction: Fun, Fast, Foundational (NordiCHI 2014), pp. 531–540. Association for Computing Machinery, New York (2014)
7. Dwivedi, N., Purao, S., Straub, D.W.: Knowledge contributions in design science research: a meta-analysis. In: Tremblay, M.C., VanderMeer, D., Rothenberger, M., Gupta, A., Yoon, V. (eds.) DESRIST 2014. LNCS, vol. 8463, pp. 115–131. Springer, Cham (2014). https://doi.org/10.1007/978-3-319-06701-8_8
8. Gregor, S., Hevner, A.R.: Positioning and presenting design science research for maximum impact. MIS Q. **37**, 337–355 (2013)
9. vom Brocke, J., Maedche, A.: The DSR grid: six core dimensions for effectively planning and communicating design science research projects. Electron. Mark. **29**(3), 379–385 (2019). https://doi.org/10.1007/s12525-019-00358-7
10. Woo, C., Saghafi, A., Rosales, A.: What is a contribution to IS design science knowledge? In: International Conference on Information Systems, 15 December 2014
11. Lee, A.S., Thomas, M., Baskerville, R.L.: Going back to basics in design science: from the information technology artifact to the information systems artifact. Info Syst. J. **25**, 5–21 (2015)
12. Iivari, J.: Information system artefact or information system application: that is the question. Info Syst. J. **27**, 753–774 (2017)
13. Cascavilla, G., Conti, M., Schwartz, D.G., Yahav, I.: The insider on the outside: a novel system for the detection of information leakers in social networks. Eur. J. Inf. Syst. **27**(4), 470–485 (2017)
14. Orlikowski, W.J., Iacono, C.S.: Research commentary: desperately seeking the "IT" in IT research–a call to theorizing the IT Artifact. Inf. Syst. Res. **12**, 121–134 (2001)

15. Orlikowski, W.J., Iacono, C.S.: The artifact redux: further reflections on the "IT" in IT research. In: Lyytinen, K., King, J.L. (eds.) Information Systems: The State of the Field, pp. 287–292 (2006)
16. Lyytinen, K., King, J.L.: Nothing at the center?: academic legitimacy in the information systems field. J. Assoc. Inf. Syst. **5**, 220–246 (2004)
17. Schwartz, D.G.: Research commentary: the disciplines of information: lessons from the history of the discipline of medicine. Inf. Syst. Res. **25**, 205–221 (2014)
18. Hansen, M.R.P., Haj-Bolouri, A.: Design principles exposition: a framework for problematizing knowledge and practice in DSR. In: Hofmann, S., Müller, O., Rossi, M. (eds.) DESRIST 2020. LNCS, vol. 12388, pp. 171–182. Springer, Cham (2020). https://doi.org/10.1007/978-3-030-64823-7_16
19. Vidmar, R., Kotzé, E., van der Merwe, T.M.: The suggestion of design theory artefacts for e-government in South Africa. In: Hofmann, S., Müller, O., Rossi, M. (eds.) DESRIST 2020. LNCS, vol. 12388, pp. 81–92. Springer, Cham (2020). https://doi.org/10.1007/978-3-030-64823-7_9
20. Patton, M.Q.: Qualitative research. In: Encyclopedia of Statistics in Behavioral Science. Wiley (2005)
21. Suri, H.: Purposeful sampling in qualitative research synthesis. Qual. Res. J. **11**, 63–75 (2011)
22. Abbasi, A., Zhang, Z., Zimbra, D., Chen, H., Nunamaker, J.F.: Detecting fake websites: the contribution of statistical learning theory. MIS Q. **34**, 435–461 (2010)
23. Adipat, B., Zhang, D., Zhou, L.: The effects of tree-view based presentation adaptation on model web browsing. MIS Q. **35**, 99–121 (2011)
24. Hönigsberg, S.: A platform for value co-creation in SME networks. In: Hofmann, S., Müller, O., Rossi, M. (eds.) DESRIST 2020. LNCS, vol. 12388, pp. 285–296. Springer, Cham (2020). https://doi.org/10.1007/978-3-030-64823-7_26
25. Brahma, A., Chatterjee, S., Li, Y.: Designing a machine learning model to predict cardiovascular disease without any blood test. In: Tulu, B., Djamasbi, S., Leroy, G. (eds.) DESRIST 2019. LNCS, vol. 11491, pp. 125–139. Springer, Cham (2019). https://doi.org/10.1007/978-3-030-19504-5_9
26. Prat, N., Comyn-Wattiau, I., Akoka, J.: Artifact evaluation in information systems design-science research-a holistic view. PACIS **23**, 1–16 (2014)
27. vom Brocke, J., Winter, R., Hevner, A., Maedche, A.: Special issue editorial –accumulation and evolution of design knowledge in design science research: a journey through time and space. J. Assoc. Inf. Syst. **21**, 520–544 (2020)
28. Tarpey, R.J., Mullarkey, M.T.: Extending design science research through systems theory: a hospital system of systems. In: Tulu, B., Djamasbi, S., Leroy, G. (eds.) DESRIST 2019. LNCS, vol. 11491, pp. 108–122. Springer, Cham (2019). https://doi.org/10.1007/978-3-030-19504-5_8

How Do Researchers (Re-)Use Design Principles: An Inductive Analysis of Cumulative Research

Thorsten Schoormann[1]([⊠]), Frederik Möller[2,3], and Magnus Rotvit Perlt Hansen[4]

[1] University of Hildesheim, 31141 Hildesheim, Germany
thorsten.schoormann@uni-hildesheim.de
[2] TU Dortmund University, Dortmund, Germany
Frederik.Moeller@tu-dortmund.de
[3] Fraunhofer ISST, 44227 Dortmund, Germany
[4] Department of People and Technology, Roskilde University, Roskilde, Denmark
magnuha@ruc.dk

Abstract. Accumulating prescriptive design knowledge, such as design principles (DP), is one of the fundamental goals in design science research projects. As previous studies have examined the use of DPs in practice to advance the development and communication of such principles, we argue that this attention also needs to be paid to how and for what researchers (re-)use DPs. Hence, this paper explores DP usage in cumulative (information systems) research based on the analysis and coding of a sample of 114 articles with 226 in-text citations. In doing this, we aim at contributing to the valuable discourse on DP reuse and accumulation by focusing on usage in research, present preliminary types of DP usage extracted from cumulative literature, as well as raise the awareness for guiding user and designer in how to (re-)use and how to allow for reuse of DPs.

Keywords: Design principle · Reuse · Cumulative research · Citation analysis

1 Motivation

The accumulation of design knowledge is the ultimate goal of design science research (DSR) [1] and necessary for a design to "[..] go far beyond a single success story" [2]. This accumulation requires the codification of design knowledge to make it reusable in different scenarios, by other users, and at another point in time [3]. Design principles (DP) are one of the most dominant mechanisms for codifying design knowledge [2].

The paramount position of reusability of DPs inevitably leads to the question of whether that happens [4]. Therefore, Chandra Kruse et al. hypothesized whether "[we] may expect that information system (IS) practitioners would use such design principles to produce reliable outcomes." [3] As the corresponding study and further discussions offer valuable insights into how practitioners use DPs and thereby advance the understanding of developing, evaluating, and communicating principles, we seek to complement this through a more research-driven perspective. Considering the emphasis on rigor from DSR we, in turn, question the level of rigor of which the literature has attained in reusing

© Springer Nature Switzerland AG 2021
L. Chandra Kruse et al. (Eds.): DESRIST 2021, LNCS 12807, pp. 188–194, 2021.
https://doi.org/10.1007/978-3-030-82405-1_20

and codifying design knowledge within its own paradigm so far. This is important for the field of knowledge to evolve smoothly and gradually for new as well as experienced DSR researcher's ability to ground, design, evaluate, and publish their research. To move towards an understanding of (re-)using DPs, we raised the following question: *What are the usages of design principles in cumulative research?*

In attempting to answer this, this research-in-progress makes three contributions as part of a more extensive study. First, it broadens the discourse on DP reusability onto the IS community by shedding light on the question of how and for what principles are (re-)used in research. Second, the paper provides preliminary types of DP usage—organized along with content-/methodology-driven usage—by employing citation analysis. Third, we discuss four main observations from our analysis, pointing to the need for guiding researchers and principle designers to leverage DP reuse in research. We believe that such guidance will potentially lead to supporting researchers in (re-)using, validating, and refining available principles as well as, from a designer perspective, in grounding [5, 6], positioning, and presenting [7] principles that allow for reuse.

2   Research Design: Identification of Cumulative Research

To disclose how and for what DPs are used by researchers, we performed a citation-driven content analysis, which qualitatively explores in-text citations, structured in three main steps: In **step 1**, we sought to obtain articles that propose DPs. We searched for the term "design principle" in the AIS Senior Scholars' Basket and leading IS proceedings using 'Publish or Perish'. We examined the top five-cited articles in each of the eight journals and determined whether they provide DPs or not. From those articles that provide DPs, we selected ten journal articles with the most citations. We also included three conference papers from ICIS, ECIS, and DERIST (see Table 1).

Table 1. Selection of top-cited articles that propose design principles (query in 02/2021).

ID	Reference	Citations	ID	Reference	Citations
J1	Markus et al. [8]	1.529	J8	Bygstad [9]	135
J2	Lindgren et al. [10]	560	J9	Seidel et al. [11]	86
J3	Gosain et al. [12]	550	J10	Corbett [13]	85
J4	Kohler et al. [14]	457	C1	Gnewuch et al. [15]	147
J5	Day et al. [16]	192	C2	Nærland et al. [17]	79
J6	Siponen & Ivari [18]	162	C3	El-Masri & Tarhini [19]	48
J7	Granados et al. [20]	147			

In step 2, to find papers that potentially (re-)use DPs for their research, we selected citing articles from the initial sample of 13 articles (see step 1). From each article, we again identified the ten most citing articles (amounting to 130 articles).

In **step 3**, from the 130 articles, we excluded non-English/non-German, duplicates, etc. The final sample contains 114 citing articles (available upon request), including a total number of 226 in-text citations (i.e., an article's sentence in which the primary DP article's citation appears). To analyze these in-text citation sentences, we employed a coding schema—inductively specified after analyzing the first articles—that differentiates between binary categories (yes/no), which is as follows: *Content-driven usage* (e.g., citing for the specification of a domain or providing definitions for a particular field); *Methodology-driven usage* (e.g., citing for the adoption of their research design). Moreover, we qualitatively added codes, including reasons and comments of why a DP article was cited for creating more specific usage insights. Finally, the obtained codes were examined and clustered within the author team to arrive at initial usage types.

3   Results: Preliminary Types of Design Principle Usage

Based on our sample, we developed eight types of usage, among two major clusters. First, **content-driven usage** refers to authors who cite a DP article because they conduct research that is related to the phenomenon the principles address. We found 181 from the 226 in-text citations—143 from journals and 47 from conferences—that can be assigned to this cluster, including four different types of usage, for instance, articles that simply emphasize the availability of DPs for a particular field or articles that make use of DPs to instantiate their artifacts. Second, **methodology-driven usage** refers to authors that cite a DP article because they adopt methodological guidance from that article. Forty-nine in-text citations from our sample—46 from journals and three from conferences—can be classified into this cluster. Usually, authors use DP articles to adopt an article's research design or point out that DPs help to achieve specific goals.

In 192 in-text citations, however, authors use DPs neither content-wise nor methodology-wise (citing a DP article not for the principles *per se*). We do not consider these relevant for our study. Table 2 summarizes the eight types of usage that have been extracted from our sample, citing DP articles.

Other types—which do not meet this study's goals—are citing articles exclusively for the phenomenon captured by a DP article (e.g., citing [15] for conversational agents) or for methods used within a DP article (e.g., citing [16] for performing interviews).

Table 2. Types of design principle usage in cumulative literature.

Type of usage		Description of type and example from our sample
Content	Availability of principles	Authors highlight the availability of DPs in a certain domain/field. In doing this, they mostly refer to principles but do not directly build upon them. *For example,* [21] *referred to and listed* [11]*'s DPs on sensemaking within their literature review on Green IS*
	Implementation of principles	Authors use available DPs to implement and/or instantiate their design knowledge/artifact. *For example,* [22] *derived a set of four DPs for Blockchain technology and implemented one of these principles by reusing* [17]*'s practices on reducing Blockchain risks*
	(Meta-)requirements	Authors refer to (meta-)requirements underpinning DPs to stress their availability and compare their insights with existing knowledge. *For example,* [23] *analyzed Chabot projects and compared their observations with* [15]*'s issues and requirements for service bots*
	Instantiation	Authors refer to a specific instantiation that has been developed based on DPs. *For example,* [24] *described* [8]*'s tool 'TOP Modeler' to illustrate that artifact instantiation help demonstrating the feasibility of the design process and the design product*
Methodology	Development methods	Authors adopt the methods for developing DPs. *For example,* [14] *used* [10]*'s work to indicate the suitability of action design research for the development of DPs*
	Development steps	Authors adopt the steps for developing DPs. *For example,* [25] *described* [11]*'s procedure for the development of DPs. Thereby, they used* [11] *as an illustrative example for their design instantiation*
	Theoretical lens	Authors reuse an underpinning (kernel) theory that is appropriate for a certain domain. *For example,* 21] *stressed that Affordance theory provides a useful theoretical lens and referred to* [11]*'s work*
	Positioning and formulation	Authors position their DPs with regard to design theories. *For example,* [26] *referred to* [8]*'s work in order to state that DPs are an important component of design theories*

4 Discussion, Conclusion, and Future Research

From analyzing DP (re-)use in cumulative literature, four main **observations** emerged.

- First, there are only a few articles in our sample that directly build upon available DPs, which is crucial to support knowledge accumulation—see also knowledge production modes for 'building on and contribution to design theory' from [1].

- Second, we observed an inconsistent use of DPs and different purposes for citing DP articles ranging from referring to a specific instantiation to abstract (meta-)requirements. Hence, there seems to be a need for additional guidance on particular *design knowledge movements* [1] for DPs, such as instantiating, advancing, and extending them. Enabling rigor in the use of DPs will potentially lead to more validation, for instance, through peer reviews and internal validation through the IS community.
- Third, some articles in our sample developed design knowledge by grounding it on available DPs. In general, to enable knowledge reuse, DSR projects need to be transparent regarding their *grounding* [1]. Since DPs can be classified as 'nascent design theory' [27], reusing them would especially contribute to the *theoretical grounding* in which "we are justifying the practical knowledge of the design theory with theoretical knowledge" [5], corresponding to the concept of 'kernel theories' [6].
- Fourth, we observed that articles presenting DPs as their primary contribution are more frequently used for the principles themselves. Those articles that propose, for instance, a design theory, are cited more frequently for other reasons than the DPs.

Drawing on these preliminary observations, we asked ourselves 'why there is scarce usage?' This could be attributed to the fact that DPs are intended to primarily help practitioners in instantiating artifacts. To investigate this, **further research** might shed light on the following questions: What are *other usage* types? (content/methodology); What are the actual *target user* groups of DPs? (practice vs. academia); How to facilitate the *evolution* of DPs? (e.g., integrating underpinning development steps for reviewing available DPs, [27]); What are possible *types/knowledge movements* of DP reuse?; How to *communicate* DPs to enable reuse in academia? (visual tools [28]).

In **summary**, our work contributes to the core of the 'practical ethos' of DSR that requires its products to be reusable [4] by broadening the scope of reusability onto the academic domain and aim for a fruitful discussion on how to grow the body of prescriptive design knowledge. We outline our initial findings that conceptualize types of how others can use DPs to enhance their effectiveness and maturity. Overall, we argue that the limited and inconsistent (re-)use of DPs in research indicates a need for further guidelines that help to leverage the full potential of design knowledge reuse. Our future work will focus on (1) further synthesizing good practices. Since we concentrate on top-cited journals, the next steps should also examine random, up-to-date, and top-cited articles. Also, we plan to include outlets beyond the top-ranked ones as they might have more applied/domain-specific research (re-)using available DPs. Moreover, we (2) plan to verify and refine our preliminary types of DP usage (e.g., by means of Q-sorting) and seek to develop guidelines for reusing such principles in research.

References

1. vom Brocke, J., Winter, R., Hevner, A., Maedche, A.: Accumulation and evolution of design knowledge in design science research: a journey through time and space. J. Assoc. Inf. Syst. **21** (2020)
2. Chandra Kruse, L., Seidel, S.: Tensions in design principle formulation and reuse. In: Presented at the Proceedings of the 12th International Conference on Design Science Research in Information Systems and Technology, Karlsruhe, Germany (2017)

3. Chandra Kruse, L., Seidel, S., Purao, S.: Making use of design principles. In: Parsons, J., Tuunanen, T., Venable, J., Donnellan, B., Helfert, M., Kenneally, J. (eds.) Tackling Society's Grand Challenges with Design Science, pp. 37–51. Springer Publishing, Cham (2016)
4. Iivari, J., Hansen, M.R.P., Haj-Bolouri, A.: A proposal for minimum reusability evaluation of design principles. Eur. J. Inf. Syst., 1–18 (2020)
5. Goldkuhl, G.: Design theories in information systems-a need for multi-grounding. J. Inf. Technol. Theory Appl. **6**, 59 (2004)
6. Walls, J.G., Widmeyer, G.R., El Sawy, O.A.: Building an information system design theory for vigilant EIS. Inf. Syst. Res. **3**, 36–59 (1992)
7. Chandra Kruse, L., Seidel, S., Gregor, S.: Prescriptive knowledge in IS research: conceptualizing design principles in terms of materiality, action, and boundary conditions. In: Proceedings of the 48th Hawaii International Conference on System Science, Kauai, Hawaii, USA, pp. 4039–4048. IEEE (2015)
8. Markus, M.L., Majchrzak, A., Gasser, L.: A design theory for systems that support emergent knowledge processes. MIS Q. **26**, 179–212 (2002)
9. Bygstad, B.: Generative innovation: a comparison of lightweight and heavyweight IT. J. Inf. Technol. **32**, 180–193 (2017)
10. Lindgren, R., Henfridsson, O., Schultze, U.: Design principles for competence management systems: a synthesis of an action research study. MIS Q. **28**, 435–472 (2004)
11. Seidel, S., Chandra Kruse, L., Székely, N., Gau, M., Stieger, D.: Design principles for sensemaking support systems in environmental sustainability transformations. Eur. J. Inf. Syst. **27**, 221–247 (2018)
12. Goasin, S., Malhotra, A., Sawy, O.A.El.: Coordinating for flexibility in e-business supply chains. J. Manage. Inf. Syst. **21**, 7–45 (2004)
13. Corbett, J.: Designing and using carbon management systems to promote ecologically responsible behaviors. J. Assoc. Inf. Syst. **14** (2013)
14. Kohler, T., Fueller, J., Matzler, K., Stieger, D., Füller, J.: Co-creation in virtual worlds: the design of the user experience. MIS Q. **35**, 773–788 (2011)
15. Gnewuch, U., Morana, S., Maedche, A.: Towards designing cooperative and social conversational agents for customer service. In: Proceedings of the International Conference on Information Systems, Seoul, Korea (2017)
16. Day, J., Junglas, I., Silva, L.: Information flow impediments in disaster relief supply chains. J. Assoc. Inf. Syst. **10** (2009)
17. Nærland, K., Müller-Bloch, C., Beck, R., Palmund, S.: Blockchain to rule the waves-nascent design principles for reducing risk and uncertainty in decentralized environments. In: Proceedings of the International Conference on Information Systems, Seoul, Korea (2017)
18. Siponen, M., Ivari, J.: Six design theories for IS security policies and guidelines. J. Assoc. Inf. Syst. **7**, 19 (2006)
19. El-Masri, M., Tarhini, A., Hassouna, M., Elyas, T.: A design science approach to gamify education: from games to platforms. In: Proceedings of the European Conference on Information Systems, Münster, Germany (2015)
20. Granados, N., Gupta, A., Kauffman, R.J.: Research Commentary—information transparency in business-to-consumer markets: concepts, framework, and research agenda. Inf. Syst. Res. **21**, 207–226 (2009)
21. Henkel, C., Kranz, J.: Pro-environmental behavior and green information systems research - review, synthesis and directions for future research. In: Proceedings of the International Conference on Information Systems, San Francisco, CA, USA (2018)
22. Chanson, M., Bogner, A., Bilgeri, D., Fleisch, E., Wortmann, F.: Blockchain for the IoT: privacy-preserving protection of sensor data. J. Assoc. Inf. Syst. **20**, 1274–1309 (2019)
23. Wessel, M., et al.: The power of bots: characterizing and understanding bots in OSS projects. Proc. ACM Hum. Comput. Interact. **2**, 182:1–182:19 (2018)

24. Bichler, M.: Design science in information systems research. Wirtschaftsinformatik **48**(2), 133–135 (2006). https://doi.org/10.1007/s11576-006-0028-8
25. vom Brocke, J., Fettke, P., Gau, M., Houy, C., Morana, S.: Tool-support for design science research: design principles and instantiation. SSRN Electron. J. (2017)
26. Hanseth, O., Lyytinen, K.: Design theory for dynamic complexity in information infrastructures: the case of building internet. In: Willcocks, L.P., Sauer, C., Lacity, M.C. (eds.) Enacting Research Methods in Information Systems: Volume 3, pp. 104–142. Springer, Cham (2016). https://doi.org/10.1007/978-3-319-29272-4_4
27. Möller, F., Guggenberger, T.M., Otto, B.: Towards a method for design principle development in information systems. In: Hofmann, S., Müller, O., Rossi, M. (eds.) DESRIST 2020. LNCS, vol. 12388, pp. 208–220. Springer, Cham (2020). https://doi.org/10.1007/978-3-030-64823-7_20
28. Schoormann, T., Behrens, D., Fellmann, M., Knackstedt, R.: On your mark, ready, search: a framework for structuring literature search strategies in in-formation systems. In: Proceedings of the International Conference on Wirtschaftsinformatik, Virtual (2021)

Emerging Methods and Frameworks
for DSR

Designing Software for Online Randomized Controlled Trials

Jonas Sjöström$^{(\boxtimes)}$ and Mohammad Hafijur Rahman

Department of Informatics and Media, Uppsala University, Uppsala, Sweden
{jonas.sjostrom,hafijur.rahman}@im.uu.se

Abstract. Researchers in psychosocial care paid an increasing interest in providing treatment online, e.g., self-help and cognitive behavioral therapy for patients with different conditions. Consequently, they need to design both complex interventions and conduct research online. There is little research on how to design appropriate support for complex online randomized controlled trials (RCTs) – a prevalent approach for investigating the effectiveness of psychological treatment. In this paper, we report from a decade-long design science research initiative conducted within an eHealth research environment. Drawing from the design experiences and literature, we present design reflections and conceptual models supporting the design of software for online RCTs. We evaluate the ideas by accounting for the long-term use of the system by various research groups, signaling proof-of-concept, proof-of-use, and proof-of-value. Our results contribute to designers of online RCT solutions and add to the discourse on tool support for design science research.

Keywords: Randomized controlled trial · Design · Research tool

1 Introduction

In Sweden, based on a proposal from the government (proposition 2008/09:50), a plan to support large strategic research environments was launched from the main public research funding agencies. The overall aim was to strengthen Sweden's position as a research nation and thereby increase its scientific competitiveness in the world. It also explicitly promoted multidisciplinary research on eHealth. Uppsala University Psychosocial Care Programme (U-CARE) was one of the 43 programs that were funded for 5 years based on this proposition. U-CARE's vision is to increase cost-effective access to participatory mental health care in connection with somatic illness by using eHealth technology.

A key activity in U-CARE is to develop, test, and evaluate online complex interventions consisting of self-help and cognitive behavioral therapy (CBT) for emotional distress experienced by individuals in relation to somatic disease. Life-threatening diseases such as cancer can cause depression and anxiety [19] both for the individual and for their loved ones. This distress may not only cause human suffering but can also negatively impact the treatment of the somatic disease and bring about other issues for

© Springer Nature Switzerland AG 2021
L. Chandra Kruse et al. (Eds.): DESRIST 2021, LNCS 12807, pp. 197–208, 2021.
https://doi.org/10.1007/978-3-030-82405-1_21

the individual and society. For example, a depressive state may cause a patient to engage in less physical activity [25], contribute to sleeping problems, and non-adherence to prescribed medications [9]. How disease is psychologically managed can also impact societal costs, e.g., due to longer, more complicated and frequent visits in healthcare. U-CARE engages researchers from psychology, medicine, information systems, caring sciences, and economics, as well as health practitioners. Around 25 people were employed in the U-CARE research group, and another 25 researchers were actively engaged in the research but employed elsewhere. For convenience, as of now, we refer to the whole group as *the U-CARE community*.

As IS researchers within the U-CARE community, we designed and developed a system to support the other researchers in providing care and conducting randomized controlled trials (RCTs) online. Our work was conducted as design science research (DSR) over a period of 10 years. During design, we noticed a lack of literature on designing software to support a *fuller* research process, including major components of an RCT. The lack of design-oriented literature on the topic complicated the design process.

This paper aims to account for our design experiences and reflections from a longitudinal process of designing RCT support for a multi-disciplinary research environment for psychosocial care.

The paper proceeds as follows. In Sect. 2, we present our research approach. In Sect. 3, we focus on the design of online RCTs by articulating *design reflections* and *conceptual models* for such software. In Sect. 4, we present and discuss the use of our artifact in a series of RCTs (and other research studies) over almost a decade. Finally, Sect. 5 highlights the contributions and concludes the paper. The paper thus follows the DSR publication schema [8] with one exception: The literature review was is integrated into Sect. 3 to save space and improve the readability of the text.

2 An Agile Action Design Research Approach

Since the inception of the U-CARE program in 2010, we have gone through initial ideation, an iterative process with bi-weekly design sprints leading to an emerging software used in practice. The U-CARE software as a whole has been developed using an agile software development process [6, 14]. There were 154 sprint meetings from November 2010 to December 2018. First, a design and development phase (2011–2012) concerned with the initial design of the software, spiking the architecture, and implementing its architectural core and basic features. Second, the production and refinement phase (2013–2015) concerned with using the software to conduct trials, and continually improving the software, and adapting it for new use cases. A mobile-first approach was adopted to design the system for both computer-based web clients and smartphones. Third, from 2016 and forward, trials continued, and the system has been subject to bug-fixing and continuous improvement by a team of three employed professional software developers.

The meetings included developers or information systems researchers and psychologists or clinical researchers. The product owner in the process was a psychology researcher, and the scrum master was an information systems researcher. The U-CARE research environment as a whole had 50 staff with whom the development team and the product owner interacted frequently. Also, Patient and public involvement (PPI) is recognized as an important strategy to ensure the relevance and legitimacy of health research activities and findings. Several activities were organized to expose emerging designs to different patients groups [12] to improve treatment protocols and user experience.

When there was a need, the agile sprints were 'hardened' as outlined by Conboy et al. [5] – i.e., sprints down-prioritizing new feature development in favor of strengthening the design either theoretically or technically. Such sprints could include a complete focus on writing new test code, ingraining the design with new theoretical insights, or doing refactoring of critical system parts such as the event management systems to send reminders to participants.

Taking place in the U-CARE community, these development sprints were strongly research–oriented, including continuous reflection, formalization of learning, and literature-based discussions along with practical needs articulated by the psychology practitioners. Design reflections were articulated continually as well as on dedicated research sessions to formalize learning [26]. Similarly, following action design research, software and knowledge emerged in cycles of build, intervention, and evaluation. While our process is best understood as action design research, we still want to emphasize our appreciation of the three-cycle view on DSR [13]. We found it highly rewarding in the agile R&D work to conceive of the process as a continual focus shift between cycles of relevance, design and evaluation, and rigor. Our contribution is both technological and theoretical [4]. Also, our work as such concerns novel research and evaluation techniques, which have also been suggested as important contribution types for DSR [13].

3 Designing Online RCTs

In this section, we describe the software designed to support RCTs. Our description is structured in a top-down manner, starting with an overview, followed by more detailed descriptions of various aspects of online RCT provision. Throughout the text, we will emphasize design reflections (DR#1–DR#6).

The foundation of an RCT is that a sample from a population is randomized into two groups [1]. By providing different treatment to the two groups (e.g., a psychosocial intervention v. no treatment at all), the treatments can be contrasted to each other using statistical methods.

Crucial elements are the inclusion of individuals into the study (making sure they are representative of the population of interest), and the randomization. The random assignment of treatment is the key in the experimental design of an RCT [32]. Below, we expand on our abstracted view on important considerations when designing software support for RCTs.

3.1 Overview

Figure 1 is a simplified static model showing the core of RCT configuration in the U-CARE software. The U-CARE community expressed a need for configurability: The idea of the software was to support multiple research trials, examining different treatment protocols for patients with various somatic issues. Earlier publications provide an in-depth view of the research environment and the design challenge complexity [27, 29].

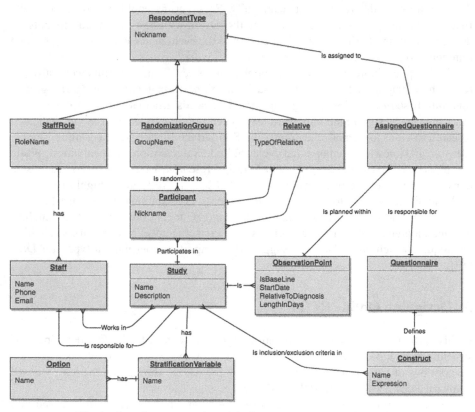

Fig. 1. A static conceptual model of the core of RCT configuration

At the heart of the model, there is the *study* class. Each study may have several observation points (one and only one is the baseline of the study, i.e., the first observation point). In each observation point, the researcher can specify what questionnaires to include. Each questionnaire is assigned to a type of respondent, that can be either a staff role (e.g., "health staff", "moderator", or "therapist"), a participant in the study (e.g., "control group participant"), or a relative to a participant (e.g., "mother"). The design of the feature to assign questionnaires for a participant to different roles was driven by requirements from researchers in U-CARE, based on their needs to collect data from different actors at different times. This leads us to DR#1: *In complex research trials, we need to collect data about a subject by conducting surveys to various stakeholders, including the subject, family members, and various health staff roles.*

For each study, the researcher can also specify inclusion/exclusion criteria, which are further elaborated in Sect. 3.3. For the software to assess eligibility to participate in a study, there is a need to define constructs and evaluate expressions based on questionnaire results. To support automated randomization, the researcher can specify stratification variables and optional values. For instance, a stratification variable may be "site" and optional values may be the various towns where patients are recruited. The rationale for Fig. 1 is further elaborated below.

Questionnaire design is an essential part of designing an RCT. To a large extent, we conceive of this part of the software as routine design [8] that will not be reported here due to space limitations. Essentially, the questionnaire design tool allows for the same question types and skip logic [33] that can be found in well-known survey tools such as Google Docs, SurveyGizmo, SurveyMonkey, and LimeSurvey. Patient-reported outcome measures (PROMs) [4] are prevalent in health research. One example is the hospital anxiety and depression scale (HADS) [32], which will be used below as an example. The survey design tool was built and tested with numerous PROMs to ensure that all common patient-reported outcome measures were available for the researchers.

In this context, our focus is on the bigger picture of integrating questionnaires into an overarching RCT. The ambition to automate RCTs causes a need for features to evaluate expressions based on questionnaire results. Below, we will demonstrate how such expression evaluation support is used in combination with well-defined inclusion and exclusion criteria to determine whether or not a participant matches the inclusion criteria in a study (see next section). *DR#2 suggests: The definition of constructs, and automated expression evaluation, in questionnaire design is a necessary foundation to trigger various types of RCT logic whenever a questionnaire is submitted.* The design reflection will be further clarified below.

Table 1. Example constructs used for inclusion in the HADS questionnaire

Construct	Expression
Anxiety	@q1@ + @q3@ + @q5@ + @q7@ + @q9@ + @q11@ + @q13@
Depression	@q2@ + @q4@ + @q6@ + @q8@ + @q10@ + @q12@ + @q14@
Inclusion	(@anxiety@ > 7 || @depression@ > 7) ? true: false

3.2 Inclusion and Randomization

There are various ways to recruit participants to a research trial. In U-CARE, recruitment was typically setup at various Swedish hospitals. For instance, if a patient at a hospital were admitted due to a myocardial infarct, a research nurse at that hospital would app-roach the patient, inform about a study, and ask the patient if she/he wanted to participate. If so, the patient would sign a consent form, then be provided with information on how to access the study online. At this point, the research nurse has created a user account for the individual, and the automated processes outlined below begin. To increase support for various types of recruitment, *DR#3 states that the software needs to support multiple modes of recruitment and multicenter recruitment.*

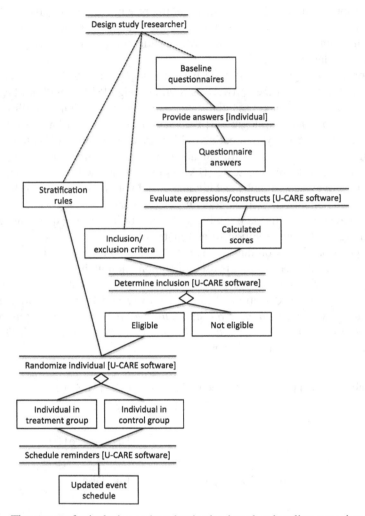

Fig. 2. The process for inclusion and randomization based on baseline screening results.

Figure 2 illustrates the process for randomization and inclusion. Once a recruited individual logs on for the first time, the screening will begin. That is; the individual answers the baseline questionnaire(s). Each time a questionnaire is submitted, the constructs in the questionnaire are evaluated. When all questionnaires in the observation point are completed, the software determines the eligibility of the individual to participate in the study (see Table 1). If eligible, the individual is randomized. Our fifth reflection, *DR#4, is that the software should automate the screening process.*

Randomization occurs following the stratification rules defined by the researchers. One important requirement from the U-CARE community was the use of block randomization [1] for each stratum to make sure that after every N randomized participant, there is an equal number of participants in the control and treatment group. An important requirement from the U-CARE researchers was that they shouldn't know the number N, "but it should be somewhere in the interval $4 \leq N \leq 10$". The software was built to facilitate allocation concealment [1] to prevent selection bias. We thus articulate *DR#5 – The software should randomize the participants following a block randomization principle, and prevent selection bias by hiding randomization sequences from the researchers.*

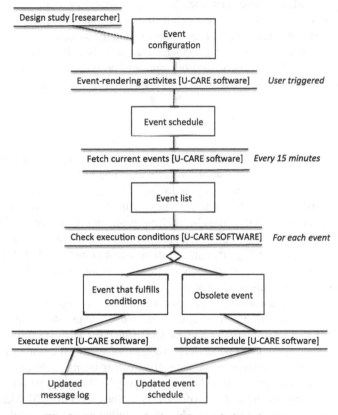

Fig. 3. The process logic of the reminder subsystem

3.3 Automated Reminders

Response frequency is an important issue in all surveys, and retention is a critical issue in any randomized controlled trial. The online setting allows for reminders at a low cost and with minimal effort [3]. A majority of participants in randomized controlled trials (RCTs) appear to accept reminders and find them harmless and useful. There is, however, little evidence about the effectiveness of reminders to increase retention [16, 21]. Nevertheless, in the U-CARE context, reminders were considered highly important to promote retention and increase the response frequency in the observation points.

Figure 3 shows the dynamics of the event scheduling and event processing (reminders are types of event in the software). Events are scheduled based on the event design made by the researchers in a study and triggered by user actions: (i) When an individual is added to a study, baseline reminders are scheduled, and (ii) when a participant is randomized, observation point reminders are scheduled. The event schedule is periodically examined for reminders to send. For a reminder to be sent, certain conditions must be met. For instance, an individual being part of a study on psychosocial support for cancer patients may no longer be alive. There must clearly be a thorough process to avoid sending repeated reminders via SMS. If an event fulfills the conditions, it is fired (e.g., reminder sent). For accountability reasons, all messages sent via the system need to be properly logged. The work on the reminder mechanisms leads to *DR#6: Reminders are essential in RCT. The software should support multiple optional recipients and modes of delivery, needs to meet well-defined conditions before being sent, and messages should be logged.*

4   Evaluation

There has been extensive use of the U-CARE software, and various research groups published research based on the use of the software. The U-CARE software has been used for ~10 years by researchers, psychologists, and patients, in 11 research trials. Approximately 3000 patients located at 27 hospitals in Sweden have participated in studies using the software. Within the U-CARE program an infrastructure, that is, logistics, structures, and policies, for delivering care and psychological treatment online has been created. Several research groups have been associated with the U-CARE program to use the U-CARE portal and the self-help programs developed within U-CARE. Table 2 shows an overview of trials conducted using the software.

Following Nunamaker and Briggs [24] we reason about the qualities of the software from three points of view: Proof-of-concept, proof-of-use, and proof-of-value. Regarding proof-of-concept, the software has been in use and refined for a decade, implementing all the features reflected upon in this paper. Regarding proof-of-use, the studies presented in Table 2 demonstrate the continued use of the software. Regarding proof-of-value, we can see that multiple research groups have been conducting RCTs and other types of studies through different configurations of the software. See Norlund et al. [23], Mattsson et al. [18], Ander et al. [2], and Hauffman et al. [12] for detailed accounts of studies designed using the software. Several recent publications [10, 11, 15, 17, 22, 30, 31] report on results from complex trials, showing that the use of the U-CARE software to conduct research supports randomized controlled trial standards in par with peer reviewer expectations in top-tier health journals.

Table 2. Studies designed and conducted using the U-CARE software

Research Trial	Period	#
RCT investigating the efficacy of a psychosocial health intervention for adults with cancer	2013–2016	1117
RCT investigating the efficacy of a psychosocial health intervention for adults who suffered a myocardial infarct	2013–2016	1052
RCT comparing two different methods for treating fear of childbirth in pregnant women	2014–2016	270
RCT investigating the efficacy of a psychosocial health intervention for patients with pelvic pain	2014–2019	356
RCT studying the effect of relapse prevention for people who take antidepressant medication but who still show residual symptoms	2014–2016	105
Two connected RCTs comparing how a varied degree of therapeutic support and variations in multimedia richness affects adherence to treatment	2014, 2016	185 + 100
Two connected RCTs examining the effect of CBT online to help women and couples cope better after having negative or traumatic experiences in connection with childbirth	2015–2018	401
Participatory action research to inquire into the needs for psychosocial support among parents with cancer-struck adolescents	2016	6
Qualitative inquiry into teenage impressions of online psychosocial care and supporting technologies	2012–2015	9
Observational study aimed at getting an overall view of the physical and mental health in young adults born with an extremely low birth weight	2018–2019	170

5 Concluding Discussion

In this paper, we have reported from a longitudinal DSR initiative in a multi-disciplinary research environment. We have presented a set of design reflections to support the design of software for online RCTs. In addition to static and dynamic models depicting key processes in conducting an RCT, we summarize our key findings as follows:

- DR#1: In complex research trials, we need to collect data about a subject by conducting surveys to various stakeholders, including the subject, family members, and various health staff roles
- DR#2: The definition of constructs, and expression evaluation, in questionnaire design is a necessary foundation to trigger various types of RCT logic whenever a questionnaire is submitted.
- DR#3: Online RCT software should preferably support multiple modes of recruitment and multicenter recruitment
- DR#4: The software should automate the screening process.

- DR#5: The software should randomize the participants following a block randomization principle, and prevent selection bias by hiding randomization sequences from the researchers.
- DR#6: Reminder functionality is essential. The software should handle multiple optional recipients and modes of delivery. Reminders needs to meet well-defined conditions before being sent, and should be logged.

These reflections are thoroughly justified empirically, and resonate well with literature on RCTs. We have shown that the implementation of the U-CARE software has worked well to support 11 research trials, many of them with complex RCT design. The substantive use of the software over a long period (i) serves as a proof-of-concept and proof-of-use of the design at hand, and (ii) also shows the technological contribution of this work: An instantiation of software that has created practical value in a multidisciplinary research community. Further, proof-of-value for researchers is derived from the growing number of publications from RCTs conducted using the software.

We recognize that the term *design reflections* is a bit vague. We contemplated articulating anatomically correct design principles [7], but the page limitations prevented us from doing so in this paper. Future work may include more elaborate design principle presentations. Furthermore, we have left out several important design reflections from this paper, such as the importance of comparability between paper-based and online questionnaires, and the logging of paradata to whitebox user behaviors. Future research will report further on such aspects of online RCTs.

Finally, we wish to highlight this research as a contribution to the tool-oriented discourse in DSR. Our contribution to the design of software for RCTs relates clearly to the discourse on an ecosystem of tools to support design science research [20] and to the idea of software-embedded evaluation in DSR [28]. Similar built-in evaluation mechanisms as those reported here may be relevant for a broad range of design experiments outside of the health sector. Also, while the software presented here – as well as the RCT process models and design reflections –are grounded in an eHealth context, we propose that they may be useful in RCTs in other settings such as education and e-commerce.

References

1. Akobeng, A.K.: Understanding randomised controlled trials. Arch. Dis. Child. **90**(8), 840–844 (2005)
2. Ander, M., et al.: Guided internet-administered self-help to reduce symptoms of anxiety and depression among adolescents and young adults diagnosed with cancer during adolescence (U-CARE: YoungCan): a study protocol for a feasibility trial. BMJ Open **7**, 1 (2017)
3. Andriopoulos, A., et al.: Commencement of and retention in web-based interventions and response to prompts and reminders: longitudinal observational study based on two randomized controlled trials. J. Med. Internet Res. **23**(3) e24590 (2021)
4. Baskerville, R., et al.: Design science research contributions: finding a balance between artifact and theory. J. Assoc. Inf. Syst. **19**(5), 3 (2018)
5. Conboy, K., et al.: Agile design science research. In: International Conference on Design Science Research in Information Systems, pp. 168–180 (2015)
6. Conboy, K.: Agility from first principles: reconstructing the concept of agility in information systems development. Inf. Syst. Res. **20**(3), 329–354 (2009)

7. Gregor, S., et al.: Research perspectives: the anatomy of a design principle. J. Assoc. Inf. Syst. **21**(6), 2 (2020)
8. Gregor, S., Hevner, A.R.: Positioning and presenting design science research for maximum impact. MIS Q. **37**(2), 337–355 (2013)
9. Grenard, J.L., et al.: Depression and medication adherence in the treatment of chronic diseases in the United States: a meta-analysis. J. Gen. Intern. Med. **26**(10), 1175–1182 (2011)
10. Hauffman, A., et al.: Cocreated internet-based stepped care for individuals with cancer and concurrent symptoms of anxiety and depression: results from the U-CARE AdultCan randomized controlled trial. Psycho-Oncology **29**(12), 2012–2018 (2020)
11. Hauffman, A., et al.: Experiences of internet-based stepped care in individuals with cancer and concurrent symptoms of anxiety and depression: qualitative exploration conducted alongside the U-CARE AdultCan randomized controlled trial. J. Med. Internet Res. **22**(3) e16547 (2020)
12. Hauffman, A., et al.: The development of a nurse-led internet-based learning and self-care program for cancer patients with symptoms of anxiety and depression—a part of U-CARE. Cancer Nurs. **40**(5), E9–E16 (2017)
13. Hevner, A.R., et al.: Design science in information systems research. MIS Q. **28**(1), 75–105 (2004)
14. Highsmith, J., Cockburn, A.: Agile software development: the business of innovation. Comput. **34**(9), 120–127 (2001)
15. Igelström, H., et al.: User experiences of an internet-based stepped-care intervention for individuals with cancer and concurrent symptoms of anxiety or depression (the U-CARE AdultCan Trial): qualitative study. J. Med. Internet Res. **22**(5) e16604 (2020)
16. Kannisto, K.A., Adams, C.E., Koivunen, M., Katajisto, J., Välimäki, M.: Feedback on SMS reminders to encourage adherence among patients taking antipsychotic medication: a cross-sectional survey nested within a randomised trial. BMJ Open **5**(11), e008574 (2015)
17. Larsson, B., et al.: Birth preference in women undergoing treatment for childbirth fear: a randomised controlled trial. Women and Birth **30**(6), 460–467 (2017)
18. Mattsson, S., et al.: U-CARE: internet-based stepped care with interactive support and cognitive behavioral therapy for reduction of anxiety and depressive symptoms in cancer--a clinical trial protocol. BMC Cancer **13**(1), 414 (2013)
19. Mitchell, A.J., Ferguson, D.W., Gill, J., Paul, J., Symonds, P.: Depression and anxiety in long-term cancer survivors compared with spouses and healthy controls: a systematic review and meta-analysis. Lancet Oncol. **14**(8), 721–732 (2013)
20. Morana, S., et al.: Tool support for design science research—towards a software ecosystem: a report from a DESRIST 2017 workshop. Commun. Assoc. Inf. Syst. **43**(1), 17 (2018)
21. Neff, R., Fry, J.: Periodic prompts and reminders in health promotion and health behavior interventions: systematic review. J. Med. Internet Res. **11**(2), e16 (2009)
22. Norlund, F., et al.: Internet-based cognitive behavioral therapy for symptoms of depression and anxiety among patients with a recent myocardial infarction: the U-CARE heart randomized controlled trial. J. Med. Internet Res. **20**(3), e88 (2018)
23. Norlund, F., et al.: Treatment of depression and anxiety with internet-based cognitive behavior therapy in patients with a recent myocardial infarction (U-CARE Heart): study protocol for a randomized controlled trial. Trials **16**(1), 1–8 (2015)
24. Nunamaker, Jr, J.F., Briggs, R.O.: Toward a broader vision for Information Systems. ACM Trans. Manag. Inf. Syst. **2**(4), 20 (2011).
25. Roshanaei-Moghaddam, B., et al.: The longitudinal effects of depression on physical activity. Gen. Hosp. Psychiatry. **31**(4), 306–315 (2009)
26. Sein, M.K., et al.: Action design research. MIS Q. **35**(1), 37–56 (2011)
27. Sjöström, J., et al.: Mutability matters: baselining the consequences of design. In: MCIS 2011 Proceedings, Limassol, Cyprus (2011).

28. Sjöström, J., Kruse, L.C., Haj-Bolouri, A., Flensburg, P.: Software-embedded evaluation support in design science research. In: Chatterjee, S., Dutta, K., Sundarraj, R.P. (eds.) DESRIST 2018. LNCS, vol. 10844, pp. 348–362. Springer, Cham (2018). https://doi.org/10.1007/978-3-319-91800-6_23

29. Sjöström, J., von Essen, L., Grönqvist, H.: The origin and impact of ideals in eHealth research: experiences from the U-CARE research environment. JMIR Res. Protoc. 3(2), e28 (2014)

30. Ternström, E., et al.: A randomized controlled study comparing internet-based cognitive behavioral therapy and counselling by standard care for fear of birth–a study protocol. Sex. Reprod. Healthc. 13, 75–82 (2017)

31. Wallin, E., et al.: Treatment activity, user satisfaction, and experienced usability of internet-based cognitive behavioral therapy for adults with depression and anxiety after a myocardial infarction: mixed-methods study. J. Med. Internet Res. 20(3) e87 (2018)

32. White, H., Sabarwal, S., de Hoop, T.: Randomized controlled trials (RCTs). Methodological Briefs: Impact Evaluation 7, UNICEF Office of Research, Florence (2014). http://home.cerge-ei.cz/kaliskova/files/policy_eval/White_Sabarwal_de_Hoop_2014.pdf

33. Wiersma, W.: The validity of surveys: online and offline. Oxf. Internet Inst. 18(3), 321–340 (2013)

Knowledge is Power: Provide Your IT-Support with Domain-Specific High-Quality Solution Material

Simon L. Schmidt[2](✉) , Mahei Manhai Li[2] , Sascha Weigel[2] ,
and Christoph Peters[1,2]

[1] University of St. Gallen, St. Gallen, Switzerland
christoph.peters@unisg.ch
[2] University of Kassel, Kassel, Germany
{simon.schmidt,mahei.li,weigel,christoph.peters}@uni-kassel.de

Abstract. As more and more business processes are based on IT services the high availability of these processes is dependent on the IT-Support. Thus, making the IT-Support a critical success factor of companies. This paper presents how this department can be supported by providing the staff with domain-specific and high-quality solution material to help employees faster when errors occur. The solution material is based on previously solved tickets because these contain precise domain-specific solutions narrowed down to e.g., specific versions and configurations of hard-/software used in the company. To retrieve the solution material ontologies are used that contain the domain-specific vocabulary needed. Because not all previously solved tickets contain high-quality solution material that helps the staff to fix issues the de-signed IT-Support system separates low- from high-quality solution material. This paper presents (a) theory- and practical-motivated design requirements that describe the need for automatically retrieved solution material, (b) develops two major design principles to retrieve domain-specific and high-quality solution material, and (c) evaluates the instantiations of them as a prototype with organic real-world data. The results show that previously solved tickets of a company can be pre-processed and retrieved to IT-Support staff based on their current queries.

Keywords: DSR · IT-support · High-quality retrieval · AI · Ontology

1 Introduction

More and more information technologies (IT) are getting deployed in organizations and so increase the complexity of infrastructures. While the day-to-day operations are dependent on the continuous availability of these complex IT services the IT-Support is under high pressure when fixing all issues as fast as possible. Whenever IT services stop operating or fail the user can often not continue to work. In other words: The company loses money. To fix an issue, general solution materials are often not sufficient as they do not apply to company-specific errors. Instead, domain-specific solution materials

© Springer Nature Switzerland AG 2021
L. Chandra Kruse et al. (Eds.): DESRIST 2021, LNCS 12807, pp. 209–222, 2021.
https://doi.org/10.1007/978-3-030-82405-1_22

are needed. We define domain-specific solution materials as descriptions of solutions that take specific software versions, special configurations for companies, company-specific hardware equipment, dependencies between soft-/hardware components, and country-specific properties/laws into account. To decrease downtime and to provide the IT-Support staff, also called agents, with domain-specific high-quality solution material an IT-Support Support System (SUSY) is built in this paper and instantiated as an artifact. A typical workflow after an error occurred to get the IT services running again is as follows. First, the user opens a support request, also called a ticket, and describes the (un)precise error that occurred. The agent then seeks all information needed to identify the problem, categorizes the ticket, and may ask for additional relevant data and communicates with the user. Based on all information the agent tries to solve the problem either by their domain-expert-knowledge or by consulting documentation of the company. Latter often takes a lot of time due to manually searching information in various databases. During the process of solution-finding, all relevant data are being written down in the ticket, making tickets potentially high-quality solution materials that contain the domain knowledge of the organization with step-by-step solutions. This research paper will focus on previously solved tickets to retrieve solution material because (a) they contain precise domain knowledge and (b) are a good complement next to often outdated and resource-intensive knowledge bases. To provide agents with solution material the information retrieval (IR) literature can be used. Nevertheless, while general-purpose solutions also retrieve general solution materials that are not applicable for agents, this paper builds a domain-specific solution material retrieval system. Further, the retrieval system is combined with an algorithm that ensures that agents are only provided with high-quality solution material because thousands of tickets are written every day and most of them do not contain useful information, e.g., "solved the issue". Therefore, solution materials with useful information need to be separated from the ones without. Hence, we define high-quality solution material in this paper as the solution material which was separated from low-quality solution material that does not contain useful information to help solve issues.

Based on relevant literature requirements for the agents during the solution-finding process are identified and design principles (DPs) for the development of SUSY are derived. SUSY will help agents by providing them with domain-specific and high-quality solution material. Finally, this will support agents to find solution material fast and to have more time for documentation of new issues and communication to users. The goal of this paper is to develop DPs that will show researchers and practitioners how to build a SUSY e.g., for rebuilding and improving IT-Support systems. Hence, we formulated the following research question: *How can we use previously solved tickets to provide agents with domain-specific and high-quality solution material?* To achieve the goal and generate the output Fig. 1 shows the DSR process accordingly to Peffers et al. [23] to design and evaluate the DPs following the problem-centered approach. First, an overview of related work will be given that – next to the introduction – motivates the study and shows the objective of the solution. Second, SUSY will be designed and developed based on design requirements (DRs) and DPs which will be instantiated as design features (DFs). Third, the DRs and DPs will be demonstrated as a prototype to multiple focus groups. Last, the DPs and the DFs will be evaluated before a discussion and the conclusion will close the paper.

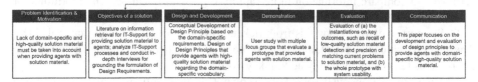

Fig. 1. DSR approach according to Peffers et al. [23]

2 Related Work and Theoretical Background

IT-Support departments are a critical success factor for continuous delivery of IT services for companies and the costs of missing availability can be enormous [12]. There are different data-driven approaches for IT-Support that draw from an interdisciplinary field, such as software engineering, data management, and statistics [12].

By analyzing future events, the failure of systems can be predicted through online failure prediction methods like failure tracking, symptom monitoring, undetected error auditing, and detected error reporting [32]. Many companies route tickets to the corresponding team based on a classification. This classification can be automatized, e.g. by classifying labels in issue tracking systems based on the textual description of an issue [1]. The time needed to fix an issue is an important key performance indicator. Following, predicting the time needed to resolve an incident [15] can help to prioritize work, to allocate resources, to calculate a budget, and to communicate with customers about the time when an issue is fixed [37].

In this paper, we will focus on providing agents with solution material with attention to previously solved tickets. Only a few studies [38, 39] focus on this topic and use ticket summaries to recommend a solution. First, the authors analyze the quality of the possible resolutions to rank them higher/lower according to the quality of the ticket. Second, to recommend a solution, they use a deep neural network ranking model that uses similarity of the summary of the ticket and all possible previously solved tickets together with the measured textual quality from step one. While these studies [38, 39] work with automatically generated incident logs, we focus on user-generated unstructured textual data in the form of tickets making it potentially more complex to compare issues as humans describe the same scenarios in different ways than machines.

The used real-world datasets are company IT-Support tickets and represent organic data [36], which can be leveraged for higher design knowledge relevance. State-of-the-art text classification can be done with Bidirectional Encoder Representations from Transformers (BERT) [6]. However, to analyze our organic data we turn to IR Literature for suitable techniques on how to retrieve solution materials [2]. IR encompasses techniques to find information based on unstructured data. They range from indexing, filtering, to searching techniques [2, 30]. Filtering techniques are based on natural language processing (NLP) and e.g., remove punctuations, or lemmatize words. Indexing techniques map documents and their content (words) to specific numbers that represent the document (e.g., a keyword score that denotes the importance of a word for a document). These indices summarize the information in a document and allow searching techniques to retrieve and compare information more rapidly e.g., with linear search algorithms, or brute force search [30]. These IR techniques can be applied as general-purpose solutions to IT-Support to extract keywords from tickets to find relevant solution materials [18]. These keywords can be maintained (e.g., protégé editor [20]) and extended by word2vec approaches [27] or by manually adding keywords.

Because many previously solved tickets do not contain useful information, we turn to NLP techniques and machine learning (ML) algorithms to detect the quality of solution materials. As shown in [17, 21, 29] the quality of a text can be assessed by extracting text features with NLP (e.g., number of words, timeliness, relevancy, length of the text, the ratio of number of characters to the number of sentences, the ratio of stop words to the number of words, uniqueness measured by term frequency-inverse document frequency (tf-idf), readability measured by Coleman-Liau score), labeling the text quality (e.g., experts, crowdsource), and training an ML algorithm (e.g.: support vector machine, k-nearest neighbor, logistic regression) with the labels and text features.

Overall, to the best of our knowledge, there do not exist IT-Support systems that (a) use domain-specific vocabulary when retrieving solution material and (b) differentiate between high-/low-quality solution material. However, some similarities have been identified with peer support systems, which focus more on the social interaction among its systems, and especially among its peers, and less on the quality issues of each element [16]. To contribute to the existing literature on IT-Support we guide the development of our holistic system that takes domain-specific and high-quality solution material into account and present SUSY.

3 Designing SUSY

3.1 Developing Design Requirements

To ensure that the real-world problems of all IT-Support stakeholders will be considered we (a) conducted literature research about IT-Support and its related problems and challenges, especially in day-to-day routines, and (b) conducted 21 in-depth interviews with stakeholders of the IT-Support e.g., agents, knowledge managers, global managers, etc. To generalize our outcome, we conducted the in-depth interviews with stakeholders from three different IT-Support departments around the globe. Through the formulated DRs the first part of the objectives of the DSR approach according to Peffers et al. [23] is addressed.

While agents are under high pressure and the complexity of infrastructures rises, they often struggle to find appropriate solution material. Automatically retrieved knowledge (**DR1**) would help them find solutions faster because in most cases they still search manually in different databases. This would especially help low-skilled agents. These are often found in external IT-Support departments that have been outsourced [4, 13, 22]. The manual search often takes a long time with up to 30 min until information about a specific error has been retrieved, opening a huge potential for automatically supplying agents with solution material. Nevertheless, different companies offer different IT services that vary in complexity and configuration. The retrieved solution material needs to take this domain-specific vocabulary of the company into account when providing agents with solution material of the exact error (**DR2**). This domain-specific solution material needs to be found especially when the IT-Support is outsourced [4, 10].

Not all tickets are useful as solution material to solve tickets. A ticket might address the same problem but might not be suitable as a guide for solution-seeking agents resulting in wasted time reading the low-quality solution materials that may only contain "solved the problem on phone. Ticket closed". Hence, these low-quality solution materials need to be found and separated (**DR3**) from the high-quality solution materials. As the basis of the problem space, all derived DRs were evaluated in a formative artificial way to match the real-world problems of the IT-Support stakcholders. Accordingly, we asked the stakeholders in the in-depth interviews as well as in subsequent meetings and received great approval after iteratively adapting the DRs several times according to the high-quality feedback gained. After receiving no additional new feedback to further develop the DRs the interview series was stopped after 21 in-depth interviews. The DRs can be found in Fig. 2 together with the derived DPs and instantiated DFs.

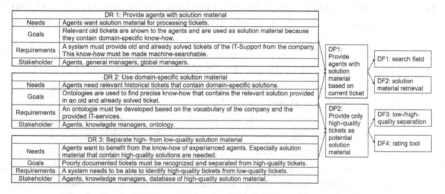

Fig. 2. Derived DRs with the developed DPs and instantiated DFs

3.2 Design Principles for Solution Material Retrieval

Based on the design requirements, we developed two major DPs to (a) provide agents with domain-specific and (b) high-quality solution material based on previously solved tickets. With these DPs we want to address scholars as well as practitioners to build and improve a

SUSY for the IT-Support. The DPs follow the anatomy of Gregor et al. [9] to ensure better reusability and describe the aim, users, implementer, context, mechanism, and rationale. Further, a recommendation that summarizes the whole DP, a visual representation to better understand the core of the DP, and an exemplary technology for implementation to increase the reusability, was added. Ultimately, two DPs were formulated.

DP1 (see Table 1) is informed by the IR literature (e.g.: [2, 19, 20, 27, 30]). It describes how to provide agents with solution material automatically based on their current ticket. In this paper, NLP is used in combination with an ontology. Different NLP techniques are used: (1) Tokenization, (2) removal of numbers, (3) removal of punctuation, (4) lower casing, (5) lemmatization, and (6) stop word removal. We created our ontology using a semi-automated approach. Since the ticket data we use for our project already contains tags that relate tickets to categories (e.g., "password"), we used these tags to initially populate our ontology. Furthermore, we applied keyword extraction methods (tf-idf) and used word embeddings to extend the ontology. To be able to find new terms, we trained a word2vec model on the ticket data. We used this model to find similar terms (or nearest neighbors) to the words already present in the ontology (using cosine similarity) as proposed by [25]. The identified candidate terms were shown to domain experts to evaluate the quality of the results. If deemed relevant the new terms were added to the ontology. These new terms included previously missing concepts and synonyms (e.g., "PW" as an acronym for password) or translations of already known terms. The newly added terms were then appended to the similarity queries on the word2vec model, allowing us to find even more candidate words through this iterative approach. The procedure was discontinued after no new candidate terms were found through the described similarity query. We clustered all ontology terms based on their word vectors derived from word2vec using k-means to segregate the data into meaningful categories. We determined the optimal number of clusters using the within-cluster sums of squares and average silhouette methods. To ensure quality, these clusters were once again evaluated by domain experts.

DP2 (see Table 2) is informed by the literature of text mining and ML (e.g.: [7, 17, 21, 26, 29]) and describes how to separate low-/high-quality solution material to provide agents with high-quality solution material only. In a first step, a set of previously solved tickets needs to be labeled manually according to their solution material quality, e.g., $1 =$ high-quality, $0 =$ low-quality. Next, the first feature readability is extracted based on the Coleman-Liau score. NLP then pre-processes tickets (Tokenization, removal of numbers, removal of punctuation, lower casing, and lemmatization) and automatically extracts more text features, that are, number of sentences, number of verbs, number of nouns, number of stop words, and individuality measured by the sum of the tf-idf indices of a ticket. In the next step, these features have to be compared to select the most appropriate ones for the classification task, e.g. with a Chi-square test. With the final text features and the labels, ML algorithms are trained and then detect low-/high-quality solution material in new sets of tickets. In the last step, the low-quality solution materials are deleted from the set of solution materials, resulting in providing agents with high-quality solution material only. Through continuous feedback from agents during the operation of SUSY, the low-/high-quality solution material detection can further learn resulting in potentially better results the more agents use SUSY.

Table 1. DP1: Provide agents with problem-solution material based on current ticket

Aim, users, and implementer

To provide agents (users) with solution material to solve new issues, similar tickets have to be found from a system (aim) developed by a programmer (implementer)

Context, mechanism

A set of previously solved tickets needs to be compared to a new ticket (context) to retrieve the solution material. This is done by comparing the similarity between new and previously solved tickets considering the domain-specific vocabulary. To do this, an ontology can be built e.g., with a semi-automatic approach that creates the ontology based on frequently occurring terms (e.g., tf-idf algorithm). The ontology can be extended by word embeddings (word2vec), adding similar neighboring terms, or by manually adding words to the ontology (e.g., by agents or knowledge manager). To further improve an ontology its terms can be structured and grouped using clustering algorithms. When comparing tickets, the tickets can be reduced to their most important domain-specific terms. Viewing tickets as a set of those terms, similarity can be measured through metrics like Jaccard similarity

Rationale

Overall, new and previously solved tickets are compared because already solved similar tickets can provide the needed solution material for the current ticket and manual search for solution materials is time-consuming. Next to the ontology, NLP has to be used for various pre-processing steps [14, 31]. These include tokenization, lemmatization, stop word removal [34], part-of-speech tagging [28], dotation removal, number handling, lowercasing, and stemming [5]

Recommendation

Find similar previously solved tickets to a new ticket, extract the solution material, and provide it to agents

Visual representation

Technology for implementation

For NLP we recommend using Python with its' powerful libraries e.g., Stanza for 66 languages [26]. Servers from Microsoft Azure can be used to deploy the code online e.g., the free Azure App Service "F1" with 1 GB RAM, shared kernels, 1 GB storage, and Linux as the operating system. If the whole code-base is saved on GitHub one can build a "pipeline" e.g., between GitHub and the Microsoft Azure App Service to automatically deploy code online when pushing it to GitHub. To create and maintain an ontology one can use the Protégé editor [20]. It allows for the easy creation of ontologies using the web ontology language (OWL) [19]. Furthermore, new classes and instances can be imported using spreadsheets. More advanced text mining techniques like the mentioned word2vec can be applied using the Python library Gensim [27], but it should be kept in mind that they need a vast amount of textual data to produce reasonable results. Clustering and feature extraction (e.g. tf-idf) can be done with scikit-learn [7]

Table 2. DP2: Provide only high-quality tickets as potential solution material

---

Aim, users, and implementer

To provide the domain-specific solution material retrieval system (user, see DP1) with high-quality solution materials (aim) a programmer (implementer) must develop an algorithm that detects the low-quality solution materials and separates them from the high-quality solution materials (aim)

Context, mechanism

A set of previously solved tickets (context) needs to be processed with NLP to create text features that are used within ML algorithms that assess the quality of solution materials (mechanism)

Rationale

The high- and low-quality solution materials need to be separated because only the latter contain well-documented step-by-step solution materials in a way that is understandable for agents. Only the consideration of several text features leads to a selection of the right tickets for the database. According to Otterbacher [21], for measuring the quality of product reviews, the number of sentences and number of words are strongly correlated with the relevance of the review, which is the most important of five criteria for assessing quality. Similar results of the length of a post about its quality were found by Rhyn & Blohm [29] for crowdsourcing texts; it was their strongest predictor. Liu et al. [17] examined the quality of product reviews based on the characteristics of informativeness, subjectivity, and readability

---

Recommendation

Use an algorithm (e.g., logistic regression, k nearest neighbor) for identifying low-quality tickets that considers the most relevant features (e.g., uniqueness, number of verbs, readability, and number of stop words) in terms of ticket quality

---

Visual representation

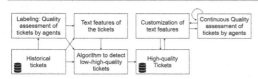

Technology for implementation

For NLP we recommend Python and Stanza [26]. Several different ML algorithms, e.g., from scikit-learn [7], should be tested with different combinations of the extracted text features according to the domain-specific tickets. To measure uniqueness, one can take the sum of the tf-idf indices of a ticket. For readability, the Python package readability 0.3.1 can be used for readability grades such as Coleman-Liau score as well as for further sentence information such as characters per word, word per sentence, etc. To identify the most likely feature candidates that are irrelevant for classification the Chi-squared method from scikit-learn can be used [7]. To label the data, multiple agents should be asked to assess the quality of the tickets to train the algorithms. To measure inter-rater reliability Cohen's kappa can be used

3.3 SUSY and its Design Features

The DPs were applied to design SUSY and its core DFs. Figure 3 illustrates the built DFs derived from the DPs. SUSY is deployed on two Microsoft Azure Web Apps. While the backend is deployed on a Linux-based Web App and written in Python, the frontend is deployed on a Windows-based Web App and written in PHP/Node.JS. The frontend communicates with the backend by an application programming interface.

Whenever agents need solution material, they can simply go to the website of the frontend and either paste the query of the user or search for specific terms (**DF1**: search field). The matching system of SUSY then uses its domain-specific knowledge base and understands the company-specific content of the request. To match the request with a potential solution material the ontology uses the vocabulary and tags the request with the relevant terms. Then, the ontology compares the tags of the request with the potential solution materials and displays the top five matches. We call these matches highly relevant because they are semantically similar and contain the domain-specific information an agent needs to resolve an issue (**DF2**: solution material retrieval). A total of five solution materials are presented to the agents and are of high quality only (**DF3**: low-/high-quality separation). This is provided by the data logic of the backend that pseudonymizes all tickets accordingly to the general data protection regulation and analyzes all potential solution material whether they contain high-quality solution material. Only the pseudonymized tickets of high quality are stored as solution material for the company/agents. To see the perceived quality of solution material agents are given the opportunity to rate solution materials (**DF4**: rating tool). This helps twofold: Firstly, the agents can see which provided solution materials contain perceived high-quality solutions briefly. Secondly, the algorithm that evaluates the quality of the solution material (**DF3**) automatically receives feedback and can learn through the human-in-the-loop design. Thus, the agents receive potentially more high-quality tickets the more they use the system.

Fig. 3. The user interface of SUSY and corresponding design features

4 Evaluation of the DPs and Artifacts

The DPs were evaluated according to the FEDS framework from Venable et al. [35] following the evaluation strategy technical risk and efficacy. The design principles were evaluated (a) via a technical experiment by instantiating the DP1 and DP2 as specific design features (**DF2** and **DF3**, see Fig. 4) and evaluating the performance of the algorithms using real-world data as a summative-naturalistic evaluation, and (b) via an initial prototype evaluation that demonstrates the useability of the instantiated DPs in a summative-naturalistic evaluation (all DFs) with future users of SUSY [24, 35]. According to [11] the evaluation is analytical and experimental to highlight the practical relevance, usefulness, and performance of the artifact in a real-world scenario.

DF2 (solution material retrieval), which is mainly based on **DP1**, matches a query to potential solution material. To prove the value of **DF2** a database of 963 unique tickets of high-quality solution material was used. We searched solution material for 40 different random queries that are based on previously solved tickets to make the evaluation as realistic as possible. Because it is from high interest that agents are provided with very precisely matched solution materials we decided for precision as the key metric. **DF2** presents the agents with a maximum of five solution materials. These retrieved solution materials have been evaluated whether they would help to solve the query or not. The ontology was refined by iteratively adding new terms to its vocabulary using the method described in **DP1**. After several iterations, our final artifact reached a precision of 0,87 for matching high-quality solution material to domain-specific queries. In comparison, a tf-idf search algorithm has been evaluated to the same queries and data set and only reached a precision of 0,29 which shows the applicability of the ontology-based retrieval.

DF3 (low-/high-quality separation), which is mainly based on **DP2**, detects low-quality solution material based on extracted text features and deletes the low-quality solutions. First, a total of 800 tickets were labeled from two different persons with a Cohen's kappa of 0,71, suggesting a substantial agreement between the annotators. Next, the dataset was split into a training (n = 480) and an evaluation (n = 320) dataset, and the algorithms k nearest neighbor, logistic regression, decision tree, support vector machine, and two-class-Bayes were evaluated. Because it is important to detect as many low-quality solution materials as possible, we decided for the recall of low-quality solution materials as the key metric. The final model (logistic regression with the features number of verbs, uniqueness, readability, and number of stop words) reached a recall of 0,91 for detecting the class of low-quality solution material as indicated in Table 3. This table also shows the accuracy, F1, recall, and precision based on the weighted average as well as the precision for the class of low-quality solution materials.

To further evaluate the DPs through instantiations SUSY was evaluated as a summative-artificial evaluation through five focus groups with stakeholders of the IT-Support of five to six people each. To analyze the strengths and weaknesses of SUSY qualitative techniques were used. Based on these results of the "start, stop, continue" exercise the DPs, as well as the DFs, were further developed. Last, the System Usability Scale [3] to evaluate the overall usability of SUSY was used. The dataset of the participants was limited to the participants of the focus groups because they are the alpha tester. The data provides preliminary evidence to suggest that the alpha version of SUSY already has good usability, with a score of 76,4 (n = 18) [3]. Overall, the DPs have been

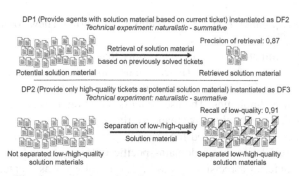

Fig. 4. Evaluation of the instantiations of DP1 and DP2

Table 3. DF3 Evaluation – class of low-quality (lq) and weighted average (wa)

Algorithm	Rec_{lq}	$Prec_{lq}$	Acc	Rec_{wa}	$Prec_{wa}$	$F1_{wa}$	$F1_{wa[Train]}$
k-nn	0,81	0,70	0,68	0,68	0,67	0,67	0,82
Log. Reg.	0,91	0,72	0,74	0,74	0,73	0,73	0,63
Dec. Tree	0,81	0,74	0,71	0,71	0,70	0,70	0,71
SVM	0,80	0,79	0,75	0,73	0,73	0,73	0,70
2Class Bayes	0,88	0,68	0,68	0,68	0,67	0,62	0,59

evaluated as instantiations in summative-naturalistic ways using real-world data. While SUSY is still in the alpha phase the prototype proves preliminary evidence for good useability, and DF2 and DF3 already show sufficient results regarding previous studies: **DF2** reached a precision of 0,87 based on 40 queries. For comparison, in [33] ten queries were evaluated with an ontology-based retrieval system for IT-Support that reached a precision of 0,86 compared to a keyword-based approach that reached a precision of 0,13. **DF3** reached a recall of 0,91 to detect low-quality solution materials while in a similar study [29] crowd-support texts were analyzed and the detection of low-quality texts reached a recall of 0,75.

5 Discussion, Implications, and Future Work

This paper presents a way to provide the IT-Support with domain-specific (DP1) and high-quality (DP2) solution material based on previously solved tickets and a domain-specific ontology. Based on issues from the IT-Support we generated DRs applicable for agents during the solution-finding process. These DRs describe the call for solution material (DR1), considering the domain-specific vocabulary (DR2), and the detection of low-quality solution material to separate them from the high-quality data (DR3). Based on these DRs DPs were derived and DFs were instantiated as a prototype while all outputs of the DSR paper were constantly evaluated during all stages. There is a known body of knowledge to retrieve solution material for the IT Support e.g., from IR, ML, and data mining communities. By combining these known solutions the identified novel problems were solved making SUSY an exception that shows a new solution to a known problem [8].

The DPs are formulated based on an anatomy that gives deep insides into the theoretical and practical decisions done. Hence, we not only share design knowledge in the form of DPs but also give relevant tips for the implementation and present examples for the selection of technologies. The used data is based on an organic [36] real-world dataset of tickets that companies have made available to us. This means that the data is not designed and was not generated for research purposes. The instantiated DP1 provides preliminary evidence that a domain-specific ontology is well suited to retrieve precise solution material (precision = 0,87). The ontology was created with a semi-automatic approach based on frequently occurring terms and was extended by manually adding important keywords. In future research, we want to extend the ontology with word-embeddings. DP2 provides that text mining techniques in combination with ML algorithms predict low-quality solution material with a high recall (recall = 0,91). In specific, logistic regression with four text features was used. In future studies, we want to add non-text features, e.g., the total time to fix and the number of involved agents to further improve the algorithm.

The derived DPs allow future research in that direction and so are not without limitations. The DPs and DFs were only evaluated with alpha testers and SUSY will soon be rolled out to more testers to gain deeper insights. In upcoming works, we also want to show that the derived DPs increase the productivity of agents and want to derive more DPs that focus on highlighting the unstructured text in different parts (e.g.: solution, problem, noise) to analyze the unstructured text faster.

In conclusion, we focused on (1) deriving theoretically and practically grounded DRs, (2) developing DPs and their artifacts, (3) evaluating each instantiation, and (4) evaluating the summative-naturalistic design of SUSY. Addressing these four steps, a set of DPs to support the development and instantiation of future support systems for the IT-Support were presented. Through the DPs and DFs, we hope to inspire researchers to rebuild/further develop SUSY to solve the day-to-day problems of the IT-Support when searching for solution material as the IT-Support is one of the most important departments of a company and keeps all IT services running.

This research is funded by the German Federal Ministry of Education and Research (BMBF) and supervised by PTKA (Project HISS - 02K18D060).

References

1. Alonso-Abad, J.M., López-Nozal, C., Maudes-Raedo, J.M., Marticorena-Sánchez, R.: Label prediction on issue tracking systems using text mining. Prog. Artif. Intell. **8**(3), 325–342 (2019). https://doi.org/10.1007/s13748-019-00182-2
2. Baeza-Yates, R., Ribeiro-Neto, B.: Modern Information Retrieval. ACM press, New York (1999)
3. Brooke, J.: SUS: A "Quick and Dirty" usability scale. In: Jordan, P.W., Thomas, B., Weerdmeester, B.A., et al. (eds.) Usability Evaluation in Industry, pp. 189–194. Taylor & Francis, London (1996)
4. Chagnon, C., Trapp, A., Djamasbi, S.: Creating a decision support system for service classification and assignment through optimization. In: AMCIS 2017 Proceedings (2017)

5. Denny, M., Spirling, A.: Text preprocessing for unsupervised learning: why it matters, when it misleads, and what to do about it. Polit. Anal. **26**, 168–189 (2018)
6. Devlin, J., Chang, M.-W., Lee, K., et al.: BERT: Pre-training of Deep Bidirectional Transformers for Language Understanding. arXiv preprint arXiv:1810.04805 (2018)
7. Pedregosa, F., Varoquaux, G., Gramfort, A., et al.: Scikit-learn: machine learning in Python. J. Mach. Learn. Res. **12**, 2825–2830 (2011)
8. Gregor, S., Hevner, A.R.: Positioning and presenting design science research for maximum impact. MIS Q. **37**, 337–355 (2013)
9. Gregor, S., Kruse, L.C., Seidel, S.: The anatomy of a design principle. J. Assoc. Inf. Syst. Forthcoming (2020)
10. Grupe, F.H.: Outsourcing the help desk function. Inf. Syst. Manag. **14**, 15–22 (1997). https://doi.org/10.1080/10580539708907040
11. Hevner, A.R., March, S.T., Park, J., et al.: Design science in information systems research. MIS Q. **28**, 75–105 (2004). https://doi.org/10.2307/25148625
12. Kubiak, P., Rass, S.: An overview of data-driven techniques for IT-Service-Management. IEEE Access **6**, 63664–63688 (2018). https://doi.org/10.1109/ACCESS.2018.2875975
13. Lacity, M.C., Khan, S.A., Willcocks, L.P.: A review of the IT outsourcing literature: insights for practice. J. Strateg. Inf. Syst. **18**, 130–146 (2009)
14. Lamkanfi, A., Demeyer, S., Soetens, Q.D., et al.: Comparing mining algorithms for predicting the severity of a reported bug. In: 15th European Conference on Software Maintenance and Reengineering, pp. 249–258 (2011)
15. Lee, Y., Lee, S., Lee, C.-G., et al.: Continual prediction of bug-fix time using deep learning-based activity stream embedding. IEEE Access **8**, 10503–10515 (2020)
16. Li, M.M., Peters, C., Leimeister, J.M.: Designing a peer-based support system to support shakedown. In: International Conference on Information Systems (2017)
17. Liu, J., Cao, Y., Lin, C.-Y., et al.: Low-quality product review detection in opinion summarization. In: Proceedings of the 2007 Joint Conference on Empirical Methods in Natural Language Processing and Computational Natural Language Learning, pp. 334–342 (2007)
18. Manning, C.D., Raghavan, P., Schütze, H.: Introduction to Information Retrieval. Cambridge University Press, Cambridge (2008)
19. McGuinness, D.L., Van Harmelen, F.: OWL Web Ontology Language Overview. W3C Recommend 10 (2004)
20. Musen, M.A.: The protégé project: a look back and a look forward. AI Matters **1**, 4–12 (2015). https://doi.org/10.1145/2757001.2757003
21. Otterbacher, J.: 'Helpfulness' in online communities. In: Proceedings of the SIGCHI Conference on Human Factors in Computing Systems, pp. 955–964 (2009)
22. Patil, S., Patil, Y.S.: A review on outsourcing with a special reference to telecom operations. Procedia. Soc. Behav. Sci. **133**, 400–416 (2014)
23. Peffers, K., Tuunanen, T., Rothenberger, M.A., et al.: A design science research methodology for information systems research. J. Manag. Inf. Syst. **24**, 45–77 (2007)
24. Peffers, K., Rothenberger, M., Tuunanen, T., et al.: Design science research evaluation. In: International Conference on Design Science Research in Information Systems, pp. 398–410 (2012)
25. Pembeci, İ: Using word embeddings for ontology enrichment. Int. J. Intell. Syst. Appl. Eng. **4**, 49–56 (2016). https://doi.org/10.18201/ijisae.58806
26. Qi, P., Zhang, Y., Zhang, Y., et al.: Stanza: A Python Natural Language Processing Toolkit for Many Human Languages. arXiv preprint arXiv:2003.07082 (2020)
27. Radim, R., Sojka, P.: Software framework for topic modelling with large corpora. In: Proceedings of the LREC 2010 Workshop on New Challenges for NLP Frameworks, pp. 45–50 (2010)

28. Rajman, M., Besançon, R.: Text mining: natural language techniques and text mining applications. In: Spaccapietra, S., Maryanski, F. (eds.) Data Mining and Reverse Engineering. ITIFIP, pp. 50–64. Springer, Boston, MA (1998). https://doi.org/10.1007/978-0-387-35300-5_3

29. Rhyn, M., Blohm, I.: A machine learning approach for classifying textual data in crowdsourcing. In: Wirtschaftsinformatik 2017 Proceedings (2017)

30. Roshdi, A., Roohparvar, A.: Review: information retrieval techniques and applications. Int. J. Comput. Netw. Commun. Secur. **3**, 373–377 (2015)

31. Runeson, P., Alexandersson, M., Nyholm, O.: Detection of duplicate defect reports using natural language processing. In: International Conference on Software Engineering, pp. 499–510 (2007)

32. Salfner, F., Lenk, M., Malek, M.: A survey of online failure prediction methods. ACM Comput. Surv. **42**, 1–42 (2010). https://doi.org/10.1145/1670679.1670680

33. Shanavas, N., Asokan, S.: Ontology-based document mining system for IT support service. Procedia Comput. Sci. **46**, 329–336 (2015). https://doi.org/10.1016/j.procs.2015.02.028

34. Srividhya, V., Anitha, R.: Evaluating preprocessing techniques in text categorization. Int. J. Comput. Sci. Appl. **47**, 49–51 (2010)

35. Venable, J., Pries-Heje, J., Baskerville, R.: FEDS: a framework for evaluation in design science research. Eur. J. Inf. Syst. **25**, 77–89 (2016). https://doi.org/10.1057/ejis.2014.36

36. Xu, H., Zhang, N., Zhou, L.: Validity concerns in research using organic data. J. Manag. **46**, 1257–1274 (2020). https://doi.org/10.1177/0149206319862027

37. Yedida, R., Yang, X., Menzies, T.: When SIMPLE is better than complex: a case study on deep learning for predicting Bugzilla issue close time. arXiv preprint arXiv:2101.06319v1 (2021)

38. Zhou, W., Tang, L., Zeng, C., et al.: Resolution recommendation for event tickets in service management. IEEE Trans. Netw. Serv. Manage. **13**, 954–967 (2016). https://doi.org/10.1109/TNSM.2016.2587807

39. Zhou, W., Xue, W., Baral, R., et al.: STAR: a system for ticket analysis and resolution. In: Proceedings of the 23rd ACM, pp. 2181–2190. https://doi.org/10.1145/3097983.3098190 (2017)

'Caution – Principle Under Construction' a Visual Inquiry Tool for Developing Design Principles

Frederik Möller[1,2]([⊠]), Thorsten Schoormann[3], and Boris Otto[1,2]

[1] TU Dortmund University, Dortmund, Germany
{frederik.moeller,boris.otto}@tu-dortmund.de
[2] Fraunhofer ISST, 44227 Dortmund, Germany
[3] University of Hildesheim, 31141 Hildesheim, Germany
thorsten.schoormann@uni-hildesheim.de

Abstract. Researchers and practitioners often face challenges in structuring larger design projects and, therefore, struggle to capture, discuss, and reflect on essential components that should be considered. These first steps are, however, of great importance because decisions such as in terms of selecting an underpinning (kernel) theory, following certain development approaches, or specifying knowledge sources impact the resulting design solution. To provide a frame for developing one of the dominant forms of prescriptive knowledge in information systems (IS), we present the 'Principle Constructor' that seeks to support the iterative endeavor of formulating design principles. This so-called visual inquiry tool is grounded in previous research on design knowledge and an empirical analysis of IS articles that present principles, built according to available guidance for this class of tools, and evaluated through several workshops. Doing this, we provide an underlying structure with building blocks for creating design principles and complement research on their anatomy and development procedures.

Keywords: Visual inquiry tool · Design principles · Design knowledge

1 Problem Awareness

The primary goal of Design Science Research (DSR) is to accumulate prescriptive design knowledge that explains how something *should be* [1–4]. Design principles are the prevailing mechanism in IS to codify such knowledge [5], and thus are an essential outcome of DSR projects [6–8], even though there has been an ongoing discussion on the topic of valid results of DSR (i.e., material artifacts versus design theory) [9].

To arrive at an adequate set of design principles, novice researchers frequently navigate the literature on design science and design theory to identify and distill methodological guidance on how to develop such principles. They are tasked with publishing design-oriented research transparently and understandably to their peers and reviewers to, for example, allow knowledge accumulation. From our analysis and personal experiences, we know the former to be a significant challenge. This is also evident by

© Springer Nature Switzerland AG 2021
L. Chandra Kruse et al. (Eds.): DESRIST 2021, LNCS 12807, pp. 223–235, 2021.
https://doi.org/10.1007/978-3-030-82405-1_23

statements of participants in this study's design cycles (see, for example, Sect. 3 and 5) who stressed hurdles in terms of planning design projects (e.g., considering the main parts at the beginning of a project to be able to derive well-grounded design knowledge afterward), following an underlying structure, collaborating with different roles and stakeholders, translating principles into practice.

Since design principles are an increasingly published meta-artifact [10] and gain importance for DSR, we propose a tool—the *'Principle Constructor'*—that seeks to support design principle development and communication to enrich papers with a clear structure and an argumentative bedrock. For that purpose, we draw from the notion of *visual inquiry tools*, which are appropriate to make complex design endeavors understandable, transferable, and communicable. In addition to existing methodological guidance, visual inquiry tools foster intuitive collaboration (e.g., academic-practice teams) and can contribute to the standardization of how design principles are developed and published [11, 12]. These tools give researchers a 'checklist', enabling them to keep in mind what they should reflect when developing principles. Hence, we argue that the artifact will be a significant extension of the accessibility of design principle development and complement existing approaches in this field (e.g., [8, 13, 14]). Hence, we formulate the following research question (RQ): *How to design a visual inquiry tool to structure design principles development and communication?*

For answering this, we utilized the DSR framework from Hevner et al. [15], applied the general build-evaluate pattern, and derived our artifact, the 'Principle Constructor'. In terms of building, we grounded our artifact in available research on design knowledge (deduction), reviewed IS articles presenting design principles (induction), and iteratively designed/refined our tool within the author team. Furthermore, as design principles, *per se*, have a "(...) practical ethos" [16 p. 1] and should be reused, we draw from the design principles for visual inquiry tools as proposed by [12]. For evaluation, we conducted a workshop with several IS researchers in which we reflected on typical challenges, ranked the importance of building blocks, and discussed possible tool designs. With this, we hope to leverage the full potential of design principles by contributing to the joint development (e.g., academic-practice collaboration), the structure and building blocks to be considered, and the reporting of the findings.

Our paper is structured as follows. Following the Introduction, Sect. 2 briefly outlines the background of design principles. Section 3 describes this study's research design. Section 4 illustrates our findings, which are evaluated in Sect. 5. Finally, Sect. 6 presents our contributions, limitations, and avenues for further research.

2   Research Background

Design principles help to codify design knowledge in prescriptive linguistic statements [17]. There are various ways to generate design principles, foundationally, differing between reflective *ex-post* and supportive *ex-ante* approaches [13]. Design principles can be classified as the *theory of design and action* in [18]'s taxonomy of theory and follow the basic paradigm of prescriptions of [19]'s *technological rules*. Rather than addressing a single instance of a problem or a solution, design principles should be adequately abstract to address a class of problems and artifacts [17].

Fundamentally, design principles are a key element of *design theory* [17, 20], for which reason we draw from [21]'s concepts of an *Information Systems Design Theory*. They require a *solution objective* that describes what the intended artifact is supposed to do [22]. From solution objectives, one can derive *meta-requirements* using a variety of underlying knowledge bases (e.g., empirical evidence [13] that addresses the class of goals rather than the instance [23]). Recent research proposes different formulation templates in terms of the actual linguistic formulation [24].

3   Research Design

To achieve our overall goal, designing a visual inquiry tool, we follow the DSR paradigm as an iterative framework that oscillates between *rigor* and *relevance* [15] (see Fig. 1) and ran through two main design cycles. We decided to create such a type of tool because they promote joint innovation, improvement, and communication (e.g., based on a non-verbal and shared understanding across disciplines), and some of them are of increasing interest in academia and practice alike [12]. Accordingly, we believe that a visual inquiry tool is fruitful for design principles as well, especially to allow communication of (interim) results with all stakeholders, to plan and reflect on important project decisions before and during a design project (see aforementioned challenges in Sect. 1), and address the iterative nature of developing principles.

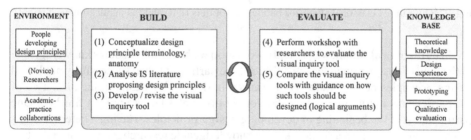

Fig. 1. Research framework based on [15] and [25].

In terms of **building** the first version of our artifact, we performed three main activities for (1) conceptualizing available knowledge (see Sect. 2), (2) analyzing articles that publish design principles, and (3) developing a visual inquiry tool. The knowledge we are looking for is engraved in the literature on DSR and design principles.

Subsequently, we opt for a systematic literature review [26]. Our literature search strategy strives to collect a *representative sample* that adequately gives insight into how design principles are developed and published [27]. We construct the sample consisting of both high-quality papers from journals and conference proceedings. We draw from the recently published sample of papers publishing design principles in [25] to obtain journal articles. We completed this by using *AISeL* and *Scopus* to search for articles in *ICIS, ECIS,* and *DESRIST*. We used the keyword "design principle" in *Title* and *Abstract* to find papers. We then screened each paper's full-text and excluded those that do not explicitly report on design principles. We collected a sample of 156 (see Fig. 2) articles that we have randomized and reduced to a sub-sample of 40 conference papers and 20 journal articles. Based on that search strategy, we analyzed inductively for design principle development components until theoretical saturation [28].

Subsequently, we formulated a strategy for analyzing the data. Two researchers analyzed each paper using an initial *a priori* defined coding scheme. The initial codes stem from our experience in design principle development and include, for example, a *knowledge base* for the design principles. We then refined the coding scheme through inductive analysis. Through the generation of codes, we develop initial building blocks.

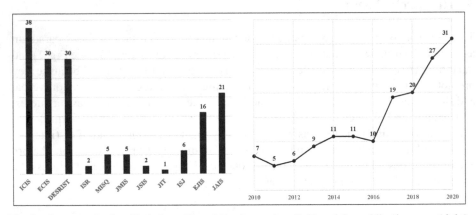

Fig. 2. Our sample classified alongside publication outlets (left) and the publication year (right).

In terms of **evaluation**, we (4) held a workshop with six PhD-students knowledgeable in the field of design principles [29]. Three of the participants had successfully published design principles before or are very advanced in developing design principles. Two of the participants are in the midst of developing principles but are not yet finished. One participant is at the beginning of developing design principles. Having a heterogeneous group enables us to gather feedback from knowledgeable researchers that can reflect on their individual (sometimes multiple) design principles projects and give feedback on our artifact's usefulness. Additionally, having participants that are currently developing design principles enables us to collect feedback from potential users of the visual inquiry tool in the early stages of their projects. After giving a short introduction (purpose of the workshop, definitions of terminology, questions) and discussing typical challenges within the group, we asked the participants to rank and sort building block candidates that we have identified in the literature.

In design cycle 2, based on the lessons learned obtained from the evaluation episodes performed during the first cycle, we refined our canvas and (4) discussed how the guidelines for visual inquiry tools from [12] are addressed by our artifact.

4   A Visual Inquiry Tool for Design Principles

4.1   The 'Principle Constructor' and Its Building Blocks

Based on our initial, mainly conceptually driven understanding of design principle development, the advancement of this understanding through examining IS articles reporting design principles, and our evaluation, we present the current version of the 'Principle Constructor' (see Fig. 3). Our tool comprises 16 building blocks arranged across four major and interrelated areas, namely 'foundation and grounding', 'problem and goal', 'solution', and 'design and evaluation'. We decided to incorporate more building blocks to allow a more specific and in-depth reflection and communication of design principles—which is also requested by the participants during the evaluation.

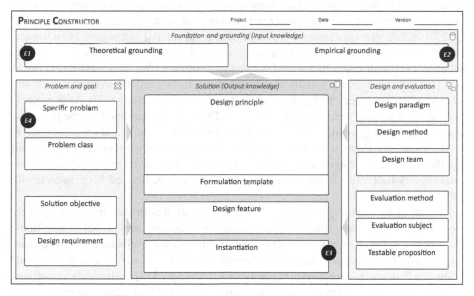

Fig. 3. A visual inquiry tool for design principles.

In the following, we describe the areas and the building blocks in more detail. Thereby, we provide references to our approach for identifying the blocks: We first identified pertinent literature concepts that conceptualize the design principles' nature and how they are developed (i.e., *deduction*), and then used these concepts as a theoretical lens to analyze papers proposing design principles (i.e., *induction*) [30].

The heart of our inquiry tool addresses the actual **solution** (i.e., output knowledge) and distinguishes between building blocks for *design principle, formulation template, design feature*, and *instantiation*. We begin with the design principles addressing the requirements and goals. Some authors use pre-defined templates to formulate their principles, e.g., by [17]. To guide how to operationalize design principles, studies provide *design features* (e.g., [31]) that bridge the gap between abstract knowledge and concrete/situated implementations. We integrated a block for instantiation, taking different forms such as a software prototype (e.g., [32]) or a process (e.g., [33]).

To arrive at those solutions, the **foundation and grounding** (i.e., input knowledge) area capture two building blocks for a *theoretical* and an *empirical* grounding of the design principles [4]. In this spirit, the grounding of design principles follows a *bottom-up strategy* that draws on empirical data engraved, for instance, in existing literature use cases, artifacts, documents, and in the experience of experts/users; or a *top-down* strategy in which principles build upon a theoretical foundation such as a kernel theory that explains why the prescriptive design knowledge should work [21]. In our sample, diverse kernel theories were used, e.g., *sensemaking* [32] or *organizational learning theory* [34]. Additionally, in line with knowledge accumulation and evaluation, the theoretical-driven approach can draw from existing design principles or general design knowledge (e.g., [35]) to develop new or extended (e.g., [36]) design principles.

The area **problem and goal** differentiate in the problem space between building blocks for a *specific problem* and the more abstract *problem class* and, from a solution-oriented view, between *solution objective* (i.e., the goal the artifact is supposed to fulfill [13, 22]) and *design requirement*. We can observe substantial heterogeneity in the terminology used to describe elements of design principles in our sample, for instance, key challenge [37], user requirement [38], design requirement [39], and meta-requirement [40]. That differentiation is usually associated with a dichotomy between theory-driven and practice-driven research (e.g., through the point of artifact design [13]). ADR projects typically do not elicit meta-requirements [13]. That can be explained by the inductive nature of ADR that generates design principles from a design study and specific cases [8, 13, 41]. Even though the term meta-requirement is often used for requirements derived from theory and user/design requirements for requirements derived from empiricism, our visual inquiry tool refers to design requirements that can be derived both theoretically and/or empirically.

Regarding the actual goal of a study, research articles in our sample frequently report research questions. Based on the analysis, we obtained three types of questions: First, *principle-driven question* (what) asking specifically for "[w]hat are the appropriate design principles for (…)?" (e.g., [42]). Second, *requirements-driven questions* (what) asking "[w]hat are the meta-requirements of (…)" (e.g., [43]). Third, *design-driven questions* (how) asking "[h]ow can we develop (…)" (e.g., [12]). Although most papers in our sample use *what*-questions, we recommend using the *how*-questions to emphasize the overarching goal of a design study.

Design and evaluation comprise building blocks for developing principles, including *design paradigm, design method, design team, evaluation method, evaluation subject*, and *testable proposition*. The design paradigm describes the underlying strategy to develop design principles, e.g., whether they are reflected from a design process or a case study. Next to ADR [8], the two dominant *DSR methods* in our sample are [44, 45]. For *evaluation*, the articles in our sample draw on the rich body of DSR methods and thus use, for example, *instantiations to demonstrate* the principle's applicability (e.g., [39]), *focus groups to discuss* the expected usefulness with practitioners (e.g., [46]), and *case studies* (e.g., [47]). Subsequently, the *evaluation method* refers to 'how' the design principles are evaluated, and the *evaluation subject* specifies with and for 'whom'. *Testable propositions* refer to short statements that guide the user of design principles to be tested against the meta-requirements [48]. Table 1 explains each 'building block' through formulating key questions that they address.

4.2 Recommendations for Using the 'Principle Constructor'

We present exemplary key questions that should be reflected during the inquiry tool's application (see Table 1), which we have derived during its construction and evaluation phase. Moreover, we propose entry points (see E1–E4, Fig. 3) to start a project.

In line with other DSR methodologies [44], we deduced four entry points from our sample, from which the rest of the fields should be filled out:

- *E1 (theory-driven de-abstraction)*: Deductive approach translating theoretical knowledge (e.g., kernel theory) into requirements and design principles.
- *E2 (empiricism-driven abstraction)*: Inductive approach generalizing empirical knowledge (e.g., interview transcripts) into more abstract design principles.
- *E3 (artifact-driven abstraction)*: Inductive approach generalizing knowledge obtained from (using) a specific instance into more abstract design principles.
- *E4 (use case-driven abstraction)*: Inductive approach reflecting on interventions and activities within a specific use case/problem scenario to generalize specific knowledge into more abstract design principles.

5 Demonstration and Evaluation

For ensuring the applicability and usefulness of our artifact, we next summarize selected results and observations that emerged from the evaluation (see also Sect. 3) and discuss how our artifact addresses the guidelines for visual inquiry tools from [14].

During our *evaluative workshop*, participants agreed and supported several challenges when developing design principles, such as the 'start dilemma', which refers to the planning stage of design projects' complexity; important design decisions need to be carried out. After ranking our tool's building blocks and discussing a preliminary version, participants stressed the relevance and expected usefulness. They argued, for instance, that the tool will be beneficial in the early stages to creatively and jointly plan design projects with different stakeholders from both academia and practice. Moreover, they highlighted the kit-inspired functionality of our tool that helps novice researchers reflect on important decisions such as selecting methods and underpinning theories and getting impulses on what components should be considered. Based on a five-point Likert scale (from 1 not agree to 5 agree), several building blocks were ranked as highly important with an average over 4.3: empirical foundation, (meta) requirement, design principle, solution objectives, formulation template, underlying paradigm, development method, and evaluation method. In a nutshell, all blocks suggested were classified as necessary, which is evident by an overall average value of 4.05.

Additionally, for evaluating our artifact by means of *logical arguments*, we compare our artifact with the general principles for visual inquiry tools (see. Table 2).

Table 1. Building blocks and exemplary key questions.

Area	Building block	Key questions
Problem and goal	Specific Problem	What is the actual problem to be addressed? Which use case/scenario raises a specific problem?
	Problem class	To which class of problems does a specific problem belong? Which class of problems is addressed?
	Solution Objective	What is the artifact supposed to do (intended effects)? For whom is a corresponding solution important?
	Design requirement	Which are the main requirements for a solution? From what sources can the requirements be extracted?
Foundation	Theoretical grounding	Which (kernel) theories support the phenomena investigated? Which available design knowledge can be (re-)used?
	Empirical grounding	Which sources can be used to inform the design? What data is available and can be (re-)used to inform the design?
Design and evaluation	Design paradigm	What is the underpinning research paradigm? How do I enter the design process?
	Design method	Which basic structure (procedure model) can be followed? Which (research) method can be used and why?
	Design team	Who develops the design principles (academic/practice)? What experts can be consulted?
	Evaluation method	What are quantitative and/or qualitative methods can be used? What are the potential benefits and shortcomings of a method?
	Evaluation subject	Which are the main solution's target user groups? Who evaluated the design principles and why?

(continued)

Table 1. (*continued*)

Area	Building block	Key questions
	Testable proposition	What are the effects occurring from using the solution? How can an effect be tested and/or measured?
Solution	Design principle	What is the intended principle's level of abstraction? Which class of artifact do the design principles address?
	Formulation template	How can the design principles be formulated? Which design principle anatomy components are addressed?
	Design feature	How can the design principles be operationalized? What is needed to further guide the operationalization?
	Instantiation	What are exemplary instantiations of the design principles? How does an instantiated artifact look like?

6 Conclusions, Limitations, and Outlook

There are many ways to develop design principles [13]. Complementing existing methodological guidance, the 'Principle Constructor' is helpful for researchers that endeavor to publish design principles and use it as a 'checklist'. Subsequently, we **contribute** to the overall corpus of DSR as we enable researchers in all stages of their academic careers to develop design principles more rigorously and transparently. Our framework can innovate new ways of design principle development, challenge existing approaches, and intuitively communicate findings to reviewers. A significant advantage to existing methodological (e.g., [13, 14]) or formulating guidance (e.g., [17, 20]) is the accessibility of the visual inquiry tool, which, intuitively, represents the most essential building blocks for design principle development that need to be 'filled out'. Methods and formulation schemes both have a place in our tool, rather than making it an umbrella that complements, contextualizes, structures, and organizes design principle development. Other visual inquiry tools for DSR (e.g., [49] or [50]) are scoped to represent a complete DSR process, while our tool narrowly and explicitly focuses on the meta-artifact *design principle*. Whereas other approaches are rather methodic and rigid, our tool has the same benefits as any visual inquiry tool, fostering innovation through collaborative and iterative design. It allows for freely innovating and planning and also gives clear conceptual borders particular to design principles. The visual inquiry tool contributes to the broader discussion on tool-support for design science research [51].

Our work is subject to **limitations**, opening avenues for future research. Even though we reached *theoretical saturation*, naturally, the sample can be extended. While we

Table 2. Design principles of visual inquiry tools as proposed by [12, p. 22].

DP		Implementation in this study's artifact
Conceptual model	Frame	The tool has mutually exclusive/collective exhaustive blocks
	Rigor & relevance	The tool builds on available knowledge and practices on developing and communicating design principles from IS literature
	Parsimony	The tool consists of 16 building blocks across four areas, more than other canvas-based approaches. Participants during evaluation asked for more guidance on what should be reflected
Shared visualization	Functionality	The tool's building blocks are represented as empty problem spaces to support the directions for use
	Arrangement	The tool draws on logical flow, e.g., in the solution area, from abstract knowledge in the top to specific knowledge. The areas themselves are summaries of interrelated 'building blocks'
	Facilitation	The tool has small icons for graphical support
Directions	Ideation	The tool provides four different entry points that guide users in a certain situation or objective within a project. Ideas, problems, and (interim) results can be stored and jointly refined
	Prototyping	
	Presentation	

incorporated knowledge from researchers, there is room for further testing in future research projects. Also, naming our building blocks is a consensus of the authors. Others might use different terminology (e.g., instead of *design requirements,* one might use *meta-requirements*), making it a product, to some extent, of our interpretation on how to develop design principles and the constructs in that process. Moreover, our work is restricted to the timespan of its development and thus is a snapshot in time. In the **next steps**, we plan to set up additional evaluation studies (e.g., longitudinal studies), employ them in academic-practice collaborations, and gather feedback on their performance.

We hope to complement the valuable stream of research on guiding design principle development (e.g., anatomy, formulation, methods) that is already available within the IS discipline by shedding light on what components should be reflected during corresponding projects. The initial evaluations indicate promising results, especially supporting novice researchers to perform, develop, and report design principles jointly.

References

1. van Aken, J.E.: Management research as a design science: articulating the research products of mode 2 knowledge production in management. Br. J. Manag. **16**, 19–36 (2005)
2. Vom Brocke, J., Winter, R., Hevner, A., Maedche, A.: Accumulation and evolution of design knowledge in design science research - a journey through time and space. J. Assoc. Inf. Syst. **21**, 520–544 (2020)

3. Legner, C., Pentek, T., Otto, B.: Accumulating design knowledge with reference models: insights from 12 years' research into data management. J. Assoc. Inf. Syst. **21**, 735–770 (2020)
4. Niiniluoto, I.: The aim and structure of applied research. Erkenntnis **38**, 1–21 (1993)
5. Chandra Kruse, L., Seidel, S.: Tensions in design principle formulation and reuse. In: Proceedings of the 12th International Conference on Design Science Research in Information Systems and Technology (2017)
6. Gregor, S., Hevner, A.R.: Positioning and presenting design science research for maximum impact. MIS Quart. Manag. Inform. Syst. **37**, 337–355 (2013)
7. Chandra Kruse, L., Seidel, S., Purao, S.: Making use of design principles. In: Proceedings of the 11th International Conference on Design Science Research in Information Systems and Technology, pp. 37–51 (2016)
8. Sein, M.K., Henfridsson, O., Purao, S., Rossi, M., Lindgren, R.: Action design research. MIS Quart. Manag. Inform. Syst. **35**, 37–56 (2011)
9. Baiyere, A., Hevner, A., Gregor, S., Rossi, M., Baskerville, R.: Artifact and/or theory? Publishing design science research in IS. In: Proceedings of the 36th International Conference on Information Systems (2015)
10. Iivari, J.: Towards information systems as a science of meta-artifacts. Commun. Assoc. Inf. Syst. **12**, 568–581 (2003)
11. Chandra Kruse, L., Nickerson, J.: Portraying design essence. In: Proceedings of the 51st Hawaii International Conference on System Sciences, pp. 4433–4442 (2018)
12. Avdiji, H., Elikan, D.A., Missonier, S., Pigneur, Y.: A design theory for visual inquiry tools. J. Assoc. Inf. Syst. **21**, 695–734 (2020)
13. Möller, F., Guggenberger, T., Otto, B.: Towards a method for design principle development in information systems. In: Hofmann, S., Müller, O., Rossi, M. (eds.) DESRIST 2020. LNCS, vol. 12388, pp. 208–220. Springer, Cham (2020). https://doi.org/10.1007/978-3-030-64823-7_20
14. Kuechler, W., Vaishnavi, V.: A framework for theory development in design science research: multiple perspectives. J. Assoc. Inf. Syst. **13**, 395–423 (2012)
15. Hevner, A.R., March, S.T., Park, J., Ram, S.: Design science in information systems research. MIS Quart. Manag. Inf. Syst. **28**, 75–105 (2004)
16. Iivari, J., Hansen, M.R.P., Haj-Bolouri, A.: A framework for light reusability evaluation of design principles in design science research. In: Proceedings of the 13th International Conference on Design Science Research in Information Systems and Technology (2018)
17. Chandra Kruse, L., Seidel, S., Gregor, S.: Prescriptive knowledge in IS research: conceptualizing design principles in terms of materiality, action, and boundary conditions. In: Proceedings of the 48th Hawaii International Conference on System Sciences (2015)
18. Gregor, S.: The nature of theory in information systems. MIS Quart. Manag. Inf. Syst. **30**, 611–642 (2006)
19. Bunge, M.: Scientific Research II: The Search for Truth. Springer, Berlin Heidelberg (2012). https://doi.org/10.1007/978-3-642-48138-3
20. Gregor, S., Chandra Kruse, L., Seidel, S.: The anatomy of a design principle. J. Assoc. Inf. Syst. **21**, 1622–1652 (2020)
21. Walls, J.G., Widmeyer, R.G., Sawy, O.A.: Building an information system design theory for vigilant EIS. Inf. Syst. Res. **3**, 36–59 (1992)
22. Heinrich, P., Schwabe, G.: Communicating nascent design theories on innovative information systems through multi-grounded design principles. In: Tremblay, M.C., VanderMeer, D., Rothenberger, M., Gupta, A., Yoon, V. (eds.) DESRIST 2014. LNCS, vol. 8463, pp. 148–163. Springer, Cham (2014). https://doi.org/10.1007/978-3-319-06701-8_10

23. Koppenhagen, N., Gaß, O., Müller, B.: Design science research in action - anatomy of success critical activities for rigor and relevance. In: Proceedings of the 20th European Conference on Information Systems, pp. 1–12 (2012)

24. Cronholm, S., Göbel, H.: Guidelines supporting the formulation of design principles. In: Proceedings of the 29th Australasian Conference on Information Systems (2018)

25. Schoormann, T., Behrens, D., Fellmann, M., Knackstedt, R.: On your mark, ready, search: a framework for structuring literature search strategies in information systems. In: Proceedings of the 16th International Conference on Wirtschaftsinformatik (2021)

26. Webster, J., Watson, R.T.: Analyzing the past to prepare for the future: writing a literature review. MIS Quart. Manag. Inf. Syst. **26**, xiii–xxiii (2002)

27. Cooper, H.M.: Organizing knowledge syntheses: a taxonomy of literature reviews. Knowl. Soc. **1**, 104–126 (1988)

28. Randolph, J.J.: A guide to writing the dissertation literature review. Pract. Assess. Res. Eval. **14**, 1–13 (2009)

29. Tremblay, M., Hevner, A., Berndt, D.: Focus groups for artifact refinement and evaluation in design research. Commun. Assoc. Inf. Syst. **26**, 599–618 (2010)

30. Niederman, F., March, S.: The "Theoretical lens" concept: we all know what it means, but do we all know the same thing? Commun. Assoc. Inf. Syst. **44**, 1–33 (2019)

31. Hönigsberg, S.: A platform for value co-creation in SME networks. In: Hofmann, S., Müller, O., Rossi, M. (eds.) DESRIST 2020. LNCS, vol. 12388, pp. 285–296. Springer, Cham (2020). https://doi.org/10.1007/978-3-030-64823-7_26

32. Schoormann, T., Behrens, D., Knackstedt, R.: The noblest way to learn wisdom is by reflection: designing software tools for reflecting sustainability in business models. In: Proceedings of the 39th International Conference on Information Systems (2018)

33. Wiethof, C., Tavanapour, N., Bittner, E.: Design and evaluation of a collaborative writing process with gamification elements. In: Proceedings of the 28th European Conference on Information Systems (2020)

34. Kolkowska, E., Karlsson, F., Hedström, K.: Towards analysing the rationale of information security non-compliance: devising a value-based compliance analysis method. J. Strateg. Inf. Syst. **26**, 39–57 (2017)

35. Babaian, T., Lucas, W., Xu, J., Topi, H.: Usability through system-user collaboration. In: Winter, R., Zhao, J.L., Aier, S. (eds.) DESRIST 2010. LNCS, vol. 6105, pp. 394–409. Springer, Heidelberg (2010). https://doi.org/10.1007/978-3-642-13335-0_27

36. Parsons, J., Wand, Y.: Extending principles of classification from information modeling to other disciplines. J. Assoc. Inf. Syst. **14**, 245–173 (2013)

37. Feine, J., Morana, S., Maedche, A.: Designing a chatbot social cue configuration system. In: Proceedings of the 40th International Conference on Information Systems (2019)

38. Wambsganss, T., Rietsche, R.: Towards designing an adaptive argumentation learning tool. In: Proceedings of the 40th International Conference on Information Systems (2019)

39. Chanson, M., Bogner, A., Bilgeri, D., Fleisch, E., Wortmann, F.: Blockchain for the IoT: privacy-preserving protection of sensor data. J. Assoc. Inf. Syst. **20**, 1274–1309 (2019)

40. Meier, P., Beinke, J.H., Fitte, C., Behne, A., Teuteberg, F.: FeelFit–design and evaluation of a conversational agent to enhance health awareness. In: Proceedings of the 40th International Conference on Information Systems (2019)

41. Iivari, J.: Distinguishing and contrasting two strategies for design science research. Eur. J. Inf. Syst. **24**, 107–115 (2015)

42. Pan, S.L., Li, M., Pee, L.G., Sandeep, M.S.: Sustainability design principles for a wildlife management analytics system: an action design research. Eur. J. Inf. Syst., 1–22 (2020)

43. Herterich, M.M.: On the design of digitized industrial products as key resources of service platforms for industrial service innovation. In: Maedche, A., vom Brocke, J., Hevner, A. (eds.) DESRIST 2017. LNCS, vol. 10243, pp. 364–380. Springer, Cham (2017). https://doi.org/10.1007/978-3-319-59144-5_22

44. Peffers, K., Tuunanen, T., Rothenberger, M.A., Chatterjee, S.: A design science research methodology for information systems research. J. Manag. Inf. Syst. **24**, 45–77 (2007)

45. Kuechler, B., Vaishnavi, V.: On theory development in design science research: anatomy of a research project. Eur. J. Inf. Syst. **17**, 489–504 (2008)

46. Horlach, B., Schirmer, I., Drews, P.: Agile portfolio management: design goals and principles. In: Proceedings of the 27th European Conference on Information Systems (2019)

47. Nguyen, A., Tuunanen, T., Gardner, L., Sheridan, D.: Design principles for learning analytics information systems in higher education. Eur. J. Inf. Syst., 1–28 (2020)

48. Gregor, S., Jones, D.: The anatomy of a design theory. J. Assoc. Inf. Syst. **8**, 312–335 (2007)

49. Morana, S., et al.: Research prototype: the design canvas in mydesignprocess. In: Proceedings of the 13th International Conference on Design Science Research in Information Systems and Technology (2018)

50. vom Brocke, J., Maedche, A.: The DSR grid: six core dimensions for effectively planning and communicating design science research projects. Electron. Mark. **29**(3), 379–385 (2019). https://doi.org/10.1007/s12525-019-00358-7

51. Morana, S., et al.: Tool support for design science research-towards a software ecosystem: a report from a DESRIST 2017 workshop. Commun. Assoc. Inf. Sys. **43**, 237–256 (2018)

Design Principles for Shared Maintenance Analytics in Fleet Management

Christian Janiesch[1,2]($\boxtimes$) (iD), Jonas Wanner[1] (iD), and Lukas-Valentin Herm[1] (iD)

[1] Julius-Maximilians-Universität Würzburg, Würzburg, Germany
{christian.janiesch,jonas.wanner,
lukas-valentin.herm}@uni-wuerzburg.de
[2] HAW Landshut, Landshut, Germany

Abstract. Many of today's production facilities are modular in design and therefore to some degree individual. Further, there is a variety of differing application contexts that impact the operation of machines as compared to the manufacturer's test cases. However, knowledge for their maintenance at the place of operation is typically limited to the manufacturer's (digitally) printed technical documentation delivered with the product. Even with local knowledge, this requires extensive time and fault data to understand and prevent machine failures. Thus, there is a need for shared maintenance analytics, a scalable, networked learning process that address these issues in fleet management. Despite partial success, which mainly stems from individual use cases, there is no generalizable architecture for a broader adoption or practical use as of yet. To address this issue, we derive design requirements, design principles, and design features to specify a system architecture for shared maintenance analytics in fleet management.

Keywords: Design principles · System architecture · Shared maintenance analytics · Fleet management

1 Introduction

Today's industry is characterized by complex production plants that require sophisticated maintenance systems to guarantee human safety, high reliability, and low environmental risks [1]. For this purpose, modern maintenance strategies increasingly focus on data-driven approaches, as the ubiquitous use of IT and enhanced sensor technology facilitate the generation of large amounts of data, providing an ideal starting point for knowledge discovery and improved decision support [2]. However, the problem is that the effort required for initializing such data-based monitoring is time and resource-intensive.

Despite its potentials, instantaneous monitoring for maintenance purposes is therefore not possible. The situation is aggravated by the fact that such systems are optimized for local machine problems today, so that reusability of existing maintenance information at other sites is not possible, and thus there are few to no corresponding synergy effects. In parallel, there is a trend is toward the modular design for machines in industrial manufacturing. That is, the machines and production modules are often similar.

L. Chandra Kruse et al. (Eds.): DESRIST 2021, LNCS 12807, pp. 236–247, 2021.
https://doi.org/10.1007/978-3-030-82405-1_24

Knowledge of similar machines that can be used across the board is being researched in the field of *fleet management*. In line with that, Al-Dahidi et al. [3] argue that such approaches have the potential to increase the overall efficiency of the entire maintenance process.

Many organizations already possess both, the capabilities and resources to deploy fleet-wide approaches in-house. However, current maintenance practices neglect the considerable potential of deploying peer-production in industrial maintenance and, thus, do not take full advantage of current technological and organizational resources as they lack guidance in terms of architecture and procedure on how to establish shared maintenance analytics. That is, the global analysis of locally acquired data for maintenance purposes. To address this, our research is guided by the following research question (RQ):

RQ: What are design requirements, design principles, and design features of a system architecture for shared maintenance analytics in fleet management?

To approach this RQ, our paper is organized as follows: In Sect. 2, we provide an overview of maintenance and fleet management, before we outline our research methodology in Sect. 3. Section 4 comprises the specification of design requirements and design principles, which we map to concrete design features to develop an architecture for shared maintenance analytics. Section 5 comprises an architecture proposal based on said features and illustrates it with an exemplary use case. Section 6 provides a short summary and an outlook.

2 Fundamentals

2.1 Traditional and Cloud-Based Maintenance

Maintenance either corrects or prevents abnormal machine behavior [4] to minimize machine downtime by error detection and analysis [5]. With the aim to minimize opportunity costs, each manufacturer usually sets up an individual maintenance policy [6]. However, due to its focus on local optimizations, the know-how is only generated per machine or module and does not consider any behavior or errors that have already been recorded or even been solved beforehand [3]. According to Medina-Oliva et al. [5] current maintenance approaches can significantly benefit from sharing a local machine's historical data and behavior against the backdrop of joint data analysis.

Here, cloud manufacturing is an emerging integrated and service-oriented manufacturing paradigm. It belongs to the domain of the Industrial Internet of Things (IIoT) [7]. In a cloud-based platform, participants form a smart network to coordinate the transformation of manufacturing resources and capabilities into manufacturing services. Framed as Maintenance-as-a-Service (MaaS), cloud manufacturing also implements a sharing paradigm to enable the use of disparate data sources [8].

2.2 Fleet Management

A fleet-wide approach aggregates and categorizes historical data stemming from other instances of similar machine types deployed under comparable or differing conditions within a knowledge database [3, 5] (cf. Fig. 1, left). In this way, it becomes possible to exploit economies of scale by continually complementing new knowledge generated during maintenance of similar machines or machine modules. Thus, one can exchange information, reconstruct known issues, and detect similar errors, while simultaneously having access to an integrated database that provides any technician with initial information on likely causes of a machine's error state and corresponding instructions for troubleshooting.

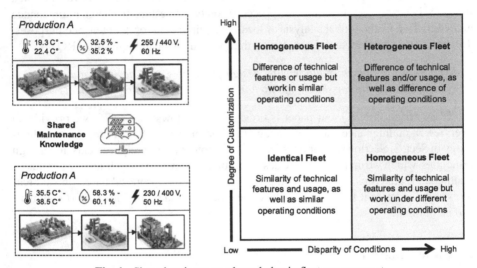

Fig. 1. Shared maintenance knowledge in fleet management

Based on the level of similarity between systems in a fleet, the fleet can be categorized either identical, homogeneous, or heterogeneous (cf. Fig. 1, right). Identical fleets are meant to have identical technical features and use, and work in the same operating conditions [9], as for example a fleet of identical diesel engines located in one ship [5]. A Further example can be found in [10]. Homogeneous fleets can either share some identical technical features and use, but they work under different operating conditions. Alternatively, they differ in their technical features or usage but work in similar operating conditions [3]. An example would be a fleet of trains sharing a common route [11]. Further examples can be found in [11, 12]. A heterogeneous fleet is showing differences in both, the technical features and/or use, as well as in their environmental and operational conditions [9]. An example is a fleet of customized steam turbines of pressurized water reactors in nuclear power plants [3]. Further examples can be found in [13, 14].

3   Methodology

3.1   Design Science Research Approach

We apply design science research (DSR) to develop our artifact and specify our design knowledge [15]. Despite the general technical feasibility of the problem at hand [9], there is limited research to implement a so-called fleet-wide maintenance solution [3]. Through a literature search and exchange with practitioners, we have identified a lack of concrete design principles for an architecture of shared data analytics to pass knowledge between individual or modularized industrial systems in the context of industrial maintenance.

To emphasize practical implications, we have conducted an expert interview study and a small quantitative survey to derive general industry requirements for modern manufacturer's machines. In the stage of design and development, we used this knowledge and the inherent meta requirements to determine design requirements before we derived design principles and design features that guide the exchange of analytical knowledge between customized fleets in a disparity of circumstances. The design requirements, design principles, and design features were developed and refined in an iterative process of five experts in the field of industrial maintenance. When a consensus of experts was reached and changes to the set became marginal, we did not start a new iteration.

During the demonstration phase, we formalized our design and describe each underlying aspect of our proposed architecture. Ultimately, we illustrate the benefit and quality of our research artifact by applying it to an exemplary use case. While demonstration covers the artifact's feasibility to solve a problem, an evaluation assesses its performance. Thereby, one can generally choose from multiple techniques, including observational methods (e.g., case studies or field studies), analytical methods (e.g., static analysis or optimization), experimental methods (e.g., controlled experiments or simulations), testing methods (e.g., functional testing and structural testing), and descriptive methods (e.g., informed argument and scenarios) [15, 16]. As our research is conceptual by nature, we use descriptive methods to evaluate the resulting system architecture [17].

3.2 Interview Study and Expert Survey

In order to understand the conditions in today's production facilities, we carried out six expert interviews, which we reevaluated in a quantitative survey at the Hanover exhibition 2019 ($n = 32$). Both studies were conducted in a personal exchange as semi-structured interviews. While we kept the questions more open-minded during expert study, the survey at the fair included possible answers to ensure a quick feedback. For the participants at the expert study, we have mainly focused on industrial service providers in Germany, dealing with various customers and each with at least five years of relevant experience. Two of the experts were from an industrial automation service provider (head of R&D and engineer), one expert each was a managing director of an industrial manufacturing company for sawmills, a product manager at a high-performance vibration sensor manufacturer, and a marketing manager from a configure price quote software provider for industrial manufacturers, and the founder and managing director of a Belgian data analytics service provider for industrial facilities in the context of maintenance. For the survey, we addressed industrial manufacturers and data analytics service providers. Half of the participants we interviewed had a marketing or administrative background, the other half had an engineering background.

In terms of the survey's content, we have aimed at answering the following three key questions: *(1)* How are today's production facilities constructed, especially regarding the degree of mechanical individualization? *(2)* Is corresponding hardware for data extraction (i.e., sensor technology) already installed? *(3)* To what extent is data analysis already used for today's maintenance purposes?

Question *(1)* revealed that the construction of a modern production facility is almost exclusively based on standardized modules that are combined in a way that suits customer requirements. The experts' statements only differed on opinion about an average degree of individualization in production facilities. We confirmed this at the fair for industrial mass production. Question *(2)* confirmed an increasing demand for industry 4.0 capable hardware. This has only become an apparent issue in the last years. Answers differed from limitations due to simple sensor technology such as light barriers to high-end sensors tracking vibration, humidity, temperature, gyro, or pressure. In general, we confirmed a high demand for innovative data measurement equipment in the sense of IIoT readiness. Question *(3)* was answered in dissimilar ways. Some engineers spoke of little to no actual implementation of data analytics but were interested. Others already talked about concrete applications in practice, which underlines the general benefit and upcoming necessity for all.

4 Design Requirements, Principles, and Features for an Architecture for Shared Maintenance Analytics

4.1 Design Requirements

In a first step, we formulated meta design requirements from the concept of fleet management as a starting point for our research. We consolidated these meta requirements with data from our interview study and expert survey. Thus, the design requirements were the direct result of our own research and discussions with experts and project partners. FDR1 emphasizes the goal to enhance the performance of shared maintenance analytics in fleet management [18]. Similarly, we seek an approach to enhance knowledge reusability for maintenance (FDR2) to avoid the cold start problem [19]. For an overview, see Fig. 2.

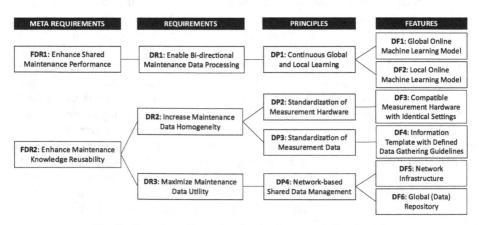

Fig. 2. Overview of mapping fleet concepts to design features

From a data-centric perspective, any maintenance service can be improved by sensor data and related analytical efforts [20]. For shared maintenance analytics, the core challenge is that most data is acquired and analyzed only locally, but needs to be shared between similar systems for global analysis to improve fleet management [3]. Hence, any increase in the learning process relies primarily on the amount and the technical feasibility of similar systems that are participating and sharing data. While this results in an iterative learning process, it is essential to decrease the effort in the long term. Against this backdrop, we derive our design requirements:

DR1: Enable Bi-directional Maintenance Data Processing. Running multiple sites, for example factories or service points, generates a lot of production and use data. Following FDR1, shared maintenance performance can be enhanced by enabling bi-directional data processing. That is, sites post their monitoring data to the system and the system makes available these observations to compatible sites to enhance their performance [21]. Further, this data can be used to build analytical models centrally, which can be refined by the users and vice versa [22].

DR2: Increase Maintenance Data Homogeneity. The effort for shared maintenance should be reduced by fleet management [3]. In this context, the use of homogeneous data stemming from similar hardware and software within the different sites reduces the effort required to operate shared maintenance data analytics in the long term. While in early development phases, shared maintenance causes higher effort compared to isolated maintenance, the use of homogeneous components for the scaling of and across sites reduces future effort [13].

DR3: Maximize Maintenance Data Utility. While there are many benefits to advanced data analytics approaches such as machine learning, there are several limitations that must be addressed. Since machine learning models require a large amount of data to work effectively [23], building the initial analytical model from scratch is a time-consuming process. A lack of comprehensive data to train the models is known as the cold start problem [19]. Therefore, initialization costs must be minimized by maximizing data utility. An infrastructure that shares data across multiple sites allows shared maintenance analytics based on advanced AI algorithms to build their analytical models better as more training data is available.

4.2 Design Principles

In several iterations, we translated the aforementioned design requirements into design principles following the recommendations of Chandra et al. [24]. The collective boundary condition for all design principles is *"for shared maintenance analytics in fleet management"*. In principle, the design principles are independent of each other and could be activated or deactivated individually. Nevertheless, DP1 constitutes the system architecture's core principle of form and function and can hardly be forwent. We assume that any configuration of fewer design principles will result in an inferior system architecture.

DP1: Provide the system architecture with the functionality to continuously learn globally and locally in order for the system to improve the system's own analytical model as well as assist users with updating their local models. Advanced analytics for example, based on machine learning offer many opportunities to learn from raw maintenance data but also from maintenance experience. By enabling the system to process data from different sites globally, the resulting analytical model can become more accurate and robust in their performance [22]. Consequently, sites can not only use the system's global analytical model but also those collected observations from other compatible sites to improve their own local models [3]. This answers the design requirement posed by DR1.

DP2: Provide the system architecture with standardized measurement hardware in order for the system to monitor data uniformly independent of the hardware's placement. To address design requirement DR2, there is a need for the standardization of hardware such as sensors and production modules across sites. Using a set of pre-defined identical hardware allows to reduce the selection process, enables knowledge sharing about monitoring hardware, and improves data uniformity and thus enables comparability [5]. This reduces the need for data processing and cleansing and enables data integration across disparate circumstances [25].

DP3: Provide the system architecture with standardized measurement data in order for the system to receive complete and uniform data independent of the measurement's origin. Adding the DP2, DR2 does not only require identical or at least comparable hardware, but it also requires identical or at least compatible data measurements [3, 5]. That is, as circumstances at sites may vary and a minimum of context data such as temperature, humidity, etc., may need to be reported as well as data points of a certain accuracy in a defined interval [25].

DP4: Provide the system architecture with network-based shared data management in order for the system to store data and exchange data with users conveniently. The use of multiple data sources from different sites requires consolidated data management based on a trusted network infrastructure to maximize data utility [8]. As not every site may have the possibility to store and process large datasets, the network infrastructure enables them to send and receive data to and from other sites [6].

4.3 Mapping Design Principles to Design Features

Design features are specific artifact capabilities that instantiate design principles [26]. In the following, we propose several design features for our design principles. Most design features can be implemented independent of each other even though DF1 shares strong dependencies with DF2 and DF6.

DF1: Global Online Machine Learning Model. Taking advantage of large, shared repositories, the system can build advanced analytical models automatically with machine learning algorithms to improve the accuracy over handcrafted maintenance models that would be created through explicit programming [23] to implement DP1. In doing so, these models act as a template for local use through transfer learning. Moreover, these models can be continuously improved with the data from the different sites. Currently, online machine learning models are used for this approach, but further technologies may emerge.

DF2: Local Online Machine Learning Model. Following DF1, companies can use the globally trained advanced analytical model for each of their sites. To ensure adaptation to their specific circumstances, local data from operations can be used to further sophisticate the pretrained global model for situated application (by transfer learning). Since the global model is trained based on data from other trusted sites, compliance and trust issues should not be of concern.

DF3: Compatible Measurement Hardware with Identical Settings. Resulting from DP2, using compatible measurement hardware such as sensors and automation systems enable companies to build up further sites more quickly by reusing preexisting knowledge. For very sensitive measurements products of the same charge or at the very least of the same manufacturer should be used while for less critical readings products should be at least compatible in their capabilities. Naturally, they should be set to the same settings.

DF4: Module Information Template with Defined Data Gathering Guidelines. The use of information templates with mandatory fields for all modules ensures the sustainability of data across sites (DP3). Here, the definition of required data such as date and sensor value are necessary to allow merging of data into a larger database, as individual customization makes scaling of data analysis difficult. Further, using predefined measurement scales and measurement precision enables companies to make the production steps from sites comparable and further allows to combine data across multiple sites.

DF5: Network Infrastructure. Implementing a network infrastructure across multiple sites enables information sharing and thus shared maintenance analytics without the necessity for local data hubs. This implements DP4. For example, sites can use the network to share local operations data with the global data store or receive (updated) versions of the global analytical model. Network infrastructure can be rented in a cloud model where available.

DF6: Global (Data) Repository. The global repository collects all operation data from the various sites. From this repository, the global analytical model is (constantly) trained, stored, and checked for drift. The data repository does not have to reside in one data center but can be based on federated cloud infrastructure or blockchain technology.

5 A System Architecture and Application for Shared Maintenance Analytics

5.1 System Architecture Proposal

Based on the design requirements, design principles, and design features, we present a multi-layered architecture for shared maintenance analytics. The production and maintenance layer as well as the local data analytics layer are implemented at every site in the network. See Fig. 3 for an overview.

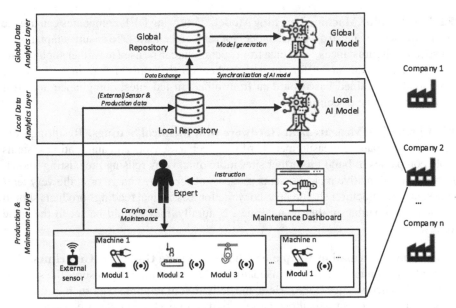

Fig. 3. Architecture for shared maintenance analytics in fleet management

Production and Maintenance Layer. Within this layer, the production and corresponding maintenance take place. Production is a combination of multiple modules with additional sensors. To ensure standardization, similar modules use compatible hardware with identical settings (DF3). All data generated during production is forwarded to the local repository within the local data analysis layer, while adhering to predefined information templates (DF4). As a result of the subsequent layers, an expert receives briefings on the maintenance process via a maintenance dashboard, which he or she can perform at the modules.

Local Data Analytics Layer. As the production and maintenance layer, the local data analysis layer is situated at each participating company (DF2). Here, the local repository stores the production data from the previous layer. Based on this data and the pre-trained AI model from the global data analytics layer, a local AI model is generated for the specific production circumstances.

Global Data Analytics Layer. Contrary to the previous layers, the global data analytics layer is not situated at a specific site. Instead, this layer is accessible to any participating company using a dedicated network structure (DF5) for example implemented as a cloud solution. Production data from each site is stored in the global repository (DF6) and used to train and continuously update the online global analytical model (DF1). When this model is trained or updated, the new version is propagated to the local data analytics layer of each company.

5.2 Scenario-Based Illustration

Above, we have demonstrated our system architecture by describing its main components as well as their relationships. In the following, we evaluate the system architecture following Venable, et al. [17] to assess its usefulness and to control for undesirable side effects. Due to the novelty of the technology, we evaluate our architecture based on a realistic scenario, derived from a current research project on industrial maintenance, not on a workable implementation.

A company specialized in punching machines is setting up several production facilities in Germany. While each production facility uses similar modules to perform the same production process, there are some differences due to local conditions. For example, the average temperature at one production facility is two degrees Celsius lower than at another. However, since each production facility uses similar hardware and measurement settings, the resulting data is compatible. Because of the high similarity, the generated data from different production facilities can be used by merging it to generate enough data to train an AI-based analytical model. This shared production data enables rapid mapping of data to identify potential production errors that are not yet known, such as an error when metal glue is not properly applied when joining to form punched-out parts. The global repository, shared via cloud infrastructure, provides production plants with a well-performing machine learning model to predict and control future maintenance. Still, the different plants need to add their locally accrued data to adapt the global AI model to their specific local needs. While the different production plants are running, the monitored data is constantly sent to the cloud solution. Here, the globally trained analytical model is continuously updated and improved. Subsequently, the various production plants receive the updated version and can adapt it to their local needs.

While this is happening in the background, a construction worker receives recommendations via his or her maintenance dashboard, if an error occurs while punching out. While the AI model can only reactively deal with errors at the beginning of the production run, the constantly accumulating data enables the model to make predictive maintenance recommendations eventually.

6   Conclusion and Outlook

In this paper, we have developed and demonstrated a system architecture for shared maintenance analytics. It is a high-level architecture to provide principles of a workable solution for fleet management independent of any domain. With the derivation of three design requirements and their translation into four design principles and six design features, we provide unique prescriptive knowledge to approach the problem of shared analytics for any fleet category, which is helpful for researchers and practitioners alike to establish shared maintenance analytics. So far, we also have not yet discussed the possibilities of services based on shared analytics knowledge or related problems such as fraud detection and data sovereignty. Neither, have we discussed technical aspects of transfer learning data exchange policies, and the role of AI-as-a-Service platforms that can implement such an architecture. Both aspects are subject to further research.

Acknowledgement. This research and development project is funded by the Bayerische Staatsministerium für Wirtschaft, Landesentwicklung und Energie (StMWi) within the framework concept "Informations- und Kommunikationstechnik" (grant no. DIK0143/02) and managed by the project management agency VDI+VDE Innovation + Technik GmbH.

References

1. Muchiri, P., Pintelon, L., Gelders, L., Martin, H.: Development of maintenance function performance measurement framework and indicators. Int. J. Prod. Econ. **131**, 295–302 (2011)
2. Fabri, L., Häckel, B., Oberländer, A.M., Töppel, J., Zanker, P.: Economic perspective on algorithm selection for predictive maintenance. In: Proceedings of the 27th European Conference on Information System, pp. 1–16. AIS, Stockholm (2019)
3. Al-Dahidi, S., Di Maio, F., Baraldi, P., Zio, E., Seraoui, R.: A framework for reconciling data clusters from a fleet of nuclear power plants turbines for fault diagnosis. Appl. Soft Comput. **69**, 213–231 (2018)
4. Henriquez, P., Alonso, J.B., Ferrer, M.A., Travieso, C.M.: Review of automatic fault diagnosis systems using audio and vibration signals. IEEE Trans. Syst. Man Cybern. Syst. **44**, 642–652 (2013)
5. Medina-Oliva, G., Voisin, A., Monnin, M., Leger, J.-B.: Predictive diagnosis based on a fleet-wide ontology approach. Knowl.-Based Syst. **68**, 40–57 (2014)
6. Li, Z., Wang, Y., Wang, K.-S.: Intelligent predictive maintenance for fault diagnosis and prognosis in machine centers: Industry 4.0 scenario. Adv. Manuf. **5**(4), 377–387 (2017). https://doi.org/10.1007/s40436-017-0203-8
7. Li, B.-H., et al.: Further discussion on cloud manufacturing. Comput. Integr. Manuf. Syst. **17**, 449–457 (2011)
8. Ren, L., Zhang, L., Tao, F., Zhao, C., Chai, X., Zhao, X.: Cloud manufacturing: from concept to practice. Enterp. Inf. Syst. **9**, 186–209 (2015)
9. Al-Dahidi, S., Di Maio, F., Baraldi, P., Zio, E.: Remaining useful life estimation in heterogeneous fleets working under variable operating conditions. Reliab. Eng. Syst. Saf. **156**, 109–124 (2016)
10. Olsson, E., Funk, P., Xiong, N.: Fault diagnosis in industry using sensor readings and case-based reasoning. J. Intell. Fuzzy Syst. **15**, 41–46 (2004)
11. Umiliacchi, P., Lane, D., Romano, F., SpA, A.: Predictive maintenance of railway subsystems using an ontology based modelling approach. In: Proceedings of the World Conference on Railway Research, pp. 22–26 (2011)
12. Rigamonti, M., Baraldi, P., Zio, E., Astigarraga, D., Galarza, A.: Particle filter-based prognostics for an electrolytic capacitor working in variable operating conditions. IEEE Trans. Power Electron. **31**, 1567–1575 (2015)
13. Voisin, A., Medina-Oliva, G., Monnin, M., Leger, J.-B., Iung, B.: Fleet-wide diagnostic and prognostic assessment. In: Proceedings of the Annual Conference of the Prognostics and Health Management Society, New Orleans, LA, pp. 521–530 (2013)
14. Saxena, A., Goebel, K., Simon, D., Eklund, N.: Damage propagation modeling for aircraft engine run-to-failure simulation. In: Proceedings of the 2008 International Conference on Prognostics and Health Management, Denver, pp. 1–9. IEEE, (2008)
15. Hevner, A.R., March, S.T., Park, J., Ram, S.: Design science in information systems research. MIS Quart. 28, 75-105 (2004)
16. Venable, J., Pries-Heje, J., Baskerville, R.: A comprehensive framework for evaluation in design science research. In: Peffers, K., Rothenberger, M., Kuechler, B. (eds.) DESRIST 2012. LNCS, vol. 7286, pp. 423–438. Springer, Heidelberg (2012). https://doi.org/10.1007/978-3-642-29863-9_31

17. Venable, J., Pries-Heje, J., Baskerville, R.: FEDS: a framework for evaluation in design science research. Eur. J. Inf. Syst. **25**, 77–89 (2016)
18. Bokrantz, J., Skoogh, A., Berlin, C., Wuest, T., Stahre, J.: Smart maintenance: a research agenda for industrial maintenance management. Int. J. Prod. Econ. **224**, 107547 (2020)
19. Lika, B., Kolomvatsos, K., Hadjiefthymiades, S.: Facing the cold start problem in recommender systems. Expert Syst. Appl. **41**, 2065–2073 (2014)
20. Ma, J., Jiang, J.: Applications of fault detection and diagnosis methods in nuclear power plants: a review. Prog. Nucl. Energy **53**, 255–266 (2011)
21. Mahyari, A.G.: Robust predictive maintenance for robotics via unsupervised transfer learning. In: Proceedings of the International FLAIRS Conference Proceedings, vol. 34 (2021)
22. Weiss, K., Khoshgoftaar, T.M., Wang, D.: A survey of transfer learning. J. Big Data **3**(1), 1–40 (2016). https://doi.org/10.1186/s40537-016-0043-6
23. Janiesch, C., Zschech, P., Heinrich, K.: Machine learning and deep learning. Electron. Markets 1–11 (2021)
24. Chandra, L., Seidel, S., Gregor, S.: Prescriptive knowledge in IS research: conceptualizing design principles in terms of materiality, action, and boundary conditions. In: Proceedings of the 48th Hawaii International Conference on System Sciences, Kauai, pp. 4039–4048. IEEE (2015)
25. Broy, M., Gleirscher, M., Merenda, S., Wild, D., Kluge, P., Krenzer, W.: Toward a holistic and standardized automotive architecture description. Computer **42**, 98–101 (2009)
26. Meth, H., Mueller, B., Maedche, A.: Designing a requirement mining system. J. Assoc. Inf. Syst. **16**, 799–837 (2015)

Respondent Behavior Logging: A Design Science Research Inquiry into Web Survey Paradata

Mohammad Hafijur Rahman and Jonas Sjöström[✉]

Department of Informatics and Media, Uppsala University, Uppsala, Sweden
{hafijur.rahman,jonas.sjostrom}@im.uu.se

Abstract. This paper introduces a framework for Respondent Behavior Logging (RBL), consisting of static and dynamic models that conceptualize respondent behavior when filling in online questionnaires, and visualization techniques and measurement constructs for RBL data. Web survey design may benefit from paradata logging as a technique for evaluation, since such data may prove useful during the re-design of questionnaires. Although other aspects of online surveys have attracted considerable attention both in the industry and in literature, it is still underexplored how the Web may leverage new and innovative techniques to support survey design. The RBL framework is evaluated using a focus group and through an experimental survey with 120 participants. We elaborate on implications for research and practice in an informed argument.

Keywords: Questionnaire design · Web survey · Evaluation · Paradata · Behavior logging · Design science research

1 Introduction

Research in information systems (IS), as well as in other disciplines, often includes data collection through surveys [20, 25]. As stated by Krosnick & Presser [13], "the heart of a survey is its questionnaire" (p. 263). The importance of well-designed questionnaires cannot be understated. Flaws in questionnaire design may lead to response errors [13] that may negatively impact the entire study. For example; question-wording problems may lead to confusion about the meaning of the question and misinterpretation of essential terms, and unintuitive skip logic may lead to missed responses and frustration among respondents [3].

There are several methodological guidelines to support questionnaire design. Following [13], we divide these guidelines into three broad categories: (i) the design of questions and the options provided to answer the questions. The design focuses on different types of open and closed questions, and how to appropriate suitable rating scales given the knowledge interest of the researcher. (ii) The structure of the questionnaire as a whole. Such guidelines address the order of questions, and various strategies to improve the interpretability of respondents' answers, e.g., through the use of vignette questions. (iii) Guidelines for the process of formative testing of questionnaires, as a means to prototype and improve the questionnaires before going live in a full-scale survey. For online

© Springer Nature Switzerland AG 2021
L. Chandra Kruse et al. (Eds.): DESRIST 2021, LNCS 12807, pp. 248–259, 2021.
https://doi.org/10.1007/978-3-030-82405-1_25

surveys, particular design guidelines have been discussed [15]. In this paper, we argue that questionnaire evaluation has not yet exploited the potential of the online medium. A literature review from the areas of IS, human computer-interaction (HCI) shows a scarcity of research on understanding and evaluating the use of online questionnaires. Meanwhile, in a broader context of social science and eHealth, the notion of web paradata [10, 14, 18] in survey design has emerged: Behavioral and contextual respondent behavior data. The paradata literature, however, typically presumes to analyze standard web logs [29], and rarely considers the conceptualization and capture of paradata from a design perspective.

We employ an action design research (ADR) approach [8, 11, 23] that resulted in the Respondent Behavior Logging (RBL) framework. The RBL framework allows us to scrutinize the respondents' process of answering questions in online surveys. The framework consists of static and dynamic models of respondent behavior, visualization techniques, and constructs to measure various aspects of respondent behavior. Our work contributes to previous work on web survey paradata, software-embedded evaluation support [26], and tool support for design science research [19].

RBL – if repeatedly used in online research where common instruments are applied – may support fine-tuning of survey instruments over time, based on extensive data sets of respondent behavior. Further, as suggested by [8], innovation-type design science research (DSR) contributes through its conceptualizations that increase the understanding of the problem domain, and one possible goal for design science research is to explore new evaluation strategies for research [11].

2 Knowledge Base

Our literature review focused on three different streams of literature: Logging in IS, logging in HCI, and paradata – a concept to denote user behavior in eHealth.

The conducted IS literature review shows that there is indeed value in carefully conceptualizing people's behaviors concerning IT use [1, 2, 6, 12, 24]. Despite a fair amount of literature on user behavior, virtually no literature has focused on the study of respondent behavior in the context of filling in online questionnaires. Previous research focuses on achieving a concrete outcome that would be valuable in some IT-reliant *practice* context, but none of the publications has focused on how the concept of respondent behavior data could be used to improve the quality of the *research* itself. The extant IS research uses self-report surveys to elicit study respondents' behavior; while this paper flips the coin to inquire into conceptualizing and analyzing respondent behavior based on log data.

The HCI literature focused on how to use log data to improve user experiences, e.g., through recommendations and personalization of user interfaces. Often, relating to the big data trend of applying data science and data analytics to investigate behavioral patterns of customers. A publicly interesting example is the use of 'clickstream' analysis on the World Wide Web, used (for instance) to tailor the display of ads on web pages [17]. Such tailoring draws from aggregated user behavior data, collected from several websites to enable profiling of users through inferences from multiple data points. The HCI literature, however, did not focus on drawing from log data to analyze or improve online surveys.

Instead, our design draws from the *paradata* discourse taking place primarily among eHealth researchers and in the general social science discourse (outside IS and HCI). Paradata concerning surveys is categorized as metadata, auxiliary data (obtained from external sources), passive data (e.g., geolocation data from a mobile device), and web paradata [14]. In this context, our focus is on web paradata (e.g., device-type information and user behavior that is available in the IP and HTTP protocols). Web survey paradata has been defined as "data describing the web survey data collection process, which can be generated and captured in the act of fielding a web survey" [18, p. 199]. Such paradata may be collected for a single questionnaire, but it may also be collected repeatedly (which is the case in the eHealth practice at hand).

From a technical point of view, the literature distinguishes between paradata collected on the client-side (the web browser) and paradata collected on the server side [10]. Client-side logging offers more detail (anything that can be captured using javascript, e.g., mouse movements) but also risks slowing down the web browser, thus disturbing the user. Server-side logging provides the data available in the HTTP request [29], and also, depending on the design of the application, additional contextual data connected to the user's web session.

The paradata discourse has primarily taken place in non–computing disciplines, thus black-boxed the logging process. Also, it presumes the use of standard web logs [29] when logging paradata on the server-side.

3   Research Setting and Research Approach

This research is part of a research setting in which a multi-disciplinary team of researchers and practitioners designed and developed software that was used to conduct randomized controlled trials in the context of online psychosocial care. The team included practitioners as well as academics. The practitioners were doctors, nurses, psychologists, and IS professionals. The academics were scholars from psychology, economics, IS, and caring sciences. We refer to the practice context as *the eHealth practice* from this point forward.

Since 2010 we have gone through an iterative process with bi-weekly design sprints leading to an emerging software used in practice. The software as a whole has been developed using an agile software development process [4]. There were 154 sprint meetings from November 2010 to December 2018. The meetings included developers or information systems researchers and psychologists or clinical researchers. The eHealth practice had among 50 staff with whom the development team and the product owner interacted frequently.

Following action design research [23], RBL was conceptualized in a series for build-intervene-evaluate (BIE) cycles. The initial concepts and conceptual models were designed (corresponding to Sect. 4.1) in the first cycle in 2012. The *design* aimed at logging behavior to allow for a detailed reconstruction of how respondents filled in questionnaires. The concepts were built and implemented into the production software. Drawing from the requirements emerging from the eHealth practice, we conceptualized user actions related to filling in questionnaires. A conceptual data model was designed to capture respondent behavior. Evaluation in the first stage consisted of a proof-of-concept implementation, and respondent behavior data has been collected since then.

In the second BIE cycle, a set of visualization techniques (Sect. 4.2) were crafted, built, and implemented into the production software. Questionnaire evaluation and paradata literature were factored in, primarily, drawing from [13], the idea of being able to assess phrasing/quality of single questions, structural issues with the questionnaire. Also, time aspects were considered essential, drawing from discussions with stakeholders and paradata literature [10, 14, 18]. The visualizations were integrated into the software used in the eHealth practice, and evaluated using a focus group approach (see Sect. 5.1).

In the third BIE cycle, a set of constructs were designed, built, and implemented into the production software. An evaluation was conducted through an experiment designed to study the utility of RBL as a means to improve survey design and interpret survey results (see Sect. 5.2).

4 A Framework for Respondent Behavior Logging

Here, we detail our conceptualization of respondent behavior in the context of online surveys. We refer to the full set of findings as the RBL framework, consisting of a *dynamic* model of respondent behavior, a *static* model of respondent behavior, *visualization* techniques, and *constructs* for respondent behavior. In the following subsections, we account for each aspect of the framework in the order listed above.

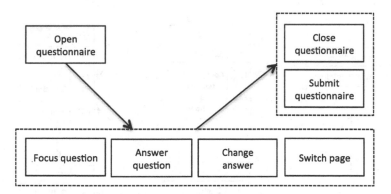

Fig. 1. Dynamic model of respondent behavior

4.1 Conceptual Models of Respondent Behavior

A logical first step in development was to identify what user actions to log. During the design process, drawing from the pragmatist interest in action-oriented conceptual modeling [1], we identified a set of user actions that the software can trace at the server-side through the HTTP requests client browsers make to the webserver. The flowchart in Fig. 1 shows the dynamic model of user behavior.

Figure 1 shows seven detectable action types in the web survey context. The action types 'open questionnaire', 'close to continue later', and 'submit questionnaire' need no further explanation. The 'focus on question' action type means that there is some indication that a question is currently in the focus of the user, e.g., by hovering a question area with the mouse pointer or setting focus on a text field by clicking it. The 'answer unanswered question' occurs when a user answers a question that has not been previously answered, differentiating it from the 'revise answer to question' action type. It is also possible to track when users switch to another page in the questionnaire. The dynamic model, despite its simplicity, is an important concept to understand better what types of user actions we may trace in the context of online questionnaires. A central idea of tracking these actions is that a rich account of actions taken serves to indicate how the respondent interprets various situations when filling in a questionnaire.

We want to stress that the distinction between server-side and client-side logging [10] is insufficient. Contemporary web applications using Ajax [7] calls allow us to design of what to log in a much more granular way than the paradata literature suggests. *Asynchronous background requests, e.g., using Ajax, allow us to make balanced trade-offs between richness in log data and a disturbance-free user experience.*

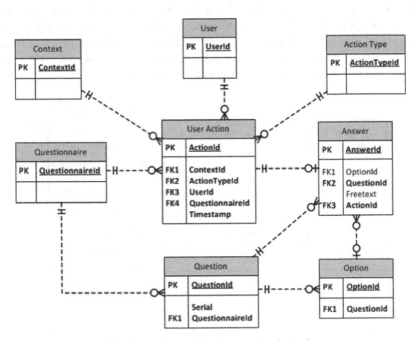

Fig. 2. Static model of respondent behavior

The entity/relationship diagram below (Fig. 2) shows a static model to keep track of user actions as shown in Fig. 1. The purpose of the design is to allow traceability, i.e., that we can reconstruct how a respondent filled in a questionnaire. Also, there is a need to keep track of the respondent's (i.e., user's) identity, to allow us to make queries related to a particular individual.

'User Action' defines the actual log record. It shows how a user, at a particular point in time, performs an action of some type while answering a specific questionnaire. This action may include an answer to a question, which may be free text, but it may also point out an optional answer to a question. Keeping track of context is imperative, since a research protocol may include the use of a questionnaire at different times, e.g., in a baseline as well as a follow-up point of measurement. This is the case in many randomized controlled trials where the same questionnaire is typically used repeatedly to measure the same construct (e.g., depression or anxiety) at different times in the study. By including action type, we facilitate queries of user behavior based on a grouping by the type of action performed.

4.2 Visualization Techniques

Visual aids are often effective methods of communication in organizational research [5], supporting interpretation of complex data [21].

There are various ways to query into the RBL database to render reports and visualizations of RBL data. Here we will present three types of visualization techniques (Table 1) to convey the idea of visualizing respondent behavior. We differentiate between structural questionnaire qualities and question qualities [15]. Each visualization technique aims at disclosing a quality dimension of a questionnaire – either targeting the structure dimension or the question dimension of the questionnaire. We will return to the answer matrix visualization in the evaluation section below to illustrate its use and interpretation by focus group participants.

Table 1. RBL visualization techniques

Visualization technique	Quality dimension	Description
Activity Chart	Question	The number of activities (answer, delete, change answer) per question in a questionnaire
Time Chart	Time	Time taken to answer each question in a questionnaire
Answer Matrix	Structure	Shows how a respondent moves between questions in a questionnaire

4.3 Respondent Behavior Constructs

As a contrast to visualization techniques – i.e., supporting people to *interpret* complex data – we also propose that RBL data may be quantified to support statistical analyses to reveal flaws in questionnaire design. Building on the three aspects used for visualization techniques – question-level aspects, questionnaire level aspects, and time aspects – a set of measures were designed to analyze respondent behaviors on question level:

- Change Frequency (**CF**). The number of times the answer to a question is changed before the questionnaire is submitted.
- Question Response Time (**QRT**). The time taken to complete a single question.

- PingPong Frequency In (**PFI**). The number of jumps to a question in focus from other questions.
- PingPong Frequency Out (**PFO**). The number of jumps from a question in focus to other questions.
- PingPong Frequency Total (**PFT**). PFI + PFO.

These measures have been proposed before in the paradata literature [14], but their practical use is rare. Also, we crafted corresponding measures for the questionnaire level. There are fewer questionnaire level constructs, due to the logical conflation of the PFI, PFO, and PFT measure into a total measure (OPF):

- Overall Change Frequency (**OCF**). The number of times an answer has been changed in the questionnaire as a whole before it is submitted.
- Overall Response Time (**ORT**). The response time for the whole questionnaire.
- Overall PingPong Frequency (**OPF**). The number of jumps between questions in the questionnaire, excluding the number of necessary jumps to move through the questionnaire sequentially.

5   Evaluation

Our evaluation highlights the three aspects proof-of-concept, proof-of-value, and proof-of-use [22]. Our software implementation serves as a first proof-of-concept. Drawing from DSR evaluation literature [11, 28], we further demonstrate proof-of-concept and to some degree proof-of-value through a focus-group evaluation (Sect. 5.1) and an experimental evaluation (Sect. 5.2) of the RBL constructs.

5.1   Focus Group Evaluation

Rationale. The goal of the focus group evaluation was to assess the reactions from active researchers, and to what extent they gained new insights from interpreting RBL visualizations. In doing so, we received stakeholder feedback about the value of RBL visualizations for researchers. Part of the evaluation was also to implement software that produced the visualizations, i.e., a proof-of-concept [22] or expository instantiation [9] demonstrating the feasibility to apply the RBL visualizations in practice.

Evaluation Overview. We organized a focus group consisting of experts from *the eHealth practice*. We presented the visualizations to the focus group, and the participants were encouraged to reflect on the utility of these representations to (i) identify design flaws and suggestions for improvements of the questionnaire and (ii) discuss if they would interpret the collected data differently given the way they made sense of the RBL visualization. We thus based the evaluation on qualitative data collected in the focus group session, focusing on if and how RBL visualizations were considered meaningful and valuable to the focus group participants.

Data Collection. We presented a series of slides with visualizations of RBL data from ongoing research in *the eHealth practice*. The visualizations were made based on how respondents answered the HADS questionnaire; an instrument used to measure depression and anxiety [30]. In *the eHealth practice*, HADS is used both for screening and for subsequent follow-ups of the participants' depression and anxiety. We made an audio recording of the entire session (approximately one hour) and took notes.

Data Analysis. The authors interpreted the audio recording to identify how focus group participants made sense of the RBL visualizations, and how they ascribed meaning to them. Below we account for the results of the analysis. Due to space limitations, we will just give a brief example from the analysis here, and then summarize the lessons learned.

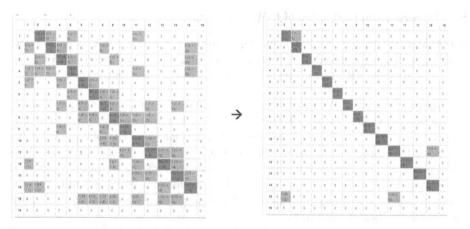

Fig. 3. Visualization showing behavior filling in HADS at two different measurement points

The RBL visualizations rendered some results related to the repeated use of a questionnaire in randomized controlled trials. A visualization of the time taken for an individual to answer each question, compared to the meantime for all participants to answer each question. One participant stated, "This chart can be very useful if we combine the same chart time to time of a specific patient to compare a patient's situation when the same patient takes HADS later in their treatment process." Another participant responded to a visualization of how an individual respondent changed their answers to each question, in relation to the mean number of changes of answers to each question: "I am not sure this brings any ambiguity because users when attending HADS for the second time, they already have learned about the questions, [..] but what should be interesting is that, the users who consistently had same results from both [times they filled in] HADS". We can see from these statements, that RBL visualizations stimulated the focus group members to interpret their data in new ways; and to start thinking about new types of analyses to understand the development of their patients over time better.

Figure 3 is an answer matrix (see Table 1) that shows how many times users 'jumped' from one question to another. The axes represent the question numbers as they appear to the users. The gray boxes show the most common path or sequence the users have answered the questions. We compare Fig. 3 further shows the same plot the second time the same questionnaire was answered, at a later stage in the study.

Lessons Learned. The focus group evaluation shows that the visualizations support researchers to reflect in new ways about the design of their questionnaires. We have shown examples of how the focus group members have (i) reflected on new ways of understanding the use of questionnaires at different observation points and (ii) how the visualization of RBL data correctly helped researchers identify a problem with the HADS questionnaire. Hence, the evaluation has shown proof-of-value [23] of the RBL visualization techniques in an actual research setting.

5.2 Experimental Evaluation of RBL Constructs

Rationale. The goal of the experimental evaluation is to evaluate if RBL data in combination with statistical analyses can be used to detect 'flaws' in questionnaire design and to assess if the RBL measurement constructs support questionnaire evaluation.

Evaluation Overview. We based the experimental design on an original questionnaire design using guidelines from the Harvard University Program on Survey research (Q1). In addition to Q1, we designed two derivate questionnaires with planted flaws: Q2 has embedded flaws on the question level, while Q3 has embedded structural flaws. To have a useful baseline questionnaire, we proceeded with the well-established USE questionnaire [16] for usability evaluation. The questionnaire concerns online learning platforms, making it relevant for the intended respondents, who were students at the various campuses at the university.

Data Collection. Students (N = 120) were approached and asked to fill in the questionnaire using tablets provided by the researcher. The process was double-blind (neither the researchers nor the respondents knew which version of the questionnaire they were filling in).

Data Analysis. A series of statistical analysis methods were used to analyze RBL data. Due to space limitations, we will here present one hypothesis and the results of the analyses. To analyze the data and draw inferences from the same, descriptive statistics were calculated separately for the metrics in each hypothesis. One-way MANOVA was performed using SPSS to test the hypothesis and results were analyzed to conclude on the same. All the assumptions of one-way MANOVA were also tested using SPSS.

Hypothesis: Questionnaire one has open-ended questions placed at the end whereas questionnaire three has open-ended questions put in the middle of the questionnaire. We tested the null hypothesis 'Mean response time and change frequency for open-ended questions is the same between questionnaire one and three.' The null hypothesis was rejected, demonstrating that response time and change frequency of open-ended questions are significant discriminating variables for questionnaires 1 and 3. We placed open-ended questions at the end of questionnaire one whereas we placed them in the middle of questionnaire three. Based on the result of the hypothesis we can also conclude that placement of open-ended questions in a questionnaire has a significant impact on their response time and change frequency. We anticipated that open-ended questions placed at the end of a questionnaire have less response time and change frequency compared to placement in the middle of the questionnaire.

A limitation is that the variables in each category were not normally distributed and that could have impacted the results of the analysis. Another limitation is that there are multiple instances, especially in questionnaire three, where the respondents' response time for numerous questions is 0 s. That is; Respondents chose not to respond to questions that were placed out of order or were not properly contextualized, and this could have impacted the results of the evaluation.

Lessons Learned. We have demonstrated how the RBL constructs prove feasible to use in statistical analysis. We have also shown that the collection of RBL data, and subsequent analysis using RBL measurement constructs, facilitates ex-post analyses of questionnaire design. Note that we have not investigated the in-depth meaning of the experimental results; e.g., attempted to correlate the characteristics of the free-text answers with the CF or time taken measures. Further, other researchers in the eHealth practice are currently using the RBL constructs to investigate various issues of respondent behavior, e.g., correlations to other measures such as question readability and emotional demand. The uptake of the concept by others indicates the value of RBL for their research practice.

6 Concluding Discussion

In this paper, we have presented RBL; a set of interrelated concepts to capture, visualize and statistically analyze paradata in the context of online surveys.

Our work is grounded in literature and in a design process in the context of eHealth and eHealth research. We provided a proof of concept through a software implementation. The software, being used in live eHealth trials, is used to collect data for respondent behavior while filling in questionnaires. Two evaluation activities demonstrate the qualities of RBL. First, a focus group in which we presented RBL visualizations to stakeholders in the eHealth research practice. In doing this, we showed proof-of-concept for the RBL framework. Also, the focus group evaluation demonstrated proof-of-value for RBL visualizations. Second, we conducted an experimental evaluation including 120 participants in which the RBL measures were used to test hypotheses about questionnaire flaws. The evaluation serves as a proof-of-concept that these measures support questionnaire evaluation by statistical means. The results show a value of RBL as a means to identify questionnaire design issues, but also to make sense of data collected in the trials, and to conduct ex-post evaluations of questionnaire design. Other researchers in the eHealth practice are using RBL constructs in their continued work.

In sensitive environments such as the eHealth research context, the extensive use of built-in web server logging mechanisms may be problematic. When managing sensitive information, we want to keep potentially sensitive within a confined environment [27]. In the current empirical context, all collected data resides in a well-encrypted database, to prevent unauthorized access. Also, going beyond standard web server logging [29] gives the researchers control over the conceptualization of respondent behavior the paradata collection. For instance, if paradata collection is part of our application, we have a better opportunity to store contextual data.

The RBL framework presented here captures data on the server-side due to an early identified risk that client-side logging might slow down the client web browser. However, we have questioned the dichotomous view on server-side v. client-side paradata. As design science researchers, we have the opportunity to affect log data collection by design, e.g., by using Ajax calls from the client to the server strategically. This is a big contrast to researchers in non-computing disciplines that may have to rely on using data that is available in the web infrastructure.

As DS researchers, we should embrace the opportunity of integrating evaluation support into our artifact design – we see this work as an example of software-embedded evaluation support [26], and, more generally as a contribution to the discourse on tools to support design science research [19].

References

1. Arroyo, E., et al.: Usability tool for analysis of web designs using mouse tracks. In: 2006 Extended Abstracts on Human Factors in Computing Systems, pp. 484–489 (2006)
2. Atterer, R., et al.: Knowing the user's every move: user activity tracking for website usability evaluation and implicit interaction. In: Proceedings of the 15th International Conference on World Wide Web, pp. 203–212 (2006)
3. Brancato, G., et al.: Handbook of recommended practices for questionnaire development and testing in the European statistical system. European Statistical System (2006)
4. Conboy, K.: Agility from first principles: reconstructing the concept of agility in information systems development. Inf. Syst. Res. 20(3), 329–354 (2009)
5. Davison, J., et al.: (Im) perfect pictures: snaplogs in performativity research. Qual. Res. Organ. Manag. Int. J. 7(1), 54–71 (2012)
6. Dewan, S., Ramaprasad, J.: Research note-music blogging, online sampling, and the long tail. Inf. Syst. Res. 23(3-Part-2), 1056–1067 (2012)
7. Garrett, J.J.: Ajax: a new approach to web applications (2005)
8. Gregor, S., Hevner, A.R.: Positioning and presenting design science research for maximum impact. Mis Q. 37(2), 337–355 (2013)
9. Gregor, S., Jones, D.: The anatomy of a design theory. J. Assoc. Inf. Syst. 8(5), 312–335 (2007)
10. Heerwegh, D.: Internet survey paradata. In: Social and Behavioral Research and the Internet, pp. 325–348. Routledge (2011)
11. Hevner, A.R., et al.: Design science in information systems research. Mis Q. 28(1), 75–105 (2004)
12. Koch, H., et al.: Bridging the work/social divide: the emotional response to organizational social networking sites. Eur. J. Inf. Syst. 21(6), 699–717 (2012)
13. Krosnick, J.A., Presser, S.: Question and questionnaire design. In: Marsden, P.V., Wright, J.D. (eds.) Handbook of Survey Research, pp. 263–313. Emerald Group Publishing Limited (2010)
14. Kunz, T., Hadler, P.: Collection and use of web paradata. Mannheim, GESIS-Leibniz-Institut für Sozialwissenschaften (GESIS Survey Guideline) (2020). https://doi.org/10.15465/gesis-sg_037

15. Lumsden, J., Morgan, W.: Online-questionnaire design: establishing guidelines and evaluating existing support (2005)
16. Lund, A.M.: Measuring usability with the use questionnaire. Usability Interface **8**(2), 3–6 (2001)
17. Martin, D., et al.: Hidden surveillance by web sites: web bugs in contemporary use. Commun. ACM. **46**(12), 258–264 (2003)
18. McClain, C.A., et al.: A typology of web survey paradata for assessing total survey error. Soc. Sci. Comput. Rev. **37**(2), 196–213 (2019)
19. Morana, S., et al.: Tool support for design science researchtowards a software ecosystem: a report from a DESRIST 2017 workshop. Commun. Assoc. Inf. Syst. **43**(1), 17 (2018)
20. Newsted, P.R., et al.: Survey instruments in information systems. MIS Q. **22**(4), 553–554 (1998)
21. Nulty, D.D.: The adequacy of response rates to online and paper surveys: what can be done? Assess. Eval. High. Educ. **33**(3), 301–314 (2008)
22. Nunamaker, J., Jay, F., Briggs, R.O.: Toward a broader vision for Information Systems. ACM Trans. Manag. Inf. Syst. **2**(4), 1–12 (2011)
23. Sein, M., et al.: Action design research. MIS Q. **35**(1), 37–56 (2011)
24. Sen, R., et al.: Buyers' choice of online search strategy and its managerial implications. J. Manag. Inf. Syst. **23**(1), 211–238 (2006)
25. Sivo, S.A., et al.: How low should you go? Low response rates and the validity of inference in IS questionnaire research. J. Assoc. Inf. Syst. **7**(6), 351–414 (2006)
26. Sjöström, J., Kruse, L.C., Haj-Bolouri, A., Flensburg, P.: Software-embedded evaluation support in design science research. In: Chatterjee, S., Dutta, K., Sundarraj, R.P. (eds.) DESRIST 2018. LNCS, vol. 10844, pp. 348–362. Springer, Cham (2018). https://doi.org/10.1007/978-3-319-91800-6_23
27. Sjöström, J., Ågerfalk, P.J., Hevner, A.R.: The design of a multi-layer scrutiny protocol to support online privacy and accountability. In: Tremblay, M.C., VanderMeer, D., Rothenberger, M., Gupta, A., Yoon, V. (eds.) DESRIST 2014. LNCS, vol. 8463, pp. 85–98. Springer, Cham (2014). https://doi.org/10.1007/978-3-319-06701-8_6
28. Venable, J., et al.: FEDS: a framework for evaluation in design science research. Eur. J. Inf. Syst. **25**(1), 77–89 (2016)
29. W3C: Extended log file format. https://www.w3.org/TR/WD-logfile.html
30. Zigmond, A.S., Snaith, R.P.: The hospital and anxiety depression scale. Acta Psychiatr. Scand. **67**(6), 361–370 (1983)

A Microservice-Based Reference Architecture for Digital Platforms in the Proteomics Domain

Marwin Shraideh[1]([⊠]) [iD], Patroklos Samaras[2] [iD], Maximilian Schreieck[1] [iD],
and Helmut Krcmar[1] [iD]

[1] Technical University of Munich, Boltzmannstr. 3, 85748 Garching bei München, Germany
{marwin.shraideh,maximilian.schreieck,helmut.krcmar}@tum.de
[2] Technical University of Munich, Emil-Erlenmeyer-Forum 5, 85354 Freising, Germany
patroklos.samaras@tum.de

Abstract. Proteomics holds huge innovations for healthcare such as personalized medicine to tremendously increase people's health. Due to its rapid growth, its multidimensional data sets and the related need for the latest technologies and huge computing capacities, a diverse and scattered tool and repository landscape evolved in an uncontrolled manner. Therefore, tool usage is complicated, time consuming and almost impossible without expert IT skills. To create the conditions for new innovations in the proteomics domain and making first steps towards personalized medicine, digital platforms are needed. However, designing such a system is complex and was not yet supported by information systems. Consequently, we will design and implement a sustainable microservice-based reference architecture for digital platforms in the proteomics domain based on the example of ProteomicsDB that focuses on maintainability, extendibility, and reusability by following the design science requirements. With our reference architecture, we extend evidence-based design knowledge in real-world information systems contributing to information systems research and provide proteomics researchers, but also practitioners a foundation for establishing new business models and enhancing existing or developing new services or platforms.

Keywords: Reference architecture · Proteomics · Digital platform · Microservices · Design science · Information systems engineering

1 Introduction

Proteomics has become increasingly important in the context of personalized medicine and healthcare [1–4]. "Proteomics refers to the study of proteomes, but is also used to describe the techniques used to determine the entire set of proteins of an organism or system, such as protein purification and mass spectrometry." [5]. Since "[p]roteins are the major effectors of cell functions" [6] in the human body, they reflect "the actual workforce of the cell and are thus highly suited for studying the mechanism of disease development and progression" [6]. Consequently, it is increasingly utilized in clinical practice to conduct proteomics analysis on individual patients to identify complex diseases such as cancer [7] more effectively, efficiently, and reliably, but also to offer a more

© Springer Nature Switzerland AG 2021
L. Chandra Kruse et al. (Eds.): DESRIST 2021, LNCS 12807, pp. 260–271, 2021.
https://doi.org/10.1007/978-3-030-82405-1_26

effective and gentle personalized treatment by informing drug selection and dosage [1, 6, 8]. This is also known as personalized medicine. Personalized medicine customizes disease treatment and post-treatment based on individual differences of patients [9]. The goal of personalized medicine is to ultimately prevent diseases instead of having to react upon its occurrence resulting in an overall improvement of people's health [4]. For personalized medicine, biomarkers are key as they "are defined as objectively measured indicators of biological processes or response to a therapeutic intervention." [10]. They inform about disease risk and status as they reflect specific characteristics of a disease and allow searching for similar characteristics in a patient's sample to identify diseases easily and for appropriate drugs to treat the disease. Consequently, proteomics has the potential to bring new innovations to healthcare and medicine [4]. For example, it contributed to important insights to understand the COVID-19 virus and revealed potential therapy targets [11]. However, analyzing complex and multi-dimensional proteomcis data requires interdisciplinary expert knowledge and a specialized set of analytics tools that can be automized to a limited extent only.

For this reason and due to the proteomics rapid evolution in the past years, the landscape of proteomics data repositories and tools has grown in an uncontrolled manner making data integration and tool usage complicated, time consuming and almost impossible without expert IT skills. Furthermore, there is no guidance for developing new tools and repositories and no standards for easier tool and repository integration. Most tools and repositories are only created to serve the purpose of publishing results from proteomics research and thus rarely offer seamless reusability by other labs and institutions.

To create the conditions for new innovations in the proteomics domain and making first steps towards personalized medicine, information systems (IS), in particular digital platforms, are a potential solution to integrate different proteomics repositories and tools and to cope with the many related challenges. Here, IS research can help with its knowledge in handling big data and information system and service system design [12–17]. However, designing such a system is complex and was not yet supported by information systems and service (systems) engineering in the proteomics domain. Existing solutions rarely provide a deep insight into the architecture of these systems and tools.

Consequently, we will design and implement a reference architecture for digital platforms based on the example of ProteomicsDB. ProteomicsDB is a big data, multi-omics and multi-organism resource for life science research initially developed for hosting the first mass spectrometry-based draft of the human proteome [18, 19]. It is built upon the in-memory database platform of SAP HANA and publicly accessible. The many users of ProteomicsDB include people from both the academic and industrial setup. ProteomicsDB tries to evolve to a digital platform to solve aforementioned challenges and to provide a "one-stop-shop" for solutions in daily issues in life science research. Therefore, ProteomicsDB already offers first online analytics services for experiments as well as search and visualization functionalities to enable the online exploration, analysis, and comparison of (imported) protein expression datasets; for example, to find appropriate cell lines or drugs for an experiment or for hypothesis generation.

However, incomplete documentation as well as a missing guidance on how to create new features makes development of new features or endpoints in ProteomicsDB time consuming and arbitrary. This resulted in a complex landscape of island solutions that is hard to update and adapt to new challenges and utilizes existing features only to a limited extent hindering rapid integration of new tools and repositories.

With our reference architecture, we want to address these challenges and pitfalls by providing a clear structure and guidance that allows tools and repositories in the proteomics domain to stay maintainable, extendable, reusable and managable in the long run. It also allows a fast and unified development approach for new tools, repositories, and proteomics resources, such as ProteomicsDB, to evolve themselves to a digital platform that can integrate most important tools and repositories of the proteomics domain to provide a maximum of utility for proteomics research and enabling and accelerating new innovations in the proteomics domain.

We structured our paper as follows: First, we provide a brief introduction to microservice architectures and reference architectures in Sect. 2, then describe our research approach in Sect. 3 and present our results in Sect. 4. Finally, we conclude this paper by discussing our results and describing the limitations of our research.

2   Theoretical Background

2.1   Microservice Architectures

According to [20], microservices is an architectural style that aims at developing applications based on small services where each service has a single purpose. Microservices are well suited for big software systems [21]. It avoids software systems from becoming rigid, hard to maintain and extendable, and uneconomical due to growing functionalities and complexity [22]. Here, it pays special attention to interchangeability of single software components, interoperability of microservices and avoiding dependencies to other components [20, 23]. Due to its simple extendibility and concept of immutability (replacing components instead of adjusting them), it simplifies development while accepting an increasing complexity of the overall architecture which can be handled by additional tools and automatization [24]. Therefore, it is used by big tech companies such as Netflix, Google and other software platforms [25].

2.2   Reference Architectures

According to [26], a reference architecture is an abstract architecture, that simplifies the development of systems, solutions, and applications by providing knowledge and defining the frame for development. It is characterized by its (re)usable object or content that is used for constructing a concrete architecture for a system to develop. A reference architecture contains a technical focus but combines it with related domain knowledge. With its expression and content, it builds a common framework allowing to have detailed discussions of all stakeholders that are involved in development [26]. Especially in highly dynamic environments with specific requirements to integration in open systems, reference architectures support in coping with increasing complexity and scale [27]. They increase quality by using best practices and lower development cost and time due to reusability of modules of the reference architectures [28].

3   Research Approach

For designing our reference architecture, we follow the 8-step approach of [29] which is based on the design science requirements [30].

1. Defining the purpose and goal of the reference architecture
2. Literature Review
3. Situation and requirements from industry
4. Standardizing terms and creating a domain description
5. Extracting generic and optional requirements
6. Transferring identified requirements to n:1 functional and logical modules
7. Creating reference processes
8. Feedback cycles and implementation of reference architecture

Step one defines what aspects the reference architecture focuses on and how it is visualized and presented to be understandable for future users of the reference architecture. To do so, we used the classification schema of [29]. This phase is equivalent to the framing of research activities and determining the focus of the planned research. The focused aspects were selected in a way that they also accomplish the goals the reference architecture is built for. In step two, the current body of knowledge in research and available technologies must be searched to build a foundation for designing the reference architecture [29]. Since we focus on microservices, we conducted a literature review according to [31] and [32] to find the status quo of requirements towards designing, implementing, and maintaining microservices. The goal is to support the develop and build phase before starting with the first design science cycle by drawing from existing knowledge from previous information systems research about microservices and thus assuring a rigor design. In total, we found 52 unique requirements from 31 relevant articles out of 1439 after we coded the extracted requirements according to [33]. Goal of step three is to gather requirements from the proteomics domain and related industry [29]. Therefore, we conducted a qualitative study based on seven semi-structured expert interviews with 5 researchers, 3 developers and the professor of the Chair for Proteomics and Bioanalytics of the Technical University of Munich according to [34] to ensure relevance of our reference architecture for practice and the proteomics domain. Here, we focused on technical requirements rather than user requirements. Step four aims at standardizing descriptions of the domain and used terms to have a common understanding of sections and terms used in the reference architecture for all involved stakeholders [29]. Since we use terms common to microservices and stick to the terms and wording used in the interviews, step four does not need special attention. In step five, the results of step two and three must be aggregated to a list of unique requirements and separated in generic and optional requirements. Generic requirements are universally applicable and should be generally fulfilled. Optional requirements should be considered only for specific use cases [29]. We only aggregated our identified requirements to a list of unique requirements and did not differentiate between generic and optional requirements since we could not clearly separate them as we already focused on a narrowed set of requirements. Therefore, we considered all our requirements as generic requirements. Based on step five, every identified requirement must be transferred into one logical module in step six [29]. However, one module can fulfill multiple requirements, where every module must be a closed unit that is responsible for a specific purpose or functionality in the system according to the separations of concerns of [35]. If one requirement cannot be fulfilled by one module, it must be split up into multiple smaller requirements. These modules must be categorized as generic or optional based on how many generic or optional requirements they include [29]. As we decided to consider all requirements as generic in the previous step, we could only identify optional modules after implementing the prototype. All modules that were not implemented were categorized as optional. In total, we identified 20 modules. The derived modules and the identified requirements from the previous steps represent the foundation for designing the first version of our reference architecture in step seven. Lastly, in step eight, multiple feedback rounds must be conducted with developers and stakeholders in the context of requirements elicitation to improve the requirements and the reference architecture iteratively [29]. Since evaluation should be conducted as often as possible according to design science requirements [36], we integrated evaluation cycles where possible.

Once we designed the reference architecture and included requirements from literature and researchers, we finished the first design science iteration by conducting the phase "develop and evaluate". We then presented our first version of our reference architecture to developers of ProteomicsDB and considered their feedback in our second version. Afterwards, we implemented the second version of our reference architecture at the example of a prototype in ProteomicsDB. Here, the goal was to evaluate whether the designed reference architecture is applicable and usable. Furthermore, we wanted to get valuable insights from the implementation itself as well as feedback from experts for a second time to improve the overall design.

4   Results

For step one, we classified our reference architecture according to [29]. Our final reference architecture will have a mixed abstraction level, will be technology neutral, industry-specific and have a cross-product focus as well as a cross-company focus. Furthermore, we agreed upon that the reference character of our architecture will focus on researchers and developers in the proteomics domain as a reference point. There will also be variation points and the technical focus considers information from the proteomics domain. Therefore, our reference architecture is driven by research and practice. We also do not claim to design a holistic and complete reference architecture. The goal is to not only standardize the architecture of tools and repositories in the proteomics domain, but also to make it easier to use, extend, maintain, and integrate tools and repositories. For creating the reference architecture, we use a combination of an inductive and deductive approach [37]. With our reference architecture, we provide knowledge about the architecture and guidelines.

From the requirements we identified in step two and three, we only considered those from literature and the interview partners that were relevant for informing the reference architecture design. The only requirement of users was the possibility to use the same tool, feature or data set for multiple different purposes and fields for an interdisciplinary approach. Consequently, most important requirements came from the developers.

Figure 1 shows our reference architecture that was created in step seven and considers all 20 modules identified in step six based on step five and the feedback of all described evaluation cycles of step eight.

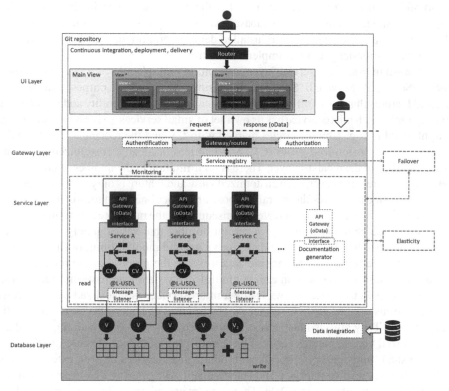

Fig. 1. Reference architecture

The reference architecture is divided in four layers: database layer, service layer, gateway layer, and UI layer. The database layer consists of the data schema and includes an abstraction layer which is demonstrated by the circles marked with a V, further referred to as view. These can be SQL views or other views that only allow read access to the tables so that database tables are not directly exposed to read operations. This layer also makes the database layer more flexible. Especially, when the data schema changes frequently as it is often the case in the proteomics domain. Since every view always provides the content of one table, it reflects the latest version of a table. Given the condition that columns in database tables and tables itself are not deleted and only new added and for every change in a table a new version of the view is created as depicted by V_2, it is possible to make changes in the database schema without affecting services that access older versions of the view. Therefore, extensibility and maintainability are increased since only new services must use the latest view version. Also, the effort for developers is decreased as they do not have to migrate all changes to the services that do not use this data (the additional column) if they would directly access the database table. This also allows a user-friendly versioning for the API since only major changes will affect older versions and therefore provide API users more time to migrate to the latest version. However, if an existing view needs the new data or must be updated due to important changes in the data schema, all services that access this view must be adjusted, too. As the possibility of integrating data is crucial in the proteomics domain, data integration must be possible. Ideally on the database layer directly due to performance reasons. Also, some databases come with preinstalled data integration tools that should be used because of its simplicity and fast implementation.

As shown in Fig. 1, the service layer can contain multiple microservices where each service (Service A, Service B, Service C and further) has a specific purpose, functionalities, and features that it also offers to other services enabling reusability and capsulation. Consequently, each microservice has its own set of small services and components which is highlighted in Fig. 1 by the circles marked with CV and the rectangles marked with f, further called customized views (CV) and feature (f). Ideally, customized views are created already in the database layer. There is no limitation in the number of customized views and features. However, each customized view and feature is only allowed to be part of a microservice if it serves the overall purpose and functionality of this microservice. If not, a new microservice must be created. Consequently, the number of customized views and features are naturally limited to a certain number that varies greatly. Customized views get the needed data from the database views and modify, limit, or filter the data as needed by the features or to provide data to serve the purpose of the microservice. Therefore, customized views can access multiple views and can have multiple hierarchies of reuse of customized views inside a microservice, as visualized by the arrows between the customized views in service A. The features of a microservice never directly access views. They always must access customized views to work with required data. As customized views, features can also have multiple hierarchies of reuse of other features. To share functionality and data with other microservices or even external users, each service has its own interface and standardized API gateway that messages over a standardized protocol such as oData. Therefore, every microservice can control which customized views or features it offers to other microservices via its interface and which of these customized views or features it offers to external users or services via its API Gateway by registering it in the service registry. To also wait for specific messages from other microservices in the service layer, every microservice has a message listener. This message listener allows to react upon messages sent by other microservices to also enable advanced automatization and communication between microservices. To keep an overview of the growing amount of microservices, their purpose, offered customized views and features, and their dependencies to other microservices, a proper documentation is crucial to keep them maintainable. Consequently, every microservice must be documented on code-level using standardized documentation languages such as unified service definition language (USDL) or linked unified service definition language (L-USDL). This allows to use an automated documentation generator that reads specific flags in the code of the microservices to collect information about their functionalities, offered data entities and analyzes the relationships in between microservices but also used database views. The collected information is provided to either internal developers or external API users to a restricted extent also via a standard API gateway. Goal of this documentation generator is to reduce the necessary effort to create documentations for microservices and the API manually after the implementation. It also prevents incomplete documentations already on code-level because continuous integration and deployment checks automatically detect missing or empty flags and prohibit productive deployment or merging a branch on the git repository.

Since not all microservices work dependent of other microservices, outages might not be recognized immediately. Therefore, a permanent monitoring of every microservice, its customized views, and features is required for availability by a microservice in the service layer. In case of an outage, failover must deploy a clone of the affected microservice and inform the service registry to reroute to the newly deployed microservice. If a microservice needs more or less computing power due to increased or decreased use, an elasticity service must assign hardware capacities appropriately. The failover service and the elasticity service are both external services that can manage the hardware directly. As mentioned before, the service registry holds all microservices and the customized views and features they offer for public use by the frontend or by external users. The Gateway/router represents the central component that can be accessed externally and receives all user and frontend requests. As all microservices have their own API, requests can simply be routed to the appropriate destination through the service registry once authentication was successful and authorization granted. The requested information is routed back to the Gateway/router by the microservice and the response is sent to the user interface or the user. In case of critical outages, the service registry is informed about the status of the requested resource and gets additional information from the failover service to inform the user accordingly.

The UI layer is separated from the overall complexity of the structure underneath the gateway layer through the API as the single point of access. The user interface (UI) itself consists of one main view and multiple views, component-wrappers and components. Components represent the smallest part of the UI and reflect visualization components, such as a table, bar chart or other types of charts that should be used once or multiple times. Therefore, each component exists only once, can only accept data, and provides status data about itself. Consequently, each component must come with one component-wrapper, that takes care of requesting data from the API, adjusting it as needed and handing its data over to the component. Also, one component-wrapper can only feed one component. A component-wrapper and a component are an independent unit that can be used and reused by any view making UI development more efficient. Since views follow the same principle, UI components can be built and reused in different context without having to write new code accelerating UI development.

Finally, a central router is responsible for navigating site requests to the respective view.

After implementing the reference architecture in ProteomicsDB, we resulted in the architecture shown in Fig. 1 without dotted elements. The most important requirements of the developers of ProteomicsDB were an overall design that heavily utilizes reuse of already implemented functionalities and features, sticking to one hardware stack and making maintainability and extendibility as easy and fast as possible with at least development effort possible. For this reason, we were not able to fulfill all microservice principles and adapted the architecture accordingly. For example, loosely coupled services with rather code duplications than dependencies between microservices for the sake of reusability. Also, failover and elasticity could not be realized due to the single hardware stack where one outage would affect all microservices. Consequently, monitoring is also not needed anymore since all microservice operations are tracked by the system. As ProteomicsDB is an open resource, we also left out authentication and authorization in the gateway layer. However, since authorization was already managed on the database level, all API requests are checked against the authorization of the database layer. Lastly, we also did not implement the message listener since it was not needed in the prototype. The documentation generator can be implemented any time since all microservices must be documented with L-USDL. According to the feedback from the developers, we met those requirements that are most important for fast development and easy maintainability with a small ruleset that does not limit a developer's coding flexibility.

5 Discussion and Limitations

The current reference architecture went through one complete iteration of a design science cycle with multiple evaluations with proteomics researchers and developers including interviews and feedback from prototyping. Therefore, it is a rigorous and relevant design artifact of design science [38]. However, we do not claim the reference architecture to be holistic and to consider all perspectives. We want to encourage to extend our reference architecture by using it as a foundation for further design science cycle iterations considering more perspectives from related stakeholders and information from the domain. For example, information from pharma companies or the already existing tool and repository landscape. Ultimately, creating a reference architecture for digital platforms in the proteomics domain that considers as much domain knowledge as possible to accelerate implementation of such platforms, overcome related challenges and pitfalls and thus enabling new innovations in the proteomics domain that improve the overall healthiness of people.

Proteomics requires huge computing capacities and therefore extraordinary expensive hardware which cannot be separated to virtualize the hardware and assign computing resources as needed. Consequently, a pure microservices architecture is not applicable in the proteomics domain due to the requirements of the domain, for practical applicability and economic reasons. Also, for the sake of maintainability, creating separated microservices that do not have the same code structure and are developed independently and individually, the problem of a landscape of island solutions that evolves uncontrolled cannot be solved. Especially in an environment where the development team changes every three to four years but the team-size remains constant over time, the effort of extending or maintaining existing services increases and becomes increasingly complex to a point where it cannot be handled anymore. Also because of the cross-expertise needed that cannot be built up under such circumstances. This led us to an interesting question for future research, whether following all microservice principles strictly is sustainable, manageable, and economic over the long run or only some of the most important principles are. Therefore, a more precise separation of strictly-to-follow and optional microservice requirements is necessary depending on the context they are implemented in.

With our research we contribute to both information systems research and proteomics research: We extended evidence-based design knowledge in real-world information systems by implementing and evaluating the designed microservice-based reference architecture in a cyclical design science approach for a digital platform in the proteomics domain [39, 40] and highlighting necessary adaptations. Our reference architecture guides proteomics and information systems researchers to systematically develop digital platforms in the proteomics domain in a unified way that also keeps its services maintainable, reusable, and adaptable in the long run. Proteomics or even bioinformatics and information systems researchers can use this reference architecture as a foundation for future research and a fast development blueprint. Pharma companies and startups can also benefit from these contributions by using the reference architecture for establishing new business models and enhancing existing or developing new services or platforms.

Acknowledgements. We thank the German Federal Ministry of Education and Research for funding this research as part of the project 031L0168 (DIAS). We explicitly thank Prof. Dr. Bernhard Küster, Prof. Dr. Mathias Wilhelm, Sascha Ladewig and all involved people for actively supporting our research.

References

1. Li, N., Zhan, X.: Signaling pathway network alterations in human ovarian cancers identified with quantitative mitochondrial proteomics. EPMA J. **10**(2), 153–172 (2019)
2. Duarte, T.T., Spencer, C.T.: Personalized proteomics: The future of precision medicine. Proteomes **4**(4), 29 (2016)
3. Parker, C.E., Borchers, C.H.: The special issue: clinical proteomics for precision medicine. Prot. Clin. Appl. **12**(2), 1600144 (2018)
4. Buriani, A., Fortinguerra, S., Carrara, M.: Clinical perspectives in diagnostic-omics and personalized medicine approach to monitor effectiveness and toxicity of phytocomplexes. In: Pelkonen, O., Duez, P., Vuorela, P.M., Vuorela, H. (eds.) Toxicology of Herbal Products, pp. 385–476. Springer, Cham (2017). https://doi.org/10.1007/978-3-319-43806-1_16
5. Nature: Proteomics - Latest research and news (2021). https://www.nature.com/subjects/proteomics. Accessed 15 Mar 2021
6. Giudice, G., Petsalaki, E.: Proteomics and phosphoproteomics in precision medicine: applications and challenges. Brief. Bioinform. **20**(3), 767–777 (2019)
7. Bozorgi, A., Sabouri, L.: Osteosarcoma, personalized medicine, and tissue engineering; an overview of overlapping fields of research. Cancer Treat. Res. Commun. **27**, 100324 (2021)
8. Drew, L.: Pharmacogenetics: the right drug for you. Nature **537**, S60–S62 (2016)
9. ESF Forward Look: Personalised Medicine for the European Citizen. Towards more precise Medicine for the Diagnosis, Treatment and Prevention of Disease (iPM) (2012). http://archives.esf.org/fileadmin/Public_documents/Publications/Personalised_Medicine.pdf. Accessed 04 Apr 2021
10. Firestein, G.S.: A biomarker by any other name.... Nat. Clin. Pract. Rheumatol. **2**(12), 635 (2006)
11. Bojkova, D., et al.: Proteomics of SARS-CoV-2-infected host cells reveals therapy targets. Nature **583**, 469–472 (2020)
12. Chekfoung, T., Sun, L., Kecheng, L.: Big data architecture for pervasive healthcare: a literature review. In: European Conference on Information Systems (ECIS) 2015 Proceedings, Münster, Germany (2015).

13. Chen, T., Lu, P., Lu, L.: Design of ASD subtyping approach based on multi-omics data to promote personalized healthcare. In: Proceedings of the 53rd Hawaii International Conference on System Sciences (HICSS), Maui, Hawaii (2020)
14. Simons, L.P.A.: Health 2050: Bioinformatics for rapid self-repair; a design analysis for future quantified self. In: BLED 2020 Proceedings, Bled, Slovenia (2020)
15. Jarvenpaa, S., Markus, M.L.: Genetic platforms and their commercialization: three tales of digital entrepreneurship. In: Proceedings of the 51st Hawaii International Conference on System Sciences (HICSS). Hilton Waikoloa Village, Hawaii (2018).
16. de Reuver, M., Lessard, L.: Describing health service platform architectures: a guiding framework. In: Americas Conference on Information Systems (AMCIS) 2019 Proceedings, Cancún, Mexico (2019)
17. Vassilakopoulou, P., et al.: Building national eHealth platforms: the challenge of inclusiveness. In: International Conference on Information Systems (ICIS) 2017 Proceedings, Seoul, South Korea (2017)
18. Samaras, P., et al.: ProteomicsDB: a multi-omics and multi-organism resource for life science research. Nucleic Acids Res. 48(D1), D1153–D1163 (2019)
19. Wilhelm, M., et al.: Mass-spectrometry-based draft of the human proteome. Nature 509, 582–587 (2014)
20. Di Francesco, P., Malavolta, I., Lago, P.: Research on Architecting Microservices: Trends, Focus, and Potential for Industrial Adoption. In: 2017 IEEE International Conference on Software Architecture (ICSA), Gothenburg, Sweden, pp. 21–30 (2017)
21. Josélyne, M.I., Tuheirwe-Mukasa, D., Kanagwa, B., Balikuddembe, J.: Partitioning microservices: a domain engineering approach. In: Proceedings of the 2018 International Conference on Software Engineering in Africa, Association for Computing Machinery, Gothenburg, Sweden, pp. 43–49 (2018)
22. Schwartz, A.: Microservices. Informatik-Spektrum 40(6), 590–594 (2017). https://doi.org/10.1007/s00287-017-1078-6
23. Garriga, M.: Towards a taxonomy of microservices architectures. In: Cerone, A., Roveri, M. (eds.) SEFM 2017. LNCS, vol. 10729, pp. 203–218. Springer, Cham (2018). https://doi.org/10.1007/978-3-319-74781-1_15
24. Fu, G., Sun, J., Zhao, J.: An optimized control access mechanism based on micro-service architecture. In: 2018 2nd IEEE Conference on Energy Internet and Energy System Integration (EI2), Beijing, China, pp. 1–5. IEEE (2018)
25. Alshuqayran, N., Ali, N., Evans, R.: A systematic mapping study in microservice architecture. In: 2016 IEEE 9th International Conference on Service-Oriented Computing and Applications (SOCA), Macau, China, pp. 44–51. IEEE (2016).
26. Reidt, A., Pfaff, M., Krcmar, H.: Der Referenzarchitekturbegriff im Wandel der Zeit. HMD Praxis der Wirtschaftsinformatik 55(5), 893–906 (2018). https://doi.org/10.1365/s40702-018-00448-8
27. Cloutier, R., Muller, G., Verma, D., Nilchiani, R., Hole, E., Bone, M.: The concept of reference architectures. Syst. Eng. 13(1), 14–27 (2009)
28. Trefke, J.: Grundlagen der referenzarchitekturentwicklung. In: Appelrath, H.-J., Beenken, P., Bischofs, L., Uslar, M. (eds.) IT-Architekturentwicklung im Smart Grid, pp. 9–30. Springer, Heidelberg (2012). https://doi.org/10.1007/978-3-642-29208-8_2
29. Reidt, A.: Referenzarchitektur eines integrierten Informationssystems zur Unterstützung der Instandhaltung. Universitätsbibliothek der TU München, München (2019)
30. Hevner, A.R., March, S.T., Park, J., Ram, S.: Design science in information systems research. MIS Q. 28(1), 75–105 (2004)
31. Vom Brocke, J., Simons, A., Niehaves, B., Riemer, K., Plattfaut, R., Cleven, A.: Reconstructing the giant: on the importance of rigour in documenting the literature search process. In: European Conference on Information Systems (ECIS) 2009 Proceedings, Verona, Italy (2009)

32. Webster, J., Watson, R.T.: Analyzing the past to prepare for the future: writing a literature review. MIS Q. **26**(2), xiii–xxiii (2002)
33. Mayring, P., Fenzl, T.: Qualitative inhaltsanalyse. In: Baur, N., Blasius, J. (eds.) Handbuch Methoden der empirischen Sozialforschung, pp. 543–556. Springer, Wiesbaden (2014). https://doi.org/10.1007/978-3-531-18939-0_38
34. Gläser, J., Laudel, G.: Experteninterviews und qualitative Inhaltsanalyse als Instrumente rekonstruierender Untersuchungen, 4th edn. VS Verlag für Sozialwissenschaften, Wiesbaden (2010)
35. Laplante, P.A.: What Every Engineer Should Know about Software Engineering, 1st edn. Taylor and Francis Group, Boca Raton (2007)
36. Peffers, K., Rothenberger, M., Tuunanen, T., Vaezi, R.: Design science research evaluation. In: Peffers, K., Rothenberger, M., Kuechler, B. (eds.) Design Science Research in Information Systems. Advances in Theory and Practice. DESRIST 2012. LNCS, vol. 7286, pp. 398–410. Springer, Heidelberg (2012). https://doi.org/10.1007/978-3-642-29863-9_29
37. Rehse, J.-R., Hake, P., Fettke, P., Loos, P.: Inductive Reference Model Development: Recent Results and Current Challenges. In: Mayr, H.C., Pinzger, M. (eds.) Informatik 2016, pp. 739–752. Gesellschaft für Informatik e.V., Bonn (2016)
38. Baskerville, R., Baiyere, A., Gergor, S., Hevner, A., Rossi, M.: Design science research contributions: finding a balance between artifact and theory. J. Assoc. Inf. Syst. **19**(5), 358–376 (2018)
39. Brax, S.A., Bask, A., Hsuan, J., Voss, C.: Service modularity and architecture – an overview and research agenda. Int. J. Oper. Prod. Manag. **37**(6), 686–702 (2017)
40. Böhmann, T., Leimeister, J.M., Möslein, K.: Service systems engineering. Wirtschaftsinformatik **56**(2), 83–90 (2014). https://doi.org/10.1007/s11576-014-0406-6

An Unsupervised Algorithm for Qualitative Coding of Text Data: Artifact Design, Application, and Evaluation

Alysson De Oliveira Silveira⑩ and Anol Bhattacherjee(✉)⑩

University of South Florida, Tampa, FL 33620, USA
{alysson,abhatt}@usf.edu

Abstract. This study presents an artifact for qualitative coding of large volumes of text data using automated text mining techniques. Coding is a critical component of qualitative research, where the "gold standard" involves human coders manually assigning codes to text fragments based on their subjective judgment. However, human coding is not scalable to large corpora of text with millions of large documents. Our proposed method extends the latest advancements in semantic text similarity using sentence transformers to automate qualitative coding of text for predefined constructs with known operationalizations using cosine similarity scores between individual sentences in the text documents and construct operationalizations. We illustrate our approach by coding corporate 10-K reports from US SEC filings for two organizational innovation processes: exploration and exploitation.

Keywords: Text mining · Text analytics · Natural language processing · Qualitative research · Coding · Organizational innovation · Semantic text similarity

1 Introduction

Thematic coding of text documents, such as interview transcripts, is a core process in qualitative research [1]. This process involves searching for key concepts or themes (called "codes") in blocks of texts. The coding process may be concept-driven or data-driven [1]. In concept-driven coding, we search the text for patterns of words that match a predefined set of concepts. In data-driven coding, we approach the text without any predefined conceptualization, letting the text speak for itself and allowing concepts to emerge from the text. Data-driven coding, also called open coding in grounded theory research, is used to inductively build theories, while concept-driven coding is typically used to deductively test hypotheses [1]. This study provides an algorithm for concept-driven coding of text data using automated text mining techniques.

The "gold standard" of qualitative text coding is using human coders, who must manually comb through text documents to search for relevant themes or concepts, and assigned codes to text fragments based on their subjective interpretation of the text. This

© Springer Nature Switzerland AG 2021
L. Chandra Kruse et al. (Eds.): DESRIST 2021, LNCS 12807, pp. 272–284, 2021.
https://doi.org/10.1007/978-3-030-82405-1_27

process has two limitations. First, human coding is laborious, resource-intensive, and not scalable to thousands or millions of text documents. Consequently, qualitative research tends to employ small samples, which limits the generalizability of such research. Second, while human coding works for research projects, where the data collection process is purposively designed to extract core themes relevant to the phenomenon of interest, it does not work very well for secondary text data, such as corporate reports, published news articles, or social media posts. Because secondary data are not designed for research data collection, they tend to be extremely "noisy" (with low signal content), rendering them inefficient for human coding.

Nonetheless, secondary text corpora offer interesting possibilities for information systems [2] and organizational research [3, 4]. First, large volumes of such data already exist in the form of electronic mails, social media posts, online reviews, text messages, and such. If properly mined, such huge datasets may allow for the detection of small effects, the investigation of complex relationships, comparison of sub-samples, and the study of rare phenomena [2]. Second, because secondary data are not created for research purposes, they are unbiased by researchers and the research process (e.g., Hawthorne effect), which often exists in primary data, for example, when a researcher's questions may lead an interviewee to respond in a "socially desirable" manner.

Researchers are increasingly turning to automated tools like Linguistic Inquiry and Word Count (LIWC) for coding text into predefined constructs. These are "bag of words" approaches, because they require specifying a bag of similar words (e.g., synonyms) representing a construct of interest, and the algorithm will count the number of words in that bag in a text corpus. However, words are often ambiguous and mean different things (e.g., "Apple" could refer to a technology company or a fruit), different words (e.g., automobile, car, "wheels," or "Toyota") may refer to the same object, an dthe same idea can be represented using different combinations of words (e.g., "AT&T merges with Time-Warner" and "Time-Warner is bought by AT&T"). Further, the semantic meaning of a word depends on its context in use (e.g., "battery" means very different in "My cell phone battery is low" and "He was charged of battery"). Hence, word-based automated coding like LIWC tend to do a poor job at deciphering the semantic meaning and context of text. In addition, word-based approaches suffer from high dimensionality and high sparsity, requiring substantial computational resources to process, while producing inferior results due to low signal-to-noise content.

In this paper, we present an alternative approach, where the unit of textual analysis is sentences, rather than words. As evident from the examples above, sentences provide a much better representation of semantic meaning and context than words, and help us make more sense of ambiguous natural languages than word-based approaches. Recent developments in deep learning involving sentence transformers offer new possibilities in our ability to compare sentences in large corpora of secondary text data with minimal human intervention, that were not feasible even a couple of years ago.

Although industry leaders like Google and Facebook have made tremendous progress in the development of pretrained language models, these models are largely unknown in academic research. In this paper, we demonstrate how a sample of annual 10-K reports filed by publicly traded corporations in the USA can be mined for concept-based coding of research constructs, such as exploration and exploitation – two popular types of organizational innovation. We evaluate our semantic text similarity (STS) based approach by comparing the automated coding with a manually coded subsample of the same data. The resulting codes represent whether or not the companies in our sample are engaging in exploration and/or exploitation activities, which can be used as dummy variables in statistical models to test research hypotheses involving these constructs. Our research lies at the interface of design science and qualitative research, and the automated coding approach that we developed can be extended to coding of other research constructs with minimal human intervention.

2   Related Literature

Text mining techniques, such as sentiment analysis, topic modeling, dimensionality reduction, classification, and clustering, are still novel in academic research. In one of the earliest studies in this area, Abbasi et al. [5] analyzed 300,000 web pages (and 30,000 images) to extract fraud cues from word phrases using similarity metrics, which were then used to identify fake web pages. Among more recent studies, Muller et al. [2] used topic modeling and classification to identify which aspects of product reviews users find "helpful." Others have employed similar techniques to predict stock price movements based on published news articles [6], forecast tourism demand by analyzing online travel forum data [7], identify smoking status based on online forum posts [8], identify helpful content from online knowledge community posts [9], assess user sentiments toward products or services [10, 11], identify fake online reviews [12], categorize users of online communities [13], categorize products competing for the same market [14], and analyze social interaction among top management members [15] or between guests and hosts [16]. A more detailed literature review is not presented here to conserve space but is available from the authors upon request.

The dominant approach of feature extraction in the above studies is the bag of words approach (e.g., [6–8, 10, 12, 14, 17, 18]). In this approach, the text corpus is tokened into words, followed by stopword removal, punctuation removal, text normalization (lowercasing and/or stemming or lemmatization). The remaining words are then converted into a term frequency-inverse document frequency (TF-IDF) matrix based on word co-occurrence frequency within and across documents. This approach helps identify influential words but does not preserve the ordering or semantic meaning of words. A variation of this approach uses n-grams (word sequences) instead of individual words for TF-IDF vectorization (e.g., [9, 11, 19]), which may provide slightly better performance than word-based TF-IDF in large text corpora.

Two drawbacks of the TF-IDF-based bag of words approach are (1) high-dimensional sparse vectors (with many zeroes) that are computationally inefficient to process, and (2) their inability to store the semantic content of language. To address these problems, in the mid-2010s, researchers (e.g., [16, 20]) developed pre-trained word vector models by using dense vectors that are computationally more efficient and can compare words using metrics such as Euclidean distance or cosine similarity. However, words often have multiple meanings (e.g., Apple: a fruit or a technology company?), which cannot be interpreted if a word is divorced from its context of use. As linguist Ludwig Wittgenstein once said, the meaning of a word lies in its use. Hence, sentences are a more appropriate unit of linguistic interpretation than words. However, we did not find any prior instance of sentence-based vectorization in the literature, and understandably so, given that sentence models are just about two years old and are still being developed. Our study is one of the earliest to apply this technique to information systems research.

Secondly, much of prior research has been inductive, searching for latent topics or features from text and using them to classify or cluster text documents. There is little instance of using text mining for deductive research, for example, to score specific theoretical constructs of interest for hypotheses testing. Our goal in this research is not to discover new patterns but to use text mining as a tool to support classical theory-driven, hypotheses testing research. We propose a semantic text similarity (STS) method that uses sentence as the unit of analysis, computes cosine similarity between sentence vectors in a text corpus and those in predefined operationalizations of theoretical constructs to code sentences, to mimic human coding.

3 Problem Context

We demonstrate our STS approach in the context of organizational innovation research. Two key innovation processes described in the organizational literature are exploration and exploitation. *Exploration* refers to discovering new products, new resources, new knowledge, and new opportunities that may lead to new product or service offerings or new markets. In contrast, *exploitation* refers to better utilization of existing products, existing resources, existing knowledge, and existing competencies to reduce production costs or improve efficiency [21]. The two approaches require diametrically opposite organizational structures, processes, capabilities, and cultures. Exploration requires risk-taking, experimentation, improvisations, radical changes, and chaos, while exploitation requires risk avoidance, incremental refinement, focus on efficiency, stability, and order. Exploration is generally associated with organic structures, loosely coupled systems, autonomy and chaos, and breaking new grounds, while exploitation is associated with mechanistic structures, tightly coupled systems, control and bureaucracy, and stable markets and technologies [22].

Consequently, organizations that excel in exploitation tend to struggle with exploration and vice versa. However, both approaches are important for organizations because exploitation generates current revenues, which is needed to fuel exploration for future revenues. Hence, a key theme in strategic management research is that organizations that are "ambidextrous" or can concurrently manage exploration and exploitation processes, outperform those that excel only at exploration or exploitation [23].

Empirical research have measured exploration and exploitation using multi-item, Likert-scaled instruments. A representative instrument for measuring exploration and exploitation, adapted from He and Wong [24], is shown in Table 1.

Two typical problems in survey research are common method bias and social desirability bias. Common method bias stems from the use of a common instrument (the same survey form) for measuring independent and dependent variables at the same time, while social desirability bias is a tendency among respondents to portray a positive view of themselves and their organizations, irrespective of the ground reality. Moreover, cross-sectional surveys provide a snapshot of contemporaneous levels of exploration and exploitation in organizations, but cannot provide any information on historical trajectories of such constructs in their organizations, or the extent to which organizations have built or lost exploration and exploitation capabilities over time. Mining historic 10-K reports filed by public corporations to the United States Securities and Exchange Commission (SEC) can help us reconstruct a historical fossil record of organizations and analyze innovation patterns within and across industry sectors, while avoiding common method bias and social desirability bias.

Table 1. Operational measures of exploration and exploitation

Exploration measures	Exploitation measures
Introduce new generation of products	Improve existing product quality
Extend product range	Improve production flexibility
Open up new markets	Reduce production cost
Enter new technology fields	Improve yield or reduce material consumption

*Adapted from He and Wong [24]

However, exploration and exploitation metrics are not readily available on financial statements. Although some researchers have considered research & development (R&D) expense as a measure of innovation, it is unclear whether R&D refers to exploration, exploitation, or both. Moreover, R&D is not comparable across industry sectors and many organizations, such as banks, do not have R&D expense, but still innovate in the form of online or mobile banking or new financial products. However, it may be possible to "infer" exploration and exploitation from "business" and "management discussions & analysis" (MD&A) sections of 10-K reports, where corporate management may discuss new product or market developments, product extensions, and/or internal process improvement initiatives for the benefit of their shareholders. If we can use text mining techniques to efficiently mine these text sections, we may be able to create corporate profiles of innovation across time and industry sectors.

4 Method

4.1 Data Sourcing

Data for our analysis was sourced from SEC's Electronic Data Gathering, Analysis, and Retrieval (EDGAR) website, which makes available all 10-K reports filed with the agency in HTML and text files. Starting with companies that filed 10-K reports with SEC during 2020, we had 5,573 reports from 5,505 unique companies. Using Standard Industrial Classification (SIC) codes, we dropped finance, insurance, and real estate, public administration, non-classifiable companies, and those with unassigned SICs. From the remaining pool of 4,147 companies, we randomly chose a sample of 201 companies. We then searched the EDGAR website for 10-K reports of these companies for each fiscal year between 2016 to 2020 to create a five-year longitudinal panel for each company's innovation activities. Companies that did not have 10-K reports for the entire five-year period were dropped, leading to a final sample of 134 companies and 670 10-K documents. The "business" section of these documents were parsed to remove XML tags and extract the text for our text mining.

4.2 Artifact Design

Our deductive coding pipeline is shown in Fig. 1. We adopted He and Wong's [24] eight exploration and exploitation measures (Table 1) as the ontology for our automated coding process.

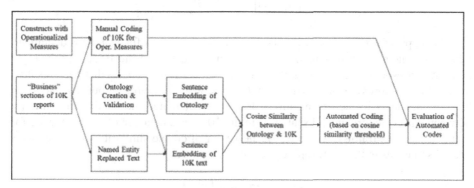

Fig. 1. Automated deductive coding of text

The extracted text was tokenized into sentences for coding. Unlike the generic wording in our exploration and exploitation ontologies, we found that products (or services) were usually addressed in 10-K reports by their specific names, such as "iPhone 12". Because the STS model did not show good match between generic "product" and specific product names like "iPhone 12" to the generic "product", we employed a named entity recognition (NER) model to replace all product names with a generic "product".

Our next decision choice was selecting a sentence transformer model for encoding each sentence in the 10-K reports and our ontologies. Transformers are pretrained deep learning models for transforming an input sequence (e.g., text) into a different output sequence (e.g., vector) using an attention mechanism that learns contextual relations in the input sequence [25]. Among different classes of sentence transformers, Bidirectional Encoder Representations from Transformers (BERT), developed by Google AI Lab in 2019, are particularly suited for STS tasks [26]. Initially intended for language translation, the BERT model uses multi-layer bidirectional architecture and shows excellent performance across various tasks, including STS, text summarization, and autocompleting search queries [27]. Robustly optimized BERT approach (RoBERTa), retrained with a much larger text corpus, more compute power, and improved training methodology, demostrate significantly improved performance over the original BERT model [28]. SRoBERTa is further retuning of the RoBERTa model to enhance its computational efficiency. With a 10,000 sentences collection, SRoBERTa reduced the time to find the most similar pair of sentences from 65 h to about 5 s and computed cosine-similarities in approximately 0.01 s [26]. Because of the above reasons, SRoBERTa was chosen as the desired sentence embedding model in this study.

We used RoBERTa to generate sentence embeddings for each sentence in the business section of 10-K reports and the eight ontology categories for exploration and exploitation, and computed cosine similarities between text and ontology sentence vectors, with and without NER replacements (for comparison). Cosine similarity is a measure of semantic similarities between two encoded sentences obtained using Eq. 1, where $\vec{a}$ and $\vec{b}$ vectors representing sentences that we are comparing:

$$\cos\theta = \frac{\vec{a} \cdot \vec{b}}{||\vec{a}|| \, ||\vec{b}||} = \frac{\sum_1^n a_i b_i}{\sqrt{\sum_1^n a_i^2} \sqrt{\sum_1^n b_i^2}} \tag{1}$$

The outputs from our processing stages were a m × 8 matrix for each 10-K document, where m is the number of sentences in the business section of the 10-K, and the eight columns correspond to eight categories in our ontology. Table 2 shows that NER resulted in significant improvement in cosine similarity scores. To aggregate our analysis from the sentence-level to the organizational level, we calculated the maximum similarity between each category and all sentences in the 10-K as a measure of category code for that document as follows, where $v_{i,j}^x$ is the vector of cosine similarities for category x and all sentences in the 10-K report of company i in year j:

$$m_{i,j}^x = \arg \max \left(\vec{v}_{i,j}^x \right) \tag{2}$$

Table 2. Effect of NER on Similarity Score

Sentence without NER [Sentence with NER]	Cosine similarity	
	Without NER	With NER
During 2020, the Company released an updated iPad Pro [During date, the Company released an updated product.]	0.4285	0.8215
During 2020, the Company released AirPods Pro® [During date, the Company released product.]	0.4181	0.7210
(…) released Apple Watch Series 6 and a new Apple (…) [released product and a new product]	0.3510	0.8080

We assigned company i to belong to category x in year j if its maximum similarity $m_{i,j}^x$ with category x equaled or exceeded a certain threshold.

$$c_{i,j}^x \begin{cases} 1 \; if \; m_{i,j}^x \geq threshold \\ 0 \; if \; m_{i,j}^x < threshold \end{cases} \tag{3}$$

Determining an appropriate threshold in Eq. (3) was an important part of our methodology. To identify what threshold value would yield the best classification performance, we manually coded a randomly chosen subsample of twenty 10-K documents (3,742 sentences) in our sample into the eight categories of interest (see Fig. 2 for our sample manual coding). We used these manual codes as benchmark to assess the performance of our automated coding at different cosine similarity thresholds from 0.0 to 1.0, with intervals of 0.1. Confusion matrices for each threshold level were used to compute recall, precision, and F1-score as metrics of our classification performance. These performance metrics for exploration and exploitation are shown in Fig. 3. These plots suggested an optimum similarity threshold of 0.50 for best automated classification performance.

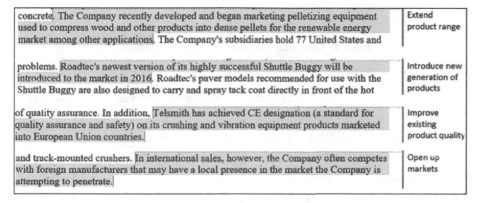

Fig. 2. Manual coding of text segments of 10-K Report

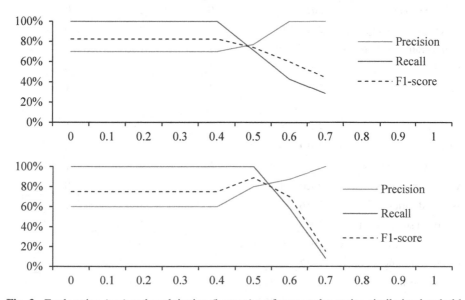

Fig. 3. Exploration (top) and exploitation (bottom) performance by cosine similarity threshold

Lastly, we classified company *i* as "explorative" in year *j*, if it belonged to at least one of the four categories: (1) introduce new generation of products, (2) extend product range, (3) open up new markets, or (4) enter new technology fields, and "exploitative" if it belongs to at least one of the categories: (5) improve existing product quality, (6) improve production flexibility, (7) reduce production cost, or (8) improve yield or reduce material consumption. This classification can be used for inductive theory building or deductive theory testing.

$$exploration_{i,j} = \arg\max(c_{i,j}^1, \ c_{i,j}^2, \ c_{i,j}^3, \ c_{i,j}^4) \tag{4}$$

$$exploitation_{i,j} = \arg\max(c_{i,j}^5, \ c_{i,j}^6, \ c_{i,j}^7, \ c_{i,j}^8) \tag{5}$$

Table 3. Classification comparison and performance

Company	Year	Exploration		Exploitation	
		Manual	Automated	Manual	Automated
Teradata	2018	1	1	1	1
Currency works	2018	1	1	0	0
Soligenix Inc.	2018	1	0	1	1
Beazer homes USA	2020	1	1	1	1
Cedar fair	2020	0	0	0	1
Citrix systems	2020	1	1	1	1
Defense technologies	2019	1	0	0	0
Concierge technologies	2017	0	0	0	0
Moneygram international	2016	0	1	1	1
Pc Tel	2018	1	1	0	0
Strattec security	2018	1	1	1	1
Zynga	2017	1	1	1	1
Union Pacific	2020	0	0	0	1
Telos	2019	0	1	1	1
Pattern wwnergy group	2017	1	0	1	1
Applied energetics	2020	1	0	0	0
Astec industries	2016	1	1	1	1
American superconductor	2016	1	1	1	1
Houston American energy	2019	0	1	0	1
Superior Drilling products	2017	1	1	1	1
Overall recall		0.714		1.000	
Overall precision		0.769		0.800	
Overall F1-score		0.741		0.889	

4.3 Design Evaluation

Using the cosine similarity threshold of 0.50, our manual and automated exploration and exploitation coding for our subsample of 20 companies, along with the overall recall, precision, and F1-score, are shown in Table 3. Overall F1-score for exploration was 0.74, and that for exploitation was 0.89 using our designed artifact.

A closer examination of classification performance by category reveals substantial variations in performance across categories. Among exploration measures, Category C1 (introduce new generation of products) had the highest F1-score of 0.74, while Category 4 (enter new technology fields) had the lowest F1-score of 0.33. Exploitation categories showed slightly better results, with F1-scores ranging between 0.957 for Category 5 (improve existing product quality) and 0.43 for Category 8 (improve yield or reduce material consumption). Terms like "yield" and "material consumption" did not appear to be referenced in most corporate 10-K reports.

Table 4. Performance measures by ontology category

Categories	Precision	Recall	F1-score
C1	63.64%	87.50%	73.68%
C2	71.43%	45.45%	55.56%
C3	33.33%	80.00%	47.06%
C4	28.57%	40.00%	33.33%
C5	91.67%	100.00%	95.65%
C6	33.33%	75.00%	46.15%
C7	85.71%	75.00%	80.00%
C8	27.27%	100.00%	42.86%

Note: C1 = introduce new generation of products; C2 = extend product range; C3 = open up new markets; C4 = enter new technology fields; C5 = improve existing product quality; C6 = improve production flexibility; C7 = reduce production cost; and C8 = improve yield or reduce material consumption

Given these variations, it may be prudent to use a different threshold to separately classify each of the eight categories, and then aggregate those binary classifications into ordinal measures of exploration and exploitation, rather than classify at the aggregate level of exploration and exploitation for each company. Given conference submission deadlines, we were unable to complete this analysis, but plan to present it at the conference, if accepted. We also plan to expand our manual analysis from 20 to 40 companies and employ two coders to assure intersubjectivity in our manual coding.

5 Implications and Conclusions

The goal of this study was to create an artifact that could be used to automatically code text documents for theoretical constructs with predefined operationalizations. We described the process of creating such an artifact for coding corporate 10-K filings for two types of organizational innovation: exploration and exploitation. We evaluated our artifact using a subsample of 20 manually coded organizations.

Our study proposed an unique method, employing pretrained sentence transformers for automatic coding of text documents into theoretical constructs. We view this as an important methodological contribution as it extends the labor-intensive manual coding process to large text corpora. Unlike prior word count based automated approaches like LIWC, our approach is based on sentences that captures semantic meaning and context better than words can, and is not sensitive to improper specification of bags of words. This is a very promising technique, given our large and growing corpora of user-generated text content such as SEC filings, online reviews, social media posts, and so forth.

Our proposed method (artifact) leverages known operationalizations of research constructs (e.g., exploration and exploitation) an as ontology to look for sentences in text corpora that are semantically close to sentences in the ontology. This sentence-based approach is also novel to academic research.

Of course, coding is just one step in the research process. The final goal of research is to understand phenomena of interest. Qualitative codes generated from our method can be linked to other constructs to support inductive theory building or may be used as dummy variables in statistical models for deductive theory testing.

Though this paper was a proof-of-concept for our proposed artifact, it raised several questions on its application to text coding that we want to explore next. For example, we do not know the sensitivity of our approach is to the size of input text documents. We also do not know how well this approach works if we increase the number of categories. Lastly, though we found NER to significantly improve matching of text entences to ontology, it may be argued that sentence transformers should ideally be able to match the word product with names of products and that NER may be unnecessary. Our current sentence transformer models are not yet able to match product with product names; however as we develop better pretrained models, NER may become unnecessary. We plan to explore these issues, with a bigger sample of manually and automatically coded 10-K documents in our subsequent research.

References

1. Gibbs, G.R.: Analyzing Qualitative Data, 6th edn. Sage, Thousand Oaks (2007)
2. Müller, O., Junglas, I., Brocke, J.V., Debortoli, S.: Utilizing big data analytics for information systems research: challenges, promises and guidelines. Eur. J. Inf. Syst. **25**, 289–302 (2016). https://doi.org/10.1057/ejis.2016.2
3. Kobayashi, V.B., Mol, S.T., Berkers, H.A., Kismihók, G., Den Hartog, D.N.: Text Mining in Organizational Research. Org. Res. Methods **21**, 733–765 (2018). https://doi.org/10.1177/1094428117722619
4. Janasik, N., Honkela, T., Bruun, H.: Text Mining in Qualitative Research. Organ. Res. Methods. **12**, 436–460 (2009). https://doi.org/10.1177/1094428108317202

5. Abbasi, A., Zhang, Z., Zimbra, D., Chen, H., Nunamaker, J.F.: Detecting fake websites: the contribution of statistical learning theory. Manag. Inf. Syst. Quart. **34**, 435–461 (2010). https://doi.org/10.2307/25750686

6. Nam, K.H., Seong, N.Y.: Financial news-based stock movement prediction using causality analysis of influence in the Korean stock market. Decis. Support Syst. **117**, 100–112 (2019). https://doi.org/10.1016/j.dss.2018.11.004

7. Colladon, A.F., Guardabascio, B., Innarella, R.: Using social network and semantic analysis to analyze online travel forums and forecast tourism demand. Decis. Support Syst. **123**, 113075 (2019). https://doi.org/10.1016/j.dss.2019.113075

8. Wang, X., et al.: Mining user-generated content in an online smoking cessation community to identify smoking status: a machine learning approach. Decis. Support Syst. **116**, 26–34 (2019). https://doi.org/10.1016/j.dss.2018.10.005

9. Liu, X., Alan Wang, G., Fan, W., Zhang, Z.: Finding useful solutions in online knowledge communities: a theory-driven design and multilevel analysis. Inf. Syst. Res. **31**, 731–752 (2020). https://doi.org/10.1287/ISRE.2019.0911

10. Chatterjee, S.: Explaining customer ratings and recommendations by combining qualitative and quantitative user generated contents. Decis. Support Syst. **119**, 14–22 (2019). https://doi.org/10.1016/j.dss.2019.02.008

11. Xu, X.: What are customers commenting on, and how is their satisfaction affected? examining online reviews in the on-demand food service context. Decis. Support Syst. **142**, 113467 (2021). https://doi.org/10.1016/j.dss.2020.113467

12. Hu, N., Bose, I., Koh, N.S., Liu, L.: Manipulation of online reviews: an analysis of ratings, readability, and sentiments. Decis. Support Syst. **52**, 674–684 (2012). https://doi.org/10.1016/j.dss.2011.11.002

13. Hwang, E.H., Singh, P.V., Argote, L.: Jack of all, master of some: information network and innovation in crowdsourcing communities. Inf. Syst. Res. **30**, 389–410 (2019). https://doi.org/10.1287/isre.2018.0804

14. Pan, Y., Huang, P., Gopal, A.: Storm clouds on the horizon? New entry threats and R & D investments in the U.S. IT industry. Inf. Syst. Res. 30, 540–562 (2019). https://doi.org/10.1287/isre.2018.0816.

15. Zhang, T., Liu, F.C., Gao, B., Yen, D.: Top management team social interaction and conservative reporting decision: a language style matching approach. Decis. Support Syst. **142**, 113469 (2021). https://doi.org/10.1016/j.dss.2020.113469

16. Wu, J., Cai, J., Luo, X.R., Benitez, J.: How to increase customer repeated bookings in the short-term room rental market? a large-scale granular data investigation. Decis. Support Syst. **143**, 113495 (2021). https://doi.org/10.1016/j.dss.2021.113495.

17. Cao, Q., Duan, W., Gan, Q.: Exploring determinants of voting for the "helpfulness" of online user reviews: a text mining approach. Decis. Support Syst. **50**, 511–521 (2011). https://doi.org/10.1016/j.dss.2010.11.009

18. Goes, P., Lin, M., Yeung, Ching-man Au.: "Popularity Effect" in user-generated content: evidence from online product reviews. Inf. Syst. Res. **25**(2), 222–238 (2014). https://doi.org/10.1287/isre.2013.0512

19. Singh, P.V., Sahoo, N., Mukhopadhyay, T.: How to attract and retain readers in enterprise blogging? Inf. Syst. Res. **25**, 35–52 (2014). https://doi.org/10.1287/isre.2013.0509

20. Zhang, L., Yan, Q., Zhang, L.: A text analytics framework for understanding the relationships among host self-description, trust perception and purchase behavior on Airbnb. Decis. Support Syst. **133**, 113288 (2020). https://doi.org/10.1016/j.dss.2020.113288

21. March, J.G.: Exploration and Exploitation in Organizational Learning. Organ. Sci. **2**, 71–87 (1991)

22. Lewin, A.Y., Long, C.P., Carroll, T.N.: The coevolution of new organizational forms. Organ. Sci. **10**, 535–550 (1999). https://doi.org/10.1287/orsc.10.5.535

23. Tushman, M.L., O'Reilly, C.A.: Ambidextrous organizations: managing evolutionary and revolutionary change. Calif. Manage. Rev. **38**, 8–29 (1996). https://doi.org/10.2307/41165852
24. He, Z-L., Wong, P-K.: Exploration vs. exploitation: an empirical test of the ambidexterity hypothesis. Organ Sci. **15**(4), 481–494 (2004). https://doi.org/10.1287/orsc.1040.0078
25. Vaswani, A., et al.: Attention is all you need. In: 31st Conference Neural Information Processing System (2017). https://doi.org/10.1109/2943.974352.
26. Reimers, N., Gurevych, I.: Sentence-BERT: sentence embeddings using siamese BERT-networks. In: 2019 Conference Empirical Methods Natural Language Processing 9th International Jt. Conference Natural Language Processing Proceedings Conference, pp. 3982–3992 (2020). https://doi.org/10.18653/v1/d19-1410.
27. Devlin, J., Chang, M.W., Lee, K., Toutanova, K.: BERT: pre-training of deep bidirectional transformers for language understanding. In: 2019 Conference North American Chapter Association Computer Linguistics Human Language Technology - Proceedings Conference, vol. 1, pp. 4171–4186 (2019)
28. Liu, Y., et al.: RoBERTa: A robustly optimized BERT pretraining approach. arXiv (2019)

DSR and Governance

Is Trust Shapeable? Design Requirements for Governing Sharing Networks

Marvin Jagals$^{(\boxtimes)}$ [ID], Erik Karger [ID], and Frederik Ahlemann [ID]

University of Duisburg-Essen, Essen, Germany
{marvin.jagals,erik.karger,frederik.ahlemann}@uni-due.de

Abstract. Driven by digitization and the accompanying attempt to compensate for a lack of resources and capabilities, the number of inter-organizational collaborations in which resources are shared increases rapidly. The individual actors within such sharing networks (SN) form the foundation for the success of these collaborations. Successful collaborations have a high level of trust between these individual actors. However, it is still unclear how to design roles and relationships in networks in order to develop and foster trust. Thus far, scholars have done very little research investigating the relationship between structural properties of sharing network configurations and trust within them. By applying design science research (DSR), this study intends to shed light on design requirements (DR) to govern successful SN. We describe the review's findings as four meta-requirements, which set the cornerstone for our journey toward a holistic information systems (IS) design theory aimed at shaping roles and relationships to govern SN effectively.

Keywords: Inter-organizational sharing networks · Design requirements · Design science research · DSR

1 Introduction

Research has produced unique explanations of sharing networks (SN). These explanations partly overlap and partly contend [1, 2]. There are many different conceptions of networks, even among those concerned with organizations linked by resource exchange [3, 4].

Several researchers have discussed the idea that SN lead to improved performance, such as lower supply chain costs or an increase of revenues [5, 6]. Besides, the coordination of a complex ecosystem grounded on individual business relationships that exist between parties involved in the SN is critical to the success of a firm and the whole network [7]. In this regard, one can categorize the idea of focusing on individuals as well as their fulfilled roles and relationships under the relational governance concept. This concept, which recognizes the weaknesses of traditional, contract-based governance by governing an SN through an informal structure, is a suitable approach to addressing these challenges [8]. Inter-organizational exchanges are typically repeated exchanges that are

L. Chandra Kruse et al. (Eds.): DESRIST 2021, LNCS 12807, pp. 287–292, 2021.
https://doi.org/10.1007/978-3-030-82405-1_28

embedded in social relationships. Governance emerges from the values and agreed-upon processes found in social relationships [9], which may minimize transaction costs compared with formal contracts [8].

Derived from this approach, the key to successful network collaboration is based on trust. Trust is an essential relational part of resource sharing, as it helps with successful communications and procedures [10]. Working in collaboration across company boundaries can be testing for companies who are not accustomed to functioning throughout their corresponding jurisdictional and business boundaries [11]. A relational governance and focus on individual actors, their roles, and their relationships are, therefore, crucial for the overall network performance.

Furthermore, many contributions have already addressed roles and relationships in the context of governing inter-organizational sharing networks. Oliveira et al. [12] provide a detailed study of structural research on inter-organizational, data-related roles and responsibilities. They also define functions with a governance character, but these functions are only partially defined precisely. Moreover, Peterman et al. [13] as well as Knight and Harland [14] set a focus on inter-organizational roles and relationships. Although there is a partial link to role theory for explaining the behavior of the individual management roles, there is no holistic framework based on prescriptive design knowledge. Furthermore, they also do not consider trust as crucial variable of successful networks in this context.

In sum, none of the publications focus on how to separately design roles and relationships among network actors and, moreover, none of the publications address the relationship of different participants and their functional roles in an SN. Furthermore, there is no design-oriented approach attempting to develop design knowledge that places trust as the central variable of research, although academics accept this as an element success factor of SN in IS research [15, 16]. These problem statements lead to our research question: *How should one design roles and their relationships to encourage building a trustful data ecosystem?*

This study aims to utilize the importance of organizational design as a resource sharing enabler by growing reusable prescriptive design knowledge in form of an information systems (IS) design theory. To efficiently reach this target, we applied Gregor and Hevner's [17] guidance on how to structure a design-oriented research paper for maximum impact.

To configure our design process, we follow Peffers et al.'s [18] contribution. Absent generalized design knowledge on designing roles and relationships in data-sharing environments acts as our research entry point and constitutes our research motivation. We then defined our objective within the introduction section. We developed our design requirements through an initial literature review conducted within major IS and IS-related databases (AISeL, ScienceDirect, ProQuest, ACM, IEEE, and Business Source Premier). The conclusion section ventures ahead and explains the next milestones on the road to a well-developed design theory.

2 Design Requirements

In the following, we derive appropriate design requirements (DR) based on extant IS and IS-related literature. These theory requirements are general. They are not the requirements for a specific example of a system theory, offering theory-based principles in a prescriptive nature instead [19, 20]. To address, on the one hand, the concept of relational governance within inter-organizational networks and, on the other hand, the individual SN roles and their behavior, we have to discuss different constructs (Fig. 1).

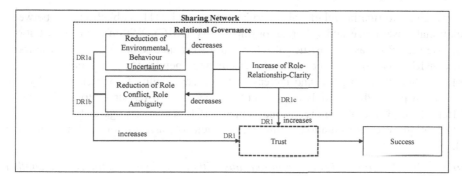

Fig. 1. Research framework

Since trust is the key to reduce or even avoid uncertainty, relational governance, also known as trust-based governance, offers a suitable approach for establishing trust as a central governance mechanism [21]. The grounding of governance as a whole hinges on agency theory. In this context, transaction cost economics has emerged as a typical structure for comprehending governance-mode-choice economic activities based on contracts [22]. These contracts are, however, the main criticism in the framework of the traditional, contractual governance [3]. Especially within inter-organizational networks, the relational aspect of governance has become crucial, as the network's coordination mode mainly relies on social contracts between network actors [23]. Besides, inter-organizational exchanges are observably repeated exchanges embedded in social relationships. Moreover, governance emerges from the values and agreed-upon processes found in social relationships [9], which may minimize transaction costs compared to formal contracts [8]. Generally, social mechanisms play a crucial role here to balance the lacking elements of contractual governance [24].

IS and IS-related literature assessed trust as crucial for sharing assets within these networks [25], and assessed the circulation of trust as vital for comprehending a network's interactions and whether trust is reciprocated amongst SN actors [15]. Trust between actors, and trust in the whole network plays a crucial role [26]. Trust, therefore, operates as a governance mechanism that reduces opportunism in sharing relations, and endorses cooperation [27].

DR1: *The design of roles and relationships within SN should foster the increase of trust between DE participants.*

Uncertainty, in contrast, decreases trust. Uncertainty initially describes the unpredictability that incomplete knowledge of alternative courses of action brings about [28]. Many SN do not work or succeed because actors cannot deal with two primary forms of uncertainty: behavioral and environmental [29]. Behavioral uncertainty occurs in the context of the possibility of sharing partners concealing or falsifying information. Environmental uncertainty takes place as a result of unpredictable environmental changes [30].

DR1a: *The design of roles and relationships within SN should minimize the adverse effects of both behavioral uncertainty and environmental uncertainty.*

Within investigating relational governance, Goo et al. [31] establish a nexus between relational governance and role-relationship-clarity (RRC). Within their contribution, they defined RRC as a construct of relational governance. Goo et al. [31] describe a lack of RRC as a direct function of the discrepancy between two functions, avoiding role conflict and ambiguity, and increasing trust. The origin of conflict generally can vary from power differentials or competitors over limited resources to tendencies to differentiate [32]. Role ambiguity may emerge if function settings lack role-relevant information, when information is limited, or when role assumptions are not specified [33].

DR1b: *The design of roles and relationships within SN should minimize role conflict and role ambiguity.*

Research already studied the interdependencies of role conflict, ambiguity, and clarity. Generally, scholars agree that RRC is kind of an antecedent to role conflict and ambiguity [34]. In this context, RRC describes the level to which required information is offered about how exactly the participant is expected to fulfill a role [35].

Participants develop trust in what they need to do and what they should expect from other participants, as they have a shared picture of what needs to be achieved to accomplish mutual goals in an SN [36]. Explicitly putting effort into creating a cross-boundary community that better collaborates, coordinates, and interacts among its members was apparent. The more these individuals interacted, organized, and partnered with one another, the clearer their roles and responsibilities were established [37].

DR1c: *The design of roles and relationships within SN should endorse to increase RRC.*

3   Conclusion

In this research-in-progress paper, we have identified four design requirements for governing SN. We gathered the requirements from IS and IS-related literature, focusing on the constructs of role clarity, uncertainty, role conflict, and trust. This study provides the foundation for further developing an IS design theory for a trust-based governance of SN. This generalized prescriptive knowledge could be beneficially reused by IS research in a future design science project; moreover, this knowledge could possibly refine existing kernel theories too. The next steps should therefore be to draft design principles, which address the given design requirements. These principles are grounded on kernel theories or related knowledge. Evaluation iterations in form of case study research, as well as the derivation of testable design propositions, will also follow.

References

1. Alter, C., Hage, J.: Organizations Working Together. Sage Publ, Newbury Park (1993)
2. Mizruchi, M.S., Galaskiewicz, J.: Networks of interorganizational relations. Sociol. Methods Res. **22**, 46–70 (1993)
3. Ebers, M.: Explaining inter-organizational network formation. Format. Inter-Organ. Netw. **1**, 3–40 (1997)
4. Snehota, I., Hakansson, H.: Developing Relationships in Business Networks. Routledge, London (1995)
5. Cachon, G.P., Fisher, M.: Supply chain inventory management and the value of shared information. Manage. Sci. **46**(8), 1032–1048 (2000)
6. Fuller, M.B., Porter, M.E.: Competition in Global Industries. Harvard Business School Press, Boston (1986)
7. Lambert, D.M., Cooper, M.C.: Issues in supply chain management. Ind. Mark. Manage. **29**, 65–83 (2000)
8. Dyer, J.H., Singh, H.: The relational view: Cooperative strategy and sources of interorganizational competitive advantage. Acad. Manag. Rev. **23**(4), 660–679 (1998)
9. Macneil, I.R.: The New Social Contract. Yale University Press, New Haven (1980)
10. Das, T.K., Teng, B.-S.: Between trust and control: developing confidence in partner cooperation in alliances. Acad. Manag. Rev. **23**, 491–512 (1998)
11. Dawes, S.S.: Interagency information sharing: expected benefits, manageable risks. J. Policy Anal. Manage. **15**, 377–394 (1996)
12. Oliveira, M.I.S., Lóscio, B.F.: What is a data ecosystem? In: Proceedings of the 19th Annual International Conference on Digital Government Research: Governance in the Data Age, pp. 1–9 (2018)
13. Peterman, A., Kourula, A., Levitt, R.: Organizational roles in a sustainability alliance network. Bus. Strateg. Environ. **29**, 3314–3330 (2020)
14. Knight, L., Harland, C.: Managing supply networks: organizational roles in network management. Eur. Manag. J. **23**, 281–292 (2005)
15. Provan, K.G., Kenis, P.: Modes of network governance: structure, management, and effectiveness. J. Public Adm. Res. Theory **18**(2), 229–252 (2008)
16. Jones, C., Hesterly, W.S., Borgatti, S.P.: A general theory of network governance: exchange conditions and social mechanisms. Acad. Manag. Rev. **22**(4), 911–945 (1997)
17. Gregor, S., Hevner, A.R.: Positioning and presenting design science research for maximum impact. MIS Q. **37**(2), 337–356 (2013)
18. Peffers, K., Tuunanen, T., Rothenberger, M.A., Chatterjee, S.: A design science research methodology for information systems research. J. Manag. Inf. Syst. **24**(3), 45–78 (2007)
19. Gregor, S., Jones, D. (eds.): The anatomy of a design theory. J. Assoc. Inf. Syst. (JAIS) **8**(5), 312–335 (2007)
20. Gregor, S.: The nature of theory in information systems. MIS Q. **30**(3), 611–642 (2006)
21. Krishnan, R., Geyskens, I., Steenkamp, J.-B.E.M.: The effectiveness of contractual and trust-based governance in strategic alliances under behavioral and environmental uncertainty. Strateg. Manag. J. **37**, 2521–2542 (2016)
22. Williamson, O.E.: The Economic Institutions of Capitalism. Free Press. Douglas, New York (1985)
23. Dekker, H.C.: Control of inter-organizational relationships: evidence on appropriation concerns and coordination requirements. Acc. Organ. Soc. **29**(1), 27–49 (2004)
24. Poppo, L., Zenger, T.: Do formal contracts and relational governance function as substitutes or complements? Strateg. Manag. J. **23**(8), 707–725 (2002)

25. Sayogo, D.S., Gil-Garcia, J.R., Cronemberger, F.A., Widagdo, B.: The mediating role of trust for inter-organizational information sharing (IIS) success in the public sector. In: 18th Annual International Conference on Digital Government Research, pp. 426–435 (2017)
26. Gil-Garcia, J., Pardo, T., Burke, G.: Conceptualizing information integration in government. Adv. Manage. Inf. Syst. **17**, 179 (2010)
27. Uzzi, B.: Social structure and competition in interfirm networks: The paradox of embeddedness. Adm. Sci. Q. **42**(1), 35–67 (1997)
28. Knight, F.H.: Risk, Uncertainty and Profit. Houghton Mifflin, Boston (1921)
29. Gulati, R., Singh, H.: The architecture of cooperation: Managing coordination costs and appropriation concerns in strategic alliances. Adm. Sci. Q. **43**(4), 781–814 (1998)
30. Wholey, D.R., Brittain, J.: Characterizing environmental variation. Acad. Manag. J. **32**(4), 867–882 (1989)
31. Goo, J., Kishore, R., Rao, H.R., Nam, K.: The role of service level agreements in relational management of information technology outsourcing: an empirical study. MIS Q. **33**, 119–145 (2009)
32. Deutsch, M.: Conflicts: Productive and destructive. J. Soc. Issues **25**, 7–25 (1969)
33. Lyons, T.F.: Role clarity, need for clarity, satisfaction, tension, and withdrawal. Organ. Behav. Hum. Perform. **6**(1), 99–110 (1971)
34. Hartenian, L.S., Hadaway, F.J., Badovick, G.J.: Antecedents and consequences of role perceptions: a path analytic approach. J. Appl. Bus. Res. (JABR) **10**(2), 40–50 (1994)
35. Teas, R.K., Wacker, J.G., Hughes, R.E.: A path analysis of causes and consequences of salespeople's perceptions of role clarity. J. Mark. Res. **16**(3), 355–369 (1979)
36. Thomson, A.M., Perry, J.L.: Collaboration processes: inside the black box. Public Adm. Rev. **66**(1), 20–32 (2006)
37. Suter, E., Arndt, J., Arthur, N., Parboosingh, J., Taylor, E., Deutschlander, S.: Role understanding and effective communication as core competencies for collaborative practice. J. Interprof. Care **23**(1), 41–51 (2009)

LEGIT Methodology: Towards Capturing Legal Compatibility of Design Science Artifacts

Ernestine Dickhaut[1]([envelope]) [ID], Andreas Janson[2] [ID], and Jan Marco Leimeister[1,2] [ID]

[1] University of Kassel, Kassel, Germany
{ernestine.dickhaut,leimeister}@uni-kassel.de
[2] University of St. Gallen, St. Gallen, Switzerland
{andreas.janson,janmarco.leimeister}@unisg.ch

Abstract. Higher legal standards with regards to the data protection of individuals such as the General Data Protection Regulation (GDPR) are increasing the pressure on developers of IT artifacts. Typically, when developing systems, we subsequently evaluate them with users to elaborate aspects such as user experience perceptions. However, nowadays, other evaluation aspects such as legality and data policy issues are also important criteria for system development. For this purpose, we introduce LEGIT (legal design science evaluation), which provides developers with guidance when considering legal requirements. We use the case of the GDPR to illustrate the feasibility, applicability, and benefit to the development process. With this novel method adapted from law research, we are able to derive actionable guidance for developers to evaluate developer efforts in increasing legal compatibility. To illustrate our methodological approach, in this paper, we describe the key steps of the method with respect to the evaluation of a learning assistant. We develop an AI-based learning assistant for university students to demonstrate the application of the novel evaluation method. We briefly discuss how this procedure can serve as the foundation for a new evaluation method of legally compatible systems in design science research.

Keywords: Legal compatibility · Evaluation methodology · Design science

1 Introduction

One major goal of design science research (DSR) is the development of innovative and novel artifacts to solve real-world problems of business and society. However, these novel IT artifacts bring new risks, e.g., legal risks, which are sometimes not anticipated correctly beforehand [1]. Consider the practical cases during the COVID-19 pandemic to illustrate this area of conflict between useful IT artifacts and legal risks quite well: video conferencing tools such as Microsoft Teams or ZOOM were (and still are) facing legal disputes questioning their legality and legal compatibility. Numerous COVID-19 tracing apps have dealt with conflicts related to how to balance the usefulness in tracking and meethind regulation rules such as the GDPR. Thus, legal and data policy aspects have always been important for many companies to avoid reputational risks but gaining

© Springer Nature Switzerland AG 2021
L. Chandra Kruse et al. (Eds.): DESRIST 2021, LNCS 12807, pp. 293–298, 2021.
https://doi.org/10.1007/978-3-030-82405-1_29

importance due new conditions such as novel IT artifacts, negative media reports and increasing end-user interest in legal aspects.

Typically, when developing systems, we subsequently evaluate them with users to elaborate on if our system design is appropriate, e.g., regarding usability, user experience perceptions, or outcomes of IT use, which we evaluate through evaluation frameworks such as [2] or [3]. However, nowadays, other evaluation aspects, such as legality and data policy issues, have also become important criteria for system development. Nonetheless, we usually do not evaluate legal aspects when deploying these systems, oftentimes caused by the lack of appropriate evaluation methodologies for legal aspects when considering novel systems. In this context, simulations are a great support for IT development. They help to visualize and play through abstract content quickly and without great effort [4]. As a rule, individual parameters can be easily varied to achieve the best possible results. In consequence, we draw on these advantages for evaluating legal aspects by imitating real-world usage of systems. With the possibility to play through different system development parameters under realistic conditions, changes can be made relatively easily during the development. Thus, the simulation study introduced by the law discipline [5] provides a method-based foundation to evaluate technology in a practical manner concerning legally compatibility.

Therefore, we propose in the following a comprehensive evaluation methodology, which we call LEGIT (legal design science evaluation), that provides developers with guidance when considering the legal requirements in DSR, especially related to the GDPR. For the application of the novel evaluation methodology, we develop an AI-based learning assistant for university students, with two overarching but somewhat conflicting design goals: (1) a high user experience that offers as much support during learning processes as possible but (2) also considers legal compatibility, i.e., achieving a higher legal standard than is required by law. LEGIT allows us to implement and evaluate our ideas for a legally compatible AI-based assistant to get feedback at an early stage, which can be used for the further development of the AI-based assistant.

2 Theoretical Background and Related Work

2.1 Legal Compatibility

We have to pay attention to the requirements from various disciplines to develop design science artifacts, such as user experience, ethical, and legal requirements. Requirements such as user experience are given much attention during the development, while legal requirements are often addressed to a minimum extent in order to be compliant with the minimal requirements of law [6]. Today, higher legal standards with regards to the data protection of individuals increase the pressure on development [7]. Data protection is gaining importance, and thus the storage and processing of personal data are becoming an integral part of system design. Legality decides on the market approval of novel technologies, which means the fulfillment of minimum legal requirements, and is still common practice in many system developments projects. Legal compatibility goes further than mere legality and is defined as the greatest possible compliance with higher-order legal goals to minimize the social risks from technical system use [6].

However, the technology neutrality of law always leaves some room for maneuvering in the implementation and interpretation of the legal requirements, which leaves developers and companies uncertain about whether they have achieved legality. In times where data policy issues have been gaining in importance for developers, especially since 2018 due to the GDPR, there is a growing body of literature that recognizes the importance of the relevance of the consideration of data protection in technical systems, so we should keep legal aspects in mind early on in the development [8–10].

2.2 Legal Evaluation Methodologies in Design Science Research

In DSR, evaluation is a central and essential activity in conducting rigorous research [11]. According to Sonnenberg et al. [2, p. 386], "Prior work already pointed out that evaluation in DSR may address either the artifact design (i.e., the artifact characteristics) or the actual artifact as it is used by some relevant stakeholders". Aspects critical to law are only revealed through real use; thus, the use of the artifact in a real-world scenario by relevant stakeholders should be an evaluation under real-world conditions. Peffers et al. [12] distinguish between ex-post evaluation methodologies in DSR that provide the foundation for an evaluation of legal disputes in real-world scenarios. Combining these real-world conditions with the previous influence on the boundary conditions of the real-world use by simulating a real-world case setting, we demonstrate how to consider legal requirements in the up-front design of the DSR evaluation.

In contrast, from the legal discipline, we know the approaches of [13], and [1] and how simulating legal violations can be used as a method to evaluate technology in a practical manner in regard to their legal compatibility, which is well-known as a simulation study among lawyers in European law [13]. Similar forms of the simulation study are already used in legal education in America and are called moot courts. In contrast to moot courts, the simulation study involves real judges and lawyers with practical experience and does not pursue the education of lawyers but rather the evaluation of novel technologies. Along these lines, the simulation study, as a form of preventive technology design, can make a substantial contribution towards socio-technical design [5]. In the following, we adapt the simulation study to achieve our goal–the introduction of LEGIT as an evaluation of DSR artifacts to capture legal compatibility.

3 Key Steps of LEGIT

In the following, we describe how we deduced our LEGIT methodology on evaluating the legal compatibility for DSR projects (see Fig. 1). Thus, the first part of LEGIT is characterized by the fact that it allows the simulation of realistic usage scenarios while real (user) damage is prevented. This was achieved by letting participants use the technology under real-world conditions that were as realistic as possible [1]. However, as there were no imminent dangers in the fictional usage situations for the participants, it was desirable to provoke critical situations and situations of conflict that would not occur in such a high concentration [5].

In summary, conducting the user study should have two things in mind. First, by provoking critical situations, the user study will provide insights into the handling of the situations by the user. Second, through the interaction with the artifact in a real-world situation critical situation can also arise that were not previously considered.

In the second part of LEGIT, we move slightly away from the users to get a reliable judgment on the legal compatibility of the developed artifact. In this part, legal violations based on the user study are derived. As described above, the violations were either provoked by designing the evaluation setting, in which case some violations may occur, but some that are expected do not occur in reality, or the legal variations were derived from usage without expecting them in advance. Thereupon, legal experts create court infringements to negotiate in court.

Fig. 1. Key steps of LEGIT

The third part of LEGIT includes simulated court cases based on the deducted legal violation. Thus, the legal assessment can be conducted as realistically as possible with claims that could arise from the practical use. The simulated court cases are built on the outcomes of the first part of our study. The situations of conflict that were previously provoked will be discussed and judged by legal experts, simulating a real court trial. The selection of a range of cases to trial during the legal assessment that are of high importance in the daily use of the technology is an important step towards the success of the evaluation. Early evaluations (especially smaller projects) should use at least one experienced legal expert for this purpose. Extensive and advanced projects, on the other hand, should evaluate the simulated court cases as realistically as possible in several proceedings in order to avoid subsequent legal violations. The legal experts should have completed at least the second state examination and have initial practical experience.

4   Application of LEGIT

In this section, we demonstrate the application of LEGIT that was embedded in a larger AI-based assistant development project (see [14, 15]. The developed AI-based assistant should support a university course by providing individual learning support. A special feature of these systems is the individual adaptation to the user, which requires a large amount of user data. Among the user data are also personal data that are considered particularly worthy of protection according to GDPR guidelines. Consider, for example, the case of Amazon's Alexa, which activates itself when nobody is home or serves, as a consequence of its data collection efforts, as a witness in court (see also [16]). Thus, AI-based assistants are a good way to apply LEGIT to evaluate the legal compatibility of this novel class of systems (see Fig. 2).

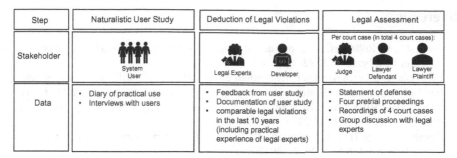

Step	Naturalistic User Study	Deduction of Legal Violations	Legal Assessment		
Stakeholder	System User	Legal Experts Developer	Per court case (in total 4 court cases): Judge	Lawyer Defendant	Lawyer Plaintiff
Data	• Diary of practical use • Interviews with users	• Feedback from user study • Documentation of user study • comparable legal violations in the last 10 years (including practical experience of legal experts)	• Statement of defense • Four pretrial proceedings • Recordings of 4 court cases • Group discussion with legal experts		

Fig. 2. Application of LEGIT in the case of AI-based learning assistants

The goal of our evaluation is to evaluate an AI-based assistant. Our use case for deploying the learning assistant was a course for business administration that was taken by about 150 students. Thus, in the first part of our evaluation, we offerred a course that, in addition to the lecture, allowed students to prepare for the upcoming exam together with the learning assistant. The user study allowed us to capture possible conflicts with the law beforehand. The deduction of legal violations included legal experts as well as the developer team. One exemplary cause of action was the disclosure of the learning data of individual students beyond the actual purpose—the use in preparation for the exam—for the decision of a job posting at the university. The legal assessment included four court cases in which the developed claims were negotiated.

5 Further Work and Expected Contribution

Our next steps include the establishment of LEGIT as an evaluation methodology in IS research. Thus, we will apply the methodology in different scenarios to derive adjustments to the methodology. For this purpose, we are working closely with legal experts. We contribute to DSR by transferring a method from law science to application development to anticipate the legal constraints both within the design process and after prototyping the use context of the future application. We furthermore add to the DSR methods a novel evaluation approach that has high external validity for anticipating the legal compatibility of novel applications before actually bringing them to market or even before building them. The application of LEGIT in a large development project demonstrates how legal requirements and their implementation may be evaluated early on and thus may derive feedback on the implementation and possible legal infringements. So far, the method has been limited to European law, which goes hand-in-hand with the fact that the European legal system is one of the strictest in terms of data protection [17]. Nevertheless, as part of the new scenarios, we will adapt the methodology for a legal system that is as international as possible.

Acknowledgements. This paper presents research that was conducted in context of the projects AnEkA (project 348084924), funded by the German Research Foundation (DFG) and Nudger (grant 16KIS0890K), funded by the German Federal Ministry of Education and Research.

References

1. Pordesch, V., Roßnagel, A., Schneider, M.: Simulation Study Mobile and secure communication in Healthcare. DuD **23**(2), 76–80 (1999)
2. Sonnenberg, C., vom Brocke, J.: Evaluations in the science of the artificial – reconsidering the build-evaluate pattern in design science research. In: Peffers, K., Rothenberger, M., Kuechler, B. (eds.) DESRIST 2012. LNCS, vol. 7286, pp. 381–397. Springer, Heidelberg (2012). https://doi.org/10.1007/978-3-642-29863-9_28
3. Venable, J., Pries-Heje, J., Baskerville, R.: FEDS: a framework for evaluation in design science research. Eur. J. Inf. Syst. **25**, 77–89 (2016)
4. Borges, G.: Legal framework for autonomous systems, pp. 977–982 (2018)
5. Roßnagel, A., Schuldt, M.: The simulation study as a method of evaluating socially acceptable technology design, pp. 108–116 (2013)
6. Hoffmann, A., Schulz, T., Zirfas, J., Hoffmann, H., Roßnagel, A., Leimeister, J.M.: Legal compatibility as a characteristic of sociotechnical systems. Bus. Inf. Syst. Eng. **57**(2), 103–113 (2015). https://doi.org/10.1007/s12599-015-0373-5
7. Barati, M., Petri, I., Rana, O.F.: Developing GDPR compliant user data policies for internet of things. In: Proceedings of the 12th IEEE/ACM International Conference on Utility and Cloud Computing, pp. 133–141 (2019)
8. Bourcier, D., Mazzega, P.: Toward measures of complexity in legal systems. In: Proceedings of the 11th International Conference on Artificial Intelligence and Law, pp. 211–215 (2007)
9. Spiekermann, S.: The challenges of privacy by design. Commun. ACM **55**, 38–40 (2012)
10. van der Sype, Y.S., Maalej, W.: On lawful disclosure of personal user data: what should app developers do? IEEE, Piscataway (2014)
11. Venable, J., Pries-Heje, J., Baskerville, R.: A comprehensive framework for evaluation in design science research. In: Peffers, K., Rothenberger, M., Kuechler, B. (eds.) DESRIST 2012. LNCS, vol. 7286, pp. 423–438. Springer, Heidelberg (2012). https://doi.org/10.1007/978-3-642-29863-9_31
12. Peffers, K., Rothenberger, M., Tuunanen, T., Vaezi, R.: Design science research evaluation. In: Peffers, K., Rothenberger, M., Kuechler, B. (eds.) DESRIST 2012. LNCS, vol. 7286, pp. 398–410. Springer, Heidelberg (2012). https://doi.org/10.1007/978-3-642-29863-9_29
13. Roßnagel, A.: Simulationsstudien zur Gestaltung von Telekooperationstechnik. GMD Spiegel Nr. 2 (1993)
14. Dickhaut, E., Janson, A., Leimeister, J.M.: The hidden value of patterns – using design patterns to whitebox technology development in legal assessments. In: 16th International Conference on Wirtschaftsinformatik (WI 2021) (2021)
15. Dickhaut, E., Li, M.M., Janson, A., Leimeister, J.M.: Developing lawful technologies – a revelatory case study on design patterns. In: HICSS 54 (2021)
16. Rüscher, D.: Alexa, Siri and Google as digital spies on behalf of the investigation authorities?, pp. 687–692 (2018)
17. Li, H., Yu, L., He, W.: The impact of GDPR on global technology development. J. Glob. Inf. Technol. Manag. **22**, 1–6 (2019)

DELEN – A Process Model for the Systematic Development of Legitimate Digital Nudges

Torben Jan Barev[1](✉) ⓘ, Sofia Schöbel[1] ⓘ, Andreas Janson[2] ⓘ,
and Jan Marco Leimeister[1,2] ⓘ

[1] University of Kassel, Kassel, Germany
{torben.barev,sofia.schoebel,leimeister}@uni-kassel.de
[2] University of St. Gallen, St. Gallen, Switzerland
{andreas.janson,janmarco.leimeister}@unisg.ch

Abstract. Digital nudging is a promising approach from behavioral economics. In decisions where individuals tend to struggle, nudges can support users of digital systems by aligning their behavior with their preferences. Despite their wide use, most digital nudges are designed to support the intended behavior from the perspective of a company while neglecting potential legal, ethical, or individual constraints or preferences. With modern technologies such as artificial intelligence or big data, these issues multiply and with the increasing effectiveness of digital nudges and use of new technologies, this has become even more critical. Thus, in this paper we follow a Design Science Research approach to develop a process model for the systematic development of legitimate nudges (DELEN). Legitimacy requires that dealings between different entities shall be fair. Unlike other models, we set normative boundaries derived from literature, expert interviews, and target group segmentation as integral elements. Target group segmentation increases nudge effectiveness and avoids unnecessary burdens for other individuals. By doing so, the DELEN process model paves the way for legitimate and effective digital nudges.

Keywords: Nudging · Design science research · Process model · Legitimacy

1 Introduction

Government policy makers and companies have increasingly adopted insights from behavioral economics to solve a wide range of behavioral issues [11, 27]. One approach to achieve this at little costs and with the potential to promote economic and other goals is nudging. Nudging is defined as a liberty-preserving approach that intends to "alter people's behavior in a predictable way without forbidding any options or significantly changing their economic incentives" [28 p. 6]. The concept of nudging has received great attention from academics and practitioners and has found its way into the digital environment. In the digital environment, nudging is described as the use of user-interface design elements to guide people's behavior in digital choice environments [33]. For instance, the indication of popular energy-saving options or austerity plans on

© Springer Nature Switzerland AG 2021
L. Chandra Kruse et al. (Eds.): DESRIST 2021, LNCS 12807, pp. 299–312, 2021.
https://doi.org/10.1007/978-3-030-82405-1_30

digital platforms are considered nudge elements. In this case, the majority's decision influences the perception and behavior of individuals in a way [31] that makes others try to imitate the behavior of the majority [5].

Critically, despite the wide use of digital nudges, many nudging concepts appear that harm ethical or legal standards. Thaler and Sunstein explain that nudges should be designed to make an individual's life safer, easier and of greater benefit [28]. In decisions where individuals tend to choose an alternative against their preferences, nudges should support individuals to align their behavior with their intention [28]. To this day, this standard is not being considered sufficiently in current nudging concepts. Many individuals are nudged in a direction that supports the needs of a company but not necessarily the needs of users [13]. For instance, in the online shopping environment, nudges can be advantageous from the seller's point of view but manipulate an individual to unintentionally enter into a contract or to accept an excessive price (for example, [17]).

Furthermore, the design of a digital nudging concept is complex, and many different aspects need to be considered. For instance, the nudge should be transparent and visible to the users, as, otherwise, critics may conclude that nudges could be of manipulative character and undermine an individual's autonomy [4]. A greater practice and accessible design knowledge of morally legitimate digital nudges is therefore urgently needed. Legitimacy is defined as a "generalized perception or assumption that the actions of an entity are desirable, proper, or appropriate within some socially constructed systems of norms, values, beliefs and definitions" [25 p. 574]. To be better guided in the digital nudging concept development, researchers and practitioners can work with process models that ensure legitimate designs [10]. Importantly, current digital nudge processes do not sufficiently take ethical and legal standards into account [15, 16], which are essential for the design of legitimate digital nudges [24]. These two aspects are of high relevance because nudging can alter an individual's behavior yet increase or decrease an individual's welfare. When the triggered behavior is not aligned with the individual's preferences, nudges can compromise the individual's life in the short or long term.

With the increasing effectiveness of digital nudges and use of new technologies such as big data and artificial intelligence, these issues multiply, and ethically designed systems are even more necessary. This is the case, as nudges can dynamically initiate an individual's behavior and can manipulate behavior more effectively than ever before [24]. For instance, with modern technology, once visiting a website, a user can be analyzed in real time, and the site can determine to nudge users to enroll for a specific service before leaving the site. Consequently, it is important that digital nudge development processes set these normative boundaries, as an integral element in a systematic development process model being able to create legitimate digital nudges. With this work, we aim to contribute to theory and practice by answering the following research question: *How can a nudging process model foster an effective and legitimate creation of digital nudges.* To achieve our goal, we selected an established and eminent Design Science Research (DSR) approach that suits our purpose exactly to tackle the proposed research question. We follow the DSR approach by Peffers et al. [18]. To carve out a process model for the development of legitimate digital nudges (named DELEN) being the proposed artifact, we follow a specific research approach, which is presented in Fig. 1.

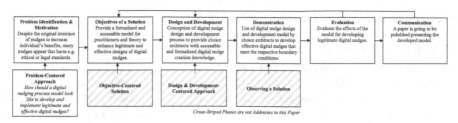

Fig. 1. Research approach adapted from Peffers et al. [18].

With the development of the DELEN model, we contribute to theory and practice by providing a digital nudging process model that fosters a legitimate and effective design and development of digital nudges. We provide systematic guidance for the creation of digital nudges that meet ethical, legal, psychological, and societal normative boundary conditions.

2 Theoretical Background

2.1 Legitimate Digital Nudges and Normative Boundary Aspects

In digital environments, nudging typically uses design elements in the user interface to influence behavior [33]. Nudging is based on the principle of libertarian paternalism to influence decisions, letting individuals freely choose a decision option (liberalism component). The individual's freedom of choice is not restricted since none of the options are prohibited and the economic incentive of the alternatives is not significantly changed. However, the individual is nudged towards a decision option that represents the supposedly greatest benefit for them (paternalism component) [28]. To be considered as nudge, Lembcke et al. state three important considerations for digital nudges: preserving individuals' freedom of choice / autonomy, transparent disclosure of nudges and individual (pro-self) as well as (pro-social) goal-oriented justification of nudging [12]. This is important, as in offline environments, online environments offer no neutral way of presenting choices. Any user interface, from organizational websites to mobile apps, can thus be viewed as a digital choice environment and nudges can be implemented [33].

Yet, not all digital nudges embody legitimate designs. Whitworth and de Moor point out that *legitimacy* considers that dealings between different entities are fair [34]. Many nudges exploit the fact that individuals often act irrationally due to social, cognitive, or emotional factors. In these cases, nudges can unconsciously drive individuals to harmful consequences such as financial exploitation, unwanted surveillance, and unhealthy behavior. As nudges can trigger behavior that sometimes is not in line with the individual's preferences, these nudges are not fair. In online environments, especially, many nudges are designed to support the needs of a company while supplanting the preferences of the users [13]. A prominent example is the framing of decisions to accept internet cookies. Framing can be done in two ways: to support the collection of user data or to protect user data by framing the legal and ethically compliant alternative. Although data-protection-friendly defaults are set in accordance with legal requirements, more and more internet platforms are framing the decision in such a way that it is easier for users to agree to additional cookies than to keep the actual default. If designers design and implement nudges that do not meet specific legal standards, companies may be confronted with high fines. Additionally, if nudges do not meet ethical standards such as fostering transparency and autonomy, and counteracting informational self-determination, these mechanisms could be linked to manipulating and harming the individual [21]. Digital nudges that act to the disadvantage of the individual make it clear that a multitude of different aspects play a role in the design of digital nudges [16]. Legitimacy is very context dependent and must be assessed in each design process specifically [34]. Hence, designers of digital nudges are asked to identify and set normative boundaries in each nudge's design process individually before operating a digital nudge concept.

2.2 State-of-the-Art of Processes for the Digital Nudge Development

To analyze the current digital nudge development processes and to craft design requirements for effective and legitimate digital nudges, we conducted a systematic literature review (SLR) following a methodology proposed by vom Brocke et al. as well as Webster and Watson [29, 32]. The literature was organized *conceptually* addressing *general scholars* on digital nudging and *practitioners* who are developing digital nudges. Our perspective on the literature was not completely neutral, as we selected those research papers and insights that could be used for the process model based on our prior knowledge. We chose to include a *representative* volume of research papers in our analysis, as contents, and especially nudge elements especially, were often mentioned redundantly. For the SLR we used the following search string: ("digital nudging" AND "model" OR "process") and used all variations of the keywords – singular, plural, hyphenated, or not hyphenated. We used the Basket of Eight and relevant IS journals and conferences to consider journals and conference proceedings at the intersection of Information Systems (IS) and Human Computer Interaction (HCI) that provided an overview of high-quality and relevant research in the respective research field. From our analysis, we identified 23 relevant papers from the field of IS and 18 relevant papers from the field of HCI. Our analysis showed, that various researchers have proposed models on how to craft nudges [6, 15, 16, 19, 22]. Weinmann et al. highlight, for example, how designers can create digital nudges by creating a design cycle [22]. Another approach to provide an easier access to digital nudging is proposed by Meske and Potthoff, named the Digital Nudging Process Model (DINU Model). In this model, the creation of digital nudging is divided into three generic phases: (1) analyzing, (2) designing and (3) evaluating, including a feedback loop [15]. In connection to this, in 2018, Mirsch et al. proposed the Digital Nudge Design Method (DND Method), presenting a universal four-step approach for how to systematically design digital nudges [16].

An analysis of the current design and implementation models is presented in Table 1. We analyzed whether the nudge development process models take both the design and the implementation into account. Additionally, we focused our analysis on ethical, legal, and psychological considerations as they are seen as essential requirements for a legitimate design [24]. Ethical considerations state that legitimate nudges should, for instance, promote transparency, voluntariness, and autonomy for reversibility. Legal standards can, for example, be based on the fact that nudges are designed in accordance with the European Union-wide General Data Protection Regulation. Psychological factors can consider that individuals who are exposed to the nudge are not left shocked, disturbed, or angry. Furthermore, we took a target group segmentation into account as our literature review results stated that nudges have to be targeted and personalized to achieve higher effectiveness [6, 19].

Table 1. Existing models for the design and implementation of digital nudges.

Existing Digital Nudge Models	Design	Implementation	Ethical Guidelines	Legal Considerations	Psychological Considerations	Target Group Segmentation
Mirsch et al., 2018 [16]	✓	✗	✗	✗	✗	✗
Meske and Potthoff, 2017 [15]	✓	✓	✗	✗	✗	✗
Schneider et al., 2018 [22]	✓	✓	✗	✗	✗	✗
Dalecke and Karlsen, 2020 [6]	✓	✗	✗	✗	✗	✓
Purohit and Holzer, 2019 [19]	✓	✓	✗	✗	✗	✓

The models listed above build on an understanding of the general user for better nudge effectiveness. Nevertheless, segmenting the target group of the nudge recipients is not an integral element in the design process. The models mainly address the average user and do not sufficiently integrate elements of targeting and segmentation [8]. The effectiveness of digital nudges can be highly individual-dependent, and these models can only serve as a scaffold [6, 8]. On the flipside, the DND and Digital Nudge Design Cycle consider design and implementation conjointly, whereas several models do not combine these steps. However, as Durlak and DuPre argue, this is urgently needed [7]. In most models, it does not become clear for nudge designers what the key elements are that can be triggered to influence implementation effectiveness. Most importantly, the presented models do not sufficiently ensure that ethical and moral directives are thoroughly considered, making practitioners prone to design societally reprehensible nudges. For instance, ethical guidelines are proposed by Meske and Amojo, but without an integration in a process model for the design and implementation of digital nudges. Thus, we have developed a model for the **de**velopment of **le**gitimate **n**udges (DELEN) for the digital environment.

3 Development of the DELEN Process Model

We deduced requirements for the development of the DELEN process model from theory and practice. To extend and validate the results of our literature review stated above and to practically enrich our requirements, we conducted semi-structured explorative interviews with German industry experts (n = 14). We interviewed digital nudging experts and researchers from various fields, such as IT developers, user interface designers and cognitive work process experts, ensuring that various perspectives and a fundamental understanding of the subject were brought together. The experts were recruited based on their specific experience and thorough knowledge in this field. Table 2 provides an overview of the interviewed experts and researchers.

In our interviews we evaluated the decision and user context, the alignment of the nudge and nudged user, the legitimacy of the nudge, the nudge effectiveness, the systems usability, and the evaluation of the nudge. We consolidated our interview results with

Table 2. Overview of interviewed experts and researchers.

ID	Expertise	Interviewee's position	ID	Expertise	Interviewee's position
1	Software development	IT developer	8	Commercial law	Director of research institute
2	Software development	IT developer	9	Commercial law	Associated researcher
3	Software development	IT developer	10	Digital marketing	Marketing manager
4	Information systems	Director of research institute	11	Business consulting	IT consultant
5	Information systems	Research group leader	12	Cognitive engineering	Business process manager
6	Information systems	Research group leader	13	Cognitive engineering	Business process manager
7	Information systems	Digital business manager	14	Ethics and information systems	Research group leader

the results of our systematic literature review to derive requirements for our model. More than 26 design requirements (DR) were collected, tested for redundancy, and encapsulated to 15 tentative model requirements. They were condensed and simplified for easier understandability, ensuring their utility for choice architects. A summary of the key findings and our requirements can be found in Table 3.

With the carved-out design requirements, we were able to derive a process model that supports ethical and legal standards and that allows for an individual adoption of digital nudge concepts. Next, the crafted requirements are presented regarding the DELEN process model and its realization.

4 The DELEN Process Model

The general process of creating digital nudges starts with a problem identification phase and an objective setting phase. In these phases, choice architects should identify and focus on the specific behavior that they want to change. In our model, we focus on the design and development processes and present these in detail, as these are the keys when creating digital nudges. After each process, the developed nudges can be assessed and revised in an artificial environment. Next, the developed nudges can be implemented into a system and evaluated in a real environment. The full model is presented in Fig. 2:

To foster practical usability, the model is condensed and simplified enough to enable easier access. The model flows in a systematic structure and avoids complex visuals, representing an easy-to-grasp approach. Furthermore, we followed the framework proposed by Renaud and van Biljon to increase communicative power [20]. The model was revised and adapted accordingly. This was crucial for usage and applicability (see

Table 3. Design requirements for the design and implementation of digital nudges.

Issue category	Design requirement (DR)	Source
Context of the decision	DR1: Creation process should consider context of the digital nudge	Expert Interview and Literature e.g. [1]
Alignment of nudge with adjoining entities	DR2: Digital nudges should be aligned with supporting activities, business processes and overall strategy DR3: The enhancement of the nudge should be considered e.g. by artificial intelligence DR4: Nudge designers must understand the user's goals, values and preferences. Nudges should be aligned accordingly	Expert Interviews and Literature e.g. [23]
Adaptability of the nudge	DR5: Different user characteristics should be considered DR6: Different technology characteristics should be considered	Expert Interviews and Literature e.g. [3, 6, 8]
Legitimacy of the nudge	DR7: Digital nudges should reflect high ethical standards DR8: Digital nudges should reflect on high legal standards DR9: Nudges should reflect on high psychological standards DR10: Digital nudges should reflect on high societal stand-ards	Expert Interviews and Literature e.g. [2, 12, 14, 30]
Effectiveness of the nudge	DR11: Process should connect design and implementation of digital nudges DR12: Nudge designers should consider timings as success of some digital nudges relies on their timely delivery	Expert Interviews and Literature e.g. [19]
Usability of the nudge in system	DR13: Creation processes should be easy to grasp and accessible in practice DR14: Cost-Benefit analysis should be considered	Expert Interviews and Literature e.g. [20]
Evaluation of the nudge	DR15: (User) feedback and new insights should be continuously integrated into the process	Expert Interviews and Literature e.g. [16]

DR13). Thus, this model paves the way for leveraging the potentials of digital nudges. Below, we will describe the model's phases in detail.

Design Process
The design process describes how digital nudges can be systematically created. It includes five steps, which should be performed consecutively and are explained below.

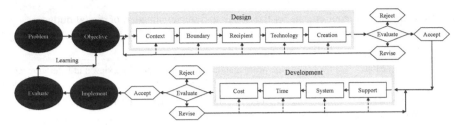

Fig. 2. Creation of legitimate nudges model.

Assessing the Context. First, choice architects should map out the user journey of the individual (see *DR1*). This helps to determine at what point individuals make decisions and to identify optimal timings to implement interventions. At the same time, the processes in which no intervention has to be implemented should be identified in order to not interfere with other processes. In doing so, the specific choice architecture should be analyzed to identify relevant context factors that determine the individual's decision-making. For instance, the decision context differs in terms of privacy-related decisions and health-related decisions.

Setting the Normative Boundaries. To craft legitimate nudge designs, choice architects should assemble the ethical (see *DR7*), legal (see *DR8*), psychological (see *DR9*), and societal standards (see *DR10*) that frame the digital nudge. It is important to highlight that these elements might differ, according to the choice architecture and are highly context dependent. For instance, different legal boundaries apply for companies and governments. Yet, nudge designers should identify and set normative boundaries regarding the assessed context.

Targeting the Recipients. Many nudges show decreased effectiveness, as they do not sufficiently target the right individuals. Thus, it is important to get an understanding of the user's cognitive and affective processes as well as which of the user's heuristics are accessible (see *DR5*). Sundar et al. state that individuals with a stronger belief in the internal logic of a given heuristic are more likely to invoke that heuristic when presented with a cue, compared to individuals with a weaker belief [26]. Hence, to achieve higher nudge effectiveness, the users should be segmented and targeted accordingly, as some individuals can be addressed by digital nudges in greater detail than others. The target group should be sufficiently narrow, as ineffective nudges can slow down work processes or stimulate the individual negatively. It is important to ensure that the intended behavior resonates with the nudged person's preferences and values (see *DR4*). This is crucial, as these are important aspects of ethical justification and legitimacy of digital nudge designs.

Adapting to Technology. Choice architects should build on special characteristics of the used technology and should consider how the individual interacts with it (see *DR6*). Nudges should be designed differently when the technology can provide visual, auditory, or haptic feedback. For example, a stop signal can be transmitted to the individual by a red button (visual), an alarm sound (auditory) or a shaking impulse (haptic). Furthermore, a nudge may look different on a stationary device than a mobile device.

Creating the Digital Nudge. Based on prior analysis, choice architects can now select the suitable nudge element. Nudge elements in digital user interfaces can be, for instance, default settings that preselect a specific option. Other elements can include the framing of a decision. Options that are beneficial for an individual can be highlighted in a green color.

Development Process

The development process consists of four elements and is a pre-stage of the implementation phase, which considers the factors that need to be set for an effective implementation. The development is closely linked with the nudge design, so choice architects should consider these processes in correlation (see *DR11*).

Support: Nudges can, despite careful design, lead to unintended or conflicting behaviors. Nudges may jeopardize other significant goals, for example, when a nudge, designed to reduce pollution, ends up increasing another factor, e.g., the energy costs for the most disadvantaged members of society [27]. Thus, from the beginning, further supporting mechanisms can be implemented to counter any harmful behaviors (see *DR2*). Individuals who show unintended behavior can be recaptured and redirected. To achieve this, a variety of mechanisms may be used. This is crucial, as leading to an alternative can happen by alternative mechanisms. Nudges are described as soft-paternalistic instruments. Choice architects may even consider other soft or even harder mechanisms, such as laws or regulations. Overall, the implemented mechanism should be aligned with the overall strategy and the existing business processes to ensure that the overall goal is met.

System: Today, there is a wide range of systems available that can influence the effectiveness of the nudges. Choice architects should decide to what extent, e.g., artificial intelligence (AI) or big data can enhance digital nudges. For instance, Ferreyra et al. state that AI can enhance digital nudges to make them dynamic, e.g., referring to smart or hyper nudges [9].

Time: The success of some digital nudges relies on their timely delivery. Various researchers have presented evidence on how the different timings of nudges have an impact on their effectiveness [6]. Thus, it is essential to consider when the nudge is implemented in the system and when it is exposed to the individual (see *DR12*). This can be at any time of day, such as in the morning, at noon, in the evening or after special events (e.g., data protection scandals).

Cost: When implementing digital nudges, choice architects should weigh the costs and benefits. It should be decided whether other alternatives have a better cost-benefit ratio, and which behavioral change mechanism should be used (see *DR14*).

Revision and Optimization Processes

After the design and development phase, a phase of testing and evaluation follows, and the nudge should be adjusted if necessary (see *DR15*). After the development, the designed nudge should be tested. At this stage, choice architects should assess whether the developed nudge meets e.g., the boundary conditions and how the users are interacting with it. After the deployment process, nudge designers should test how the nudge works for instance in collaboration with supporting mechanisms or at different times in the system. After the evaluation, choice architects can adjust the different factors accordingly and can take specific learnings into account for another cycle of design and development, if necessary. This means that even when the designed and implemented nudges fail (are adjusted or rejected), choice architects now have a method to better analyze what went wrong and then gain insight into improvements in the future.

5   Model Application and Criteria Based Evaluation

The DELEN process model was applied and evaluated by a group of interdisciplinary choice architects. This group used the DELEN process to design cookie acceptance consent forms, which were positioned on the first page of a fictional online page. An exemplary privacy nudge is presented below (Fig. 3).

Fig. 3. Exemplary privacy nudge developed by deploying the DELEN process model.

Here, the nudge focuses on presenting relevant information for privacy friendly decision making. The nudge is personalized and uses, from a legal perspective, a General Data Protection Regulation (GDPR) compatible default option. Ethical directives are considered in terms of transparency, as this choice architecture encourages informational self-determination. This developed cookie consent form visually highlights further information and supporting contacts. It can be smoothly integrated in the user interface of a digital work system.

Following, it is presented how the specific features are developed phase by phase using the DELEN process model (see Table 4). The digital nudge is split up in its components, explained and assigned to the respective phase.

In a concluding step, we proved the suitability of our model by taking the criteria presented in Sects. 2 & 3 for another evaluation cycle. This is in line with Peffers et al. [18]. We presented the developed model and assessed it in semi-structured interviews with 14 experts of the legal, ethical and IS field (see Table 2). We tested and discussed how well the model serves its main purpose of supporting choice architects in designing and implementing effective and legitimate digital nudges. Furthermore, we tested if the model incorporates multi-stakeholder perspectives and is accessible to various choice architects. This ensured usability and application.

Multi-stakeholder Perspective: The consideration of overarching stakeholders is implemented to prevent a one-sided focus, e.g., on only focusing on company interests while also taking ethical, legal, and societal interests into account.

Fostering Nudge Effectiveness: To ensure nudge effectiveness choice architects are encouraged to assess the context (e.g., mapping out the user journey), targeting the recipients specifically, adapt the nudges to individual characteristics and support their effects with supporting mechanisms. Unlike other models, a thorough process is presented that fosters not only on the design but also on the implementation of the nudge as an integral element.

Fostering Nudge Legitimacy: The process model specifically ensures that normative boundary conditions are considered. Choice architects are encouraged to assemble the ethical, legal, psychological, and societal standards that frame the digital nudge. Furthermore, by setting normative boundaries regarding the used technology, designs are crafted that meet standards across different technologic channels. This is important, as legal rules vary in terms of technology. Thus, ensuring that the developed nudges are crafted as legitimate designs.

Accessibility to Nudge Designers: To foster practical usability for various user groups, the DELEN process model is condensed and simplified. The model flows in a systematic

Table 4. Developed digital nudge components phase by phase of DELEN process model.

Component	Rationale of component	Development in associated section	
User behavior influence	Object Oriented Behavior Influence to disclose less personal information	Objective	
User support	Intervention is placed when user enters page for first time	Context	Design process
Normative boundaries	Meeting GDPR regulations as default is set in the right direction. Ethical directives are considered in terms of transparency, encouraging informational self determination	Boundary	Design process
Personalization	Recipient is addressed and message adjusted for specific target audience appeal	Recipient	Design process

(continued)

Table 4. (*continued*)

Component	Rationale of component	Development in associated section	
Visual cues are carved out	Visual cues highlight important components for faster recognition and processing	Technology	Design process
Nudge design	The option of cookie preferences is preselected as default, colour coding is used to symbolize the best alternative, and additional information is given to foster acceptance and trust	Creation	Design process
Further information and contacts are provided	Supporting mechanisms are linked to message such as further information about cookie settings, link to IT-department is set for further contact	Support	Development process
Technical enhancement	Artificial intelligence or big data can enhance digital nudges	System	Development process
Timing	The intervention is closely presented to the time of the decision	Time	Development process
Cost assessment	Implementation of this digital nudge is cost effective as system adjustments are rather small	Cost	Development process

structure and avoids complex visuals, representing an easy-to-grasp approach. Thus, even with different levels of prior knowledge the model to accessible enough for application and usability.

6   Contributions, Limitations and Future Research

With the developed DELEN model, we contribute to theory and practice by providing a digital nudging process model that fosters a legitimate and effective design and development of digital nudges. We provide systematic guidance for the creation of digital nudges that meet ethical, legal, psychological, and societal normative boundary conditions. Our structured process model is condensed and formalized to provide choice architects with easy-to-grasp and accessible knowledge about how to design digital nudges that meet important legal and ethical standards. Unlike other models, we implement normative boundaries as integral elements for our model as well as propose target group segmentation as a key element. Target group segmentation increases nudge effectiveness and avoids unnecessary burdens for other individuals. By doing so, our model paves the way for legitimate and more effective digital nudges. By following our systematic model, choice architects can more easily compare and improve nudge designs. Even when digital nudges fail, the choice architects can systematically go through every element of the systematic model and assess their execution. Even though, our digital nudge model offers directives within a digital environment, transferring and testing these directives in an offline environment and adapting this model may be a fruitful endeavor in the future.

Acknowledgement. The research presented in this paper was funded by the German Federal Ministry of Education and Research in the context of the project Nudger (www.nudger.de), grant no. 16KIS0890K. The third author also acknowledges funding from the Basic Research Fund (GFF) of the University of St. Gallen.

References

1. Abouzied, A., Chen, J.: CommonTies. In: CSCW 2014. 2014, Baltimore, MD, USA, pp. 1–4. ACM, New York (2014)
2. Barev, T., Schwede, M., Janson, A.: The dark side of privacy nudging. In 54th HICSS. Maui, Hawaii, USA (2021)
3. Barev, T.J. Janson, A.: Towards an integrative understanding of privacy nudging – systematic review and research agenda. In: 18th Annual Pre-ICIS Workshop on HCI Research in MIS (ICIS) (2019)
4. Blumenthal-Barby, J.S.: Choice architecture. In: Coons, C., Weber, M. (eds.) Paternalism. Theory and Practice, pp. 178–196. Cambridge University Press, Cambridge (2013)
5. Coventry, L.M., Jeske, D., Blythe, J.M., Turland, J., Briggs, P.: Personality and social framing in privacy decision-making. Front. Psychol. **7**, 1341 (2016)
6. Dalecke, S., Karlsen, R.: Designing dynamic and personalized nudges. In: 10th WIMS 2020. Biarritz, France, pp. 139–148. ACM. New York (2020)
7. Durlak, J.A., DuPre, E.P.: Implementation matters. Am. J. Commun. Psychol. **41**(3–4), 327–350 (2008)
8. Egelman, S., Peer, E.: The myth of the average user. In: New Security Paradigms Workshop on ZZZ - NSPW 2015, pp. 16–28. ACM Press, New York (2015)
9. Ferreyra, N., Aïmeur, E., Hage, H., Heisel, M., van Hoogstraten, C.: Persuasion meets AI: ethical considerations for the design of social engineering countermeasures. In: 12th IJCKDKEKM. Science and Technology Publications, pp. 204–211 (2020)
10. Indulska, M., Green, P., Recker, J., Rosemann, M.: Business process modeling: perceived benefits. In: Laender, A.H.F., Castano, S., Dayal, U., Casati, F., de Oliveira, J.P.M. (eds.) ER 2009. LNCS, vol. 5829, pp. 458–471. Springer, Heidelberg (2009). https://doi.org/10.1007/978-3-642-04840-1_34
11. Johnson, E.J., Goldstein, D.: Medicine. Do defaults save lives? Science (New York, N.Y.) **302**(5649), 1338–1339 (2003)

12. Lembcke, T.-B., Engelbrecht, N., Brendel, A. B., Kolbe, L.: To nudge or not to nudge: ethical considerations of digital nudging based on its behavioral economics roots. In 27th ECIS, Stockholm & Uppsala, Sweden, 8–14 June 2019 (2019)
13. Mathur, A., Acar, G., Friedman, M.J., Lucherini, E., Mayer, J., Chetty, M., Narayanan, A.: Dark patterns at scale. In: Proceedings of ACM HCI, vol. 3, pp. 1–32. CSCW (2019)
14. Meske, C., Amojo, I.: Ethical guidelines for the construction of digital nudges. In 53rd HICSS. Maui, Hawaii, USA (2020)
15. Meske, C., Potthoff, T.: The DINU-model - a process model for the design of nudges. In: 25th ECIS, Guimarães, Portugal, pp. 2585–2597 (2017)
16. Mirsch, T., Lehrer, C., Jung, R.: Making digital nudging applicable: the digital nudge design method. In International Conference on Information Systems (2018)
17. Nouwens, M., Liccardi, I., Veale, M., Karger, D., Kagal, L.: Dark patterns after the GDPR: scraping consent pop-ups and demonstrating their influence. In: 2020 CHI, [S.l.], pp. 1–13. ACM (2020)
18. Peffers, K., Tuunanen, T., Rothenberger, M.A., Chatterjee, S.: A design science research methodology for information systems research. JMIS **24**(3), 45–77 (2007)
19. Purohit, A.K., Holzer, A.: Functional digital nudges. In: CHI 2019, Glasgow, Scotland UK, pp. 1–6. ACM, New York (2019)
20. Renaud, K., van Biljon, J.: A framework to maximise the communicative power of knowledge visualisations. In: 2019 SAICSIT Skukuza, Kruger National Park, South Africa. ICPS, pp. 1–10. ACM, New York (2019)
21. Ryan, R.M., Deci, E.L.: Self-regulation and the problem of human autonomy. J. Pers. **74**(6), 1557–1585 (2006)
22. Schneider, C., Weinmann, M., Vom Brocke, J.: Digital nudging. Commun. ACM **61**(7), 67–73 (2018)
23. Schöbel, S., Barev, T., Janson, A., Hupfeld, F., Leimeister, J.M.: Understanding user preferences of digital privacy nudges – a best-worst scaling approach. In: 53rd HICSS. Maui, Hawaii, USA (2020)
24. Spiekermann, S.: Ethical IT Innovation. CRC Press, Boca Raton (2016)
25. Suchman, M.C.: Managing legitimacy. AMR **20**(3), 571–610 (1995)
26. Sundar, S.S., Kim, J., Rosson, M.B., Molina, M.D.: Online privacy heuristics that predict information disclosure. In: 2020 CHI, [S.l.], 1–12. ACM (2020)
27. Sunstein, C.R., Reisch, L.A.: Green by Default. Kyklos **66**(3), 398–402 (2013)
28. Thaler, R.H., Sunstein, C.R.: Nudge. Penguin, New York (2008)
29. Vom Brocke, J., Simons, A., Riemer, K., Niehaves, B., Plattfaut, R., Cleven, A.: Standing on the shoulders of giants (2009)
30. Vugts, A., van den Hoven, M., de Vet, E., Verweij, M.: How autonomy is understood in discussions on the ethics of nudging. Behav. Public Policy **4**(1), 108–123 (2020)
31. Wang, C., Zhang, X., Hann, I.-H.: Socially nudged. ISR **29**(3), 641–655 (2018)
32. Webster, J., Watson, R.T.: Analyzing the past to prepare for the future. MIS Q. **26**(2), 13–23 (2002)
33. Weinmann, M., Schneider, C., Vom Brocke, J.: Digital nudging. BISE **58**(6), 433–436 (2016)
34. Whitworth, B., de Moor, A.: Legitimate by design. Behav. IT **22**(1), 31–51 (2003)

Sourcing the Right Open Data: A Design Science Research Approach for the Enterprise Context

Pavel Krasikov$^{(\boxtimes)}$, Christine Legner , and Markus Eurich

Faculty of Business and Economics (HEC), University of Lausanne, 1015 Lausanne, Switzerland
{pavel.krasikov,christine.legner,markus.eurich}@unil.ch

Abstract. Open data has become increasingly attractive for users, especially companies, due to its value-creating capabilities and innovation potential. One essential challenge is to identify and leverage suitable open datasets that support specific business scenarios as well as strategic data goals. To overcome this challenge, companies need elaborate processes for open data sourcing. To this end, our research aims to develop prescriptive knowledge in the form of a meaningful method for screening, assessing, and preparing open data for use in an enterprise setting. In line with the principles of Action Design Research (ADR), we iteratively develop a method that comprises four phases and is enabled by knowledge graphs and linked data concepts. Our method supports companies in sourcing open data of uncertain data quality in a value-adding and demand-oriented manner, while creating more transparency about its content, licensing, and access conditions. From an academic perspective, our research conceptualizes open data sourcing as a purposeful and value-creating process.

Keywords: Open data · Data sourcing · Design science · Knowledge graph

1 Introduction

Open data is known to be free for use, reuse, and redistribution by anyone [1]. This definition encompasses the supply (e.g. by governments) and consumption (e.g. by enterprises) perspectives, where open data can be seen as "a process that can appear on different levels of organization or society" [2]. As the availability of open data sources increases, so do companies' expectations for open data to fuel advanced analytics, optimize business processes, enrich data management, or even enable new services [3–5]. However, as simple as the easy and free availability of open data may appear, open data consumers have hurdles to overcome, for example uncertainty about the data quality, lack of transparency about its content, or unclear licensing and access conditions [6–8]. These hurdles prevent companies from using open data to generate value [9] and lead to a "mismatch between the needs and expectations of the users and the possibilities offered by available datasets" [10].

One lever to counteract this mismatch is designing a structured sourcing process for open data that would support enterprises in identifying the right data for the given purpose and preparing it for use. Data sourcing is a complex and largely unaddressed phenomenon

© Springer Nature Switzerland AG 2021
L. Chandra Kruse et al. (Eds.): DESRIST 2021, LNCS 12807, pp. 313–327, 2021.
https://doi.org/10.1007/978-3-030-82405-1_31

[11], encompassing procuring, licensing, and accessing the data, followed by its use. To the best of our knowledge, suitable processes and methodological approaches for open data do not yet exist, at least not in a well-structured, holistic, and rigorously scientific manner. It therefore remains uncertain which process steps and actions qualify to identify and source open data successfully.

To this end, we draw upon design science research (DSR) as it is concerned with "the systematic creation of knowledge about, and with (artificial) design" [12]. In line with DSR in its facet of intentional, intellectual, and creative activities for problem solving, [13] our research focuses on the design of an open data selection and sourcing process. We aim to address the existing void in the information systems research related to data sourcing [11] and focus on the enterprise context of open data use. This leads to the research question: *How can companies be helped to source open data systematically?* The findings of this study support enterprises by providing methodological guidance for screening, assessing, and preparing open data for use. The proposed method ensures that the specific purpose and relevant aspects, such as provenance, access conditions, and quality of sources and datasets are taken into account and that the most suitable open data is finally selected. The scientific community can also benefit from the insights, as the proposed method helps to allocate research activities along the process chain and builds a foundation for future research on the semantics of open datasets.

The remainder of this paper is structured as follows: Sect. 2 introduces the related work about open data and adoption barriers. Section 3 elaborates on our research objectives and the research process. Section 4 presents our method to screen, assess, and prepare open data for use. In Sect. 5, we present our concluding remarks.

2   Related Work

Open data has been addressed in the literature, predominantly in a limited scope of open government data. Numerous national open data initiatives have led to more than 2,500 open data portals worldwide [14], with data.europa.eu and data.gov combined providing access to almost 300,000 open datasets [15, 16]. Despite these impressive numbers, open data use by enterprises remains below expectations [3]. This has motivated researchers to study barriers to open data adoption and open data processes.

2.1 Open Data and Adoption Barriers

Contrary to a widespread perception of open data being only public information assets published by official authorities, in reality it refers to data that is "freely available and can be used as well as republished by everyone without restrictions from copyright or patents" [17]. It yields growth for national economies [18] and offers business and innovation potential for companies [3, 19]. One of the major myths [19] around open data is the assumption that the mere fact of making data available is sufficient for its successful reuse. Nonetheless, open data platforms and their underlying services, as means to ease open data use [20–24], are not sufficient and "the success of open data systems requires more than the simple, provision of access to data" [19]. Open data's definition alone pinpoints some of the many impediments towards its seamless adoption. A meta-analysis by Krasikov et al. [6] reviews the existing studies on open data adoption from both a consumption and a supply side. It identifies three main challenges in using open data from an enterprise perspective: lack of transparency, heterogeneity, and unknown quality of open datasets. The first barrier (transparency) refers to the difficulties of identifying "the right data" [19], understanding its content and the consistency of conclusions that can be drawn by analyzing it. The second (heterogeneity) challenges the discrepancies of how open data is made available in terms of access conditions, licenses, use permissions, file formats, and data structure [20, 25]. The third barrier (quality) mentions the deficiency of open datasets' information quality on multiple levels: inaccurate or incomplete data, obsolete or non-valid data, and simply unclear purpose for use [6, 19]. With regards to the latter, researchers have suggested various assessment techniques [7, 24, 26], but often with a limited focus on platforms and the underlying metadata, ignoring the content and the use context.

Despite the rising expectations towards open data use [20], enterprises encounter the abovementioned barriers. They lack enabling mechanisms for an enterprisewide open data strategy implementation [9], implying a need for a strategic shift with elaborate processes for open data use.

2.2 Open Data Processes from Publisher and Consumer Perspectives

To improve open data adoption, researchers have suggested processes that address some of the issues associated with open data publishing and use. These studies predominantly target open data publishers and focus on identification and selection processes to choose the data to publish. Only two of the existing studies explicitly address the underlying processes from the consumers' perspective (Table 1). Even though the context of these papers differs, they outline similar processes for open data users, namely finding (identifying), analyzing, and processing (integrating and validating) open data.

Ren and Glissmann [27] propose a five-phase process to identify open data information assets to drive open data initiatives. This structured approach focuses on concrete steps to harvest value from open data, taking a governmental perspective: define business goals, identify stakeholders, identify potential information assets, assess quality, and select. Although this approach does not reflect a user perspective, the authors consider selecting information assets as a key decision to ensure the subsequent positive impact from open data use. They also highlight the need for guidelines that would help to increase publishers' return on investment when engaging in open data initiatives.

Zuiderwijk and Janssen [28] investigate sociotechnical barriers and developments in open data processes from both perspectives – publishers (governments) and users (citizens) – with six highly dependent steps for the open data processes: creating, opening, finding, analyzing, processing, and discussing. While creating and publishing open data refer to data providers, open data consumers are involved in the finding and using steps. "The data that are published are usually not published in a format that makes it easy to reuse the data" [28].

Continuing the exploration of open data barriers, Crusoe and Melin [31] expand the open government data process [28], where publishers are additionally involved in assessing the suitability of open data, and releasing it. From the users' perspective, open datasets lack context interpretations, are difficult to find, hard to understand, and often do not consider open data users' needs. Businesses are often positioned as both publishers and consumers of open data [34–36], and are equally impacted by the sociotechnical barriers linked to open data use.

These impediments are encountered along the distinctives phases of providers' as well as consumers' interaction with open data. In a later work, Zuiderwijk et al. [3] depict corporate activities for commercial open data use: search for open data, find, use, and enrich open data, and interpret findings. We can also note that governments, as opposed to other open data consumers, undertake steps for publishing open data that resonate with their counterparts' actions in using open data. In the context of data analytics, Hendler [30] distinguishes three major steps for using heterogeneous online datasets: discovery, integration, and validation. Finally, Abella et al. [32] suggest that open data reuse, as

Table 1. Open data processes from publisher and consumer perspectives

Source	Context	Research method	Perspective
Ren and Glissmann, 2012 [27]	Identifying and incorporating information assets for open data initiatives	Based on principles of business architecture and information quality	Open data publisher (government)
Masip-Bruin et al., 2013 [29]	Systematic value creation process, enabled by a middleware, to identify suitable information to be used	Scenario- and practice-driven	Open data publisher (city council)
Hendler, 2014 [30]	Integration techniques for structured and unstructured online data, exemplified with open data	Explorative analysis	Big data user
Zuiderwijk et al., 2015 [3]	Commercial open data use for creating competitive advantage	Multi-method study: scenario development, semi-structured interviews (n = 2), and survey (n = 14)	Open data user
Crusoe and Melin, 2018 [31] based on [28]	Investigating and systematizing open government data research	Literature review (n = 34)	Open data publisher (government) and user
Abella et al., 2019 [32]	Impact generation process of open data	Practice-driven analysis	Open data publisher and user
Abida et al., 2020 [33]	Integrating and publishing linked open government data	Illustrative case study	Open data publisher

a concluding step of the proposed open data process, will have a social and economic impact on the surrounding society.

In order to benefit from open data, its consumers (enterprises in particular) need to establish and improve their practices related to open sourcing [9]. Besides initial attempts to define open data consumption processes (Sect. 2.2), there are only a few guidelines that help enterprises to identify and prepare open datasets for use. This offers opportunities for design science researchers to develop prescriptive knowledge, in the form of methodological guidelines, that help companies to overcome the existing barriers (lack of transparency, heterogeneity, and unknown quality of open datasets).

3   Methodology

3.1   Research Objectives

Our research aims to develop prescriptive knowledge in the form of a meaningful method to screen, assess, and prepare open data for use in an enterprise setting, in adherence to the concepts of action design research (ADR). A method explains "what to do in different situations" [37] in a stepwise structure, while also including additional constituents such as notation, procedural guidelines, and concepts [38], specifying and documenting the "what" and "how" of the work to be done. It can be considered as a type V theory in Gregor's [39] taxonomy of IS research.

In order to accumulate prescriptive knowledge with the due scientific rigor in an iterative research process, we adhere to the methodological stages Sein et al. [40] suggested. Open data proposes a welcoming setting for ADR, which guides the process of building artifacts of organizational relevance in a rigorous manner and is based on insights from practical implementations. Since our artifact purports to solve the problems related to open data identification and sourcing, the interactions with practitioners are critical for a successful IS research outcome [41]. By combining the design-based research with action research, we aim to create rigorous and relevant business knowledge that will help to develop "specific solution(s) in specific situation(s)" [42] and learn from the instantiations.

3.2   Research Process

Our research activities (Table 2) begin with a problem formulation stage, aligned to the principles of practice-inspired research and theory-ingrained artifacts [40]. The artifact development was iterative, in line with the principle of guided emergence [40]. The method was developed in a close industry-research collaboration by a team of researchers (two PhD students, two senior researchers and three master's students) who worked with a data service provider and data experts from more than 15 multinational companies. Our method thereby formalizes learnings gained from building platforms that support companies in using open data and implement several use cases that are relevant for multinational firms. In accordance with the principle of generalized outcomes [40], our method proposes universal guidelines to open data screening, assessment, and use.

The *first building, intervention, and evaluation (BIE) cycle* was part of a multiyear research project that resulted in a productive platform for data quality services, operated by the data service provider. This platform focuses on business partner curation. Over time, more than 40 open datasets were onboarded onto the platform to validate and enrich business partner data. In the formalization of learning stage following the first BIE cycle, we aimed to convert the situated learning into general solution concepts that support the identification and integration of open datasets. In this phase, the first version of our method was developed based on analyzing the practices the service provider established to select and prepare datasets and integrating them with heterogenous target systems. This version comprises the method's nominal steps and the supporting use of knowledge graphs to explicate business concepts and link related datasets. It was evaluated with practitioners during the focus group discussions.

The *second BIE cycle* was a two-year research project that aimed to build an open data catalog for business purposes and resulted in a prototype implementation. It encompasses a broader scope of research that focuses on an extensive number of use cases, generated with a research team and three companies, and elaborated on by the data service provider specialists. We applied the method in more than 10 business scenarios (e.g. marketing and international trade) to identify 40 open data use cases, screen and assess relevant open datasets, and map their data models. The discussion of potential use cases for open data led to a systematic approach to use case generation. From our experiences in applying the method to use cases in marketing (such as social events and customer targeting), we made several key additions to the method, including the development of the assessment phase. In the formalization of learning, these steps were fully documented, demonstrated, and evaluated in two focus groups with 12 participants from 8 companies and 14 participants from 11 companies.

Subsequently, the method was further consolidated, and its separate components (assessment, documentation, and reference ontology model for the selected use cases) were discussed and evaluated in three individual sessions with practitioners from three companies. The sessions were concluded with a questionnaire, where the approach was evaluated by using a five-point Likert scale. Generally, the participants fully agreed (3/3) that the proposed approach supports the discovery or relevant dataset for selected business purposes, agreed (2/3) and fully agreed (3/3) that it supports the assessment and comparison of existing datasets, and agreed (1/3) and fully agreed (2/3) that it supports the mapping of the dataset's attributes to business concepts. They also agreed (1/3) and fully agreed (2/3) that the proposed approach to open data integration helps companies to make better use of open data and could be implemented in their company.

Table 2. Design cycles and contribution to method development

	First BIE cycle	Second BIE cycle
Context	Productive platform for data quality services, integrating open data for validation and enrichment	Open data catalog for enterprises (research prototype)
Use cases	Business partner curation, 43 datasets	Ten business scenarios, 46 use cases, assessment of 23 data domains, 220+ datasets
Method development	Development of the method's main phases, focus on phase 3 (preparation for use)	Addition of preparatory phase 0 (use case generation) and refinement of all phases
Main methodological contributions	Knowledge graph to define business concepts, map external datasets, and integrate into internal systems	Assessment approach comprising metadata, schema, and dataset level

4   Method to Screen, Assess, and Prepare Open Data for Use

4.1 Purpose and Overview

The method aims to support companies to identify and prepare suitable open datasets for use in specific business scenarios. It addresses the three issues that are highlighted in literature and were confirmed by the practitioners involved in our research: lack of transparency, heterogeneity, and unknown quality of open datasets. The method comprises four core phases, starting with use case documentation and encompassing the screening, assessment, and preparation of open data. Based on the insights gained in the first design cycle, we were guided by several design considerations:

- Open data identification should be facilitated and guided by specific use context that is relevant for the company (screening).
- The method should help companies gain transparency on relevant datasets and assess their fitness for use (assessing).
- Open data integration needs to consider the existing systems and platforms and map open datasets to internal data models (preparing for use).

Given the heterogeneity of the open datasets and the complexity of their integration, the method relies on knowledge graphs and the concepts of linked data powered by semantic web technologies [3, 21–23]. This common practice is based on the conceptual mapping of various datasets with identical entities through a graph-based representation of this knowledge, where "the entities, which are the nodes of the graph, are connected by relations, which are the edges of the graph ... and entities can have types, denoted by *is a* relations" [43]. In an enterprise setting, this approach helps companies to deal with the heterogeneity of open datasets and integrating them in internal systems.

4.2 Phases and Illustration

The method comprises a procedural model that includes documentation templates (when appropriate) for the introduced steps. Each phase has one or more steps, with descriptions of the main activities and outcomes (Table 6). In this section, we present each phase with its steps, as well as the relevant concepts and embedded approaches.

Phase 0 – Use Case Documentation. This phase is a mandatory preparation to understand how open data could complement the enterprise data and help to address specific business problems. In order to define the context, a company should document different aspects of how open data is intended to be used. For this purpose, we propose a template to capture the idea and key notions about the desired use of open data with four main building blocks: open datasets and providers, data objects (internal and external business concepts/attributes), data management impact, and business impact invoked by the use case. Table 3 shows these building blocks for two selected use cases: business partner

Table 3. Example of use case documentation

Use case name	Description	Open datasets and providers	Internal data objects	Data management impact	Business impact
Business partner data curation	Leverage on open corporate data to increase the quality and knowledge of our business partners (suppliers and consumers)	National corporate registers, global open data company registers (GLEIF, OpenCorporates)	Business partner master data: identification, address details, etc.	Validation of new entries and existing records; Enrichment with new business partner data from open sources; Curation of current business partner data	Prevent billing errors; Automation of data quality activities; Reduced time for data maintenance and entry
Customs clearance	Improve customs clearance process by using universal standardized codes for product/service classification, tax tariffs, dangerous goods, etc.s	World customs organization; Customs offices, United Nations, ISO, industry classification (SIC, NACE, EU)	Product data (item name, identifiers, transported quantities, units)	Enrichment of product and supplier data with classification codes; Adherence to international standards; Automation of data maintenance (pre-filled fields)	Reduction of operational cost and customs fees; Improved coordination with customs authorities

data curation and customs clearance. It supports drafting the potentially appropriate sources and datasets for the use cases, requirements towards them, and derive relevant concepts (or entities) that can correspond to the typical attributes in the open datasets.

Phase 1 – Screening. With a defined context for using open data, this phase aims to identify suitable data sources and datasets. Open data is available from various providers, such as governments, non-governmental organizations, and companies. While open government initiatives offer access to a large number of open datasets via open data portals (e.g. data.gov, U.S. Census Bureau, or data.europa.eu), some of these open datasets are also discoverable via traditional search engines or dedicated dataset search engines (e.g. Google dataset search or Socrata). In this regard, open data users not only have to identify relevant datasets but must also verify the authoritativeness (publisher details) of the source by the means of provided metadata, if available. The absence of such information raises concerns about the source and content of the underlying data. For the use case of business partner data curation, Table 4 shows examples of identified datasets with the acknowledged data sources and publisher information. It is interesting to note that for corporate registers, multiple sources lead to the desired dataset.

Table 4. Example of identified open data sources and datasets

Dataset	Publisher	Data source
French Register of Companies	National Institute of Statistics and Economics Studies (France)	Sirene.fr, GLEIF
OpenCorporates	OpenCorporates	OpenCorporates
Swiss UID Register	Federal Statistical Office (Switzerland)	Admin.ch, GLEIF
UK Companies House	Companies House (UK)	Gov.uk, Google dataset search
Wyoming Business Register	Secretary of the State of Wyoming (USA)	Data.gov, Wyo.gov, GLEF

Phase 2 – Assessment. In this phase, candidate datasets are analyzed to understand their suitability for the defined use case. This process is threefold and is conducted on metadata, dataset schema, and datasets' content levels (Table 5). Each of the subphases comes with specific criteria and may lead to a dataset being rejected or selected.

Subphase 2.1. This subphase begins with the high-level analysis of metadata, typically available at the source level. Relevant metadata attributes comprise the minimal information related to identifying a dataset, such as the access conditions (format, access login, lookup service), licensing presence, publishing details (publisher, publishing date, update cycle), and general content-related information (resource language, geographic coverage, number of records, and number of diverse attributes). With this information at hand, simple rejection criteria can be verified (e.g. no access to the data, no machine-readable formats, non-open license). Violating these criteria will lead to the dataset being removed from further investigation. If available, descriptive statistics of the datasets' contents can also be considered at the source level, for example number of downloads, ratings, number of rows and attributes in a dataset, as well as file size.

Subphase 2.2. Upon completing the metadata assessment, an initial investigation into the datasets can be done, starting with their data model. In this subphase, the datasets' schemas are further analyzed, allowing to verify the presence of the mandatory attributes, defined as "business concepts" in Phase 0. This assessment can be conducted using the schema completeness functional form, "which is the degree to which entities and attributes are not missing from the schema" [44]. This step is crucial to understand whether each dataset's content is sufficient to realize the use case, and to comprehend if the mapping between the concepts present in internal and external datasets can be established. For instance, datasets from corporate registers contain information about enterprises' identification codes and address details (Table 3), but the availability of concrete attributes (e.g. VAT numbers and postal codes) should be verified.

Subphase 2.3. To finalize the assessment and solidify the selection of open datasets for the use case, a thorough assessment of their content must be conducted. This assessment focuses on datasets' content in terms of typical data quality dimensions, such as completeness, uniqueness, validity, and the related metrics. Such approaches are covered it literature [7, 24], but need to be adapted for open datasets' domains in different use cases. After the assessment, a final decision can be made if the open dataset is suitable for the intended use case.

Table 5. Example of assessment phase documentation

Dataset name	French register of companies	Wyoming corporate register
Metadata	Identification: RA000189 Format: CSV, API available License: Open License V2.0 Publishing date: 19.08.18 Update cycle: 1d Geographic coverage: National # of records: 21'059'740 # of attributes: 118	Identification: RA000644 Format: CSV License: Open Government Publishing date: 19.03.14 Update cycle: N/A Geographic coverage: State # of records: 522'691 # of attributes: 87
Schema assessment	17/21 mandatory attributes	14/21 mandatory attributes
Content assessment	Completeness: score in % Uniqueness: score in % Validity: score in %	Completeness: score in % Uniqueness: score in % Validity: score in %

Phase 3 – Preparation for Use. This phase requires integrating identified and assessed open datasets in a company's internal system. The identified business concepts in Phase 0 are key for the concept mapping, in line with the knowledge graph principles, specifying the links between the sources fueled by relations between the entities.

Subphase 3.1. The method suggests thoroughly documenting the selected open datasets and providing complete metadata information. Certain open data sources (e.g. open data portals) already adhere to well-known metadata vocabularies and standards (e.g. DCAT, DCT, DQV, SDO), which simplify the documentation process by having standardized RDF vocabularies for metadata description. A common metadata model for open datasets' documentation helps to harmonize them, increase transparency, and document additional aspects, such as quality and dataset attributes. In addition, documentation of attributes should contain the associated business concepts (as seen in Phase 0), which allows beginning the construction of the knowledge graph.

Subphase 3.2. This final subphase focuses on integrating open datasets by means of a knowledge graph (Sect. 2.1). The previous subphase emphasized the links between open dataset attributes and the common entities (business concepts), that denote the construction of an ontological model for a given use case. For instance, a company's internal data objects need to be associated with similar entities, as the ones in open datasets. This entity-linking process is a common way of integrating heterogeneous datasets [3, 21–23]. As a result, a company will be able to locate open datasets containing attributes that correspond to business concepts, which then relate to their internal data.

Table 6. Overview of the method to screen, assess, and prepare open data for use

Phase 0	**0. Use case documentation**	
	Goal	Define and document the use case for open data
	Main activities	• Specify the context for which new data is needed in the company • Collect potentially relevant sources, decide on relevant business concepts located in open data and their counterpart in internal data • Estimate the business impact to concretize the motivation to use open data
	Outcomes	Documented use cases (based on template, comprising potential open sources and datasets, business and management impact)
Phase 1	**1. Use case-driven identification of relevant open data sources and datasets**	
	Goal	Identify relevant sources and underlying datasets
	Main activities	• Search for and select suitable datasets from open data portals, dedicated search engines, metasearch engines, or expert knowledge of concrete relevant sources • Search for authoritative sources or the ones that are fit for the purpose of the use case
	Outcomes	A list with names of datasets, publishers, and data sources
Phase 2	**2.1 High-level assessment of metadata**	
	Goal	Assess the metadata available at the source
	Main activities	• Analyze the metadata provided at source level • Check descriptive statistics of the dataset (if available at the source level) • Verify minimal requirements toward the datasets
	Outcomes	Shortlist of selected datasets
	2.2 Schema-level assessment	
	Goal	Understand the use case feasibility
	Main activities	• Assess schema completeness for the required attributes predefined for the use case • Analyze required attributes presence for use case feasibility
	Outcomes	Business concept mapping in knowledge graph
	2.3 Dataset content analysis	
	Goal	Assess the dataset content
	Main activities	• Assess content quality based on applicable data quality dimensions
	Outcomes	Decision on which open datasets can be considered for further use in the defined use cases
Phase 3	**3.1 Semantic documentation of open datasets**	
	Goal	Document open datasets
	Main activities	• Provide full metadata documentation, including access, licensing, and provenance • Document the dataset attributes
	Outcomes	Detailed dataset documentation
	3.2 Integration of open datasets with internal data	
	Goal	Prepare the datasets for further use by mapping open data with internal data
	Main activities	• Associate the identified attributes with existing business concepts • Formulate the mapping and transformation rules for the open data attributes • Link open dataset attributes with company entities, using the knowledge graph
	Outcomes	Integrated open datasets

5 Conclusion

To the best of our knowledge, this is one of the first pieces of research that leverage design science to develop prescriptive knowledge and address the widespread sociotechnical barriers and challenges in open data adoption. The designed artifact consists of a method that comprises four phases and supports companies in all steps from deciding on the suitable use cases for open data to preparing them for actual use. Compared to the few existing approaches in prior literature, the method suggests a context-specific open data assessment approach that comprises metadata, schema, and content levels. The method is enabled by using semantic concepts – a knowledge graph and reference ontologies – that allow mapping open datasets to internal data objects.

Our method contributes to research as well as practice. For practitioners, it provides a systematic approach by which to identify and screen open datasets. For academics, our research conceptualizes open data sourcing as a purposeful and value-creating process. It contributes to closing the gap recent studies [9] outlined, namely the elaborate processes for open data use and mechanisms for enterprise-wide open data strategy implementation. The suggested method also demonstrates how semantic technologies resulting from the technical open data research streams can be systematically applied and how they complement organizational processes for open data assessment and use.

Nevertheless, this work has limitations in terms of the proposed method's versatility and our specific research context, which may limit the generalizability of the findings. Although our method synthesizes practitioner knowledge from various open data use cases and firms, large-scale demonstrations and evaluation would be beneficial. Since the method comprises context-specific elements, it would benefit from pre-existing reference ontologies for specific business contexts. This offers interesting potential for future design science research in the information systems field.

References

1. The Open Definition: Defining Open in Open Data, Open Content and Open Knowledge. https://opendefinition.org/. Accessed 27 May 2021
2. Tammisto, Y., Lindman, J.: Definition of open data services in software business. In: Cusumano, M.A., Iyer, B., Venkatraman, N. (eds.) ICSOB 2012. LNBIP, vol. 114, pp. 297–303. Springer, Heidelberg (2012). https://doi.org/10.1007/978-3-642-30746-1_28
3. Zuiderwijk, A., Janssen, M., Poulis, K., van de Kaa, G.: Open data for competitive advantage. In: Proceedings of the 16th Annual International Conference on Digital Government Research, pp. 79–88 (2015)
4. Schatsky, D., Camhi, J., Muraskin, C.: Data ecosystems: how third-party information can enhance data analytics. Deloitte (2019).
5. Enders, T., Benz, C., Satzger, G.: Untangling the open data value paradox. In: Proceedings of Wirtschaftsinformatik 2021 (2021)
6. Krasikov, P., Obrecht, T., Legner, C., Eurich, M.: Is open data ready for use by enterprises? In: Proceedings of the 9th International Conference on Data Science, Technology and Applications, pp. 109–120. SCITEPRESS (2020)
7. Vetrò, A., Canova, L., Torchiano, M., Minotas, C.O., Iemma, R., Morando, F.: Open data quality measurement framework. Gov. Inf. Q. **33**, 325–337 (2016)

8. Bachtiar, A., Suhardi, Muhamad, W.: Literature review of open government data. In: Proceedings of the 2020 International Conference on Information Technology Systems and Innovation, pp. 329–334 (2020)

9. Enders, T., Benz, C., Schüritz, R., Lujan, P.: How to implement an open data strategy? Analyzing organizational change processes to enable value creation by revealing data. In: Proceedings of the 28th European Conference on Information Systems (2020)

10. Ruijer, E., Grimmelikhuijsen, S., van den Berg, J., Meijer, A.: Open data work: understanding open data usage from a practice lens. Int. Rev. Adm. Sci. **86**, 3–19 (2018)

11. Jarvenpaa, S.L., Markus, M.L.: Data sourcing and data partnerships: opportunities for is sourcing research. In: Hirschheim, R., Heinzl, A., Dibbern, J. (eds.) Information Systems Outsourcing. PI, pp. 61–79. Springer, Cham (2020). https://doi.org/10.1007/978-3-030-458 19-5_4

12. Baskerville, R., Pries-Heje, J., Venable, J.: Evaluation risks in design science research: a framework. In: Proceedings of the 3rd International Conference on Design Science Research in Information Systems and Technology (2008)

13. Chandrasekaran, B.: Design problem solving: a task analysis. AI Mag. **11**, 59–71 (1990)

14. Opendatasoft: A Comprehensive List of 2600+ Open Data Portals in the World. https://opendatainception.io/. Accessed 19 Apr 2021

15. EU Open Data Portal. https://data.europa.eu/euodp/en/data/. Accessed 19 Apr 2021

16. Data.gov. https://www.data.gov/. Accessed 19 Apr 2021

17. Braunschweig, K., Eberius, J., Thiele, M., Lehner, W.: The state of open data. In: Proceedings of 21st World Wide Web Conference, pp. 1–6. ACM (2012)

18. Manyika, J., Chui, M., Groves, P., Farrell, D., Van Kuiken, S., Doshi, E.A.: Open data: unlocking innovation and performance with liquid information. McKinsey (2013)

19. Janssen, M., Charalabidis, Y., Zuiderwijk, A.: Benefits, adoption barriers and myths of open data and open government. Inf. Syst. Manag. **29**, 258–268 (2012)

20. Zuiderwijk, A., Janssen, M., Choenni, S., Meijer, R., Alibaks, R.S.: Socio-technical Impediments of Open Data. Electron. J. e-Govern. **10**, 156–172 (2012)

21. Bizer, C., Heath, T., Berners-Lee, T.: Linked data - the story so far. Int. J. Semant. Web Inf. Syst. **5**, 1–22 (2009)

22. Auer, S., Bizer, C., Kobilarov, G., Lehmann, J., Cyganiak, R., Ives, Z.: DBpedia: a nucleus for a web of open data. In: Aberer, K., et al. (eds.) ASWC/ISWC -2007. LNCS, vol. 4825, pp. 722–735. Springer, Heidelberg (2007). https://doi.org/10.1007/978-3-540-76298-0_52

23. Zaveri, A., Rula, A., Maurino, A., Pietrobon, R., Lehmann, J., Auer, S.: Quality assessment for linked data: a survey. Semant. Web. **7**, 63–93 (2016)

24. Zhang, R., Indulska, M., Sadiq, S.: Discovering data quality problems: the case of repurposed data. BISE **61**, 575–593 (2019)

25. Martin, S., Foulonneau, M., Turki, S., Ihadjadene, M.: Risk analysis to overcome barriers to open data. Electron. J. e-Govern. **11**, 348–359 (2013)

26. Stróżyna, M., Eiden, G., Abramowicz, W., Filipiak, D., Małyszko, J.: A framework for the quality-based selection and retrieval of open data. Electron. Mark. **28**, 219–233 (2018)

27. Ren, G.-J., Glissmann, S.: Identifying information assets for open data. In: 2012 IEEE 14th International Conference on Commerce and Enterprise Computing, pp. 94–100. IEEE (2012)

28. Zuiderwijk, A., Janssen, M.: Barriers and development directions for the publication and usage of open data. In: Gascó-Hernández, M. (ed.) Open Government, vol. 4, pp. 115–135. Springer, New York (2014). https://doi.org/10.1007/978-1-4614-9563-5_8

29. Masip-Bruin, X., Ren, G.-J., Serral-Gracia, R., Yannuzzi, M.: Unlocking the value of open data with a process-based information platform. In: 2013 IEEE 15th Conference on Business Informatics, pp. 331–337. IEEE (2013)

30. Hendler, J.: Data integration for heterogenous datasets. Big Data **2**, 205–215 (2014)

31. Crusoe, J., Melin, U.: Investigating open government data barriers: a literature review and conceptualization. In: Parycek, P., et al. (eds.) Electronic Government. LNCS, vol. 11020, pp. 169–183. Springer, Cham (2018). https://doi.org/10.1007/978-3-319-98690-6_15
32. Abella, A., Ortiz-de-Urbina-Criado, M., De-Pablos-Heredero, C.: The process of open data publication and reuse. JASIST **70**, 296–300 (2019)
33. Abida, R., Belghith, E.H., Cleve, A.: An end-to-end framework for integrating and publishing linked open government data. In: Proceeding of the 29th International Conference on Enabling Technologies, pp. 257–262. IEEE (2020)
34. Jaakkola, H., Mäkinen, T., Eteläaho, A.: Open data: opportunities and challenges. In: Proceedings of the 15th CompSysTech, pp. 25–39. ACM (2014)
35. Immonen, A., Palviainen, M., Ovaska, E.: Requirements of an open data based business ecosystem. IEEE Access **2**, 88–103 (2014)
36. Buda, A., Ubacht, J., Janssen, M.: Decision support framework for opening business data. In: Proceedings of the 16th European Conference on e-Government, pp. 29–37 (2016)
37. Goldkuhl, G., Lind, M., Seigerroth, U.: Method integration: the need for a learning perspective. In: IEE Proceedings – Software, p. 113 (1998)
38. Sandkuhl, K., Seigerroth, U.: Method engineering in information systems analysis and design. Softw. Syst. Modell. **18**, 1833–1857 (2019)
39. Gregor, S.: The nature of theory in information systems. MIS Q. **30**, 611–642 (2006)
40. Sein, M.K., Henfridsson, O., Purao, S., Rossi, M., Lindgren, R.: Action design research. MIS Q. **35**, 37–56 (2011)
41. Hevner, A.R., March, S.T., Park, J., Ram, S.: Design science in information systems research. MIS Q. **28**, 75–105 (2004)
42. Andriessen, D.: Combining design-based research and action research to test management solutions. In: Towards Quality Improvement of Action Research, pp. 125–134 (2008)
43. Paulheim, H.: Knowledge graph refinement. Semant. Web. **8**, 489–508 (2016)
44. Pipino, L.L., Lee, Y.W., Wang, R.Y.: Data quality assessment. Commun. ACM **45**, 211 (2002)

Designing a Risk Assessment Tool for Artificial Intelligence Systems

Per Rådberg Nagbøl[1]($\boxtimes$) (ID), Oliver Müller[2] (ID), and Oliver Krancher[1] (ID)

[1] IT University of Copenhagen, Rued Langgaards Vej 7, 2300 Copenhagen, Denmark
{pena,olik}@itu.dk
[2] Paderborn University, Warburger Str. 100, 33098 Paderborn, Germany
oliver.mueller@upb.de

Abstract. Notwithstanding its potential benefits, organizational AI use can lead to unintended consequences like opaque decision-making processes or biased decisions. Hence, a key challenge for organizations these days is to implement procedures that can be used to assess and mitigate the risks of organizational AI use. Although public awareness of AI-related risks is growing, the extant literature provides limited guidance to organizations on how to assess and manage AI risks. Against this background, we conducted an Action Design Research project in collaboration with a government agency with a pioneering AI practice to iteratively build, implement, and evaluate the Artificial Intelligence Risk Assessment (AIRA) tool. Besides the theory-ingrained and empirically evaluated AIRA tool, our key contribution is a set of five design principles for instantiating further instances of this class of artifacts. In comparison to existing AI risk assessment tools, our work emphasizes communication between stakeholders of diverse expertise, estimating the expected real-world positive and negative consequences of AI use, and incorporating performance metrics beyond predictive accuracy, including thus assessments of privacy, fairness, and interpretability.

Keywords: AI · Risk assessment · Risk management · Interpretability · Envelopment

1 Introduction

Artificial Intelligence (AI) technologies such as machine learning (ML) allow an increasing number of organizations to improve decision-making and automate processes [1]. Notwithstanding these potential benefits, organizational AI use can lead to undesired outcomes, including lack of accountability, unstable decision quality, discrimination, and the resulting breaches of the law [2]. For instance, media and academia have revealed cases of algorithmic discrimination concerning facial recognition [3], crime prediction [4], online ad delivery [5], and skin cancer detection [6].

Drawing on the risk management literature [7, 8], we refer to such potential undesired outcomes as *risks*. Given the increasing adoption of AI, a key challenge for organizations these days is implementing procedures that prevent or mitigate risks from organizational

© Springer Nature Switzerland AG 2021
L. Chandra Kruse et al. (Eds.): DESRIST 2021, LNCS 12807, pp. 328–339, 2021.
https://doi.org/10.1007/978-3-030-82405-1_32

AI use. A critical task in this regard is to *assess* (i.e., identify, analyze, and prioritize) [8] the risks associated with a new AI system (i.e., a software system based on AI) before its go-live. Risk assessment is critical for responsible organizational AI use because it allows organizations to make informed decisions grounded in a thorough understanding of the risks and benefits of using a specific AI system and because risk assessment is the foundation for risk control [8] after go-live.

The risk management literature, governmental frameworks, and the AI literature provide some foundations for understanding how organizations should assess risks from organizational AI use. Two key insights from the risk management literature are that risk management is a knowledge integration process involving business and technical stakeholders [9, 10] and that risk management operates within a tension between template-based deliberate analysis and expert intuition [8, 11]. Governmental frameworks, such as Canada's Directive on Automated Decision-Making [12], provide blueprints for risk assessment templates. The AI literature provides methods for data and model documentation [13, 14], for improving the interpretability of ML models [15], and for identifying biases [16, 17]. The AI literature has recently also advanced the concept of envelopment [18–20] to explain how organizations can address risks by limiting the agentic properties of AI technologies [21].

Although these foundations are valuable, the existing literature provides limited guidance to organizations on assessing AI risks because of two fundamental limitations. First, there is little research that explicitly takes a risk management perspective on AI. While most AI research does not explicitly draw on risk management theory [13, 14], the risk management literature does not focus on AI, examining instead risks associated with information system (IS) projects [8, 9] or with traditional software and hardware [22]. However, AI systems differ from these two in that AI systems are software (unlike IS projects) with agentic qualities (unlike traditional hardware and software) [21]. Second, given the conceptual nature of most work [20], there is a lack of *empirical* research that is grounded in the experience of real organizations in assessing AI-related risks. Given these gaps, our paper addresses the following research question: *How should procedures be designed to assess the risks associated with a new AI system?*

We address this research question through an Action Design Research (ADR) study [23]. We worked together with a governmental agency with a pioneering AI practice to iteratively build, implement, and evaluate the AI Risk Assessment (AIRA) tool. Our key contributions are theory-engrained and empirically validated design principles for assessing risks associated with new AI systems.

2 Literature Background

2.1 The AI Literature

There is a rapidly growing body of research from computer science and IS on AI, defined as *"systems that display intelligent behavior by analyzing their environment and taking actions – with some degree of autonomy – to achieve specific goals."* [24]. Although AI research has rarely paid explicit attention to risk assessment of new AI systems, three streams within AI research provide important perspectives on this issue: research on interpretability, on envelopment, and on dataset and model documentation.

Interpretability. The main argument why we grounded our artifact in the literature on interpretable AI is that insights into the process of algorithmic decision making enable the early detection of unintended outcomes and side-effects, hence lowering overall risk. We rely on Lipton's [15] conceptualization of interpretability with the subcategories transparency and post-hoc interpretability. Transparency refers to AI systems that are inherently understandable for humans, such as linear models and decision trees. It comprises the criteria simulatability of the model as a whole (e.g., whether a human can trace how the model transforms inputs into outputs), decomposability of its individual components (e.g., the decision rules and parameters of a model), and transparency of the learning algorithm (e.g., how a model learns its decision rules or parameters) [15]. Post-hoc interpretability is an alternative to inherent transparency. For complex and opaque AI systems, it might be possible to construct a faithful abstraction of the original black-box model that is understandable for humans (e.g., a visualization, an example-based explanation) [15]. Such post-hoc explanations can focus on an individual prediction (local explanations) or on the general patterns the model has learned (global explanations) [15].

Envelopment. Envelopment theory provides conceptual guidance for enhancing the safety of AI systems in production environments. Envelopment—a term borrowed from the field of robotics—describes how micro-environments are enveloped around robots' three-dimensional space enabling them to achieve their purpose successfully while preventing damaging people or material [20, 25, 26]. Although the concept is originally from the physical space, Robbins suggested that the areas to be addressed by an AI system can also be enveloped into a confined virtual space. These areas are training data (its suitability for production environments), boundaries (expected scenarios and possible inputs including data types), input (how all sensed data are combined), function (the purpose of the AI), and output (the AI's production utilized to fulfill its function) [20]. For instance, an organization may envelop training data by stipulating that the model needs to be retrained with new training data if significant environmental changes question the suitability of the training data for the current production environment [20].

Model Documentation. Datasheets for datasets guides the communication between dataset creators and dataset consumers to enhance transparency and accountability. Datasets are accompanied by a datasheet documenting key aspects such as composition, collection, and cleaning [13]. Model cards for model reporting has been developed to supplement datasheets for datasets and follows a similar logic. Model cards are documentations that accompany trained ML models. The model cards contain information related to the application domain [14]. Reactive approaches are developed to audit the performance of facial recognition classifiers performance across different genders and skin colors [16, 17].

2.2 Risk Management

We draw on the risk management literature as one foundation for understanding how organizations can assess potential undesired outcomes of using an AI system. Risk management is frequently conceptualized as a process that starts with risk assessment, consisting of risk identification, risk analysis, and risk prioritization, followed by risk control [7, 8]. Our paper focuses on risk assessment. Although most of the IS risk management literature focuses on risks associated with IS projects, the literature offers two key ideas that are potentially relevant for the risk assessment of AI systems.

First, risk management is a knowledge integration process involving business and technical stakeholders. Wallace et al. [10] showed that problems in IS projects often have their origin in social-subsystem risks (e.g., unstable environments, user resistance), which translate into technical risks and project management risks. In line with these ideas, it has been shown that knowledge integration between technical and business stakeholders is key for addressing risks in IS projects [9]. Although IS projects are different from organizational AI use, organizational AI use is, like an IS project, a socio-technical system in which users delegate their work to AI systems and the development of these AI systems to developers and data scientists [21], presenting thus a need for knowledge integration between users and data scientists.

Second, risk management operates within a tension between template-based deliberate analysis and expert intuition. The bulk of academic risk management research suggests that deliberate efforts to identify, analyze, and prioritize risks are beneficial because they help to capture a wider range of risks [8] efficiently. For instance, risk managers were shown to capture a wider range of risks when they performed a deliberate risk analysis based on templates [27]. However, another strand of the risk management literature emphasizes the key role of expert intuition for mindfully identifying and focusing on relevant risks [28], suggesting that risk assessment often requires a balance between document-based and expertise-based approaches.

3   The Action Design Research Project

The Action Design Research (ADR) project described in this paper is a university-government collaboration between the Danish Business Authority (DBA) and the IT University of Copenhagen. The DBA is a Danish government agency with approximately 700 employees. The DBA offers services like the cross-governmental platform virk.dk, Covid-19 compensation, the central business register, and annual reporting to Danish and foreign businesses. It has deployed 22 AI systems to support employees in operational decision-making and automation of routine tasks. The DBA presented an ideal setting for our study given its intensive use of AI, the high level of digitization in Denmark [29, 30], and the strategic priority of ensuring responsible AI use in the Danish public sector [31].

The artifact developed in this ADR project was the AI Risk Assessment (AIRA) tool. The AIRA is designed to be the first out of four artifacts in the X-RAI framework [32]. Its key purpose was to assess the risks associated with a new AI system. We developed the AIRA tool between April 2019 and March 2021 through three iterations of building, evaluating, and testing (see Table 1) [23]. During this time, the first author of this paper spent approximately every other week at the DBA. Everyday interactions and meetings with DBA employees, especially around 30 meetings, including 12 one-on-one sessions with the ML lab team leader, shaped its design. These interactions have led to a rich empirical base consisting of transcripts, field notes, documents, and artifacts.

Table 1. Overview for application, test and evaluation of AIRA on AI systems

AI systems	Test approach (artifact version)
Business document compliance validator	Framework (v1) filled out at the meeting
Document preprocesing filter	Framework (v1) filled out at the meeting
Identification check	Framework (v1) filled during two meetings
Compensation	Framework (v2.1.1) filled out during two recorded Microsoft Teams interviews
Fraud	Framework (v2.1.3) filled out at the meeting
Industry code selector	Framework (v3.0.1. ML part) filled out pre meeting and evaluated at the meeting
Identification check	Framework (v3.0.1. ML part) filled out
Bankruptcy report	Frameworks (v3.0.1. Business part and v3.0.1. ML part) filled out before the meeting for discussion and evaluated at the meeting (recorded)
Fixed costs compensation	Frameworks (v3.0.2. Business part, v3.0.4. ML part, and v3.0.3. Facilitator part) filled out before the meeting and discussed at the meeting
Salary compensation	Frameworks (v3.0.2. Business part, v3.0.4. ML part, and v3.0.3. Facilitator part) filled out before the meeting and discussed at the meeting
Self-employed compensation	Frameworks (v3.0.2. Business part and v3.0.4. ML part) filled out before the meeting and discussed at the meeting

Iteration #1: The initial design of the AIRA tool was inspired by the Algorithmic Impact Assessment (AIA) tool of the Canadian government. Although the AIA tool served as a blueprint, key stakeholder at the DBA found that the AIA tool did not focus enough on algorithms and data, lacked clear roles and responsibilities, and was tailored to Canadian law. Hence, using the AIA tool as a source of inspiration, the ADR team *built* an initial alpha version of the AIRA tool consisting of ten questions. The questions addressed areas such as algorithms (e.g., underlying learning algorithms and used libraries), training data (e.g., types and sources of data), predictive performance (e.g., a confusion matrix incl. description of the consequences of each cell, the existence of ground truth), interpretability (e.g., use of post-hoc explainability methods), and decision making (e.g., is there a human-in-the-loop?). The organizational *intervention* occurred by applying the tool on three AI systems in collaboration with data scientists from the DBA. The *evaluation* happened in the form of feedback from the team leader of the DBA's ML Lab. The evaluation found that the general idea was likely to work in the context of the DBA and that the tool should be expanded to include user stories from a business perspective and data privacy. In addition, the desire to calculate a risk score, just like in the Canadian AIA tool, was articulated.

Iteration #2: The second iteration focused on expanding the contents of the tool. The *building* phase concentrated on identifying further relevant areas which need to be covered for risk assessment (e.g., a more detailed description of the purpose of the AI system from a business perspective). In addition, the level of detail for assessing the training data aspect was increased considerably. The *intervention* occurred by applying the artifact to two additional AI systems. The concurrent *evaluation* yielded two key findings. First, it was important to acknowledge the knowledge differences between different people and roles involved. Data scientists had problems answering questions related to business objectives and the business need for model interpretability, as one data scientist formulated it: *"...The need for transparency is defined by the business unit. I just try to build the best model for a given need of transparency. It is business who needs to define the requirements for transparency and how these requirements need to be understood."* (Data scientist 1). Second, it was found that going through the questionnaire from start to end was too time-consuming and that different stakeholders should contribute to different parts. Henceforth, the artifact should be filled out before the meeting and discussed at the meeting. The ADR team also realized that the original idea of automatically calculating a risk score, like in the Canadian AIA tool, was complicated by numerous context dependencies and interdependencies between questions.

Iteration #3: Based on the feedback from the previous iteration, we focused the *building* phase on restructuring the questionnaire into self-contained modules for distinct stakeholders and improving the overall user experience in terms of required time and knowledge. The first module initiated the assessment process and is to be filled out by a future user of the AI system (i.e., the business unit). The second module was filled out by those building the model (i.e., data scientists). The third module was filled out in collaboration between the user (domain experts) and data scientists in a physical meeting moderated by a facilitator. The *intervention* phase included applying the tool to six AI systems. The *evaluation* suggested potential for improvement regarding the readability of some questions and the preparation time required for participants.

4   The Artificial Intelligence Risk Assessment Tool

Figure 1a provides a schematic overview of the final version of the AIRA tool. The tool contains three modules, each targeted at a different audience. We will now describe the structure and contents of these modules in more detail.

The first module is targeted at the business unit that will use the AI system and focuses on eliciting requirements from a business perspective. Amongst others, the module contains a consequences matrix showing potential positive and negative consequences of deploying the AI system (see Fig. 1b for an example). Inspired by the concept of a confusion matrix, it asks domain experts for a qualitative description of the consequences of these four types of outcomes. Following the idea of expected utility theory [33, 34] the combination of this information with quantitative data from a classical confusion matrix (which is included in the second module of the tool, see Fig. 1) allows assessing the chances and risks of deploying the AI system. The assessment is complemented by information describing if a human receives the output of the AI system and if a human can instantly verify the truthfulness of the output.

The second module is meant to be filled out by the data scientist responsible for developing the AI system. The main themes covered in this module are the predictive performance, training data, interpretability of the model and its outputs, and its interfaces and boundaries. The interpretability part is based on the concepts and categorizations proposed by Lipton. With regards to transparency, the data scientist is, for instance, asked whether they are able to describe how the algorithm discovers decision rules (algorithmic transparency) and how these rules are later used to make predictions for specific cases (simulatability). If the AI system is based on a black box algorithm, questions regarding local and global post-explainability are asked. Another important part of the module is related to the processing of personal data. Drawing on the EU GDPR, it is checked whether the AI system processes protected personal attributes (e.g., gender, ethnicity, age) and if the model has been checked for potential biases and discrimination against these groups. At this, six types of biases (historical, representation, measuring, aggregation, evaluation, and implementation) [35] and metrics for their detection (e.g., Equal Opportunity Difference, Disparate Outcomes) are considered. Finally, the interface of the AI system to other downstream models (e.g., to discover potential chain reactions if the model fails) and potential boundary conditions (e.g., In which situations should be the model not be used?) are documented.

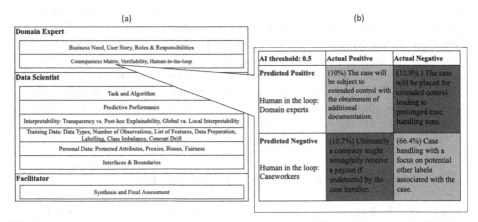

Fig. 1. (a) Schematic overview of the artificial intelligence risk assessment tool with (b) an Example of a consequence matrix

The third module comprises a synthesis and final assessment of the business and technical perspectives. This qualitative assessment, which should be conducted collaboratively by domain experts, data scientists, and a facilitator, replaces the original idea of a quantitative risk score (like in the Canadian AIA tool). Exemplary questions include "Does the model solve the business need?", "Is the model interpretable enough?", or "Is the model free from discriminating biases?". The AI system cannot be put into production before every question in this section is answered with a yes.

5 Reflection, Learning, and Formalization of Design Principles

Going beyond the concrete and situated IT artifact described in Sect. 4, we also derived more general theoretical statements from our ADR project and formalized them in the form of design principles (see Table 2). These prescriptive statements should enable others to build instances of the here presented class of IT artifacts (i.e., AI Risk Assessment tools). According to the idea of ADR, these design principles constitute the main scientific contribution of our work. We describe design principles using a recently proposed schema[1] [36].

The first three design principles are grounded in risk management theory and focus on eliciting input and feedback from a diverse group of motivated stakeholders. More specifically, the risk assessment should involve both ML designers and users in the assessment process (DP #1). Support for this principle comes both from the risk management literature [9, 10] and from the issues encountered in the second integration when we used one document that did not cater for the needs of specific stakeholders. We also made the experience that it can be difficult to involve experts in the risk assessment, which they may perceive as a formality with little business value [8]. To not burden experts with too many forms and rules and allow for advances in technology and domain-specific approaches, we decided not to prescribe precisely which methods and metrics to use during the assessment but instead to rely on their expertise in choosing the right tools (DP #2). The predictions made by the AI systems deployed at the DBA can have critical real-world consequences for businesses and citizens. Hence, in line with the focus on both probability and impact in risk management [7], it is not sufficient to evaluate their performance purely in terms of statistical measures (e.g., accuracy, precision, or

Table 2. Design principles for an artificial intelligence risk assessment tool

Principle of...	Aim, implementer, and user	Mechanism	Rationale
1: Multi-perspective expert assessment	To perform a multi-perspective risk assessment (aim), organizations using AI should ...	... ensure that the AI system is jointly assessed by users (domain experts) and developers (data scientists)	Risk assessment in socio-technical systems implies integrating knowledge from business and technical perspectives [9, 10]
2: Structured intuition	To motivate and engage diverse stakeholders to participate in risk assessment (aim), organizations using AI (implementers) should ...	... prescribe aspects that need to be assessed, but not the specific methods or tools to be used for that assessment	Risk assessment needs to strike a balance between deliberate analysis and structure to ensure motivation and coverage of key risks [8]

(continued)

---

[1] As the Context element did not vary between our design principles ("In organization with values similar to the European Union where AI is used to aid or make decisions.") we decided to omit it from the table. We also omitted the optional Decomposition element.

Table 2. (*continued*)

Principle of...	Aim, implementer, and user	Mechanism	Rationale
3: Expected consequences	To make risk assessments based on expected real-world consequences instead of lab results (aim), organizations using AI (implementers) should ...	... combine probabilities of outcomes of algorithmic decisions (e.g., true positive/negative rate) with their respective costs and benefits	Considering both risk probabilities and their impacts is a common practice in risk management [7, 8]. Drawing on expected utility theory [33], we extend this idea to also take positive outcomes into consideration
4: Beyond accuracy	To account for risks beyond "false predictions" (aim), organizations using AI (implementers) should ...	... evaluate AI systems not only in terms of predictive accuracy but also in terms of dimensions like interpretability, privacy, or fairness	We draw on Lipton's [15] desiderata of interpretable ML (trust, causality, transferability, informativeness, and fair and ethical decision making) and the accompanying properties of interpretable models in terms of transparency and post-hoc explainability. The principle is further backed up by the EU GDPR
5: Envelopment of black boxes	To leverage the superior predictive power of complex "black box" AI systems with minimal risks, organizations using AI (implementers) should ...	... envelop the training data, inputs, functions, outputs, and boundaries of their AI systems	In robotics, envelopes are three-dimensional cages built around industrial robots to make them achieve their purpose without harming human workers or destroying physical things [25]. The idea has recently been transferred to ML by Robbins [20] and Asatiani et al. [19]

recall). Instead, decision-makers should assess the expected consequences in terms of the probabilities of correct and erroneous decisions and their costs and benefits in the downstream business processes (DP #3).

The last two design principles are grounded in the literature on interpretable and safe ML. In line with the previous principle, a purely technical evaluation in terms of predictive accuracy will not capture all possible risks stemming from the use of AI in governmental contexts. Algorithmic decisions must be precise *and* interpretable for audiences with varying levels of ML knowledge (e.g., citizens, caseworkers, lawyers, politicians) and comply with a country's legal frameworks and ethical values (DP #4). Finally, we realized that in some situations, it might not be possible to use inherently transparent AI systems (e.g., because a deep neural network offers drastically superior predictive performance on text or image data over a simple statistical model). Adopting the idea of envelopment from the field of robotics, we propose to build virtual envelopes acting as safety nets around parts of an AI system to detect and mitigate risks (DP #5). Examples include putting a human in the loop to check the outputs of an AI system or to monitor if the distribution of input data at production time is still compatible with the data the model was trained on.

6 Discussion

In this paper, we asked the research question: *How should procedures be designed to assess the risks associated with a new AI system?* We addressed this research question through an ADR project where we built, implemented, and evaluated the AIRA tool at a public sector organization with pioneering AI use. Our key outcomes are an artifact—the AIRA tool—and five design principles for AI risk management.

Although there is little research on the specific topic of AI risk management, the closest research is work on AI model documentation, including the Canadian AIA tool, Datasheets for datasets [13], Model cards for model reporting [14], and auditorial approaches [16, 17]. Our work goes beyond this existing research in four important ways. First, our work puts greater emphasis on guiding the communication between stakeholders of diverse expertise, focusing on the interaction between AI systems builders and users. This emphasis manifests in questionnaires for three distinct user groups (domain expert, data scientist, facilitator) and in design principle #1. Second, the AIRA tool goes beyond existing approaches by its greater focus on establishing a joint understanding of the consequences of AI use among involved stakeholders, helping the participants to assess risks relative to the benefits of the AI system. This manifests in design principle #3. Third, the AIRA tool emphasizes incorporating model performance metrics beyond accuracy, including assessments of bias, fairness, and interpretability. This balanced assessment is important because the interpretability of AI is essential for preproduction risk identification and for postproduction risk monitoring. Fourth, we contribute to a stronger theoretical grounding of literature on AI documentation and assessment by discussing how the broader risk management literature and envelopment theory can inform AI documentation and assessment efforts.

Our research is not without limitations. First, the artifact has not been subject to summative evaluation. It was not possible to compare the undesired outcomes when using the AIRA tool to undesired outcomes when not using the tool. Second, the AIRA tool might not transfer without adjustments to other countries and the private sector. Third, the AIRA tool is a proactive measure, helping ensure that compliance requirements are met when implementing a new AI system; but it does not address the changing nature of society, including AI systems impact on own environment. A false sense of security can occur if the AIRA tool is applied with a once-and-for-all mindset due to e.g., data drift issues that can impact the model performance and responsibility when running in production. Given that the focus of the AIRA tool is on risk assessment and not on risk response planning, the AIRA tool would need to be complemented by proactive measures such as an evaluation plan before production and reactive measures in production such as evaluation and retraining [32].

References

1. Benbya, H., Davenport, T., Pachidi, S.: Special issue editorial: artificial intelligence in organizations: current state and future opportunities. MIS Q. Executive **19**, ix–xxi (2020)
2. Mayer, A.-S., Strich, F., Fiedler, M.: Unintended consequences of introducing ai systems for decision making. MIS Q. Executive **19**, 239–257 (2020)
3. Hill, K.: Wrongfully Accused by an Algorithm. https://www.nytimes.com/2020/06/24/techno logy/facial-recognition-arrest.html (2020)
4. Angwin, J., Larson, J., Mattu, S., Kirchner, L.: Machine Bias. https://www.propublica.org/art icle/machine-bias-risk-assessments-in-criminal-sentencing?token=1B8jKuq-H9G4ZEq4_ 95FZ7ZaZ9a3rKDs. Accessed 11 Oct 2020
5. Sweeney, L.: Discrimination in online ad delivery: google ads, black names and white names, racial discrimination, and click advertising. Queue **11**, 10–29 (2013). https://doi.org/10.1145/ 2460276.2460278
6. Lashbrook, A.: AI-Driven Dermatology Could Leave Dark-Skinned Patients Behind. https:// www.theatlantic.com/health/archive/2018/08/machine-learning-dermatology-skin-color/ 567619/. Accessed 12 Oct 2020
7. Boehm, B.W.: Software risk management: principles and practices. IEEE Softw. **8**, 32–41 (1991). https://doi.org/10.1109/52.62930
8. Moeini, M., Rivard, S.: Sublating tensions in the IT project risk management literature: a model of the relative performance of intuition and deliberate analysis for risk assessment. J. Assoc. Inf. Syst. **20** (2019). https://doi.org/10.17705/1jais.00535.
9. Barki, H., Rivard, S., Talbot, J.: An integrative contingency model of software project risk management. J. Manag. Inf. Syst. **17**, 37–69 (2001)
10. Wallace, L., Keil, M., Rai, A.: Understanding software project risk: a cluster analysis. Inf. Manage. **42**, 115–125 (2004). https://doi.org/10.1016/j.im.2003.12.007
11. Baskerville, R.L., Stage, J.: Controlling prototype development through risk analysis. MIS Q. **20**, 481–504 (1996). https://doi.org/10.2307/249565
12. Treasury Board of Canada Secretariat: Directive on Automated Decision-Making. https:// www.tbs-sct.gc.ca/pol/doc-eng.aspx?id=32592. Accessed 17 Oct 2020
13. Gebru, T., Morgenstern, J., Vecchione, B., Vaughan, J.W., Wallach, H., Daumé III, H., Crawford, K.: Datasheets for Datasets. arXiv:1803.09010 [cs] (2020)
14. Mitchell, M., et al.: Model cards for model reporting. In: Proceedings of the Conference on Fairness, Accountability, and Transparency - FAT* 2019, pp. 220–229 (2019). https://doi.org/ 10.1145/3287560.3287596
15. Lipton, Z.C.: The mythos of model interpretability: in machine learning, the concept of interpretability is both important and slippery. Queue **16**, 31–57 (2018). https://doi.org/10. 1145/3236386.3241340
16. Buolamwini, J., Gebru, T.: Gender shades: intersectional accuracy disparities in commercial gender classification. In: Proceedings of Machine Learning Research, vol. 81:1–15, p. 15 (2018)

17. Raji, I.D., Buolamwini, J.: Actionable auditing: investigating the impact of publicly naming biased performance results of commercial AI products. In: Proceedings of the 2019 AAAI/ACM Conference on AI, Ethics, and Society, pp. 429–435. ACM, Honolulu HI USA (2019). https://doi.org/10.1145/3306618.3314244

18. Asatiani, A., Malo, P., Nagbøl, P.R., Penttinen, E., Rinta-Kahila, T., Salovaara, A.: Challenges of explaining the behavior of black-box AI systems. MIS Q. Executive 19, 259–278 (2020)

19. Asatiani, A., Malo, P., Nagbøl, P.R., Penttinen, E., Rinta-Kahila, T., Salovaara, A.: Sociotechnical envelopment of artificial intelligence: an approach to organizational deployment of inscrutable artificial intelligence systems. J. Assoc. Inf. Syst. 22, 325–352 (2021). https://doi.org/10.17705/1jais.00664

20. Robbins, S.: AI and the path to envelopment: knowledge as a first step towards the responsible regulation and use of AI-powered machines. AI Soc. 35(2), 391–400 (2019). https://doi.org/10.1007/s00146-019-00891-1

21. Baird, A., Maruping, L.M.: The next generation of research on IS use: a theoretical framework of delegation to and from agentic IS artifacts. Manage. Inf. Syst. Q. 45, 315–341 (2021). https://doi.org/10.25300/MISQ/2021/15882

22. Badenhorst, K., Eloff, J.: Computer security methodology: risk analysis and project definition. Comput. Secur. 9, 339–346 (1990)

23. Sein, M., Henfridsson, O., Purao, S., Rossi, M., Lindgren, R.: Action design research. Manag. Inf. Syst. Q. 35, 37–56 (2011)

24. European Commission: Communication from the commission to the european parliament, the European council, the council, the European economic and social committee and the committee of the regionS Artificial Intelligence for Europe, Brussels (2018)

25. Floridi, L.: Children of the fourth revolution. Philos. Technol. 24, 227–232 (2011). https://doi.org/10.1007/s13347-011-0042-7

26. Floridi, L.: Enveloping the world: the constraining success of smart technologies. In: CEPE 2011: Crossing Boundaries Ethics in Interdisciplinary and Intercultural Relations, p. 6. INSEIT (2011), Milwaukee Wisconsin (2011)

27. Keil, M., Li, L., Mathiassen, L., Zheng, G.: The influence of checklists and roles on software practitioner risk perception and decision-making. J. Syst. Softw. 81, 908–919 (2008). https://doi.org/10.1016/j.jss.2007.07.035

28. Bannerman, P.L.: Risk and risk management in software projects: a reassessment. J. Syst. Softw. 81, 2118–2133 (2008). https://doi.org/10.1016/j.jss.2008.03.059

29. United Nations: United Nations E-Government Survey 2018. United Nations (2018)

30. United Nations: Department of Economic and Social Affairs: United Nations e-government survey 2020: digital government in the decade of action for sustainable development. United Nations, Department of Economic and Social Affairs, New York (2020)

31. The Danish Government: National Strategy for Artificial Intelligence. Ministry of Finance and Ministry of Industry, Business and Financial Affairs (2019)

32. Nagbøl, P.R., Müller, O.: X-RAI: a framework for the transparent, responsible, and accurate use of machine learning in the public sector. In: Proceedings of Ongoing Research, Practitioners, Workshops, Posters, and Projects of the International Conference EGOV-CeDEM-ePart 2020, p. 9 (2020)

33. Morgenstern, O., Von Neumann, J.: Theory of Games and Economic Behavior. Princeton University Press (1944)

34. Briggs, R.: Normative Theories of Rational Choice: Expected Utility. https://plato.stanford.edu/entries/rationality-normative-utility/ (2014)

35. Suresh, H., Guttag, J.V.: A Framework for Understanding Unintended Consequences of Machine Learning. arXiv:1901.10002 [cs, stat] (2020)

36. Gregor, S., Kruse, L.C., Seidel, S.: Research perspectives: the anatomy of a design principle. J. Assoc. Inf. Syst. 21, 1622–1652 (2020). https://doi.org/10.17705/1jais.00649

The New Boundaries of DSR

The Digital Science Field of Design Science Research

Veda C. Storey$^{(\boxtimes)}$ (iD) and Richard L. Baskerville (iD)

Computer Information Systems, J. Mack Robinson College of Business, Georgia State
University, Atlanta, GA, USA
vstorey@gsu.edu, baskerville@acm.org

Abstract. With all aspects of sciences quickly becoming digital, this paper proposes digital science as a new area of inquiry for design science research. Scientists, in every field, design and develop digital systems as artifacts to support their research, resulting in all of science now becoming what Herbert Simon called the *Sciences of the Artificial*. There are many significant software engineering challenges of digital science, including poor or unreliable artifacts, errors in coding, and unclear requirements. Software engineering solutions are not enough, but many digital science challenges can be addressed by the methodologies created by research in design science over the past two decades.

Keywords: Digital science · Computational science · Digitalization of science · Scientific artifacts · Digital systems · Design science research · Sciences of the Artificial

1 Introduction

In information systems, there are now two main types of research: behavioural and design science. Design science research has contributed methodologies, generalizability, and evaluation guidelines, and recognized the existence of various types of knowledge that deal with design and with science. It should now be feasible to extend the results of the diligent work on design science research to other disciplines. After all, Simon [1] proposed that the *Sciences of the Artificial* should primarily design and create artifacts that can be used by society.

Today, scientists in every field are increasingly challenged to design and develop digital systems to accomplish their work. The natural sciences have "gone digital," with scientists engaged in designing and assembling tools and equipment. Scientists have always been engaged in these activities. However, in the era of digitalization, when many consumer and personal activities now involve a digital process or procedure, science is increasing its dependence on complex digital assemblies of computational devices, software, and data. Much more of science occurs *in silico:* within a digital system with sensors, calculations, displays, etc. Science thus needs to make its digital artifacts first, and make them well. These needs apply in natural science fields such as chemistry, physics, and biology. But a science does not become a science of the

© Springer Nature Switzerland AG 2021
L. Chandra Kruse et al. (Eds.): DESRIST 2021, LNCS 12807, pp. 343–355, 2021.
https://doi.org/10.1007/978-3-030-82405-1_33

artificial just because it uses artificially-made measurement tools. Instead, a science of the artificial has the artificial products of humankind, and the design of these artifacts, as its object of study.

In this paper we argue that *all of science* is rapidly becoming what Simon regarded as sciences of the artificial. For example, the BioNTech/Pfizer vaccine was not discovered by experimenting in a lab with cellular matter on petri dishes. It was *designed* by Dr. Uğur Şahin, in Germany, using computer systems, on January 25th 2020 [2]. The vaccine (and its MessengerRNA) is an artifact. The record for vaccine development was shortened from five years to eight months. The biochemistry subfields of genetics and genetic engineering are now designing artifacts, and studying the artifacts they have inserted into our environments. Whether we like it or not, design science is becoming about everything. This is because of the now heavy reliance on digital artifacts to support almost all aspects of society.

This situation matters to design science research because natural scientists are increasingly dependent on computer-based systems to conduct their work. These systems are often poorly designed, which can lead to errors in science. Design science research adds theorizing and methods to artifact development while maintaining the innovation and creativity needed to address complex, real-world problems. Information systems broadly, and design science, specifically, delivers the kind of theory-based designs, with well-validated digital artifacts, that science needs. The objectives of this research are to: define and describe digital science; identify the challenges associated with digital science; and propose how design science research can contribute to digital science. The contribution is to identify digital science as a new area of inquiry for research in design science.

2   Computational Science: The Digitalization of Science

We live in a digital world with the digitalization of science part of the broader digitalization of human existence. Digitalization entails assemblies of big data, consumerized devices, robotics, artificial intelligence, and so forth. The digital world is potentially more transformative than any previous disruptive technology [3]. While the public has been entranced by social networks, driverless cars, and 3-D printing [4], science has spawned the computational sciences: computational physics, computational biology, computational chemistry, *in silico* medicine, and so forth.

Computational science is the use of computers, software, and algorithms to solve complex problems and needs [5]. It holds promise as a third paradigm for scientific discovery. That is, in the form of computational science, digitalization is transforming science with rapid advances via simulations (e.g., astronomy), mining of massive data sets (e.g., bioinformatics and medicine), and other technology-based discovery techniques. However, these natural science advances needed groundwork: development of essential, specialized, devices and software.

Research, traditionally considered as basic, pure, or fundamental, now involves a basis many considered applied; that is, applying computer and information systems to develop specialized, novel computing artifacts. *System medicine,* for example, creates specialized computer applications to integrate big data from multiple sources, in an effort to provide healthcare on an individual basis [6]. *Computational biology tools* deal with a large amount of data being generated to understand the challenges of comparative genomics [7]. The *3D printing of body parts* has created, and continues to create, previously unavailable medical options: fabricated mandible calvarial (skullcap) bone, cartilage, and skeletal muscle; replacement body parts (bone, cartilage, and a trachea); and biological soft materials (coronary arteries, embryonic hearts) [4]. A *pressure sensor* measures only the normal pressure, even under extreme bending conditions [8]. The tool, *MetaDrug* TM, identifies structurally exact or similar components and provides information on proteins with which they interact, to predict biological effects [9]. These contemporary examples demonstrate that it is, simply, no longer possible to advance science without first making digital artifacts.

The digitalization of science extends to the opening of the scientific community. This opening, described as *Science 2.0* [10], combines open scientific outputs, citizen science [11], and data-intensive science. Science 2.0 is a shift from the current state of science which includes predictive models, hypothesis testing, and the need for validity, replicability, and generalizability. Science 2.0 is composed of the new kinds of science needed to study problems in interdisciplinary collaboration. The main distinction is its methods. In Science 1.0, methods contained equations to identify and define scientific relationships. In Science 2.0, the methods study variables such as trust, empathy, responsibility, and privacy, by measuring and predicting interactions among these variables. Observational and case study methods build evidence for hypotheses for the interactions among variables. These types of methods are believed to ultimately be more effective in promoting advancement in scientific discovery and innovation. The move to Science 2.0 requires efforts to advance "integrative thinking that combines computer science know-how with social science sensitivity" [12].

Science 2.0 is a paradigm shift which, if successful, will result in computational science becoming as equally significant as other existing fields in the history of scientific discovery. However, the big challenge of Science 2.0 is the fact that research problems cannot be studied in traditional laboratories that are not able of capturing the context of collaboration, the variables that interact, and the interactions between people and technology. *Digital science* refers to scientific endeavors that require the development of a digital artifact.

3   Software in Digital Science

For decades, the natural sciences have already been stumbling over poorly designed or badly constructed digital artifacts. Software errors were prominent for potentially significant or catastrophic effects in pioneering space exploration [13]. For example, 387 software errors occurred in Voyager and Galileo spacecraft (87 for Voyager, 122 for Galileo). During the process of system testing and integration, discrepancies were identified between the computed, observed, or measured value and what should have been the true or theoretically correct value. These were documented by describing both the problem and further analysis needed. The errors were categorized as negligible, significant, or potentially catastrophic, such as safety hazards, but these sets of code took years and teams of developers to program.

3.1 A Venue with Software Issues

Doubtlessly there are many excellent software developers and project managers working in digital science. Nevertheless, the available research indicates that much of the scientific software is developed by subject scientists themselves, not software professionals. Even though most scientists lack extensive programming skills, they still are required to develop software and assemble digital systems needed for their research [5, 14]. Scientific programming involves computer software, often written by researchers with extensive training and experience in their field of science, but little programming training. These important software products are used "to model biological structures, simulate the early evolution of the Universe and analyze past climate data, among other topics" [14], p.775. There have been well-meaning efforts by hard-working scientific researchers who attempt to harness modern computing power as an increasing part of their overall research toolkit. This has sometimes resulted in poorly programmed code written by researchers, creating very large problems for entire research projects. These problems range from issues with programs that do not work properly to scientific results that are dramatically different from the accurate results that would have been obtained had the program been written properly. An example is the results from a "structural-biology group led by Geoffrey Chang of the Scripps Research Institute" where a program changed a minus sign by mistake and invalidated the research data, forcing the group to retract five published journal papers [14].

The digital artifacts that underlie computational science are often complex, badly designed, badly constructed, and badly tested. At best, the artifacts cripple the falsifiability, repeatability, and reproducibility of the results [15]. At worst, the conclusions are simply wrong. Some cases are embarrassing, such as the exposure of shabby research artifacts in the "Climategate" scandal [5]. Other cases are more injurious. When Robiou-du-Pont et al. [16] tested a popular web-based bioinformatics tool, SNAP (for single nucleotide polymorphisms (SNPs)), they found instances of 17.6% and 36.6% false negatives. The Duke cancer research scandal, in which the data analysis ranged across a complicated set of graphical and spreadsheet tools, yielded questionable and incorrect results [17]. That led to a full retraction of 10 articles and correction or partial retraction of seven others [18].

The cause of known cases of errors in scientific experiments is usually attributed to software errors, caused by scientists being self-taught programmers [14], debunking the notion of science 2.0 [10]. Within science, there is a well-recognized technical deficit that comes from writing suboptimal code under time pressure, knowing that the code will need to be rewritten. The rewriting does not improve the software's utility and, therefore, considered not worth the effort. This concept, known as *technical debt* describes "future obligations that are the consequence of technical choices made for a short-term benefit" [19]. At some point, the poor code will need to be fixed, reminding scientists of the potential long-term impact of their decisions. For computational science, there is a great deal of infrastructure consisting of supercomputers, software development tools, programming languages, etc., each of which can add to technical debt. The way to decrease this technical debt, or at least make a difference in it, is through education and training of scientists.

Reproducibility, so important in scientific research, requires documentation of how a research project is carried out. Computational science, in general, is often poor at showing reproducible results due to the: 1) use of immature technology; 2) large volumes of information required; and 3) obsession with performance [19]. If the technology is immature, it will not be maintained. Large volumes of information can lead to heavy computation and unnecessary complexity in computing programs. It is the performance issue, however, that can lead to technical debt. Focusing on optimization and performance can lead to programming practices that involve writing code for performance only, but do not involve good coding practices, such as thorough and systematic error checking [19].

When a scientist works in a highly risk-averse application domain, software mistakes can potentially have a very high negative impact on health or safety [20]. Scientists must possess a great deal of knowledge of both the software environment in which they work, and their application domain. Their mindset will affect how they address issues related to knowledge sharing and long-term maintainability [20]. Their focus is much narrower than someone trying to create a general solution to a set of problems for multiple people.

The importance of independently, and systematically, assessing the validity of outputs of bioinformatics tools is shown by the invalid outputs from SNAP [16]. When SNAP was used to assess the availability of SNPs in the Cardio-Metabochip custom genotyping array, the outputs from SNAP had drastically different SNP levels than a comparison Cardio-Metabochip file. The study concluded that the SNAP outputs were invalid, highlighting the importance of proper evaluation of this digital artifact.

These issues demonstrate that the relatively new disciplines of computational science may be considered "troubling immature" with design choices that may be "absurd" [5].

3.2   How Better Software Engineering Can Help

For over a decade, the software engineering literature has reported how essential problems in computational science are more than just poor programming; they are poor software engineering. From a design science perspective, these problems are poor systems design. Even when software engineering problems are resolved, poorly designed artifacts remain.

The software engineering field does have solutions, which is a reasonable conclusion if one's only training in digital systems has been programming. There is no doubt that poor programming habits may be present. The numerical discrepancy between expected and computed results increases by approximately 1% per 4,000 lines of code [5]. As software becomes larger and more complex, its accuracy diminishes. Initially, this concern was underestimated, but it has become more important as the complexity of digital scientific artifacts increase. In fact, there are numerous studies that demonstrate the results of poor programming in science [15]. These problems are not new to software engineering. There are essential principles that can be applied in digital science to correct many of these issues. Table 1 identifies significant software engineering problems facing the computational sciences, along with references and common software engineering solutions.

Table 1. Software engineering issues and resolutions in digital science

Scientific software engineering issues	Scientific field references	Software engineering resolutions
Digital artifact: software Issue: Software not routinely "released for inspection/verification" Impact: complexity of software used in climate science makes "interaction between software defects and scientific results difficult to interpret." [21] Results: Incorrect findings	Climatic Research Controversy over software, data, email at University of East Anglia in United Kingdom [15]	Verification of code [22]; complexity management (scope, context, decomposition) [23]
Digital artifact: software Issue: programming defects in widely-cited analysis; miscalculated ratios on public debt Impact: Incorrect findings Results: Refutation of results [24]	House of Commons Science and Technology Committee [25, 26]	Software evaluation, quantitative measurement, documentation [27]
Digital artifact: software Issue: Trivial Programming errors Cause: software designed by specific researcher, not challenged or checked Impact: Error-ridden software used by other researchers in publications Results: Influential articles retracted	5 years of research work lost; future related articles scrutinized heavily [15, 28]	Validation [29] Artifact evaluation [30]
Digital artifact: software Issue: code problems in published research Impact: publications in computing sciences conferences problematic Results: Only ¼ of research capable of being reproduced; public funding Obstacles revealed, funding efforts futile	Attempts to measure repeatability of computing science results; researchers examine source code for computing science conferences [31]	Source code availability [32]

(continued)

Table 1. (*continued*)

Scientific software engineering issues	Scientific field references	Software engineering resolutions
Digital artifact: software Issue: Characteristics unique to scientific software development create obstacles preventing scientists from using advanced tools and methods Impact: Creates "chasm" between software engineering and computational science; credibility and productivity crisis Results: Attempts to address "chasm" problem ineffective; recommend further research into scientific software	Difficult forms of verification/validation; formal software processes restrictive; scientific software lacks value; scientists not trained and disregard best practices	User requirements solicitation, representation, traceability [33]
Digital artifact: software Issue: practices in software engineering (e.g., generality) hinder ability to work effectively with computational scientists Impact: tolerance for inadequacy in programming knowledge makes crisis of unproductivity and reputation/credibility Results: Software engineering assists computational science Impact: adoption of techniques	Mutually ignorant ideas in software engineering and computational science disciplines [5] Software Engineering: generality Computational Science: productivity crisis Credibility Crisis: ability to reproduce results in question	Methods/techniques for implementation; must be performed correctly; model-driven software engineering, modular architectures, could benefit both fields; more software with longer life spans, easier maintenance
Digital artifact: code Issue: Certain scientific domains did not make source codes available (commonly commercial products) Impact: Diminishes transparency Results: "Black box" software poses risk for correct implementation of models	Software in science domains with unavailable source code [15]	Source code management; code reviews [34]

(*continued*)

Table 1. (*continued*)

Scientific software engineering issues	Scientific field references	Software engineering resolutions
Digital artifact: customized tool support (FCM) for change management and compilation Issue: group configuration management practices	Software development practices at U.K. Meteorological Office configuration management [15, 26]	Software standards and documentation requirements [35]
Digital artifact: software Issue: Scientists do not learn software engineering techniques despite necessity of software for their work Impact: poor communication of potential negative effects of bad software; Results: unavailability of tools and methods for scientific programming	Empirical investigation of software development by scientists [36, 37]	Formal approach for information gathering; documentation [36]; software engineering developed tools [38]
Issue: Developers dependent on decentralized and informal information gathering approaches Impact: poor software development practices adopted Result: Standardized information acquisition approaches needed	Comparison of software development practices of computing science and molecular biology professionals, focus on information gathering practices [15, 36]	Process model for scientific software development [39]
Digital artifact: software Issue: Use of prototyping practices while software being written for production Result: software of low quality, highly complex, duplication	Review of scientific programming projects [15, 38]	Use case studies [40]
Digital artifact: software Issue: Linear, plan-based engineering methods not effective; no common process for requirements specification Impact: poor code	Informal evaluation; contracted external team to create library for software components [15, 39]	Collaboration of scientist and software developers; bridge chasm of code vs engineering [41]

(*continued*)

Table 1. (*continued*)

Scientific software engineering issues	Scientific field references	Software engineering resolutions
Digital artifact: software Issue: Software engineering error Impact: Mission failure Result: Experiment lost	Loss of Mars Rover	Multi-level testing [42]

4   A Venue for Design Science Research: Digital Science

We have seen that better software engineering can address many of the software issues in digital science. But given the past decades' advances in design science research, will improved software engineering go far enough? There are serious risks accompanying the digitalization of science. The challenge is how to address, and more importantly, avoid them [43]. Design science research provides an ideal paradigm for investigating and resolving these risks because it produces proven artifacts and brings scientific rigor to the process of artifact production. It embodies methods for designing, building, and evaluating artifacts, thereby ensuring the reliability of the knowledge in the artifacts. Scientists often design their own devices, taking the design and development of these artifacts for granted. They fail to recognize that the scientific enterprise is becoming wholly dependent upon the scientific production of digital artifacts. Poor software engineering is one symptom of the problem. The problem itself is more than this symptom. The problem is poor design science.

When the production of digital artifacts occurs as design science research, such artifacts are theory-driven and verifiable. When applied to digital science, the production of digital artifacts for science itself becomes a relevant kind of science. This form of science, *design science research*, merges practice, research, and design into a coherent set of goals that generate digital artifacts and acquire knowledge using methodical procedures [44]. The use of design science research in the fields of computational science extends Simon's (50-year-old) vision of the *science of design* to all branches of science. From Acarology to Zythology, all of science is developing digital artifacts for use in research; all are branching into the realm of design science research; all are becoming, at least partly, sciences of the artificial.

Of course, many of these branches of science have yet to realize that they have begun this transformation because the immediate task at hand is one of natural science: biology, physics, chemistry, etc. Better design science can seem like an unnecessary sidetrack. At this point in the history of science, it can only be the knowledgeable custodians of design science research that rise to the service of the other sciences. The field of information systems is one of the greatest of these custodians. Therefore, it should develop an agenda for research in design science that envelopes its application in other branches of science. This broad expansion of design science applications can enable other scientific disciplines to more effectively continue to develop an understanding of the nature and role of digitalization in science through the development of their own artifacts.

At first glance, it might seem that the field of information systems has little to contribute to the development of natural sciences such as biology, chemistry, and physics. However, when these fields are viewed as collectives of organizations such as universities, research agencies, and governments, the importance of their information systems becomes more obvious. There are research information systems, but the scope of these systems envelopes only research administration such as grant proposals, compliance, or public data repositories. Yet natural science researchers often develop complicated information systems that exchange, process, and visualize vast amounts of data for analysis, simulation *in silico* experimentation. It becomes especially obvious that these systems are growing essential for the validity and reliability of the signal organizational products, scientific knowledge and not merely the administrative data for the laboratory's organization.

The investigation into how scientific disciplines can improve the development of their artifacts would prove to be a blue ocean research strategy [45] for the field of information systems. These disciplines use underdeveloped methods that yield many errors and create little reuse of their digital artifacts (i.e., digital exhaust). By applying a design science research paradigm to improve a computational science, we broaden the flow of information systems contributions to knowledge in two directions, as shown in Fig. 1. The first (top) direction is from design science research to digital science. The traditional contributions found in design science research, namely, its artifacts, principles, and design theories, are applied to a larger segment of society: the sciences. The second direction (bottom) is the contributions that will benefit design science research from exploring new applications.

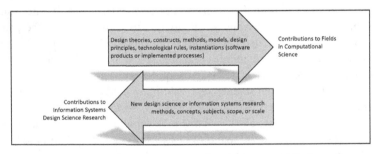

Fig. 1. Two-way flow: contributions between digital science and design science research

Using design science research in scientific disciplines contributes to the *digital science perspective,* by applying well-developed and comprehensive methods, yielding fewer errors, and increasing the potential reuse of scientific digital artifacts. For the *design science research perspective,* applications in digital science provide an ideal setting to further review design science research itself *while creating more broad societal impacts for both information systems and design science research.* Table 2 details some of the ways in which design science research can help address the known problems in digital science.

Table 2. Contributions of design science research to digital science problems

Digital science problem	Design science solutions	Examples
Narrow view of computing	Achieving both rigor and relevance in research	Hevner et al. [46]
Informal/incomplete technical training	Developing technical knowledge for systems management	Aken [47, 48]
Technical debt	Better project management that tracks work done, work undone, testing, and future scaling issues	vom Brocke and Lippe [48]
Chasm between computational science and software engineering	Agile design science	Conboy et al. [49]
Poor adoption of new or emerging technologies	Action Design Research	Sein et al. [50]
Culture/Communications gap	Design Ethnography	Baskerville & Myers [51]

Design science research contributes to methodologies, generalizability, and evaluation guidelines, and recognizes the existence of various types of knowledge production (e.g., contributions to design and science [52]). The methodologies are widely applied to develop artifacts (e.g., [53]). These general methodologies can be applied to the development of scientific artifacts, thus, delineating digital science as a design science research arena.

5 Conclusion

This research has proposed that the digitalization of science, as it transforms into *digital science*, can be supported by design science research, which has contributed to deepening our understanding of Simon's *Science of the Artificial*. Design science researchers can help to address the risks that arise in the natural sciences by applying the design science knowledge and methodologies that have been gained over the past two decades of design science research. This contribution reveals broad new arenas, *viz.* the natural sciences, for information systems design science researchers.

References

1. Simon, A.: The Science of the Artificial/Herbert. Cambridge (1969)
2. Linebaugh, K., Knutson, R.: The creator of the record-setting Covid vaccine. J. Wall Street J. Podcast (2020)
3. Larsen, H.: The crisis of public service broadcasting reconsidered: commercialization and digitalization in Scandinavia. Digit. Future 43–58 (2016)

4. Kirkpatrick, K.: 3D-printing human body parts. Commun. ACM **60**(10), 15–17 (2017)
5. Johanson, A., Hasselbring, W.: Software engineering for computational science: past, present, future. Comput. Sci. Eng. **20**(2), 90–109 (2018)
6. Apweiler, R., et al.: Whither systems medicine? Exp. Mol. Med. **50**(3), e453 (2018)
7. Commins, J., Toft, C., Fares, M.A.: Computational biology methods and their application to the comparative genomics of endocellular symbiotic bacteria of insects. Biol. Proced. Online **11**(1), 52 (2009)
8. Lee, S., et al.: A transparent bending-insensitive pressure sensor. Nat. Nanotechnol. **11**(5), 472 (2016)
9. Ruiz, P., et al.: Integration of in silico methods and computational systems biology to explore endocrine-disrupting chemical binding with nuclear hormone receptors. Chemosphere **178**, 99–109 (2017)
10. Szkuta, K., Osimo, D.: Rebooting science? Implications of science 2.0 main trends for scientific method and research institutions. Foresight **18**(3), 204–223 (2016)
11. Lukyanenko, R., Wiggins, A., Rosser, H.K.: Citizen science: an information quality research frontier. Inf. Syst. Front. **22**(4), 961–983 (2019). https://doi.org/10.1007/s10796-019-09915-z
12. Shneiderman, B.: Science 2.0. Science **319**(5868), 1349–1350 (2008)
13. Lutz, R.R.: Analyzing software requirements errors in safety-critical, embedded systems. In: Proceedings of the IEEE International Symposium on Requirements Engineering (1993)
14. Merali, Z.: Computational science: error, why scientific programming does not compute. Nature **467**(7317), 775–777 (2010)
15. Storer, T.: Bridging the chasm: a survey of software engineering practice in scientific programming. ACM Comput. Surv. **50**(4), 32 (2017)
16. Robiou-du-Pont, S., et al.: Should we have blind faith in bioinformatics software? Illustrations from the SNAP web-based tool. PLoS ONE **10**(3), 8 (2015)
17. Fienen, M.N., Bakker, M.: Repeatable research: what hydrologists can learn from the Duke cancer research scandal. Hydrol. Earth Syst. Sci. **20**(9), 3739–3743 (2016)
18. Califf, R.M., Kornbluth, S.: Establishing a framework for improving the quality of clinical and translational research. J. Clin. Oncol. **30**(14), 1725–1726 (2012)
19. Hinsen, K.: Technical debt in computational science. Comput. Sci. Eng. **17**(6), 103–107 (2015)
20. Kelly, D.: Scientific software development viewed as knowledge acquisition: towards understanding the development of risk-averse scientific software. J. Syst. Softw. **109**, 50–61 (2015)
21. Shackley, S., et al.: Uncertainty, complexity and concepts of good science in climate change modelling: are GCMs the best tools? Clim. Change **38**(2), 159–205 (1998)
22. Oberkampf, W.L., Roy, C.J.: Verification and validation in scientific computing (2010)
23. Kaul, M., Storey, V.C., Woo, C.: A framework for managing complexity in information systems. J. Database Manag. (JDM) **28**(1), 31–42 (2017)
24. Reinhart, C.M., Rogoff, K.S.: Growth in a time of debt. Am. Econ. Rev. **100**(2), 573–578 (2010)
25. Britain, G.: House of Commons Science and Technology Committee. Forensic Science on Trial (2005)
26. Matthews, D., et al.: Configuration management for large-scale scientific computing at the UK Met office. Comput. Sci. Eng. **10**(6), 56–64 (2008)
27. Pries-Heje, J., et al.: Advances in information systems development: from discipline and predictability to agility and improvisation. In: IFIP World Computer Congress, TC 8 (2008)
28. Miller, G.: A scientist's nightmare: software problem leads to five retractions. American Association for the Advancement of Science (2006)
29. Lynch, C.J., et al.: A content analysis-based approach to explore simulation verification and identify its current challenges. PloS One **15**(5), e0232929 (2020)

30. Venable, J., Pries-Heje, J., Baskerville, R.: FEDS: a framework for evaluation in design science research. Eur. J. Inf. Syst. **25**(1), 77–89 (2016)
31. Moraila, G., et al.: Measuring reproducibility in computer systems research. Technical report, University of Arizona (2014)
32. Stodden, V., Guo, P., Ma, Z.: Toward reproducible computational research: an empirical analysis of data and code policy adoption by journals. PloS One **8**(6), e67111 (2013)
33. Ramesh, B., et al.: Requirements traceability: theory and practice. Ann. Softw. Eng. **3**(1), 397–415 (1997)
34. Kelly, D., Hook, D., Sanders, R.: Five recommended practices for computational scientists who write software. Comput. Sci. Eng. **11**(5), 48–53 (2009)
35. Erickson, J., Lyytinen, K., Siau, K.: Agile modeling, agile software development, and extreme programming: the state of research. J. Database Manag. (JDM) **16**(4), 88–100 (2005)
36. Chilana, P.K., Palmer, C.L., Ko, A.J.: Comparing bioinformatics software development by computer scientists and biologists: an exploratory study. In: 2009 ICSE Workshop on Software Engineering for Computational Science and Engineering. IEEE (2009)
37. Hannay, J.E., et al.: How do scientists develop and use scientific software? In: 2009 ICSE Workshop on Software Engineering for Computational Science and Engineering. IEEE (2009)
38. Morris, C.: Some lessons learned reviewing scientific code. In: Proceedings of the 30th International Conference Software Engineering (iCSE08) (2008)
39. Segal, J.: Models of scientific software development (2008)
40. Jacobson, I.: Object-Oriented Software Engineering: A Use Case Driven Approach. Pearson (1993)
41. Baxter, A., et al.: Agile Scrum Development in an ad hoc Software Collaboration. arXiv preprint arXiv:2101.07779 (2021)
42. Brat, G., et al.: Experimental evaluation of verification and validation tools on Martian rover software. Formal Methods Syst. Des. **25**(2), 167–198 (2004)
43. Sanders, R., Kelly, D.: Dealing with risk in scientific software development. IEEE Softw. **25**(4), 21–28 (2008)
44. Walls, J.G., Widmeyer, G.R., El Sawy, O.A.: Building an information system design theory for vigilant EIS. Inf. Syst. Res. **3**(1), 36–59 (1992)
45. Kim, W.C., Mauborgne, R.A.: Blue Ocean Strategy, Expanded Edition: How to Create Uncontested Market Space and Make the Competition Irrelevant. Harvard Business Review (2014)
46. Hevner, A.R., et al.: Design science in information systems research. MIS Q. 75–105 (2004)
47. van Aken, J.E.: Management research based on the paradigm of the design sciences: the quest for field-tested and grounded technological rules. J. Manag. Stud. **41**(2), 219–246 (2004)
48. vom Brocke, J., Lippe, S.: Taking a project management perspective on design science research. In: Winter, R., Zhao, J.L., Aier, S. (eds.) DESRIST 2010. LNCS, vol. 6105, pp. 31–44. Springer, Heidelberg (2010). https://doi.org/10.1007/978-3-642-13335-0_3
49. Conboy, K., Gleasure, R., Cullina, E.: Agile design science research. In: Donnellan, B., Helfert, M., Kenneally, J., VanderMeer, D., Rothenberger, M., Winter, R. (eds.) DESRIST 2015. LNCS, vol. 9073, pp. 168–180. Springer, Cham (2015). https://doi.org/10.1007/978-3-319-18714-3_11
50. Sein, M.K., et al.: Action design research. MIS Q. 37–56 (2011)
51. Baskerville, R., Myers, M.D.: Special issue on action research in information systems: making IS research relevant to practice: foreword. MIS Q. **28**(3), 329 (2004). https://doi.org/10.2307/25148642
52. Baskerville, R.L., Kaul, M., Storey, V.C.: Genres of inquiry in design-science research. MIS Q. **39**(3), 541–564 (2015)
53. Peffers, K., et al.: A design science research methodology for information systems research. J. Manag. Inf. Syst. **24**(3), 45–77 (2007)

PlanDigital: A Software Tool Supporting the Digital Transformation

Andreas Hermann[✉] [iD], Torsten Gollhardt [iD], Ann-Kristin Cordes [iD],
and Paul Kruse [iD]

European Research Center for Information Systems, University of Münster, Münster, Germany
{andreas.hermann,torsten.gollhardt,ann-kristin.cordes,
paul.kruse}@ercis.uni-muenster.de

Abstract. Due to the plethora of possible digital technologies, companies face difficulties in selecting appropriate technologies to innovate their business model. Therefore, we introduce PlanDigital: a software tool supporting the digital transformation. PlanDigital combines existing tools and concepts in an integrated manner to support the identification, evaluation, and selection of potential digitalization ideas. Thereby, the application helps practice and academia in managing digitalization ideas in the early phase of a company's digital transformation. In the tool, the user models and organizes goals, the current business model, digitalization ideas, as well as digitalization roadmaps, which ultimately represent a company-specific digital transformation agenda. The paper accounts for the technological and visual design as well as the features of the tool.

Keywords: Web tool · Software design · Digital transformation · Idea management · Technology roadmap

1 Introduction

In the course of the Digital Transformation (DT), companies from various sectors are urged to digitally transform their businesses as a response to internal and external drivers, such as increased customer expectations or inefficient processes [1]. In this pursuit, it is crucial for companies to manage, i.e., identify, evaluate, and select promising innovation ideas, to begin with [2, 3]. An effective Idea Management (IM) may prevent the implementation of unsuitable ideas while allowing companies to implement successful innovations. To support these IM activities, research and practice have come up with a number of solutions. For instance, research has proposed dedicated procedures [4] and revealed a variety of idea evaluation criteria (cf. [3]). Furthermore, the use of specialized software has been shown to be valuable in this context.

Existing IM software often focuses on one or a few specific activities (e.g., evaluating ideas) and is embedded in a company's (product) innovation management and not necessarily focusing on the peculiarities of the DT. However, a successful DT approach requires a profound integration of IM activities with business-related facets (e.g.,

L. Chandra Kruse et al. (Eds.): DESRIST 2021, LNCS 12807, pp. 356–361, 2021.
https://doi.org/10.1007/978-3-030-82405-1_34

company goals or business model). In addition, IM is best performed in collaboration, potentially integrating external ideators. Thus, the relevance of IM software for
supporting the DT of organizations depends on the integration of DT-specific features.

In the light of this context, we propose a web application (PlanDigital) that combines
existing tools (e.g., the business model canvas [5]) and concepts of IM and DT. The tool
mirrors the IM activities identification, evaluation, and selection, which are augmented
by DT-specific concepts. PlanDigital allows managing digitalization ideas in the early
phase of a company's DT in a structured manner.

2   Artifact Design

2.1   Technology Stack and Database Design

The core of the application has been implemented utilizing the Python web framework
Django (cf. Fig. 1). This choice is mainly motivated by the framework's popularity, the
large community, the thorough documentation, and its built-in modular architecture. As
a web server, we made use of the Nginx web server, which is open source and commonly employed in Django-based web applications. In addition, the Web Server Gateway
Interface Gunicorn, responsible for running the Django application, is integrated into
the architecture. The database of the application is a PostgreSQL database, which seamlessly integrates with the Django web framework. More specifically, Django comes with
an Object Relational Mapper, which provides an interface for mapping data from a relational database table to objects that can easily be accessed within the Django application.
All previously mentioned components have been containerized using Docker to increase
modularity, consistency, and ease the roll-out process.

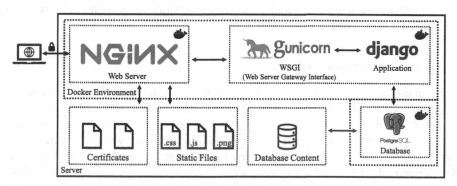

Fig. 1. Architecture overview.

The implementation of the tool is informed by a data model that integrates essential
DT and IM concepts into a holistic database design. To depict the database design,
we constructed an Entity Relationship Model (ERM) (cf. Fig. 2). In an ERM, real-life
concepts are modeled as entities (rectangles) and relationships (diamonds) among these.

At the center of any DT endeavor is the company itself. A SWOT analysis can
be conducted to inform the subsequent idea generation and evaluation. A company

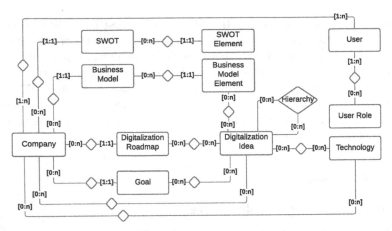

Fig. 2. Excerpt from the Entity Relationship Model (ERM) of the tool's data model.

can document (different versions of) its business model (components). The DT of a company is progressing by the realization of digitalization ideas. Digitalization ideas can be implemented based on a variety of different digital technologies [4, 6]. A critical aspect of a company's DT progress is the effects of implemented digitalization ideas on its business model (components). Additionally, digitalization ideas are aligned to at least one company goal to frame the IM activities further. Digitalization ideas are arranged on a digitalization roadmap, which can be understood as a company-specific DT agenda. A digitalization roadmap lists already realized ideas as well as planned idea realizations. Also, it is possible to collect digitalization ideas on an ideation space, i.e., digitalization ideas are not necessarily assigned to a digitalization roadmap. A simplified authorization concept with respect to the user and the company is integrated to account for the different user roles in the software tool.

2.2 Features and Visual Design

To illustrate the tool's main features, we introduce a fictional workshop use case. To convey the general idea of the visual design, a clickable mockup set is available online.[1]

The CEO of a small "furniture retail" enterprise wants to elaborate on potential digitalization opportunities for her company. She schedules a workshop with a local consultancy agency. Before the workshop, a consultant prepares the workshop in the PlanDigital tool. The consultant is assigned to the user role digitalization coach. Thus, she is able to create a new company (i.e., "furniture retail") and sets up a regular user for the company's CEO, who can now access the authorized company in the tool.

In the workshop, the CEO and the consultant agree to start with an as-is analysis of the company. Therefore, they model the current business model in the tool and enter as well as prioritize the company's goals. Afterward, the consultant creates a digitalization roadmap. While preparing the workshop, the consultant already created three digitalization ideas in the tool's ideation space. Both CEO and consultant agree to add two

---

[1] https://www.voil.eu/en/PlanDigital.

of them onto the digitalization roadmap. Moreover, the CEO adds one additional idea. Each digitalization idea is linked to affected business model elements, goals, enabling technologies, and related ideas (i.e., predecessor & successor). This link guarantees a company-specific identification of digitalization ideas. After the identification of new ideas, the CEO and the consultant evaluate these ideas in terms of selected evaluation criteria, such as cost factor or implementation effort. Next, the digitalization ideas can be assigned to short-term, mid-term, long-term, and as-is. The roadmap resembles a composition of selected digitalization ideas and serves as a company-specific DT agenda. At the end of the workshop, the digitalization roadmap is exported and sent to the CEO as a workshop protocol. Besides, the CEO can access PlanDigital after the workshop when she wants to view, edit, add, or delete certain ideas.

3   Significance to Practice and Research

The success of any DT endeavor is governed by a variety of factors along the entire transformation process. Generally, a well-structured and comprehensive preparation and ideation prior to the implementation of selected ideas are among the most crucial success factors in the early stages of a company's DT [4]. In fact, research and practice have proven the impact of early orientation activities such as understanding a company's business model, analyzing the as-is situation in terms of digital maturity, or investigating environmental drivers or trends [4]. An integrated IM (i.e., identifying, evaluating, and selecting ideas) which operates based on those contextual factors (e.g., business model, goals) paves the road to successful idea implementations.

Against this backdrop, the main contribution of the proposed tool prototype is to support an integrated IM to prepare a company's DT endeavors in a structured and comprehensive fashion. Therefore, PlanDigital complements the portfolio of DT tools by re-combining existing concepts and tools to provide a better basis for early orientation activities. More specifically, the tool enables the identification, evaluation, and selection of digitalization ideas while incorporating the particular company context. Besides, the tool can ease the communication among stakeholders and create a shared understanding of the DT of an organization. Resulting digitalization roadmaps serve as a tailored agenda to be followed as a flexible guide throughout a company's DT. Afterward, other tools, e.g., from the domains of project management or business process management, might support companies in conceptualizing and realizing individual ideas. However, since DT is an ongoing process [4], PlanDigital is designed to be used both in the beginning as well as repeatedly within the DT endeavors of a company.

Although the focus is to support companies in their DT, the tool addresses a number of relevant research topics as well. First, one central aspect is the unique combination of the research areas IM and DT. Traditionally, IM has been discussed in a much broader sense, especially in the context of product innovations (e.g., [7]). For this tool prototype, we adopt central aspects of IM (e.g., a collaborative idea identification, the possibility to persist ideas in an idea database, etc.) and incorporated DT-specific aspects. Second, through wide dissemination and continuous application of the tool in company settings, valuable data can be gathered and analyzed. This data, in turn, may be of interest to future research efforts. For instance, researchers may study collected data on the digital maturity of a sector, recently trending technologies, or digitalization ideas that have been proven to align well. Third, the tool can be considered as an ex-post evaluation of proposed DT procedures (cf. [8]). Many researchers have previously focused on the actual dynamics of the DT in real-world settings [4]. In particular, procedure models were developed to describe and prescribe the process of IM [3] and DT in companies [4]. The proposed tool essentially instantiates the major phases of such procedures and augments these by selected tools (e.g., the business model canvas). Thus, the tool extends the conceptual knowledge on the dynamics of IM and DT from a practically relevant perspective.

4 Evaluation and Concluding Discussion

The evaluation of the prototype has been accomplished twofold. First, we conducted a focus group discussion with practitioners and potential end-users of the tool. Second, we collected individual feedback in dedicated testing sessions.

The focus group discussion aimed at evaluating the overall design choices [8]. In a related research effort, we systematically derived a set of Design Principles from implemented case projects that informed the development of the prototype (cf. [9]). These Design Principles address the tool's requirements within four meta-dimensions, i.e., general design, modeling, collaboration, and technical. For instance, Design Principles regarding the general design intend to reuse existing concepts or integrate external supporters. Four experts from the case projects with wide expertise in digitalization projects were recruited. Two of them can be considered end-users of the tool. For the focus group discussion, we translated the Design Principles into mockups to mimic the tool's features. Overall, the participants confirmed the usefulness and usability in the context of the DT. The participants highlighted the importance of simple assessment functions for digitalization ideas to make them comparable. Moreover, they emphasized the importance of integrated annotation and assessment features to augment digitalization ideas. One participant suggested including an "ideation space" to document ideas before being mapped onto the digitalization roadmap (cf. Subsect. 2.2).

The second type of evaluation was continuously conducted along the course of the implementation phase. The team conducted both moderated (i.e., with pre-defined tasks) and exploratory testing with a total of five IS master students as testers. All testers had various practical experiences gained through different digitalization projects. Each testing session lasted about two hours. In the beginning, the testers were given a quick introduction to the prototype. The testers were encouraged to provide feedback as they performed the tasks. After the sessions, the feedback collected was aggregated and prioritized to ensure meaningful improvements. As presented exemplary in the following, results of the various testing sessions were manifold and significantly improved the tool. For example, almost all the testers voiced the need for a back button on all screens. One tester was slightly irritated that the side navigation bar could not be collapsed intuitively. Besides, a help feature was integrated to navigate the user through the tool.

In conclusion, the proposed tool contributes to both research and practice by merging selected concepts of IM and DT to support an integrated identification, evaluation, and selection of promising digitalization ideas in the early phase of a company's DT. Thereby,

PlanDigital complements the portfolio of tools for supporting companies' DT endeavors. Future research could focus on extending the tool and its underlying Design Principles, as well as its dissemination and application in real-world settings.

Acknowledgment. This paper has been written in the context of the research project VOIL - "Virtual Open Innovation Lab". The project received funding from the Erasmus+ Programme (2019-1-DE01-KA203-005021).

References

1. Wall, B., Jagdev, H., Browne, J.: A review of ebusiness and digital business - applications, models and trends. Prod. Plan. Control **18**(3), 239–260 (2007)
2. Brem, A., Voigt, K.-I.: Innovation management in emerging technology ventures - the concept of an integrated idea management. Int. J. Technol. Policy Manag. **7**(3), 304–321 (2007)
3. Gerlach, S., Brem, A.: Idea management revisited: a review of the literature and guide for implementation. Int. J. Innov. Stud. **1**(2), 144–161 (2017)
4. Barann, B., Hermann, A., Cordes, A.-K., Chasin, F., Becker, J.: Supporting digital transformation in small and medium-sized enterprises: a procedure model involving publicly funded support units. In: Proceedings of the 52nd Hawaii International Conference on System Sciences, pp. 4977–4986 (2019)
5. Osterwalder, A., Pigneur, Y.: Business Model Generation: A Handbook for Visionaries, Game Changers, and Challengers. John Wiley & Sons, New Jersey (2010)
6. Vandenbosch, B., Saatcioglu, A., Fay, S.: Idea management: a systemic view*. J. Manag. Stud. **43**(2), 259–288 (2006)
7. Ferioli, M., Dekoninck, E., Culley, S., Roussel, B., Renaud, J.: Understanding the rapid evaluation of innovative ideas in the early stages of design. Int. J. Prod. Dev. **12**(1), 67–83 (2010)
8. Sonnenberg, C., vom Brocke, J.: Evaluation patterns for design science research artefacts. In: Helfert, M., Donnellan, B. (eds.) EDSS 2011. CCIS, vol. 286, pp. 71–83. Springer, Heidelberg (2012). https://doi.org/10.1007/978-3-642-33681-2_7
9. Möller, F., Guggenberger, T.M., Otto, B.: Towards a method for design principle development in information systems. In: Hofmann, S., Müller, O., Rossi, M. (eds.) DESRIST 2020. LNCS, vol. 12388, pp. 208–220. Springer, Cham (2020). https://doi.org/10.1007/978-3-030-64823-7_20

A Conceptual Design for Digital Industrial Symbiosis Ecosystems

Linda Kosmol🅳 and Christian Leyh(✉)🅳

Technische Universität Dresden, 01062 Dresden, Germany
{linda.kosmol,christian.leyh}@tu-dresden.de

Abstract. Conceptualizing, developing, and using digital platforms to support industrial symbiosis has gained momentum to facilitate sustainable industrial development. However, current research provides little insight and scarce guidance for the design of platform-supported industrial symbiosis. Furthermore, experiences and viewpoints of (potential) platform users and providers are hardly captured. Moreover, the actors' roles and the suitability of platforms for different industrial symbiosis settings remain neglected. These aspects are relevant for providing, maintaining, continuously developing, accepting, and using the platforms themselves. Therefore, within a long-term research project, we developed the Digital Industrial Symbiosis Ecosystem (DISE) concept as an artifact to guide developing and disseminating industrial symbiosis platforms (ISP). This research is embedded in a design science research approach focusing on design criteria for ISPs. In this paper, we present how we developed and evaluated the DISE concept from the perspective of design science.

Keywords: Industrial symbiosis · Ecosystem · Platform design · Design science

1 Introduction

While companies, government authorities, and organizations individually engage in sustainable innovation, they have the greatest impact when they work together [1]. In the industrial sector, this teamwork manifests itself in the concept of circular economy, which aims at the transition from linear to circular supply chains, networks, and ecosystems. An inter-firm approach to drive this transition on a primarily local or regional scale is *industrial symbiosis*. The increasing number of scientific publications on the subject (see [2]), its incorporation into political programs (e.g., [3]), and the expansion of consulting initiatives in practice (e.g., International Synergies - www.international-synergies. com) show that industrial symbiosis is perceived as a promising path toward sustainable industrial development. By exchanging or sharing underutilized or excess resources such as waste materials and energy, infrastructure, services, logistics, and expertise between different industries, industrial symbiosis aims to create sustainable industrial networks of various geographic scales and to foster eco-innovation [4, 5].

There is a widespread and increasing consensus in the scientific community on the merits and (anticipated) benefits of information technology (IT) to support and accelerate

© Springer Nature Switzerland AG 2021
L. Chandra Kruse et al. (Eds.): DESRIST 2021, LNCS 12807, pp. 362–374, 2021.
https://doi.org/10.1007/978-3-030-82405-1_35

the emergence of industrial symbiosis by supporting all involved parties: practitioners; intermediaries; and facilitators [6–8]. Especially, platform-supported industrial symbiosis is considered a promising way to accelerate sustainable industrial development [8, 9]. Platforms can facilitate the exchange or sharing of the aforementioned resources between different actors (e.g., resource buyer and supplier) by, for example, enabling the exchange of necessary information whilst reducing transaction costs. Therefore, the conception and development of digital platforms to facilitate industrial symbiosis has gained momentum in recent years [2, 6, 9, 10].

However, the diffusion and maturity of both industrial symbiosis and its corresponding platforms are still low in practice. As results of two analyses (see [2, 11], we could show that although IT support for industrial symbiosis is studied, often only its functionality is examined. Research on design aspects of industrial symbiosis platforms (ISPs) and their implications for practice is scarce. Specifically, the role of the platform provider and platform management, the actual contribution of ISPs to the creation of industrial ecosystems, and their implementation in existing industrial structures and processes are insufficiently investigated.

To remedy this, we initiated a research project following the design science research (DSR) paradigm. We aim to design an IT artifact (the concept for a Digital Industrial Symbiosis Ecosystem (DISE)) to support the transition to industrial symbiosis through the diffusion and application of IT support for this domain. In this paper, we present how we applied design science approaches during the development and evaluation of our DISE concept.

In the next section, we present a short, theoretical background to consider when designing and implementing ISPs. Subsequently, we describe our research methodology in line with DSR. Doing so, we briefly place steps that have already been carried out in our research project into the overall process and, in particular, present the procedure and results of the next steps. The paper concludes with a summary and further research.

2 Theoretical Background

Industrial symbiosis encompasses various economically and ecologically motivated collaborative business models between industrial companies from different sectors across traditional supply chains [4, 12]. These models are either based on exchanging resources, i.e., substituting raw materials with waste or by-products (e.g., sewage sludge for fuel), or sharing resources, i.e., utilities, infrastructure, and services (e.g., joint warehousing). The associated transactions can be supported by digital platforms, with the diversity of resources posing a challenge for appropriate design.

Implementing these business models on a larger scale creates industrial ecosystems, in which industries gradually form a community with shared values and commit to sustainable development and collective value creation by adopting symbiotic behavior [4, 13]. Ecosystems are characterized by interconnectedness, interdependence, and self-organization [14]. Industrial ecosystems differ in their geographical scope, involved actors, and applied sustainability practices. We distinguish two types:

- *Eco-industrial park* (EIP): regional, strongly coupled systems whose members recognize or possess a common network identity; and

- *Industrial symbiosis network* (ISN): spatially distributed systems with a high degree of flexibility, but less continuity and a lower sense of community among members.

The geographic scope and type of ecosystem imply different requirements for IT support in terms of users, functionality, and governance. For example, geographic distance affects the transport feasibility of certain resources and especially the number of potential network participants, which in turn affects the probability of finding a match of resources and business partners. This *network effect* is an important factor in the vitality and success of a supporting digital platform; the value of a service/platform to an individual user increases as more users adopt the service/platform [15, 16]. For example, if more companies offer waste on an ISP, the matching service becomes more valuable as the user is more likely to find suitable matches among other users.

The implementation of industrial symbiosis usually requires four roles [11]: *Resource providers* and *resource consumers*, typically from the process industry, who offer or buy resources; *intermediaries* who enable transactions between consumers and providers by offering services like logistics, recycling or expertise; and *facilitators* who have a coordinating and brokering role, establishing relationships and trust between firms and intermediaries, and support the removal of barriers.

Digital platforms can form the core of industrial ecosystems and support the aforementioned roles. Platforms, from a software engineering or technical viewpoint, offer a core functionality and modular architecture that enables a flexible recombination of technical/software components and an adaptable information infrastructure [17]. From an economic viewpoint, platforms can act as inter-organizational systems or multi-sided markets facilitating third-party complements and relationships between different user groups of a platform [18]. From establishing services and different roles around the platform, *platform ecosystems* can emerge [19]. Fundamental roles are: the *platform provider*, who provides the basic infrastructure and common platform components (e.g., hardware, operating system, architecture); *demand-side users*, who use the platform's solutions and services; and *supply-side users* or *third-party software developers*, who add complementary services to the platform for demand-side users.

3 Development of the Artifact "DISE Concept"

3.1 Overall Research Approach

To tackle current drawbacks and research gaps of IT supporting industrial symbiosis, we aim to provide a holistic approach to the design and development of ISPs. We therefore pursue designing an artifact that can serve as a guide for the design of ISPs and for the different actors potentially involved in the development, operation, and use of IT for industrial symbiosis, such as researchers, practitioners, or facilitators. Hence, we follow the design science paradigm. In detail, our research approach aligns with the Design Science Research genre Design Science Research Methodology (DSRM) as described in Peffers et al. [20] and is positioned as one of several DSR genres in Peffers et al. [21]. The steps of our overall approach are shown in Fig. 1. In addition, our research steps align to Hevner et al.'s [22] guidelines and Hevner's [23] research cycles. Our steps also correspond to the thinking of March and Storey [24], who summarize four required steps for design science in IS research: Identifying the problem; Demonstrating a novel artifact; Evaluating the artifact; and Communication.

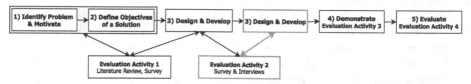

Fig. 1. DSRM process model (adapted from [20, 25])

Since IT support specifically designed for industrial symbiosis is a rather new perspective, literature studies and empirical case studies are quite limited. Accordingly, to ascertain existing concepts and considerations, as well as ISPs' perspectives and opinions on design criteria, we studied the academic literature and conducted exploratory surveys and interviews. In the following, we describe how we proceeded in the individual DSR steps. Currently, we are in the final stages of Step 3 (highlighted in red in Fig. 1) of our research project on IT-supported industrial symbiosis.

3.2 Problem Identification & Definition of Objectives

We initiated our research by identifying the problem (industrial symbiosis) and a solution space (IT and/or platform support) through comprehensive literature reviews. First, we identified problem areas of industrial symbiosis—in particular, informational and managerial issues—that can be addressed through IT artifacts (Step 1). These reviews revealed manifold barriers to the development and use of ISPs by potential practitioners (see [2, 26]). In a further analysis, we investigated the solution space, namely ISPs, derived further issues to be addressed, and first conceptual design requirements (Step 2). Through two systematic literature reviews (see [11, 27]), we obtained a profound understanding of the design (e.g., scope, actors, components) of existing or conceptual ISPs. We noticed in particular that the design concepts themselves, necessary development steps, and especially the roll-out as well as the operation of digital platforms in the context of industrial symbiosis have not yet been greatly considered deeply and comprehensively enough. Furthermore, the tool/platform is often only considered in isolation, without addressing the contextual conditions or the (industrial and platform) ecosystem in which the tools are embedded, or which can result from these tools. This leads to untapped potentials of ISPs. Accordingly, we moved to Step 3 of the DSR process, using platform theory as our theoretical foundation.

DSR perspective: With the literature reviews, we identified problems in the field per Hevner et al.'s [22] second guideline and verified the relevance of addressing and solving those problems in future research per Hevner's [23] recommendations. Additionally, we derived first requirements for the use of digital platforms in the field of industrial symbiosis.

3.3 Design and Development

Within Step 3, we deepened the investigation of ISPs by identifying further requirements to consider when designing ISPs and extended the scope of our initial platform concept from a technical viewpoint. As part of Step 3 (see [28]), we derived and discussed issues limiting the number/diffusion of these platforms in practice and proposed the adoption of a platform ecosystem perspective to address these issues. Based on this, we came up with the conceptual design of an industrial symbiosis platform builder. This platform builder is a digital tool to establish and facilitate industrial and corresponding platform ecosystems in industrial symbiosis. The main objective of the proposed artifact is to push the diffusion and maturity of ISPs to create industrial ecosystems through platform ecosystems and vice versa. Our next activities in Step 3 were to identify the requirements of potential platform users and providers (e.g., platform modules, interaction mechanisms) to propose a more specific ISP design concept. Since, most academic studies (identified in Step 2) reporting barriers are largely literature-based and conceptual, without providing practice-oriented insights into the viewpoints of potential users, providers, or developers, we decided to set up an empirical study to deepen the identification of requirements and also to evaluate our concept. Therefore, we chose a mixed-method approach combining a quantitative approach in the form of an online survey and a qualitative approach in the form of in-depth expert interviews.

The online survey had an exploratory character. It was first tested in a pre-study with ten participants [27] and then slightly revised to increase the fit toward our objectives in terms of the intended requirements identification for the DISE concept as part of Step 3 (see Fig. 1). The purpose of the online survey was to obtain user perspectives on ISPs by: (i) investigating the state of the art regarding awareness and practice of industrial symbiosis and its IT support; and (ii) determining preferences regarding design criteria of IT support as well as identifying unresolved problems. The online questionnaire contained the following four sections and was provided in German and English: company data (e.g., company size); industrial symbiosis awareness and practice (e.g., exchange of by-products); information and knowledge availability/sharing (e.g., confidential information); and IT awareness and design preferences (e.g., awareness of existing tools). Randomly chosen European companies from the manufacturing sectors were invited by e-mail to participate in the survey from April to September 2020. A total of 231 complete and valid participant records were generated. Of the 231 participants, 95% belong to manufacturing companies, including supply and disposal contractors. Another 3% of the participants are from the service sector and 2% of the respondents are from park/network management organizations.

The interviews were conducted to obtain opinions and actual experiences of experts involved in the development and use of ISPs for industrial symbiosis within research projects (researchers, facilitators, IT developers). Thereby, a further user perspective (facilitators) and the platform provider perspective is considered. The aims were: to (i) identify critical factors for the implementation; and use of digital platforms to support industrial symbiosis via project insights and lessons learned, and (ii) evaluate our conceptual design for ISPs developed prior to this study – the DISE concept (see [28]). Eleven experts from seven different research projects participated in an interview. The projects in which the interviewees participated included the following: *BEN collaboration platform* [29], *E-Simbioza* [30], *EPOS* (www.spire2030.eu/epos), *eSymbiosis* (http://esymbiosis.clmsuk.com), *MAESTRI* (https://maestri-spire.eu), *SHAREBOX* (http://shareboxproject.eu) and *Simbiosy* (https://www.simbiosy.com). The interviews were conducted as online meetings in the form of semi-structured interviews. The interviews were divided into two parts: first, an in-depth case study; and secondly, an evaluation of the DISE concept. For the evaluation, the original DISE concept [28] was explained to the interviewees to evaluate its usefulness and ability to mitigate issues in IT-supported industrial symbiosis.

A detailed result presentation of the online survey and the expert interviews is provided in [31] or is provided upon request by the first author. Finally, the results from the survey and the interviews were incorporated into the initial model of the DISE concept to improve it. The resulting evaluated concept (described below) incorporates technical components and different actors and their roles in the emerging platform and industrial ecosystems or industrial symbiosis communities.

Technical Components. The primary technical components of our approach are a *Meta-Platform* (MP) providing the *Industrial Symbiosis Platform Builder* (ISPB) to create multiple *ISP instances* (Fig. 2).

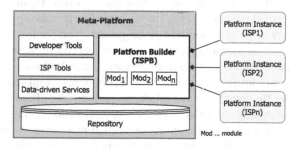

Fig. 2. Technical components of the DISE

The MP is the technical foundation of our approach. It provides the basic infrastructure, tools and services for its users, and the ISPB to set up any platform and functionality for different user groups. ISP tools serve handling instantiated ISPs (e.g., search for existing ISPs), while developer tools enable supply-side users to develop or improve ISP modules (e.g., matching module,), which can then be deployed by the ISPB. This is especially applicable for clustering, i.e., assigning or inviting platform participants according to certain criteria (e.g., region, industry) to other ISPs (e.g., local and national ISP), as it can facilitate access to information and knowledge networks beyond the scope of a specific locality. Connecting communities whilst maintaining a regional focus serves to ultimately accelerate the diffusion of industrial symbiosis [2, 4, 32]. Moreover, this approach would help create a critical mass for the entire platform ecosystem since one ISP may either have limited network size and limited economies of scale or may be too "broad" to offer value for a specific region. Another vital component is the *data repository*. By feeding back (declassified) information (e.g., synergy data) from the ISP instances into the repository, data-driven services, statistics, and module development can be advanced. The potential of existing data can be leveraged, for example, as general evaluations regarding synergy possibilities can expand the knowledge base of the meta-platform and in turn be incorporated into the modules provided by the ISPB. The fact that 79% of the 231 survey respondents declared their willingness to share anonymized data (e.g., synergy data, material, and energy flow data) in an ISP for the purpose of analysis and evaluation (e.g., characterization of established synergies, identification of infrastructure needs, dissemination of best practices) with a third-party supports this idea.

The ISPB offers tools and services to instantiate and configure individual ISPs, i.e., specific platform instances. It enables and supports the development and configuration of several different platforms for different industrial symbiosis communities. A modular built allows adjusting, adding, or removing modules on the created ISP, which enables a user-oriented development and step-by-step introduction of an ISP. The interviewees pointed out the necessity to align the tool development and/or provision to the parties (industrial companies, software developers or facilitators) willing to act in industrial symbiosis environments. The interviewees agreed that a network-specific design, which has not been considered to date, is valuable to the participants. Thereby, uncertainties regarding the cost-benefit ratio (e.g., time and personnel resources for development, maintenance and use) of an ISP, expressed by the survey participants, are considered by a fairly simple and fast development of ISPs via the ISPB. From a technical point of view, the ISPB provides advantages in the reuse and further development of already developed ISP components and a reduced development effort for ISPs.

The ISPs can serve as infrastructure to operate industrial symbioses in an industrial park or for communication, business, and collaboration in an ISN and enable a more effi-cient marketplace for industrial symbiosis. With a common, central space for symbiotic activities, it is easier for companies to explore the possibilities of industrial symbiosis. Furthermore, by promoting the success of the exchange and sharing of resources by a small group of early adopters through the individual platforms, the interest of other companies in industrial symbiosis and participation in ISPs could be sparked. Moreover, a federal structure, i.e., operating parts of the ISP under one's own control without being excluded from other parts—and thus from the overall benefit of the platform—could increase willingness to participate and uncertainties regarding information disclosure stated by the survey participants.

Actors and Roles. As indicated in Section 2, the users and roles around the platform make a platform worthwhile and can result in platform ecosystems. Our concept dis-tinguishes two types of platform providers: the one who provides the meta-platform including the ISPB (MP provider) and the one(s) operating a specific platform instance (ISP provider). For the MP provider, two options have emerged in the course of our research work: a government authority or a facilitating organization. Regarding the ISP provider(s) the survey results reveal that most companies (58%) are in favor of a local or regional network management entity (e.g., industrial park management or business association), followed by a public actor (e.g., municipality) (48%).

The **demand-side users** of ISPs and the ISPB include industrial actors within the various industrial ecosystems and communities and third-party actors such as intermedi-aries, private facilitators and governmental entities. *Industrial manufacturers* are at the core of industrial symbiosis acting as resource providers and consumers. While some interviewees stated that an ISP should not be intended for use by industrial actors but by intermediaries, others stated that this should be precisely the goal. As many as 42% of respondents said they or their company would likely use ISPs to pursue industrial symbiosis activities, while 48% were unsure about this matter. Only 10% would not opt for an ISP, i.e., 90% of the participants do not reject the idea of an ISP. We think they should be able to use the ISP but the initial success of the DISE should not rely on industrial users but on the facilitator(s). In case a company does not have the necessary capacities to pursue industrial symbiosis activities, "if a company is interested, they will contact their facilitator". The presence of a *facilitating third party* supporting the implementation of industrial symbiosis is recognized as crucial by the survey participants and evident from the interviews. Industrial symbiosis networks are highly case-specific due to differences in waste types, waste volumes, logistical issues or industries required for waste reception and recovery. This requires experts who are familiar with the existing (local/regional) conditions, i.e., a regional facilitator (e.g., environmental agency) to be users of the platform (and optimally the platform designer). Also, *intermediaries* (e.g., logistics service providers) need to be incorporated into the ISP and industrial symbiosis community as well. Interviewees mentioned explicitly that in case of by-product or utility matching, it is important to follow up by providing the required transportation to actually implement a synergy. The involvement of *governmental/political actors* is beneficial for industrial symbiosis and its IT support as they influence decisions that industrial companies make by setting regulations and granting subsidies. Moreover, government agencies have a wealth of data from companies that could be used to populate the platform. The government can also be a beneficiary of the data on various ISPs or the meta-platform to ensure that policies are appropriate to advance regional development. The survey participants' willingness to make data available to a regional governmental actor further supports them being users of ISPs or even providers of specific ISPs. Table 1 summarizes the roles and stakeholders participating in the DISE, and Fig. 3 illustrates the DISE concept in its entirety.

DSR perspective: Given Hevner's [23] recommendation that the design cycle should include the iterative construction and evaluation of the artifact, we conducted an initial demonstration and evaluation of our DISE concept by presenting the solution to business experts during the interviews. In doing so, we comply with Sonnenberg's and vom Brocke's proposal to conduct evaluation cycles in the early phase of research [25]. The holistic approach of DISE received excellent feedback, and the interviewees confirmed that the concept covers the requirements for IT tool support in industrial symbiosis environments. The evaluation also represents our first applicability assessment, as recommended by Rosemann and Vessey [33] to investigate the relevance of our research to practical needs, which was confirmed.

Table 1. DISE roles and stakeholders

DISE Role	Stakeholders
MP provider	Governmental authority; national facilitator; Private Public Partnership
	→ sustainable platform provision and continuous improvement
ISP provider	Governmental authority; regional facilitator
	→ ISP delivery coupled with additional services by the respective facilitator who knows location specifics and defines ISP business model
Demand-side users	Intermediaries, especially logistic service providers; facilitators; industry; governmental authorities
	→ Exploitation of network and community knowledge and data
Supply-side users	Software developers; researchers
	→ Continuous improvement of modules and functionality

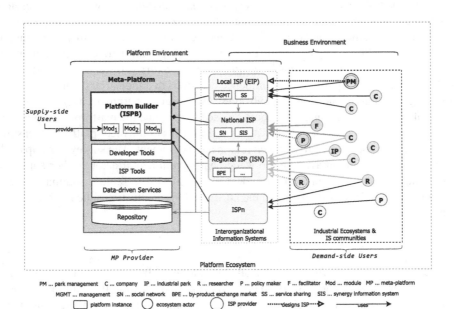

Fig. 3. Concept of the DISE with exemplary platform instances and ecosystem participants

4   Conclusion and Further Research

In our research project presented in this paper, we applied DSR in the domain of platform-supported industrial symbiosis. By following a DSR process, we developed a conceptual design—the DISE concept—to guide the development and diffusion of industrial symbiosis platforms and leverage the potentials of ISPs.

The DISE concept describes technical components and shows the roles of the different ecosystem actors. The concept's technical core concepts are a Meta-Platform, an

Industrial Symbiosis Platform Builder and the ISP instances. The relevant platform and industrial ecosystem participants are the provider of the Meta-Platform, the respective ISP provider, and the users. With these components and actors, the DISE concept focuses on networking and community building to establish industrial and platform ecosystems as well as on technical development efficiency and accessibility of ISPs to support practitioners and other stakeholders. The DISE concept takes up existing platform approaches to support industrial symbiosis, enables the reuse of IT components and extends them to achieve a larger diffusion of industrial symbiosis among different communities and to create more value offered by ISPs. It emphasizes that IT should be oriented for the use cases and not as IT itself. Thereby, the DISE concept attempts to counteract problems such as: neglect of stakeholders and unclear roles, lack of critical mass, limited access, fit and know-how regarding IT support, and insufficient transfer of data, information, and knowledge.

For the IS community, this paper additionally shows how DSR can be applied in a domain-specific environment, namely the digital platform ecosystems supporting industrial symbiosis. We present a research approach with a strong practical background represented in the different research steps involving knowledge and experience of practitioners in early phases of the artifact's development. Therefore, a contribution of this paper is to demonstrate how such a research project can be performed—from problem identification to first evaluation of the artifact—by presenting which research methods we chose for each step and the respective results. By showing how we addressed DSR guidelines in our research project, we share our experience on how DSR can be conducted in strong collaboration with practice.

For next steps in our research project, we need to complete, "the last research mile of IS research" according to Nunamaker et al. [34]: the proof of concept regarding functional feasibility, the proof of value showing that the DISE concept can create value and the proof of use to demonstrate that practitioners can gain value from their own instances of our solution. This means in general, from a content point of view, the DISE concept needs to be further elaborated. In particular, more detailed technical specifications are required to develop a prototype for a proof of concept in a next step. In this context, another interesting focus lies in the identification of "ISP templates" to propose specific platform configurations that match the industrial symbiosis setting or community and its users (ISN, EIP, etc.). From the proof of values viewpoint, the topic of platform-based business models in industrial symbiosis is important and has to be addressed in research. There are large differences in the exchange of material by-products, energy waste, local services, sharing of personnel and knowledge, etc. in terms of suitability for trading via a platform. Therefore, it is necessary to examine what is relatively easy to trade or can potentially be standardized, and also what should not be transacted through a platform. Furthermore, for the platform to be economically viable and to create incentive systems for participation, the business models of the providers and new business opportunities of the participants on the platform have to be investigated based on further platform theory (e.g., [35]). In this context, collaborative data-based business models could be a win-win option for platform providers and users, creating incentives to share data and generating added value for those involved. Questions that arise are the following:

- How to motivate participants to share their data?

- How to monetize (shared) data?
- How to determine and distribute the profit generated by collective data provision?
- How to ensure that the data is used exclusively and securely by those entitled to it?

Ultimately, IT support is only one advantageous condition of many to facilitate and accelerate the emergence of industrial symbiosis. To promote participation in industrial symbiosis and ISPs, further contextual conditions must be created. However, our proposed approach contributes to placing IT support in the context of relevant stakeholders and provide a framework for IT components to enable the emergence of IT-enabled industrial symbiosis. Our DISE concept echoes the basic tenor that sustainable innovations have the most reach and impact when the stakeholders work together.

References

1. Carter, C.R., Liane Easton, P.: Sustainable supply chain management: evolution and future directions. Int. J. Phys. Distrib. Logist. Manag. **41**, 46–62 (2011). https://doi.org/10.1108/096 00031111101420
2. Kosmol, L.: Sharing is caring - information and knowledge in industrial symbiosis: a systematic review. In: Proceedings of 2019 IEEE 21st Conference on Business Informatics (CBI 2019), pp. 21–30 (2019). https://doi.org/10.1109/CBI.2019.00010
3. European Union: Roadmap to a Resource Efficient Europe (2011)
4. Lombardi, D.R., Laybourn, P.: Redefining industrial symbiosis: crossing academic-practitioner boundaries. J. Ind. Ecol. **16**, 28–37 (2012). https://doi.org/10.1111/j.1530-9290. 2011.00444.x
5. Deutz, P.: Food for thought: seeking the essence of industrial symbiosis. In: Salomone, R., Saija, G. (eds.) Pathways to Environmental Sustainability, pp. 3–11. Springer, Cham (2014). https://doi.org/10.1007/978-3-319-03826-1_1
6. Grant, G.B., Seager, T.P., Massard, G., Nies, L.: Information and communication technology for industrial symbiosis. J. Ind. Ecol. **14**, 740–753 (2010). https://doi.org/10.1111/j.1530-9290.2010.00273.x
7. van Capelleveen, G., Amrit, C., Yazan, D.M.: A literature survey of information systems facilitating the identification of industrial symbiosis. In: Otjacques, B., Hitzelberger, P., Naumann, S., Wohlgemuth, V. (eds.) From Science to Society, pp. 155–169. Springer, Cham (2018). https://doi.org/10.1007/978-3-319-65687-8_14
8. Yeo, Z., Masi, D., Low, J.S.C., Ng, Y.T., Tan, P.S., Barnes, S.: Tools for promoting industrial symbiosis: a systematic review. J. Ind. Ecol. **23**, 1087–1108 (2019). https://doi.org/10.1111/jiec.12846
9. Fraccascia, L.: Quantifying the direct network effect for online platforms supporting industrial symbiosis: an agent-based simulation study. Ecol. Econ. **170**, 106587 (2020). https://doi.org/10.1016/j.ecolecon.2019.106587
10. Scafá, M., Marconi, M., Germani, M.: A critical review of industrial symbiosis models. In: Peruzzini, M., Pellicciari, M., Bil, C., Stjepandić, J., and Wognum, N. (eds.) Transdisciplinary Engineering Methods for Social Innovation of Industry 4.0, pp. 1184–1193. IOS Press (2018). https://doi.org/10.3233/978-1-61499-898-3-1184
11. Benedict, M., Kosmol, L., Esswein, W.: Designing industrial symbiosis platforms - from platform ecosystems to industrial ecosystems. In: Proceedings of PACIS 2018 (2018)
12. Chertow, M.R.: Uncovering industrial symbiosis. J. Ind. Ecol. **11**, 11–30 (2007). https://doi.org/10.1162/jiec.2007.1110

13. Lowe, E.A., Evans, L.K.: Industrial ecology and industrial ecosystems. J. Clean. Prod. **3**, 47–53 (1995). https://doi.org/10.1016/0959-6526(95)00045-G
14. Jacobides, M.G., Cennamo, C., Gawer, A.: Towards a theory of ecosystems. Strateg. Manag. J. **39**, 2255–2276 (2018). https://doi.org/10.1002/smj.2904
15. Gawer, A., Cusumano, M.A.: Industry platforms and ecosystem innovation: platforms and innovation. J. Prod. Innov. Manag. **31**, 417–433 (2014). https://doi.org/10.1111/jpim.12105
16. de Reuver, M., Sørensen, C., Basole, R.C.: The digital platform: a research agenda. J. Inf. Technol. **33**, 124–135 (2018). https://doi.org/10.1057/s41265-016-0033-3
17. Tiwana, A., Konsynski, B., Bush, A.A.: Research commentary - platform evolution: coevolution of platform architecture, governance, and environmental dynamics. Inf. Syst. Res. **21**, 675–687 (2010). https://doi.org/10.1287/isre.1100.0323
18. David, R., Aubert, B.A., Bernard, J.-G., Luczak-Roesch, M.: Critical mass in interorganizational platforms. In: Proceedings of AMCIS 2020 (2020)
19. Tiwana, A.: Platform Ecosystems: Aligning Architecture, Governance, and Strategy. Morgan Kaufmann, Amsterdam, Waltham, MA (2014)
20. Peffers, K., Tuunanen, T., Rothenberger, M.A., Chatterjee, S.: A design science research methodology for information systems research. J. Manag. Inf. Syst. **24**, 45–77 (2007). https://doi.org/10.2753/MIS0742-1222240302
21. Peffers, K., Tuunanen, T., Niehaves, B.: Design science research genres: introduction to the special issue on exemplars and criteria for applicable design science research. Eur. J. Inf. Syst. **27**, 129–139 (2018). https://doi.org/10.1080/0960085X.2018.1458066
22. Hevner, A.R., March, S.T., Park, J., Ram, S.: Design science research in information systems. MIS Q. **28**, 75–105 (2004)
23. Hevner, A.R.: A three cycle view of design science research. Scand. J. Inf. Syst. **19**, 87–92 (2007)
24. March, S.T., Storey, V.T.: Design science in the information systems discipline: an introduction to the special issue on design science research. MIS Q. **32**(4), 725–730 (2008). https://doi.org/10.2307/25148869
25. Sonnenberg, C., vom Brocke, J.: Evaluation patterns for design science research artefacts. In: Helfert, M., Donnellan, B. (eds.) Practical Aspects of Design Science. CCIS, vol. 286, pp. 71–83. Springer, Heidelberg (2012). https://doi.org/10.1007/978-3-642-33681-2_7
26. Kosmol, L., Otto, L.: Implementation barriers of industrial symbiosis: a systematic review. In: Proceedings of HICSS 2020 (2020). https://doi.org/10.24251/HICSS.2020.741
27. Kosmol, L., Leyh, C.: Perspectives on industrial symbiosis implementation: informational, managerial, and it aspects. In: Ziemba, E. (ed.) Information Technology for Management: Current Research and Future Directions. LNBIP, vol. 380, pp. 192–213. Springer, Cham (2020). https://doi.org/10.1007/978-3-030-43353-6_11
28. Kosmol, L., Leyh, C.: A vision for industrial symbiosis: build your platform (Ecosystem). In: Proceedings of ECIS 2020 (2020)
29. Raabe, B., et al.: Collaboration platform for enabling industrial symbiosis: application of the by-product exchange network model. Procedia CIRP. **61**, 263–268 (2017). https://doi.org/10.1016/j.procir.2016.11.225
30. Fric, U., Rončević, B.: E-simbioza – leading the way to a circular economy through industrial symbiosis in Slovenia. Soc. Ekol. **27**(2), 119–140 (2018). https://doi.org/10.17234/SocEkol.27.2.1
31. Kosmol, L.: Platforms as Enablers for Industrial Symbiosis. Dissertation, Technische Universität Dresden, Dresden. (will be published in Fall 2021)
32. Fric, U., Rončević, B., Uršič, E.D.: Role of computer software tools in industrial symbiotic networks and the examination of sociocultural factors. Environ. Prog. Sustain. Energy **39**(2), e13364 (2020). https://doi.org/10.1002/ep.13364

33. Rosemann, M., Vessey, I.: Toward improving the relevance of information systems research to practice: the role of applicability checks. MIS Q. **32**, 1–22 (2008). https://doi.org/10.2307/25148826

34. Nunamaker, J.F., Briggs, R.O., Derrick, D.C., Schwabe, G.: The last research mile: achieving both rigor and relevance in information systems research. J. Manag. Inf. Syst. **32**, 10–47 (2015). https://doi.org/10.1080/07421222.2015.1094961

35. Song, P., Xue, L., Rai, A., Zhang, C.: The ecosystem of software platform: a study of asymmetric cross-side network effects and platform governance. MIS Q. **42**, 121–142 (2018). https://doi.org/10.25300/MISQ/2018/13737

Design Principles for Digital Transformation in Traditional SMEs - An Antipodean Comparison

Sarah Hönigsberg[1]([⊠]) [iD], Malshika Dias[2] [iD], and Barbara Dinter[1] [iD]

[1] Chemnitz University of Technology, Chemnitz, Germany
{sarah.hoenigsberg,barbara.dinter}@wirtschaft.tu-chemnitz.de
[2] Queensland University of Technology, Brisbane, Australia
malshika.dias@qut.edu.au

Abstract. Digital transformation (DT) in companies is becoming a focal theme in information systems research and practice. However, we often overlook the transformation in traditional industries, particularly in small and medium-sized enterprises (SMEs). To address this gap in the literature, we ask, what are the design principles for developing DT methods for SMEs in traditional industries? Using an "antipodean" case comparison of two longitudinal action design research projects in Germany and Australia, we show the intertwined character of the learning and doing cycles of the researcher's action design research study and the firm's DT process. We propose five design principles: (DP1) goal orientation, (DP2) iterative character, (DP3) synchronized learning and transfer, (DP4) cyclic transformation and imprinting, and (DP5) impact measurement and revisiting goals. By formalizing learning and design principles, we contribute to the design-oriented knowledge base on DT in traditional SMEs.

Keywords: Digital transformation · Design principles · Small and medium-sized enterprises · Traditional industries

1 Introduction

Digital transformation (DT) in companies is becoming a focal theme in information systems (IS) research and practice [1, 2]. DT describes the extensive change process that a company experiences when integrating new digital technologies, often with the goal of improvement [1]. Global competition and new business models and ecosystems of born-digital players like Amazon or Google changed the market over the last decades, leading to the value proposition of traditional businesses being threatened [3].

Small and medium-sized enterprises (SMEs) in traditional industries, which often have many centuries of history, are shrinking rapidly under pressure to change [4]. This phenomenon can be seen in traditional industries such as textile [5, 6], construction [7–9], and finance [4, 10]. The effect is mainly due to the digitalization of global supply chain networks and the faster reach of affordable regions via more transparent online

© Springer Nature Switzerland AG 2021
L. Chandra Kruse et al. (Eds.): DESRIST 2021, LNCS 12807, pp. 375–386, 2021.
https://doi.org/10.1007/978-3-030-82405-1_36

marketplaces, which became a stress factor for traditional businesses [11]. The remaining traditional SMEs, also known as Mittelstand firms [12], show similar characteristics. They are small and medium-sized and strongly locally networked within their communities, including suppliers, manufacturers, and customers [12]. An important characteristic is their resilience to respond to market changes [13]. This survival strategy of traditional SMEs, which is often based on advances in knowledge and local network connections, is insufficient to survive in the long run in the globalized digital economy. In the digital economy, they face the challenge of adopting digital technologies and managing the transformation across tradition-bound networked businesses [4, 14]. These companies can benefit significantly from a small technological change compared to big companies [5].

In recent research, the influence of tradition on DT of such companies as an aggravating factor is recognized, and the question of how they develop appropriate DT methods (a set of steps with defined outputs to support a specific task [15]) is being examined [cf. 3, 4]. Because of the traditional practices and resource-constrained nature of such SMEs, their DT challenges are particularly significant. However, there is still little known about how traditional SMEs manage this task since DT in this type of company is vastly under-researched [4, 11, 12]. This research gap is particularly severe in conventional economies where SMEs account for a significant percentage of all economic units [10, 16]. Recent literature argues that managers in traditional firms adopt different strategies and methods compared to born-digital companies to navigate through DT, primarily aiming to preserve their tradition [17, 18]. Emphasizing the business strategy, this stream of literature has overlooked the DT approaches of traditional SMEs. In fact, we believe that design principles (DP) for DT methods when accompanying action design research (ADR) projects could be beneficial for traditional SMEs because the impact ADR studies can make in such companies is significant compared to big corporations. The DT process in traditional SMEs is very individual, and therefore a DT method tailored to a specific company is advisable. This study aims to offer support for the development of a company-specific DT method. We, therefore, ask what are the DPs for developing DT methods for SMEs in traditional industries?

To answer this question, we have conducted a retrospective analysis of two longitudinal ADR studies [19] in two traditional SMEs in Germany and Australia, which we call 'an antipodean comparison.' We chose these two SMEs because of their similar characteristics regarding tradition, size, and local networks. We compare the case settings as well as the opposing ADR and DT approaches of the cases. Through the comparison, we see that the DT approaches in both organizational contexts are inverse to our ADR approaches. We synthesize DPs for developing DT methods as organizational contexts complement to the researcher's ADR method. We contribute to research and practice by identifying the similarities and differences of DT practices in the antipodean cases and proposing DPs that practitioners could adopt in traditional SMEs.

2 Foundations

In recent years, DT literature has gained attention in traditional SMEs [3, 18]. DT is defined as "a process that aims to improve an entity by triggering significant changes to its properties through combinations of information, computing, communication, and connectivity technologies" [1]. Companies go about DT in two main approaches: forming a digital strategy [2] or implementing IT [20]. If the managers decide to develop a strategy first, the significant changes may follow a roadmap to improve existing IT systems or introduce new technologies [4]. Alternatively, DT may arise when an organization decides to implement a new IT system disrupting the traditional practices [7]. Thus, in addition to the strategy-driven DT, which follows a top-down approach [21], there is an implementation-driven DT, which pursues a bottom-up approach [20] and a continuum between the two extremes.

The growing literature on digital strategy has emphasized the transformative role digital technologies play in traditional companies [2, 22]. Digital strategy formulation and implementation are especially challenging for those companies because of persisting practices from their foundations in the pre-digital economy [3]. However, some managers have found innovative ways and strategies to transform their companies using digital technologies [9, 23]. For example, Dremel et al. [24] show how AUDI, a traditional car manufacturing company, transformed its decision-making process from experience-based to evidence-based by using big data analytics. Chanias et al. [4] explain how a DT strategy is being formulated and implemented by a traditional financial service provider using top-down development of a digital roadmap and bottom-up development of new digital products. The financial provider's two-year DT journey started formulating the strategic direction by recognizing the need and assessing the DT readiness of the company [4].

Opposite to the discussed focus on strategy in DT literature, networked SMEs' approaches and their path through DT require a less strategic, more learning-by-doing-oriented approach [7]. Shifting the level of analysis in Vial's [1] conceptualization of the DT processes to organizational networks means a network-level strategy is necessary to realize DT. Instead, to initiate network-level DT, SMEs often choose an operational-driven process of exploring new digital technologies leading to managerial learning processes and, if successful, initiating additional digitalization projects [7]. Strategically driven top-down approaches and operationally driven bottom-up approaches are thus only two sides in the DT cycle, with SMEs often starting with the latter. As Wang et al. [25] rather pointedly formulated: "Compared with large firms which have greater resources, [SMEs] are sometimes struggling with survivals rather than peacefully planning long-term strategies."

Practice-oriented research where scholars actively engage in solving organizational problems is currently a prominent stream in IS research [26]. In particular, ADR with its interventional character represents an important practice- and design-oriented research method [19]. When intervening in an organizational strategizing or change process, scholars are "viewing field problems (as opposed to theoretical puzzles) as knowledge-creation opportunities [...] at the intersection of technological and organizational domains" [19]. The recurring alternation between the deductive-theoretical design and empirical-inductive forming from the perspective of an empirical case represents the learning- and doing-cycle of this research approach [27]. We believe that the approach described by Sein et al. [19] is particularly well suited for designing for DT because ADR recognizes the role of the organizational context that shapes the design and the artifact instance. Further, the transformation that the new artifact triggers in the organization becomes visible in the internal context and can be considered and investigated by the researchers. When, as in the studies described in this paper, researchers study a domain practice (e.g., DT approaches) and use a specific research practice (e.g., ADR) and maybe intervene to improve the domain practice, an imbrication of research and domain practice occur [28]. Thus, the learning and doing cycles in the researcher's ADR study and the organization's DT process are intertwined. Therefore, the scholars are becoming impactful field researchers and play a strategic role by investigating problems, identifying DT potential, reconstructing business models [18], or collecting ideas to develop DPs [29].

3   Research Approach

We present a retrospective analysis of two longitudinal ADR studies conducted separately from each other in traditional companies. Both studies see the overburdening of traditional SMEs with previous DT approaches (too costly, time-consuming, too little assurance of success) as a class of problems, and this problem leads to the hesitation of these companies to engage in DT initiatives. We analyzed the case settings and research approaches besides the DT approach. For each case setting, we collected data on the DT and approaches taken, before conducting the analysis to identify common DPs [19, 29]. Our ADR study settings are two traditional SMEs in Germany and Australia.

The first case is a traditional SME involving four textile companies that jointly develop and produce in the German technical textile industry (hereinafter 'TexNet'). The companies (a weaver, a knitter, a finisher, and a coater) each form essential parts of the textile value chain. In some instances, strong dependency relationships (e.g., knitter to finisher) and in others substitution relationships (e.g., weaver and knitter) can be observed in TexNet. The companies were founded in East Germany in 1888, 1900, 1920, and 1994. Three of them were expropriated by the state and reprivatized by the founding families.

The second case is a traditional SME involving 25 retail stores in the Australian building and construction industry (hereinafter 'MasonNet'). Founded between 1960 to 1990, this network of retailers is regarded as one of Australia's largest suppliers of hardware, building construction, plumbing, and renovation products to retail and industrial customers. Starting from one corner store in 1960, MasonNet has expanded to 25 stores across the state, each specializing in one or a few areas of the construction supply chain. In 2019, MasonNet handled over 140,000 construction supplies and was dealing with over 750 local and international stakeholders regularly.

Therefore, both cases represent traditional SMEs that have experienced disruptions such as changes in the political system, expropriation, and market-driven shifts because of digital technologies and globalization. The idea to compare these two cases came through when the authors perceived a common ground of traditional SMEs regarding the DT and ADR approaches.

At TexNet, the data collection included several qualitative questionnaires, over 35 h of semi-structured interviews, several hours of group interviews or workshops, over ten hours of primary and secondary observations per company, internal documents, and a panel survey. At MasonNet, the data collection included 30 h of semi-structured interviews, 25 h of observations, four workshops, and archival material. The archival material comprises more than 750 double-spaced pages, including internal strategy documents, newspaper articles on the organizational history, and technical documents on the IT systems. Additionally, to have a broader understanding of the two studies, we shared and analyzed the reports and presentations formulated during the ADR approach.

Combining the data and analyses of the two ADR studies, we conducted a retrospective analysis to answer the research question following the example of [30]. We re-analyzed the data in three stages, aiming to develop common DPs for DT method in traditional SMEs. First, we shared our experience in the individual ADR studies among the researchers. We reflected on each other's learnings during the discussions and developed a common understanding of the studies. Second, through re-analysis by unrelated researchers, the requirements of the cases and the design features of the DT methods could be validated. Finally, in the reflection, the DPs were derived by comparing the design features and reflecting them against the corresponding knowledge base (see rationale of the DPs). We used Gregor et al.'s anatomy of a DP [29] to formulate our DPs.

We revealed an antipodean view of DT initiatives guided by the ADR studies conducted in Germany and Australia through the analysis. Based on the analysis, we present an antipodean comparison for investigating how SMEs in traditional industries approach DT by adopting an approach similar to previous IS cross-studies [30–32].

4   Antipodean Case Comparison

Our comparison of the case settings of the two cases is inspired by the building blocks of the DT process (left column) of Vial [1], as summarized in Table 1. We focus on the companies' DT's procedural aspect and therefore omit the affecting aspects (structural changes and organizational barriers) in our comparison [cf. 1]. Both studies are multi-year ADR studies, whereas in TexNet, design decisions were derived rather theory-driven and adapted to the organizational context.

In contrast, MasonNet's design decisions were derived strongly from the organizational context, and theoretical assumptions were used for adjustment. When comparing the two cases, we noticed that the context in which the class of problems is situated differs slightly. While TexNet focuses on networks of SMEs, MasonNet considers tradition, but both cases look at the DT approaches. However, additional data revealed that TexNet also concerns tradition and MasonNet also consists of networked businesses, even if this was not the primary focus of the respective ADR studies.

Remarkably, industry disruptions have triggered both cases, but the two cases show different IT-related responses to them. While TexNet reacts more operatively and bottom-up with a project for IT introduction, MasonNet initiates a top-down reaction with a strategic plan for IT adoption. Accordingly, once an operational issue and once a more future-oriented objective is addressed. Although the cases and the researcher's ADR are somewhat different, the observed DT approaches are comparable.

TexNet used a bottom-up approach for DT, and the ADR method was aligned to achieve the IT development goals. First, TexNet researchers and practitioners formulated a network-wide vision and value co-creation indicators. Second, they defined a

Table 1. Antipodean comparison of the cases

DT building blocks	TexNet	MasonNet
Characteristics of the operating industry	Textile production: expansion of geographical boundaries for better economies of scale	Building and construction sales: rise of industrial warehouses and online retail markets
Need for DT	IT helps to prioritize innovation in production and re-establish the brand	IT helps to better compete with the new players and regain the market position
Relationship of units	Loosely coupled independent family businesses	Tightly coupled stores operated as a single family-owned business
Traditions and organizational culture	Intensive local collaboration, personal contact, and knowledge-intensive custom-made developments	Community attachment, family-vested interests, and industry-specific trade expertise
Triggering disruption	High competitive pressure leading to a shrinking market and perceived pressure towards IT	High competitive pressure leading to slowing of growth and perceived industrial change through DT
Strategic response	Niche strategy with specialization in knowledge-intensive service and flexible value chains. Decision to start a DT project (bottom-up approach)	Niche strategy with specialization on industry-specific expert services and flexible value chains. Decision to develop a DT strategy (top-down approach)
Objectives of the digitization initiative	To counteract inhibition of innovation /development processes through coordination problems	To attract the digital-savvy generation of suppliers and customers to the traditional stores
Main artifact/Use of digital technology	A shared digital value co-creation platform	A roadmap to guide SMEs in the retail sector toward DT
Changes in value creation	Tighter and more efficient interlinking of the value network via the platform as a new partner and customer channel. Faster textile development as a value proposition	Streamlining of business processes across the stores utilizing existing and new digital technologies. Faster supply chain and more efficient services to customers
Impact	Increased trust in the network, enhanced network reach, and competitiveness	Increased customer satisfaction, new tech-savvy customers, and paperless offices

(*continued*)

Table 1. (*continued*)

DT building blocks	TexNet	MasonNet
Research approach	ADR with strong embedding in theoretical assumptions (slightly deductive focus) and context focus on DT in SME networks	ADR with strong empirical orientation (inductive focus) and context focus on DT in traditional organizations

digitalization plan after identifying the potential processes to digitalize through synthesizing and prioritizing new IT initiatives. Third, TexNet used agile methods for IT implementation and adaptation. Finally, we focused on launching and acceptance testing of the platform while ensuring the network vision and value co-creation indicators are met.

MasonNet researchers and practitioners started the DT and ADR, focusing on formulating a DT strategy. First, they focused on understanding the field problem and outlining the strategic priorities. Second, MasonNet streamlined network-wide business processes and revised the organizational policies accordingly. Third, the managers and researchers shared their knowledge and experience to assess the IT-based value creation opportunities. Finally, we developed a DT roadmap including a timeline, activities, and evaluation protocols. These steps were executed iteratively in both TexNet and MasonNet, although MasonNet used a top-down approach.

Although one case follows a bottom-up and one case a top-down approach, both cases were goal-oriented in their DT efforts. Another similarity is that phases of the internal reshaping of the company (e.g., process adaptation) occur, which is associated with a reflection on the company's tradition - these phases alternate with phases of synchronization, learning, and alignment with other network partners. Finally, in both cases, it was evident that the effectiveness of the digitalization measures is being evaluated and that the repetitive or continuous nature of the DT approach can be observed.

5 Design Principles for Digital Transformation Method in Traditional SMEs

When reflecting on the comparison, we find one remarkable similarity. There is a symmetrical countermovement of the deductive-inductive orientation of research and the top-down vs. bottom-up approach of the company. Since the companies under consideration are SMEs, the ADR studies have automatically influenced and guided their transformation processes. The researcher thus becomes a sort of advisor. If the SME already has strategic plans for the DT, the researcher must adapt to these guidelines. On the other hand, if the SME starts without strategic planning, it makes sense for the researcher to rely more on theoretical assumptions as a guideline. Based on our comparison (see Fig. 1), we conceptualize the DPs addressing the ADR Team below:

(DP1) Principle of Goal Orientation: To allow owners and leaders of SMEs in a traditional industry to envision a future state when they start to transform their organization using new digital technologies to solve business problems. Formulation of a network-wide vision or a DT strategy to achieve that is important because "a digital transformation strategy is supposed to coordinate, prioritize, and implement a traditional SME's transformation efforts and, as a long-term objective, to govern its journey to achieve the desired future state of being digitally transformed" [4]. For example, TexNet's goal was to develop an IT system, whereas MasonNet's was to develop a digital strategy.

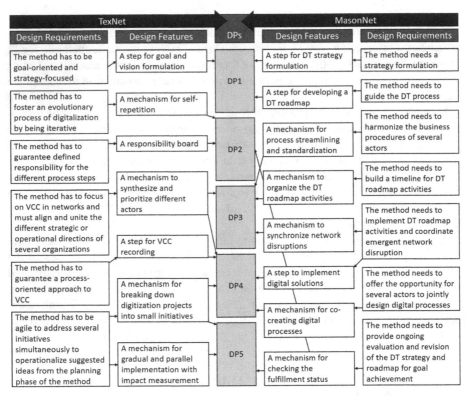

Fig. 1. Derivation of design principles for a digital transformation method

(DP2) Principle of Iterative Character: To allow owners or leaders of SMEs in a traditional industry to change and improve the organization with new digital technology by recurring, consecutive cycles of activity for solution approximation ("iteration"), because DT is an ongoing process of constant change and improvement of an organization, which is closely linked to trial and error as well as a learning and doing cycle [4, 21]. For example, both TexNet and MasonNet approached their DT in subsequent initiatives allowing gradual adoption of the new technologies.

(DP3) Principle of Synchronized Learning and Transfer: To allow owners or leaders of SMEs in a traditional industry to exchange knowledge and insights with network partners and researchers to help them build the necessary capabilities to transform their organization. Particularly SMEs with limited resources must first develop new capabilities during DT in order to be able to exploit new technology [7]. For extensive transformations, dynamic capabilities must be established at the management level in a learning process [33]. For example, TexNet started IT system implementation with the most resourceful SME and transferred the learnings throughout the network.

(DP4) Principle of Cyclic Transformation and Imprinting: To allow owners and leaders of SMEs in a traditional industry to reimagine the past of their trade and communities amid DT. Invoking the tradition-driven worldview during the transformation triggers an iterative imprinting process that brings back memories and remnants of the traditional arrangements in networked SMEs. This principle appears as a network-level organizational inverse because "the social technology available during the establishment of intercorporate community networks continues to influence contemporary network structure and behavior" [14] alongside cyclic processes of DT. For example, MasonNet revised its traditional policies to assess their applicability in the digital strategy.

(DP5) Principle of Impact Measurement and Revisiting Goals: To allow owners and leaders of SMEs in traditional industries to measure the impact of their DT efforts taken together with external change agents. Revisiting the goals to assess the outcomes of business problems addressed needs a "multidimensional view (i.e., that more than one way to make an impact)" [34] across networks. This principle offers researchers to assume a more active role as "change agents" within traditional SMEs because of our focus on real-world problem solving toward realizing business goals. For example, both TexNet and MasonNet had measurement matrices as a part of their DT method.

6 Discussion

With the antipodean case comparison, we addressed the research question of which DPs arise for DT methods for SMEs in traditional industries. We have derived five DPs from our long-term ADR studies, which address an important class of problems. In particular, we highlight the importance of cyclic transformation and imprinting in SMEs when they approach DT. Managers and ADR researchers must be aware of the organizational history, network structures, and technologies used during organizational evolution and consider the tradition-driven worldview in the network level organizational inverse [14]. Carefully understanding and managing the imprints throughout the cycles of DT was necessary for SMEs.

We believe that this observation demonstrates that the learning and doing cycles of the researcher's ADR study and the organization's DT process are intertwined, as suggested by [28]. Thus, the DT approaches of the SMEs are the organizational inverse method to our research method in the studied cases. Suppose one imagines the intervention interface between the research sphere and the organizational sphere as a semi-permeable boundary. In that case, the two groups move towards each other to exchange knowledge and move away from each other into their respective research or organizational context to act on the obtained insights. Thus we see that the reciprocal shaping takes place not only between the dyad of the organizational context and the artifact [19] but between a triad that includes the research context.

The semi-permeable boundary represents the junction between the research sphere and the organizational spheres. The scope of action of the participants overlap here, and knowledge and insights diffuse into the other sphere. According to our observation, the border is semi-permeable since knowledge from the field is limited and filtered by the researcher's worldview (e.g., critical realism vs. positivism or qualitative vs. quantitative) and only partially reaches him/her [35, 36]. On the other side, knowledge from research in the interactions also diffuses only partially into the sphere of the organization limited and filtered by its worldview (e.g., tradition- vs. technology-driven) [37]. The traditions of the organization determine the precipitation of the diffused knowledge from the adjacent spheres. According to our observations, the organization's internal conditions determine how it manages the external impulses.

The organizational inverse occurs for each organization in the network, and the semi-permeable boundary connects their spheres as well. Thus, we could observe a similar cross-boundary exchange of knowledge between the organizations. In their sphere, all participants process the exchanged knowledge. This interlinking of research and DT activities represents our theoretical assumption drawn from the retrospective analysis on the DT approaches in the TexNet and MasonNet cases and the resulting DPs for a DT method for SMEs. The method's DPs are juxtaposed with the principles of ADR (shown as P1 - P7 in Fig. 2) to emphasize their intertwined character.

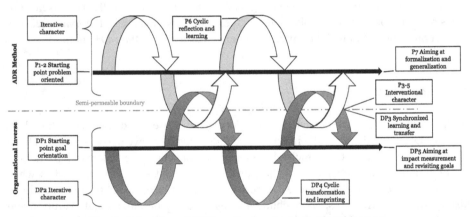

Fig. 2. Principles of ADR method and organizational inverse

As shown in Fig. 2, the cycles of the observed organizational inverse start with a goal and end with impact measurement by revisiting those goals defined at the beginning. The iterative character directly reflects the intertwined nature, as it is common to both the ADR method and the organizational inverse. We observed the emergence of synchronized learning and transferring at the semi-permeable boundary where the interactive cycles cross each other. Within the iterative cycles, networked traditions invoked and imprinted over the transformation processes.

7 Conclusion

In this study, we aimed to understand the DT in traditional SMEs through an antipodean case comparison. We present the antipodean view through a retrospective analysis, but we note that the ADR studies conducted independently, by different research teams in Germany and Australia, as a limitation. Despite the limitations, we believe that our results can help with the problem of the missing guidance and overload the SMEs face during their first steps in DT. Guidance is provided which is flexible enough to allow SMEs to create their own suitable DT method, regardless of whether top-down, bottom-up or co-existing DT strategies [20, 21] are realized in the SME. In addition to the owners, this is especially interesting for ADR researchers, who can design this method together with the traditional SMEs to help them manage the ADR outcome considering their tradition [17]. By doing so, we contribute to the design-oriented knowledge base on DT in SMEs. Future research can examine the relationships between the DPs.

Acknowledgment. PROFUND was supported by a grant from the German Ministry for Research and Education (BMBF), no: 03ZZ0618C.

References

1. Vial, G.: Understanding digital transformation: a review and a research agenda. J. Strateg. Inf. Syst. **28**, 118–144 (2019)
2. Bharadwaj, A., El Sawy, O.A., Pavlou, P.A., Venkatraman, N.: Digital business strategy: toward a next generation of insights. MIS Q. **37**, 471–482 (2013)
3. Sebastian, I.M., Mocker, M., Ross, J.W., Moloney, K.G., Beath, C., Fonstad, N.O.: How big old companies navigate digital transformation. MIS Q. Exec. **16**, 197–213 (2017)
4. Chanias, S., Myers, M.D., Hess, T.: Digital transformation strategy making in pre-digital organizations: The case of a financial services provider. J. Strateg. Inf. Syst. **28**, 17–33 (2019)
5. Marschinski, R., Martinez Turegano, D.: Reassessing the decline of EU manufacturing : A GLOBAL value chain analysis, EUR 29999 EN., Luxembourg (2019)
6. Hönigsberg, S., Dinter, B.: Toward a method to foster the digital transformation in SME networks. In: 40th International Conference on Information Systems, pp. 1–8, Munich (2019)
7. Li, L., Su, F., Zhang, W., Mao, J.Y.: Digital transformation by SME entrepreneurs: a capability perspective. Inf. Syst. J. **28**, 1129–1157 (2018)
8. Soluk, J., Kammerlander, N.: Digital transformation in family-owned Mittelstand firms: a dynamic capabilities perspective. Eur. J. Inf. Syst. 1–36 (2021)
9. Dias, M., Pan, S., Tim, Y., Land, L.: Digital imprinting: the role of history in digital strategising at a predigital organisation. In: Twenty-Third Pacific Asia Conference on Information Systems, Dubai, pp. 1–8 (2020)
10. Mills, K.: Fintech, Small Business & The American Dream. Palgrave Macmillan, Cham (2018)
11. Rogers, D.L.: The Digital Transformation Playbook: Rethink Your Business for the Digital Age. Columbia University Press, New York (2016)
12. Kammerlander, N., Dessì, C., Bird, M., Floris, M., Murru, A.: The impact of shared stories on family firm innovation: a multicase study. Fam. Bus. Rev. **28**, 332–354 (2015)
13. Stoian, M.-C., Rialp, J., Dimitratos, P.: SME networks and international performance: unveiling the significance of foreign market entry mode. J. Small Bus. Manag. **55**, 128–148 (2017)

14. Marquis, C.: The pressure of the past: Network imprinting in intercorporate communities. Adm. Sci. Q. **48**, 655–689 (2003)
15. March, S.T., Smith, G.F.: Design and natural science research on information technology. Decis. Support Syst. **15**, 251–266 (1995)
16. ASBFE Ombudsman: Small business counts: Small business in the Australian economy (2019)
17. Erdogan, I., Rondi, E., De Massis, A.: Managing the tradition and innovation paradox in family firms: a family imprinting perspective. Entrep. Theory Pract. **44**, 20–54 (2020)
18. Remane, G., Hanelt, A., Nickerson, R.C., Kolbe, L.M.: Discovering digital business models in traditional industries. J. Bus. Strategy. **38**, 41–51 (2017)
19. Sein, M.K., Henfridsson, O., Purao, S., Rossi, M., Lindgren, R.: Action design research. MIS Q. **35**, 37–56 (2011)
20. Gregory, R.W., Kaganer, E., Henfridsson, O., Ruch, T.J.: It consumerization and the transformation of it governance. MIS Q. Manag. Inf. Syst. **42**, 1225–1253 (2018)
21. Kane, G.C., Palmer, D., Phillips, A.N., Kiron, D., Buckley, N.: Strategy, not technology, drives digital transformation. MIT Sloan Manag. Rev. Deloitte Univ. Press. **14**, 1–25 (2015)
22. Hanelt, A., Bohnsack, R., Marz, D., Marante, C.A.: A systematic review of the literature on digital transformation: Insights and implications for strategy and organizational change. J. Manag. Stud. **1**, 1–39 (2020)
23. Yeow, A., Soh, C., Hansen, R.: Aligning with new digital strategy: a dynamic capabilities approach. J. Strateg. Inf. Syst. **27**, 43–58 (2018)
24. Dremel, C., Herterich, M., Wulf, J., Waizmann, J.-C., Brenner, W.: How AUDI AG established big data analytics in its digital transformation. MIS Q. Exec. **16**, 81–100 (2017)
25. Wang, Y.C.W., Chang, C.-W., Heng, M.: The levels of information technology adoption, business network, and a strategic position model for evaluating supply chain integration. J. Electron. Commer. Res. **5**, 85–98 (2004)
26. Pan, S.L., Pee, L.G.: Usable, in-use, and useful research: a 3U framework for demonstrating practice impact. Inf. Syst. J. **30**, 403–426 (2020)
27. Sein, M.K., Rossi, M.: Elaborating ADR while drifting away from its essence: a commentary on Mullarkey and Hevner. Eur. J. Inf. Syst. **28**, 1–5 (2018)
28. Ågerfalk, P.J., Karlsson, F.: Artefactual and empirical contributions in information systems research. Eur. J. Inf. Syst. **29**, 109–113 (2020)
29. Gregor, S., Chandra Kruse, L., Seidel, S.: The anatomy of a design principle. J. Assoc. Inf. Syst. (2020, in press)
30. Haj-Bolouri, A., Östlund, C., Rossi, M., Svensson, L.: Work-integrated learning as an outcome of using action design research in practice. In: Tulu, Bengisu, Djamasbi, Soussan, Leroy, Gondy (eds.) DESRIST 2019. LNCS, vol. 11491, pp. 92–107. Springer, Cham (2019). https://doi.org/10.1007/978-3-030-19504-5_7
31. Kvasny, L., Keil, M.: The challenges of redressing the digital divide: a tale of two US cities. Inf. Syst. J. **16**, 23–53 (2006)
32. Levina, N., Vaast, E.: The emergence of boundary spanning competence in practice: implications for implementation and use of information systems. MIS Q. **29**, 335–363 (2005)
33. Teece, D.J.: Business models and dynamic capabilities. Long Range Plan. **51**, 40–49 (2018)
34. Wiener, M., et al.: Information systems research: making an impact in a publish-or-perish world. Commun. Assoc. Inf. Syst. **43**, 26 (2018)
35. Mingers, J.: Realizing information systems: critical realism as an underpinning philosophy for information systems. Inf. Organ. **14**, 87–103 (2004)
36. Venkatesh, V., Brown, S.A., Bala, H.: Bridging the qualitative-quantitative divide: guidelines for conducting mixed methods research in information systems. MIS Q. **37**, 21–54 (2013)
37. Dacin, M.T., Dacin, P.A., Kent, D.: Tradition in organizations: a custodianship framework. Acad. Manag. Ann. **13**, 342–373 (2019)

Business Model Design and Ecosystem Innovation: A Method for Visualizing Interactions

Deborah Glassey-Previdoli[1](✉) ⓘ, Riccardo Bonazzi[1] ⓘ, and Gianluigi Viscusi[2] ⓘ

[1] University of Applied Sciences Western Switzerland, HES-SO, Sierre, Switzerland
{deborah.glassey,riccardo.bonazzi}@hevs.ch
[2] Imperial College Business School, London, UK
g.viscusi@imperial.ac.uk

Abstract. In this article, we consider the existing literature in business ecosystem design and business model design to propose a method called *Bifocals*. The method aims to align the two ecosystem and business perspectives. We illustrate how to use Bifocals by describing how we supported the creation of a new service, which adapts to recent evolution in the business ecosystem of nursing homes. The access to the field for the instantiation of the method is provided by an ongoing research project, which is mainly addressed to managers of nursing homes. Indeed, recent events have obliged nursing homes to redefine the interactions among stakeholders in their business ecosystem. In the end, we claim that our method (a) allows representing in greater details the niche ecosystem where the firm is located, (b) it offers a more structured way to respond to an ever-evolving ecosystem, and (c) it underlines a coherent way to build and test new business model features to restructure the firm, in response to its ecosystem.

Keywords: Business ecosystem · Business model design · Innovation ecosystems · Nursing homes · Design science

1 Introduction

This article investigates the relationships between business model innovation in one or more organizations and the evolution of the ecosystems that are connected to them. In particular, we are interested in how those relationships and changes can be represented for the involved organizations may eventually respond in a satisficing way, by redefining the interactions among stakeholders in their business ecosystem. In this article, we consider a *business ecosystem* as an "economic community supported by a foundation of interacting organizations and individuals—the organisms of the business world" [1]. Business ecosystems focus on customer value creation, and the actors have several reasons to stay together or actively participate in the orchestration of their ecosystem [2]. Hence, our research questions guiding the research are:

Q1: How to represents the changes in business ecosystems due to the adoption of new business models

© Springer Nature Switzerland AG 2021
L. Chandra Kruse et al. (Eds.): DESRIST 2021, LNCS 12807, pp. 387–398, 2021.
https://doi.org/10.1007/978-3-030-82405-1_37

Q2: How to adopt that representation to assess a business ecosystem for an organization willing to conceive new services with new business models?

Moreover, we consider the business ecosystem of nursing homes as the substantive domain of the research. The access to the field is provided by an ongoing research project, which is mainly addressed to managers of nursing homes. Indeed, recent events have obliged nursing homes to redefine the interactions among stakeholders in their business ecosystem. We refer to [3] to define a *nursing home* as a facility that provides 24-h functional support for people who have identified health needs and require assistance with activities of daily living (ADLs) and instrumental activities of daily living (IADLs). Such a place may or may not be staffed with health care professionals and it provides long-term care and/or rehabilitation as part of hospital avoidance or to facilitate early hospital discharges. In recent years, European countries have explored new forms of nursing homes, such as day-care services as well as retirement communities and flats built close to but not in care homes [4]. Such movement towards decentralization of hosting solutions for patients might require new transportation solutions and the changes in the business ecosystem may offer new opportunities for innovation. Thus, in our case, the focus is on conceiving a "new transportation service". In particular, we consider the use of digital platforms as, for example, Uber for the access of healthcare services from a specific part of the aging population. Services like GoGo grandparent allow seniors, who are not familiar with smartphones to book their Uber or Lyft by phone, whereas specialized drivers from SilverRide escort riders out of their homes, help them transfer into and out of the car, and then accompany them to their specific destinations. Taking the above issues and questions into account, in this article we consider the existing literature in business ecosystem design and business model design to propose a method called *Bifocals* that aims to align those two perspectives.

The rest of the paper proceeds as it follows. Section 2 reviews the relevant literature to answer our research question and underlines a research gap. Section 3 describes how we applied design science to develop an artifact that addresses the research gap. Section 4 describes our artifact in the shape of a method to switch from ecosystem design to business model design. Section 5 offers an example or *instantiation* of how the process can be used to develop new services to adapt to an evolving business ecosystem. Section 6 illustrates our preliminary results and Sect. 7 concludes the paper by highlighting its contributions and limitations.

2   Theoretical Background

Among the early scholars that introduced the notion of ecosystem in the management literature, Moore [5] claimed that "in a business ecosystem, companies co-evolve capabilities around an innovation: they work cooperatively and competitively to support new products, satisfy customer needs, and eventually incorporate the next round of innovations." Since then a vast literature has been produced on the topic of ecosystems [6–9]. Among the different definitions, [6] considered an ecosystem as "the alignment structure of the multilateral set of partners that need to interact for a focal value proposition to materialize" further proposing two views for its conceptualization. The first view (*ecosystem-as-affiliation*), focuses on the association of actors based on their affiliations to networks or platforms; the second view (*ecosystem-as-structure*) emphasizes the configurations of activity guided by a value proposition [6]. As to those issues, [8] outlined the differences between market networks and ecosystems, which are characterized by the management of "non generic complementarities in the absence of full hierarchical control". Furthermore, [9] has identified through a comprehensive literature review a set of characteristics that jointly distinguish ecosystems from other collecting forms of organizing: the participants' heterogeneity, the facilitation of collective outputs greater than individual participants outputs, their technological, economic, and cognitive interdependence, and the specific of governance that allows for co-alignment among ecosystem participants with specific roles not formally established by formal contracts. According to [9], a business ecosystem is a specific type of innovation ecosystem that can be generally defined as "a community of hierarchically independent, yet interdependent heterogeneous participants who collectively generate an ecosystem output and related value offering targeted at a defined audience". Also, [10] pointed out the need for studying ecosystems from an open innovation perspective, thus extending the focus of the scholars interested in that field from a focal firm-based perspective to an extensive consideration of other participants in the networks opened up for innovation purposes. As to these issues, [11] lists a set of recommended principles on how to successfully innovate in ecosystems related to the circular economy by performing three relevant processes: (a) *collaboration*, (b) *experimentation* and (c) *platformization*. This latter point is particularly relevant for the role attributed to digital platforms as the locus of interaction, collaboration, and experimentation for innovation ecosystems [12, 13]. The connection between business model and ecosystems has been considered especially by the literature that has questioned business model design for innovation [14–17]. In this article, we consider the following definition of business model innovation as "as the design and implementation of an activity system that is new to the focal firm or new to the product–market space in which the focal firm competes" [18]. However, notwithstanding the linkages to ecosystem's actors and elements in the available conceptual models and software/tools for the design of business models [18–20], business model and ecosystems design has followed different and often separated paths.

In order to create and capture more value from the innovation of existing ecosystems [21], an increasing number of authors have engaged in providing frameworks and techniques to map their different actors and interactions. Among them, [22] have specifically considered the alignment between the different layers that characterize the activities within an innovation ecosystem and that can be distinguished as *explorative* or *exploitative*. Moreover, from a strategic management perspective, [23] proposed to move from identifying value propositions to put them into action through a value blueprint that aims to map the impacted ecosystem. A recent technique called *Ecosystem Pie Model - EPM* [24] allows to visualize (a) the strategies for aligning the actors to the value proposition of the ecosystem [25], (b) the interfaces of collaboration between parties [26], (c) the types of complementarity between the different actors [7]. Accordingly, the structure of their resulting model [24] is composed of six constructs that determine the risk of the project: an "Actor", who has a "Dependence" to the ecosystem, has access to "Resources" that are used in "Activities" to produce "Value addition" and enable "Value Capture". Finally, in their analysis concerning care coordination, [27] identify three capacities for firms in a changing ecosystem: (i) the capacity to understand the ecosystem; (ii) the capacity to respond to an ever-evolving ecosystem; and (iii) the capacity to structure itself in response to its ecosystem.

Accordingly, we argue that it seems possible to (a) assess the environment with the process of [11] and find new collaboration in the ecosystem niche, (b) use the EPM to perform experimentation, and (c) restructure the firm to develop a platform by using existing business model design tools such as the value proposition canvas or the business model canvas [28]. Moreover, we refer to [29] to adapt the classics risks addressed by design thinking into business model components: lack of product/service desirability (a problem-solution fit), lack of technical feasibility (à product-market fit), or lack of economic viability (à business model fit). Nonetheless, a single coherent process to do these three steps appears to be missing in the literature.

3   Research Method

In this Section, we position our study in the field of design science research [30] and we describe how we developed an artifact under the shape of a design science research method, by following the steps outlined by [31].

(1) **Identify the problem and motivate:** As described in Sect. 1, we center our analysis around the evolution of nursing homes, and we look for new transportation services that involve multiple actors in the business ecosystem.
(2) **Define objectives of the solution:** As shown in Sect. 2, we intend to combine existing literature from business ecosystem innovation and concepts for business model design in one single method.
(3) **Design and development:** Section 4 illustrates how we combined tools in ecosystem design and business model design, to (i) visualize the evolution of the ecosystem, (ii) find new solutions to respond to an ever-evolving ecosystem; and (iii) suggest the changes to implement and the testing strategy to validate the business hypotheses.
(4) **Demonstration:** Section 5 illustrates an example of how to use the BiFocals method to visually describe a transportation service that follows new trends in the business ecosystem of nursing homes.
(5) **Evaluation:** Section 6 describes the preliminary feedback received by a startup offering the service conceived, by using the Bifocals method.
(6) **Communication:** We have started sharing the preliminary results via academic conferences and we plan to submit our full report once the first phase of data collection will be completed.

4   The Artifact

In this Section, we illustrate how we created our method, which we called *Bifocals*, to underline the fact that it allows to bridge business ecosystem to business model design. To this end, we consider two of the approaches mentioned in the previous Section, the principles proposed by [11] for ecosystems innovation and the EPM by [24] together with the perspective by [29] and Osterwalder et al., 2020 [28] for business model design. Those contributions ground the key components of the Bifocals method, whose conceptual model is shown in Fig. 1 and that we discuss in what follows by using the details provided by Table 1.

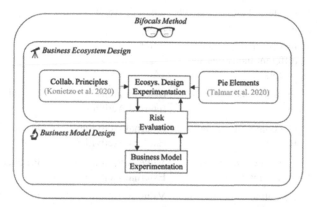

Fig. 1. The Bifocals method: a conceptual model

In the first column of Table 1 we follow the principles proposed by [11] and we represent them by linking together the elements of the EPM [24] in the second column, which deals with experimentation. In particular, as the substantive domain of interest, we take the point of view of the nursing home and we make a distinction between internal and external resources/activities/value addition components. This allows focusing on the niche ecosystem mentioned by [25], while visualizing the flow of information, goods, and money. That leads to the first testable proposition: **(P1)**: *the ecosystem component of the Bifocals method allows representing in greater details the niche ecosystem where the firm is located.*

By observing the links among components shown in the EPM canvas, it is possible to underline features that can be "Eliminated", "Reduced", "Raised" or "Created" [32]. In addition to that, the process of [11] allows addressing the right questions in the right order. That leads to our second testable proposition **(P2)**: *the value alignment component of the Bifocals method offers a more structured way to respond to an ever-evolving ecosystem.* For each step of the process, the third column assigns a type of risk derived from the literature on business model design [28, 29]. That leads to our third testable proposition: (P3): *the business model component of the Bifocals method underlines a coherent way to build and test new business model features to restructure the firm, in response to its ecosystem.*

Table 1. Steps of the method including the considered items.

Collab. step (C)	Item: Business Ecosystems Design Principles [11]	Item: Elements in the EPM [24]	Item: Types of Business Model Design Risks [28, 29]
C1	Define a partner selection process	Internal Resource/ Actor	–
C2	Involve new actors from different industries and sectors	Actor	–
C3	Establish and maintain trust	External Activities > Internal Activities	Technical Feasibility
C4	Get commitment and buy-in	External Activities > External Activities	Product Desirability
C5	Align individual and shared interests	Value Addition > External Activity	Product Desirability
C6	Re-define actor roles and responsibilities	Value Addition > External Activity	Product Desirability
C7	Develop a decentralized and collaborative governance structure	Internal Activity > Internal Resource	Technical Feasibility
C8	Develop joint strategies and goals	Ecosystem Value Proposition (EVP)	Product Desirability
C9	Ensure fair value capture among involved actors	External Activity > Internal Value Capture	Economic Viability

5 Demonstration

In this Section, we present the current situation in Switzerland concerning nursing homes, we briefly describe some of the trends for the future and we move on to illustrating the resulting Ecosystem Pie obtained with our method (Fig. 2).

In Switzerland, nursing homes (*Etablissement Médico-Social* in French and *Pflege-heim* in German) have hosted 122'000 people in 2017 for long-term stays of 3.5 years on average [33]. According to the Swiss Federal Statistics Office [34], a Swiss nursing home exchanges data with five stakeholders: (A) the Federal Offices of Public Health and Social Insurance, (B) the insurers (D) the Cantonal public health services, as well as social welfare offices and statistical offices, (E) the research institutions and (H) the service and hosting providers concerned with the nursing home. Previous attempts to visualize the innovation ecosystem in healthcare, such as the one done by [35], allows us to add those stakeholders to Fig. 2 together with (C) the social and interest groups, (F) the suppliers, (G) the collaborators, such as the healthcare providers, which are usually separated from the hosting providers, (I) the customers and consumers that surround the immediate customer, that will be named here *informal caregivers*, (J) the immediate "customers", which will be named *Elderly people*.

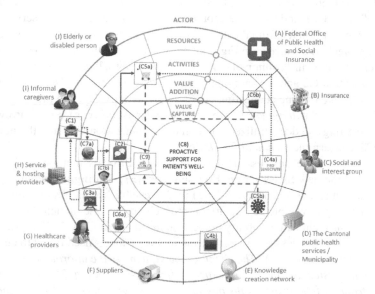

Fig. 2. Ecosystem pie for a nw transportation service offered to elderly people

The first principle proposed by [11] led us to select a niche of actors, who were in contact with the elderlies while they were not hospitalized. That led to the inclusion of informal caregivers as a resource for transportation (shown in Fig. 2 as step C1 and a taxi icon). Inspired by Uber, we thought if we could create a crowdsourced transportation system for elderly people. Indeed, it turned out that it already existed for disabled people [36]; nonetheless, it is offered by professionals instead of professionally trained volunteers. That led to the creation of a new component for value addition of the ecosystem (named C2 in the Fig. 2): drivers trained by care providers might be able to use the time spent driving to support the elderly people and collect information about their wellbeing. The fact of being trained by healthcare providers (named C3a in Fig. 2 and a blackboard icon), will establish trust among ecosystem actors interacting with the service, whereas Social and interest groups (such as pro-senectute in Switzerland, named C4a) will support the service by promoting its services to elderly people and research institutes (C4b in Fig. 2) will offer the technological know-how to manage the platform.

The new value created will be linked to the current activities of other actors, such as doing daily shopping for elderly people (item C5a, which refers to the step) and helping the municipality to improve the nursing homes during the Covid-19 pandemics (item C5b). Moreover, a service that collects data while performing transportation might be important for doctors (item C6a) who can receive relevant data about their patients from professionally trained personnel and insurance firms (item C6b), who are willing to reposition themselves by sharing with their clients' data about their health risk (in Switzerland, this is currently possible as long as the health risk data is not used by the insurance to assess the financial risk of each client). Finally, the internal activities management of the network (item C7a) and decentralized autonomous organization (item C7b) will assure the decentralized governance suggested by step 7. Consequently, the joint goal of the niche ecosystem can be summarized as *"proactive support for patient's well-being"* (item C8), and the value capture activity to finance the new service would be a yearly subscription fee from the three actors, thus getting support for their activities (Item C9). Moreover, the arrows in Fig. 2 allows to assess the different types of business risk, expressed in the third column of our table: a) full arrows, like the one connecting the new value addition C2 and the shopping activity C5a, concern *product desirability*; b) dashed arrows, like the one connecting the shopping activity C5a and the value capture activity C9, concern *willingness to pay* and *business viability*; c) dotted arrows, like the one connecting the decentralized autonomous organization C7b and the new value addition C2, concern the *technical feasibility*.

An example of the business model side of our Bifocals method is the project Match'NGo of the new Swiss startup ErgoSum Sarl [37]. During the beginning of the Covid-19 pandemics, the team has used the Fig. 2 to establish a minimum viable product made of a network of volunteers (C1) to transport elderly people in their daily activities (C5a) and test the technical feasibility of the system (link C3a-C1-C7-C2). To assess the economic viability and desirability of the system, the team has used Fig. 2 to define two business hypotheses to test: *(A) The clients of the system are the informal caregivers and the users of the system are the elderly citizens (link C2-C5a in Fig. 2) and (B) The most important feature of the system is the possibility to receive a personalized diagnostic by using a certified checklist (element C2).*

Accordingly, four rounds of interviews have been conducted to assess their willingness to pay and their likelihood to suggest the service to a friend/relative (the Net Promoter Score). The first group (ALL AGES – DIAGNOSTIC) was composed of people of different ages, and it received the description of the transportation service with the possibility to receive a diagnostic of the personal well-being, which was done by a driver trained by professional nurses. For example, the pink dot in square 1 (on the top left corner of Fig. 3) shows that one participant aged around 50 years old (x-axis) was willing to pay up to 50 Swiss francs for the service (y-axis), and he/she was very likely to recommend the system to a friend (as shown by the color scale for the net promoter score or NPS dimension). Accordingly, the results presented in square 1 show that the willingness to pay on the y-axis decreases as the age increases; in the meantime, the net promoter score of respondents in square 01 is fairly high across all the interviewed sample. The second group in square 2 (ALL – NO DIAGNOSTIC), did not receive the information about the possibility to receive a personalized diagnostic and commented on a transportation service done by a driver trained by professional nurses. The third group in square 3 (FOCUS – NO DIAGNOSTIC) was focused on informal caregivers, who mentioned that the system was not much needed by them and they didn't see the value for their parents.

The last group represented by square 4 in the bottom right corner (FOCUS – DIAGNOSTIC) was composed of informal caregivers, who confirmed their intention to promote the service among their personal contacts, and their willingness to pay is considerably higher than groups 2 and 3. Therefore, we can confirm in Fig. 2 that the clients are

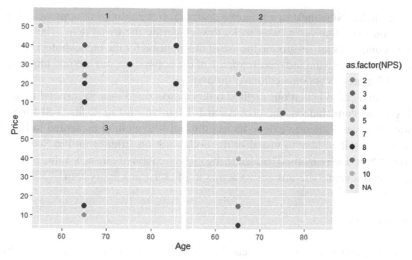

Fig. 3. Economic viability (price) and desirability (NPS) for a new transportation service

the informal caregivers and the users are elderly citizens and that the personalized diagnostics is a game-changer in the willingness to pay of the potential clients. The idea has already won a startup competition [38] that took place at the end of May 2020 and which gave Match'NGo visibility across other actors in the ecosystem. The project managers are currently discussing with the Pro-Senectute association (item C4a) and they have received a small grant from the Swiss confederation to work with a research institution (C4b). In the meantime, they are working closely with different municipalities (C5b) to fine-tune their services.

6 Discussion

In this Section, we discuss our preliminary results by following the argumentative model of [39]. Considering the background that describes the problem and the research questions, as shown in Sect. 1, our research question concerns how to assess the business ecosystem of a nursing home and design new transportation services that are desirable, feasible, and economically viable. The relevance of this research question is grounded in longstanding socioeconomic trends (the increase of lifespan and the consequent expansion of healthcare expenses), recent shifts linked to new technologies (business model changes of insurance firms linked to recent developments in machine learning algorithms), and unexpected events (new safety guidelines following the worldwide spread of covid-19).

Our first claim is that our method allows to represent in greater detail the niche ecosystem where the firm is located. The reason for our claim is described in Sect. 2: previous scholars have described the innovation ecosystem in healthcare, but they have not used the EPM. In Sect. 5 we offered as evidence the description of how we managed to visually assess the interactions among actors, once we include informal caregivers. Compared to previous visualizations, our representation allows to see more in detail the ecosystem niche. Nonetheless, a possible reservation regarding our approach concerns the focus on one main actor, who seeks to orchestrate the ecosystem. Therefore, our boundary conditions are set around the use of this method for the orchestrator: if multiple actors want to obtain a unified representation of the ecosystem, our method might require additional features to obtain a common ground.

Our second claim is that our method offers a structured way to respond to an ever-evolving ecosystem. Indeed, the ecosystem PIE shown in Fig. 2 fits well for experimentation, but we wanted to extend its use through the method presented in Fig. 1. In Sect. 4, we described how to visualize the collaboration strategy and in Sect. 5 we're have shown how such a method had led to the identification of one new value proposition and additional revenue streams across actors in the business ecosystem.

7 Conclusion

This article describes an ongoing research project, which describes how nursing homes can adapt to changes in their ecosystem by offering new services. Recent events have obliged nursing homes to redefine the interactions among stakeholders in their business ecosystem, and by combining the existing literature in business ecosystem design and business model design, we propose a method called *Bifocals* to align the two ecosystem and business perspectives. We claim that our method (1) allows representing in greater details the niche ecosystem where the firm is located, (2) it offers a more structured way to respond to an ever-evolving ecosystem, and (3) it underlines a coherent way to build and test new business model features to restructure the firm, in response to its ecosystem. We illustrate how to use Bifocals by describing how we supported the creation of a new service that adapts to recent evolution in the business ecosystem of nursing homes. Although the paper shows promising insights, our research project is currently ongoing and it has its limitations, as discussed in Sect. 6. The Bifocals method so far has led to the development of a single business idea, and we are planning to use it in the future to structure our discussion with owners of nursing homes and health department officers. The Bifocals method is a bridge between existing techniques in business ecosystem design and business design, and it cannot be used as stand-alone. Therefore, future research will continue to work on how to seamlessly integrate such tools into one coherent approach. The Match'NGo project has passed the first round of tests concerning product desirability and technical feasibility, but it is still at its initial stage. Nonetheless, such limitations allow future directions of investigations and future work will develop a more advanced prototype to validate product-market fit and business model fit.

References

1. Moore, J.F.: The Death of Competition: Leadership and Strategy in the Age of Business Ecosystems. HarperCollins, New York (1996)
2. Valkokari, K.: Business, innovation, and knowledge ecosystems: How they differ and how to survive and thrive within them. Technol. Innov. Manag. Rev. **5**, 17–24 (2015)

3. Sanford, A.M., et al.: An international definition for "nursing home". J. Am. Med. Dir. Assoc. **16**, 181–184 (2015)
4. The Economist: The pandemic shows the urgency of reforming care for the elderly (2020)
5. Moore, J.F.: Predators and prey: a new ecology of competition. Harv. Bus. Rev. **71**, 75–86 (1993)
6. Adner, R.: Ecosystem as structure: an actionable construct for strategy. J. Manag. **43**, 39–58 (2017)
7. Jacobides, M.G., Cennamo, C., Gawer, A.: Towards a theory of ecosystems. Strateg. Manag. J. **39**, 2255–2276 (2018)
8. Shipilov, A., Gawer, A.: Integrating research on interorganizational networks and ecosystems. Acad. Manag. Ann. **14**, 92–121 (2019). https://doi.org/10.5465/annals.2018.0121
9. Thomas, L.D.W., Autio, E.: Innovation ecosystems in management: an organizing typology (2020). https://oxfordre.com/business/view/10.1093/acrefore/9780190224851.001.0001/acr efore-9780190224851-e-203
10. Yaghmaie, P., Vanhaverbeke, W.: Identifying and describing constituents of innovation ecosystems: A systematic review of the literature. EuroMed. J. Bus. **15**(3), 283–314 (2020). https://doi.org/10.1108/EMJB-03-2019-0042
11. Konietzko, J., Bocken, N., Hultink, E.J.: Circular ecosystem innovation: an initial set of principles. J. Clean. Prod. **253**, 119942 (2020)
12. Drewel, M., Özcan, L., Koldewey, C., Gausemeier, J.: Pattern-based development of digital platforms. Creat. Innov. Manag. caim.12415 (2020). https://doi.org/10.1111/caim.12415
13. Trabucchi, D., Buganza, T.: Fostering digital platform innovation: from two to multi-sided platforms. Creat. Innov. Manag. **29**, 345–358 (2020). https://doi.org/10.1111/caim.12320
14. Foss, N.J., Saebi, T.: Fifteen years of research on business model innovation: how far have we come, and where should we go? J. Manag. **43**, 200–227 (2016). https://doi.org/10.1177/0149206316675927
15. Foss, N.J., Saebi, T.: Business models and business model innovation: between wicked and paradigmatic problems. Long Range Plann. **51**, 9–21 (2018). https://doi.org/10.1016/j.lrp.2017.07.006
16. Frankenberger, K., Weiblen, T., Csik, M., Gassmann, O.: The 4I-framework of business model innovation: a structured view on process phases and challenges. Int. J. Prod. Dev. **18**, 249–273 (2013)
17. Hacklin, F., Björkdahl, J., Wallin, M.W.: Strategies for business model innovation: how firms reel in migrating value. Long Range Plann. **51**, 82–110 (2018). https://doi.org/10.1016/j.lrp.2017.06.009
18. Zott, C., Amit, R.: Business model innovation: toward a process perspective. In: Shalley, C., Hitt, M.A., Zhou, J. (eds.) The Oxford Handbook of Creativity, Innovation, and Entrepreneurship. Oxford University Press (2015)
19. Massa, L., Hacklin, F.: Business model innovation in incumbent firms: cognition and visual representation. In: Sund, K.J. (ed.) New Horizons in Managerial and Organizational Cognition, pp. 203–232. Emerald Publishing Limited (2020)
20. Szopinski, D., Schoormann, T., John, T., Knackstedt, R., Kundisch, D.: Software tools for business model innovation: current state and future challenges. Electron. Mark. **30**(3), 469–494 (2019). https://doi.org/10.1007/s12525-018-0326-1
21. Adner, R., Kapoor, R.: Value creation in innovation ecosystems: how the structure of technological interdependence affects firm performance in new technology generations. Strateg. Manag. J. **31**, 306–333 (2010). https://doi.org/10.1002/smj.821
22. Visscher, K., Hahn, K., Konrad, K.: Innovation ecosystem strategies of industrial firms: a multilayered approach to alignment and strategic positioning. Creat. Innov. Manag. Caim. 12429 (2021). https://doi.org/10.1111/caim.12429

23. Adner, R.: The Wide Lens. Penguin Books Ltd., London, New York (2012)
24. Talmar, M., Walrave, B., Podoynitsyna, K.S., Holmström, J., Romme, A.G.L.: Mapping, analyzing and designing innovation ecosystems: the ecosystem pie model. Long Range Plann. (2020). In Press
25. Walrave, B., Talmar, M., Podoynitsyna, K.S., Romme, A.G.L., Verbong, G.P.: A multi-level perspective on innovation ecosystems for path-breaking innovation. Technol. Forecast. Soc. Change. **136**, 103–113 (2018)
26. Davis, J.P.: The group dynamics of interorganizational relationships: collaborating with multiple partners in innovation ecosystems. Adm. Sci. Q. **61**, 621–661 (2016)
27. Raynor, J., Cardona, C., Knowlton, T., Mittenthal, R., Simpson, J.: Capacity building 3.0: how to strengthen the social ecosystem. N. Y. TCC Group (2014)
28. Osterwalder, A., Pigneur, Y., Smith, A., Etiemble, F.: The Invincible Company: How to Constantly Reinvent Your Organization with Inspiration From the World's Best Business Models. Wiley, Hoboken (2020)
29. Amarsy, N.: Survival of the fittest (2014). https://www.strategyzer.com/blog/posts/2014/11/10/survival-of-the-fittest
30. Hevner, A., March, S., Park, J., Ram, S.: Design science in information systems research. Manag. Inf. Syst. Q. **28**, 75–105 (2004)
31. Peffers, K., Tuunanen, T., Rothenberger, M.A., Chatterjee, S.: A design science research methodology for information systems research. J. Manag. Inf. Syst. **24**, 45–77 (2007). https://doi.org/10.2753/MIS0742-1222240302
32. Kim, W.C., Mauborgne, R.: Eliminate-Reduce-Raise-Create Grid (ERRC Grid) (2004). https://www.blueoceanstrategy.com/tools/errc-grid/
33. Swiss Federal Statistics Office: Population des établissements médico-sociaux, en 2017 (2019)
34. Office fédéral de la statistique: Statistique des institutions médico-sociales - Conception détaillée | Publication. https://www.bfs.admin.ch/bfs/de/home/statistiken/gesundheit/erhebungen/somed.assetdetail.303721.html
35. Phillips, M.A., Srai, J.S.: Exploring emerging ecosystem boundaries: defining 'the game'. Int. J. Innov. Manag. **22**, 1840012 (2018). https://doi.org/10.1142/S1363919618400121
36. THV: Courses & Transports. https://transporthandicapvaud.ch/courses-transports/
37. Registre du commerce du Canton de Fribourg: ErgoSum Sàrl. https://adm.appls.fr.ch/hrcmatic/hrcintapp/externalCompanyReport.action?companyOfsUid=CHE-139.395.750
38. EPFL Innovation Park: YES YOU CAN – Relançons l'économie locale. https://epfl-innovationpark.ch/relancons-l-economie-locale
39. Toulmin, S.E.: The Uses of Argument. Cambridge University Press, Cambridge (2003)

Correction to: RefineMind: A Mobile App for People with Dementia and Their Caregivers

Beenish Moalla Chaudhry(iD) and Joy Smith(iD)

Correction to:
**Chapter "RefineMind: A Mobile App for People
with Dementia and Their Caregivers"**
in: L. Chandra Kruse et al. (Eds.): *The Next Wave*
of Sociotechnical Design, **LNCS 12807,**
https://doi.org/10.1007/978-3-030-82405-1_2

The originally published chapter 2 contained multiple errors in data, the name of the first author was incomplete. The errors have been corrected in Abstract and sections 2.1, 2.2, 2.3, 3.1, 3.2, and 4. The name of the first author has been corrected as "Beenish Moalla Chaudhry".

The updated version of this chapter can be found at
https://doi.org/10.1007/978-3-030-82405-1_2

Author Index

Printed in the United States
by Baker & Taylor Publisher Services